WORLDCOMP'13
July 22-25, 2013
Las Vegas Nevada, USA
www.world-academy-of-science.org

PROCEEDINGS OF THE 2013 INTERNATIONAL CONFERENCE ON INTERNET COMPUTING AND BIG DATA

ICOMP 2013

Editors

Hamid R. Arabnia
Victor A. Clincy
Leonidas Deligiannidis
Ashu M. G. Solo
Fernando G. Tinetti

FIREWALL MEDIA
(An Imprint of Laxmi Publications Pvt. Ltd.)
An ISO 9001:2008 Company
BENGALURU • CHENNAI • COCHIN • GUWAHATI • HYDERABAD
JALANDHAR • KOLKATA • LUCKNOW • MUMBAI • RANCHI • NEW DELHI
BOSTON (USA) • ACCRA (GHANA) • NAIROBI (KENYA)

This volume contains papers presented at The 2013 International Conference on Internet Computing and Big Data (ICOMP'13). Their inclusion in this publication does not necessarily constitute endorsements by editors or by the publisher.

Branches

✆	Bengaluru	080-26 75 69 30	
✆	Chennai	044-24 34 47 26,	24 35 95 07
✆	Cochin	0484-237 70 04,	405 13 03
✆	Guwahati	0361-254 36 69,	251 38 81
✆	Hyderabad	040-27 55 53 83,	27 55 53 93
✆	Jalandhar	0181-222 12 72	
✆	Kolkata	033-22 27 43 84	
✆	Lucknow	0522-220 99 16	
✆	Mumbai	022-24 91 54 15,	24 92 78 69
✆	Ranchi	0651-220 44 64	

PUBLISHED IN INDIA BY

FIREWALL MEDIA
(An Imprint of Laxmi Publications Pvt. Ltd.)

An ISO 9001:2008 Company
113, GOLDEN HOUSE, DARYAGANJ,
NEW DELHI - 110002, INDIA
Telephone : 91-11-4353 2500, 4353 2501
Fax : 91-11-2325 2572, 4353 2528
www.laxmipublications.com info@laxmipublications.com

C—
Printed at:

Foreword

It gives us great pleasure to introduce this collection of papers to be presented at the 2013 International Conference on Internet Computing and Big Data (ICOMP'13), July 22 through 25, 2013, at The New Tropicana Hotel, Las Vegas, USA.

An important mission of the World Congress in Computer Science, Computer Engineering, and Applied Computing (a federated congress to which this conference is affiliated with) includes *"Providing a unique platform for a diverse community of constituents composed of scholars, researchers, developers, educators, and practitioners. The Congress makes concerted effort to reach out to participants affiliated with diverse entities (such as: universities, institutions, corporations, government agencies, and research centers/labs) from all over the world. The congress also attempts to connect participants from institutions that have* ***teaching*** *as their main mission with those who are affiliated with institutions that have* ***research*** *as their main mission. The congress uses a quota system to achieve its institution and geography diversity objectives."* By any definition of diversity, this congress is among the most diverse scientific meeting in USA. We are proud to report that this federated congress has authors and participants from 82 different nations representing variety of personal and scientific experiences that arise from differences in culture and values. As can be seen (see below), the program committee of this conference as well as the program committee of all other tracks of the federated congress are as diverse as its authors and participants.

The program committee would like to thank all those who submitted papers for consideration. About 65% of the submissions were from outside the United States. Each submitted paper was peer-reviewed by two experts in the field for originality, significance, clarity, impact, and soundness. In cases of contradictory recommendations, a member of the conference program committee was charged to make the final decision; often, this involved seeking help from additional referees. In addition, papers whose authors included a member of the conference program committee were evaluated using the double-blinded review process. One exception to the above evaluation process was for papers that were submitted directly to chairs/organizers of pre-approved sessions/workshops; in these cases, the chairs/organizers were responsible for the evaluation of such submissions. The overall paper acceptance rate for regular papers was 32%; 12% of the remaining papers were accepted as poster papers (at the time of this writing, we had not yet received the acceptance rate for a few individual tracks.)

We are very grateful to the many colleagues who offered their services in organizing the conference. In particular, we would like to thank the members of the Program Committee of ICOMP'13, members of the congress Steering Committee, and members of the committees of federated congress tracks that have topics within the scope of ICOMP. Many individuals listed below, will be requested after the conference to provide their expertise and services for selecting papers for publication (extended versions) in journal special issues as well as for publication in a set of research books (to be prepared for publishers including: Springer, Elsevier, BMC, and others).

- *Dr. Alireza Abbasi; University of New South Wales (UNSW), Canberra, Australia*
- *Dr. Selim Aissi (World Congress Steering Committee); formerly, Chief Strategist - Security, Intel Corp., USA; Senior Business Leader & Head of Global Enterprise Security Architecture, Visa Corporation, USA*
- *Prof. Babak Akhgar (World Congress Steering Committee); Fellow of the British Computer Society, CITP; Professor of Informatics; Co-Director of CENTRIC (Centre of Excellence in Terrorism, Resilience, Intelligence & organised Crime research), Sheffield Hallam University, Sheffield, UK*
- *Prof. Nizar Al-Holou (World Congress Steering Committee); Professor and Chair, ECE Department; Vice Chair, IEEE/SEM-Computer Chapter; University of Detroit Mercy, Detroit, Michigan, USA*
- *Prof. Hamid R. Arabnia (World Congress Steering Committee); Professor, Computer Science; Editor-in-Chief, The Journal of Supercomputing (Springer); Elected Fellow, Int'l Society of Intelligent Biological Medicine (ISIBM); The University of Georgia, Department of Computer Science, USA*
- *Peyman Arebi; Assistant Professor, Technical and Vocational University, Bushehr, Iran*
- *Prof. Ezendu Ariwa (Publicity Vice-Chair); Chair, IEEE Consumer Electronics Chapter, UK&RI; Visiting Professor, Gulf Univ., Bahrain; Visiting Professor, University of Lagos and Kano State Polytechnic, Nigeria*
- *Prof. Juan Jose Martinez Castillo; Director of The Acantelys Research Group and Coordinator of the Computer Engineering Department, Universidad Gran Mariscal de Ayacucho, Venezuela*

- *Dr. Hsi-Ya (Jerry) Chang; Division Chief, National Center for High-Performance Computing, Taiwan; Secretary General of ACCTA; Member, Council of the Taiwan Association of Cloud Computing (TACC); Taiwan, ROC*
- *Prof. Victor A. Clincy; Professor of Computer Science, College of Science and Mathematics, Kennesaw State University, Georgia, USA*
- *Prof. Kevin Daimi (World Congress Steering Committee); Director, Computer Science and Software Engineering Programs; Department of Mathematics, Computer Science and Software Engineering; University of Detroit Mercy, Detroit, Michigan, USA*
- *Prof. Leonidas Deligiannidis; Professor, Computer Science, Wentworth Institute of Technology, MA, USA*
- *Somdip Dey; St. Xavier's College (Autonomous), Kolkata, India*
- *Prof. George A. Gravvanis; Democritus University of Thrace, Greece*
- *Dr. Hicham H. Hallal (SAM); Fahad Bin Sultan University, Saudi Arabia*
- *Dr. Shaikh Abdul Hannan (SAM); Vivekanand College, India*
- *Dr. Bing He (PDPTA); Cisco System Inc., San Jose, California, USA*
- *Prof. George Jandieri (World Congress Steering Committee); Georgian Technical University, Tbilisi, Georgia; Chief Scientist, The Institute of Cybernetics, Georgian Academy of Science, Georgia; Editorial Board Member: International Journal of Microwaves and Optical Technology, Georgia*
- *Prof. Seifedine Kadry (PDPTA); School of Engineering, American University of the Middle East, Kuwait*
- *Prof. Dong Hwa Kim; Department of Electronic and Control Engineering, Hanbat National University, Korea; Visiting Professor, Budapest University of Technology and Economic, Hungary; International Einstein awardee for Scientific achievement (2010)*
- *Prof. Dattatraya V. Kodavade (World Congress Steering Committee); Head of Computer Science and Engineering, D.K.T.E Society's Textile & Engineering Institute, Ichalkaranji, Maharashtra State, India*
- *Prof. B. Raja Sarath Kumar; Principal, Lenora College of Engineering, Andhra Pradesh, India*
- *Prof. Kun Chang Lee (World Congress Steering Committee); Professor of MIS and WCU Professor of Creativity Science, Business School and Department of Interaction Science, Sungkyunkwan University, Korea*
- *Arshad Mansoor (EEE); Pakistan Aeronautical Complex, Pakistan*
- *Prof. Gevorg Margarov; Head of Information Security and Software Development Department, State Engineering University of Armenia, Armenia*
- *Prof. George Markowsky (World Congress Steering Committee); Professor and Associate Director, School of Computing and Information Science; Chair International Advisory Board of IEEE IDAACS; Director 2013 Northeast Collegiate Cyber Defense Competition; Cooperating Professor Math and Statistics Department UMaine and School of Policy & International Affairs UMaine; University of Maine, Orono, Maine, USA*
- *Dr. Ali Mostafaeipour; Industrial Engineering Department, Yazd University, Iran*
- *Dr. Saurabh Mukherjee; Associate Professor, Banasthali University, India*
- *Prof. Prashant R. Nair; Vice-Chairman, Information Technology & Accreditation; Faculty, AMRITA-TIFAC Centre of Excellence in Cyber Security; Amrita University, Tamil Nadu, India*
- *Prof. Noel De Palma; Associate Vice President for Research, Computer Science; Leader, ERODS Research, LIG Labs.; Board of Directors, OW2 Consortium; Department of Computer Science; University Joseph Fourier (UJF), Grenoble, France*
- *Prof. G. N. Pandey (World Congress Steering Committee); Vice-Chancellor, Arunachal University of Studies, Arunachal Pradesh, India; Adjunct Professor, Indian Institute of Information Technology, Allahabad, India*
- *Prof. James J. (Jong Hyuk) Park (World Congress Steering Committee); Professor of Computer Science and Engineering, Seoul National University of Science and Technology (SeoulTech), Korea; President, KITCS; President, FTRA; Editor-in-Chiefs: HCIS, JoC and IJITCC Journals*
- *Dr. Liang Shi; Senior Researcher, McAfee, USA*
- *Ashu M. G. Solo, (Publicity Chair); Fellow of British Computer Society, Principal/R&D Engineer, Maverick Technologies America Inc., USA*
- *Prof. Fernando G. Tinetti (World Congress Steering Committee); School of Computer Science, Universidad Nacional de La Plata, La Plata, Argentina; Co-editor, Journal of CS and Technology (JCS&T)*
- *Dr. Predrag Tosic (World Congress Steering Committee); Microsoft, Washington, USA*
- *Prof. Vladimir Volkov (World Congress Steering Committee); The Bonch-Bruevich State University of Telecommunications, Saint-Petersburg, Russia*
- *Dr. Wei Wei; School of Computer Science and Engineering, Xi'an University of Technology, P. R. China*
- *Dr. Alexander Wohrer; Program Manager ICT at Vienna Science and Technology Fund, Schlickgasse, Vienna, Austria*
- *Prof. Dr. Bernd E. Wolfinger; Telecommunications and Computer Networks Division, University of Hamburg, Germany*

As Sponsors-at-large, partners, and/or organizers each of the followings (separated by semicolons) provided help for at least one track of the World Congress: Aldebaran Robotics Inc., USA (http://www.aldebaran-robotics.com); Altera Corporation, USA (http://www.altera.com/); Computer Science Research, Education, and Applications Press (CSREA); Impulse Accelerated Technologies, Inc., USA (http://www.impulseaccelerated.com/); NVIDIA Corporation, USA (http://www.nvidia.com/object/about-nvidia.html); Parallella Community, Supercomputing for Everyone, USA (http://forums.parallella.org/); Pico Computing, Inc., USA (http://picocomputing.com/); SemiWiki.com, The Semiconductor Wiki Project, USA (http://www.semiwiki.com/); Solarflare Communications, Inc., USA (http://www.solarflare.com/); Stream Computing, Performance Engineers, The Netherlands (http://streamcomputing.eu/); Taylor & Francis, UK (http://www.taylorandfrancis.com/); US Chapter of World Academy of Science (http://www.world-academy-of-science.org/) ; and WEBestSOL & Webest Solutions Ltd, UK (http://webestsol.com/). In addition, a number of university faculty members and their staff (names appear on the cover of the set of proceedings), several publishers of computer science and computer engineering books and journals, chapters and/or task forces of computer science associations/organizations from 5 countries, and developers of high-performance machines and systems provided significant help in organizing the conference as well as providing some resources. We are grateful to them all.

We express our gratitude to keynote, invited, and individual conference/tracks and tutorial speakers - the list of speakers appears on the conference web site. We would also like to thank the followings: UCMSS (Universal Conference Management Systems & Support, California, USA) for managing all aspects of the conference; Dr. Tim Field of APC for managing the printing of the proceedings; and the staff of the New Tropicana Hotel in Las Vegas for the professional service they provided. Last but not least, we would like to thank the Co-Editors of ICOMP'13: Prof. Hamid R. Arabnia, Prof. Victor A. Clincy, Prof. Leonidas Deligiannidis, Ashu M. G. Solo, and Prof. Fernando G. Tinetti.

We present the proceedings of ICOMP'13.

Steering Committee, 2013
http://www.world-academy-of-science.org/

Contents

SESSION: SECURITY + COMMUNICATION SYSTEMS + RECOMMENDER SYSTEMS + HIGH PERFORMANCE COMPUTING

SESSION: SOCIAL NETWORKS + BLOGS + TEXT MESSAGING SYSTEMS AND RELATED ISSUES

SESSION: POSTERS

SESSION: LATE BREAKING PAPERS: GAME TECHNOLOGIES, BIG DATA, WEB MINING, DATABASES, RESOURCE DISCOVERY AND WEB SERVICES, TIME-SERIES ANALYSIS, AND DATA WAREHOUSES

SESSION

BIG DATA: DATA MANAGEMENT AND STORAGE + SIMULATION + APPLICATIONS

Chair(s)

TBA

Creation of a Habit Model from GPS Data and Algorithms for Providing Awareness Services

Nobuo Matsuo
Graduate School of Engineering, Soka University
1-236 Tangi-cho, Hachioji-shi, 192-8577 Japan
e10m5235@soka.ac.jp

Kazumasa Takami
Graduate School of Engineering, Soka University
1-236 Tangi-cho, Hachioji-shi, 192-8577 Japan
k_takami@t.soka.ac.jp

***Abstract*—Big data including life logs, are attracting attention because of a number of recent developments: ever-increasing volume of data being generated every day due to advances in the broadband environment, increasing sophistication of mobile terminals, and growth of social networking services. If these can be fully exploited, useful added value can be created. Collecting, analyzing and managing such a huge volume of diverse data require innovative ideas and technologies. As an example of life log-based services, this paper proposes a "awareness" service, which provides a reminder for the user of a cellular phone or smartphone based on his/her particular situation (time, location, etc.) in order to encourage him/her to take a certain action. A convenient feature of life logs is that the user's location can be determined easily, even without requiring his/her conscious action, because the global positioning system (GPS) is normally installed in these mobile terminals. The algorithms for analyzing the user's GPS data to identify significant data in them, and for deriving his/her habit model from the identified data have been proposed. These algorithms have been implemented and evaluated. The awareness services have been compared with corresponding existing services, and the volume of data that can be reduced by using the habit data has been calculated.**

Keywords*—*GPS; big data; location information; a habit model: awareness service

I. Introduction

Big data are attracting attention because of a number of recent developments: ever-increasing volume of data being generated every day due to advances in the broadband environment, increasing sophistication of mobile terminals, and growth of social networking services. Big data is a huge volume of diverse and indeterminate data, such as a life log, which records the activities of an individual. Useful added value can be created if big data is fully exploited. However, big data is so big, amounting to 1.8 trillion GB in 2011, and so diverse that it is not easy to link, analyze and manage big data. Innovative ideas and technologies are required to execute these. A life log that records the entire life of a person can be as big as 3 TB, and contains wide-ranging types of data. A technology to record life log data continuously must be devised. One of the main items of a life log is location information. This information can be obtained easily because the global positioning system (GPS) is normally installed in cellular phones and smartphones, and because the information is recorded even without requiring the user's conscious action. In this paper, we have limited the scope of a life log to GPS data, and studied how to analyze, manage and utilize GPS log data.

The goal of this research is to develop a life log service for cellular phone and smartphone users. We have proposed algorithms for a awareness service, a service that analyzes the user's GPS data to identify significant data in them, derives his/her habit model from the identified data, and provides a reminder for the user based on the habit model and his/her context (time, location, etc.). These algorithms have been implemented and evaluated. The awareness services have been compared with corresponding existing services, and the volume of data that can be reduced by using the habit data has been calculated.

Section II discusses related studies. Section III outlines the habit model used in this research and the proposed awareness services. Section IV identifies the issues that need to be addressed to develop this service. Section V provides algorithms that address these issues. Section VI evaluates the proposed algorithms and the proposed service. Finally, Section VII summarizes this paper, and presents issues that need to be studied.

II. Related Work

The scope of research on life logs encompasses the collection, analysis, management and utilization of life logs. Although the collection and analysis of life logs have been studied widely [1][2], there are few studies on the management and utilization of life logs [3][4]. Some studies on the collection and analysis of GPS log data focused on identifying user locations, and developing a model that indicates transitions of user locations. For example, Ashbrook et al. determined the user's location from GPS data using the k-means clustering, and proposed to predict the his/her future movement using a Markov model by assigning a probability to each possible transition from his/her current location [5].

Nishino et al. determined the user's location using the DBSCAN clustering, accumulated data in which the transitions of locations are sorted chronologically, and applied sequential mining to the accumulated data to develop a model that indicates transitions of the locations frequented by the user [6]. Both studies determined the user's location and developed a model that indicates the transition from the determined location. They focused on the analysis of GPS data, but did not go further to study how to manage and utilize the analysis result. Neither did they consider the means and routes of movements, information that is related to transitions of the user's locations.

Our study differs from these studies in a number of respects. First, in our study, the granularity of locations is buildings (and their premises). We have not only developed a model for transitions of the user's location but also used the model for data management. Second, we consider not only the user's location and the duration of stay at a location but also other time data, such as day of the week, and the means and routes of movements, which constitute a part of the information about transitions of the user's location. Third, our study encompasses the entire scope of log data handling, from the collection to the management and utilization of log data.

III. Habit Model And Awareness Service

A. Habit model and Awareness

A habit model represents the user's behavior in the form of transitions of his/her locations. It is created by accumulating and synthesizing data on daily transitions of the user's locations. "Awareness" is meant in this paper to encourage the user to take an action that he/she is expected to take next, or to alert him or her to a certain event. Figure 1 shows a conceptual diagram of a habit model.

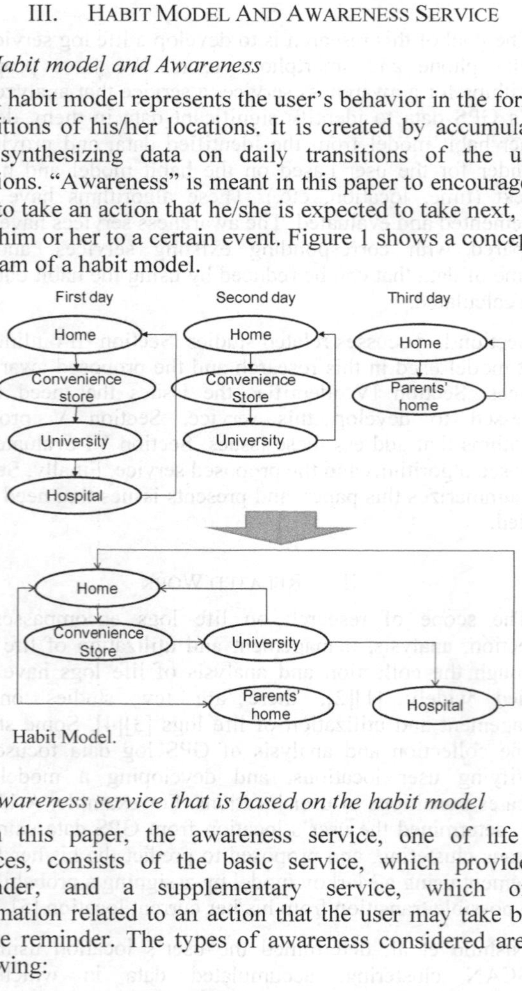

Fig. 1. Habit Model.

B. Awareness service that is based on the habit model

In this paper, the awareness service, one of life log services, consists of the basic service, which provides a reminder, and a supplementary service, which offers information related to an action that the user may take based on the reminder. The types of awareness considered are the following:

- Awareness that informs the user of the approaching departure time of the last train or bus.
- Reminder that informs the user to the approaching deadline for returning DVDs to a rental shop or books to a library.
- Awareness that informs the user of a certain event (relocation of a shop, etc.)
- Awareness that helps the user avoids daily life risk.

IV. Study Issues

The main issues that need to be addressed in developing the awareness service are as follows.

A. How to Identify Significant Information in a GPS Log

A GPS log simply contains time, latitude and longitude data. It is necessary to study how to identify significant information in a GPS log and how to obtain it.

B. How to Define and Derive a Habit Model

A habit model is used to predict the user's next action and to support him/her in taking that action. To define a habit model, it is necessary to study how information taken from a GPS log can be translated into an expression of action, and how a particular habit model can be derived. It is also necessary to study how to determine the direction of each transition from the user's location in the habit model in order to predict the user's next action.

C. How to Provide the Awareness Service Based on the Habit Model

It is necessary to study the algorithms with which the reminder service can be provided based on the derived habit model and context (time, location, etc.) of the user.

V. Solutions

A. Experiment of Collecting a GPS Log and Findings

Humans repeat the cycle of moving, staying at a location, and moving again. We have collected a GPS log experimentally focusing on this cycle, analyzed it, and gained some insight into the speeds and directions of movements. Figure 2 shows the movements of a subject before and after he stopped at New Loire (cafeteria in Soka University), as plotted on the Google earth and the Google map.

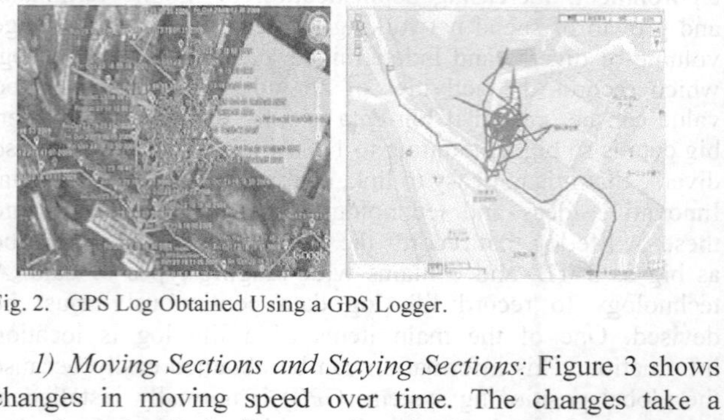

Fig. 2. GPS Log Obtained Using a GPS Logger.

1) Moving Sections and Staying Sections: Figure 3 shows changes in moving speed over time. The changes take a waveform that looks like a series of pulses. The higher levels indicate the speed in moving sections, the sections in which the subject is moving from one building to another while the lower levels indicate the speed in staying sections, the sections in which the subject stays within a building (or its premises). Naturally, the speed is higher in moving sections than in

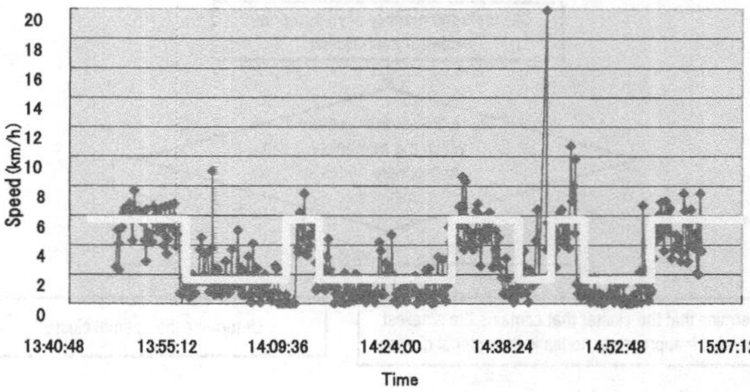

Fig. 3. Changes in moving speed over time.

2) Findings about the directions of movements: The difference in the latitude values between two points can be classified into plus, zero and minus. The difference in longitude values can also be classified in the same way. When these categories of differences in latitude and longitude values are combined, there can be 9 direction patterns as shown in Table I. Table II shows actual latitude and longitude values in both moving and staying sections recorded in the above-mentioned experiment. It can be observed that the movement directions are stable in moving sections, but unstable in staying sections.

TABLE I. CLASSIFICATION OF MOVEMENT DIRECTIONS

9 patterns of movement direction		
Pattern name	Difference in latitude value	Difference in longitude value
A	+	+
B	+	-
C	+	0
D	-	-
E	-	+
F	-	0
G	0	0
H	0	+
I	0	-

B. Algorithms for Identifying Significant Information

1) Significant Information to be Identified: Information included in a GPS log can be broadly classified into three categories:

- Temporal information (date, day of the week, time)
- Staying building information (information about the building where the user is staying, such as building location and name, duration of stay, number of stays, etc.)
- Transition-related information (means, route, time and frequency of movement)

To identify staying building information and transition-related information, it is necessary to divide items of information in a GPS log into those in moving sections and those in staying sections. Staying building information can be found in information in staying sections while transition-related information can be found in information in moving sections. The algorithm for finding staying building information is described in this paper.

TABLE II. COMPARISON OF MOVEMENT PATTERNS BETWEEN THE MOVING AND STAYING SECTIONS

Differences in latitude and longitude values in moving sections		
Difference in latitude value	Difference in longitude value	Direction pattern
0.00005720	-0.00013730	B
0.00005340	-0.00013730	B
0.00004200	-0.00016790	B
0.00005340	-0.00013730	B
0.00004950	-0.00015260	B
0.00001910	-0.00015260	B
0.00004580	-0.00015260	B
0.00003060	-0.00013730	B
0.00002290	-0.00010680	B
0.00004580	-0.00006110	B
0.00006110	-0.00009160	B

Differences in latitude and longitude values in staying sections		
Difference in latitude value	Difference in longitude value	Direction pattern
-0.00004580	0.00000000	F
0.00002290	0.00000000	A
0.00003050	0.00003060	A
0.00002670	-0.00003060	B
0.00005340	0.00007630	A
0.00006100	0.00000000	C
0.00004580	-0.00007630	B
-0.00001530	-0.00001520	D
-0.00011060	-0.00003060	D
-0.00018320	0.00016790	E
0.00003430	0.00000000	A

2) Algorithm for Determining Moving and Staying Sections: The algorithm for determining moving and staying sections has been derived based on the findings described in Section V.*A*. Figure 4 shows the proposed algorithm.

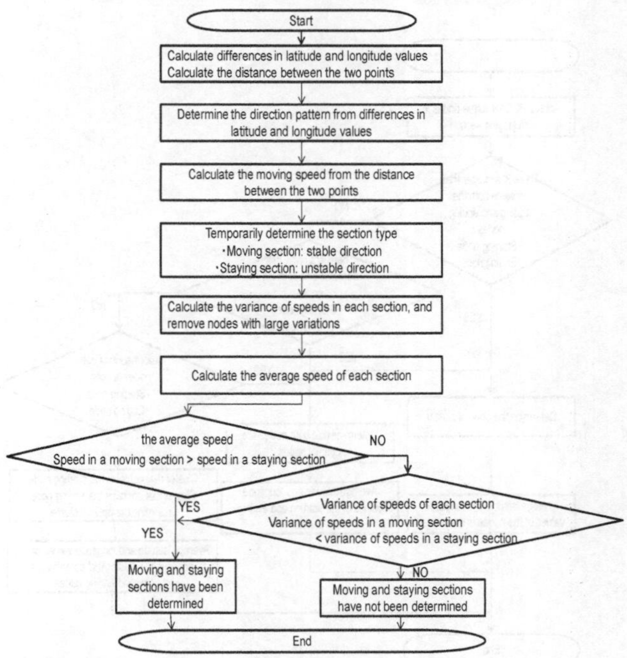

Fig. 4. Algorithm for Determining Moving and Staying Sections.

3) Algorithms for Determining the Latitude and Longitude Values of a Staying section: A staying section can contain several nodes, which are points in a building. Three alternative algorithms for selecting the optimal node whose location can be used to represent the location of the staying section are proposed below. In Alternative *A*, nodes with large errors are removed, and the average latitude and longitude values of the remaining nodes are used as the location of the section. In Alternative *B*, DBSCAN [7] is applied to the nodes to develop clusters, and the average latitude and longitude values of the nodes within the cluster that contains the nodes through which the user entered the building (starting node) and the node through which the user exited the building (ending node) are used as the location of the section. In Alternative *C*, the average latitude and longitude values of the nodes in the cluster in which the number of nodes with large errors is the smallest are used as the location of the section. These alternatives are shown in Figs. 5 to 7.

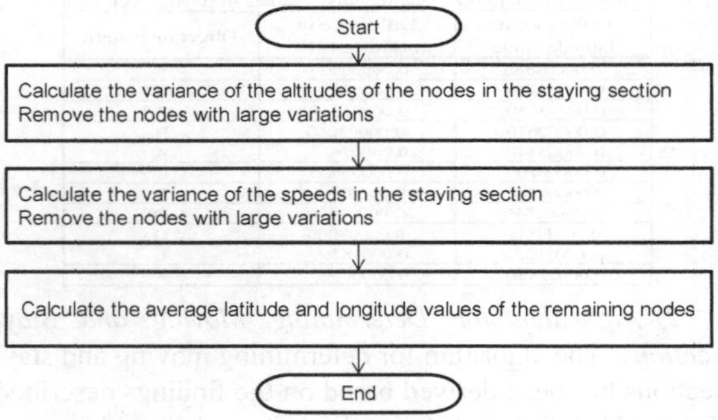

Fig. 5. Alternative A.

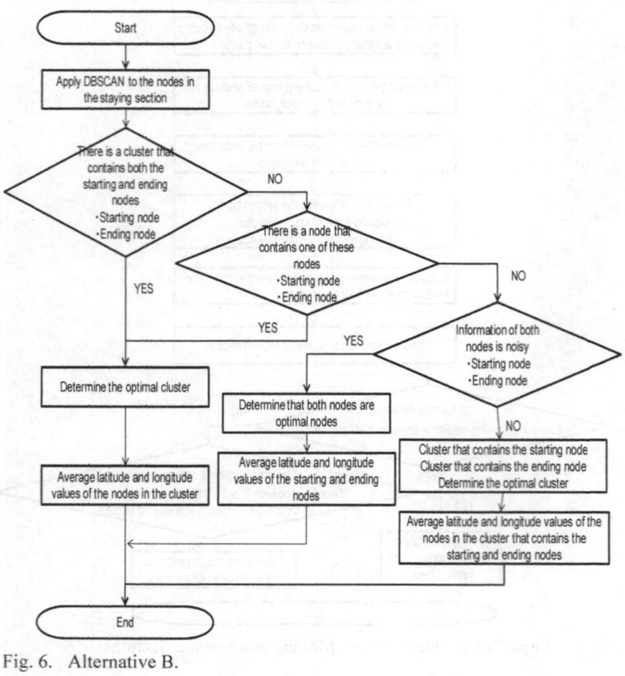

Fig. 6. Alternative B.

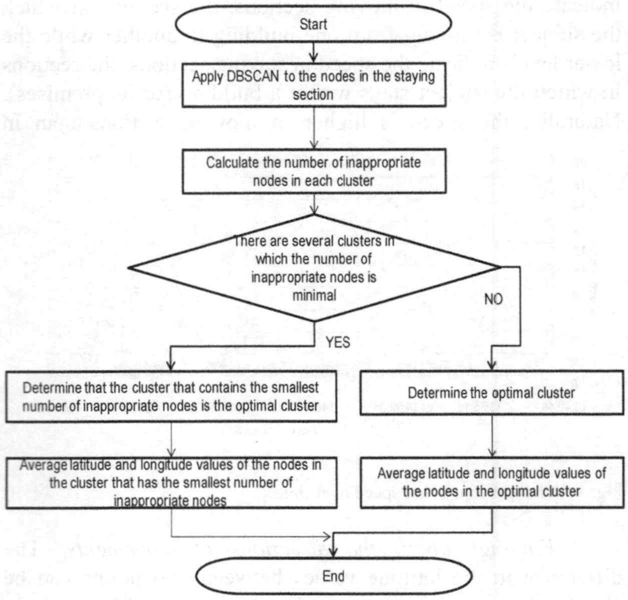

Fig. 7. Alternative C.

C. Definition of a Habit Model and Algorithm for Deriving the Habit Model

1) Definition of a Habit Model: Human behavior may be represented by transitions of his/her locations. A habit model is defined as shown in Fig. 8 based on the locations where he/she stayed and the transitions from these locations.

As shown in Fig. 8, our habit model has a hierarchical structure. The upper layer consists of the original data while the lower layer stores processed data. Information about the location of stay are classified into STATE elements. Information about movement are classified into LINK elements. The elements that influence the selection of the destination are classified into TREE elements. "Log" stores all the processed data elements. The proposed awareness service is normally provided using only the information in the upper layer but information in the lower layer may be used as necessary.

2) Definition of a Habit Model: The habit model is derived as follows. First, Log-DB is built, followed by the construction of State-DB, Link-DB, and Tree-DB. New log data to be entered in a particular database is compared with data in the database, and if there is matching data in the database, the update frequency is changed. If there is no matching data, it is entered in the database. Duration of stay, etc., are obtained by referring to data in Log-DB. The steps for constructing State-DB, Link-DB, and Tree-DB are shown in Figs. 9, 10 and 11.

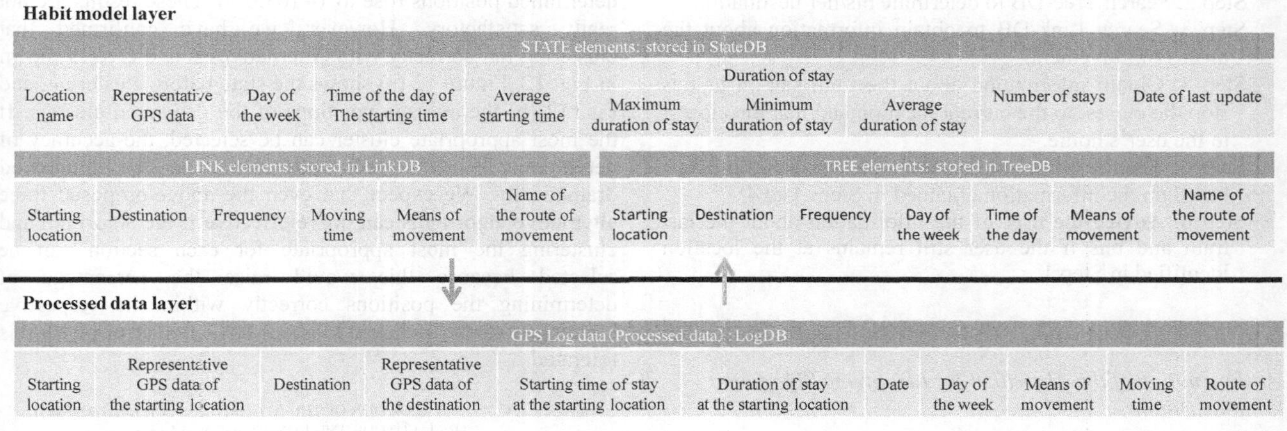

Fig. 8. Definition of a Habit Model.

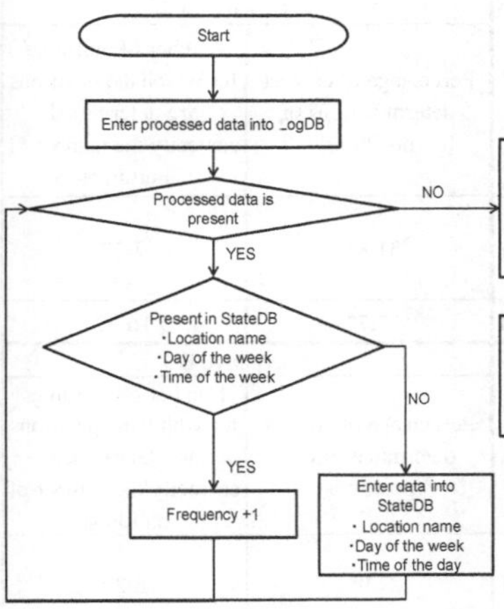

Fig. 9. Steps of constructing StateDB.

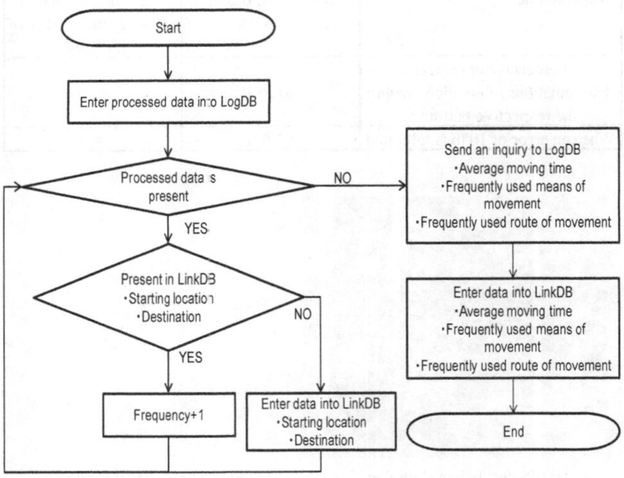

Fig. 10. Steps of constructing LinkDB.

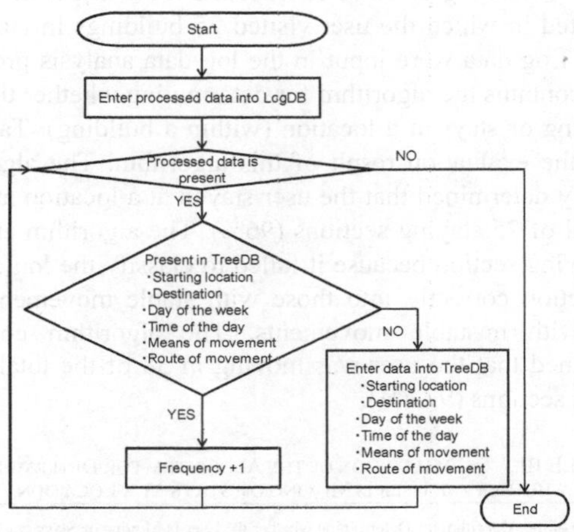

Fig. 11. Steps of constructing TreeDB.

3) Determination of Destinations in the Habit Model: Since this habit model is a transition model of locations, it resembles a state transition model. The destination of a transition can be determined based the current state of the user. In this paper, destinations are determined based on data in Tree-DB, which contains well-defined transition conditions derived from empirical data. Specifically, the next destination of the user is determined based on information about the day of the week, time of the day, means of movement available and route of movement. Data elements in Tree-DB are shown in Fig. 8. In Tree-DB, *destination* is a prediction result while *day of the week, time of the day, means of movement*, and *name of the route of movement* are transition conditions.

D. How to Provide the Awareness Service Using the Habit Model

An example of awareness services that use the habit model is the provision of the information about the last train and bus. This service is provided as follows:

Step 1: Search State-DB for information about the building in which the user stays.

Step 2: Search Tree-DB to determine his/her destination.

Step 3: Search Link-DB to obtain information about the means of movement.

Step 4: Obtain information about the train station or bus stop the closest to the current location and that the closest to the user's home.

Step 5: Obtain information about the last train and bus based on the information obtained in Steps 1 to 4.

Step 6: Advice the user of the information about the last train and bus if the user still remains at the location identified in Step 1.

VI. Evaluation

A. *Evaluation of the Algorithm for Identifying Significant Information*

1) Evaluation of the algorithm for determining whether the user is moving or stays at a location: An experiment was conducted in which the user visited 25 buildings in Hachioji, Tokyo. Log data were input in the log data analysis program, which contains the algorithm for determining whether the user is moving or stays at a location (within a building). Table III shows the evaluation result of this algorithm. The algorithm correctly determined that the user stayed at a location at 24 of the total of 25 staying sections (96%). The algorithm erred in one staying section because it failed to classify the log data of that section correctly into those with stable movements and those with unstable movements. The algorithm correctly determined that the user was moving in 38 of the total of 39 moving sections (97.4%).

TABLE III. Evaluation of the Algorithm for Determining Whether the User is Moving or Stays at a Location

Evaluation of the Algorithm for Determining whether the User is Moving or Stays at a Location		
Criteria / Evaluation Item	Percentage of correct determinations	Number of the correctly determined sections/total number of sections
Determination of staying sections	96.0%	24/25
Determination of moving sections	97.4%	38/39

2) Evaluation of the algorithms for determining the latitude and longitude values: Out of the 24 staying sections where the above algorithm correctly determined that these were staying sections, two sections in which Google map had not been updated were excluded in the evaluation of the algorithms for determining the latitude and longitude values. Table IV shows the result of the evaluation of the three alternative algorithms described in Section *V.B.3)*.

Table IV reveals the following. Out of the 22 staying sections, 7 positions determined by Alternative *A* correctly fell within the respective buildings. The percentage of correct positions was 31.8%. If an error of 10 m is tolerated, 16 positions were correctly determined (72.7%). With Alternative *B*, 6 positions were within the respective buildings (27%). If we allow an error of 10 m, the algorithm determined 14 positions correctly (63.6%). Alternative *C* determined 7 positions within the respective buildings (31.8%). With the tolerance of an error of 10 m, the number of correctly determined positions rose to 14 (63.6%). These results are not really satisfactory. However, we have confirmed that clustering ran correctly with Alternatives *B* and *C* as is shown in Fig. 12. Figure 12 (a) shows the state before clustering, and Fig. 12 (b) the average positions of the generated clusters. If the most appropriate cluster can be selected, the accuracy of determining the correct positions can be improved dramatically. We expect that even the above-proposed three alternative algorithms can prove effective if the algorithm and clustering the most appropriate for each section can be selected because this would raise the percentage of determining the positions correctly within the respective buildings to 50%, and even to about 80% if an error of 10 m is tolerated.

TABLE IV. Evaluation of the Algorithms for Determining the Latitude and Longitude Values

Evaluation of the Algorithms for Determining the Latitude and Longitude values		
	Alternative A	
Aalternative / Evaluation Item	Percentage of correct determinations of positions	Number of buildings for which the positions are determined correctly/the number of buildings
Percentage of correct determinations of positions within the respective buildings	31.8%	7/22
When an error of 10 m is tolerated	72.7%	16/22
	Alternative B	
Aalternative / Evaluation Item	Percentage of correct determinations of positions	Number of buildings for which the positions are determined correctly/the number of buildings
Percentage of correct determinations of positions within the respective buildings	27.0%	6/22
When an error of 10 m is tolerated	63.6%	14/22
	Alternative C	
Aalternative / Evaluation Item	Percentage of correct determinations of positions	Number of buildings for which the positions are determined correctly/the number of buildings
Percentage of correct determinations of positions within the respective buildings	31.8%	7/22
When an error of 10 m is tolerated	63.6%	14/22

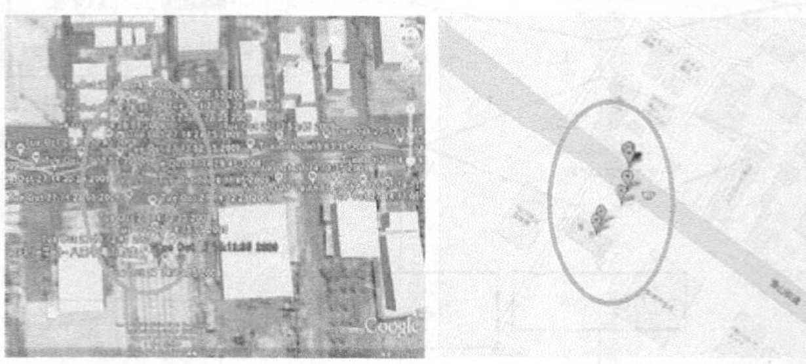

(a) GPS data before clustering (b) GPS data after clustering

Fig. 12. Result of clustering.

B. Evaluation of the Algorithm for Identifying Significant Information

1) Evaluation of the Effectiveness of the Habit Model: To evaluate how effective the proposed habit model for the awareness service is, we have compared it with two corresponding existing services shown in Table V. The functions provided by the three services are compared in Table VI.

TABLE V. FUNCTIONS PROVIDED BY CORRESPONDING EXISTING SERVICES

Name of existing service	Functions provided
i-concierge [8] automatic GPS function (last train alarm)	The user pre-registers up to three destination stations. This service informs him/her of the departure time of the last train from the nearby station to the destination station at the time when he/she can still walk to the nearby station before the departure time.
i-concierge [8] automatic GPS function (bus operation state)	The user pre-registers the bus stop he/she uses to go to work or school. This service informs him/her of the arrival time of the next bus and that of the last bus at the bus stop.

TABLE VI. COMPARISON WITH EXISTING SERVICES

	i-concierge (last train)	i-concierge (last bus)	Proposed habit model
Initialization	Needed	Needed	Not needed
Scope of service	From the current location to home	Pre-registered bus line	From the current building to home or parent's home
Provision of linked information	Information about the last train only	Information about the last bus only	It is possible to link the information about the last train to information about the last bus

To confirm that the habit model shown in Table VI is indeed more desirable than the existing services, we have implemented a part of the last train informing service. Since the habit model contains information about means of movements, it has been possible to link the information about the last train to information about the last bus.

2) Evaluation of how much the use of the habit model can reduce the volume of data that has to be managed: In using life logs, it is important to reduce their sizes as much as possible. Since the habit model manages data that have been processed from row GPS log data, the volume of data it manages is much smaller than that of the row data. The comparison of the volume of row GPS log data and the volume of data in the habit model is shown in Fig.13.

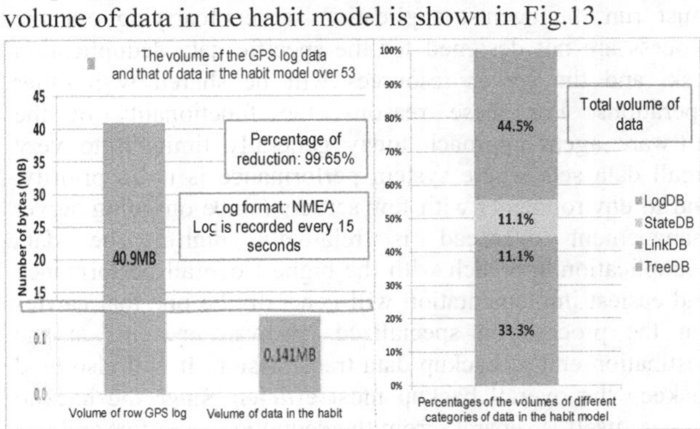

(a) Reduction in the volume of data from

(b)Percentages of the volumes of different categories of data in the habit model

Fig. 13. Reduction the Volume of Data.

Using a GPS Logger (tripmate850), we have collected GPS data every 15 seconds over 53 days from the middle of March to early April and from early September to the middle of November. The format of the collected data was that of NMEA (National Marine Electronics Association). Figure 13 (a) shows that the use of the habit model dramatically reduces the volume of data that has to be managed, from 40.9 MB of the row GPS data to 0.141 MB of the habit model -- a reduction of 99.65%. This reinforces the effectiveness of using the habit model. Figure 13 (b) shows the percentage of the size of each database in the habit model (Log-DB, State-DB, Link-DB, and Tree-DB). The largest database is Log-DB. Since it stores all processed data, its size will grow as the collection of GPS log continues. In contrast, other databases, State-DB, Link-DB, and Tree-DB, only update the same items of data. The volume of such update data tends to decrease as the collection of GPS log continues. Therefore, the proportion of Log-DB will continue to increase.

VII. CONCLUSIONS

We have identified significant information in GPS data, built a habit model from this information, and proposed a awareness service using this habit model. An experimental system for providing this service has been developed, and used to compare this service with corresponding existing services. The comparison result has confirmed the effectiveness of the habit model. The use of the habit model also reduces the volume of data that has to be managed.

The issues that need to be studied include improvement of the algorithm for identifying various types of significant information, a service that makes use of the habit models of multiple persons, and possible services that can be provided by linking not only GPS data but also other types of data in life logs.

REFERENCES

[1] Kazuya Okada, Teruaki Yokoyama, Youki Kadobayashi, and Suguru Yamaguchi , "Estimating Location Relationship from User Trajectories and its Application," pp1120-1126, DICOMO symposium 2009.7.

[2] Naoharu Yamada, Yoshinori Isoda, Masateru Minami, and Hiroyuki Morikawa, "Movement Prediction based on Route History for GPS-enabled Cellular Phones," B-15-23 IEICE General Conference 2010.3.

[3] Daisuke Kamisaka, Takeshi Iwamoto, and Hiroyuki Yokoyama, "Estimation Method of Homes and Offices from Location Data Obtained by Mobile Phones, " B-20-29 IEICE General Conference 2010.3.

[4] Manabu Motegi, Hirohisa Tezuka, Yukihiro Nakamura, Shin-ichiro Eitoku, Shun-ichi Seko, Masaaki Nishino, Shin-yo Muto, and Masanobu Abe, "Field Trial of the System using Life Logs," D-9-12 IEICE General Conference 2010.3 .

[5] Ashbrook D and Starner T, "Using GPS to learn significant locations and predict movement across multiple users," Personal and Ubiquitous Computing, Vol.7, NO.5, pp.275-286, 2003.

[6] Nishino Masaaki, Shunichi Seko, Masakatsu Aoki, Tomohiro Yamada, Shinyo Muto, and Masanobu Abe, "A Study on Extracting Movement Patterns from Transition Data," IPSJ SIG Technical Report UBI 2008(110),pp.57-64,2008.11.

[7] Martin Ester, Hans-Peter Kriegel, Jörg Sander, and Xiaowei Xu, "A density-based algorithm for discovering clusters in large spatial databases with noise, " KDD'96,1996.

[8] i-concierge, http://www.nttdocomo.co.jp/service/customize/iconcier/, (2013/3/10)

Data De-duplication in Storage Management

R. Dornala[1], **K. Akingbehin**[2], **D. Yoon**[2]
[1]Healthfirst, New York, NY, USA
[2]CIS Department, University of Michigan – Dearborn, Dearborn, MI, USA

***Abstract** - In many large organizations, the huge amount of data is generated beyond their imagination and companies need to invest a great deal of money in securing and retaining the data. Most of the time, the data is repeatedly written into several different locations and causing the system administrators and management a hard time to restore the data during the disaster. The backup timing window is increasing daily with the new amount of data being added to the system. The same documents are copied at various locations on the network with big data coming at big storage costs. One way to store less is simply not to store the same data twice. In this background, there has been lot of research effort in deduplication.*

In this paper, the various methods of deduplication will be discussed in details and their merits behind each method. Also the techniques and algorithms will be presented with explanations. Deduplication is one of the fastest emerging trends in reducing the backup data. The Data duplication systems detect redundancies between data blocks to either reduce storage needs or to reduce network traffic. A class of deduplication systems splits the data stream into data blocks or chunks and then finds exact duplicates of these blocks. Data Duplication is the process of eliminating duplicate copies of data. With current deduplication technologies, it is possible to reduce the storage requirements by up to 20:1, depending on your data, which saves both money and disk write overheads.

Keywords: Clouds, deduplication Fundatmentals, deduplication approaches

1 Introduction

Data deduplication refers to the removal of what is technically known as redundant data [1]. As part of the deduplication process, duplicate or repeated data is deleted and only one copy of the relevant data remains stored. However, deduplication never removes the vital indexing of all data in order that it can be retrieved should it be required.

Deduplication is a task of detecting record replicas in a data repository that refer to the same real world entity or object and systematically substitutes the reference pointers for the redundant blocks; also known as storage capacity optimization.

Data deduplication reduces the required storage capacity since only unique data is stored. This significantly improves the run times and performance capabilities of various pieces of software, storage systems and computers. Essentially, with data deduplication, only one instance of any piece of any given data is retained so that the user has more free space to work with.

There are many benefits of data deduplication including reducing start-up infrastructure costs, power, physical space, and even cooling measures. When it comes to putting the theory of deduplication into practice, there are typically two different methods of deduplication to choose from; 'Source Deduplication' and 'Target Deduplication'.

2 Data deduplication architecture

The data deduplication operation certainly introduces some amount of overhead and often involves multiple processes at the solution level, including compression. This means that the choice of where and how deduplication is carried out (over LAN or WAN) can affect the speed of a backup process. The deduplication process can be applied to data in a stream (during inline) or to data at rest on disk (post-processing). It can also occur at the target side of a backup operation or at the source side.

Wherever the data deduplication is carried out, just as in the case of processes like compression or encryption, the fastest performance will in most cases be attained from purpose-built systems optimized for the specific process. An alternative approach that uses software agents running on general purpose operating platforms can also carry out deduplication but it has some its own shortcomings.

All operations are software based; all protected servers must run the agents, application servers carrying out the process are not designed for the specific data deduplication task, and the server resources will be shared with other operations. For these reasons, the functionality of the software agent approach today generally limits it to very small data sets where system performance is not a priority, and to environments with few servers (since on-going server management overhead is relatively high). The data deduplication approach with the highest overall performance and easiest implementation will generally be one that carries out the process on specialized hardware systems at the destination end of backup data transmission. It will also tend to keep the overall backup most efficient since the backup process itself is separate from the deduplication effort and can operate at high efficiencies with any backup software package.

Deduplication uses a hashing algorithm to compare data. A Signature Generation Module computes the hashed signature for each object/block and then compares it with the existing signatures maintained in the Deduplication Store to determine whether it is identical. Based on the comparison for duplicated data, it performs one of the following operations:

- If the signature is unique, the data is stored and an entry added to the deduplication store for subsequent comparisons.
- If the signature is identical to an existing signature, additional entries are created in the deduplication store with pointers to the existing storage.

3 Data deduplication methods

Data deduplication can generally operate at the file, block or byte level thus defining minimal data fragment that is checked by the system for redundancy. Hash algorithm generates a unique identifier and hash number – for each analyzed chunk of data. It is then stored in an index and used out duplicates – the duplicated fragments will have the same hash numbers.

Theoretically, the more detailed analysis is, the higher deduplication rate of storage should be obtained. In actual practice, all three levels have their peculiarities. The file-level deduplication can be performed most easily. It requires less processing power since files' hash numbers are relatively easy to generate. However, there is the reverse side of a medal: if only one-byte of a file is changed, its hash number also changes. As a result both file versions will be saved to storage.

When deduplication operates at the block level, every file is split into multiple block-sequences of fixed or variable length. If we make minor changes to a large file, the system will only store its changed fragments. In average, file deduplication allows disk space savings as high as 5:1, while block deduplication performs the deduplication rate at the level of 20:1

Block deduplication requires more processing power than the file deduplication, since the number of identifiers that need to be processed increases greatly. Correspondingly, its index for tracking the individual iterations gets also much larger. Using of variable length blocks is even more source-intensive. Moreover, sometimes the same hash number may be generated for two different data fragments, which is called hash collisions. If that happens, the system will not save the new data as it sees that the hash number already exists in the index.

Some vendors use variable block sizes that can be specified according to environment requirements – 4 or 256 Kb or any other. A larger block size requires fewer resources, but sometimes provides less compression. A smaller one provides better compression, but requires more resources. Byte-level deduplication doesn't need additional processing – in this case data chunks are compared in the most primitive way – byte by byte. It performs checks for redundant fragments even more accurately. Byte-level deduplication takes quite much time and as a rule is applied to in post-process deduplication.

4 Data deduplication fundamentals

Deduplication is similar to data compression, but it looks for redundancy of large sequences of bytes. Sequences of bytes identical to those previously encountered and stored are replaced with smaller references to the previously encountered data. This is all hidden from users and applications. When the data is read, the original data is provided to the application or user.

Deduplication performance is dependent on the amount of data, bandwidth, disk speed, CPU, and memory or the hosts and devices performing the deduplication.

4.1 Hashes and fingerprints

Deduplication typically uses hashing algorithms. Hashing algorithms [2] yield a unique value based on the content of the data being hashed. This value is called the hash or fingerprint, and is much smaller in size than the original data being deduplicated. Since different data contents yield different hashes, each hash can be checked against previously stored hashes.

4.2 File-Based deduplication

In file-based deduplication only the original instance of a file is stored. Future identical copies of the file use a small reference to point to the original file content. File-based deduplication is sometimes called single-instance store (SIS).

In this example four files are being deduplicated. Files A and C are identical, but each has its own copy of the file content. Files B and D also have their own copy of identical content. After deduplication there are still four files. Files A and C point to the same content which is stored only once on disk. This is similar for files B and D. If each file is 20 megabytes, the file-based deduplication has reduced the storage required from 80 megabytes to 40.

4.3 Variable-length segment deduplication

Variable-length segment deduplication evaluates data by examining its contents to look for the boundary from one segment to the next. Variable-length segments are any number of bytes within a range determined by the particular algorithm implemented.

4.4 Effect of change in deduplication storage pools

When a dataset is processed for the first time by a data deduplication system, the number of repeated data segments within it varies widely depending on the nature of the data (this includes both the types of files and the applications used to create them). The effect can range from negligible benefit to a gain of 50% or more in storage efficiency. However when multiple similar datasets are written to a common deduplication pool—such as a sequence of backup images from a specific disk volume—the benefit is typically very significant because each new write operation only increases the size of the total pool by the number of new data segments that it introduces. In data sets representing conventional business operations, it is common to have a data segment-level difference between two backup events of only 1% or 2% although higher change rates are also seen frequently. [4]

The number of new data segments introduced in any given backup event will depend on the data type, the rate of change between backups, and the amount of data growth from one backup job to the next. The total number of data segments stored over multiple backup events also depends to a very great extent on the retention policies set by the user—the number of backup jobs and length of time they are held on disk. The difference between the amount of space that would be required to store the total number of backup datasets in a conventional disk storage system and the capacity used by the deduplication system is referred to as the deduplication ratio.

The below formula used to derive the data deduplication ratio, and Figure 3 shows the ratio for four different backup datasets with different overall compressibility and different change rates. Figure 3 also shows the number of backup events required to reach the 20:1 deduplication ratio widely used in the industry as a working average for a variable-length data segment-based data reduction system. In each case, for simplicity we are assuming a full backup of all the primary data for each backup event. With either a daily full model or a weekly full/daily incremental model, the size of the deduplicated storage pool would be identical since only new data segments are added during each backup event under either model. The deduplication ratio would differ, however, since the space that would have been required for a non deduplicated disk storage system would have been much greater in a daily full model—in other words the storage advantage is greater in a full backup methodology even though the amount of data stored remains essentially the same.

$$\text{Deduplication Ratio} = \frac{\text{Total Data before Reduction}}{\text{Total Data after Reduction}}$$

What is clear from the examples is that deduplication has the most powerful effects when it is used for backing up data sets with low or modest change rates between backup events, but even for data sets with high rates of change the advantage can be significant. [5]

5 Data deduplication approaches

Despite of less expensive ATA/SATA disk drives, one of the biggest challenges for enterprise storage systems today continues to be the storage cost. The purpose of deduplication is to:

- Increase the amount of information that can be stored on disk arrays
- Increase the effective amount of data that can be transmitted over Networks

The data de-duplication operation inevitably introduces some amount of overhead and often involves multiple processes at the solution level, including compression. This means that the choice of where and how de-duplication is carried out can affect the speed of a backup process.

The de-duplication process can be applied to data in a stream (during ingest) or to data at rest on disk (post processing). The approach is:

- **In-band**: deduplicate the data as they're writing it to the array or VTL
- **Out-of-band**: deduplication is a secondary process that may run asynchronously

There are advantages and disadvantages to each method. An important differentiator among deduplication products is whether they work in-band or out-of-band. The advantage to the in-band method is that it works with the data only one time. The drawback is that, depending on the implementation, it could slow down the incoming backup. The out-of-band method has to write the original data, read it, identify its redundancies, and then write one or more pointers if it's redundant. The advantage to this is that you can apply more parallel processes (and processors) to the problem, whereas the in-band method can apply only one process per backup stream. The disadvantage is that the data is written and read more than once, multiple reads and writes. If the question is how fast we can get our data onto the box then post-processing deduplication is preferred.

5.1 Deduplication practices – selecting the right deduplication technologies

In this section, we will focus on choosing the right deduplication technology for your data backup and recovery needs. This section also discusses and compares the technologies such as source vs. target deduplication, inline vs. post-processing deduplication, and the pros and cons of global deduplication.

5.1.1 Source deduplication vs. target deduplication

All the deduplication vendors adopt either the source or target deduplication technologies. The below picture depicts how the compression occurs in source and target deduplication techniques. In target deduplication, you're using the same backup software you already have, but you are sending the data to a target, which will then deduplicate it. This deduplication technology is best for large-scale data centers. With source deduplication, you have to use different backup software that deduplicates at the source. It reduces the IP load from the very beginning, and is best suited for remote offices and branch offices.

5.1.2 Source deduplication

Source deduplication is the removal of redundancies from data before transmission to the backup target. Source deduplication products offer a number of benefits, including reduced bandwidth and storage usage. No additional hardware is required to back up to a remote site and many source deduplication products also support automation for offsite copies. On the other hand, the source-based method can be slower than target deduplication, especially for large (multiple terabyte) amounts of data. Because of the increased workload on servers, overall backup times may increase

Source deduplication works through client software that communicates with the backup server to compare new blocks of data with previously stored blocks of data. If the server has previously stored a block of data, the software does not send that block and instead notes that there is a copy of that block of data at that client. If a previous version of a file has already been backed up, the software will compare files and back up any parts of the file it hasn't seen. Source deduplication is well suited for backing up smaller remote backup sets.

5.1.3 Target deduplication

Target deduplication is the removal of redundancies from a backup transmission as it passes through an appliance sitting between the source and the backup target. The method allows you to use any backup software that the device supports. Target deduplication reduces the amount of storage required but, unlike source deduplication, it does not reduce the amount of data that must be sent across a LAN or WAN during the backup. [6]

Target deduplication requires hardware at remote sites, which is sometimes considered a major disadvantage in comparison to source deduplication products. Since, it provides faster performance for large data sets; it is most widely used in most of the companies with larger datasets and less bandwidth constraints.

5.1.4 Inline deduplication vs. post-processing deduplication

Another technology (Inline or post-process) is to consider when the data is deduplicated.

- **Inline deduplication**

With inline deduplication (also called real-time deduplication), all deduplication happens between the RAM and the processor. The data is analyzed and deduplicated before writing new data to disk. If it is new data it is written to disk. If it is data that has been previously stored then a pointer is written to disk. Hashes and hash tables are often used to identify previously stored data. The advantage with this method is that no extra space is required. Another advantage is that once the data is deduplicated and stored, the process is done, and backup data may be replicated to offsite storage. With post-processing deduplication, data must be written to storage, then deduplicated at a later time, and then replicated to offsite storage. As a result, the time to complete the entire backup process – including replicating to offsite systems – can be longer than systems that deduplicate inline. Like source deduplication, it increased the CPU load. [7]
Inline deduplication requires less disk space than post-process deduplication. There's less administration for an inline deduplication process, as the administrator does not need to define and monitor the staging space.

- **Post-Process deduplication**

In post-process deduplication, files are first written to disk in their entirety (they are buffered to a large cache). Once the files are written, the hard drive is scanned for duplicates and compressed. In other words, with post-process deduplication, deduplication happens after the files are written to disk.

For backup/storage administrators looking minimize the time it takes to back up their data, the best option is often to use a post-process method. This has the advantage of backing up data faster, reducing the backup window. The disadvantage of this method is that additional storage space is consumed. Backup data is sent to a temporary holding area in order to speed the backup process. Once that completes, the data is reexamined for duplicates, with duplicate data removed (some post systems start deduplicate the data before the whole backup is complete, so they may not require as much storage on the target).

6 A comparison of data deduplication products

Storage budgets are suffering the current economic climate, but that doesn't mean storage spending is on hold. The bonus is now on doing more with less, and one key technology that can help is data deduplication.
It's a technology that has matured over the past year, and investing in it can bring huge savings. By reducing the amount of data that needs to be backed up and stored by 20:1 and more, data deduplication can save on bandwidth and storage media. It can also allow for a massive increase in the efficiency of data restores by allowing backups to be retained on disk for far longer [8].

But there are a large number of deduplication products on the market [11], with many key differences. Things to consider during the procurement stage include whether to choose a hardware or software data deduplication product; should deduplication be part of a virtual tape library (VTL) or a NAS subsystem; does it use in-line or post-process features; is deduplication done at the source or target; and should you use SHA-1 or MD5 as your data redundancy elimination algorithm.

7 Conclusions

Data deduplication is a new trend of storage technology and has a prospect for wide applications in primary storage systems and archiving storage systems. The trend is from fixed length blocks to intelligent variable-length blocks, from traditional hash algorithms to faster hash algorithms with fewer collisions, and from static hash lookup to dynamic distributed hash lookup. In this report, by using the simulator tool, an analysis is done to predict the compressed data against the original data. An analysis has been done for the various deduplication methods and algorithms. The EMC Data domain results also show the compression statistics. In the report, a detailed analysis has been done for the VTL and NAS as storage units for the deduplication. As it was evident with the above analysis, the deduplication has lot of future and it is one of the fastest emerging trends in IT.

Data deduplication is an important new technology that is quickly being embraced by users as they struggle with issues of data proliferation. By eliminating redundant data blocks, an immediate benefit is obtained through space and cost efficiencies. When choosing a deduplication product, however, it is important to consider all aspects of design, including space savings efficiency, performance overhead, and resiliency against failure. As described, Data deduplication is a hot topic in storage and saves significant disk space for many environments, with some trade-offs.
As stated above, the future lies in data deduplication. This will be the enabler for cloud storage. It makes it practical to deploy cloud storage because the data being sent will be 10x less data over the WAN. This will have significant implications for deploying cloud-based data sets.

8 References

[1] Y. Won ,R. Kim, J. Ban, J.Hur, “Prun: Eliminating Information Redundancy for Large Scale Data Backup System”, Proc. IEEE Int’l Conf. Computational Sciences and its applications,2008.

[2] Jaehong Min, Daeyoung Yoon, and Youjip Won, “Efficient Deduplication Techniques for Modern Backup Operation,” IEEE Transactions On Computers, Vol. 60, No.6, June 2011.

[3] EMC Data Domain Training Manuals-Data Domain Training Class, Retrieved from <https://my.datadomain.com>.

[4] Mark R 4 Coppock, Steve Whitner, “Data Deduplication For Dummies, Quantum Special Edition”.

[5] Data Deduplication Background: A Technical White Paper." - *Datamation*., 19 Jan. 2010. <http://www.datamation.com/white_papers/article.php/387300/Data-Deduplication-Background-A-Technical-White-Paper.htm>.

[6] Margaret Rouse, Aug 2010. What is target deduplication? Search Databackup, Retrieved from. http://searchdatabackup.techtarget.com/definition/target-deduplication.

[7] Wendt, Jerome. "Inline vs. Post-processing Deduplication Appliances." *Inline vs. Post-processing Deduplication Appliances*. N.p., n.d. Web. 04 Oct. 2012.
http://searchdatabackup.techtarget.com/tip/Inline-vs-post-processing-deduplication-appliances.

[8] Adshead, Antony. "A Comparison of Data Deduplication Products." *A Comparison of Data Deduplication Products*. N.p., 28 Jan. 2009. http://www.computerweekly.com/news/1346197/A-comparison-of-data-deduplication-products

[9] Storage Engineering Team. “*Data Deduplication and Its benefits” Mindteck*, 9 Sep. 2009. < http://archive.ciol.com/resources/UserFiles/Technology/DataDe-duplication-Whitepaper.pdf

[10] Taylor, Steve, and Jim Metzier. "How WAN Deduplication Can Aid WAN Acceleration." *Network world*. N.p., 28 Aug. 2008. Web. 04 Oct. 2012. http://www.networkworld.com/newsletters/2008/082508wan2.html.

[11] R. Dornala, “Data De-deduplication in Storage Management and Benefits to Industry,” MS-CIS project, University of Michigan – Dearborn, 2012.

ACRE: A Method for Supporting Strong Consistency and Adaptivity in Replicated Data Storage

Scott J. Denman and Kyoung-Don Kang
Department of Computer Science
State University of New York at Binghamton
{sdenman1, kang}@binghamton.edu

Abstract

As most key-value stores partition and replicate data to support high availability with no strong consistency guarantee among replicas, users may suffer from data inconsistency. Although previous research has been done to support strong consistency among replicated data, most existing approaches suffer from potential hotspots and load imbalance. Neither do they consider dynamic data access patterns that may largely vary over time. In this paper, we propose a new approach, called ACRE (Adaptive Chain REplication), to support strong consistency among data replicas, hotspot avoidance and load balancing, and adaptivity to dynamic data access patterns.

1 Introduction

Replicated data stores are a fundamental building block for advanced online applications such as scientific computing and social networking. In these systems, data are partitioned and replicated multiple times to manage vast amounts of data in a highly available manner [5]. However, the CAP theorem [1] states that it is impossible for replicated data stores to support strong data consistency, availability, and tolerance to network partitions simultaneously. Thus, to support the high availability of service, a number of key-value stores, such as the ones used at Google [3] and Amazon [2], only support eventual consistency, providing no strong consistency among replicas. As a result, users of online applications may suffer from a nuisance or even inconsistent results. Also, developing advanced applications without strong data consistency support is cumbersome and time consuming.

A novel method called chain replication [7] has been developed to support strong consistency, while improving the availability and throughput of fail-stop storage servers. In chain replication, all nodes storing shared data objects are organized as a chain. The head node in a chain handles all write requests, while the tail processes all read requests. Writes are propagated down from the head to the tail of the chain of replicated data stores before acknowledging the client. Thus, total ordering among the versions of a data item in the chain is supported. Also, strong consistency is supported with respect to the version of the data that is successfully written (i.e., committed) at the tail. As the chain replication method is simple and lacks multi-round protocols, it supports consistency, high availability, and easy recovery. However, all read requests for a data object must be processed at the tail. Thus, the tail may become a hot spot and performance bottleneck.

CRAQ (Chain Replication with Apportioned Queries) [6] extends the chain replication method [7] to support strong consistency as well as lower latency and higher throughput for *read* requests. In CRAQ, not only the tail but any node in a chain can process reads. When a write commits at the tail, an acknowledgment (ACK) for the committed version of the data object is passed backwards, ultimately reaching the head. The head and intermediate nodes, if any, process read requests using the latest version acknowledged by the tail. If the head or an intermediate node receives a read request for a dirty version awaiting an ACK, it simply waits for the ACK or sends a version query to the tail that returns the latest version number. In this way, CRAQ enhances the read throughput, while supporting strong consistency with respect to the tail. However, CRAQ has a drawback too. A node has to query the tail first, if it wants to process a read request without waiting for the ACK. Thus, the tail may be flooded by excessive version queries and become a bottleneck especially in the presence of write-heavy workloads.

Although chain replication and CRAQ support strong consistency with acceptable throughput and availability, neither of them is effective enough to deal with *dynamic data access patterns*. This can be a serious problem, because it is known that data access patterns often vary largely over time [4]. Hence, optimizing a replication scheme for a specific data access pattern may result in undesirable performance and resource waste, while not necessarily enhancing the availability.

To shed light on this problem, we propose a new approach called ACRE (Adaptive Chain REplication). In ACRE, any node can process a read request by returning the latest acknowledged version, similar to CRAQ [6]. However, ACRE is different from chain replication and CRAQ; *ACRE autonomously adapts chain replication based on the dynamic data access patterns* that can be observed in the life cycle of data, such as new scientific data or news articles read a lot when created and gradually become dormant, while supporting *strong consistency.* More specifically, ACRE extends an existing chain by adding another node to the chain to process read requests efficiently, if the frequency of read requests increases significantly, for example, due to the increased popularity of the data.

On the other hand, if write requests dominate and read requests shrink, we shorten the chain by removing a node from the chain as long as the required minimum chain length, i.e., the number of the replicated data stores in the chain, for fault tolerance is maintained. In this way, the total number of cascading writes from the head to the tail along the chain can be decreased without affecting the required level of fault tolerance. Also, the wait time for the ACK of a write request and the frequency of version queries sent to the tail decrease. Thus, ACRE enhances not only the read performance but also the cost-effectiveness of strong consistency as well as fault tolerance considering dynamic data access patterns.

In addition, ACRE naturally supports *load balancing among the chained storage nodes.* Because any node can process reads, it is less likely for the tail to become a bottleneck. For load balancing, read requests can be evenly distributed (in an approximate sense) to the chained nodes via, for example, random distribution of reads to the nodes. Also, a write is performed by every node in the chain to support strong consistency and fault tolerance. Relatively little prior work has been done to support flexible data replication with strong consistency as well as adaptivity to dynamic data access patterns, while supporting hotspot avoidance and load balancing [7, 6, 5].

For performance evaluation, we have implemented ACRE and CRAQ and evaluated them using synthetic read/write workloads, similar to [6]. Our initial results show that ACRE decreases the average delay for data access by approximately 30 - 50% compared to the service delay provided by CRAQ by dynamically adapting the replication chain considering different data access patterns.

The remainder of this paper is organized as follows. A description of ACRE is given in Section 2. Performance evaluation results are presented in Section 3. Related work is discussed in Section 4. Finally, Section 5 concludes the paper and discusses future work.

2 Adaptive Chain Replication

In this section, the design and implementation issues of ACRE are discussed in sequence.

2.1 Design of ACRE

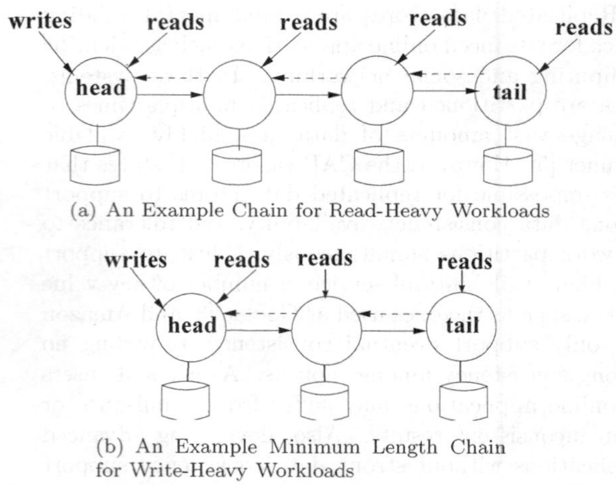

Figure 1. Adaptive Chain Replication

In ACRE, any node can process read requests as shown in Figure 1. The solid horizontal lines in Figure 1 indicate a write request performed in a cascading manner, while a dotted line represent an ACK packet carrying the version information that acknowledges a successful write of a data item at the tail. The head or an intermediate node (that is neither the head nor the tail of a chain) has to either wait for the corresponding ACK from the tail or send the tail a version query, if it receives a read request for a dirty data object. For a read request, a node in ACRE returns the latest acknowledged version.

The key advantage that sets ACRE apart from the existing approaches is the *flexibility* and *adaptation* to dynamic changes in data access patterns. In ACRE, if the frequency of read requests increases by a certain threshold, a chain is *expanded*. For example, assume that a chain initially consists of 3 nodes, but extends to 4 nodes as shown in Figure 1(a). To extend a chain, ACRE performs the following procedure:

1. ACRE appends a new node to the current tail, if necessary, to extend the chain considering dynamic data access patterns.

2. ACRE requires the current tail to forward the most up-to-date versions of the data, S, to the new node. Let t_1 indicate the time at which the tail starts sending S to the new node.

3. The new node writes S to its storage. While the new node is doing the writes, the current tail continues to work as the tail of the chain.

4. Once the new node finishes all writes, the new node announces itself as the new tail to all the other nodes in the chain via a reliable multicast. When the current tail receives the announcement at time t_2, it stops working as the tail and becomes the previous tail.

5. If some data ΔS have been written by the previous tail between t_1 and t_2, the previous tail forwards ΔS to the new tail, which treats ΔS as regular data writes to its storage and acknowledges the other nodes after finishing the writes.

ACRE repeats this process, if necessary, to support acceptable read performance, while supporting the increased availability as data become more popular. As a result, the throughput and availability of data enhance as more replicas are created for more read requests. In this paper, a node failure is handled in a similar manner to the original chain replication protocol [7].

On the other hand, the chain is *shortened* as shown in Figure 1(b), if the data access pattern becomes write-heavy. We take this approach, because a long chain is subject to large delays and overheads for write-heavy workloads, providing little opportunities to improve the performance by processing many reads in parallel. Specifically, ACRE *cuts the tail*, if necessary, to efficiently handle increasing writes. Notably, removing the tail from the chain is the simplest and fastest way to shorten a chain, since the the data stored by all the other nodes are at least as fresh as the tail's. Thus, we avoid overheads for maintaining data consistency among the nodes by cutting the tail. The leaving tail only has to process pending version queries, if any, and then announce its departure, while declaring its predecessor as the new tail to the other nodes in the chain. ACRE repeats the tail cutting process as writes become more frequent until the chain cannot be shortened any further to maintain the minimum specified number of replicas as shown in Figure 1(b). For example, the Google File System maintains three replicas for each data object by default [3].

In ACRE, adaptation is performed by adding or removing a node at the end of the chain for coordinated control with little overhead. Depending on read/write workloads, a node can be removed from and added back to the tail later; however, the newly added node only needs the latest versions acknowledged by the current tail. When a new node is added to the tail, the current tail continues to serve the data requests, while sending the latest data to the new tail in the background to minimize the impact on the performance.

2.2 Chain Adaptation

In this paper, we assume that clients are given the list of the data stores currently in the chain. In the specific implementation of ACRE evaluated in Section 3, the head node disseminates the list whenever it is updated. Also, a client submits a read request to a (pseudo) randomly selected data store for load balancing purposes, while always submitting a write request to the head node. In addition, ACRE has a number of tunable parameters, such as the chain adaptation threshold that triggers the chain to adapt to the data access pattern. One metric, two thresholds, and two constraints used for adaptation in ACRE are described in this subsection.

For performance enhancement via adaptation, we use the *read ratio* metric that measures the ratio of read requests to writes tracked at each node in the chain. This ratio is updated following every request reception at a given node. It should be emphasized that the scope of the ratio is limited to a single node but all writes to the chain will eventually touch each node in the chain. (However, this is not true for read requests). Using the read ratio measured at each node, the chain is adapted by ACRE, if all the following thresholds are exceeded and the constraints are met.

- *Extend threshold:* This is the upper bound used to determine when the chain will benefit from adding a new node. When the read ratio exceeds this threshold at any node that individual node sends the tail a request to extend the chain (provided the following adaptation constraints 1 and 2 are met).
- *Reduce threshold:* This is the lower bound used to determine when the chain will benefit from cutting the tail. When the reduce threshold exceeds the read ratio at a node, the node sends the tail a request to shorten the chain (provided the following two constraints are met).

In addition to defining the read ratio and the thresholds for adaptation, we allow adaptation only if the following two constraints are met to support *hysteresis* and avoid potential oscillations.

- *Constraint 1. Minimum request bound:* The minimum request bound imposes a lower limit on the number of requests a node has processed before allowing a chain adaptation request to be sent. This bound allows ACRE to avoid too frequent adaptation, which can result in oscillatory and unstable system behaviors.
- *Constraint 2. Minimum adaptation gap:* The minimum adaptation gap imposes a minimum wait time between two consecutive adaptation requests processed by the chain. This allows time for the previous request to take effect prior to requesting a similar adaptation. As any adaptation happens at the tail, the tail tracks the amount of time since the last adaptation. No additional adaptation will be allowed until this minimum amount of time has passed.

We observe that it is possible for the nodes in the chain may make conflicting requests for chain adaptation in an extreme case. For example, one node may request ACRE to extend the chain, while another node may request ACRE to shorten the chain

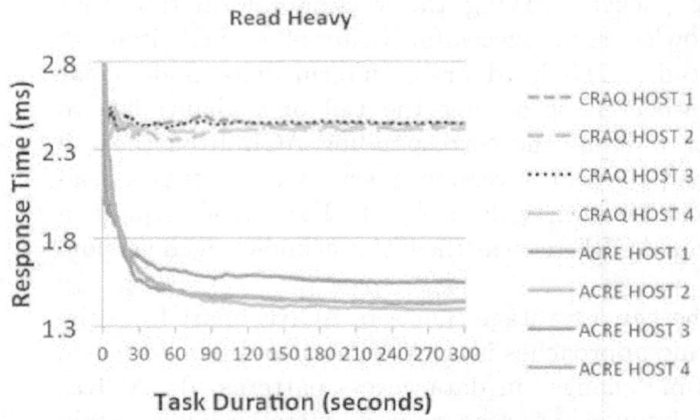

Figure 2. Response Time for Test 1

when the read load is largely imbalanced among the nodes in the chain. To address this problem, every adaptation request is sent to the tail that makes a final decision and actually adapts the chain, if necessary, to decrease the data access delay. In this paper, the tail makes a decision for adaptation based on the read ratio measured by itself, if two or more nodes send conflicting adaptation requests to the tail and the two constraints are satisfied. We take this approach, because the tail is aware of the progress of all writes and receives a roughly fair share of read requests, since clients randomly distribute read/write requests to the nodes for load balancing purposes in this paper.

3 Performance Evaluation

In this section, we implement ACRE and CRAQ using TCP/IP and evaluate their performance. We describe our experimental settings for synthetic workload generation followed by the performance results.

3.1 Experimental Settings

In this paper, we aim to evaluate CRAQ and ACRE for different synthetic read/write workloads, similar to [6]. More specifically, three tests are performed for workloads that model read-heavy, write-heavy, and mixed request streams, respectively.

- *Test 1:* In this test, data are initially written once but only read later on. Hence, the read to write ratio approaches infinity to model a read-heavy workload.
- *Test 2:* In this test, data are initially read but only written later on. Thus, the read to write ratio approaches zero, modeling a write-heavy workload.

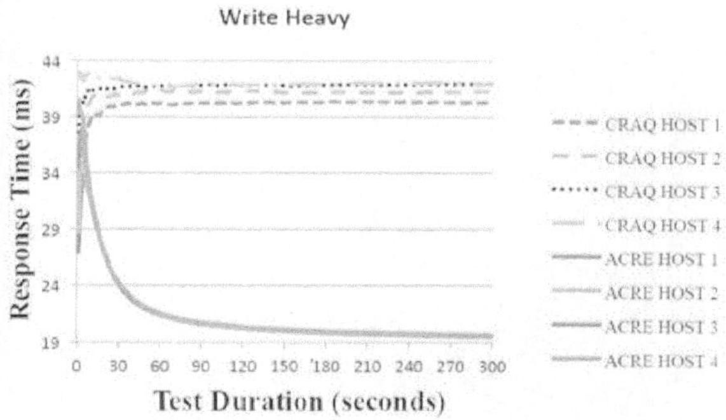

Figure 3. Response Time for Test 2

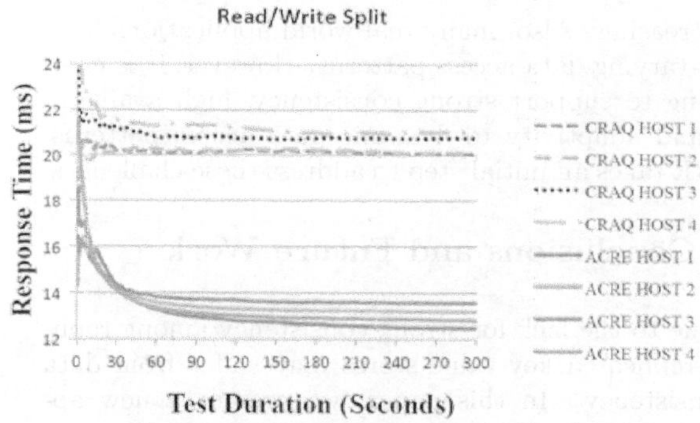

Figure 4. Response Time for Test 3

- *Test 3:* The read to write ratio set to 1 in this test. Hence, an equal number of read and write requests are issued to model a balanced read/write split.

We initially use 4, 10, and 10 storage nodes in Test 1, Test 2, and Test 3, respectively. ACRE may extend or shrink the chain between 4 and 10 nodes based on the data access pattern. Each test is run for 5 minutes. These tests were intended to demonstrate the benefits of ACRE over a short burst of extreme read to write ratios. In each test, 100 clients running on 4 physical machines submit read/write requests to the storage nodes in the chain. A write request is always sent to the head to maintain the strong consistency of the chained data nodes. A read request is submitted to one of the available nodes in the chain that is selected using a pseudo random number generator for load balancing. After sending a read/write request, a client waits for a random inter-request delay selected in the range of [0ms, 100ms]. Hence, on average, 2,000 read/write requests are submitted to the chain every second. Each read/write request reads/writes 1024 bytes. For ACRE, the minimum request bound for adaptation and minimum adaptation gap are set to 500 requests and 30s, respectively.

3.2 Performance Evaluation Results

Each data point in Figure 2 - Figure 4 shows the average response time of read/write requests processed per second measured in the four physical machines hosting the clients. (In ACRE, a chain can be extended up to 10 nodes. However, the response time in the other nodes remain similar to the ones shown in the figures.) From these figures, we observe that the response time of ACRE is considerably shorter than that of CRAQ. The response time gap becomes pronounced after 30s. As shown in the figures, the response time of ACRE is 30% - 50% shorter than that of CRAQ after 30s. By dynamically adapting the chain based on the data access patterns, ACRE reduces the service delay, while supporting strong data consistency and data availability. This contrasts to the popular data stores, e.g., [3, 2], which sacrifice strong data consistency and rely on eventual consistency, providing no guarantee on data consistency. These results show the viability of adaptive replication that provides a strong consistency guarantee, while adapting to dynamic read/write patterns.

4 Related Work

Data are partitioned and replicated to support high performance and availability. Popular key-value stores, e.g., [1, 2], only support eventual consistency among replicas. As a result, inconsistent data can be exposed to distributed clients accessing shared data.

Chain replication [7] supports strong consistency by using a chain of replicated data stores. However, the tail node in a chain can be a performance bottleneck, because only the tail has to process all reads. CRAQ [6] enhances the read performance by allowing not only the tail but also all the other nodes in a chain to process reads. However, the tail can be a bottleneck, if write-heavy workloads are given.

ACRE addresses this problem by dynamically adapting the chain in a cost-effective manner, if necessary, to improve the performance by considering data access patterns unlike static approaches, such as [3, 2, 7, 6], which support either weak consistency or strong consistency in a fixed chain. The need for strong consistency and high availability with load balancing is increasing. Also, many real world applications have time-varying data access patterns. However, it is challenging to support strong consistency, high availability, and adaptivity to dynamic data access patterns. ACRE takes an initial step to address these challenges.

5 Conclusions and Future Work

Due to the lack for strong consistency among replicas, replicated key-value stores may suffer from data inconsistency. In this paper, we present a new approach, called ACRE, to support strong consistency, load balancing, and adaptivity to dynamic data access patterns to enhance the performance. In the future, we will investigate more efficient approaches to supporting strong consistency with further enhanced performance.

Acknowledgement

This work was supported, in part, by the NSF grant CNS-117352.

References

[1] E. Brewer. Towards Robust Distributed Systems. In *PODC Keynote*, 2000.

[2] G. Decandia, D. Hastorun, M. Jampani, G. Kakulapati, A. Lakshman, A. Pilchin, S. Sivasubramanian, P. Vosshall, D. Hastorun, G. Decandia, and W. Vogels. Dynamo: Amazon's Highly Available Key-Value Store. *Symposium on Operating Systems Principles*, 2007.

[3] S. Ghemawat, H. Gobioff, and S. Leung. The Google File System. In *Proceedings of the 19th ACM Symposium on Operating Systems Principles (SOSP'03)*, 2003.

[4] R. T. Kaushik and M. Bhandarkar. GreenHDFS: Towards An Energy-Conserving, Storage-Efficient, Hybrid Hadoop Compute Cluster. In *HotPower*, 2010.

[5] W. Lloyd, M. J. Freedman, M. Kaminsky, and D. G. Andersen. Don't Settle for Eventual: Scalable Causal Consistency for Wide-Area Storage with COPS. In *ACM Symposium on Operating Systems Principles*, 2011.

[6] J. Terrace and M. J. Freedman. Object Storage on CRAQ: High-throughput chain replication for read-mostly workloads. In *USENIX Annual Technical Conference*, 2009.

[7] R. van Renesse and F. B. Schneider. Chain Replication for Supporting High Throughput and Availability. In *Operating Systems Design and Implementation*, 2004.

Performance of Mining Medium-to-Large-Scale Scientific Simulation Data

S.G. Morgan and K.A. Hawick
Computer Science, Massey University, North Shore 102-904, Auckland, New Zealand
email: scottgarrymorgan@gmail.com, k.a.hawick@massey.ac.nz
Tel: +64 9 414 0800 Fax: +64 9 441 8181

April 2013

ABSTRACT

Many scientific simulations generate bulky data sets that must be mined for observable features. It is often not computationally feasible to do this in real time and the data must be saved for subsequent "off-line" analysis either by separate software or sometimes by direct human visualisation. We present some scoping analysis and preliminary software approaches for mining medium to large scale data sets in the form of time slices or model configurations. We report on current storage and visualisation technology response and interaction times for mining scientific simulations on regular lattices using hyper-bricks of model configurations.

KEY WORDS
big data; data mining; data visualization; scientific simulations.

1 Introduction

Numerical simulations often generate relatively large data sets that need "offline" analysis. A time series analysis can generally not be conducted until the simulation sequence is completed and data-mining and visualisation tools are needed to support scientists conducting post simulation mining activities.

Computational simulations include: discrete event simulation models [12]; complex system models based on particles [16] or agents; or time-integrated field models all produce bulk data that is often stored and post processed in this manner. Often such data is spatially oriented [4] but can come in a myriad of different storage formats. In this present paper we focus on "hyper-bricks" of regular data that come from models or simulations where the key data structure is a multidimensional array or "brick" of data. The cells of such data might be simple pixels or volume element - voxels; or multi-channel data with several scalar or vector properties at each spatial location [21].

Our experience is that a semi-interactive pattern matching identification [18] of even just a visual inspection of the various "slices" of such data bricks can be very instructive as part of a numerical experiment.

Such data arises from environmental modelling [22] and geographical systems [1, 23] as well as from complex systems models in application areas like: forest fire systems [3]; lattice gases and complex fluids [10]; critical systems [8]; and ecological systems [5].

Relational or graph data [7, 20] from biological [6] and other applications [19] can also of course be mined using statistical pattern matching, but such databases tend to have their own specialist performance optimization strategies. In the present paper we focus on data that is held in simpler more "raw" formats such as rasters and hyper-bricks rather than relational and textual data.

There has been considerable interest in the literature on strategies to mine very large time series data [15] and on how to manage such data on distributed systems [13]. In this present paper we investigate practical matters concerning the manipulation of medium to large data sets that can be manipulated by post-simulation analysis software on a modern desk-top or desk-side scaled computer system.

Our article is structured as follows: In Section 2 we describe the hyperbrick data manipulation problem in detail and discuss file format and data layout issues for coping with arbitrary dimensional data. In Section 4 we report on experiments to characterise read and write performance of large contiguous bricks of such data. We discuss implications of typical read and write performance for individual and bulk data for a range of different storage devices in Section 5. We offer some conclusions and areas for further work on bulk data manipulation in Section 6.

2 Scientific Model Data Bricks

There are some sophisticated 3D solid design file formats available that are used by proprietary and some open computer aided design tools. Even for those formats that are open their complexity makes it a cumbersome burden to interface a stand-alone simulation program to them. A very simple file format family was designed to provide a bridge between the *Cubes* visualisation program and the sort of simulation code our research group regularly develops in C, C++, Java and other languages.

The hyperbrick file format – with file ending ".hbrk" – was inspired by the incredibly useful portable pixmap format family (often known as "NetPBM") designed by Poskanzer and developed by Henderson [11]. Researchers have been using ppm and pbm formats with 2D simulation programs for over two decades and their value is largely due to their simplicity. One can off the top of one's head code up C/C++/Java to generate, or read and write these formats.

In a sense therefore, the "H1" hyperbrick is a generalisation of the pgm 2D greymap image file format, for the case of 3D data.

```
H1
# a comment or header line
# another comment
1
3 64 64 32
hyper-raster-of-unsigned-chars
```

Figure 1: The .hbrk hyperbrick file format for a 3-d data set of unsigned chars with spatial extent $x = 64 \times y = 64 \times z = 32$.

Figure 1 shows the .hbrk file format, consisting of a two character textual header "H1" followed by a newline and an optional series of comment lines starting with a hash character. The subsequent integer – in this case a size of "1" denotes the number of bytes in each payload entity. If one wanted voxels to be allowed to take on 2^24 different levels - like portable pixmap pixels, then one could use a size of "3" to denote three bytes per voxel. The next line gives the dimensionality d of the hyperbrick – usually $d = 3$ for examples discussed in this document, followed by exactly d integer edge lengths in order of increasing significance – so in the example shown $L_x = 64, L_y = 64, L_z = 32$. This line is terminated by a newline and the remainder of the ".hbrk" file is a set of binary characters in the "hyper-raster" order implied by the dimensionality and lengths. So in the example thei_x index would move fastest, the i_y next fastest and so forth.

Many of the simulation codes we work with use what is known as "k-indexing" whereby a single integer indexes into the d-dimensional hyperbrick and:

$$k = i_x + L_x \times i_y + (L_x \times L_y) \times i_z \quad (1)$$

These ideas are very useful for manipulating rectilinear data independent of the dimension and are described in [9] and can be generalised to specify data transforms [14].

The Netpbm format family supports both "raw" and textual formats for pix maps and grey maps. The full "hrbk" format family is still under development but the present plan is to support together data types so that for example "H4" maps to 32-bit integer data, "H8" maps to 64-bit integer data. The "H1" unsigned-char type can also be used with data cell length 4 or 8 of course to encode this as long as you do not care about byte order within the cells.

A useful variation that is easily described here is the **sparse** version or ".sbrk" sparse hyperbrick format. We found many of our programs deal with a model that can be represented as cells of one or more values in a "sea of zeroes" and consequently it is a waste of space explicitly saving all the zeros.

```
S1
# a comment or header line
# another comment
1
3 64 64 32
63455 255
67551 128
71647 192
```

Figure 2: The .sbrk sparse hyperbrick file format for a 3-d data set of unsigned chars with spatial extent $x = 64 \times y = 64 \times z = 32$.

Figure 2 shows the .hbrk file format which is similar to the "H1" format but has "S1" as its magic prefix, and embodies the assumption that the entire hyperbrick has voxel values of zero **except** the explicitly stated (k, v) pairs giving the k-index and voxel value both encoded as unsigned integers. In the example shown, the following (x, y, z) indices give rise to the k-indices:

```
(31 31 15)->k of 63,455, voxel value 255
(31 31 16)->k of 67,551, voxel value 128
(31 31 17)->k of 71,647, voxel value 192
```

The sparse hyperbrick format could also be extended into a family of formats with different magic header characters to convey type information but the simple "S1" format with the type-code "1" stating that each voxel is limited to 2^{8^1} levels suffices for most purposes.

These sort of data files with a mixed textual header and binary or raw-readable data have rather gone out of fashion at present, with a surprising number of inappropriately large XML formats being common. The simplicity of the hbrk and sbrk formats means that they can be read using built-in language I/O capabilities without recourse to needing complicated parsers.

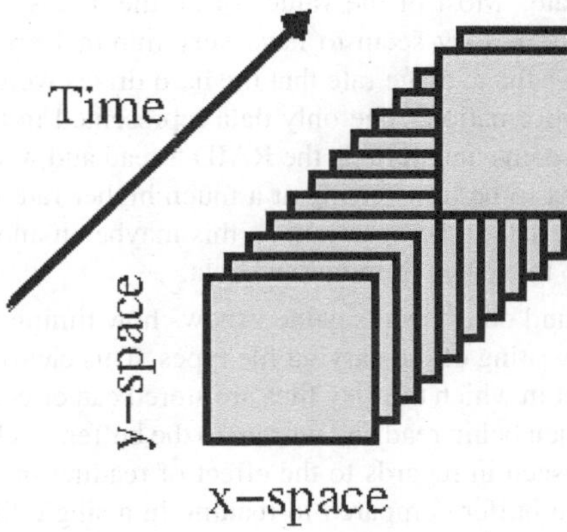

Figure 3: Time sequence of planes (which could be hyper-bricks themselves) arranged with a short window of the whole data pulled out and being analysed at once.

The k-indexing notion extends the notion of a raster contiguous image format to arbitrary dimensions. The main point is that the k-indexing allows the hyperbrick of data to be treated as a block of data that is contiguous in memory or on the storage medium. It can be read and written in a single call to a low-level read/write service call within the operating systems kernel or file systems daemon.

Figure 3 shows a time sequence of hyper-bricked data. A sub-sequence or window of the overall sequence is pulled out and analysed at once. It is therefore important to be able to read and write blocks of the overall sequence rapidly. It is therefore important to assess the current attainable performance for various storage devices.

3 Data Access Experiments

The given experiment was to test the performance on varying Hard Drive Disks and the effect of using smaller individual files in comparison to a single file totaling in equal size. A custom written program in C/C++ was used and run on the different Hard Drives and RAID formats to give full control over how the information was written and read. The physical hard drives ranges from an IDE 5200rpm based disk to a Solid State Drive. This way the variation based on physical hardware can be seen and how it can impact performance. The basis of having multiple small files being 1 Megabyte in size then totaling up to a single large file of the combined size was to assess how much the latent performance of reading and writing was affected by buffering.

Using a custom written program in C/C++ gave full control on how reading and writing were used and hence how they performed. Primarily choosing fread and fwrite as the way to read and write information to and from the hard drive, this gave the ability to be concerned with the type format the data could be. Pseudo randomly generated information was created for writing the information which was stored in a buffer then the timing was given for when the write function was called. With this implementation this helped limit any chances patterned data in which operating system could effect the timing in which random data is read or written by caching.

The test was broken down into four main parts. The initial writing of the single large file created at the set size, after the writing of the single small files. This is then followed by the reading of the same files. To make sure that no caching was done for the file so it would not effect the reading or writing time to the hard drive, commands in the terminal were used to clear the cache, for example Linux's $echo3 > /proc/sys/vm/drop_caches$. These commands where done during the test however they were not placed in when timing was done, so it will not have any effect on the timing results. The size spacing for each of the tests were done in 200MB intervals and was tested ten times each up to the limit of 2000MB.

Algorithm 1 Writing algorithm and random data generation

declare $buffer[]$
for all $unsigned\ characters$ **in** $buffer$ **do**
  randomise $buffer$[i] with $unsignedcharacter$
end for
create $emptyfile$
begin timing
write from buffer to file
end timing
close file
record timing

Algorithm 1 shows the basic constructs of how the process of writing a single large file and the generation the random data. Initially a buffer is generated and allocated the memory required for the final size of the file being created. Then the buffer is filled with randomly generated unsigned characters where the randomisation has been seeded from time using the rand function as shown in Figure 4. Once the buffer has been filled, an empty file is created in which the data from the buffer will be stored. The timing starts and will end once the writing function has ended. The function used was fwrite as shown in Figure 4. When this has completed the file is then closed and the timing is recorded and stored in a external file.

4 Performance Results

Performance between the variety of disks while reading and writing can be clearly seen. The style (using the same type of hard drive but using multiple devices with a RAID format) in which data has been stored also seems to have impacted the hard drive performance. Clear separations between the physical devices are seen as the older devices seem to be slower

```
for (int i = 0; i < dataSize; i ++) {
    cp[i] = rand() % 255;
}
FILE * fp;
for (int i = 0; i < 10; i++) {
    char file_name[200];
    sprintf(file_name,"single_large_%i.data",i);
    fp = fopen( file_name, "w");
    assert( fp != NULL );
    t1 = mytimer();
    fwrite(cp, m, dataSize, fp);
    t2 = mytimer();
    t3 = t2-t1;
    timerArray[i] = t3;
}
free(cp);
fclose(fp);
```

Figure 4: Writing function and data generation

in all areas between both large and small files in comparison to the newer technologies such as solid state drives.

The latency itself represents the time taken just for the overhead of the file without including the information based on reading or writing to and from the buffer. This would include the spin up time of the hard drive if mechanical, finding a place to put the file on the platter (or memory if a solid state drive) or anything else that would take up time that is not involved with writing or reading the information into the buffer [17]. Table 1 shows the results of all the hard drives based on information measured from reading a single file. The information that represents IDE 5400rpm, Sata 7200rpm, and RAID 1 shows a negative value essentially stating based off the line of best fit the overhead of reading a single file would be in the negative which is impossible. However all these values have a high error rate resulting in these values to become invalid. RAID 0 gave a more reliable result of stating the the initial overhead time for reading a single file resulted in the time taken to be 87ms with a standard error of 16. Most of these results seem very varied and no pattern can been seen, however the timed measured is very small compared to the total time taken for reading and writing files.

Table 2 and Table 3 represents the basic transfer speeds being recorded to and from the buffer. Table 2 shows the speed in which the files are written to the hard disk from the buffer with the randomly generated data stored in the buffer. This clearly shows that older hard drives such as the IDE 5400rpm ATA has a much slower transfer rate (being only 26.37 MB/s with a standard error of 2MB/s) than the Solid State(244MB/s with an error of 44MB/s). This same pattern can also be seen in Table 3 with the read speeds essentially mirroring its counterpart(except for the solid state which has a varying read and write speed). These results are based on just a large single file as from other data represented in Figure 9 and Figure 6 shows how being stored can effect the transfer rate. Most of the values of all the data seem to be very stable as they seem to have very minimal error rates. This shows the average rate that the hard drives were able to transfer information. The only data represented in these tables that seems unnatural is the RAID 5 read and write. This data seems to be transferring at a much higher rate than the rest of the data in comparison, so this maybe an anomaly in regards to this piece of individual data.

Figure 6 and other results gained shows how timing for both read and writing of the varying file types. This clearly shows the impact in which the way files are stored can effect performance when being read and written to the buffer. A clear definition is seen in regards to the effect of reading in multiple files to the buffer compared to reading in a single file. This seems to be far slower and takes more time on how files are read in. However reading and writing seems to be very similar, however in other results this has varied slightly with writing multiple files on average seems to be slower than writing a single file.

The RAID format clearly can increase the performance of a hard drive. This is shown with the performance increase with RAID 0 (this is being setup in which two hard drives share the load essentially increasing its performance). With two hard drives setup (SATA 3 7200rpm HDD) in RAID 0 the performance has double in comparison to just using a single hard drive as shown in Table 3. RAID 1 (mirroring the device for redundancy) showed a slight performance increase compared to the SATA 3 7200rpm single device however this is very minimal in comparison. RAID 5 format (providing increase in performance and redundancy requiring four hard drives) gave very unusual results as these systematically doubled the RAID 0 results in bandwidth through put.

Unusual anomalies have shown themselves in way different hards store information. Figure 9 shows that the time taken for it to write multiple files took longer than reading them, while all other tests represented this in the the opposite way. Figure 10 shows that writing a single file took substantially longer than all other tests taken. However as shown, the results for writing the single large file is very scattered suggesting an issue when writing as timing between the data points vary in an unusual pattern of every second point is smaller than the previous.

Device	Average Read Latency(ms)
IDE 5200rpm ATA HDD	-2926 ± 877
SATA 7200rpm HDD	-600 ± 400
RAID 0 (SATA 7200rpm)	87 ± 16
RAID 1 (SATA 7200rpm)	-471 ± 525
RAID 5 (STAT 7200rpm)	30 ± 60
Solid State HDD	421 ± 210

Table 1: Latency speeds from reading single file

Device	Average Write Speeds (MB/s)
IDE 5200rpm ATA HDD	26.37 ± 2
SATA 7200rpm HDD	132.4 ± 1.3
RAID 0 (SATA 7200rpm)	362 ± 12
RAID 1 (SATA 7200rpm)	173 ± 1.3
RAID 5 (STAT 7200rpm)	620 ± 42
Solid State HDD	244 ± 44

Table 2: Average hard drive write speeds

Device	Average Read Speeds (MB/s)
IDE 5200rpm ATA HDD	32.42 ± 1
SATA 7200rpm HDD	146.8 ± 0.5
RAID 0 (SATA 7200rpm)	349 ± 11
RAID 1 (SATA 7200rpm)	170 ± 1.1
RAID 5 (STAT 7200rpm)	692 ± 31
Solid State HDD	354 ± 2

Table 3: Average hard drive read speeds

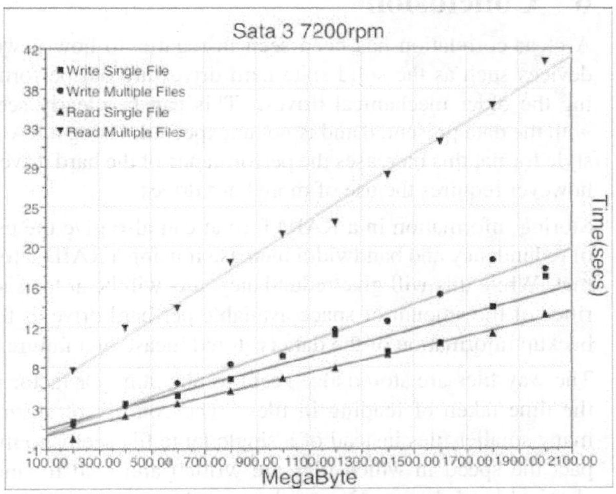

Figure 5: 7200rpm SATA 3 Drive

5 Discussion

With the results given, this shows a correlation between the way the files are stored and how being stored can effect the performance. It seems that overhead while minimal, can slowly add up to decrease performance while a file of equivalent size but stored in its entirety will have a better performance. However, issues arise with the limitation of hardware and memory to how big the file can be stored.

There are also unseen factors that can effect the performance of reading and writing and that is the current state of the disk and fragmentation. Since a hard drive needs to put information on the sectors it would be more efficient if it was able

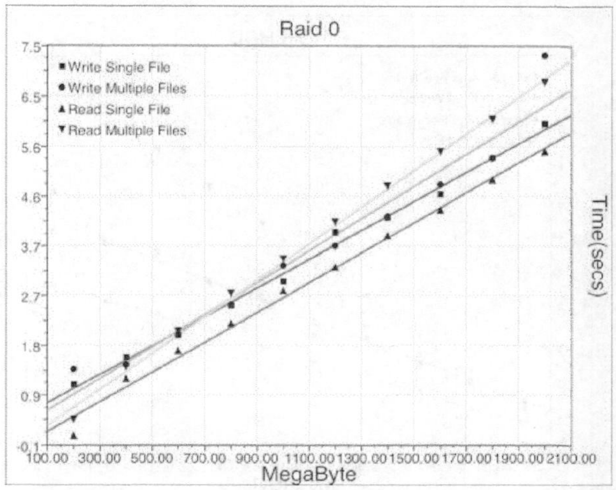

Figure 6: RAID 0 with 7200rpm SATA 3 Drives

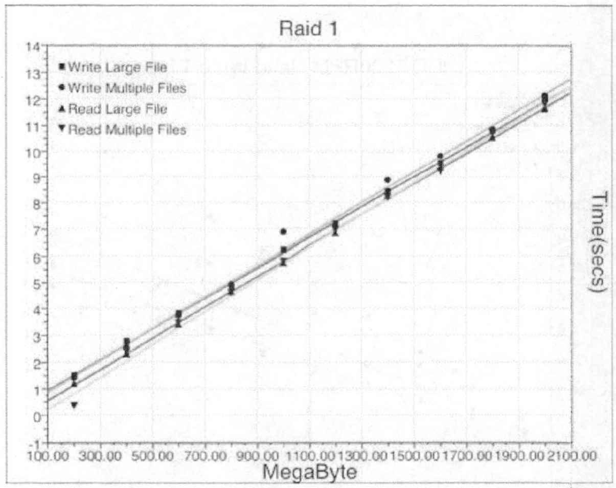

Figure 7: RAID 1 with 7200rpm SATA 3 Drives

to put the information on the same track continuously rather than having the information scattered as this would increase overhead [17]. This effect however is only for mechanical hard drives as the solid state hard drives [2] do not use platters to store the information.

Using a RAID format increased performance (for RAID styles that are meant to increase performance for example RAID 0 and 5) of the same type of hard drive as shown in Table 3, while the needed amount of physical hard drives increase (dependant on the type of RAID format this can vary), this shows that by using a format of RAID this greatly increases the bandwidth that it can pass through. Other RAID formats such as RAID 1 and 5 also give the ability for redundancy which could be useful incase of hard drive failure

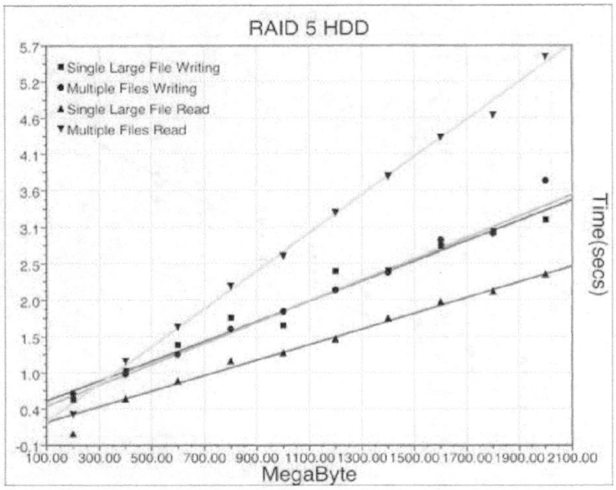

Figure 8: RAID 5 with 7200rpm SATA 3 Drives

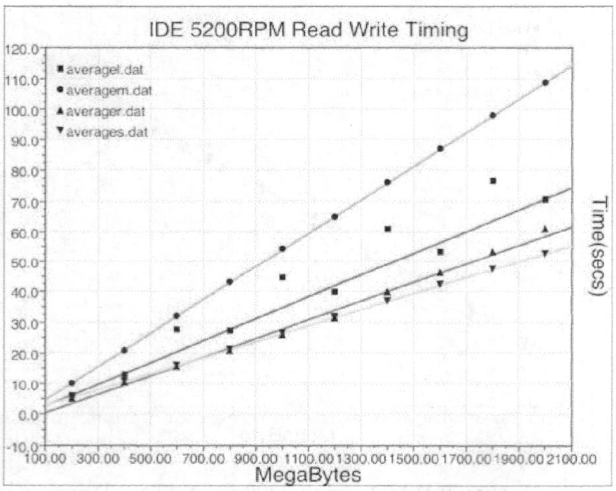

Figure 9: IDE 5200rpm ATA Drive

which if used for a single hard drive, this would result in loss of all data.

The variation in which the type of hard drive(Sata 3 7200rpm, IDE 5400rpm and Solid State) showed a complete variation on the way storing files effected time for the transfer. The Sata 3 7200rpm drives showed that reading multiple files has the longest time take (even in RAID 0 and 5 format) while with the IDE 5400rpm hard drive, writing multiple files seems to be significantly slower. The solid state hard drive had an issue with reading writing single files. This could be related each device and how they were designed and caching techniques.

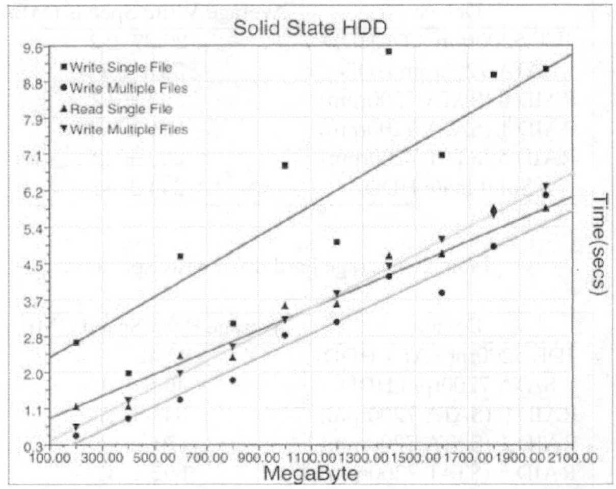

Figure 10: Solid State Hard Dive

6 Conclusion

A clear correlation has been seen in regards to how newer devices such as the solid state hard drives are out performing the older mechanical drives. This can be clearly seen with the data presented and is not unexpected. Using a RAID style format this increases the performance of the hard drives, however requires the use of more hard drives.

Storing information in a RAID format can also give the use of redundancy and bandwidth increase if using a RAID 5 format. While this will give redundancy, this will be at the sacrifice of the amount of space available per hard drive as the backup information of the data is stored incase of a failure.

The way files are stored also seem to play a major factor in the time taken of reading in files. The concept of storing many smaller files instead of a single large file seems to impact the speed in which files are written and read for mechanical hard drives. Due to the way that mechanical hard drives store information this is unsurprising that having to store multiple files will generate more overhead as having to find the individual files scattered over the platters.

Due to the nature of the solid state and the way it stores information this is not affected any mechanical parts so files are not will not be scattered and overhead is dramatically decreased with reading and writing multiple files the same as reading a single large file of equivalent size [2].

From the test given, it seems that the solid state hard drives seem to be much faster in ever aspect compared to the IDE and Sata 3 mechanical hard drives. While storing data in a RAID format using mechanical hard drives gives a very close results equivalent to a solid state, this is at the cost of using multiple hard drives.

If solid state drives are stored in a RAID format (based on the changes of bandwidth from the Sata 3 7200rpm) this would clearly increase the performance to far exceed that of the mechanical drives. However due to solid states being a far newer technology, the cost in relation to the amount of space available for the capacity of the device is higher in comparison to the current mechanical drives available.

Overall it seems that with the information given it varies on the users available equipment and the memory limitation of the computer. While It does seem with mechanical drives that storing the information as a single large file will give better speeds, this is limited to the amount of memory available to the user on the current computer they are reading it on. While devices like the solid state seem to have very minimal effect on the way the file is stored, the best choice on how the file is stored will be dependant on the physical hardware it self and what is available for the user.

In summary we have evaluated the read and write performance of several storage devices managing contiguous blocks of data suitable for simulation configuration hyperbricks. Having determined how multi-dimensional systems could be encoded in this manner we have found that desktop and desk-side devices give an adequate read and write performance for a semi-interactive data mining analysis of simulation results. In particular there is strong evidence in favour of using solid state storage devices where possible, for this sort of work.

References

[1] Coddington, P.D., m. W. Grigg, Fabbro, S.J.D., Hawick, K.A., James, S.P., Lo. E.H.S., Lut, A.K., Mason, K.D., Owen, M.J.: Interfacing to on-line geospatial imagery archives. In: Proc. 27th An. Conf. of AURISA. Leura, NSW, Australia (22-26 November 1999)

[2] Cornwell, M.: Anatomy of a solid-state drive. Communications of the ACM 55, 59–63 (2012)

[3] Gu, P., Zheng, Y.: A new data mining model for forest fire cellular automata. In: Proc. Fifth Int. Conf. on Intelligent Computation Technology and Automation (ICICTA 2012). pp. 37–40. CPS, Zhangjiajie, Hunan, China (12-14 January 2012)

[4] Guo, D., Gehagen, M.: Spatial ordering and encoding for geographic data mining and visualization. J. Intell. Inf. Sys. 27, 243–266 (2006)

[5] Hawick, K.A.: Spectral analysis of growth in spatial lotka-volterra models. In: Proc. International Conference on Modelling and Simulation. pp. 14–20. No. 685-030, IASTED, Gabarone, Botswana (6-8 September 2010)

[6] Hawick, K.A.: Applying enumerative, spectral and hybrid graph analyses to biological network data. In: Int. Conf. on Computational Intelligence and Bioinformatics (CIB 2011). pp. 89–96. IASTED, Pittsburgh, USA (7-9 November 2011)

[7] Hawick, K.A., Coddington, P.D., James, H.A., Patten, C.J.: On-line data archives. In: Proc. 34th Hawaii Int. Conf. on System Sciences. pp. 1–10. No. DHPC-021, HICSS, Hawaii, USA (January 2001)

[8] Hawick, K.A., Playne, D.P.: Modelling, Simulating and Visualizing the Cahn-Hilliard-Cook Field Equation. International Journal of Computer Aided Engineering and Technology (IJCAET) 2(1), 78–93 (2010), inderscience

[9] Hawick, K.A., Playne, D.P.: Hypercubic Storage Layout and Transforms in Arbitrary Dimensions using GPUs and CUDA. Concurrency and Computation: Practice and Experience 23(10), 1027–1050 (July 2011)

[10] Hawick, K.: Visualising multi-phase lattice gas fluid layering simulations. In: Proc. International Conference on Modeling, Simulation and Visualization Methods (MSV'11). pp. 3–9. CSREA, Las Vegas, USA (18-21 July 2011)

[11] Henderson, B.: Netpbm history. Web Site (2007), `http://netpbm.sourceforge.net/history.html`, last Visted October 2010

[12] Hossain, M., Harari, N., Semere, D., Martensson, P., Ng, A., Andersson, M.: Integrated modeling and application of standardized data schema. In: Proc. 5th Swedish Production Symposium (SPS-12). pp. 473–478. Linkoping, Sweden (6-8 November 2012)

[13] James, H.A., Hawick, K.A.: Scientific data management in a grid environment. Journal of Grid Computing 3(1-2), 39–51 (September 2005), iSSN: 1570-7873 (Paper) 1572-9814 (Online)

[14] Johnson, M.J., Hawick, K.A.: Optimising energy management of mobile computing devices,. In: Proc. Int. Conf. on Computer Design (CDES'12). pp. 1–7. WorldComp, Las Vegas, USA (16-19 July 2012)

[15] Keogh, E., Kasetty, S.: On the need for time series data mining benchmarks: A survey and empirical demonstration. Data Mining and Knowledge Discovery 7(4), 349–371 (October 2003)

[16] Mehta, S., Hazzard, K., Machiraju, R., Parthasarathy, S., Wilkins, J.: Detection and visualization of anomalous structures in molecular dynamics simulation data. In: Proc. IEEE Visualization 2004. pp. 465–472. Austin, Texas, USA (10-15 October 2004)

[17] Ng, S.W.: Advances in disk technology: Performance issues. IEEE Computer May, 75–81 (1998)

[18] Rao, C.S., Gupta, M., Murthy, K.V.S., Rajanikanth, J.: Sequetial pattern mining based on multi dimensional sequence data - a case study. Indian Journal of Computational Intelligence and Systems Sciences 1, 1–5 (2013)

[19] Sbalzarini, I.F.: Modeling and simulation of biological systems from image data. Bioessays 35, 482–490 (2013)

[20] Schietgat, L.: Graph-based data mining for biological applications. AI Communications 24, 95–96 (2011)

[21] Shekhar, S., Zhang, P., Huang, Y., Vatsaval, R.: Trends in Spatial Data Mining, chap. 3, pp. 833–851. Springer (2005), in Data Mining and Knowledge Discovery Handbook

[22] Trepos, R., Masson, V., Cordier, M.O., Gascuel-Odoux, C., Salmon-Monviola, J.: Mining simulation data by rule induction to determine critical source areas of stream water pollution by herbicides. Computers and Electronics in Agriculture 86, 75–88 (2012)

[23] Yang, H., Pathasarathy, S., Mehta, S.: A generalized framework for mining spatiotemporal patterns in scientific data. In: Proc. ACM Int. Conf. on Knowledge Discovery and Data Mining. pp. 716–721. Chicago, Illinois, USA (21-24 August 2005)

Mobility Analysis Using MapReduce to Enhance Services Improvement for an University Smart Campus

Laura Torres-López[1], **Victor M. Larios-Rosillo**[1], **José G. Robledo-Hernández**[1], **and Ignacio Silva-Lepe**[2]
[1]PhD in IT, University of Guadalajara, Zapopan, JAL, México
[2]IBM T.J. Watson R.C., Yorktown Heights, NY, U.S.A

Abstract—*The analysis of urban mobility information lets us improve different services within a city. However, due to the interaction between different systems logically interconnected generating information on a daily basis, the very large volume of data collected brings challenges for the processing, visualization and simulation of data. Moreover the people through the use of mobile devices, act as a networked sensors collecting data that are convenient to analyze in order to get valuable information about real urban dynamics.*

Trends on big data technologies have proposed the adoption of new programming models able to process the growing amount of information such as MapReduce, among others. This work presents the construction of a model for a test bed to perform analysis and simulation of urban mobility using these trends; the development of this test bed, over a University campus, is intended to scale up to a city under the scope of Smart Cities.

Keywords: Bigdata, Urban computing, Smart Cities

1. Introduction

The subject of urban mobility study is the movement of people, no matter what kind of media are used for commuting: walking, public transport, car, bicycle and so on. This makes mobility a wider concept, in terms of its study, than transport or traffic [1]. Regarding urban habitants, Pilling [2] estimated that by 2050 they will be three-quarters of the total world's population.

In that sense, a megacity is a *system of systems* that integrates interconnected subsystems such as: government services, transportation, energy and water, public safety, education and healthcare, among others; all of them are continuously generating and requiring information to work properly [3]. Instances such as governments, private entities and social organizations face problems inherent to megacities, they are taking advantage of data collected through information technologies (IT), such are the cases of London, Singapore and Stockholm that have developed systems to manage mobility situations [4] in the scope of Smarter Cities[1].

[1]http://www.ibm.com/smartercities

However, in order to support such system of systems, more advanced information technologies are required to manage efficiently big amounts of information. A city's infrastructure usually has sensor systems covering different geographical areas to collect data automatically; additionally, people are generating large amounts of data as a result of the IT adopted for daily living [5], [6], [4], these are some of the situations that propitiate the Big Data paradigm. In this regard, trends on data management technology, such as the programming model Mapreduce [7], [8], [9], are alternative solutions for traditional databases.

The contribution of this work is a model for a suitable test bed for urban mobility analysis and simulation over a controlled area, with the potential for further scale out; we chose a digital campus simulation that reflects a sample of the basic characteristics of a whole city; the experimental goal is to adopt the MapReduce programming model in order to deal with big data analytics. Mobility and services analysis over a smarter campus revealed where the points of interest are: occupancy for buildings and rooms, student density over the time. This analysis allows simulation to focus on the use of facilities and planning of maintenance events for a Smart Campus, which could eventually scale to Smart Citiy models. All of these web services technologies and mobile devices use geo-referenced digital maps via crowdsourcing.

2. Related Work

Urban Computing[2] is an emerging concept related to the interaction between computing, sensing, and technologies used in a daily basis for urban lifestyles [10].

Thus, research on Urban Computing has focused on urban mobility analysis. Yuan et al. in [11] present an approach that uses historical GPS data to extract smart driving directions. Moreover, [12] presents a system that additionally predicts traffic conditions.

Our original contribution on this paper establish a relation between a megacity infrastructure which is a complex environment against an University campus as a controlled one, both systems provides services that we would explain in further sections where we are dealing with solutions to understand mobility and related services as security, maintenance and so on.

[2]http://research.microsoft.com/en-us/projects/urbancomputing/default.aspx

On that sense, the base for mobility analysis requires a digital map, modeled as a graph because to describe interconnected paths over a geographical area of a city. The size of the graph could be very large depending on the number of streets and its mesh-like structure. Thus, the very large volume of data requires technology enabled to deal with the processing, Lin et al. in [13] points out the use of MapReduce to process large-scale graphs.

Our programming model is based in MapReduce [8], [14], which is the most adapted for processing very large datasets. This model empowers the distribution and parallelization of the dataset analytics. The main principles of MapReduce state two basic functions: *map* and *reduce*, organizing the data sets by key/value pairs as input and output of each one of the functions in order to deliver a data set as result.

However, a MapReduce-based solution can be complex to model. Thus, some approaches to simplify the coding with MapReduce include the web-based graphic user interface proposed by Shih et al. [15], and a query optimizer that transforms MapReduce queries to adopt features provided by SQL databases, as the authors present in [16]. Additionally, tools like Karmasphere Studio[3] provide a graphical environment to implement and optimize MapReduce algorithms through the well known development platform Eclipse[4], using Java[5] as the main programming language.

3. Building a digital campus simulation

The digital campus simulation was performed at Guadalajara city, located in the state of Jalisco, México, with a surface of 2,734 km^2 and a population of 4.2 millions[6], related to traffic there are an estimated of 1.5 millions of vehicles and 11,045 km of vial infrastructure [17]. It has all the characteristics mentioned above with respect to a megacity and its inherent challenges, requiring the development of information based solutions to improve the quality of life. Since the model of the city is more complex we decided to start on one of the University of Guadalajara campuses: CUCEA. We simulated the behavior of students as mobile entities over a controlled geographical area. CUCEA, the business studies campus, has a population of ~20,000, including students, academic and administrative staff, and a surface of 299,466 $m2$ from which 55,690 $m2$ are built[7]. Table I shows a comparative summary of characteristics from both Guadalajara city and University CUCEA campus.

The University CUCEA campus can be seen as a subset of the city; our algorithm contributes as a lighter manner, enabled to be adapted with minor changes at the context of the city, also campus has more controlled and detailed information that could be tested with the acceptance from the University authorities.

Table 1: Comparison: Megacity vs. University campus

Characteristic	Guadalajara city	University CUCEA
Surface	2,734 km^2	~300 km^2
Infrastructure vial	11,045.0 km streets	60.5 km streets and corridors
Population	4.2 millions	~20,000
Services	Government services, transportation, energy and water, public safety, education, healthcare	Administrative offices, library, laboratories, bank, coffee shop, security, parking, medical aid, lockers

Hence, the model to build our original digital campus simulation, shown in figure 2, has 3 stages: (A) Data sources, (B) generation of mobility data and (C) exploratory data analysis. The next sections describe each one of the stages.

3.1 Data sources

3.1.1 Student schedules

The model consists of *sequences* the set of paths that the students traverse over the campus during a week in order to attend their classes. A sequence S is $S=\{p_0, p_1, ... p_x\}$. Each p_k is a point in a route that depends on predecessor and successor points: p_{k-1}, p_{k+1}. The set of collected sequences describe the mobility behavior of users at a given time, so Δt_k is the difference between t_{k-1} and t_k.

Commonly, sequences are collected through sensor infrastructure or GPS devices by smartphone applications; however, prior to the construction of our test bed, we used as a data source the student schedules for a regular week. Traces started from one of the entrances, assigned by probability, and eventually they reach the different classrooms or laboratories according to the time scheduled for each one. The algorithms for generation the students GPS traces require the geo-referenced digital map.

3.1.2 Design a geo-referenced digital map

The foundation of a mobility analysis relies on the geo-referenced digital map as the bottom layer. Indeed, the more detailed the information about the real infrastructure, the more valuable the results. A digital map is a directed graph $G=(V,E)$ that keeps the information about a geographical region. The vertices are $V=\{v_0, v_1, ... v_n\}$ where each v_i is a tuple (latitude, longitude); the edges are $E=\{e_0, e_1, ... e_m\}$ where each e_j links two vertices and describes a segment, with their properties such as direction, lines and distance. A section of the digital map is a subgraph $G'=(V',E')$ such that $G' \subseteq G$ and the set of existing vertices $V' \subseteq V$ and edges $E' \subseteq E$ respectively.

Since our team did not have access to a proprietary digital map such as NAVTEQ[8], we adopted the one provided

[3] http://www.karmasphere.com/
[4] http://www.eclipse.org/org/
[5] http://www.java.com/
[6] http://www.inegi.org.mx
[7] http://www.cucea.udg.mx/?q=acerca/numeralia
[8] http://www.navteq.com/

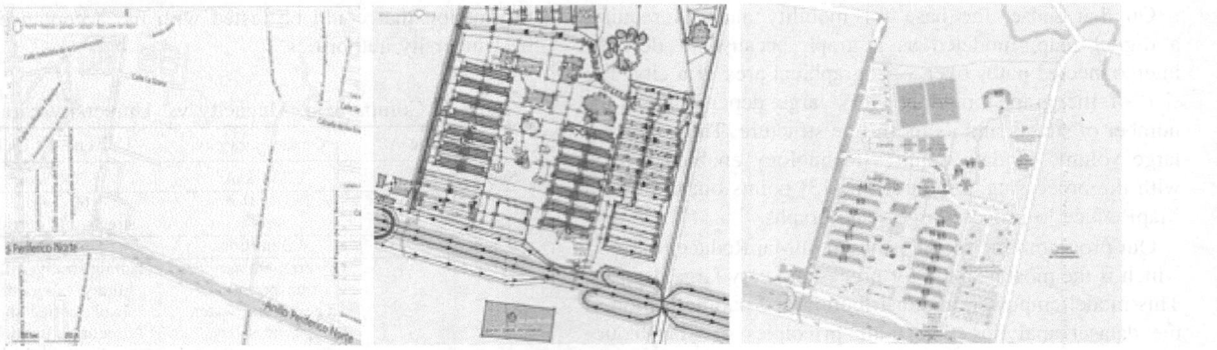

Fig. 1: Digital Map Build Process

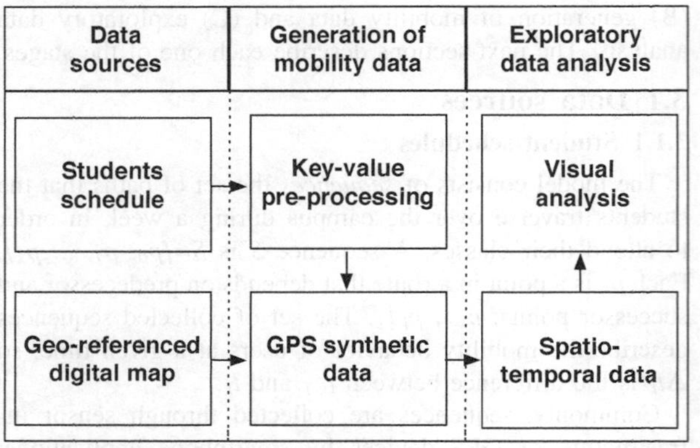

Fig. 2: Model to build the digital campus simulation

by OpenStreetMap[9] a crowdsourcing approach. For map edition, we used JOSM[10] and Potlatch2[11] online; undergraduate students worked on the design of the campus map with enough detail to include the location of classrooms, computer labs, and services such as coffee shops, library, restrooms, lockers; even more detail includes the location of energy sockets, wired and WiFi network connections, and waste baskets. Figure 1 shows some images of the resulting work.

The CUCEA digital map consist of 2,400 nodes. This constitutes 5% of the total number of nodes from a simplified graph of a Guadalajara city map. Once the design was concluded, we used Quantum GIS[12] in order to separate the layers and filter the data as well.

[9]http://www.openstreetmap.org/
[10]http://wiki.openstreetmap.org/wiki/JOSM
[11]http://wiki.openstreetmap.org/wiki/Potlatch2
[12]http://www.qgis.org/

Algorithm 1 Key-value format for schedules

Require: Students Schedule

```
Class TheMapper
    method Map(studentID id, course c)
        keyID ← id, c.dayofweek
        course ←
        c.building, c.room, c.timeInitial, c.timeFinal
    Emit(keyID k, course c)
End
Class TheReducer
    method Reduce(keyID k, courses[c1,c2,...])
        for all c_n ∈ courses[c_1, c_2, ...] do
            schedule ← schedule + c
    Emit(keyID k, schedule s)
End
```

3.2 Generation of mobility data

3.2.1 Key-value pre-processing

The data about student schedules introduced above for the current academic calendar were pre-processed. Each tuple describes one course for each student; its attributes are: StudentID, dayofweek, timeInitial, timeFinal, building and room. Given our use of MapReduce, the format of the input was pre-processed to become key-value pairs, e.g., Key = (StudentID) and Value = a list of (dayofweek, building, room, timeInitial and timeFinal), the dependence on the sequence of the values described the time along the day, we use the algorithm 1.

In the sense of Smart Cities, pre-processing would let us to prepare de the data set according with standards as Common Alerting Protocol (CAP)[13] for exchange between systems. Since the original CAP schema was provided in the form of XML, it is applicable the use of JSON[14] the data-interchange format. JSON works properly for non-relational

[13]http://docs.oasis-open.org/emergency/cap/v1.2/CAP-v1.2-os.html
[14]http://www.json.org/

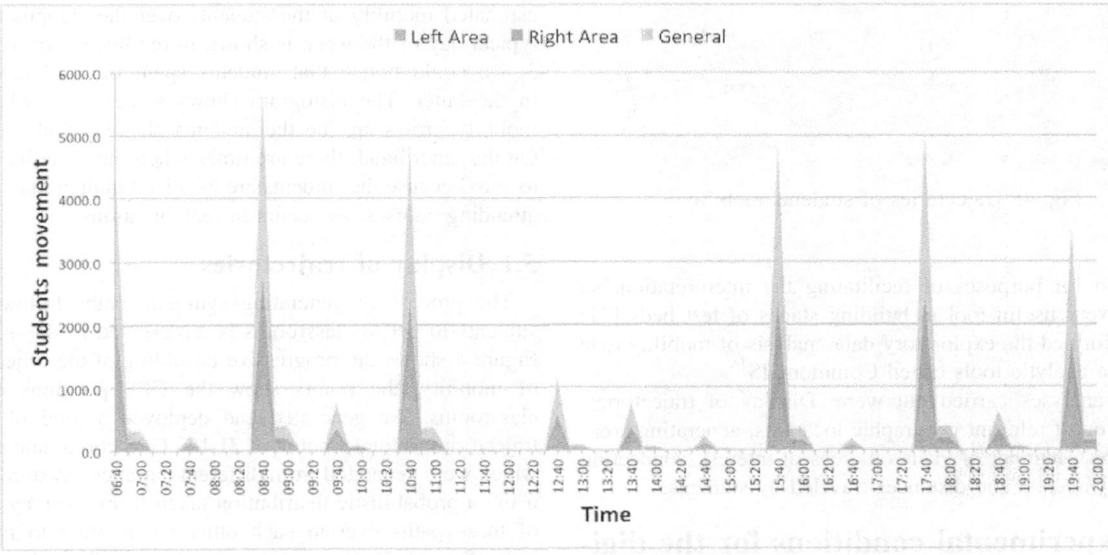

Fig. 3: Students mobility over campus facilities

Algorithm 2 Generation of GPS traces

```
Require: Graph map (map.osm), Students Schedule, pedSpeed=1.22 m/sec
Class TheMapper
    method Map(studentID id, schedule s)
        for i ← 1, s.length − 1 do
            route ← path(s(i).room, s(i + 1).room)
            timeT ← s(i).timefinal
            route(1).timestamp ← timeT
    Emit(studentID id, route r)                ▷ For each s(i)
End
Class TheCombiner
    method Reduce(studentID id, routes[r1,r2,...])
        for all r_n ∈ routes[r_1, r_2, ...] do
            for j ← 2, route.length do
                timeT ← timeT+
                (distE(route(j − 1), route(j))/
                pedSpeed)
                route(j).timestamp ← timeT
    Emit(studentID id, route r)
End
Class TheReducer
    method Reduce(studentID id, routes[r1,r2,...])
        for all r_n ∈ routes[r_1, r_2, ...] do
            trace ← trace + r
    Emit(studentID id, trace t)
End
```

data management as in the case of MapReduce.

3.2.2 GPS synthetic data

The next step used the graph from the digital map and key-value information as input to generate synthetic mobility data, shown in figure 4. The key-value format prevents the division of a sequence in different nodes during the parallelization. An additional parameter was pedestrian walking, set to 1.22 m/sec, according to [18], in order to estimate the timestamp for each visited vertex during a student's traversal of a path. We used algorithm 2.

The complexity of the MapReduce algorithms presented above based on Goel work [19] as key complexity and sequential complexity. Our algorithm 1 with S number of students, each one with C number of courses, and C_{MAX} maximum number of courses has key and sequential complexity $O(C_{MAX})$ and $O(S)$ respectively.

Additionally, algorithm 2 with the same S number of students, each one with P number of points over a GPS trace, and P_{MAX} maximum number of points has a key complexity $O(P_{MAX})$ and a sequential complexity $O(S)$ plus the complexity of path searching algorithm, we used Dijkstra $O(n^2)$ from JUNG[15] framework implementation. Regarding the complexity, it is remarkable our algorithm 2 required just one iteration which differs from others graph-based MapReduce implementation as PageRank[20].

3.3 Exploratory data analysis

Exploratory analytics provide an interesting approach to statistical results from spatio-temporal data, and their visu-

[15] http://jung.sourceforge.net/

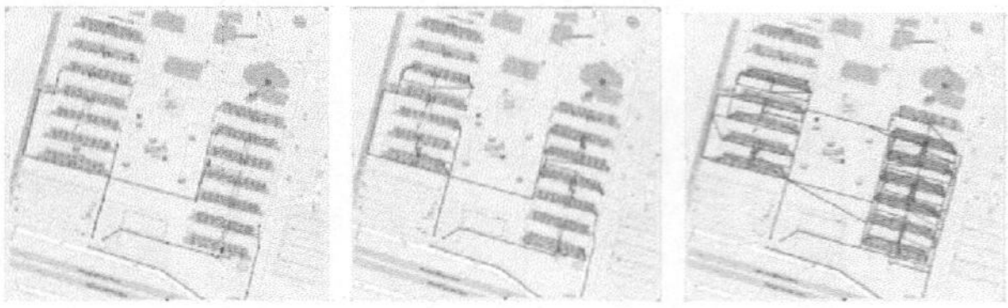

Fig. 4: Trajectories of students mobility.

alization for purposes of facilitating the interpretation, so it is a very useful tool in building stages of test beds [21] we performed the exploratory data analysis of mobility data with the analytic tools called CommonGIS[16].

The analyses carried out were: Display of trajectories, extraction of relevant geographic locations, generating areas of interest, number of visits on areas of interest, connecting areas of interest and distances traveled by students.

4. Experimental conditions for the digital campus simulation

The model was implemented as described in the above section, the digital campus simulation required the experimental settings shown in Table II. Even when the distribution and parallelization are the main advantages using MapReduce, the actual volume of information did not require the use of these. However, our Java code was generated according to the specification and tools as if it was to work for a very large data set. Once the GPS synthetic data was generated we performed the exploratory data analysis which deliver statistical and visual results describing the students behavior in order to validate the accuracy against real situations and conditions among the campus. The next section presents and discusses about our experimental results.

Table 2: Settings for experimentation

Features	Description
Memory	4Gb 1067Mhz DDR3 RAM
IDE	Eclipse
MapReduce implementation	Hadoop Cloudera CDH3b3 Karmasphere Studio 2.0
Digital map	Open Street Maps
Digital map tools	JOSM, Potlatch2, QuantumGIS
Data analysis	CommonGIS
Digital map graph	2,400 vertices/2,330 edges
Student trajectories	2,650
GPS positions	21,160

5. Results and Discussion

The campus digital map was divided in two areas: Right (8 buildings mostly classrooms and library) and left (7 buildings where are located computer laboratories). The estimated mobility of the students over the campus over a typical day of the week is shown in the histogram of figure 3, we could notice that students spent most of day time in the latter. The histogram shows some peaks when the mobility grows up due the students change of classrooms. On the other hand, there are times when the mobility trends to zero because the students are localized in their classrooms attending courses, as occurs in real situations.

[16]http://www.iais.fraunhofer.de/index.php

5.1 Display of trajectories

The process of generating synthetic paths followed by students to get to classrooms is represented in this section. Figure 4 shows the progressive unfolding of the trajectories of mobility, the points show the GPS positions of the classrooms. We generated and deployed a total of 2,650 trajectories (a total amount of 21,160 GPS coordinate points) which were generated from different entrances as start points using a probabilistic distribution taken from a survey. Many of these paths overlap each other so in order to make a separation of these we use a visualization through a space time cube where we added the time dimension to the other two dimensions that represent geographical space.

5.2 Significative Areas Extraction

This analysis consisted in generating the areas along which the moving entities meet the conditions of being stopped for at least 30 minutes. These are generalization-based clusters with a radius of 30 to 80 meters. Additionally, above the areas are displayed the lines that represent the generalization of trajectories to see the interaction between the different areas. Each circle in figure 5 represents a generalization of positions where stops are significant. The least time for the stop is 1800 seconds and the radios of the clusters are 30 and 80 meters.

5.3 Points of interest based on stop time and frequency of use

This analysis shows points of interest in terms of use, i.e. classrooms. The figure 6 is a qualitative representation where the circles pointed out the use preference level for the classroom in descending order from a qualitative colorimetry using red, yellow or green color.

Additionally, we create a representation using circular areas whose radius depends on the value of an attribute, in this case the attribute is called frequency of use. To generate this representation we use a set of points of interest containing all campus classrooms, including its corresponding node ID and geographical position. The frequency of use is obtained from the student schedule data set. Additionally we use a time parameter, in this case a date value.

The result of this analysis shows small value flow diagrams corresponding to each of the nodes that are being analyzed, in this case we refer to classrooms. This allows a simple way to observe the behavior details of performance

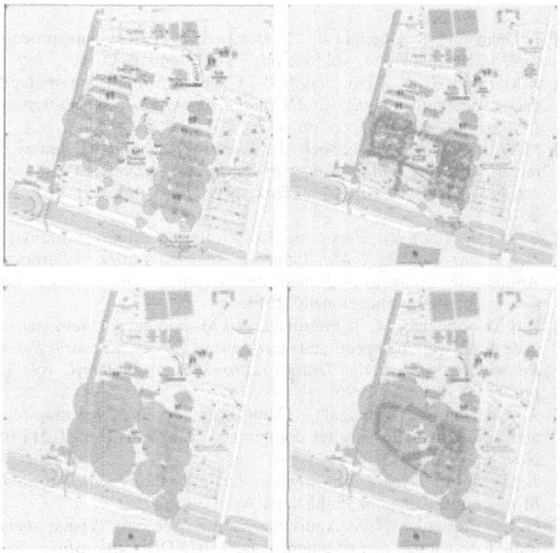

Fig. 5: Significative areas extraction

Fig. 6: Qualitative colorimetry for the use of classrooms

at each point of interest. It is possible to show a satellite view of a small section of the campus where some buildings appear as associated with each node.

6. Conclusion

The test bed worked properly and allowed us to observe the behavior of students as entities moving about a geographic area. This also allows us to observe the use made of the campus facilities, which reveals some imbalances, it shows the underutilization of some areas and secondly overuse of other resources. The synthetically generated paths have produced a set of data that we consider valid, as the exploratory analysis of the data shows patterns of student mobility with a behavior very similar to what occurs in reality. Moreover, even if the amount of data set used for this work is not very large, the MapReduce algorithms showed an accurate performance and are ready to be scaled and used with larger volumes of information.

Our analysis is stable in space and time, it is enough for us because we were interested in knowing the traces regardless of time, i.e. most used routes. We can do multiple analysis for a city, this work filtered the speed because we are focus on use of facilities, so we did source-target simulation to determine the best schemes to infrastructure maintenance. As another goal of the entire project, a team will work on speed simulation performed through lines to model the velocity of individuals that will give us a higher precision for the time, through the information of the edges; more precision in speed serves to calculate routes to make better use of the entire road network.

Finally, as a future work we plan to use the test bed with collected GPS raw data through a designed mobile application, that students could adopt to know the status of the facilities, events, as well as report issues that require some repair or maintenance. Eventually, the project is going to scale out to a Smarter Traffic system to analyze and simulate urban mobility among the city, in order to improve services in the aim of Smarter Cities[17] in collaboration with IBM.

Acknowledgment

The work described in this paper was supported by CONACYT through University of Guadalajara in collaboration with IBM on the Smarter Cities context. The authors would like to thanks to Emmanuel Barajas and Elizabeth Ramos for their technical assistance.

References

[1] E. Obra Social de Caja Madrid, "Movilidad urbana sostenible un reto energético y ambiental 2010 (www.fenercom.com/pdf/publicaciones)."

[2] D. Pilling, "Megacities (http://www.ft.com/intl/cms/s/2/6fb8a08e-0089-11e1-ba33-00144feabdc0.html)," November 4, 2011.

[3] M. Naphade, G. Banavar, C. Harrison, J. Paraszczak, and R. Morris, "Smarter cities and their innovation challenges," *Computer*, vol. 44, pp. 32 –39, june 2011.

[4] J. Bughin, M. Chui, and J. Manyika, "Clouds, big data and smart assets: Ten tech-enabled business trends to watch (http://www.mckinseyquarterly.com/)," August, 2010.

[5] D. Bollier, *The Promise and Peril of Big Data.* Communications and Society Program, One Dupont Circle, NW Suite 700 Washington, DC, USA: The Aspen Institute, 2010.

[6] R. E. Bryant, R. H. Katz, and E. D. Lazowska, "Big-data computing: Creating revolutionary breakthroughs in commerce, science and society at http://www.techrepublic.com/whitepapers/big-data-computing-creating-revolutionary-breakthroughs-in-commerce-science-and-society/2109733 (december,2008)," 2008.

[17] http://www.ibm.com/smartercities

[7] J. Dean and S. Ghemawat, "Mapreduce: simplified data processing on large clusters," in *Proceedings of the 6th conference on Symposium on Opearting Systems Design & Implementation - Volume 6*, (Berkeley, CA, USA), pp. 10–10, USENIX Association, 2004.

[8] J. Dean and S. Ghemawat, "Mapreduce: simplified data processing on large clusters," *Communication of the ACM*, vol. 51, pp. 107–113, January 2008.

[9] J. Urbani, S. Kotoulas, E. Oren, and F. Harmelen, "Scalable distributed reasoning using mapreduce," in *Proceedings of the 8th International Semantic Web Conference*, ISWC '09, (Berlin, Heidelberg), pp. 634–649, Springer-Verlag, 2009.

[10] T. Kindberg, M. Chalmers, and E. Paulos, "Guest editors' introduction: Urban computing," *IEEE Pervasive Computing*, vol. 6, pp. 18–20, 2007.

[11] J. Yuan, Y. Zheng, C. Zhang, W. Xie, X. Xie, G. Sun, and Y. Huang, "T-drive: driving directions based on taxi trajectories," in *Proceedings of the 18th SIGSPATIAL International Conference on Advances in Geographic Information Systems*, GIS '10, (New York, NY, USA), pp. 99–108, ACM, 2010.

[12] J. Yuan, Y. Zheng, X. Xie, and G. Sun, "Driving with knowledge from the physical world," in *Proceedings of the 17th ACM SIGKDD international conference on Knowledge discovery and data mining*, KDD '11, (New York, NY, USA), pp. 316–324, ACM, 2011.

[13] J. Lin and M. Schatz, "Design patterns for efficient graph algorithms in mapreduce," in *Proceedings of the Eighth Workshop on Mining and Learning with Graphs*, MLG '10, (New York, NY, USA), pp. 78–85, ACM, 2010.

[14] J. Dean and S. Ghemawat, "Mapreduce: a flexible data processing tool," *Commun. ACM*, vol. 53, pp. 72–77, January 2010.

[15] J.-M. Shih, C.-S. Liao, and R.-S. Chang, "Simplifying mapreduce data processing," *Utility and Cloud Computing, IEEE Internatonal Conference on*, vol. 0, pp. 366–370, 2011.

[16] M.-Y. Iu and W. Zwaenepoel, "Hadooptosql: a mapreduce query optimizer," in *Proceedings of the 5th European conference on Computer systems*, EuroSys '10, (New York, NY, USA), pp. 251–264, ACM, 2010.

[17] C. A. de Fomento Banco de Desarrollo de América Latina, ed., *Desarrollo Urbano y Movilidad en América Latina*. Corporación Andina de Fomento - Banco de Desarrollo de América Latina (www.caf.com/publicaciones), 2011.

[18] R. L. Knoblauch, M. T. Pietrucha, and M. Nitzburg, "Field studies of pedestrian walking speed and start-up time," *Transportation Research Record: Journal of the Transportation Research Board*, vol. 1538, pp. 27–38, January 1996.

[19] A. Goel and K. Munagala, "Complexity measures for map-reduce, and comparison to parallel computing," *CoRR*, vol. abs/1211.6526, November 11 2012.

[20] J. Lin and C. Dyer, *Data-Intensive Text Processing with MapReduce*. Morgan and Claypool Plubishers, April 30 2010.

[21] G. L. Andrienko, N. V. Andrienko, and S. Wrobel, "Visual analytics tools for analysis of movement data," *SIGKDD Explorations*, vol. 9, no. 2, pp. 38–46, 2007.

SESSION

SEARCH + INTELLIGENT DATABASES + TEXT INFORMATION MANAGEMENT

Chair(s)

TBA

Proposal on Divergent Web Search Engine with Mandal-Art

Motoichi Adachi
Dep. of Information System
Toyo University
Kawagoe, JAPAN
m-adachi@amy.hi-ho.ne.jp

Eigo Ito
Dep. of Information System
Toyo University
Kawagoe, JAPAN
e-mail@e-ito.jp

Takayuki Fujimoto
Dep. of Information System
Toyo University
Kawagoe, JAPAN
me@fujimotokyo.com

***Abstract*— There is a vast amount of information on the Internet. A user can directly access any Website listed on the pages of a search engines. However, submitting a query is integral to the use of search engines. Therefore, the accessible information largely depends on the user's own vocabulary and creativity abilities. Consequently, the user may not be able to access adequate information. To solve this problem, a search suggestion function appeared. However, this function is mainly for input support, and it is not suitable for developing a search. In this article, we propose a search assist method by developing a search engine using the "Mandal-Art", a creativity technique.**

Keywords—Keyword Search, Web Search, Search Suggest, Mandal-Art, Smartphone

I. Introduction

A. Research Abstract

A Web search is conducted by entering the keyword in the search field. The searcher carries out a keyword search using related words to access the targeted information. It is easy to carry out data processing for the keyword in a search engine and its mechanism is easily understandable. However, the choice of keywords chosen to search the targeted information and the proper refinement of the keywords inevitably relies on the user's own vocabulary and creativity abilities.

It means that the use of the keyword search engine requires those abilities. Knowledge of the proper keywords is essential in achieving an effective keyword search. In other words, it is needless to say that one cannot search the keyword which one does not know. All kinds of information is stored on a huge database of the Internet, however a paradox exists as the user can only search the keywords which are known to them.

To solve this problem, most of the Web search engines implement search suggestions. The search suggestions function displays input predictions and related keywords in real time when the user enters the search keywords. It was introduced to many internet search engines including Google Suggest in 2004 and Yahoo! Search Suggest in 2007. Systematically search suggestions are displayed directly below the text input box to compare with the entered keywords. This method is simple and suited for the Web search engines as the related keyword suggestions are placed in list form.

Thus, search suggestions enhance the convenience of the keyword search. However, this method only suggests the typical keywords related to the entered search keywords and is a case of input support and no more. Specifically, there is no support to narrow the search result and reach the targeted information.

It is said that Web search engines enable the users to access more on-target information by selecting the keywords from the list of search results and thus allows them to develop the search further. Meanwhile, the research and development of the system that offers this kind of search support is not necessarily sufficient. There are a few support systems to develop the search; however, they are not intuitive or convenient. As far as we know, there is no system or service which has considerable currency.

In this article, we propose a system using the "Mandal-Art" motif, as a new information search method designed to be used in a Web search.

Mandal-Art is a creativity technique which extends ideas divergently in an easy and systematic way by starting from one key word and using only nine cells.

This research proposes to develop a Web search engine which supports the input and search of keywords based on the creativity technique devised by Mandal-Art.

B. Related Studies・Existing Systems

1) The number of keywords used for the search

Third Door Media, Int. carried out research on the number of keywords used in a Web search in 2010[1]. U.S. search queries were measured in the survey. The Presence or absence of white space is used to separate words.

According to the results, the rate of multi-word queries is over 77%. Notably, the rate of queries which contain 2 to 5 words is more than 65%. It means that generally Web search engines are used for the more target-oriented search by query refinement.

2) Mandal-Art

One of the creativity techniques employed by Mandal-Art[2] is a 3 x 3 grid consisting of nine square cells.

First of all, one must write down the subject in the center cell. Next, in the surrounding eight cells, write down some related words. The eight keywords written in the surrounding cells could be intuitive or subjective.

Then, choose one of the eight surrounding keywords and put it in the center. As you have already done, write down eight keywords related to the center on the surrounding cells.

Repetition of this process an arbitrary number of times extends the ideas from the original keyword developmentally, and it helps you reach a surprising result.

A multidimensional perspective of the subject is realized through the effort of filling out the eight cells as indicated above.

"iMandalArt for iPhone" is one of the application-optimized examples of Mandal-Art. Mandal-Art, which is practiced on paper, has been developed as a smartphone application of this system.

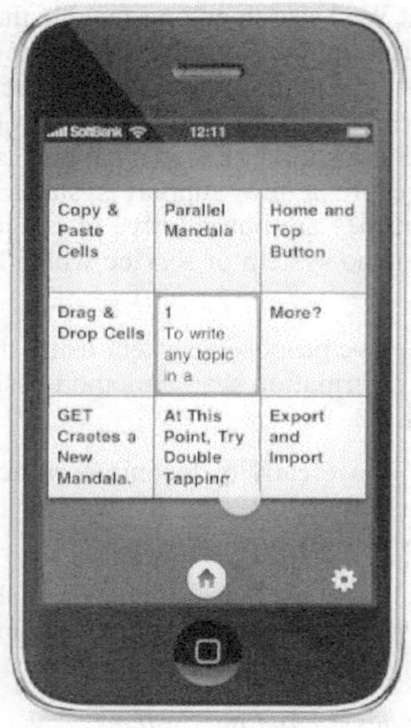

Fig. 1. The use of Mandal-Art (iMandalArt for iPhone)

This research proposes Web search support application software using the creativity technique of "Mandal-Art". In the proposed system, the search results derived from the keyword entered in the center cell are assigned to the eight cells. It facilitates the rich development of ideas based on the keywords and the intuitive information search which can be viewed with ease.

In general the current search suggestion functions display eight to ten suggestions. This number is suitable for the display of related information; hence the eight cells of Mandal-Art. Also, in the Web search, since the keywords are added by one word at a time, by way either of the key input or the search suggestion function, the added keywords are suitable for the sequential display layout of Mandal-Art.

3) Web service "What do you suggest"

"What do you suggest?" is the Web service utilizing a search suggestion function. This system displays the related keywords which are suggested based on the original keyword entry, like a mind map. It enables the multi-layered display; by clicking on the relevant keywords displayed on the screen, new search suggestions are again generated from the original keyword entry and the selected relevant keyword. If no search suggestion is available, the search results display access to applicable Web pages.

This method is excellent as it allows the user to view all of the related keywords at one time. The multi-layered display requires a broad area for the display. The refinement support system could be run by a one word entry. However, the results of search suggestions using one word are diverse, and this system seems wasteful as it is necessary to display these suggestions. Also, the displayed contents are the same as the usual search suggestions; Only the method of operation is different.

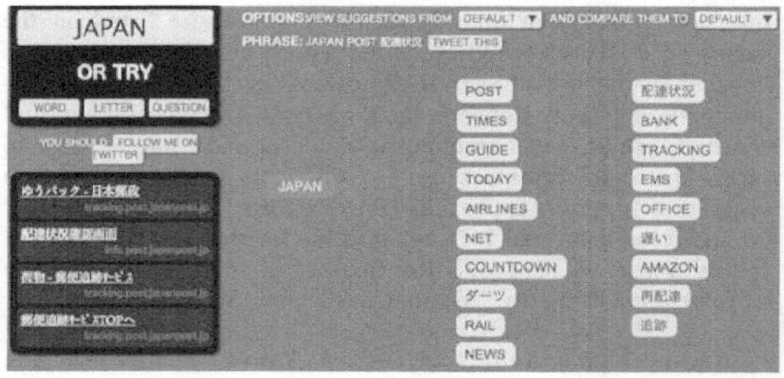

Fig. 2. The use of search suggestions Function(What do you suggest?)

II. System Proposal

A. System Summary

This system was developed with the aim of providing a service which can be used instantly and with ease. Therefore, we have developed it as smartphone application software to be used easily and intuitively.

The Web search process with this system is indicated below.

[Step1] Enter the search keyword.

[Step2] Eight keywords related to the original are displayed by the search suggestion function.

[Step3] Select one of the related eight keywords displayed.

[Step4] The original keyword and the related keyword selected are displayed in the center of the next screen.

[Step5] The Keywords are displayed. These words relate to the word in the center cell.

[Step 6 and more] Repeating the above process an arbitrary number of times supports the keyword entry and broadens the variety of keywords.

[Final step] Finally the search runs with all keywords entered /selected, and displays the result.

All of these displays/operations have to be simple.

In this system, the display processing operations show the search suggestions or the search results.

The number of the search suggestions and the search results displayed by the representative services today are indicated in the TABLE I.

TABLE I. THE NUMBER OF THE SUGGESTIONS/SEARCH RESULTS

	Google	Yahoo!	Bing	MediaWiki	Amazon
Suggests /Page	8	10	8	10	10
Results /Page	10	10	10	20	16

Representative services display eight to ten suggestions .Usually, with regard to the display, adequate visibility and a variety of the alternatives are trade-offs. However, the number of the suggestions is rarely seen to be a problem. It is considered that the display of eight to ten suggestions is no great issue.

Similarly, ten is the biggest number per page in the search results case.

In Mandal-Art, information is described in the surrounding eight cells at random, relating to the subject entry. The displays, based on Mandal-Art, of the suggestions and search results are realized by setting the search keyword as a subject entry and assigning suggestions and results to the surrounding cells. A limitation of Mandal-Art is that the number of suggestions or results is confined to eight. However, as for the display of the suggestions and search results, this number is not necessarily restrictive, when compared to the results displayed by other existing services. Therefore, this number would seem to be appropriate.

B. System Flow

This system consists of four screens.

The first screen is for the entry of the keyword to be searched. (Fig.3.).

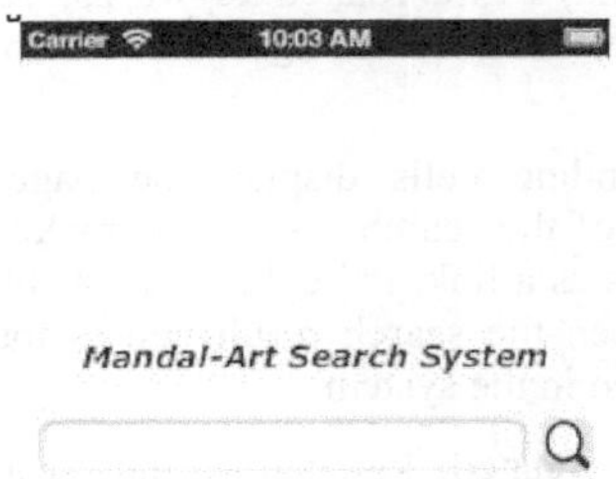

Fig. 3. Keyword Search entry screen

Only the system name, the text field to enter the search keywords, and the search button are placed in the center of this screen.

To inform the users that this is a Web search system, the screen design is simple. To proceed to the next screen simply click on the search button next to the search keyword entry field.

The second screen is for the related keyword selection (Fig.4.). A 3 x 3 grid consisting of nine cells, which is used in Mandal-Art, is displayed on this screen. The center cell displays the search keyword entry. The surrounding eight cells display the keywords related to the search keyword.

Up to eight search keywords can be added by touching the related keyword cells. In this case, all of the search keywords are displayed in the center cell. For example, if "toy" is entered as a search keyword, at first "toy" is only displayed in the center cell and the surrounding cells display the keywords related to "toy", as shown on the left side of Fig.4.. Subsequently, when "story" is touched and selected the display changes as indicated on the right side of Fig.4. "Toy" and "Story" are displayed in the center cell and the surrounding keywords are related to both of "toy" and "story".

The search result screen can be accessed by tapping on the center cell. Also, the search keyword editing screen can be accessed by pinching out the nine cells.

Fig. 4. Related keyword selection screen (left:beginning, right:added keywords)

The third screen displays the search results (Fig.5.).

This layout of this screen, like the related keywords selection screen, is based on Mandal-Art.

It is common to display the search keyword in the center cell, with the second screen and the surrounding cells displaying the Web search results. These results consist of the Web page title, summary text and URL. The related keyword selection screen can be accessed by touching the center cell.

Fig. 5. Search Result Screen

The fourth screen displays the search keyword editing function(Fig.6.). The display of this screen is also based on Mandal-Art as well as the second and third screen.

The center cell displays the original search keyword entry. The surrounding eight cells display the additional search keywords which were selected from the related keyword selection screen.

Fig. 6. Search keyword editing screen

The search keywords can be activated/deactivated by touching each cell. Once a search keyword is deactivated, a blue x icon appears and the background color becomes light gray. If a keyword is deactivated, it can be reactivated by touching it again.

In order to move to the related keyword selection screen after editing, simply pinch in the nine cells. Then, the search keywords which are deactivated are deleted. When the screen shifts to the search keyword editing screen again, those deleted search keywords are now invalid. If all of the search keywords are deactivated, the screen shifts back to the search keyword entry screen exceptionally.

The system proposed in this research supports a Web search utilizing the four kinds of screens discussed above. When the system is started, firstly the search keyword entry screen is displayed. After the search keyword entry, the screen reverts to the related keywords selection screen. This screen, where the search is refined, is the main part of the proposed system. After fully examining the search key words, the users can access Web pages through the search result screen. The search keyword editing screen is just for directional correction and the refinement of a search and it is not a fundamental component of the search. The keyword entry screen can be accessed from any screen by clicking the reset button located on each screen and a new search can be carried out from the beginning.

C. Related keywords display/selection

When the search keyword is entered, the screen transits to the related keyword selection screen. Retrieving the related keywords is done with the search keyword at this point. Suggest API does not distinguish between an input estimation search and related keyword search. Since input estimation is not necessary, the query for a Suggest API is set as a search keyword with trailing half-width white space: this request enables us to get the related keywords easily.

Retrieved results are used after eliminating the input estimations included. If one suggestion consists of multiple related keywords, only the initial word is treated as a related keyword. If the number of related keywords is less than eight, overlapping words are chosen at random and displayed. The related keywords are assigned to the cells on a random basis.

By touching the displayed related keywords, the search keywords can be added to. If this action occurs, all information on each of the nine cells is renewed.

If no related keyword is retrieved, the screen automatically reverts back to the search result screen.

D. Search result display/selection

The display of the search results is based on Mandal-Art as well as the display of the related keywords. To distinguish the former from the latter, the background color of the center cell is set as gray.

The surrounding cells display the page titles and the summary texts of the search results. To make it clear that the page title serves as a link, its' color is set as blue and it is also underlined. When the search result cell is touched, the Web page is displayed in the system.

Unlike the related keywords, the search results are distributed in clockwise direction from top left according to the search ranking. Also, if the eight sells are not filled with the results, there is no overlapping result display prepared.

By flicking the screen to the right, the lower-ranking results can be viewed. Conversely, by flicking to the left, the upper-ranking results can be viewed again.

III. System Prototype

A. Technique used in production

This system utilizes a Web search and a search suggestion function. Representative search engines like Google, Yahoo!, Bing, and et al., opens API which realize these functions. Each API has different fees and a limit on the number of searches obtainable. This system utilizes the affordable Yahoo! Search BOSS API provided by Yahoo! USA, though developers are required to display the Yahoo brand name.

This system has been developed for the Smartphone as its distinct functions such as, the minimized display layout of Mandal-Art and the intuitive input by a single touch can be realized on a Smartphone. This time, the prototype has been developed as application software which operates on the iPhone, one make of Smartphone.

B. Web Search Implement

Using Yahoo! Search BOSS, information is acquired with GetMethod over the HTTP protocol. Although a search based on multiple services is possible, this system sends a request for the search suggestion and a request for the Web search separately. This is because both the search suggestion and the Web search are carried out independently in the system.

The request for the Web search utilizes Web Service. Many value settings, including q argument value setting are possible when applying Web Service. At first, the format argument is specified to "json" to make the data output format JSON.

The Search string is encoded into UTF-8 using the method CFURLCreateStringByAddingPercentEscapes from the library, the Core Foundation and sent as the argument q. Because the number of the search results is eight at most, the count argument, the number of the results, is set as 8 and the start argument, the ordinal position of the first result, is set as 8 x p (p is the page number, the default value is 0) To narrow down the targeted information format and generate a Web page, the view argument is specified to "smfeed", and the type argument is specified to "html". To secure the sufficient number of the characters for the summary text, the abstract argument is specified to "long'.

Response is received as JSON response as specified by the format argument. The number of the search results is retrieved from a count property in the web field. Each result is stored in the result fields separately.

The page title is retrieved from the title field: the text summary from the abstract field: the URL from the clickurl field, in each result field. Received JSON is converted to NSDictionary using NSJSONSerialization.

C. Search Suggestion Function Implement

The search suggest function implement applies Related Service by Yahoo! Search BOSS.

When using Related Service, the search string encoded into UTF-8 is sent as the q argument at first and the format argument is specified to "json" in the same way as when using Web Service. To use search suggestions with editing, the count argument, the number of the suggestions, is set as 10, the maximum value. The start argument is set as 0, if the available data is insufficient, the start argument starts increasing by 10 for data addition.

Response is received as JSON response. The search suggestions are described as one string in the suggestion field. After conversion into NSDictionay in the same way as when using Web Service, the string is separated by white space. Depending on the utilization purpose, each suggestion is examined to delete and modify. The number of search suggestions can be increased by altering the start argument and repeating the request to the Related Service until the number of suggestions reaches the required number. If the count property in the related field of the response is 0, this process stops.

D. Data type conversion

Data output acquired by the Web search and the search suggestion function, is JSON. To utilize this data, it is required to process the data into the available type. iPhone applies Objective-C for the programming language. Since Objective-C provides NSJSONSerializaion class, a JSON serializer, this class is used for conversion.

IV. Conclusions

The Web search engines today operate a search based on an initial query. It is necessary for the user themselves to devise an appropriate query if they are to access the targeted information. This query is not always close to the desired information. Therefore, usually the method to refine the search with multiple words is practiced.

The proposed system is a system which generates a Web search by optimizing the use of the search suggestion function; by selecting the search keyword with a single touch.

Visibility of the search suggestions and the search results is improved by utilizing Mandal-Art to display them.

Since Mandal-Art only displays a 3 x 3 grid consisting of nine cells on the screen, the operation procedure becomes clear and therefore the ease with which it can be used is also improved.

By entering one word as the original search keyword, the user can carry out a search powered by Mandal-Art. A large display and the use of simple operations make it easy to peruse Web search results.

In Mandal-Art, which only use nine cells, it could happen that some related information is missed. However, since the displayed number of the suggestions/search results is almost the same as those displayed by the current existing services, selectivity is maintained.

Thus, by utilizing Mandal-Art, it is possible to develop a system in which users can easily take advantage of the multiple words search and search suggestion function often used by the Web search providers today. In this research, we have experimentally developed the system for use on Smartphone's which have small screens, and were able to realize the methods necessary to secure visibility and the operability.

V. Future Tasks

Mandal-Art started as a creativity technique using handwriting. The center cell is the important cell, the subject. When handwritten, this structure requires the practitioner to first, place the keyword the center cell, explicitly and consciously. However, customarily important information tends to be placed in a position close to top left, the origin of the display to secure the space for the display, in the computer system. When introducing Mandal-Art to the Web search system, the search keyword is displayed in the center cell. Whether users can recognize the importance of this layout and the significant difference it makes to visibility is a matter that requires further validation.

Also, this system was particularly developed for use on smartphones, most of which of have minimum scroll function and the screen size can be stabilized.

However, a Web search is generally conducted on a Web page through a browser.

Therefore, we feel it necessary to develop a system which can operate on any terminal through the use of a browser.

References

[1] Chris Sherman, "What The Long Tail Of Search Actually Looks Like", <http://searchengineland.com/what-the-long-tail-of-search-actually-looks-like-39639/>, Search Engine Land, Third Door Media, Inc., April 2010.

[2] Hiro Art Directions, Inc., "iMandalArt", <http://iphone.mandal-art.com/imandalart-e/>, November 2011.

[3] Simon Elvery, "What do you suggest?", <http://whatdoyousuggest.net/>, July 2010.

[4] Ingrid Hsieh-Yee, "Research on Web search behavior", Library & information science research, Vol. 23, No. 2, pp.167, 2001.

[5] K. Kozuki, A. Tsubokura, S. Harima, N. Ashida and K. Tsushima, "Cognitive Idea Processor --- Modified Mandal-Art", World Conference on Educational Multimedia, Hypermedia and Telecommunications (EDMEDIA) 2000, p.1820, 2000.

[6] K. Kozuki, N. Ashida, N. Nomura, T. Otsuka; A. Tsubokura and K. Tsuchima, "Cognitive interface for idea processor", Advanced Learning Technologies, 2000. IWALT 2000. Proceedings. International Workshop on, pp.268-269, December 2000.

[7] S. Buisine, G. Besacier, M. Najm, A. Aoussat, F. Vernier, "Computer-Supported Creativity: Evaluation of a Tabletop Mind-Map Application", Engineering Psychology and Cognitive Ergonomics, pp.22-31, July 2007.

Structured Synonym Knowledge Base Expansion by Mining from Unstructured Web Text

Yangsheng Ji[1], **Xiang Chen**[23], **Yiling Liu**[4], **Chong Gu**[4], **Shouling Cui**[4], **Jiangtao Jia**[4]
[1]CETC 28TH Institute, Nanjing 210007, China
jiyangsheng@gmail.com
[2]Nantong University, Nantong 226019, China
[3]State Key Laboratory for Novel Software Technology, Nanjing University, Nanjing 210093, China
chenxiang.nju@gmail.com
[4]Section F, Huawei Industrial Base, Bantian Longgang, Shenzhen, China
{liuyiling,guchong,cuishouling,jiajiangtao}@huawei.com

Abstract— *Recognition of semantic similarity between words plays an important role in text information management, information retrieval and natural language processing. There are two major approaches to recognizing the semantic similarity, among which one way is extracting similarity relationships based on a structured semantic dictionary, while the other way is learning the semantic similarity from a large corpus. Building a semantic dictionary is a time consuming task which also requires much expertise, while the learning method alone cannot extract precise similarity between words. This paper proposes to expand the semantic dictionary by learning the word similarity from heterogenous knowledge bases statistically. This method can not only expand the semantic dictionary from the open knowledge bases, but also achieve accurate semantic similarity. In the evaluation of semantic relatedness competition held by CCF, the proposed system ranks the* 3rd *place according to the macro average F1 and the* 2nd *place according to the micro average F1.*

Keywords: semantic similarity, heterogenous knowledge bases, statistical learning, semantic mining.

1. Introduction

Natural language has such a diversity that we have multiple choices to describe a single concept. In the domain of text information, the different descriptions of the same concept are often regarded as synonymous words. E.g., both of `(buy purchase)` and `(big large)` are synonymous word pairs. This means although the word forms of synonyms are different, they actually have the same semantic meaning.

The synonymy can give rise to "semantic gap" between words, which makes great challenges for tasks in text mining, information retrieval, and natural language processing. In opinion text, different people tend to comment on the same product attribute in different ways, which are synonymous. In order to get a comprehensive analysis on the reviews of the product, it is essential for review summarization and opinion identification systems to identify the different descriptions of the same attribute [1]. In information retrieval, the query is a kind of descriptions for the concept of users' interest, while the relevant documents of the concept may employ different kinds of descriptions. The semantic gap resulted from different descriptions leads to a mismatch between the query and relevant documents [2], [3]. In natural language processing (NLP), the machine translation system after training can be well suited for certain types of descriptions of a concept. However, the system may fail to translate unknown and different descriptions of the concept [4]. The above mentioned tasks are widely applicable in daily life. However, these applications are faced with severe challenges of semantic gap brought by synonyms. Thus, the identification of semantic word similarity has been an important research topic.

The recent research on approaches to identification of semantic word similarity mainly falls into two categories: extracting similarity relationships based on a structured semantic dictionary, and learning the semantic similarity based on a large corpus. The former approaches [5], [6], [7], [8], [9], [10] compute the word similarity according to a user-defined similarity measure, which is based on the structure of the dictionary. The dictionary is often created by Linguistic experts, who encode the word relationships as the semantic structure in the dictionary. While the dictionary based approaches are precise for identifying the synonyms, the construction of the dictionary requires much expertise and a huge amount of efforts. As the dictionary is fixed, these approaches are infeasible to extend for handling new words. The second approaches [11], [12], [13], [14], [15], [16], [17] compute the word similarity according to a statistical similarity measure based on a large corpus. These approaches can handle more words than the dictionary based approaches. However, the computed word similarity is not as accurate as the former approaches.

To solve the problems mentioned above, we propose to

extract the word similarity from heterogenous knowledge bases. The proposed approach can not only expand the semantic relationships in the dictionary, but also achieve accurate results while preserving a higher recall than the dictionary based approaches. In the evaluation of semantic relatedness competition held by CCF, the proposed system ranks the 2nd place according to the micro average F1 and the 3rd place according to the macro average F1.

In the following parts, Section 2 introduces the proposed approach, and Section 3 performs an extensive evaluation. Finally, we make a conclusion.

2. Identification of Word Similarity from Heterogenous Knowledge Bases

The heterogenous knowledge bases in the proposed approach include a structured synonym dictionary and open resources on the web. The open resources include *Douban*[1], *Baike*[2] and *Baidu-Dictionary*[3], which are heterogenous knowledge bases in the text form. The key of the proposed approach is the fusion of the knowledge bases. First, we mine the synonymous relationship patterns (syn-patterns) from the knowledge bases, respectively. Then, the unstructured information of synonyms on the web can be transformed into structures which comply with the dictionary. Finally, by combining and cleaning the structured information of the former step, the synonym dictionary can get expanded while preserving the high accuracy.

2.1 The Structured Synonym Dictionary

As *Yidian*[4], a synonym dictionary, includes a sufficient amount of synonyms, it is selected as the dictionary component of the proposed system. The formal definition of the structured synonym dictionary is as following:

Definition *1 (The Structured Synonym Dictionary):* The dictionary is denoted as $D = D_S \cup D_R$. $D_S = \{(w_i, SID_i, S(w_i))|i = 1, ..., |D_s|\}$ denotes the synonym item set, with w_i denoting the target word in the synonym item, SID_i denoting the concept ID of w_i, $S(w_i)$ denoting the set of w_i's synonyms. $D_R = \{(w_j, RID_j, R(w_j))|j = 1, ..., |D_R|\}$ denotes the item set of semantic related words, with w_j denoting the target word of the item set, RID_j denoting the related concept ID of w_j, $R(w_j)$ denoting the set of w_j's related words.

In Definition 1, the synonym means it shares the same meaning with the target word, while the related word indicates sharing a relevant meaning with the target word. In this paper, the related word is a broader concept than the synonym.

[1]http://www.douban.com
[2]http://baike.baidu.com
[3]http://dict.baidu.com
[4]http://ir.hit.edu.cn

Table 1: HTML Syn-Pattern Mining for Semantic Similarity Identification in *Douban*

Input : the target word $w \in D$, and the synonym set $S(w)$ Output: the set of candidate pattern words $pattern(w)$
Steps : 1. type w in the query box of *Douban*, get the content of the return page $page(w)$; 2. set the candidate pattern words $pattern(w) = \emptyset$; 3. for each $v \in S(w)$ 4. search for v in $page(w)$; if not found, turn to step 3; 5. extract the content segment of v in $page(w)$, delete the HTML tags, and get a string $str(v)$; 6. segment the string $str(v)$ by spaces and tabs, get a group of words, and add them into $pattern(w)$; 7. end for; 8. output $pattern(w)$.

2.2 Extraction of Syn-Patterns from the Knowledge Bases

In *Douban* and *Baike*, person names, organization names and some other items are explicitly marked with their synonyms in the HTML code of the web pages. These marks are accurate and reliable for syn-pattern mining. In *Baidu-Dictionary* and *Baike*, the unstructured text also contains much information of synonyms, which can infer the syn-patterns. However, the syn-patterns are not trivial either in the structured HTML code, or in the plain text. Thus, we need to design algorithms to mine the patterns in the knowledge bases.

2.2.1 Mining the HTML Syn-Patterns in *Douban*

In order to get the HTML syn-patterns from *Douban*, we need to carry out the following steps. First, we input the target word w in the query box of *Douban*, and get the HTML content of the return page. Then, we search for the target word in the HTML content, and extract the content segment from the HTML tag before w to the tag after w. At the same time, we record the frequency of words in the content segment. Finally, when the operations for all the target words are carried out, the words with top ranked frequencies in the content segment can be employed to build the HTML syn-patterns.

It is notable that both Chinese words and other string forms (a word attached with a punctuation) in the segment, which are separated by spaces or tabs, can be indicative for the synonymous relationship. As a result, we need to record all of their frequencies to build the patterns later on. The algorithm for mining the HTML syn-patterns in *Douban* is shown in Table 1.

We gather the candidate pattern words $pattern(w)$ for all $w \in D$, and record the frequency for each word. The words with top ranked frequencies are selected as the final syn-pattern words $pattern(D)$. In *Douban*, to compute the

Table 2: HTML Syn-Pattern Mining for Semantic Similarity Identification in *Baike*

Input : the target word $w \in D$, and the synonym set $S(w)$
Output: the set of candidate pattern words $pattern(w)$

Steps :
1. type w in the query box of *Baike*, get the content of the return page $page(w)$;
2. extract the information table $table(w)$ from $page(w)$;
3. if the extraction fails, turn to step 10;
4. set the candidate pattern words $pattern(w) = \emptyset$;
5. for each $v \in S(w)$
6. search for v in $table(w)$; if not found, turn to step 5;
7. extract the content segment of v in $table(w)$, delete the HTML tags, and get a string $str(v)$;
8. segment the string $str(v)$ by spaces and tabs, get a group of words, and add them into $pattern(w)$;
9. end for;
10. output $pattern(w)$.

synonyms of a new word w_{new}, we search for each syn-pattern word $u \in pattern(D)$ in $page(w_{new})$. If u is found, we extract the content segment from $page(w_{new})$ and remove the tags, syn-pattern words and punctuations. The remaining string is the synonym.

2.2.2 Mining the HTML Syn-Patterns in *Baike*

Baike contains a lot of items such as person names, location names and movie names. These items provides much information for synonyms, which are stored in the information tables. The table is shown as in Figure 1.

Mining the HTML syn-patterns in *Baike* requires in advance extracting the information tables, which could be extracted by matching the regular expression. When the table content is extracted, the syn-pattern mining from the information table is a similar procedure with the algorithm in Table 1. The algorithm for mining the HTML syn-patterns in *Baike* is shown in Table 2.

The above algorithm recognizes the information table in step 2, while other steps are similar with the algorithm for *Douban*. In *Baike*, to compute the synonyms of a new word w_{new}, we search for each syn-pattern word $u \in pattern(D)$ in $table(w_{new})$. If u is found, we extract the content segment from $table(w_{new})$ and remove the tags, syn-pattern words and punctuations. The remaining string is the synonym.

2.2.3 Mining the Syn-Patterns in Unstructured Text

In the open knowledge bases on the web, e.g. *Baidu-Dictionary*, *Baike*, the synonym patterns are more often contained in the plain text than in the structured HTML code. If the syn-patterns can be mined from the unstructured text, the knowledge base of synonyms can be largely expanded,

Table 3: Plain Text Syn-Pattern Mining for Semantic Similarity Identification

Input : the synonym dictionary D
Output: the syn-pattern P in the plain text

Steps :
1. initialize the candidate syn-pattern set as $T = \emptyset$;
2. for each $w \in D$
3. initialize the candidate syn-pattern set of w as $T(w) = \emptyset$;
4. type w in the query box, and get the return page content $page(w)$;
5. extract the plain text $text(w)$ from $page(w)$;
6. if $text(w)$ is empty, turn to step 2;
7. for each $v \in S(w)$
8. search for v in $text(w)$; if not found, turn to step 7;
9. extract the text segment $context(w, v)$;
10. perform Chinese word segmentation on $context(w, v)$, and get the syn-pattern $template(w, v)$ for synonym word pair (w, v) ;
11. $T(w) = T(w) \cup \{ template(w, v)\}$;
12. end for;
13. $T = T \cup T(w)$;
14. end for;
15. apply frequent pattern mining algorithm, and get $P = FrequentPattern(T)$.
16. output P.

especially the synonym dictionary.

However, the syn-patterns in the plain text is not trivial. So we need to design algorithms to discover the patterns or rules. The syn-patterns in the plain text have similar properties with the HTML syn-patterns. Along with the occurrence of the synonym, there are explicit or implicit marks for indicating the synonymous relationship. The major difference between the syn-patterns is that the syn-patterns in the plain text employ free natural language to describe the synonymous relationship, while the syn-patterns in HTML use limited descriptions. Thus, the syn-patterns in the plain text are more difficult to extract, and less reliable than the HTML syn-patterns. The extraction algorithm of syn-patterns in the plain text is shown in Table 3.

The algorithm in Table 3 describes the steps to build the plain text syn-patterns. The core idea is to extract the context template $template(w, v)$ for each synonym word pair (w, v) in the dictionary. We assume $template(w, v)$ is a set of words without the order information. The words in $template(w, v)$ are extracted from $context(w, v)$, which is the context of the words w and v. $context(w, v)$ denotes the shorter one of (1) the segment from the target word w to the synonym v, and (2) the text segment separated by the punctuations with containing the synonym v. The templates for all synonym word pairs build up a pattern database T. By applying the frequent pattern mining algorithm to T, we can get the most representative syn-patterns from the plain text. The synonym extraction of new words is the same as previous algorithms.

中文名:	关羽	出生日期:	约160年(延熹三年六月)
外文名:	GuanYu	逝世日期:	220年初(建安二十四年冬)
别名:	关长生,关云长,关公	职业:	前将军
民族:	汉族	主要成就:	阵斩颜良、打败于禁
出生地:	河东郡解县	谥号:	壮缪侯

Fig. 1: An Information Table from *Baike*

2.3 Evaluation on the Reliability of Syn-Patterns

As mentioned above, the HTML syn-patterns are more reliable than the plain text syn-patterns. Thus, reliable patterns should be assigned higher weights so that they can make more contributions. In order to evaluate the reliability of different patterns, we perform the pattern mining based on a small subset of the dictionary, and extract some new synonyms by applying the patterns. By human annotating the new synonyms, we can get the accuracy of each pattern. The higher accuracy of the syn-pattern, the larger weight the syn-pattern will get. We excerpt some results shown in Table 4.

Table 4: Weights for Different Syn-Patterns

Syn-Pattern				Weight	Type
[近义词]	又名:	简称:	别名:	1.0	HTML Syn-Pattern
也说	亦称	俗称	的别名	0.9	Plain Text Syn-Pattern
谓	泛称	亦称(	之称	0.8	Plain Text Syn-Pattern
犹				0.7	Plain Text Syn-Pattern
指	的对称			0.6	Plain Text Syn-Pattern

2.4 Synonym Information Fusion from Heterogenous Knowledge Bases

When the syn-patterns are extracted, we can apply them to the web pages, and build an open synonym dictionary $D_{open} = \{S_i^o = \{w_{i,1}, ..., w_{i,t_i}\} | i = 1, ..., k\}$. The rank j for $w_{i,j}$ is determined according to the weight of the syn-pattern, which extracts $w_{i,j}$ from the text. To expand the existing synonym dictionary D, we need to fuse D and D_{open} together. The fusion algorithm is shown in Table 5.

2.5 Synonym Computation based on Heterogenous Knowledge Bases

When the syn-patterns are extracted and the synonym dictionary D has been expanded, the proposed system can compute the synonyms of a query word effectively, which is shown in Figure 2. As abbreviations are a sort of synonyms with complicated forms, the knowledge bases can only include a few of them [19], [20]. We implement a component to deal with the problem [21] so that our system can handle more complicated scenarios.

Table 5: Synonym Dictionary Fusion from Heterogenous Knowledge Bases

Input : D and D_{open}
Output: fused dictionary D

Steps :
1. for each $S_i^o \in D_{open}$
2. initialize $R = \emptyset$;
3. for each $w_{i,j} \in S_i^o$
4. for each $(w_k, SID_k, S(w_k)) \in D$
5. if $w_{i,j} \in S(w_k)$, then $R = R \cup \{(w_k, SID_k, S(w_k))\}$
6. end for
7. end for
8. if $|R| == 0$, update $D = D \cup \{(w_{i,1}, D.tatol_sid + 1, S_i^o)\}$;
9. if $|R| == 1$, update $(w_k, SID_k, S(w_k)) = (w_k, SID_k, S(w_k) \cup S_i^o)$;
10. if $|R| > 1$, the set S_i^o contains multiple concepts, the fusion of R and D needs human annotation;
11. end for
12. output D.

3. Experiment

3.1 Data Set

The heterogenous knowledge bases include *Yidian*, and other open resources on the internet, e.g. *Baidu-Dictionary*, *Baike*, and *Douban*, etc.
The evaluation data set for the proposed system employs the data provided by CCF Conference on Natural Language Processing and Chinese Computing 2012. We use NLPCC2012 to denote the data set. NLPCC2012 includes 9455 query items.

3.2 Syn-Patterns and An Expanded Synonym Dictionary

Table 6: Patterns for Semantic Similarity

HTML Syn-Pattern	“中文名：", “别名：", “本名：", “别名昵称：", “封爵：", “谥号：", “爵位：", “别称：", “公司名称：", “庙号：", “中文名称：", “其它译名：", “粤语名：", “简称：", “外文名：",“近义词：", “同音词：", “中文学名：", “定义："
Plain Text Syn-Pattern	简称[“ 《为：](.*?)[” 》))（，、；。] 简称(.*?)[,.))（，、；。]

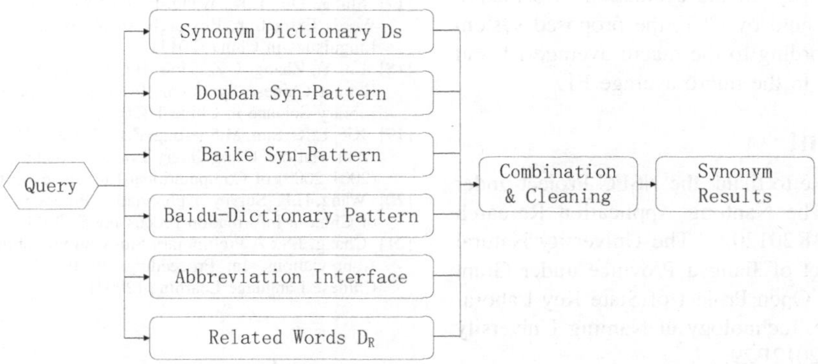

Fig. 2: Synonym Computation Based on Heterogenous Knowledge Bases

Table 7: Statistics of Expanded Synonym Dictionary

#Synonym	#Synonym Concept	#Related Word	#Related Concept
79960	28201	38096	3907

Synonymous relationship patterns (syn-patterns) are categorized into the HTML syn-patterns and the plain text syn-patterns. The HTML syn-patterns are extracted from the content of web pages based on the HTML structures. The plain text syn-patterns are extracted from the unstructured text based on the frequent pattern mining algorithm. Table 6 lists some of the syn-patterns in each category.

The statistics of the expanded synonym dictionary are listed in Table 7. It can be seen that the expanded dictionary has a large scale, which is important for real applications.

3.3 System Evaluation

We implement two systems for evaluating the proposed approach in this paper. These two systems compute the synonyms for the words in NLPCC2012, and we evaluate the systems according to accuracy, recall and F1 measure. The systems work as the following procedures:

(1) **System1**: if the components of dictionary D_S, *Douban* syn-patterns or the abbreviation interface produce results, then the system outputs the union of above three components; else if *Baidu-Dictionary* produces results, then the system outputs them; otherwise, the system outputs the results from the component of dictionary D_R.

(2) **System2**: if the components of dictionary D_S, *Douban* syn-patterns, *Baidu-Dictionary*, *Baike*, or the abbreviation interface produce results, the system output the union of above components; otherwise, the system outputs the results from the component of dictionary D_R.

Table 8: Evaluation of participant systems on the data set NLPCC2012

	Macro Accuracy	Macro Recall	Macro F1	Micro Accuracy	Micro Recall	Micro F1
System1	0.3641	0.5176	**0.3664**	0.2754	0.5829	**0.3740**
System2	0.3305	0.5506	0.3635	0.2615	0.6102	0.3662
NNU	0.3588	0.6041	**0.3968**	0.3025	0.6358	**0.4100**
ZZU1	0.2975	0.6395	0.3588	0.2530	0.6762	0.3682
ZZU2	0.3256	0.6930	**0.3919**	0.2540	0.7040	**0.3734**
CAS	0.1328	0.1034	0.1033	0.4737	0.0687	0.1199
BIT	0.1999	0.2441	0.1874	0.2115	0.2299	0.2203
BJTU	0.2878	0.3394	0.2733	0.3088	0.3737	0.3382
HQU	0.0382	0.0111	0.0151	0.2996	0.0115	0.0221
HIT	0.3225	0.3885	0.2842	0.2303	0.3676	0.2832

The major difference is that system1 doesn't include the results of *Baike*. *Baike* extracts plain text syn-patterns, which can cover a lot of synonym relationships and improve the coverage or recall of the system. The performance evaluation results are listed in Table 8. It can be seen that sytem1 ranks the 3rd place according to the macro average F1 and the 2nd place according to the micro average F1. Although system2 performs a little bit worse than system1, system2 does improve the recall. This means including the *Baike* component can improve the coverage of the synonym relationships.

4. Conclusion

The synonymy can give rise to "semantic gap" between words, which makes great challenges for tasks in text mining, information retrieval, and natural language processing. The identification of semantic word similarity has been an important research topic.

This paper proposes to expand the semantic dictionary by learning word similarity from heterogenous knowledge bases statistically. This method can not only expand the semantic dictionary from the open knowledge bases, but also achieve accurate semantic similarity. In the evaluation of semantic relatedness competition held by CCF, the proposed system ranks the 3rd place according to the macro average F1 and the 2nd place according to the micro average F1.

Acknowledgement

The authors would like to thank the NSFC Project under Grant No. 61202006; The Nantong Application Research Plan under Grant No. BK2012023; The University Natural Science Research Project of Jiangsu Province under Grant No. 12KJB520014; The Open Project of State Key Laboratory for Novel Software Technology at Nanjing University under Grant No. KFKT2012B29.

References

[1] Wang, S.G., Li, D.Y., Wei, Y.J., Song, X.L.: A Synonym-based Word Sentiment Orientation Discriminating Approach. Journal of Chinese Information Processing (2009).

[2] Cao, J.: Synonyms Recognition and Application Research in Concept-based Information Retrieval System. Master Thesis, Northeastern University (2006).

[3] Lu, Y., Hou, H.Q.: Automatic Recognition of Synonyms for Iformation Retrieval and Its Trend. Journal of Nanjing Agriculture University (Social Science Edition) **3** (2004).

[4] Li, Z.F., Yarowsky, D.: Unsupervised Translation Induction for Chinese Abbreviations using Monolingual Corpora. In: Proceedings of the Association for Computational Linguistics (2008) 425-433.

[5] Budanitsky, A., Hirst, G.: Semantic Distance in WordNet: An Experimental, Application-oriented Evaluation of Five Measures. In: Workshop on WordNet and Other Lexical Resources of the 2nd North American Chapter of the Association for Computational Linguistics. Pittsburgh USA (2001).

[6] Mei, L.J., Zhou, Q., Zang, L., Chen, Z.S.: Merge Information in HowNet and TongYiCi CiLin. Journal of Chinese Information Processing **1** (2005).

[7] Zhang, C.Z.: Research On Synonyms Dictionary - Based On Recognition of Synonyms. Journal of Huaiyin Institute of Technology **1** (2004).

[8] Tian, J.L., Zhao, W.: Words Similarity Algorithm Based on Tongyici Cilin in Semantic Web Adaptive Learning System. Journal of Jilin University (Information Science Edition) **6** (2010).

[9] Li, Y.H., Bandar, Z.A., Mclean, D.: An Approach for Measuring Semantic Similarity between Words Using Multiple Information Sources. IEEE Trans. on Knowl. and Data Eng.. Piscataway NJ USA **4** (2003) 871-882.

[10] Lin, D.K.: An Information-Theoretic Definition of Similarity. International Conference on Machine Learning. Morgan Kaufmann (1998) 296-304.

[11] Salahli, M.A.: An Approach for Measuing Semantic Relatedness Between Words via Related Terms. Mathematical and Computational Applications **1** (2009) 55-63.

[12] Pantel, P., Lin, D.K.: Discovering Word Senses from Text. In: Proceedings of the 8th ACM International Conference on Knowledge Discovery and Data Mining. New York NY USA (2002) 613-619.

[13] Bollegala, D., Matsuo, Y., Ishizuka, M.: Measuring Semantic Similarity between Words via Search Engines. In: Proceedings of the 16th International Conference on World Wide Web. New York NY USA (2007) 757-766.

[14] Turney, P.D.: Mining the Web for Synonyms: PMI-IR vs LSA on TOEFL. In: Proceedings of the 12th European Conference on Machine Learning. (2001) 491-502.

[15] Lu, Y., Hou, H.Q.: Automatic Recognition of Chinese Synonyms Based on PageRank Algorithm. Journal of Xihua University (Natural Science) **2** (2008).

[16] Song, Y.X.: The Research and Implementation of Synonyms Mining Method based on the Search Log and Click Log. Master Thesis, Beijing Jiaotong University (2011).

[17] Shi, J., Qiu, L.K., Wang, F., Wu, Y.F.: Ensemble Methods for Similar Words Extraction. Research Advances (2009-2011) of Computational Linguistics in China (2011).

[18] Lu, Y., Zhang, C.Z., Hou, H.Q.: Using Multiple Hybrid Strategies to Extract Chinese Synonyms from Encyclopedia Resources. Journal of Library Science in China **1** (2010).

[19] Xie, L.X., Sun, M.S., Tong, Z.J., Wang, C.H.: Identification of Chinese Abbreviations Using Query Log and Anchor Text. Research Advances (2007-2009) of Computational Linguistics in China (2009).

[20] Wang, H.F.: Survey: Abbreviation Processing in Chinese Text. Journal of Chinese Information Processing **5** (2011).

[21] Chang, J.S.: A Preliminary Study on Probabilistic Models for Chinese Abbreviations. In: Proceedings of the 3rd SIGHAN Workshop on Chinese Language Learning (2004).

Infocommunication systems of saturated traffic control in megalopolises

Alexander P. Buslaev[1], Andrew V. Provorov[2], Marina V. Yashina[2]
[1]Department of Mathematics, Moscow State Automobile and Road Tech. University, Russia
[2]Department of Mathematical Cybernetics, Moscow Tech. University of Communications and Informatics, Russia

Abstract—*Modern advances in computing and infocommunication technologies make it possible to obtain, process and forecast the state of megalopolis traffic for the near future, while ensuring the activity of all groups of potential users of urban road networks. In this study we are created three-tier client-server system, where clients are mobile infocommunication tools - smartphones. Problems for difficult socially-technical systems where processes are characterized by dynamics on time and distribution of a large territory are considered.*

Keywords: smartphone, client-server system, traffic flow, intelligent database

1. Introduction

The development of automobilization in the world has resulted in unpredictable traffic in the places of people concentration. First of all, it is true for urban road networks (URN) of megalopolises. Starting from the last decade of the 20th century, the problem of traffic management in Russian megalopolises has been especially urgent in view of the explosive automobilization growth, given that the capacity of urban road networks remains constant. Since the creation of modern multi-level urban road networks in Russian megalopolises lags far behind automobilization, it is necessary to create infocommunication systems for the regulation of access and regimes of use of the urban road network by automobilists. Despite the fact that legislative and executive authorities of the Russian Federation are trying to introduce prohibitive and restrictive measures, such as the zero ppm threshold of alcohol content, separation (removal) of special use lanes, the increased penalties for traffic offenses up to withdrawal of the right to drive a vehicle, it is not feasible to exercise fairly these actions technologically, while the traditional methods of supervision enhance the corruption component, which, in its turn, leads to the formula: "the severity of Russian laws is compensated by the optionality of their performance".

2. Practical problems of the infocommunication traffic support

Megalopolis traffic is a mix of numerous subsystems: public transport, special systems (medical, emergency, etc.), enterprise systems (delivery of products, diverse services, etc.) and personal systems. Despite the fact that a system user is also acted individually, the main contribution to the behavior pattern is made by target system tasks. Thus, the construction of the model of the traffic structure and behavior in urban road networks is the first major task of traffic optimization. One of the important characteristics of this model is the matrix of correspondence, which is now actively investigated in both experimental and theoretical aspects.

The observance of driving regulations by drivers is still a topical issue of the Russian traffic. It is known that traffic violations, including the so-called risky driving, lead to traffic accidents. Being random by time and place, these events, at the current technology of registration in the Russian Federation, lead to a significant hardship in traffic on the corresponding roads. The changed geometry of urban road networks implies a special traffic management in the vicinity of an accident, which can be also implemented by creation of the relevant mobile infocommunication management systems.

In the broader aspect, the urban road network may be the subject of mobile surveillance, including the effects of weather conditions, unauthorized parking, abnormal condition of the road traffic management resources, etc.

In today's Russia, there are several systems that provide traffic synchronization. First of all, it is the Yandex traffic jams web service, a system that allows specialists to evaluate the traffic speed in urban road networks of Moscow and some other megalopolises in the quasi-real time mode, as well as presence of traffic obstacles according to the classification: road construction, accidents, etc.

The Parkon [3] system, which fixes illegal parking on the lane for route vehicles, pavements and roadways where parking is prohibited by traffic signs or road markings, is also known.

The SignalGuru program [4] for smartphones monitors the turn-on time of traffic light signals with a camera and sends a signal to the driver in advance - when it is necessary to speed up to pass on a green light and when it is necessary to slow down in advance, because the green light will soon change into yellow. Such intelligent prediction can save a lot of fuel in the urban cycle, because the driver stops to make a frequent braking and the engine runs idle more rarely.

The Clique Trip [5] application allows connecting drivers and passengers in different cars when traveling as a group to a common destination. In order to establish the feeling of connectedness, the system automatically switches to an alternative navigation system when the cars tend to loose each other. In that way, the cars are following the leading car and can find each other again. Whenever the cars are within a defined distance, the system further establishes a voice communication channel between the vehicles. In order to form such a multicar traveling group, it is necessary that the trip is registered beforehand via a mobile device.

3. System architecture

The article presents the developed real time systems of remote control of vehicles, moving in the traffic flow and equipped with smartphones having special applications (data transmission + data processing), on the base of the application server running on Microsoft Windows Server. All the considered scenarios-tasks use a three-level (three-tier) client-server architecture [6], [7] (Fig. 1).

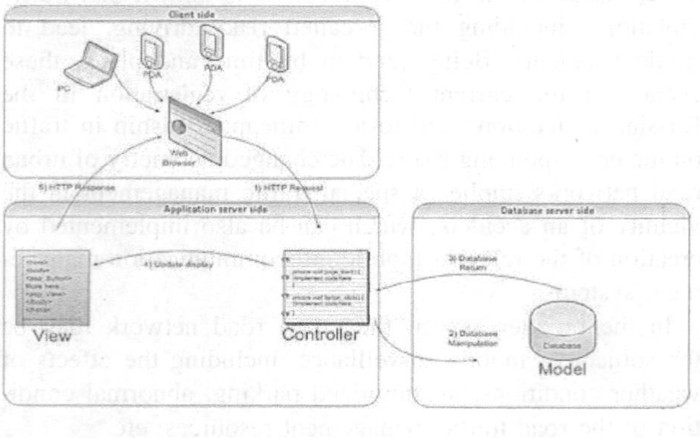

Fig. 1: The logical architecture of the system

4. Methods for solving problems of distributed control

4.1 Problem of GPS tracks monitoring of the car in real time

During movement on the urban road network, the driver of the control vehicle collects the following information by means of SSSRTrack application installed on a smartphone:

- latitude, longitude, time, instant speed (automatically);
- number of lanes in current section of road (manually);
- lane number on which the car is at the moment (manually);
- numbers of lanes which are blocked for movement at the current time and place (parking, road accident etc.) (manually).

It is supposed that the control car moves according to traffic regulations and with the speed which the condition of traffic flow allows.

4.2 Visualization of GPS tracks on the server

On the basis of data received from a problem of GPS tracks monitoring in real time it is restored flowing urban road network geometry. The quantity of lanes on sites of urban road networks is a variable, however directly influences on traffic capacity. Therefore construction the graph of urban road networks as functions of time allows to reveal potential places of the complicated movement.

For determine of urban road networks characteristics and flows on a separate fragment the database of GPS tracks and procedure of averaging of flow characteristics is created. Visualization of a GPS track and also display of percent of free lanes is developed.

4.3 Monitoring system of the road infrastructure condition

The SSSRInfr application for smartphones has been developed, which provides the real time monitoring of the urban road network condition and the traffic management structure in winter and summer.

4.4 Automatic fixation of violations of parking rules

Software for the server providing the storage of information about traffic violations has been developed. The database holds the position, date/time and other important information about the violation. A web site that makes it possible to display the received violations on the map and filter them according to certain criteria has been created.

4.5 Estimates of dynamic dimension of a vehicle in the flow

A pair of cars following one after another is considered: conducting and conducted (the leader – the follower). There is SssrDSEst software with appropriate specifications (conducting and conducted) installed in each car. The information goes on the server and then is processed. Basic numeric characteristics are the dependence of distance between smartphones on time and dependence of distance on the velocity of the second one – estimate of dynamic dimension. This information is necessary to build a dynamic model of traffic flows and estimate the capacity of roads.

4.6 Protection of a dynamic dimension

Static particle size is the minimum space occupied by a particle among similar others when the velocity of the flow $V = 0$ (extreme mode). In this case, a maximum density at the required conditions of security is provided. Laminar flow ($lamina$ — slab, strip) is a flow of particles without stirring and pulsation, a smooth flow. In this case, there are no abrupt changes of velocity, considered as a vector, neither on magnitude nor direction. In laminar flow case, minimal space for the safe movement depends primarily on the velocity and it is called dynamic dimension. One of the simplest models of the dynamic dimension is a linear function from the velocity $f(v)$. The term of dynamic dimension in the traffic flow and the first experimental estimates go back to the thirties of the twentieth century, and belong to American traffic engineers [1], [2]. Thus, in laminar flow it is necessary to control our own velocity, depending on the distance to the particle moving in front. Moreover, on the traffic line its width is determined by the static dimension, it is necessary to ensure the absence of any other movement obstacles.

Mounted on a particle (flow component), the smartphone with SssrDS application (Fig. 2, 3) can control the area of dynamic dimension and in case of any emergency situations it can transmit a signal to the server and other parts of the infocommunication system.

Fig. 2: Control of the dynamic dimension

Fig. 3: Control of the dynamic dimension on smartphone

4.7 The problem of optimization of passing through a bottleneck and traffic synchronization

A bottleneck is a road section with an obstacle that does not block traffic completely. The traffic slows down even with a relatively small number of cars. This may be a narrow bridge or tunnel, deep notch or narrow causeway, or maintenance works implemented on the road section (Fig. 4). These are the areas with traffic jams during rush hours.

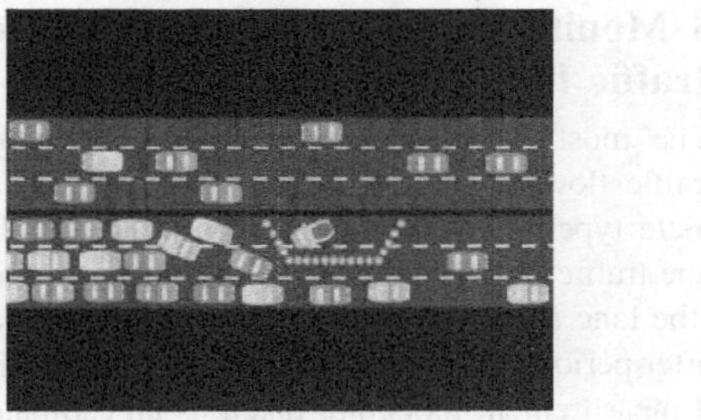

Fig. 4: Example of a bottleneck

A mobile infocommunication system for traffic management has been developed (Fig. 4). By means of SSSRBottleneck, the original flow of connectivity $r = 1$ is loosened [9] to make vehicles transform from the larger number of lanes into a smaller one.

The packet — sequence of traffic particles, each of which is on distance $d(V)$ from previous, where $V = V(t)$ – the law of movement of the leading vehicle.

- Function $d = d(V)$ is known;
- A signal about a speed mode, $V(t)$, arrives on the leading smartphone
- A signal about safety distance arrives on following smartphones.

Thus, the synchronized packet with the density corresponding $V^{-1}(V(\rho)) = \rho$ is controlled (Fig. 5).

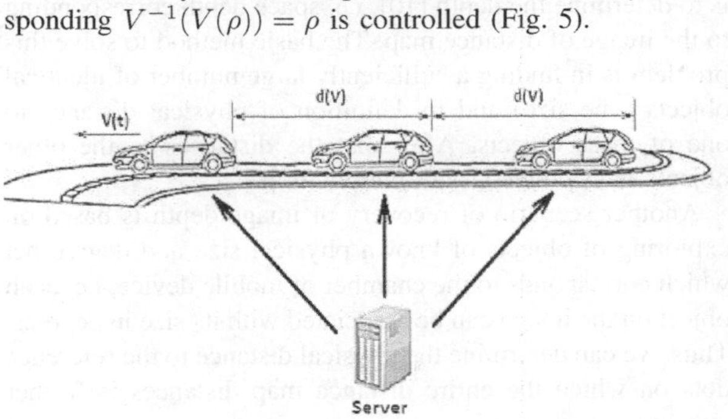

Fig. 5: The synchronized packet of vehicles

Through the server control a uniformly distributed chain of vehicles is generated, where the speed of the leader is also given by the server. This procedure makes it possible

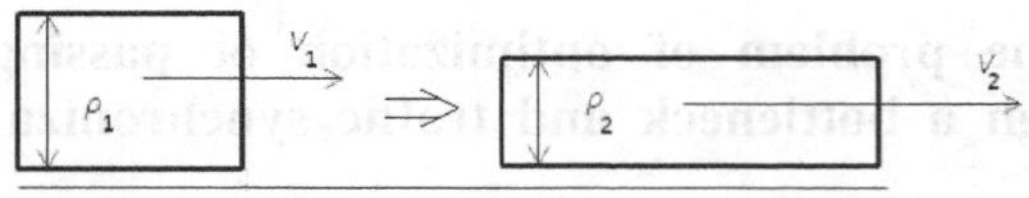

Fig. 6: Control of density of a traffic flow by means of synchronization

to remove the waves of density in the chain and improve the safety and traffic intensity in the vicinity of a bottleneck.

4.8 Monitoring of the intensity and density of a traffic flow

The most useful and frequently used characteristics of a traffic flow are the traffic flow intensity, its structure by vehicle types, flow density and traffic speed. The intensity of the traffic flow is defined as a number of vehicles passing on the lane for a unit of time. A year, month, day, hour and shorter periods of time, depending on the task of observation and measurement tools, are taken as an estimated period of time to determine the traffic intensity. The virtual detector is the part of the video stream received by the smartphone fixed on coordinates. Typically, this is a rectangular area. Standard processing consists in calculation of average value of brightness of the image and the standard output: 0 – "not", or 1 – "yes". Deeper algorithms of processing are also possible.

A typical application is the automatic evaluation of the flow intensity with the help of the SSSRInfr smartphone application. Depending on the flow parameters, both the detector size and frequency of frame processing are realized. In this way, you can restore the matrix of mixing in the node: intensity and output share for the flows incoming to the node.

4.9 Measurement and restore the image depth

One of the major components of the identification problem is to determine the depth [10], i.e. space depth corresponding to the image of distance map. The basic method to solve this problem is in finding a sufficiently large number of identical objects (one size) and in definition of physical distance to one of these objects. After that the distances to the other objects is calculated, and interpolation.

Another scenario of recovery of image depth is based on exploring of objects of known physical size and degree net which corresponds to the chamber of mobile device, i.e. each object on the image can be associated with its size in degrees. Thus, we can determine the physical distance to the reference dots on which the entire distance map distances is further restored.

The number of quantum of connected isolated multitude on the image helps to understand the square of original. This fact is important, for example, on the road, where auto traffic prevents to get a quantitative estimate of defects or patches directly. When such measurements take place, there are errors caused by discredit step of the quantized image, the curvature of the observed surface, etc. The introduction of measures on the display enables to estimate linear and spatial dimensions. At the same time to measure the volumes it is necessary to process the object image from multiple angles.

The application developed on the basis of it, is integrated into system 4.3 to automate the evaluation of the area of a paving

5. Experiments

Department of mathematical modeling of MADI(STU) since 2000 conducts scientific and practical researches by means of mobile laboratory – the Mobile Street and Road Receptor (MUDREC). For the solution of tasks, in which two and more laboratories technologically participate (simultaneous measurement of characteristics of a stream in two different points of the network, parallel processing and information transfer), is acquired one more mobile laboratory on the basis of Volkswagen Transporter (OTROK), equipped with instruments of measuring and communication, transfers of the images, remote control of devices.

5.1 Problem of GPS tracks monitoring of the car in real time

Fig. 7: Our mobile laboratory (OTROK)

Statistical data are stored on the smartphone in a format:

1) operator;
2) latitude;
3) longitude;
4) date/time;
5) instant velocity;
6) altitude
7) number of lanes in current section of road;
8) lane number on which the car is at the moment;
9) numbers of lanes which are blocked for movement at the current time and place (parking, road accident etc.);
10) number of satellites.

(1)	(2)	(3)	(4)	(5)	(6)	(7)	(8)	(9)	(10)
01	55,79279415	37,54827851	08.11.11 5:33:29	43,3	154,8	3	3	0	6(6)
01	55,79273087	37,54846612	08.11.11 5:33:30	51,8	163,4	3	3	0	6(6)
01	55,79264322	37,54863624	08.11.11 5:33:31	55,5	160,9	3	3	0	6(6)
01	55,79256128	37,5488153	08.11.11 5:33:32	55,5	160,7	3	3	0	6(6)
01	55,79247822	37,54899828	08.11.11 5:33:33	54,8	169,7	3	3	1	6(6)
01	55,7924526	37,54915225	08.11.11 5:33:34	52,4	162,1	3	3	1	6(6)
01	55,79237077	37,54933995	08.11.11 5:33:35	49,4	161,9	3	3	1	6(6)
01	55,79229719	37,54950372	08.11.11 5:33:36	47,5	163,8	3	3	1	5(6)
01	55,79221506	37,54966866	08.11.11 5:33:37	45,3	165,1	3	3	1	5(6)

Fig. 8: Obtained data

The example of data obtained from smartphone is shown on Fig. 8.

Fig. 9 shows the road which consists of three lanes. The first lane is occupied. The car is moving on the third lane.

Fig. 9: Program interface and real road

Fig. 10 shows the road which consists of three lanes. The third lane is occupied. The car is moving on the second lane.

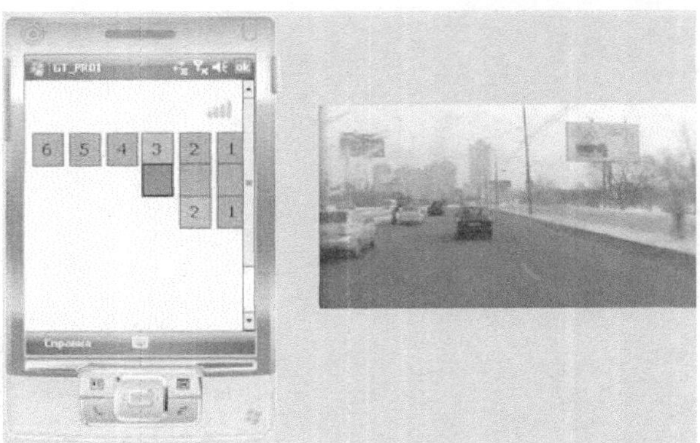

Fig. 10: Program interface and real road

5.2 Visualization of GPS tracks on the server

Data obtained from smartphone is sent to the server and displayed on the map. An example of visualization is shown on Fig. 11 and Fig. 12.

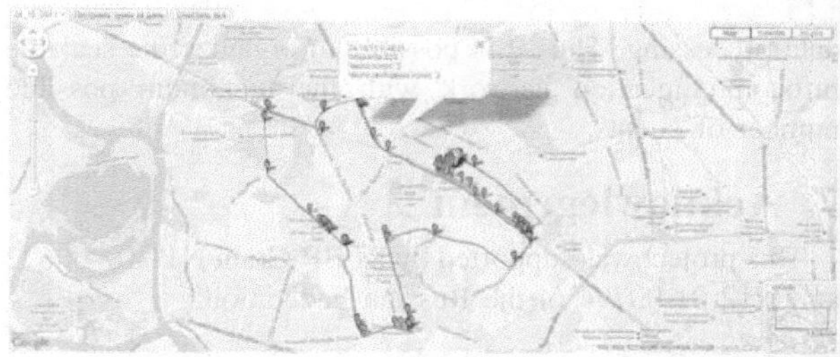

Fig. 11: Geometry of urban road network (24.10.11)

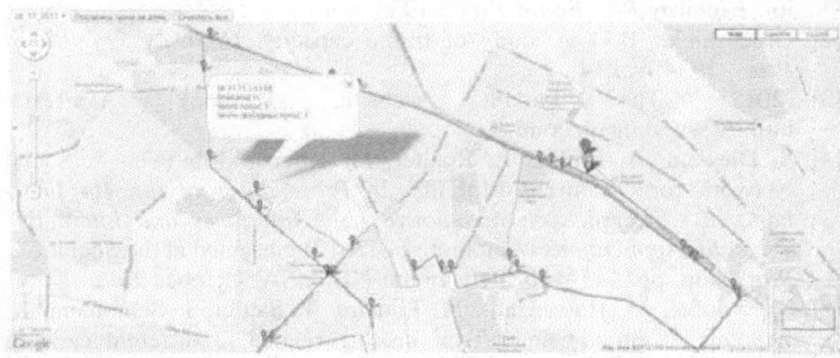

Fig. 12: Geometry of urban road network (08.11.11)

5.3 Estimations of dynamic dimension in traffic flow

Experimentally by means of the smartphones installed in cars are received dependence of distance between smartphones on time and dependence of distance on the velocity of the second one – estimate of dynamic dimension (Fig. 13).

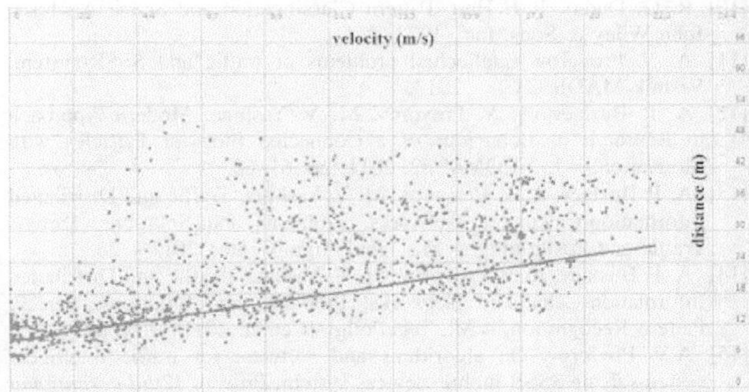

Fig. 13: Estimation of the dynamic dimension

6. Conclusion

A technology of experimental measurements of traffic based on three-tier client-server architecture is developed. The full software package which is carrying out functions of distributed infocommunication system is created. These programs can solve a wide range of traffic control problems in megalopolises. By means of this solution the typical mobile device under control of Windows Mobile and Android turns into the powerful instrument of collecting and data processing. Thus it is possible to organize the scalable infocommunication network with the maximum possible number of clients.

7. Acknowlegement

This project was supported by RFBR Grant N11-07-00622 and N12-01-00794 of the Russian Federation.

References

[1] Greenshields B.D. The photographic method of studying traffic behavior. *Highway Res. Board Proc.*, 1933, vol.13.

[2] Greenshields B.D. A study of traffic capacity. *Highway Res. Board Proc.*, 1934, vol.14.

[3] (2012) The Parkon website. [Online]. Available: http://www.simicon.com/

[4] S. Diewald, A. Moller, L. Roalter, M. Kranz. MobiliNet: A Social Network for Optimized Mobility. In *Proceedings of the 4th International Conference on Automotive User Interfaces and Interactive Vehicular Applications* (AutomotiveUI2012) presented at the Social Car Workshop, pp. 145–150, Portsmouth NH, USA, October 2012

[5] M. Knobel, M. Hassenzahl, M. Lamara, T. Sattler, J. Schumann, K. Eckoldt, A. Butz. Clique Trip: Feeling related in different cars. In *Proceedings of the 9th International ACM Conference on Designing interactive Systems*, DIS '12. Newcastle, UK, June 11 – 15, 2012.

[6] Gustavo Alonso, Fabio Casati, Harumi Kuno, and Vijay Machiraju. Web Services – Concepts, Architectures and Applications. Springer-Verlag, 2004.

[7] Ariel Ortiz Ramirez. Three-Tier Architecture, Linux Journal, July 1st, 2000.

[8] A. P. Buslaev, V. V. Dorgan, D. M. Kuzmin, V. M. Prikhodko, V. Ur. Travkin, M. V. Yashina. Image recognition and monitoring of road pavement, traffic flows and movement safety factors. Vestnik MADI(STU) ISBN - 5-79620061-5. N 4, 2005., pp. 102–109.

[9] A. P. Buslaev, A. V. Novikov, V. M. Prikhodko, A. G. Tatashev, M. V. Yashina. Stochastic and Simulation Approach to Traffic Optimization. Mir; 2003. p. 368.

[10] R. O. Duda , P. E Hart. Pattern Classification and Scene Analysis. John Wiley & Sons, Inc., 1973.

[11] A. V. Provorov. Intellectual problems of traffic and SSSR-system. Vestnik MADI(STU). – 2013.

[12] A. P. Buslaev, A. V. Provorov, M. V. Yashina. Modern Approach to Research of Behaviour of a Connected Flow of Particles with Motivation. – J. T-COMM-#2, 2011, pp. 61–63.

[13] A. P. Buslaev, A. V. Provorov, M. V. Yashina. Traffic and Distributed Information-Calculated Networks. Problems and Solutions. Part 1. Traffic and Positioning. – M., TechPoligrafCenter. 2011 – 263 p.

[14] A. P. Buslaev, A. V. Provorov, M. V. Yashina. Traffic and Distributed Information-Calculated Networks. Problems and Solutions. Part 2. Pattern Recognition. – M., TechPoligrafCenter. 2011 – 108 p.

[15] A.V. Provorov. On algorithms and software for traffic intelligent systems using SSSR mobile devices system. *Proc. of 12th International Conference on Computational and Mathematical Methods in Science and Engineering*, 2012.

SESSION

CLOUD COMPUTING + WEB SERVICES + INTERNET COMPUTING AND APPLICATIONS

Chair(s)

TBA

Eknoware: A Knowledge as a Service Platform and Application Framework

Rao Yuan[1], Dai Jun[1], Lu Shumin[2],Lv yongkang [3]

1) College of Software Engineering, Xi'an Jiaotong University, Xi'an 710049, China
2) College of Social science, Xi'an Jiaotong University, Xi'an 710049, China
3) Xi'an Jiaotong University Nation Science and Technique Park, Xi'an 710049, China

(E-mail: yuanrao@163.com)

An evolution model with requirement, personalization and knowledge solution domain was proposed for providing the creative knowledge services. Based on this model, the different between KAAS and KM from the dimension of the core technique, knowledge target, and knowledge extraction were compared and a BNF definition about KAAS was proposed. In cloud computing environment, a KAAS Cloud Architecture was introduced to make the knowledge available on a self-service, social network-based collective intelligence and on-demand service with three knowledge service layers as follows: knowledge resource layer, service delegate layer, and solution delivery layer. All these three key layers for providing knowledge services are how to improve the access of unstructured and scattered information for the non-specialist users, how to provide adequate information to knowledge workers and how to provide the information in situations requiring highly domain-specific, related and time critical information. Then, a research case about KAAS, Eknoware platform, was developed based on the architecture above-mentioned.

Keywords: Knowledge as a Service, Cloud Computing, Knowledge Cloud

1. INTRODUCTION

With the rapid development of network technology and knowledge economy, social knowledge networking, as a new methodology of network computing, provided many new knowledge sharing patterns, which is based on the Web2.0, cloud computing and some OPEN APIs to communicate with friends in communities of practices (COP) and to share some knowledge resources across different systems over Internet [1~3]. The core competitive capability and knowledge value always embody the process of technical innovation about products and services under the knowledge economy environment. More and more companies [4], such as Proctor and Gamble, Cisco, IBM and Air Products, were beginning to use social knowledge network platform to manage and share their enterprise knowledge and to acquire the competitive advantage by extending and enhancing the effectiveness of intra- and inter-enterprise collaboration. The transition from a loosely structured committee of individual contributors into a collaborative team, such as social networks (MySpace, Facebook…), professional networks (LinkedIn, Plaxo Pulse…), and shared community content development networks (Wikipedia, Del.icio.us, YouTube) and podcasts, blogs, etc., is an important progress in productivity, particularly in organizations operation in the knowledge service economy.

This paper investigated a social knowledge network and knowledge service mechanism from knowledge as a service (KAAS) and Cloud computing architecture perspective. The rest of this paper is organized as follows: Section 2 presented the features and existed problems of knowledge service and proposed knowledge as a service statement space model with requirement content, personalization and the knowledge solution to present the knowledge service economical evolution process with best results to right person in right time. Section 3 illustrated a formalized KAAS definition and architecture with multi-element and analyzed the knowledge services invocation operations to "push" the relevant services together into composited domain information. Section 4 provided a case study, EKNOWARE, which is a new social KAAS platform, to illustrate the merits of knowledge service and KAAS Cloud Architecture. Section 5 presented an overview of knowledge as a service, knowledge service cloud and related works. Finally, the conclusion and future research works were presented in Section 6.

2. KNOWLEDGE as a SERVICE CHARACTERISTICS

2.1 Knowledge service evolution model

Many research papers about knowledge management are investigated into knowledge management elements and relationship or sharing mechanism between knowledge and person [5]. A knowledge management evolution model based on knowledge model is provided as follow:

$KM = (K + P)^{S(t)}$ Where:

— KM denotes a knowledge management tool to classify and manage the domain of knowledge, which created by specially experts in various domains.

— K denotes the knowledge with some basic elements, such as title, content, UKL (unify knowledge location), tags etc.

— P denotes the person in the COP, who needs the knowledge to consume or to create new knowledge for consume.

— "+" denotes a transfer channel. Today, web technique is become the more important channel for knowledge sharing and learning, which can put the fitness knowledge achievement together for different person's requirements over Internet.

— S(t) denotes the degree of knowledge sharing with time. It means the method and capability of knowledge sharing and propagating with time.

By this definition, the first value about knowledge management is to provide the best knowledge to right person with the best channel by IT tools. The second one is how to share and propagate the right knowledge to more persons who need it. But, in new era about web2.0, the relationship between person and knowledge is changing. The person not only can consume and study the knowledge created by others, but also can provide the new knowledge created by himself under the online social network environment. Everyone is owner in social network, which needs more relevance knowledge combined with his personalized requirement and share something to others, including contents, valuation, recommendation, etc. In addition, the sharing mechanism is become from passive reading to active creating by web 2.0 method.

Therefore, the knowledge management is not effective measure, while knowledge service is becoming a new phase for personalization knowledge acquirement to yield the best solutions from e-learning to knowledge as a service for specially question. This paper proposed an evolution model from knowledge management to KAAS perspective, which can be described by a KAAS model as follow:

Definition 1: (Knowledge Service Evolution Model)

The knowledge service evolution model as follow

$\Psi_{ks} = (\zeta(k) + \Re(q))^{p}$ where:

—k denotes the knowledge, and $\zeta(k)$ denotes the solution with a set of combined or recommended knowledge. k is a finite set of knowledge with $k = \{k_i \mid 1 \le i \le n, k_i \notin \phi\}$. It means that the solution is composed of the fusion knowledge by tagging, data mining, aggregation analysis, and knowledge discovery. In addition, some recommended knowledge stems from content filter or collaboration filter based on the person profile model.

—q denotes the list of questions, and $\Re(q)$ denotes the user's knowledge requirement with a set of questions in various domains. q is a finite set of questions with $q = \{q_j \mid 1 \le j \le m, q_j \notin \phi\}$. It means that the user's requirement, from keywords searching into context understanding, is becoming the core driving force for knowledge service. All solutions provided by system must be fit to the user's requirement and questions. Meanwhile, different question brings on different solution or the same question steamed from different person maybe results in different personalization solution, which bases on the person's profile or favorites' models strongly.

— "+" also denotes a knowledge transfer channel by IT technique. It means that new social media service platform bridges the different experts and users together to share knowledge each other easily over Internet. By this platform, the KAAS is become the main knowledge sharing service.

—p denotes the degree about personalization. It means that the degree bout the best knowledge for right person in right time to solve the fixed question. With the increasing about p, the best QOS about knowledge service and the best solution will focus on the user's requirement rightly.

From the definition above-mentioned, Knowledge service, mixing knowledge and personalization service together, is a new method of knowledge sharing and propagating, whose target is to provide the value-added service with the most relevant knowledge and solution by knowledge mining and discovering to the users' question. So, knowledge service is the context of question-oriented, which the core destination pursues to solve the problem and provides one-by-one attentive service, but knowledge management is specification-oriented, which emphasizes on how to manage the knowledge document and provide unify information retrieve method to user. In general, the evolution process of the knowledge service is leveraged by knowledge service resources from three dimensions of evolution model illustrated in figure 1.

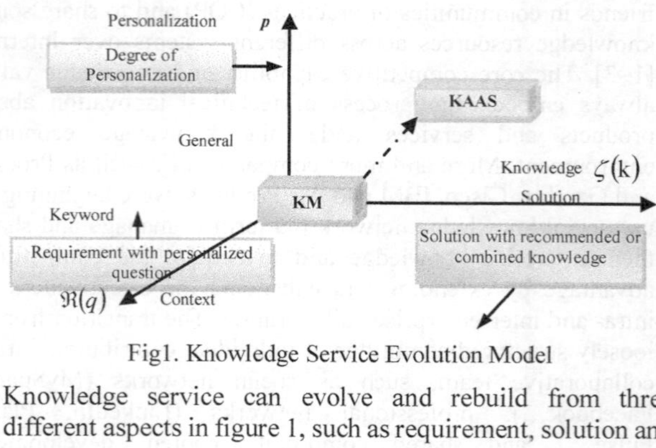

Fig1. Knowledge Service Evolution Model

Knowledge service can evolve and rebuild from three different aspects in figure 1, such as requirement, solution and degree of personalization, which also provides three knowledge service strategies. On the solution aspect, the knowledge service should support knowledge retrieval from simple knowledge to combined knowledge, and end to certain solution with fusion knowledge under user's context environment. On the requirement aspect, the knowledge service aims to solve user's personalization question from simple keywords to complex content of question under user's scenario and semantic environment. On the degree of personalization aspect, the quality of service (QoS) about knowledge service is greatly related with more personalization solution by person's profile model to satisfy the user's questions and requirements.

2.2 The Characteristics of KAAS

Many commercialized KM software have been introduced various version for different users, such as personal knowledge management application, C/S-based or B/S-based enterprise knowledge management version, etc. All these software can excavate out the potentiality of reusing existed knowledge resources to the maximum extent and promote the knowledge reused level greatly in special domain. Whereas it is obviously insufficient to provide knowledge resources for reused to solve cross-domain problem. In particularly, with the digital of information resources and the virtualization about information systems, the method about information retrieve is becoming more convenient and simplify under cloud computing environment, it is important how to acquire the content of knowledge and integrate these knowledge into a solution to form new knowledge products and services.

Knowledge as a Service (KaaS) is an on-demand, where-needed approach [6] to knowledge acquisition, who couples the knowledge and service together and turns the knowledge resources into products and service for value-added. Meantime, KAAS also is a process to solve the end-users problems and provide a utilities knowledge application products and knowledge innovation service, based on a series of activities under user's context environment from knowledge retrieval, cleaning and analysis to knowledge reorganization. S. Xu [6] proposed that KaaS can decouple help, training, and solution customization activities from monolithic projects and makes them available on a self-service, socially-networked basis through the cloud. Therefore, KAAS is next generation of knowledge management paradigm with some new characteristics illustrated in table 1.

Based on the greater change about the thought of KAAS above-mentioned, more and more knowledge service techniques have been proposed in knowledge management and discovering field with more complexity mechanism at service level, such as knowledge cloud computing, semantic-based knowledge mining, content analysis and personalization recommended service etc. In addition, knowledge services not only are simple information collection, but also put the static knowledge to flow [7] from the knowledge service providers to end-users and lessen the distance between them, then, realize how to organize the target of these service activities based on the user's behaviors. In currently, three principal problems should be solved in knowledge service process. First principle is the requirement expression, which means that there exists semantic analysis on the user's question for assembling the new knowledge. Second principle is the degree of personalization, which means that a personalization profile model must be built directed against user's needs limited by his favorites, location, and time. Third principle is the solution composition, namely, the user can obtain and utilize the combined knowledge that should be solved the user's requirements in standardized descriptions and operation methods with convenience to use. Although, many technique factors are associated with non-technique factors to realize the knowledge service, the three basic principles above-mentioned are foundation and vital elements to realize Knowledge as a service successfully.

3. SOCIAL NETWORK-BASED KNOWLEDGE SERVICE FRAMEWORK

3.1 The Definition of KAAS

Knowledge as a service is an emerging concept that integrates knowledge management, knowledge markets and

Table1. The characteristics comparison between KM and KAAS

	KM	KAAS
Target of Knowledge	Provide or transmit the relevant knowledge documents to user	Provide fitness solution to user's problem
Extraction Method	Search, retrieval knowledge	Combined or recommended knowledge
Method of requirement	Keywords matching	Term frequency or semantic analysis under context
Service method	Sharing with general knowledge	Sharing with personalization solution
Value of Service	Information provided	Value-added with integrated knowledge
Service provider	System or operators	Experts in domain
IT infrastructure	Knowledge Management system	Social network sharing platform
Interactive with users	1 : n One knowledge document to more users	1: 1 One knowledge solution to one requirement
Core technique	MIS and Searching Engine	Could, SNS and Semantic Web

knowledge organization as cloud computing. Knowledge service, which is openness, on-demand, content-based and where-needed service innovation process, is becoming core elements to propel the knowledge society and the organization unities forward. Social network expedites the turnover of knowledge and the communication among with different persons, especially, mixed the more experts' knowledge in community of practice (COP) into the product and service innovation process of enterprise. Therefore, the knowledge as a Service (KaaS), in social network environment, is a service transfer method which contains three major functions: collection and organized knowledge resources created by all users in CoP, aggregation and analysis the requirement of user's with a knowledge agent, and delivery of the personalized solution for knowledge innovation services. Then, the conception of KAAS is defined as follow:

```
<Knowledge as a Service>::= <Knowledge Resource, Service Delegate, Solution Delivery>
<Knowledge Resource>::= <Knowledge Specification, knowledge Construction>
<Knowledge Specification>::= <Provider, Knowledge Tag ,Content, Constrains>
<Knowledge Construction>::= <Atomic Knowledge>|<Composite Knowledge >
<Atomic Knowledge>::= <Knowledge Name, URI>
<Composite Knowledge >:: = <Composite Type, Instance Statement, Connection>
<Service Delegate>:: = <Requirement Specification, Service Context, Knowledge Aggregation >
<Requirement Specification>::=<Provider, Requirement Tag ,Content, Constrains>
<Solution Delivery>::=<Delivery Type, Instance Statement>
```

Fig2. The BNF definition about Knowledge as a Service

From this definition, the knowledge as a service (KAAS) has three independent parts, such as knowledge resources, service delegate and solution delivery. In addition, Knowledge resources can be divided into two elements, such as knowledge specification and knowledge construction. Knowledge specification defines the elements and relationships about knowledge services with provider information, knowledge classify tag, knowledge content and some constrains to use. We can build a user's profile model by provider's information, which can help system provides more personalized and simulated knowledge to user.

Knowledge construction describes the relationship of knowledge composition with atomic or composite knowledge. From knowledge construction perspective, the knowledge is nested hierarchy structure that can assemble the atomic knowledge together to build more complex and practical composed knowledge for reuse. Atomic knowledge includes knowledge name, description and a knowledge access entry point, e.g., URI, which is unique identity of knowledge in network. Composite knowledge can be integrated by some atomic knowledge with instance statement of atomic knowledge and reference, which can connect from atomic knowledge to composition knowledge.

Service delegate introduced a uniform mechanism for knowledge discovered with standard OWL-based description specification from lightweight knowledge service directory register center, which predigested the knowledge discovered process of reusable knowledge resources. Service delegate also is a knowledge agent, which can contact with some knowledge consumers and acquire their requirements. Therefore, Service delegate has three elements, such as requirement specification, service context and knowledge aggregation, to complete the task of requirement analysis and knowledge aggregation. Requirement specification is an important element which also includes some sub-elements as follow: requirement provider, requirements classify tag, requirements description and some constrains.

Solution delivery is the conclusion of knowledge service, which can successfully invoke the knowledge solution to satisfy the user's requirements with some different knowledge delivery type. From the viewpoint of marketplace, the KaaS marketplace offers rich opportunities to discover and purchase knowledge solution directly from producers-whether help desk analysts, implementation consultants, developers-as an alternative or precursor to traditional consulting and systems integration engagements. Moving from a knowledge delivery to a knowledge acquisition paradigm provides the end users some new capability to build their own IQs rather than depend exclusively on knowledge consultants. Furthermore, this method decreases the costs about software implementation, customization, and upgrade in enterprise.

3.2 KAAS Cloud Architecture

Based above definition, KAAS, who decouples help, training, and solution customization activities from monolithic projects, is programs that provide content-based organization by data, information and knowledge value-added, which also outputs some advices, answers or

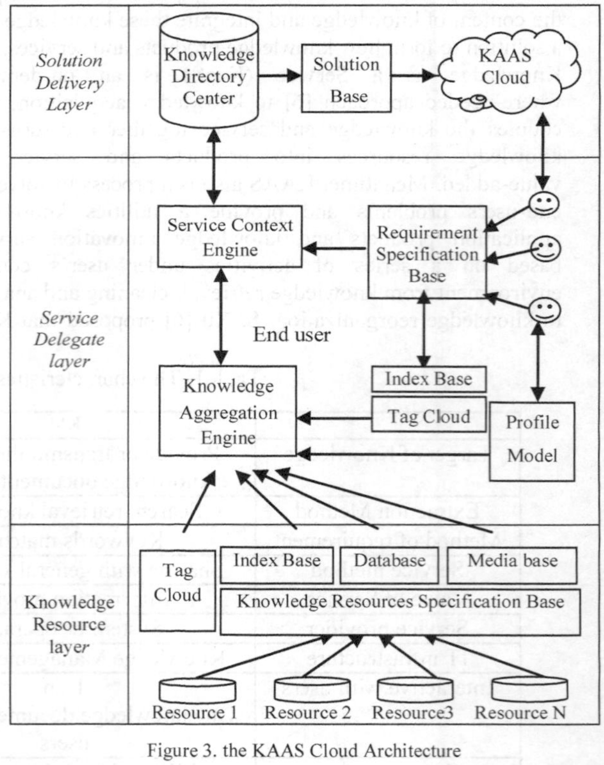

Figure 3. the KAAS Cloud Architecture

facilitations to meet external user's needs. In cloud computing environment, KaaS makes the knowledge available on a self-service, social network-based collective intelligence, and on-demand service with three knowledge service layers. First is knowledge resources layer, the various knowledge resources can be cleared and normalized by knowledge specification. The knowledge resources specification base, which built by index base, database, media base and knowledge tag cloud, is a basis of knowledge analysis and aggregation. In addition, the knowledge tag cloud can put the different knowledge with same tags into one classification contains for aggregating the knowledge together.

The second layer is service delegate layer, which put various knowledge and data resources into Knowledge Aggregation Engine. This engine can match the right knowledge solution from knowledge resources specification base, by user's profile model and user's knowledge requirement specification, which can form the requirement document index and requirement tag. The match method adopts the weighted TF/IDF algorithm, which can weight different style terms to analysis the similarity among the different requirements and knowledge base. In addition, the user's profile model can be build by an iterated mechanism, which can add the new tags from two methods with different weight mechanism as follow. First is the tags stem from the documents (including: blog, active, group, discussion and so on) created by user himself. Second is that the tags from the documents created by the other users, who are focused on by knowledge consumer. Service context engine can utilize the requirement context and semantic to optimize the order list of similarity knowledge and aggregate these knowledge into a whole knowledge service after cleaning.

The third layer is solution delivery layer, which put various aggregated knowledge into knowledge directory center to form the different solution. All these solution can pull the new knowledge to consumer by KAAS cloud with different knowledge client, such as mobile phone, mobile pc and others.

All these three key layers for providing knowledge services are how to improve the access of unstructured and scattered information for the non-specialist users, how to provide adequate information to knowledge workers and how to provide the information in situations requiring highly domain-specific, related and time critical information. Then, this paper introduces a platform of knowledge acquisition and services, named EKNOWARE, which using social knowledge network as a backbone. Based on the special design about community knowledge sharing and personal knowledge profile model, the system ensures that knowledge service could be improved the user potential business in knowledge consumption.

4. KNOWLEDGE SERVICECASE RESEARCH

In this section, a KAAS-based application platform, EKNOWARE, with knowledge sharing method and the requirement specification is introduced in the social network environment. The purpose of this application wants to reuse the legacy teaching resources, such as assignments, reference materials, and project resources developed by different teachers and other students in different periods over different departments. The system architecture is illustrated in figure 4. The Knowledge Achievement Resources Unit means that the reusable knowledge resources of the system, such as expert pool, patents pool, research paper Lib and e-training applications, which can be encapsulated to become knowledge service unit with data sources stored in database or Lucene's index files. The Creative Knowledge Service can be stored in the knowledge service pool that listed all knowledge services and published all these information into private knowledge service register and publisher center (KSRPC) for reuse. When a new knowledge creative service need to be provided, that can pass the process of analyzing the knowledge acquirement and putting the new value add in. KSRPC plays an important actor to aggregate the knowledge

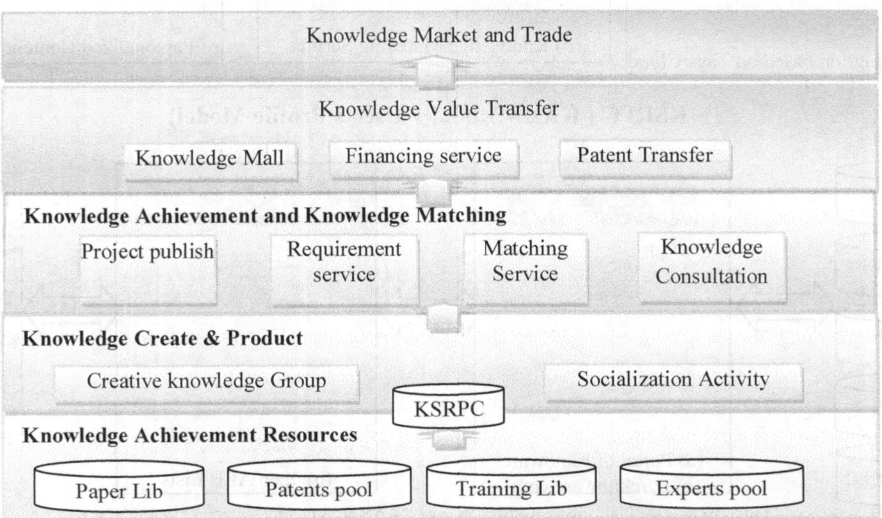

Figure4. The Core Architecture of Knowledge as a Service Platform

and put the direction of knowledge into right method for research and match. By this method, the knowledge-creative service not only reused the knowledge services, but also reused all the data resources which can be merged into a whole knowledge contents located in distributed knowledge database.

The Knowledge Create and Product Unit means that to build some socialization knowledge collaboration communities for sharing and creating new knowledge, which can provide some online knowledge groups and activities to exchange the ideas and knowledge, and then put them into certain project. The knowledge Achievement and Match Unit means that to build some key knowledge matching algorithms, which can put the most similarity knowledge or requirements together for user search. Based on these algorithms and matching service, the user can publish the project's achievements or requirements with more personalized knowledge pulled by system. In addition, the experts, registered in platform, can provide the knowledge consultation and answer the user's problems.

The Knowledge Value Transfer Unit means that to provide a knowledge exchange or trade mechanism, which can help all the people in platform to find right knowledge commodity and can pay for it easily. So, how to design an out-off-the-shelf knowledge service and build a reliable online payment, which include many relative knowledge units to output the right value in the right process to user, is a keypoint in KAAS application. Based on this unit, an online knowledge markets will be formed to pay for expert's intelligence resource, related knowledge resources, and transferred patents resources.

Based on the above-mentioned architecture, a practice knowledge as a service platform, named eknoware (http://eknoware.com), can be build in campus network environment in China. This platform provides some basic functions for knowledge sharing and learning, such as experts blog, online question and answer, discuss in a online knowledge communities, and so on. In specifically, a personal knowledgebase is provided which can not only exchange the knowledge between different persons, but share the knowledge between different knowledge groups. So, the knowledge become a flow from one person to others person with new contents and value-added. The eknoware platform, a best practice of KAAS architecture, is illustrated in figure 5.

5. Related Work

Recently, Murray [8] proposed that the knowledge cloud is "the future of the future". Many researchers focused on the knowledge as a service and promoted the new "wave" to develop the knowledge service-based application. In generally, the knowledge service strategies [9] can be divided into three aspects: knowledge management service, knowledge value-added flow and creative service and socialized knowledge trade in cloud environment. According to the principles of service science, KAAS service is to allow users "pay-per-use" access to "specialized" provider

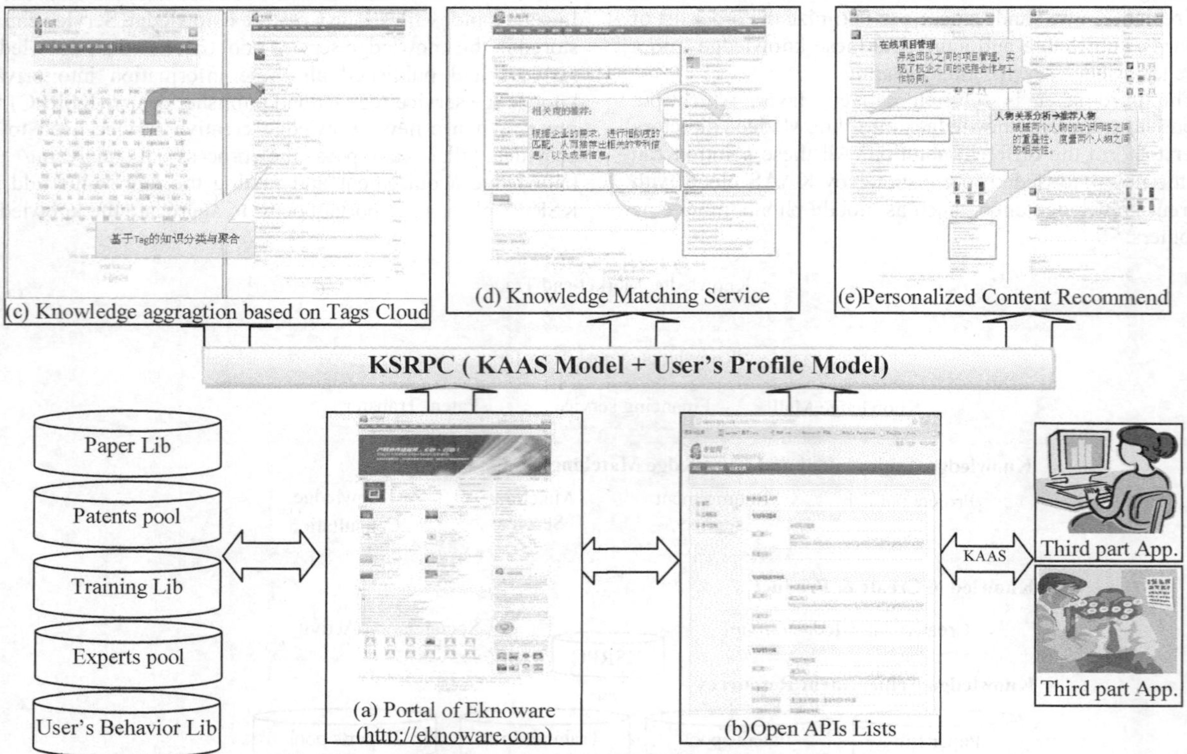

Fig.5. Eknoware Platform: a Best practice of KAAS architecture (http://eknoware.com)

knowledge, on demand, so as to integrate it with their own specific internal knowledge to create value for themselves. Eng K. Chew [10] provided a methodology about KAAS classification scheme based on the business model principles. In particulate, the knowledge embedded in software as a service (SAAS) will promote the value about software greatly. Ju [11] proposed a public knowledge service platform framework and a practice application about on-the-job learning platform in outsourcing professional development process with knowledge service. Furthermore, the knowledge service and KAAS technology were proposed to resolve the semantic problems for automated knowledge service without much manual intervention, which can put knowledge into all the business process to win huge value-added. The research about the core technique on knowledge as a service is one direction in our future work.

6. Conclusion and Future Work

The purpose of knowledge service, however, is to reuse knowledge resources and create a new value-added service method more efficiently. This paper proposed a KAAS evolution model with Requirement, Personalization and Solution domain for providing the creative knowledge services. The BNF definition about KAAS is proposed after compared the characteristics between the KM and KAAS with core technique, knowledge target, extraction, and so on. In addition, a KAAS Cloud Architecture is provided in cloud computing environment, which makes the knowledge available on a self-service, social network-based collective intelligence and on-demand service with three knowledge service layers as follows: knowledge resource layer, service delegate layer, and solution delivery layer. All these three key layers for providing knowledge services are how to improve the access of unstructured and scattered information for the non-specialist users, and how to provide adequate information to knowledge workers. Then, a case about KAAS, Eknoware platform, is developed based on the KAAS cloud architecture. The future work of us will design and describe the KAAS-Oriented Architecture with a uniform formulization description language based on the OWL, which can provide the consistency description of system and a mechanism of the semantic of knowledge service at runtime.

Acknowledgments: This paper is joint supported by "2012 National Torch Plan Project in China (2012GH571817)", "2012 the Fundamental Research Funds for the Central Universities in China (08143003)", "2012 Shanxi Province Key Scientific and Technological Project (2012K11-08, 2012K06-18)" and "2012 XI'AN Science and Technology Project (CX12178(3))".

References and Notes

1. Cheong, KFR & Tsui, The Roles and Values of Personal Knowledge Management: An exploratory study, VINE: The journal of information and knowledge management systems(2010), Vol.40, no. 2, p. 204-27.
2. Hofmann, P & Woods, D., Cloud Computing: The limits of Public Clouds for Business Applications, IEEE Internet Computing,(2010), Vol.14, no. 6,p. 90-94.
3. Malcolm, D., The five defining characteristics of cloud computing [online], ZDNet, 2010, http://www.zdnet.com/news/the-five-defining-characteristics-of-cloud-computing/287001.
4. Delic, K.A & Riley, J.F., Enterprise Knowledge Clouds : Architecture and Technologies, Handbook of Cloud Computing, 2010, Springer, NY, p.239-254;
5. Ergazakis, K., Metaxiotis, K., and Psarras, I. Knowledge Management in Enterprises: A Research Agenda. Intelligent Systems in Accounting, Finance and Management, 2005.13 (1): p. 17-26.
6. S. Xu and W. Zhang, Knowledge as a service and knowledge breaching, in SCC 200505: Proceedings of the 2005 IEEE International Conferenceon Services Computing. Washington, DC, USA: IEEE Computer Society, 2005, p. 87–94.
7. Li Junning, Chen Wei, Xie Youbai, Novel Frame System of Knowledge Service Platform for Modern design and Its Knowledge Flow Rules, Journal of XI'AN Jiaotong University [J] (in Chinese), 2012, vol.46, No.1, p:y1~y5.
8. Murray, A. & Mohamed, M, The Future of the Future: Are You Ready for the Coming Knowledge Cloud? [Online]. Available: http://www.kmworld.com/Articles/Column/Future-of-the-Future/The-Futureof-the-FutureAre-you-ready-for-the-coming-knowledge-cloud3f-66075.aspx, 2010.
9 Aurich, J. C., Mannweiler, C. and Schweitzer, E., How to design and offer services successfully, CIRP, Journal of Manufacturing Science and Technology 2, 2010, p.136–143;
10. Eng K. Chew, Towards a methodology framework for designing a KAAS system, 2011, IEEE, p.2823~2826;
11. Ju, D. & Shen, B., "A Design Framework for Public Knowledge Service Platform", Proceedings of KaaS 2010, American Scholars Press, 2010.

A Genetic Algorithm with Simplex Optimization Method for QoS-driven Cloud Service Selection

Chengwen Zhang [1], **Yan Gong** [2], **Jiali Bian** [3], **Bo Cheng** [4], **and Lei Zhang** [5]
[1]Beijing Key Laboratory of Intelligent Telecommunications Software and Multimedia, Beijing University of Posts & Telecommunications, Beijing, China
[2]Chinese Electronic Equipment System Engineering Corporation, Beijing, China
[3]Beijing Key Laboratory of Intelligent Telecommunications Software and Multimedia, Beijing University of Posts & Telecommunications, Beijing, China
[4]State Key Lab of Networking and Switching Technology, Beijing University of Posts & Telecommunications, Beijing, China
[5]Key Laboratory of Trustworthy Distributed Computing and Service (BUPT), Ministry of Education, Beijing, China

Abstract - *A special Genetic Algorithm (GA) with simplex optimization method is proposed for the problem of selecting an optimal cloud service composition plan from a lot of composite plans on the basis of some global Quality-of-Service (QoS) constraints. In this GA, some Simplex Method (SM) operations and a fitness function are provided. The design of the SM operations is made in the light of the characteristics of cloud service composition. After analyzing the types of different QoS attributes, objective function and fitness function are built. SM operations enhance local search capability of GA. Because the design of the hybrid algorithm accords with the characteristics of cloud service selection very well, excellent composite cloud service plan can be gotten from a lot of composite plans on the basis of global QoS constraints. Some tests and analyses show that the proposed algorithm can be a good method for QoS-based cloud service selection.*

Keywords: Cloud service selection, Genetic algorithm, Simplex method, QoS-aware

1 Introduction

In cloud computing technology [1-3], service is one of the most important concepts. Services in cloud computing environment are cloud services. With the rapid deployment of cloud service, the number of cloud services with same functionalities and different QoS attributes are increasing. These services can combine tens of thousands composite services with same functions and different QoS. Therefore, we need to choose service components from massive cloud services with same functions and different QoS according to user's QoS requirements.

In the field of QoS-based cloud service selection, a lot of international research works were done and some research results were obtained [4-8, 11-21]. There are two kinds of QoS properties calculation methods. One is exhaustive methods and another is approximate algorithms. It is under the scope of combinatorial optimization to find an optimal combination plan that meets some global QoS constraints. QoS-based cloud service selection is in the area of NP-hard. Therefore, approximate algorithm is a good way for cloud service selection. GA is a powerful means for combinatorial optimizing things [9-10]. In GA, a population with a fixed size is used to search the whole solution area. Each individual describes a solution in the population. In GA, the design of its operators and parameters will have significant impact on itself. GA is not advantageous for its local convergence. Thus, its efficiency is not enough and its convergence speed is slow. In order to compensate for GA's local search capability, it is necessary that GA combines a local search algorithm.

To compensate for GA's local search capability, this paper presents a hybrid algorithm of GA and SM. Some SM optimization operations and a fitness function are described.

The remaining sections of this paper are as follows. Section 2 described researches of cloud service selection based on QoS. The proposed hybrid algorithm was discussed in detail in section 3. Section 4 presented some test works and discussed test results. Section 5 came to conclusions and noted that the next step in research content.

2 Cloud service selection based on QoS

It is the area of combinatorial optimization to select the best plan from a large number of cloud service composition plans on the basis of all global QoS constraints. The calculation methods based on QoS attributes are divided into two categories. One category is exhaustive algorithm. In this kind of algorithm, all of candidate plans are calculated according to certain rules in order to choose the best plan. The methods used in [4-6, 11-12, 19-21] fall into this category. The other is approximate algorithm. In this type of algorithm, an ideal composition plan is infinitely close to the best one. At last, a plan that meets all QoS requirements but is not the best one will be gained. [7, 8, 13-18] used some approximate algorithms.

It is a representative calculation method to calculate QoS properties through the establishment of QoS matrix. [4] adopted a run-time services selection method in dynamic service composition. It could select a single better service, but it could not meet the entire QoS requirements. A local optimization algcrithm and a global optimization algorithm were proposed in [5, 6]. The local optimization algorithm could not reach a global optimal solution. When the size of composition services was large, the compution of the global computational algorithm had increased a lot. [12] analysed the conditions of triggering service re-selection. It gave the constraint expression for a stateful cloud service selection and the idea of the service re-selection.

Because a service selection problem according to QoS belongs to NP-hard problem [8], the exhaustive combinatorial optimization method is poor scalability and has large calculation. It is a good way to obtain an approximate solution. Heuristics method can be used. A multidimensional 0-1 knapsack problem model was used for multiple QoS constraints selection in [13]. [7, 8, 14-18] used GA for the optimization of service composition.

In order to compensate for the local search capability of GA itself, GA and some kind of local search algorithms need to be combined to enhance its local search capabilities.

SM is a local optimization approach. A combination of GA and SM can form a hybrid algorithm that includes a global optimization algorithm and a local optimization algorithm. The two algorithms complement each other. GA ensures that the hybrid algorithm has a global search capability and can find a global optimal point. SM can add a number of parallel searches in many local areas and it can use local search methods to direct the search. It can not only speed up the process of global optimization, but also solve the "premature" problem of GA to a certain extent. Better convergence speed and search capability can be gotten at the same time.

3 Hybrid algorithm built by GA and SM

In order to solve QoS-aware selection, a special hybrid algorithm is presented in this section. Firstly, some SM operations are proposed on the basis of the decision variable matrix. Lastly, a fitness function is built.

3.1 SM operations

In order to enhance GA's local search capability, this paper presents a hybrid algorithm that is the combination of GA and SM. The following is the main operation procedure of the hybrid algorithm.

1), building some initial simplexes. Every time a new generation of population is produced in GA, it is necessary to build some local initial simplexes. On the basis of a certain probability, *n+1* individuals in a population will be randomly selected to compose a local initial simplex in a n-dimensional space. Each individual's fitness function value shall be the function value of the corresponding vertex in the simplex. NUM_{sm} is the number of generated initial simplexes. It can be controlled by simplex probability P_{sm} . It is formula (1).

$$NUM_{sm} = floor(\frac{SIZE_{pop}}{LEN_{chm}+1} \times P_{sm}) \quad (1)$$

In the formula (1), $SIZE_{pop}$ is the number of individuals in each generation of population. The symbol LEN_{chm} is the length of a chromosome. In the case of a certain population size, the simplex probability P_{sm} determines the number of simplexes in each generation of population. Its value will have great influence on the local search ability of the hybrid algorithm and the running time of the hybrid algorithm.

2), obtaining the worst individual. Through comparing the function values of *n+1* vertices, the vertex with the smallest function value is found and its corresponding individual is denoted by I_{n+1} . $I_1, I_2, \cdots, I_n$ indicate the individuals corresponding to the remaining *n* vertices respectively.

3), constructing all decision variable matrixes. The symbol m_{ij} is a decision variable. All of decision variables m_{ij} can constitute a decision variable matrix that is denoted by *M*. In *M*, each row represents a decision variable vector of all candidate services of a task. In every decision variable matrix, m_{ij} is 1 only when the *j*th candidate service of the *i*th task is selected, otherwise m_{ij} is 0. All decision variable matrixes $M_1, M_2, \cdots, M_n, M_{n+1}$ are built respectively for $I_1, I_2, \cdots, I_n, I_{n+1}$.

4), obtaining a reflection center. *n* individuals except the worst individual I_{n+1} can decide their reflection center I_c .

5), calculating a reflection point. The reflection point I_0 of the worst individual I_{n+1} can be obtained on the basis of the reflection center I_c. M_0 is the decision variable matrix of I_0.

6), deciding the next operation. The following is to decide whether to terminate simplex operation or not. In NUM_{sm} initial simplexes, after every simplex has gained a new individual whose fitness value is better than the worst individual in the simplex and that is able to meet the global user constraints, these new individuals will replace the worst ones and added into the population to participate in the next generation of population genetic manipulations. Otherwise, if the new individual's fitness is less than the worst individual or the new individual does not meet user's global QoS constraints, the new individual will also replace the worst one in population and form a new simplex to continue with the next iteration of the simplex algorithm. We can end the operation of the simplex until a new individual's fitness is greater than the worst individual and the new individual meets user's global QoS constraints.

SM can control the evolution direction of GA to make better solutions. The "premature" problem of GA can be solved to a certain extent, because some parallel searches in a number of local solution spaces not only enhance the local search ability but also accelerate the global convergence.

3.2 Fitness calculation

The fitness of individual determines the probability of itself being copied to the next generation. Individual's fitness is obtained through a fitness function. The fitness function should take into account an objective function and all global QoS constraints.

1), objective function

The following is how to build an objective function. There are two types of QoS attributes. One is decrease-type (the smaller the value of QoS attribute is, the better the impact of the QoS attribute is. such as Price), and another is increase-type (the larger the value of QoS attribute is, the better the impact of the QoS attribute is. such as Reputation). Different QoS attributes tend to have different dimensions or units. When choosing services, it is difficult to directly compare the relative importance of various QoS attributes. Therefore, it needs for QoS attributes to be normalized. The specific practice is to map the various range of different QoS attributes to [0, 1] interval. The formula (2) is for the decrease-type QoS. The formula (3) is for the increase-type QoS.

$$Q_q' = 1 - \frac{Q_q}{Q_{qMax}} \tag{2}$$

$$Q_q' = \frac{Q_q}{Q_{qMax}} \tag{3}$$

Q_{qMax} is maximum of the qth QoS attribute among all of instances of composite cloud services.

In this paper, Wq is used to indicate the weight value of the qth QoS attribute. The value of Wq signifies different degree of importance of QoS property. After QoS properties values are normalized, the weight value calculation will be done. Then, the objective function of integrated QoS for the entire composition cloud services can be established. It is formula (4).

$$Q = \sum_{q=1}^{n} W_q Q_q' \tag{4}$$

In formula (4), n is the number of QoS properties.

Through the above steps, an objective function can be made. On the basis of the definition of the equation of the objective function, the bigger the objective function value is, the better the selection result is.

2), fitness function

Some global QoS constraints will be established on the basis of the global QoS requirements that users may bring forward. Penalty function method is a common way of dealing with constrained optimization problems. This way can ensure the population diversity to avoid the algorithm into local convergence. This paper adopts penalty function method to integrate all global constraints and the objective function together. It is formula (5).

$$Fit = Q - \lambda \sum_{j=1}^{n} (\Delta Q_j)^2 \tag{5}$$

In the formula (5), Q is the objective function, n is the number of constraint conditions, λ is a coefficient and an experience value. Q_j is the global value of the jth QoS attribute. The definition of ΔQ_j is shown as follows.

If Q_j is less than 1, the formula of ΔQ_j is (6).

$$\Delta Q_j = \begin{cases} Q_j & if\ Q_j > R_{jMax} \\ 0 & if\ R_{jMin} \le Q_j \le R_{jMax} \\ 1 - Q_j & if\ Q_j < R_{jMin} \end{cases} \tag{6}$$

If Q_j is equal to 1 or larger than 1, the formula of ΔQ_j is (7).

$$\Delta Q_j = \begin{cases} 1 - 1/Q_j & if \ Q_j > R_{jMax} \\ 0 & if \ R_{jMin} \le Q_j \le R_{jMax} \\ 1/Q_j & if \ Q_j < R_{jMin} \end{cases} \quad (7)$$

In the formula (6) and (7), R_{jMax} and R_{jMin} are maximum and minimum in the *j*th restrictive condition respectively.

4 Tests and analyses

In this paper, a more powerful and efficient hybrid search algorithm is composed by GA and SM. The hybrid algorithm will have better search ability and faster convergence speed. Through some tests and test analyses, the capacity and efficiency of presented hybrid algorithm will be validated. In order to verify the effect of services choice done by the hybrid algorithm, some comparison tests between simple GA and the hybrid algorithm were made.

4.1 Test data preparation

Aiming at a fair comparison between two algorithms, they would run in the same hardware and software operating environment, including CPU, memory, OS, development language and IDE, etc. In addition, the simple GA (SGA) and the hybrid algorithm used initialization parameters as following. The population size is 500. The crossover probability is 0.7 and the mutation probability is 0.1.

The values of specific QoS attributes were randomly generated within a certain range. Some global limits for a part of QoS properties were randomly generated. The overall limits were applied to all specific cloud service compositions through the above penalty function method. In the comparison tests, simple GA and the hybrid algorithm were run for 50 times respectively. They would all be used to solve different scale of problems (that is, the number of different tasks and different number of candidate services). In every comparison test, the two algorithms solved the cloud service selection problems with the same size of cloud services combination. The number of tasks in cloud service composition was same. Their tests and analyses will be made in three parts. One is search ability. Another is convergence ability. The last one is running time. At last, different values of simplex probability are analyzed.

4.2 Tests and analyses of search ability

Search capability is that the algorithm can find the optimal solution in a solution space. It can be measured by the quality of the solution that the algorithm searches. In GA, the algorithm search capability can be measured through the fitness value of the final selected individual. In the hybrid algorithm, the bigger the fitness value is, the better the selection result is. The average values of the final fitness values at all running time were taken. A few of test data are listed in Tab.1. In Tab.1, the value of the simplex probability p_s is 0.7.

Tab. 1. Fitness Comparison (SGA : Hybrid algorithm)

Tasks Number	Average Maximum Fitness
10	0.141:0.148
25	0.053:0.165
30	0.036:0.112

As described in Tab.1, comparison of data can fully verify that the hybrid algorithm can get better results of cloud service selection than the simple GA. The efficiency of simple GA is still unsatisfactory, although to a certain extent it solved the service selection problem. When the selection problem is the same size of combination cloud services, the hybrid algorithm can get higher average final fitness value than the simple GA. When the scale of the composition problem is small, the advantage of the hybrid algorithm is not clear. But, when there are a larger number of tasks in a combined service flow, the hybrid algorithm can get much better solutions than the simple GA. In the test conditions of this article, when the number of tasks is more than 25, the hybrid algorithm clearly has stronger search capabilities. This shows that the SM operations have better search capabilities in the larger scale of cloud service selection. Because, the more the number of tasks is, the more the number of individuals in each local initial simplex. The local search ability is stronger. Thus, the search capabilities of the hybrid algorithm are more prominent. This means that the presented hybrid algorithm has greatly enhanced the local search capability on the basis of the combination of SM and GA.

4.3 Tests and analyses of convergence ability

The test results were analyzed on their convergence speeds. Algorithm convergence rate refers to the generation where the final fitness value is reached. In order to validate whether the proposed hybrid algorithm increased the convergence speed, simple GA and the hybrid algorithm were run for many times respectively. The average running generations were taken. A few of result data are listed in Tab.2. The value of the simplex probability p_s is 0.7.

Tab. 2. Comparison of Convergence Generation (SGA : Hybrid algorithm)

Tasks Number	Average Generation
10	356:287
25	372:268
30	383:312

As described in Tab.2, comparison of data can fully verify that the hybrid algorithm has faster convergence than the simple GA. This shows that the presented hybrid algorithm has greatly quickened the local convergence rate on the basis of the combination of SM and GA.

4.4 Tests and analyses of simplex probability

The simplex probability P_S determines the number of the simplexes in each generation of population. Tab.3 shows different fitness values that the hybrid algorithm obtains when the value of P_S is different.

Tab. 3. Fitness Comparison (different Simplex Probabilities)

Tasks Num	$P_S = 0.1$	$P_S = 0.5$	$P_S = 1$
10	0.132	0.139	0. 165
25	0.089	0. 157	0. 196
30	0.056	0.082	0.157

In Tab.3, the bigger the value of P_S is, the greater the value of fitness is. Because, with an increasing value of P_S, the number of the simplex is added in each generation of population. As a result, the local search ability is stronger. But, the running time of the hybrid algorithm will be raised too. So, a median value may be accepted.

5 Conclusions

Now, more and more easily used cloud services with the stability characteristics are shared on network. A single atomic cloud services can provide limited functionalities. In order to more fully utilize the shared cloud services, it is necessary to combine shared cloud services to form a new combination of cloud services. It is inevitable for a function to appear a large number of candidate services with the same function property and different non-functional attributes (mainly referring to QoS attributes). It has become an urgent problem that how to fast and flexibly select the best services to meet user's needs from massive candidate services.

Based on the analyses of composite cloud service selection problem, a simple GA combines a local optimization algorithm – SM. In the result, the search ability and convergence speed can be improved at the same time. The proposed algorithm also includes a fitness function. Through the realization of the above-mentioned algorithm, some strong validations of the proposed algorithm in capacity and efficiency effects were done. The hybrid algorithm can be a good solution for QoS-driven cloud services selection.

The number of individuals in populations is same when the combination sizes in the above experiments are different. If the populations with different sizes can be adopted for different composition scales, the efficiency of algorithm will be greatly improved. Therefore, the next study will examine the dynamic adaptive mechanism of population size.

Acknowledgments: This work was supported by NSFC under Grant No. 60872042, the Fundamental Research Funds for the Central Universities (2011RC0203) and the Co-construction Special Funds of Beijing.

6 References

[1] B. Rochwerger, D. Breitgand and E. Levy, et al. "The reservoir model and architecture for open federated cloud computing" ; IBM Journal of Research and Development, 53, 4, 1—17, 2009.

[2] M. Armburst, et al. "Above the clouds: a berkeley view of cloud computing". Tech. report UCB/EECS-2009-28, Electrical Eng. and Computer Science Dept., Univ. of California, Berkeley, 2009.

[3] B. Hayes. "Cloud computing" ; Comm. ACM, 51, 7, 9—11, 2008.

[4] Y. Liu, A. H. Ngu and L. Zeng. "QoS computation and policing in dynamic web service selection". In Proceedings of the 13th International Conference on World Wide Web (WWW), ACM Press, New York, USA, 66—73, 2004.

[5] L. Zeng, B. Benatallah, M. Dumas and Q. Z. Sheng. "Quality driven web services composition". Proc. 12th Int'l Conf. World Wide Web (WWW), ACM Press, Budapest, Hungary, 411—421, 2003.

[6] Liang Zhao Zeng and Boualem Benatallah, etc. "QoS-aware middleware for web services composition" ; IEEE Transactions on Software Engineering, 30, 5, 311—327, 2004.

[7] Liang Jie Zhang, Bing Li and Tian Chao, etc. "On demand web services-based business process composition". IEEE International Conference on System, Man, and Cybernetics (SMC'03), Washington, USA, 4057—4064, 2003.

[8] G. Canfora, M. Di Penta and R. Esposito, etc. "A lightweight approach for Qos–aware service composition". In Proc. 2nd International Conference on Service Oriented Computing (ICSOC'04), New York, USA, 36—47, 2004.

[9] M. Srinivas and L. M. Patnaik. "Genetic Algorithm: a survey" ; IEEE Computer, 27, 6, 17—26, 1994.

[10] R. Ignacio, G. Jesús and P. Héctor, etc. "Statistical analysis of the main parameters involved in the design of a Genetic Algorithm" ; IEEE Transactions on Systems, Man, and Cybernetics—Part C: Applications and Reviews, 32, 1, 31—37, 2002.

[11] H. Chan and T. Chieu. "Ranking and mapping of applications to cloud computing services by SVD". IEEE/IFIP, 362—369, 2010.

[12] A. Danilo and P. Barbara. "Adaptive service composition in flexible processes" ; IEEE Transactions on Software Engineering, 33, 6, 369—384, 2007.

[13] T. Yu, Y. Zhang and K. J. Lin. "Efficient algorithms for web services selection with end-to-end Qos constraints" ; ACM Transactions on the Web, 1, 1, 1—26, 2007.

[14] C. M. Gao, M. L. Cai and Chen Huowang. "Qos-aware service composition based on tree-coded Genetic Algorithm". 31st Annual International Computer Software And Applications Conference COMPSAC, 1, 361—367, 2007.

[15] C. W. Zhang, S. Su and J. L. Chen. "Diga: population diversity handling Genetic Algorithm for Qos-aware web services selection" ; Computer Communications". Elsevier, 30, 5, 1082—1090, 2007.

[16] Y. H. Yan and Y. Liang. "Using Genetic Algorithms to navigate partial enumerable problem space for web services composition". 3rd International Conference on Natural Computation, 475—479, 2007.

[17] G. Canfora, M. Dipenta, R. Esposito and M. L. Villani. "A light weight approach for Qos-aware service composition". Proceedings of the 2th International Conference on Service Oriented Computing, New York, 232—239, 2004.

[18] G. Canfora, M. Dipenta and R. Esposito. "An approach for Qos-aware service composition based on Genetic Algorithms". Proceedings of the Conference on Genetic and Evolutionary Computation, Washington, 1069—1075, 2005.

[19] S. Pearson and T. Sander. "A mechanism for policy-driven selection of service providers in SOA and cloud environments". IEEE, 333—338, 2010.

[20] Z. ur Rehman, F.K. Hussain and O.K. Hussain. "Towards multi-criteria cloud service selection". 2011 Fifth International Conference on Innovative Mobile and Internet Services in Ubiquitous Computing (IMIS), 44—48, 2011.

[21] Zhao Laiping, Ren Yizhi and Li Mingchu. "Flexible service selection with user-specific QoS support in service-oriented architecture" ; Journal Of Network And Computer Applications, 35, 3, 962—973, 2012.

A Secure Agent-based Single Sign-On Scheme Supporting Web Services Home Network Environments

Woei-Jiunn Tsaur and Jia-Xin Wu
Department of Information Management, Da-Yeh University, Taiwan

Abstract - *The number of services in home network environments has been growing increasingly, and therefore users must manage multiple user names and passwords daily. The previous works like SAML (Security Assertion Markup Language) standard and the commercial software called .NET Passport provide web services' single sign-on function; however, the SAML system not only increases the heavy loading of servers but also costs the Internet flow. Furthermore, it may cause the potential attacks like the replay and man-in-the-middle attacks. Also, in .NET Passport the privacy of users may suffer the risk of eavesdropping. Therefore, this paper develops an agent-based single sign-on system in web services based home network environments. The proposed single sign-on scheme can reduce the number of communications among users and servers, enhance the security of home network services, provide the privacy of users, and promote the efficiency of system in the web services based home network environments.*

Keywords: Home network, user authentication, single sign-on, mobile agent, web services

1 Introduction

With the increasing growth of the number of services in home network environments including a wide variety of personal equipment, servers, services and networked devices in the home [1]-[5], user authentication is extremely crucial for consumers to access home servers, web and broadcasting resources in the integrated home network environments [1]. In a traditional password authentication scheme, users must manage multiple user names and passwords daily for accessing multiple servers, and therefore it cannot be efficiently used for solving the user authentication of multi-server based home network services. The objective of efficient user authentication in multi-server based home network environments emphasizes that any user can obtain service granted from multiple servers without repeating registration to each server.

More and more platforms can provide intergraded services from multiple servers with the development of web services. While each platform has its own authentication method, this will limit the efficiency of web services. Except for using the trusted third party to authenticate users, a "single sign-on (SSO)" scheme can be considered as another method. SSO allows users to log in only one site to obtain all the services provided in multiple servers. In the previous work, Jeong et al. [1] proposed an SSO scheme in which a mobile user offers his/her credential information to the home network for obtaining user authentication and access to another domain such as web servers to get related information using this authentication, based on the SAML (Security Assertion Markup Language) standard. However, because the authentication procedure of SSO is complicated, it is easily attacked by hackers, and may therefore encounter many security threats. Although the security standard SAML established by the Organization for advancement of Structured Information Standards (OASIS) can provide single sign-on function, it was pointed out that there is still some worry on security when using SAML for SSO [6], [7].

Basically, the SSO technology developed by commercial software can be practical for common enterprises to provide user authentication services. However, their SSO services are mostly based on single authentication framework, which uses one authentication server to manage a variety of user data and also to complete operations of user authentication. In such a way, the performance of the authentication server must be affected. On the other hand, SAML, Liberty Alliance and web services belong to the framework of multiple authentication centers. Their existing common platforms use the token method, but the security of token is weak because cookies must be saved in clients [8]. Therefore, in this paper we develop an agent-based SSO to enhance the security of user authentication in home network service environments. A mobile agent is a software entity that can autonomously migrate from one node to another in order to perform operations on behalf of the users in the system. Through this concept, network traffic and communication latency can be reduced. Thus, the proposed agent-based SSO scheme can minimize the number of communications among users and servers, and promote the efficiency of system as well as less delay in home network service environments.

The rest of this paper is organized as follows. In Section 2, we review the previously proposed related technologies. Then we present the proposed agent-based SSO scheme in Section 3. In Section 4, we give security and efficiency analyses of the proposed SSO scheme. Section 5 simulates the proposed agent-based SSO system to certify the results. Finally, some concluding remarks are presented in Section 6.

2 Related work

In this section, we first present several existing SSO solutions, and then several SSO schemes for web services will be discussed.

2.1 Single sign-on solutions

Existing solutions for SSO can be divided into five categories [7], [9]-[11], including (1) broker-based SSO, (2) agent-based SSO, (3) token-based SSO, (4) agent and broker-based SSO, and (5) gateway-based SSO. We will introduce them in the following. There is a server that manages the warranty and users' name in the broker-based SSO. Broker is used for electronic ID saving and reading for the next request [12]. Using of central database has decreased on management costs and provided one suitable and independent third party for authentication, like Kerberos. The advantage of this solution is the concentrated method that provides central database for users' management. However, it requires upgrading its existing program to meet its need. Besides, all the application systems and services will be affected if the authentication server cannot calibrate with this concentrated management framework.

There is an agent program to authenticate users' identities for various different application programs in the agent-based SSO [11], [13]. This agent program will need to design for different functions [14]. For example, it can use passwords or encrypted keys to remove the authentication operations of clients, and be installed in servers as the translator between the authentication system and users, such as SSH. Its advantage is easy for transplantation, but it needs to design a protocol to communicate with previous application programs. Because the authority of agent program is not easy to set up [15]-[17], it is inconvenient for the agent-based SSO to manage.

The token-based SSO is the most widely used password authentication system [18], such as the log-in authentication of FTP and mail server, which are called single-factor password authentication. This is easy and more available method fr users, but it has some incipient faults in security; such as easy to guess, seldom change of password, using same password in different systems, etc. As well, it can cause great damage if a password is stolen accidentally.

When the agent-based SSO and the broker-based SSO are combined, the flexibility and the central management existing in the former one and latter one, respectively, are the advantages, and can be also economic in modifying the web application program from the contribution of agent-based SSO.

2.2 SSO schemes for web services

1. Kerberos

Kerberos protocol is based on the trusted third party [12]. Its framework is divided into servers and clients. It assists to authenticate users' identities in open network environments. Server only needs to provide management and distribute Kerberos Ticket, while clients' calls on server according to user warrant on Kerberos Tickets for certifying ID. The time for both synchronization and its security are equally important, otherwise, attackers can re-attack by changing host time. Moreover, the internal web services of enterprises are not suitable in opening services and the complex communication program between server and client related to Kerberos.

2. SESAME

The full name of SESAME is Secure European System for Application in Multi-vendor Environment [19]. It is a European organization security project, which is considered to be a European Kerberos. SESAME is based on the GSS-API (Generic Security Services Application Programming Interface), which provides SSO and security in a distributed environment. Although SESAME and Kerberos are both based on the same model, they don't copy with each other, and SESAME is added some new characteristics. Moreover, SESAME is different from Kerberos in operating. In Kerberos, users are first authenticated by an authentication server and get tickets from the server, and then obtain authorization from a variety of servers; in SESAME, the server called privilege attribute server distributes privilege attribute certificates to users to obtain the authorization for service requirements.

3. SAML

SAML a standard developed by OASIS based on XML elements. It provides authorization and warranty of data exchange in the transactions of business. It can act as a trusted third party that provides identity verification for millions of service providers. Not only it can be used for ID verification, authorization and SSO between web services but also it can eliminate the complexity of one-to-one relationship on the networks effectively, which can be the basic platform for most ID verification. SAML defines many security validations including authentication assertion, attribute assertion and authorization assertion, which can keep the security for XML framework and achieve SSO e-business.

Although SAML is a standard for the present web services, it has a lot of security vulnerabilities. Because of mutual authentication is not required, the man-in-the-middle attack will happen. Even though the specification requires integrity and privacy that an attacker won't see or change the content, the attacker can use the browser to connect with destination sites, so the HTTP attack will happen due to the lack of verification and tag notification during transmission.

4. Liberty Alliance

Founded in 2001, Liberty Alliance is composed by more than 170 manufacturers. Its aim is to develop one specification that allows users to enter personal information once and then use several application services. At the first phase, Liberty Alliance proposed Liberty Identity Federation Framework (ID-FF), which manages user identification in enterprises and applications based on the open SAML standard. Web Services Framework (ID-WSF) is developed at the second phase, the aim of which is to build up ID service framework of inter-connection, ID attributes sharing, ID service description and search etc. Nokia and Vodafone have already developed it for B2B business. The main aim for Liberty Alliance is that all related companies will have to use the same way to achieve jointed-ID managements. But problems will happen when enterprises connect to their partners and clients whom might operate in different systems, and that will bring difficulties in management.

5. WS Security (WSS)

OASIS established WSS technology committee and related rules in July 2002. WSS simplifies the data sharing from different programs by XML. It improves connection of secure systems using XML standards and defines extended standards of SOAP to ensure privacy of information transmission between services. WS-Security can be used in different products, such as XML firewall, web service management software and web security access system.

Summarized above, commercial software and Kerberos are to use a single authentication center, while SAML, Liberty Alliance and WS-Security belong to multiple authentication centers. They all have potential threats in security.

3 Proposed agent-based single sign-on scheme

Agent programs have the ability of saving user identities and passwords when users log in a web server at the first time. Then, when users want to log in other application servers, the agent programs will retrieve the saved user identities and passwords to access these services. That is, users do not need to enter them again. In the following, we will propose an SSO scheme in which a user offers his/her credential information to the home network for obtaining user authentication and access to another domain to get related information using this authentication, based on a mobile agent.

3.1 System framework

Home network has a special server called home server. The home server manages home appliances and connects the home network to the external systems. In the home network service environments, the proposed SSO framework consists of three main parts that are shown in Fig. 1. In the following, we will introduce the details of the web site, mobile agent and user.

1. Web Sites

Web sites are the service sites providing all kinds of services for users in this framework. These web sites have their own independent manners of user authentication and authorization management, and authentication information must be recorded in the system service unit. The user authentication and authorization in these web sites have the following functions:

(1) Authenticating common users' log-in operations and managing access rights.

(2) Verifying all requests from reliable web sites.

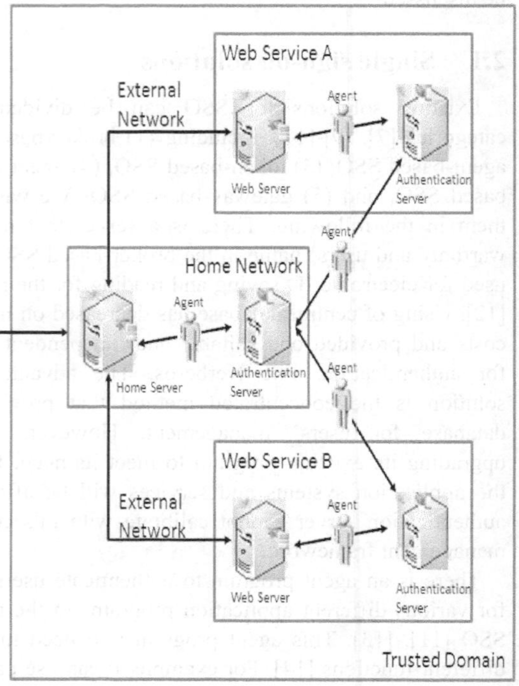

Fig. 1. The proposed SSO framework

(3) Defining users' authorization sent by reliable web sites.

2. Mobile Agent

Mobile agent can take the responsibility to transmit log-in information and authentication information from unreliable web environments instead of ones that can be relied on. It also assists users to achieve the aim of SSO by requesting services from other former servers with the authentication. The content of agent includes code, status and attributes:

Code: program that defines the actions of agent.

Status: variation of agent, such as keeping it active when the agent moves to another host.

Attributes: description of agent, including owners, resource requirement, authentication key, etc. The agent cannot modify these attributes.

The operating process by an agent between the web server and user browser is shown in Fig. 2. When the web server needs to communicate with a user, it will download the program of agent and change its status and then transmit it to the user by SOA-RPC. After the user received the agent, he/she can start and connect with the agent; when it is finished, the agent will send back to the web server, and the operating process is completed.

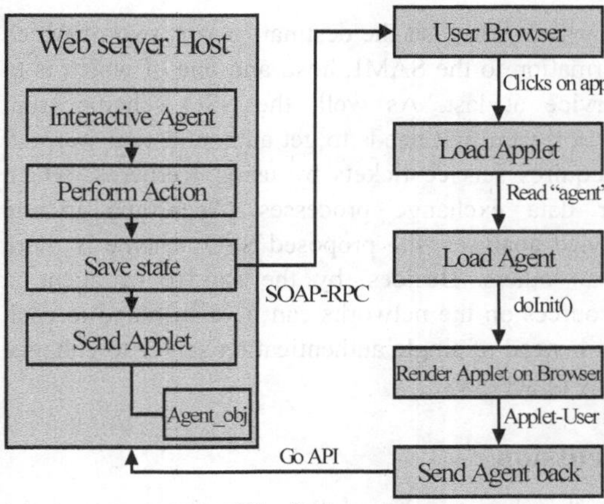

Fig. 2. Agent operations

A user can transmit one agent to a server through POST and change its status by "Get" instruction. In HTTP, transmission of data (requirement/response) is through MIME protocol. For agent transmission, the way we use here is similar to MIME but with the description of agent (including description language and agent type).

3. User

This means common users who use this type of systematic service within service web sites under this framework.

3.2 System procedure

For the convenience of description, the notations are defined as follows:

B: browser for user
S: source site
D: destination site
bs: connection from a user's browser to a source site
Cid: channel ID
S?: judging if S is a source site
bs_cid: a secure channel from a user to a source site
$A \rightarrow_c B$: data transmitted from A to B via C

The processing steps of this system are shown in Fig. 3 including the registration phase and SSO phase.

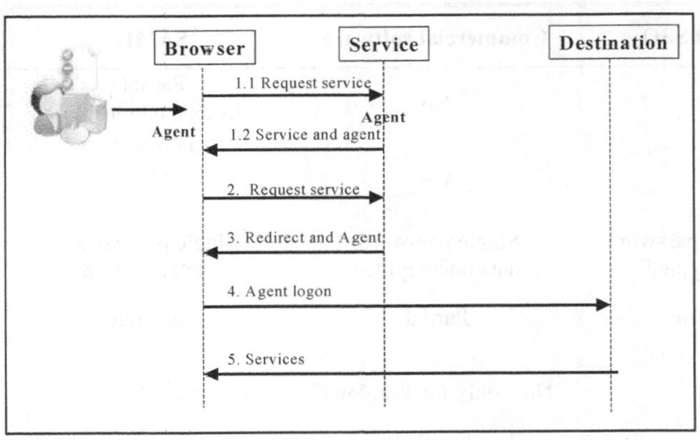

Fig. 3. System operating procedure

Summarized above, the SSO algorithm is shown below:

XML-based algorithm: authentication

Input: Sign-on request
Output: Sign-on response

1 Using IE browser to show sign-on interface for entering ID / Password.
2 User's computer requires random value for entering servers.
3 User inputs ID and password.
4 Server counts r =BHash(Random), transmits r to user's computer and sets Session("r")=r
5 User's computer counts:
6 user_spw=BHash(BHash(user_id | user_pw| S)| r)
7 User's computer transmits user's ID, role password to server by agent.
8 User signs in to source site.
9 Server judges whether SSO is successful by the following steps:
10 config = XQuery(doc("config.xml")\policy)
11 user_spw2 =XQuery(config\user_list\user[user_id=user_id]\SPW)
12 if(user_spw == BHash(user_spw2 | Session("r"))
13 return Accept
14 else
15 return Reject
16 endif
17 Server clears Session("r").
18 Server provides services.

4 Security and Efficiency Analyses

In this section, we will analyze the security and efficiency of the proposed SSO scheme.

4.1 Security analysis

In the following, we will analyze the proposed scheme can withstand possible security attacks, including the impersonation, replay, and man-in-the-middle attacks. First, several notations are defined as follows:

SA：system authority
S：source site
D：destination site
U：user
U→S：a communication from a user to a source site
U→D：a communication from a user to a destination site
IDU: user's ID
mw: warrant for mobile agent, including IDU, mobile agent ID, user's public key, valid time, routing list and list of server authorization
req: log-in request from user, including host serial number and timestamp

1. Impersonation attack

When an attacker wants to impersonate a legal user to log in a host by intercepting the log-in request {IDU, mw, req}, he/she cannot forge mw' to pass the authentication of the host, because he/she has no ability of getting the secret key shared between the legal user and SA. Besides, this system uses the warrant and timestamp to certify the validity of agent key for preventing an attacker from impersonating a legal user.

2. Replay attack

For preventing the replay attack, this system uses a timestamp to avoid attackers to replay the stolen log-in request from a legal user. No matter U→D or U→S, the host serial number and timestamp are contained in the attacker's log-in information, and thus this can prevent the replay attack effectively.

3. Man-in-the-middle attack

In this system, the agent and authentication servers encrypt messages by the public key. Unless an intruder successfully attacks the authentication server and acquires its secret key, the attacker cannot log in a site successfully within a valid time interval. The mutual authentication between an agent and a host can prevent the man-in-the-middle attack more effectively.

4.2 Efficiency analysis

This system can reduce the web transmission between a user's browser and the authentication server effectively by using the agent technology. The user just needs to enter an account and password at the first time and then he/she can visit other service sources without entering the password again. The agent uses SOAP-RPC to log in and achieve the aim of SSO by entering an account and password once and transmitting twice on the web. On the other hand, SAML has to re-verify the validity of cookie or profile by turnaround service, and this needs seven times for data transitions, three of which are to get turnaround services from the destination site, one of which is to visit the destination site, two of which is the confirmation to the SAML host, and one of which is to provide service at last. As well, the SSO scheme from commercial software first needs to get authentication warrant, and then acquires service tickets by using Kerberos, which needs four data exchange processes. According to the aforementioned analyses, the proposed SSO scheme is more efficient than others. Besides, by the service of agent, a variety of sources on the networks can be distributed to each service host instead of single authentication server to enhance the efficiency of services.

4.3 Discussion

Based on the above analyses, the comparisons among the proposed scheme, commercial software and SAML are shown in Table 1. Commercial software may damage users' privacy for enquiring his/her information, while the proposed scheme will not cause such a problem due to setting agents. Besides, SAML uses a cookie as an authentication pattern, and the cookie is usually saved in a user's browser, which can cause the replay attack or man-in-the-middle attack. The technologies of agent and encryption used in the proposed system can improve the SSO security.

Cookie is considered as the only warrant for user's log-in in SAML. Such cookies are easily to be imitated or guessed. Malicious users will be treated as legal users as long as they get the legal cookies for access authorization. The critical problem for commercial software in using Kerberos authentication is that time synchronization needs to be ensured for checking the validity of timestamp. In the proposed scheme, even thought the data of agent has been decrypted, the access can still be rejected due to insufficient valid time length provided for entering the system.

Besides, the reuse and open platform abilities of technologies are the most concerning aspects in the system development of web services. The use of the agent technology in this paper can meet these development requirements.

Table 1. Function comparisons among the proposed SSO, commercial software and SAML

Function	Proposed SSO	Commercial software	SAML
Privacy protection	Yes	No	Partial (Cookie may reveal privacy)
Central authentication	Yes	Yes	No
Security	Agent, single password, data encrypted	Single password, data unencrypted	Single password; data encrypted
Reuse of technology	Complete	Partial	Complete
Open platforms	Yes	No，only for Windows	Yes
Capability of system integration	Good	Poor	Good

5 System Simulation

The simulation includes two hosts, a web server and a application program server, each of which is equipped with 1024M RAM and installed Windows server operation systems and IIS server. The client uses Windows Internet Explorer. Java Servlet is used for HTTP request and response, and JAXP is used for supporting XML Schema for XML process. Java based SAAJ (SOAP with Attachment API for Java) is for SOAP message process, and JAXR is for UDDI communication (Java API for XML Registries). JAX-RPC (Java API for XML-based RPC) is used for SOAP communication protocol and WSDL file description when processing RPC. Besides, JADE is the development tool for agent program. All of these are listed in Table 2.

Table 2. System environment and development tools

System Environment	Development Tools
Processing HTTP Request & Response	Java Servlet
Processing XML	JAXP supported XML Schema
Processing SOAP Messaging	SAAJ
Communication with UDDI	JAXR
Processing RPC	JAX-RPC
Agent Program	JADE

In the beginning, a user registers to the home network server by http://127.0.0.1/SSOWebHomeNetwork/register.jsp, as shown in Fig. 4. After registration, the user can enter the home page of the home network services management, as shown in Fig. 5. When the user wants to enjoy the service of shopping mall, he/she may choose the "Shopping Mall" item in Fig. 5. Because this is the first sign-on, the system will turn to the sign-on interface, as shown in Fig. 6. After signing on, Fig. 7 will first show the user ID "ssodemo" has successfully passed the SSO authentication, and then the user can obtain the service of the shopping mall. When the user needs to use another service, e.g. auction, he/she may click the "Auction site" item in Fig. 5 to directly go to the auction site to enjoy its service by employing ID "ssodemo", as shown in Fig. 8.

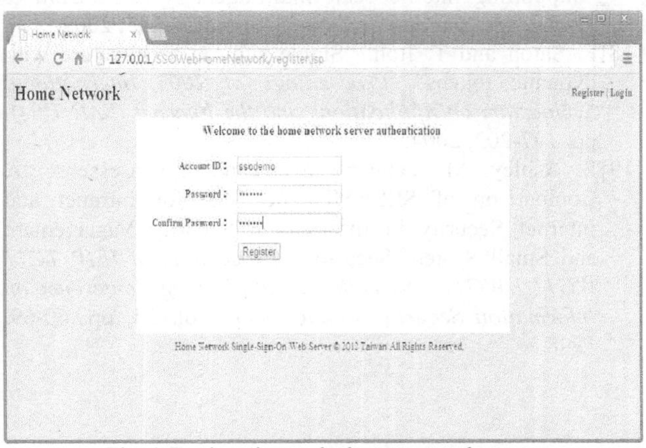

Fig. 4. Registration to the home network server

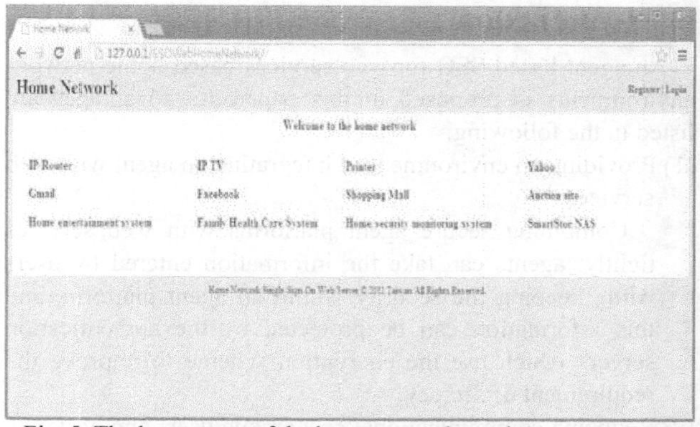

Fig. 5. The home page of the home network services management

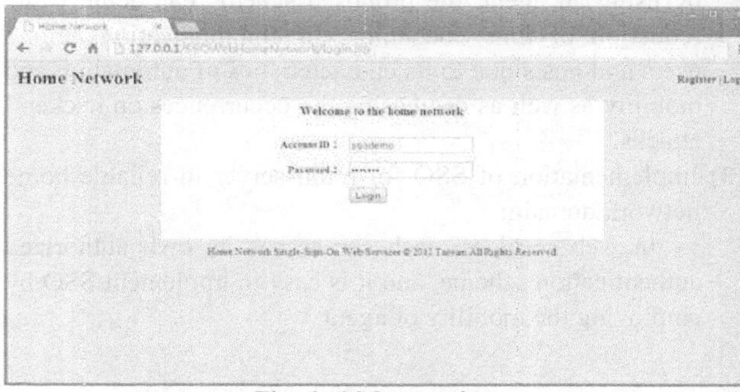

Fig. 6. SSO operation

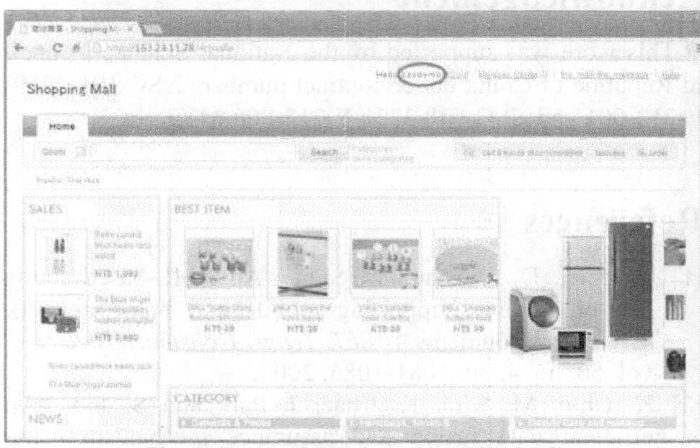

Fig. 7. Successful login to Shopping Mall

Fig. 8. Successful login to Auction site

6 Conclusion

An agent-based SSO for web services based home network environments is proposed in this paper. Its advantages are listed in the following:

(1) Providing an environment of integrating an agent with web services:

Combining secure agent platforms with web services tightly, agents can take the information entered by users while keeping the security within an agent platform, and this information can be protected by the authentication servers which use the encryption scheme to improve the requirement of secrecy.

(2) Reducing communicational cost among users and hosts:

When users want to access from one web site to another by using an agent, the proposed scheme can achieve the reduction of time consuming in communication among users and hosts due to its characteristics of automation and mobility as well as decreasing the occurrences on hackers' attacks.

(3) Implementation of SSO for multi-server in reliable home network domain:

In web services, each server has its own authorized authentication scheme, and it is easy to implement SSO by employing the mobility of agent.

Acknowledgement

This work was supported by the National Science Council of Republic of China under contract numbers NSC 101-2219-E-212-001 and NSC 101-2221-E-212-006-MY3.

References

[1] J. Jeong, D. Shin and D. Shin, "An XML-based single sign-on scheme supporting mobile and home network service environments", *IEEE Trans. Consumer Electron.*, vol. 50, no. 4, pp. 1081-1086, 2004.

[2] K. Choi, M. Kim, K. Chae, J. Park and S. Joo, "An efficient data fusion and assurance mechanism using temporal and spatial correlations for home automation networks," *IEEE Trans. Consumer Electron.*, vol. 55, no. 3, pp. 1330-1336, 2009.

[3] D. Diaz-Sanchez, A. Marin, F. Almenarez and A. Cortes, "Social applications in the home network," *IEEE Trans. Consumer Electron.*, vol. 56, no. 1, pp. 220-225, 2010.

[4] K. Han, T. Shon and K. Kim, "Efficient mobile sensor authentication in smart home and WPAN," *IEEE Trans. Consumer Electron.*, vol. 56, no. 2, pp. 591-596, 2010.

[5] A. Sleman and R. Moeller, "SOA distributed operating system for managing embedded devices in home and building automation," *IEEE Trans. Consumer Electron.*, vol. 57, no. 2, pp. 945-952, 2011.

[6] T. Gross. "Security analysis of the SAML single sign-on browser/artifact profile", *Proceedings of 19th Annual Computer Security Applications Conference (ACSAC '03)*, pp. 298-309, 2003.

[7] S. Suriadi, E. Foo and A. Jøsang, "A user-centric federated single sign-on system," *Journal of Network and Computer Applications*, vol. 32, no. 2, pp. 388-401, 2009.

[8] E. Bierman and E. Cloete, "Classification of malicious host threats in mobile agent computing", *Proceedings of SAICSIT*, pp. 141-148, 2002.

[9] M. Hansen, J. Skriver and H. R. Nielson, "Using static analysis to validate the SAML single sign-on protocol", *Proceedings of the workshop on Issues in the theory security*, pp. 27-40, 2005.

[10] R. Semancik, "Internet single sign-on system", *Proceedings of Informatics and Information Technologies Student Research Conference*, pp. 116-123, 2005.

[11] J. F. Gonzalez, M. C. Rodrıguez, M. L. Nistal and L. A. Rifon, "Reverse OAuth: A solution to achieve delegated authorizations in single sign-on e-learning systems," *Computers & Security*, vol. 28, no. 8, pp. 843-856, 2009.

[12] J. T. Kohl, B. C. Neuman, and T. Y. T'so, "The evolution of the Kerberos authentication system", *Distributed Open Systems, IEEE Computer Society Press*, pp. 78-94, 1994.

[13] S. Adabala et. al., "Single sign-on in In-VIGO: Role-based access via delegation mechanisms using short-lived user identities", *18th International Parallel and Distributed Processing Symposium*, pp. 22-29, 2004.

[14] J. Wu, S. Yuan, S. Ji, G. Zhou, Y. Wang and Z. Wang, "Multi-agent system design and evaluation for collaborative wireless sensor network in large structure health monitoring," *Expert Systems with Applications*, vol. 37, no. 3, pp. 2028-2036, 2010.

[15] N. Park, G. Lee, "Agent-based web services middleware", *Proceedings of 2003 Global Telecommunications Conference (GLOBECOM '03), IEEE*, vol. 6, pp. 3186-3190, 2003.

[16] J. Peters, "Integration of mobile agents and web services", *Proceedings of 1st European Young Researchers Workshop on Service Oriented Computing*, pp. 53-58, 2005.

[17] N.Wijngaards, B. Overeinder, M. Steen, F. Brazier, "Supporting Internet-scale multi-agent system", *Data & Knowledge Engineering*, Vol. 41, pp. 229-245, 2002.

[18] F. Satoh and T. Itoh. "Single sign-on architecture with dynamic tokens", *Proceedings of 2004 International Symposium on Applications and the Internet (SAINT'04)*, pp. 197-202, 2004.

[19] P. Ashley, M. Vandenwauver, and J. Clasessens, "A Comparison of SESAME and SSL for Intranet and Internet Security in Information Security Management and Small System Security", *Proceeding of IFIP TC11 WG11.1/WG11.2 Seventh Annual Working Conference on Information Security Management*, Vol.154, pp. 60-69, 1998.

Web Services-based Managerial Mechanisms Consideration

Zheng YANG[1], Yan FAN[1], Xuanqi ZHAO[1], Lan LAN[1], Li ZHANG[1]
[1]School of Economics,Sichuan University, Chengdu, Sichuan, China

Abstract : *The relevance of Web Services (WS) has received important interest among businesses. Along with the growing interest in WS comes also the users' concerns about reliability, security, and privacy vis-à-vis these services provided via the Web. The objective of the present paper is to discuss managerial mechanisms that may help to mitigate these issues in building a trustworthy environment over the Internet. First, an examination of the ASP decision model with its related factors is presented. Second, the Outsourcing decision model with its associated advantages and drawbacks is analyzed. Finally, the presence of Web assurance seals that aim to reduce users' concerns about security and privacy is examined. The consideration of these managerial mechanisms may helps managers to make sound decisions related to Web Services (WS), develop trust among potential and existing users of WS, and eventually lead to a decision model framework for WS.*

Keywords: Managerial mechanisms; Web services; Application Service Provider; Decision model; Level of trust;

1 Introduction

The relevance of Web Services (WS) has received important interest among businesses. WS can be defined as applications or information system (IS) resources accessible through standard Internet protocols. The possibility to utilize IS applications and computer hardware and software to operate the business without the risks of ownership is appealing and deserved consideration by decision-makers. WS can be used to integrate in a cost-effective way not related applications and IS assets, and connect business partners and customers. The opportunity to rethink and reorganize computer operations is enhanced since established providers, such as IBM, Oracle, Microsoft and SAP now offer to users various WS business applications .

Along with the growing interest in WS comes also the users' concerns about reliability, security, and privacy vis-à-vis these services provided via the Web. Some studies have examined the technical aspects of WS for instance, the verification of the quality of WS and the procedural security mechanisms, [11] but we are not aware of studies that examined the managerial aspects of WS such as the decision-making process that leads to sign up a WS contract, and the Web assurance seals aiming to enhance the level of trust for existing and potential WS users. Main reasons evoke why WS are not reaching its full potential are due to service reliability issues and the lack of trust.

The objective of the present paper is to discuss managerial mechanisms that should be taken into account to build trustworthy computing over the Internet: 1) an examination of the Application Service Provider (ASP) decision model with the related factors to consider, 2) the Outsourcing decision model with its associated advantages and drawbacks, and 3) the presence of Web assurance seals that aim to reduce users' concerns about security and privacy. The consideration of these managerial mechanisms may helps managers to make sound decisions related to WS, develop trust among potential and existing users of WS, and eventually lead to a decision model framework for WS.

The paper is organized as follows. Section 2 describes the application service provider decision model and Section 3 the IS outsourcing decision model. Section 4 examines the presence of Web assurance seals, while Section 5 covers factors facilitating the WS environment. The last section presents a conclusion.

2 The application service provider decision model

Web services are sometimes called application service providers (ASP), and ASP are sometimes called "software as a service", "on-demand computing", or "utility computing". ASP emerges around 1998 as online provision of computing services. ASP firms provide access to and usage of application programs through the Internet; ASPs own and host software. Users may "rent" the access and utilization of software remotely. The usual subscription lasts for two-year agreement which provides an incentive for ASPs to invest in the relationship with users to satisfy them and obtain the renewal at the end of the contract. Major players such as Oracle and SAP have experimented the ASP model and obtained varying success.

Table 1 summarizes the main elements considered when evaluating ASP that may apply to the decision to opt for WS.

Table 1 Elements to consider when evaluating ASP

Users' Concerns:	*Expected Benefits:*
▲Availability and reliability of services; ▲Lack of supports to problems; ▲Security and privacy of information; ▲Long-term viability of the provider.	▲Costs savings on IS operations; ▲Reduced internal IT personnel; ▲Systematic upgrading to latest version of software and hardware.

(Adaptation from Romney and Steinbart 2008, p. 58)

Users' concerns come from the risks to rely on a third party provider of WS for key business activities such as the processing and storage of data. Concerns relative to reliability of services, lack of support, and security and privacy are present. Besides, the above threats may be mitigated in dealing with an established WS firms such as IBM, Microsoft, or SAP where the long-term viability is not call into question. Reputation of the WS providers comes into play. For instance, established WS firms have resources to deploy more sophisticated security controls mechanisms to deal with sensitive data.

The service agreements between users and WS firms should contain precise performance level features such as response time, size of XML messages, frequency of backup, logical access controls, encryption protocols, and other considerations such as limit the possibility that a direct competitor may be a client of the WS firms; this aims to protect sensitive data from competition. The service agreement should also cover a dispute resolution system and financial penalties when WS firms do not meet the level of service contracted.

Accordingly, decision-makers should examine the elements of the application service provider decision model to make a wise choice on WS.

3 The IS outsourcing decision model

Reliance on outsourcing as a way to provide IS services has expanded regularly over the two past decades[1]. IS outsourcing is signing up a contract with an external organization to operate all or a segment of a firm's IS processing activities. In some outsourcing agreements, the outsourcer takes over the firm's hardware, software, communication system, and IS staff, then operate and manage the IS function. In other agreements, a specific service/function is outsourced such as payroll, data processing, or PC operations. Outsourcing contracts are usually signed for long periods, say 20 years and beyond. What drives firms to consider IS outsourcing is mainly to reduce costs. But as any business decisions, several elements have to be take into account; IS outsourcing has its advantages and drawbacks. Table 2 summarizes the main elements considered when evaluating IS outsourcing that may apply to the WS environment.

Table2 Elements to consider when evaluating IS outsourcing

Advantages:	*Drawbacks:*
▲Can reduce the IS costs; ▲Permit to focus on key skills; ▲Gain access to advanced IT expertise; ▲Take away from peak and low usage of computer capacity.	▲Poor service from outsourcers; ▲Lost control of data, system, and know-how in IS; ▲Inflexibility of contracts and lock-in situation

(Adaptation from Bahli et al. 2008; Earl 2009; McFarlan and Nolan 2009)

On the positive side, IS outsourcing may reduced the IS costs by 20 to 30 percent as outsourcers may transfer to their clients savings from 1) standard applications, such as payroll and account receivable functions, 2) purchases of IS assets, such as software and hardware, at bulk prices, 3) allocation of development and operations expenses between IS projects and 4) operating at upper data processing capacity.[9].

Outsourcing permits firms to focus attention on their key skills, knowledge, and market niches, leaving IS operations to computer providers. These providers are recognized to have better IS expertise and be at the forefront of technology. Firms that need high level of computer capacity just for certain peak periods are prime candidates for outsourcing in obtaining savings in paying only for IS utilization level.

On the negative side, a number of firms that experienced outsourcing indicated having received poor quality of service from outsourcers; poor service performance has also been recently reported for WS as well.[7] Another outcome of IS outsourcing is that firms lose certain control of their data and information systems which, among other things, placed them at risk for their sensitive data. The firm's understanding of its IS, being a necessity to respond to decision-makers information needs, becomes more problematic to manage. Finally, for outsourcing contracts signed for several years, when numerous problems come up it is very hard and costly to cancel the agreement, then bring back in-house the IS function as firms often have no more hardware, software, and IS staff with expertise. Knowing this, an outsourcer could take advantage over the firm and creates a lock-in situation where the firm has no other choice than to maintain the agreement and renew the contract at high price with the same outsourcer. Lock-in situation manifests often when there is a small number of IS providers since their bargaining power increases;[8] being short of alternative source may only lead firms to be captive and depend on their present providers.[12]

Different mitigation mechanisms exist to deal with IS outsourcing drawbacks such as 1) dual sourcing, 2) usage of external expertise, and 3) alternative methods of dispute resolution. First, dual sourcing means to find a way to deal with more than one provider to create competition, leading to lower costs, higher performance levels, and acceptable service quality.[8] Second, as outsourcing assessment require technical, legal, and management expertise,[1] IS consultants and legal representatives can make things easier for the firm in negotiating the contract and protecting its position. Finally, as dispute resolution methods, mediation (settle disputes through a facilitator) and arbitration (where an independent third-party hear the dispute and impose a final solution) can be utilized to mitigate IS outsourcing drawbacks.

Since the decision to opt or not for WS involves the assessments of computer software, hardware, and service providers, Table 3 presents a useful checklist for decision-makers. The checklist brings up relevant questions that add to the elements discussed earlier.

Table 3 Checklist for software, hardware, and IS service providers assessments

Software criteria:
▲Does the software meet all information needs and specifications?
▲Is the performance (speed and reliability) adequate?
▲Does the software contain adequate security control?
▲How many other firms use the software?
▲Are they satisfied?
▲Is the software compatible with existing information system?
▲Is the software user-friendly?
▲Can the software be demonstrated and test driven?
▲Will the provider supply software updates?
Hardware criteria:
▲Are the processing speed and capabilities adequate for the intended usage?
▲Are the input and output speeds adequate?
▲Does the system have adequate communication capabilities?
▲Is the hardware based on the most recent technology?
▲Is the hardware compatible with software and peripherals?
IS service providers criteria:
▲How long has the IS service provider been in business?
▲How large is the provider?
▲How much experience does the IS provider has with the hardware and software?
▲Does the provider has a reputation for reliability, and timely support?
▲Does the provider has responsive, quality, and experiences staff?
▲How well the IS provider stand behind its products?
▲Will the IS provider put promises in the contract?
▲Will the IS provider supply a list of customers as references?
▲Does the IS provider supply training?

(Adaptation from Romney and Steinbart 2008, p. 618)

Sections 2 and 3 discussed decision models and presented a checklist to help decision-makers to make a wise choice on WS. The next section will examine the presence of Web assurance seals which may help to reduce potential and existing WS users' concerns about security and privacy.

4 The presence of web assurance seals

Web assurance seals, such as TRUSTe or VeriSign, aimed to reassure online users that web transactions can be secure. The presence of a seal on a website intended to send a clear signal to users that the business is concrete and that online transactions are conducted securely. Accordingly, the appearance of a seal confirmed that the website has been certified by an independent third-party, thus users could be reassured that their confidential information are protected. The rationale is based on the preconceived notion that the presence of a seal can help a website foster a relationship of trust with users, which in turn leads to increased consumer traffic, transactions and ultimately, to increased revenue for the site owner.

Notwithstanding efforts by e-businesses, surveys still indicated that users are reluctant to buy services on the Web due to security and privacy concerns. Therefore, the presence of assurance seals on websites may have a positive impact on user behavior. A dozen of known seals exist but we limited our examination to two well-recognized, say VeriSign and TRUSTe.

4.1 VeriSign

The VeriSign seal authenticates a company's online business, encrypts sensitive data, and securely processes payments. It offers users the capability to click on the seal icon and link in real-time to a VeriSign server that verifies the seals' authenticity hence confirming business legitimacy. The seal supplies both the B2C and B2B market. VeriSign tracks all issued seals preventing websites from posting any revoked or expired seal. VeriSign products enable companies, from small businesses to large enterprises, to securely buy and sell products and services online. The VeriSign seal is free of charge if a business already holds a Secure Site certificate. Thousands of websites post a VeriSign seal.

4.2 TRUSTe

TRUSTe main characteristic is that it addresses the privacy concerns of users. The seal is awarded to sites that adhere to TRUSTe's established privacy policy of disclosure. The security procedures protect users' collected information from loss, misuse, or alteration. If a site collects, uses, or distributes identifiable information, acceptable transmission protocols (e.g. encryption) must be in place. Furthermore, websites that display a TRUSTe privacy seal agree to comply and endorse fair information practices with regard to the collection of information in order to promote the Internet as a trustworthy environment. Thousand of websites post the TRUSTe seal.

Accordingly, posting an assurance seal on its website may help a WS provider to reassure its potential and existing users that services offer through the web are secured and privacy is protected. Assurance seal certification is a viable business solution to build trustworthy computing over the Internet.

5 Factors facilitating the WS environment

Some other factors may facilitate the WS environment such as the growing expertise of Internet users, a firm's reputation, technological advancements, credit card industry's initiatives, and new government regulations. Each of these elements is discussed below.

5.1 The Growing Expertise of Internet Users and Reputation of a Brick and Mortar Counterpart

An important element for WS is that users view trust as a dynamic process. The more user interacts with a given website for WS, the more trust deepens and a relationship strengthens. Building trust in a WS environment can be measured as a function of time. The longer the interaction with the same site the higher is the level of trust.

Also, a firm's reputation, its size, and presence of a brick and mortar counterpart contribute to consumer confidence. [4] Established firms such as IBM and Microsoft help to build trust in the WS industry.

5.2 Technological Advancements with SET and The Credit Card Industry's Initiatives

The Secure Electronic Transaction (SET) protocol for electronic payment may facilitate the usage of WS. The objective is to allow the payment of services purchased from an e-business website with a transaction protocol that is more secure. SET encrypts the information and only the payment gateway can decrypt it; the merchant could only view the portion of the transaction that is relevant to them. Accordingly, based on the SET specifications, confidentiality, data integrity and security are provided, elements among the key aspects that users value most in Web transactions. The only issue with SET is related to its current implementation cost, an element that will be handled in a near future.

To encourage the adoption of online security measures, majors such as MasterCard and VISA launched data protection services.[13] MasterCard Site Data Protection calls for the adoption and implementation of data and network security standard for e-commerce transactions through websites. A security scanning tool assesses the vulnerability in network infrastructure and determines flaws. In the same line, VISA has developed the Account Information Security program which helps retailers to protect sensitive transaction information.[14] The program is a set of standards, best practices, and an online security tools to evaluate and improve the security of the information systems, business processes, and websites.

5.3 Government New Regulations

Existing laws address issues related to e-business transactions. For example, the Fair Credit Billing Act protects online transactions.[15] Under this law, consumers have the right to dispute charges under certain circumstances and temporarily withhold payment while the creditor investigates. Some offer a guarantee that ensures users that they will not be held accountable for any unauthorized charges made online. If fraud has occurred the user, as a victim, will not be held accountable.

In Canada, the Personal Information Protection and Electronic Documents Act states that organizations can only collect, use, or disclose information for purposes for which users have given consent in the course of any commercial activity.[16] In other words, information can only be used for purposes to which users have consented. As laws are being developed, more and more websites will have to conform or they may face severe prosecution. With time we may anticipate that more rigorous legislation on privacy will apply and be imposed. Accordingly, confidentiality and privacy issues ring up by potential or existing WS users are mitigated by new regulations.

6 Conclusions

Web services can be used to integrate in a cost-effective way not related applications and connect business partners. WS is considered as a dynamic and decentralized platform permitting to set up new types of applications, programming languages, then forms of organizations.[11] With WS, computer users have now the alternative to rent on the Web the necessary applications, hardware, and software, then pay the IS providers according to the level of usage of services.

The study of these managerial mechanisms aims to help managers to make sound decisions related to WS and develop trust among potential and existing users. In examining the Outsourcing decision model and the WS environment, some observations come out. For example, links connecting WS with a service provider can be more easily broken, and new ones created;[11] more specific, if a hotel service utilized in a travel agent application is not performing to the level of service negotiated in the contract service, the application can be transfer to another service from another provider.

Users may more easily set up and maintain services and business relationships by mutually contracting service agreements. Doing so, the presence of lock-in situation discussed with the Outsourcing model, where service providers may have more bargaining power, can be reduced considerably in a WS environment.

Another observation is that Outsourcing contracts are signed for 10 years, while the usual subscriptions in ASP agreements last for two-year. Two-year contract creates an incentive for WS providers to invest in the relationship, otherwise the service contract will not be renew. Accordingly, users may have all the benefits to sign contract for short periods of time, say 1-2 years, to make sure to get satisfying services and carry on only agreements with reliable WS providers.

All in all, it remains to the decision-makers' responsibility to perform pertinent analyses to make a wise choice on WS. The present paper aims to help them for such analyses.

7 References

[1] Bahli, B., Rivard, S., "The Information Technology Outsourcing Risks: A Transaction Cost and Agency Theory-based Perspective," Journal of Information Technology, 18, 2008, pp. 211-221.

[2] Earl, M.J., "The Risks of Outsourcing IT," Sloan Management Review, 37, 3, 2009, pp. 26-32.

[3] Larsen C.A., "How Did E-Loan's CEO Get Into the Picture?" American Banker, 168, 173, 2003, pp. 9-12.

[4] Lehmann C., McDuffie, R.S., Runyan, B., Smith, L.M., "Web Assurance Services: What Internal Auditors Need to Know," Internal Auditing, 17, 6, 2005, pp. 17-23..

[5] Mateos, C., Zunino, A., Campo,. M., "Integrating Intelligent Mobile Agents with Web Services," International Journal of Web Services Research, 2, 2, 2010, pp. 85-103.

[6] McFarlan, W., Nolan, L., "How to Manage an IT Outsourcing Alliance," Sloan Management Review, 36, 2, 2009, pp. 9-23.

[7] Metzler, J., "Web Services Take Off," Network World, 22, 7, 2010, pp. 57-58.

[8] Porter, M., "Competitive Advantage Creating and Sustaining Superior Performance," 1998, The Free Press, New York.

[9] Romney, M.B., Steinbart, P.J., "Accounting Information Systems and E-Biz, 9th Ed.," 2008, Prentice Hall, New Jersey.

[10] Systinet Corp., "Web Services: A Practical Introduction," available at www.systinet.com. 2008

[11] Tcherevik, D., "Management and Security in the World of Web Services, " White Paper, Computer Associates, 2008

[12] Williamson, O.E., "The Economic Institutions of Capitalism," 2005, Sage Free Press, New York.

[13] MasterCard International, 2008. MasterCard Security Standard Applicable to Merchants and Member Service Providers, https://sdp.mastercardintl.com

[14] Visa International,2009.http://corporate.visa.com/st/programs.jsp

[15] See http://www.ftc.gov/os/statutes/fcb/fcb.pdf

[16] Office of the privacy commissioner of Canada. http://www.privcom.gc.ca/legislation

SESSION

SECURITY + COMMUNICATION SYSTEMS + RECOMMENDER SYSTEMS + HIGH PERFORMANCE COMPUTING

Chair(s)

TBA

A Framework for Intrusion Deception on Web Servers

Constantine Katsinis[1] and Brijesh Kumar[2]
[1]Computing and Security Technology, Goodwin College, Drexel University, Philadelphia, PA, USA
[2]Security Research Group, Rapidsoft Systems, Inc., Princeton, NJ, USA

Abstract - *Threats against computer systems continue to multiply, but existing security solutions that attempt to keep the attacker out of the system are becoming unable to keep pace with these challenges. In this paper we discuss the application of military deception to defend computer systems. Deception techniques enable the defender to influence the attacker's selection of targets and thus direct him to perform actions that reveal his presence and intentions. We discuss techniques that mislead attackers and cause them to take specific actions that aid in the defense of a computer system. We then focus on web servers, that are frequently attacked often as a first step of a deeper intrusion into a computer network, and present an architecture integrating deception into a popular web server.*

Keywords: Deception, Intrusion Detection, Intrusion Response, Information Security, Information Warfare.

1 Introduction

Traditionally, security professionals have used two strategies for defending against attacks in cyberspace: identifying and fixing vulnerabilities and detecting attacks before they inflict significant damage. They have focused on keeping attackers from stealing data by actively watching for intrusions, strengthening perimeter defenses, blocking attacks with network technologies such as firewalls, protecting against malicious software with antivirus technology and relying on defensive signatures.

However, these techniques have their limits. In fact, the Internet provides attackers with a common knowledge base. They can research new vulnerabilities and find systems that exhibit these vulnerabilities. Given enough time and information an attacker can learn to circumvent a firewall. An IDS will only provide information after the attack has started, which often leaves little time to secure all vulnerable systems, in effect forcing administrators to wait until the damage is done. Then, their only option is to make defensive changes and relaunch as quickly as possible.

Recently, the thinking has evolved to the point where, while keeping the enemy out is paramount, it is assumed that attackers have gotten inside and will again. There is growing sense that organizations need to be more aggressive in fighting off intruders especially as the costs of digital espionage keep increasing.

Web servers in particular are exposed to the public and are easily examined by the outside world. An attacker can take the time to traverse the site, understand how web applications are coded and locate the defensive measures that are in place which allows them to avoid being profiled. This activity goes undetected because the server sees it as the traffic of a legitimate user. The attacker may continue the attack for example by locating dynamic pages, especially those which accept form or query input, derive boundary input cases and attempt to provoke an unintended response from the server. By repeating this process systematically, he obtains a list of all the parameters that are either properly validated by the server or not. He therefore obtains pages that are vulnerable because boundary values of their parameters produce calculation errors, fatal errors, or are injected into the response without cleansing. He then attempts to exploit these vulnerabilities by trying different attack vectors. Being detected or blocked at this point is not an issue as the attacker can continue the attack through another proxy.

Among the most important web application vulnerabilities, as they appear in the OWASP 2013 Top 10 project [17], are Cross-Site Scripting, Injection attacks and Path Traversal. Injection attacks include attacks based on input that may contain malicious code to be executed, such as the SQL injection attack. They also include Command injection, an attack that converts the application into a system shell that executes the attacker's commands on the operating system without even being logged on. If the web application runs under root permissions, then the attacker is able to run any possible command. Path Traversal attacks rely on the "insecure direct object reference" vulnerability which exposes a reference to a file or directory without proper access control check. The attacker can modify such a reference to access a file outside the web root directory.

2 Intrusion Defense Evolution

Deception is invaluable in warfare and other conflicts as it can be used to trick an adversary into taking actions that waste his resources or move his resources to make them easier to attack. Deception-based defenses in information systems have been in use for a long time, from simple techniques such as the login process asking for a password even when the supplied user account does not exist, to the extensive use of honeypots and decoys since the early 1990s.

Intrusion Deception is an extension of intrusion detection and prevention with a primary purpose to confuse, misdirect and frustrate maliciously driven attackers. Early forms of Intrusion Deception techniques include spoofing service banners, labeling system services deceptively, routing threatening traffic to honeypot networks, integrating decoy systems within critical resources and placing tracking beacons on decoy files.

Intrusion Deception can create an environment where the attacker is uncertain if he has succeeded in intruding into the network and whether he has extracted the data he was searching for. Ultimately, though, the intruder should not even be aware of the deception. The goals of Intrusion Deception can be either to keep the attacker on the system in order to trace him or to make him leave. If the goal is to make him leave then he must be induced to lose interest or believe that he was successful in his attack. In either case, if he leaves on his own, he is unlikely to come back. In the end, Intrusion Deception costs more time to the attacker (in fruitless attacks and extraction of false information) than the defender and gives the defender information about the attacker's tools and motives to prevent the attack from causing damage.

Honeypots

Honeypots were among the first deployments of network deception. Honeypots appear to be a component of a larger network architecture. In reality, though, they do not contain any useful data and are often separated from regular network resources. They serve no purpose, except collecting data about attacks on them, and have no legitimate users and consequently can be deceptive all the time. However, they offer no utility after a successful attack has already occurred.

Low interaction honeypots like Honeyd [6] basically simulate the network protocols and respond to network probes. High interaction honeypots respond to network probes and permit logins and access to resources. Honeynets are groups of honeypots, imitating an actual or fictitious network, used to study how attacks spread from one computer to computer.

Honeypots can be recognized without deception, since attackers can see a lack of normal file structure and lack of temporary files. Several techniques are provided in [4] that an attacker could use to detect honeypots. There have been many proposals of deliberately deceptive activities on honeypot networks to keep attackers busy. Such activities include configuring the router to respond to many fake IP addresses, and augmenting the honeypot with a virtual storage system. These are a simple passive form of deception. In addition, honeypots do not follow an important principle of conventional warfare, that deception should be integrated with genuine operations. As argued in [14,15], deceptive tactics are more effective on real systems.

Typical honeypot deployments include:
a) a minefield, where honeypots exist among regular servers, possibly containing some of the real server data. An example deployment is placing honeypots among servers in the DMZ to capture attacks against the public servers and also servers in the internal network. This deployment can be effective against intruder stealth scanning ("slow scans") which may not set off an IDS system but will be detected by the honeypots.
b) a shield, where each regular server is paired with a honeypot deployed in a DMZ. A firewall redirects the network traffic according to the shielding policy: regular traffic is directed to the server while any suspicious traffic destined for the server is instead sent to the honeypot shield. The honeypot typically mirrors some noncritical content of the regular server to increase its deception.

Sticky Honeypot (LaBrea) is another deception technique used to protect networks and some applications. It takes over unused IP addresses, and creates virtual servers that are attractive to worms, hackers, and other denizens of the Internet. The program answers connection attempts in such a way that the machine at the other end gets "stuck", sometimes for a very long time [5].

3 Deception Strategies

Deception in computer systems relies heavily on the principles of deception in military conflict settings. Several types of military deception have direct application in computer systems, such as feints, lies, disinformation, ruses, concealment, camouflage, and manipulation of the adversary by insight into their reasoning and goals [3]. In a similar fashion, information systems can lie, cheat, and mislead attackers to prevent them from succeeding [15]. Such deception can rely on minimal resources to be very effective in creating deceptive delays (to allow setting up a permanent defense to time-critical attacks) and defensive lies (to manipulate attackers).

Just as in military conflict, deception in computer systems is a way to foil attacks. Deception may convince an enemy to go away without any fight most probably to avoid an all out defeat. However, the ultimate success of deception in computer systems occurs when the enemy goes away thinking he has succeeded. A computer system can achieve this by relying on intrusion detection to monitor suspicious user behavior. As suspicious activity increases, the system increases its deceptive measures, keeping the attacker fooled as long as possible, tying up his resources, and allowing him to believe he is successful while reducing his chances of successful attack. Simple excuses can be combined to create deception: the file system has crashed, the required software has bugs, network parameters are incorrect, security policy is in effect, the attacker action caused the system to malfunction.

Planning is essential to deception because most often defensive lies and delays require consistency. The system needs to maintain, and be able to reason about, what has been presented to the attacker so far so it can decide what deceptive action to take next. For example, once network problems are used as an excuse to deny or delay some request, the same excuse (or similar evidence of network problems) should be given to following requests of the same type by the attacker. In other situations, an earlier excuse may not be sufficient for a subsequent refusal to a new request by the attacker. For well-defined situations resulting from known attacks a detailed plan may be constructed [10]. Otherwise alternative excuses may be ranked and selected [15]. [2] used attack graphs to guide the activities of attackers based on situation-dependent lies. The objective of the plan is to minimize damage to the system and can be characterized by the probability that the attacker goes away either having given up or thinking he has succeeded in his attack. Figure 1 shows the basic flow of engaging an attacker using a deception plan.

While planning of consistent deception actions is essential, inconsistent deceptions are also useful [13]. A consistent deception builds a fake reality that still functions under the rules of reality so the attacker does not see the deception. An inconsistent deception attempts to disorient the attacker. He will realize the inconsistency, even the deception, but will not know which of his observations relate to the real system and which to the deceptions. One possible outcome is that the attacker will leave without causing any damage to the system.

4 Decoys

Deployment of decoys in computer systems follows the basic idea of filling the attacker's search space with decoys so that detection of real targets becomes difficult. One common deployment of decoys is to defeat penetration testing tools used by attackers that probe target servers looking for vulnerabilities. Penetration testing tools identify operating system and server types and versions and provide facilities to perform attack sequences against identified vulnerabilities in the target system. However, these tools have characteristic behaviors which make them readily identifiable by the targets of their attacks. The defender can then simulate a variety of server characteristics and services (decoys) so that the attacker makes errors differentiating between real and fake targets, and is lead by the defender down defender-designed attack graphs that cause the attacker to waste resources or deceive him into thinking he is succeeding.

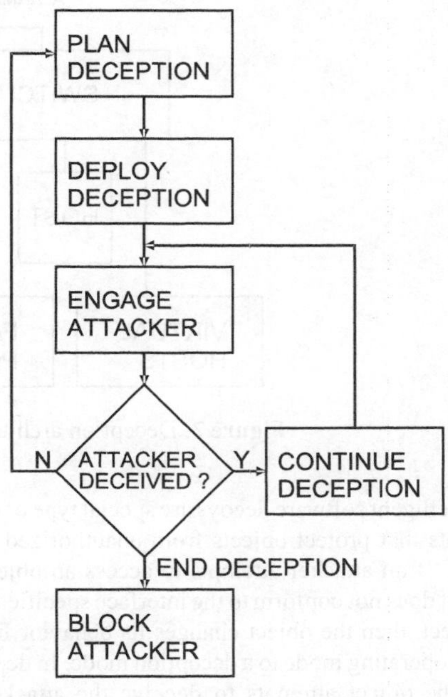

Figure 1. Deception plan deployment

In general, decoys are constructs which contain data that appears valuable but is in fact fake. They may be files, web page elements, fake data flows injected into a network, or fake but believable user activity on a server [1]. Figure 2 shows the basic network architecture. Decoys may contain random data or bait information which the attacker may attempt to use at a later time. They are effective because attackers lack the thorough knowledge of the target system which authentic users have. Authentic users can distinguish or remember which resources are real and which are fake, and have no reason to access inauthentic decoys with no useful data, while an attacker will have difficulty differentiating decoys from desirable data. Decoys are able to defeat low quality attackers without interfering with normal users and can quickly indicate the presence of an attack. The target can respond by increasing security measures against the attacker including escalating its deception profile.

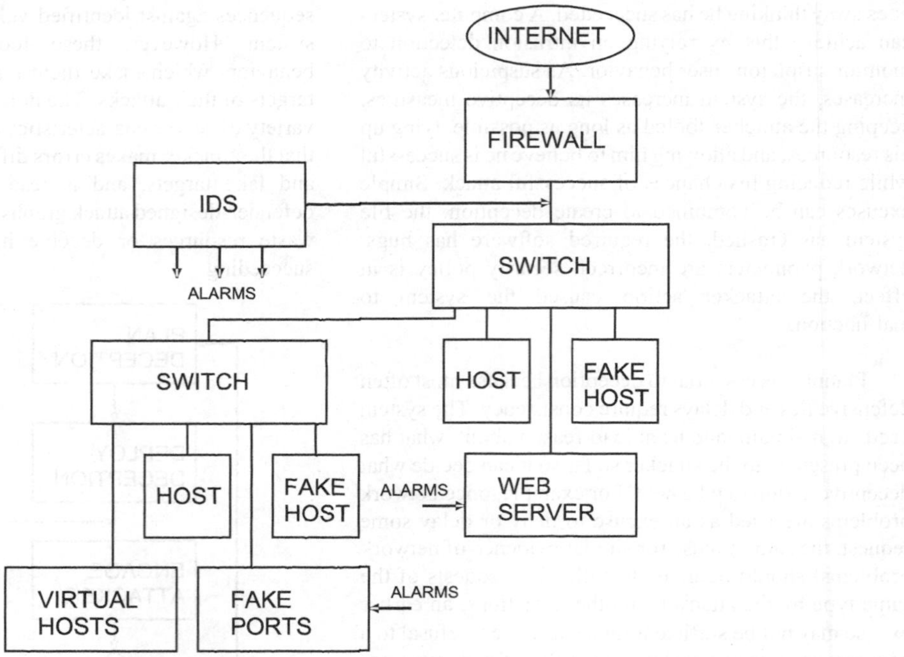

Figure 2. Deception architecture

Intelligent software decoys are special type of decoys or agents that protect objects from unauthorized access [11,12]. If an attacker attempts to access an object in a way that does not conform to the interface specification of the object, then the object changes its behavior from its normal operating mode to a deception mode. In deception mode the object attempts to deceive the attacker into concluding that its violation of the interface specification has been successful. In general, responses of such software decoys include maintaining the interaction with the attacker to learn about the nature of such interactions, terminating the interaction or even treating the attacker as a cybercombatant.

Effective decoys have certain characteristics [16] which enable them to maintain deception against attackers without affecting normal users. Decoys must be believable with name, content and attributes that are realistic; but it also must be variable, exhibiting as much variability as normal documents in the system, so that they are not easily detected by simple pattern-recognition processes. Decoys must be conspicuous and enticing so that they are located in places where the attacker will most probably search; but they also must avoid confusing the normal users or obstructing regular activities on the system. The operating system must be configured to make any decoy access detectable; use of decoy contents by the attacker can also serve as an alarm. Finally, decoys must be updated regularly to keep them believable, conspicuous and enticing.

5 The role of deception in Web attacks

There are many reasons why web servers are frequently attacked:

- Most of the application code (with vulnerabilities) is public on the website.
- The web server offers the quickest pathway to infiltrate the company network.
- The web server is largely undefended, reducing the possibility that the attacker will be detected.
- The skill level required to exploit known web server vulnerabilities is low because attack scripts are available

to download.

It is challenging to respond to Web application abuse because attacker probing is mostly invisible to intrusion detection systems, and cannot be easily distinguished from normal user behavior. Organizations maintain a layered defense in the form of network firewalls, intrusion protection systems and web application firewalls primarily based on signatures and anomaly detection. These security technologies are useful in blocking the known attacks but are not sufficient to prevent intrusions from unknown attacks for which no pattern exists.

While organizations can continue to rely on layered defenses, embedding deceptive technology into the web server can be used to block and misdirect attackers before they succeed in their attacks. Most web server attacks start with a malicious user or automated tool probing the website for information leakage or potential vulnerabilities. Subsequently, any attacker attempt to exploit a vulnerability activates an alarm that intercepts the attacker's communications and transmits back misleading information. For example an attempt by the attacker to use boundary input cases on forms and provoke an unintended response from the server causes an embedded code fragment (a code landmine) to fire and activate an alarm.

Deception in the web server relies on several components:

- The application can contain fake code, fake form fields and fake files.
- Landmine code which generates alarms when any attempt is made to access it.
- Spoofing network data sent to attackers
- Dynamic rerouting of attacker traffic for asset protection
- Identifying the attacker's actions based on his interaction with landmine code.
- Recording the attacker's actions after an alarm is activated.
- Interaction with other deployed security technologies.
- The ability to tag attacker's browser so he can be identified in future attacks.

Deceptive activities must attempt to control the attack by sending the attacker fake information such as fake file containing incorrect data, worthless password files or incorrect application responses. Furthermore, deception can be enhanced by increasing the investment in time and effort the attacker need to make to continue the attack. For example, a typical account lockout policy that blocks an attacker after five failed login attempts can be replaced by a deceptive one whereby the attacker is presented with a higher-level authentication after three failed attempts. If he attempts to defeat the authentication, the server assumes that it is under attack and slows down the response to the login attempts. Finally the server allows the attacker to login even with an incorrect password and redirects all traffic to a honeypot. As a further example, an attacker may attempt to manipulate form fields that are protected by landmine code. When unusual behavior generates an alarm, all attacker traffic is redirected to a virtual sandbox created dynamically for the attacker and presenting a fake but believable web site. Similarly, landmine code can cause an alarm when an attacker is attempting to exploit an SQL injection vulnerability. At that point, deceptive code can start leaking other fake database-related data, possibly encrypted but appearing enticing to the attacker, such as password hashes which when broken reveal passwords that either do not work or are associated with fake accounts that feed more fake information.

Decoys can be put to effective use in the protection of a web server through deception [7,8]. Decoys exist as a large collection of fake virtual machines, and detection points: fake server files, fake parameters, fake functions, fake inputs and fake configuration files that appear to end users and attackers as part of the application itself. If an attacker attempts to communicate with a decoy virtual machine the suspicious activity causes an alarm. Similarly, if while probing a web site an attacker touches a detection point an alarm is generated. Detection points include link traversal, such as searching the application for links to hidden resources; attempts to search protected directories; header abuse; illegal request method such as non-standard HTTP methods; input parameter manipulation such as form inputs, injection and cross-site scripting attacks; attempts to manipulate application behavior through query parameter abuse; error codes such as suspicious application errors or unexpected response codes; suspicious file requests such as filenames with known suspicious extensions, prefixes, and tokens; requests for directory configurations, passwords, and protected resources; login attempts with invalid credentials; attempts to crack authentication; and cookie abuse.

For example, in a directory traversal attack, an attacker uses a automated custom spider tool to create a map of all the hidden files and directories that are present on the web server, with the intention of discovering and mining sensitive information such as passwords and configuration settings. These hidden files are not linked from anywhere in the site because they are intended to be accessed by the public, but spider tools can attempt to discover them using a list of common names of these files. A decoy that triggers an alarm when a directory traversal attack is detected can respond that the requested files do exist and can cause an arbitrary number of fake files and directories to be presented to the attacker, essentially creating a loop for the attacker that can last forever.

Deception in a web server creates a layer of code that forces attackers to reveal themselves but remains invisible to normal users. Once an attacker is identified, he can be tracked or slowed down or blocked. The ultimate effect is supplying the attacker with misinformation, a sequence of fake responses and data to exploit that gives the attacker the impression that he is successful while he is attacking a deceptive server.

Figure 3 shows the architecture of a web server integrated with deception modules. The basic web server functionality draws from the Apache design as described in [9]. Apache is using a modular approach to process an HTTP request allowing a module to handle a particular task but ignore other aspects of the request that are not relevant. At its core is the content generator. Modules register content generators by defining a function referenced by a handler configured by directives in the configuration file httpd.conf. A request goes through several phases in the metadata processor before being processed by the content generator. These phases examine and change the headers of the request to verify access rules, map the request to a file or script, and determine the proper content generator. The logging phase takes place after the content generator has sent the response back. In Apache, new modules can be developed and inserted into any of the processing phases described above. A module defines a function and, through the proper hook, tells Apache to call the function at the appropriate processing phase. Figure 3 shows a single deception module inserted between the metadata processor and the content generator. However, it is possible to create multiple deception modules and insert them between different Apache phases for even finer control of the deception. Figure 3 shows the deception module communication with the decoys and the IPS to receive alarms and modify the content sent as part of the server's response to the attacker. The deception module may also decide to redirect the attacker traffic to a honeypot when it is determined that the deception has not been successful. For even finer deception control, some of the decoy functionality could become part of the content generator in the form of additional modules.

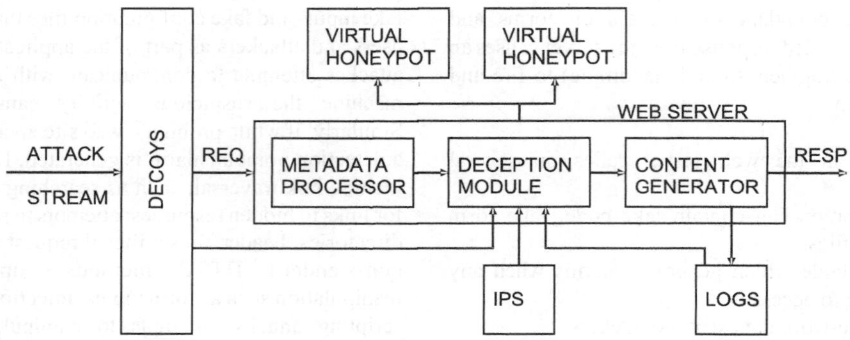

Figure 3. Deceptive web server architecture

6 Conclusion

Defense techniques based on deception can be beneficial if the deception is maintained successfully for the proper amount of time, leading the adversary to conclude that he has been successful, when in fact he is not. In this paper we examine the architecture of a deceptive web server that integrates intrusion detection, decoys, virtual honeypots and a deceptive content generator that detect the attack, trap the attacker and keep supplying him with misinformation, a sequence of fake responses and data to exploit. Deception technology is thus an additional, increasingly effective, layer of defense against ever more sophisticated attacks that succeed in bypassing the traditional defense layers of firewalls and intrusion prevention systems.

7 References

[1] Bowen, B., et. al., "Botswindler: Tamper resistant injection of believable decoys in vm-based hosts for crimeware detection", Recent Advances in Intrusion Detection, 118-137, 2010.

[2] Cohen, F., Koike, D., "Leading attackers through attack graphs with deceptions", Computers & Security, Volume 22, Issue 5, pp. 402-411, July 2003

[3] Dunnigan , J., & Nofi, A. "Victory and Deceit",

Deception and Trickery in War, 2nd Ed., San Jose, California: Writers Club Press, 2001.

[4] Holz T., Raynal F., "Detecting honeypots and other suspicious environments", Proc. 6th IEEE Information Assurance Workshop, United States Military Academy, West Point, NY, USA, 2005.

[5] http://labrea.sourceforge.net/labrea-info.html

[6] http://www.honeyd.org

[7] http://www.mykonossoftware.com/

[8] http://www.projectnova.org/

[9] Kew, N., "The Apache Modules Book: Application Development with Apache", Prentice Hall, 2007.

[10] Michael J. B., Fragkos G., & Auguston M., "An experiment in software decoy design: intrusion detection and countermeasures via system call instrumentation", Proc. IFIP 18th International [Information Security Conference, Athens, Greece, 2003, 253-264.

[11] Michael, J. B, "On the Response Policy of Software Decoys: Conducting Software-based Deception in the Cyber Battlespace," Proc. 26th Annual International Computer Software and Applications Conference, pp. 957- 962, Aug. 2002.

[12] Michael, J. B., Riehle, R. D., "Intelligent Software Decoys", Proc. Monterey Workshop on Engin. Automation for Software-Intensive Syst. Integration, June 2001, pp. 178-187.

[13] Neagoe, V. , Bishop, M., "Inconsistency in Deception for Defense," Proc. New Security Paradigms Workshop, pp. 31-38, Sep. 2006.

[14] Rowe, N. C., "Deception in defense of computer systems from cyber-attack", in Cyber War and Cyber Terrorism, ed. A. Colarik and L. Janczewski, Hershey, PA: The Idea Group, 2007

[15] Rowe, N. C., Rothstein H., "Two taxonomies of deception for attacks on information systems", Journal of Information Warfare 3 (2) (2004) 27-39.

[16] Voris, J., et. al., "Bait and Snitch: Defending Computer Systems with Decoys", Proc. 3rd Cyber Infrastructure Protection Conference (CIP), Sep. 2012.

[17] https://www.owasp.org/index.php/Category:OWASP_Top_Ten_Project

Cross-site Recommendation Application Based on the Viewing Time and Contents of Webpages Captured by a Network Router

Kazuki Masuda*, Shin-ichi Ishida*, Hiroaki Nishi*
*Dept. of Science and Technology, Keio University, Japan

Abstract - *In this study, we implemented a novel recommendation application for webpages. Our proposed application based on network traffic can recommend more valuable webpages to users. In this application, we used a special router that captured the packet stream directly. The scoring index used to make effective recommendations was based on the similarity, appearance frequency, and viewing time, which could only be captured by the network router. Thus, it was necessary to identify users to analyze their viewing time of webpages, which was achieved using their IP address and HTTP headers. We evaluated our proposed application by A/B testing and checking whether the browsing history of a user was tracked correctly. This demonstrated that our method identified users and that they preferred the recommended webpages while using our proposed application based on the viewing time.*

Keywords: recommender systems, content-based filtering, network traffic analysis, viewing time, service-oriented router

1 Introduction

The amount of information that travels across the Internet has increased dramatically in the past few decades because of the huge growth in the number of Internet users. People use the Internet to share information related to entertainment, social networking, education, and business. With the improvement in richness of Internet services, Internet users have had access to massive amounts of data. However, this can be problematic because users become confused if they are given too much information. This is why users need to limit the amount of useful information they can obtain in a day. If users cannot access useful information instantly, they may waste their time accessing useless information.

To address this problem, data mining technology has been introduced for finding valuable and newer information in large information databases both effectively and efficiently. In particular, many companies use this technology to analyze correlations and trends when mining past sales data, and they can utilize the mined data to improve their business outcomes. Data mining technology allows a particular company to capture the attention and to attract users by recommending appropriate products. A recommendation service is a method that provides suggestions for products or services that users may like. With the support of recommendation services, users can access the required information instantly.

The Amazon recommendation service is a well-known service. Amazon provides a recommendation service that recommends items to users who are looking at a particular product, i.e., “Customers who bought items like this also bought”. This recommendation service makes it easier for the user to find the product they want. Several companies that provide a recommendation service also incur additional benefits because the recommendation service shows items with a higher probability of being purchased by customers. Recommendation services are used by shopping websites and also by video-sharing websites such as YouTube and search engines such as Google. For example, the Google search engine suggests possible search queries while users are entering query keywords in the search box.

In general, there are two different methods for gathering information for recommendation services: server-based and crawler-based methods. Server-based recommendation services can obtain limited information based on the browsing history and buying history of users. In this method, the basic information used by the recommendation service can only be obtained from the server by crawling the Internet. Therefore, this method cannot use information, which is not stored on the server. If a recommendation service provider uses this method, the quality and coverage of the recommendation service can be improved by using analytical information from the servers of service providers. In addition, information is transferred over the network for sharing with different servers. However, this increases the network traffic. Special applications are also required to record a log of network transactions and to share information with servers that provide services. Crawler-based recommendation services analyze the link structure of webpages and obtain information from network itself. Indeed, this is the main cause of increased network traffic.

In this study, we propose a router that functions to route packets but that also collects the payloads of packets. This router is referred to as a Service-oriented Router (SoR) [1] (Fig. 1). SoR can capture all of the information transferred over the Internet. When packets pass through SoR, it analyzes the packets and stores selected contents of the packet as well as the timestamp and IP address of the packet. The data obtained includes information about who did what, when, and where. This can be used to provide high-quality services to Internet users.

In this paper, we propose a new recommendation service based on the features of the SoR. This service can recommend webpages to users based on the keywords they type in a form. In particular, we exploit the viewing times of webpages as an index for this application. The viewing time is the duration of a visit to a webpage. The viewing rate of TV programs is a similar metric to the viewing time. This viewing time of webpages can be regarded as a critical value for making an index of search engines and recommendation engines. This information can only be obtained when using SoR as a network router. There are alternative methods for measuring the viewing time, but other methods have limitations when gathering information. For example, the viewing time cannot be captured simply by using an access log obtained from a particular single host. SoR can measure any type of viewing time on webpages, regardless of the access log and type of service. Our proposed application uses the viewing time captured by the SoR, which can be used to provide services that will be indispensable for Internet users.

The structure of this paper is as follows. Section 2 describes related work in this study area with a focus on how to utilize access logs. Section 3 presents our method of gathering information from network traffic. Section 4 describes how we obtain the Uniform Resource Locators (URLs), titles, and viewing times of webpages. This section also introduces the algorithm used by the proposed recommendation application. Our experiments and evaluation are presented in Section 5. Finally, the conclusions are given in Section 6.

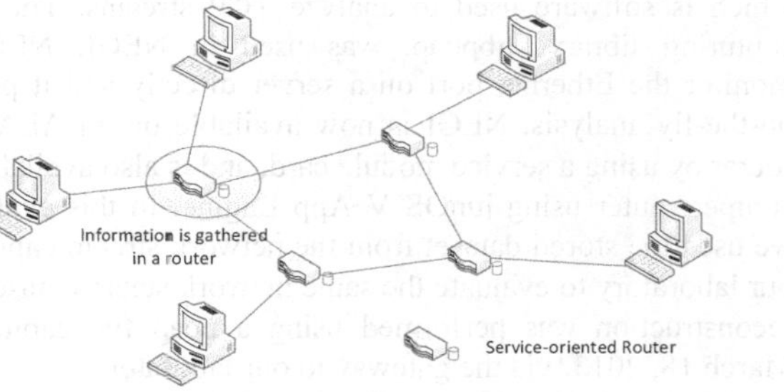

Fig. 1. Service-oriented Router

2 Related work

Mihara et al. proposed a method for measuring the viewing time by analyzing the access logs of a web server [2], where the access log of a web server was analyzed to determine the access history of a user. The timestamp, given by the intermediate time between two HTTP requests in a sequence, was used to estimate the viewing time of the webpage. The viewing time of each webpage was divided into three categories. If the viewing time was less than 30 s, the weight of the webpage was 0. If it was more than 30 s, the weight of the webpage was 1. Using this estimation method, there was a situation where it was impossible to calculate the viewing time. For example, the viewing time of the last accessed webpage could not be calculated. The weight of such webpages was 2. Based on this weight, the user's underlying essential aim of browsing could be estimated based on a comparison with a similar browsing history, except the information related to the viewing time. Based on the patterns derived, the interests of users could be determined by analyzing the webpages that users visited for longer periods. In another study, Xu et al. proposed a recommendation system that recommended webpages to users from a bunch of pages on its website [3]. The data used for making recommendations was based on the access logs captured at Dhaka University. The proposed ranking algorithm had three variations. First, a ranking algorithm conducted a sort-by-frequency among the browsed webpages. The second algorithm conducted a sort-by-frequency of the webpages that redirected to another webpage on the target server. These webpages appear in the HTTP REFERER property of the redirected webpage. The third algorithm conducted a sort-by-similarity between the visited webpages and other webpages. The similarity between webpages was based on the cosine similarity. The appearance rate of words in a page was used to calculate the vector of the cosine similarity. Internet users who employed this ranking service could access information more easily and could reduce their web viewing time. In another study [4], the browsing history of users on a certain host was obtained by analyzing the access logs of a web server. Based on the number of browsed webpages and links on a webpage from other webpages, the weighted score of a webpage was calculated. Using the weight, a primary webpage was recommended to users. In another study [5], a website was designed to explain the process of a student experiment as a class on a course. In this study, the viewing times and transitions among webpages were obtained from their access log at Tohoku Gakuin University. The author estimated how the processing of the experiment was accomplished by each student and whether the students experienced difficulty in the experiment when using the access history. The webpage described the process of the experiment. The access log included the student ID, which was added by an authentication process on the website. The viewing time of a page was calculated based on the differences between the timestamps of consecutive page accessed by the same user. This information was used to improve the context of the webpages to increase the understanding of the students. Shimizu et al. confirmed these effects by considering the viewing times of webpages [6]. For example, they assumed that pages with longer viewing times were more popular. They verified this assumption using the manually obtained viewing time and a questionnaire.

3 Layer 7 analyzer : NEGI

As described in the previous section, existing methods do not use the web access contents. Thus, it is possible to improve recommendation services using the information extracted from these contents. In a network router, it is necessary to reconstruct the packet streams to obtain the contents based on the TCP/IP streams. This reconstruction on a router can provide site-independent recommendation services because these contents are captured by a router and are not based solely on a specific server.

We implemented middleware as an API to capture and reconstruct the packet contents. This middleware was designed using C/C++ and is known as NEGI [7]. A flowchart of this software is shown in Fig. 2. The IP/Port filter determines whether the incoming packets should be processed depending on the IP address and the port number. This judgment is based on the five-tuple (source IP address, destination IP address, source port, destination port, and protocol) of each packet.

Many streams exist in a core network, and the streams arrive at a router in a perfectly mixed state. Therefore, packets that belong to a specific stream do not always arrive at a router sequentially, i.e., a situation should be considered where the packet of stream B comes after the packet of stream A. In this situation, the packet processing is frequently interrupted in a router. This interruption consumes a large amount of memory when storing all of the incomplete packet streams. To address this problem, we applied a processing scheme with a context switch to the TCP stream reconstruction process.

When the processing of a packet in stream A is finished, the ongoing status is stored in the context memory. This status is reused when a packet in stream A arrives at the router again. By repeating this context switching process, the TCP stream can be reconstructed. During the TCP stream reconstruction process, packets with the HTTP 1.1 protocol are decoded by the L7 decoder module. After HTTP 1.1 decoding, the packets are ready for the next extraction process. During this process, the important parts of the stream are extracted using a string extraction filter based on the user's query request. If the contents match the user query, the filtered content is stored in a database. The data size or range of this extraction process is also given by a user. The process used for insertion into the database is achieved without waiting for the end of the TCP stream reconstruction process. When the last packet of a stream has been processed or if the stream is incomplete, the dedicated entry into the context memory is discarded. The proposed recommendation application uses the relations in this database, which is constructed using NEGI. Table I shows the columns used by the database.

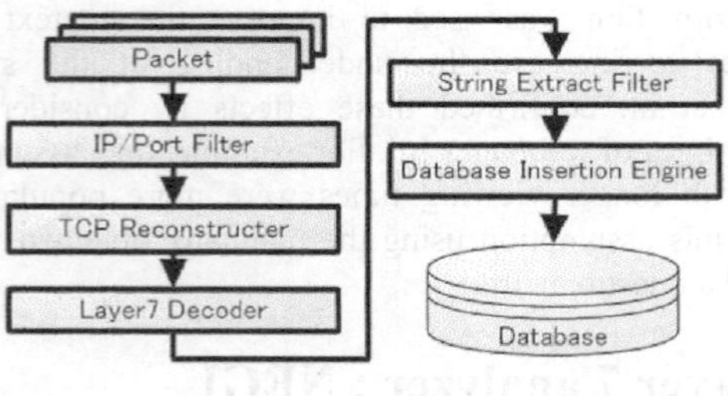

Fig. 2. Flowchart of NEGI

TABLE I. COLUMNS AND THE RESULTS IN NEGI

Column	Explanation
Stream ID	ID of each stream
Timestamp	Time of passing through a router
Source IP address	Source IP address
Destination IP address	Destination IP address
Source port	Source port number
Destination port	Destination port number
Pattern	Matching string pattern
Result	Characters stored in the database

4 Recommendation application

The proposed application employs three processing steps (Fig. 3). The first step is TCP reconstruction and the extraction of the network streams. The second step is the extraction of URLs and other information required by the proposed recommendation application. The final step is making a recommendation to users with the proposed application.

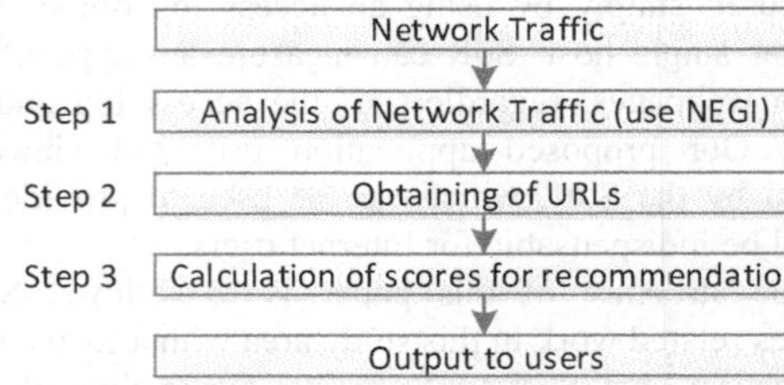

Fig. 3. Flowchart of the recommendation application

4.1 Application design

We implemented a recommendation application based on the stream contents captured by a network router. The network traffic, captured by the network router, was executed by NEGI, which is software used to analyze TCP streams. The stream capturing library, libpcap, was used in NEGI. NEGI can monitor the Ethernet port on a server directly and it provides on-the-fly analysis. NEGI is now available on an ALAXALA router by using a service module card, and is also available on a Juniper router using junOS V App Engine. In this evaluation, we used the stored dataset from the network stream captured in our laboratory to evaluate the same network steam dataset. TCP reconstruction was performed using a pcap file captured on March 18, 2013, via the gateway to our laboratory.

The goal of this application is to provide a URL recommendation service to Internet users so it should retrace URLs from the packet transactions in the captured network traces. An accessed URL can be obtained using the "Host:" header and the "GET" method in HTTP. For example, if "Host:" is "www.yahoo.com" and "GET" is "/", the obtained URL is "www.yahoo.com/". The other retrieval conditions were "<title", "<h1", and "Referer:". "<title" and "<h1" were used to estimate the similarities between a webpage and a user's query.

"Referer:" is an HTTP header field that identifies the address of the webpage, which is linked to the resource being requested. After checking the "Referer:", the new webpage can determine where the request originated. Table II describes the results of NEGI for each search condition as an example. During the practical application of these results, the useless parts of the results are omitted.

NEGI uses these retrieval conditions and its results are stored as strings in a database. NEGI obtains the URLs, the contents of a webpage linked by a URL, and the viewing time for each webpage from this database. The URLs of webpages are obtained by combining the results of "GET" and "Host:", as described earlier. In this application, the contents of a webpage are substituted by combining strings, which are tagged with "<title" and "<h1" as a retrieval condition.

It is difficult to analyze the relation between a URL and its contents. The URL can be used to analyze a request from a user to a server. The related contents of the URL can be used to analyze a reply from a server to a user. These accesses belong to two different packet streams. The proposed application should relate the request access to the reply access. To achieve this relating process, the proposed application uses the source port number and the destination port number. It memorizes the port numbers included in HTTP requests. Next, if the port numbers in the request access and the inverse port numbers in the reply access are the same, these two accesses can be regarded as a request-reply pair.

TABLE II. EXAMPLES OF EXTRACTION RESULTS

Search condition	Result
GET	/ HTTP/1.1\015\012Host: www.yahoo...
Host:	www.yahoo.com\015\012User-Agent...
Referer:	http://jp.msn.com/?rd=1&ucc=JP...
<title	>Yahoo !</title>\012\011<base href...
<h1	><a href...>Yahoo !</a></h1></div>...

4.2 User identification

Next, we present the method used to obtain the viewing time. The viewing time of a specific webpage is calculated based the difference in the access timestamps of two consecutive HTTP requests by a user. However, it is possible that people in the same domain, such as companies or schools, may have the same IP address when using Network Address Translation (NAT). In this case, this method cannot identify the individual user because a router in a middle of the Internet cannot know the private IP address.

In order to address this misidentification problem, the URL and host name are used in the access history. We propose an identification method that uses the URL and host name information based on an access example. Table III shows the access example obtained using information in the router. Three accesses have the same global address. These three accesses may have different private addresses within an NAT domain. However, a router outside of the domain cannot use the private IP addresses. The viewing time is calculated using only the difference in the global IP address and the viewing time of the first webpage is 7 s.

However, the users of #1 and #2 are different. Thus, the actual viewing time should be 18 s for the access of page #1. Therefore, we have to identify the users to obtain the correct viewing time. To facilitate this identification, "Referer:" is used, which holds the previous URL browsed by a user. Based on "Referer:", the users of #1 and #2 can be distinguished. We can identify users with the same IP address based on this technique but identification with "Referer:" is not a perfect method. When a user browses webpages from the same host, these requests do not have correct "Referer:" information. To compensate for the correctness of user identification, the host name is used in the browsing history. If the base host name of the URL (a host's Fully Qualified Domain Name) is the same as that of previously accessed page, the application assumes that a single user accessed both pages. Using these methods, the proposed application can track the access history of webpages by identifying the users.

Even if the proposed application uses these methods, there is a possibility that the viewing time of frequent webpages cannot be obtained correctly. However, the proposed methods can focus on the webpages that result from search engines rather than the pages of a search engine itself. If two different users from the same global IP address in the same NAT domain enter the same keyword into the same search engine, the two users cannot be identified correctly and the proposed application cannot obtain the correct viewing time. Moreover, if a user employs multiple browser applications or multiple tabs in a browser application, the user does not pay attention to all of the active webpages. These problems were not considered in this study.

TABLE III. EXAMPLES OF SITUATIONS USING PRIVATE IP ADDRESSES

#	URL	Timestamp
1	http://www.keio.jp/index.html	2012-10-11 10:22:30
2	http://www.westlab.jp/faq.html	2012-10-11 10:22:37
3	http://www.keio.jp/members.html	2012-10-11 10:22:48

4.3 Recommendation process

An algorithm is proposed for obtaining URLs and viewing times, which is based on the access history. Figure 4 shows the flowchart for the URLs, viewing times, and the titles of webpages. The proposed application employs SQL to use the access history managed in the database described in Table I, and it reads the access history sequentially based on the timestamp. If an access includes "Host:", "GET", or "Referer:" in the HTTP 1.1 header, it finds the next access by reading the table in the database repeatedly. This process is based on the proposed "/method using the URL and the host name because the URL of a webpage is generated by combining the results of "GET" and "Host:", as described earlier. However, there may be a situation where "Referer:" does not exist in certain HTTP requests. If it exists, the "Referer:" is memorized.

A webpage contains the HTML source file as well as pictures and advertisements. These URLs are not necessary for tracking transactions during a user's web accesses. To avoid these URLs, a URL blacklist is applied by the proposed algorithm. If strings at the end of the URL include the extensions of images files, such as ".png" and ".jpg", the URL is ignored. After checking the URL blacklist, the existence of a "Referer:" is checked. If it exists, the coordination of relevant accesses is achieved by using the "Referer:" of the target access and the URLs of webpages stored in the memory as past accesses. During this matching process, the IP addresses are also checked and they should be same. If the target access does not match any of the URLs in the database entries, the same process is used to check the host name in the database entries. If the target access does not match any of the host names, the webpage is regarded as the origin of browsing for a user.

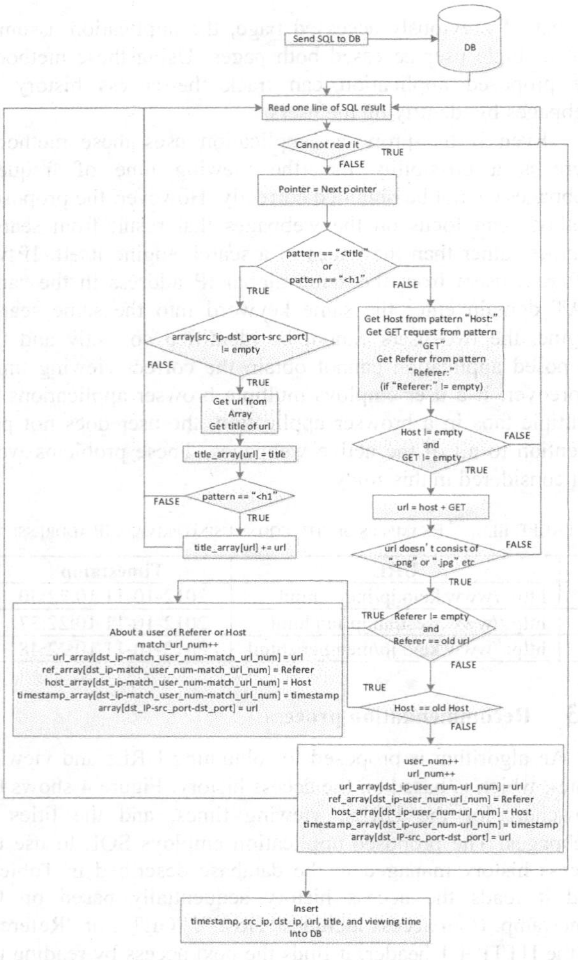

Fig. 4. Flowchart showing the acquisition of URLs and viewing times

The URL, "Referer:", host name, and timestamp are stored in the database with the key of the destination IP address, the user number (user ID), and the URL number (the number of URLs for the user). If the "Referer:" or host name of an access match entries in the database, the access contents are stored into the database with the key of the destination IP address, the number of matched users, and the number of URLs for the user + 1. In addition the URL is stored in the database with the key of the destination IP address, the source port number, and the destination port number because the packet stream of a HTTP request and that of a HTTP response are different streams. Therefore, when storing the database, the URL is associated and managed with the destination IP address, the source port number, and the destination port number.

If a webpage contains "<title" or "<h1" and it matches the key of the source IP address, the destination port number, and the source port number, the entries in the title tags are obtained and stored in the database. When matching the key, the source and destination IP address are exchanged. This is because the IP address set in a HTTP request from a client to a server is simply inverted, compared with the relevant IP address set in a HTTP response from a server to a client.

When the matching process is complete, all of the access flows for each user can be resolved. Based on this flow, the viewing time of each webpage can be calculated based on the difference in the timestamps between two consecutive accesses of the webpage. Thus, information such as the timestamp, source IP address, destination IP address, URL, contents, and viewing time of the webpage are inserted into the database. Using the information stored in the database, our proposed application provides the result as a recommended webpage.

4.4 Scoring in the proposed recommendation application

A recommendation score is calculated based on the information stored in the database. The application recommends URLs and locations to a user based on the query input as the retrieval condition. The application recommends a URL to the user, which has a higher score than others calculated by using the similarity index for the query input, the access frequency of URLs, and the viewing time of the URL. The similarity is calculated using the cosine similarity for the query and the contents (title and h1) of the URL [8]. The query and the URL are expressed as a vector and its dimension is equal to the number of query terms. Each element of the vector denotes the value of TF-IDF, which is a weight used by natural language processing. TF-IDF is the product of the Term Frequency (TF), i.e., the number of appearances of a term on a certain webpage and the Inverse Document Frequency (IDF), i.e., the log value of the Document Frequency (DF) divided by the number of documents. DF is the number of webpages that contain at least one query term. TF expresses the degree of importance of a term. However, articles, prepositions, conjunctions, and other frequently appearing terms have a high TF value because of their frequent usage. Therefore, the TF value is multiplied by the IDF, which represents the rarity of a term in all webpages. Therefore, the value of TF-IDF is larger when the term appears frequently on a webpage but rarely on other webpages. The equations used to calculate TF-IDF are as follows:

$$idf_t = \log \frac{N}{df_t} \tag{1}$$

$$tfidf_{t,d\,or\,q} = tf_{t,d\,or\,q} \times idf_t \tag{2}$$

where idf_t denotes the IDF of a term and N is the total number of documents in the original definition. In this study, documents refer to webpages tagged with a title or h1. df_t denotes the DF of the term. $tfidf_{t,\,d\,or\,q}$ denotes the TF-IDF of a term in a document or a query input submitted by a user. $tf_{t,\,d\,or\,q}$ denotes the TF of the term in a document or a query. The equations used to calculate the cosine similarity between the document and the query are as follows.

$$sim(d,q) = \frac{V(d)\cdot V(q)}{|V(d)||V(q)|},$$
$$(V(d) = (tfidf_{t_1,d}, tfidf_{t_2,d}, \cdots, fidf_{t_n,d}), \tag{3}$$
$$V(q) = (tfidf_{t_1,q}, tfidf_{t_2,q}, \cdots, fidf_{t_n,q}))$$

In these equations, sim(d,q) denotes the similarity between the document and the query. V and |V| denote the vectors of the document or the query and the size of vector V, respectively. The elements of the vector comprise the TF-IDF values of each term. To consider the number of browsed webpages and the viewing times of webpages, the frequency of accesses to a webpage is normalized using the total number of accessed webpages, which includes at least one query term. In the same way, the viewing time is normalized using the total viewing time. The score is calculated using the following equation:

$$score(d,q) = sim(d,q) \times \frac{f_d}{N_f} \times \frac{t_d}{N_t} \quad (4)$$

where score(d,q) denotes the score of each webpage that matches the given query. f_d and t_d denote the access number and viewing time of the document, respectively. N_f and N_t are the total frequency and viewing time for webpages that match the query, respectively. The application generates a list of URLs and allocates high scores using the proposed method. In the evaluation, a practical comparison was conducted that used the recommendation application without the viewing time like a conventional method and with viewing time according to the proposed method. The scoring equation ($score_{wv}(d,q)$) for a conventional recommendation without considering the viewing time is as follows.

$$score_{wv}(d,q) = sim(d,q) \times \frac{f_d}{N_f} \quad (5)$$

5 Experimental evaluation

The specifications of the host computing PC used to execute the recommendation application are shown in Table IV. In this study, two experiments were conducted. The first experiment verified the tracking correctness for the user browsing history. The other experiment was an A/B test of the recommendation application. As described earlier, a recommendation application that did not consider the viewing time was used for comparison.

TABLE IV. EXPERIMENTAL ENVIRONMENT

Machine	Intel Xeon X5650
CPU Frequency	2.67 GHz
Main memory (DDR3)	32 GB
OS	Debian 6.0.4
Development language	C++

In the first experiment, we evaluated the user identification accuracy. In this evaluation, we assumed that there were two users with one IP address. Each searched for different keywords at the same time and browsed various webpages. We actually perform the experiment based on this assumption. The network traces were captured using libpcap.

Next, we evaluated the effectiveness of the recommendations. In this evaluation, we used the network traffic of the three users. The three users browsed the Internet to obtain information using the same query keyword. Using the browsing results log, the application calculated the index. Next, the application recommended five webpages to ten users based on the proposed index. The ten users voted for the best-recommended sites to compare the proposed application with a conventional application that did not consider the viewing time.

5.1 User identification accuracy

Table V shows the URLs accessed by two users. Table VI describes the viewing time results based on the proposed method. Table V was compared with Table VI.

TABLE V. ACCESSED URLS

user_id	URL
1	www.bing.com/search?q...
1	www.nfl.com/
1	de.wikipedia.org/wiki/A...
1	www.miniclip.com/ga...
2	www.yahoo.com/
2	search.yahoo.com/sear...
2	sports.yahoo.com/mlb/
2	en.wikipedia.org/wiki/Baseball
2	espn.go.com/mlb/

TABLE VI. URLS AND VIEWING TIME BASED ON THE PROPOSED METHOD

user_id	URL	viewing time [s]
1	www.bing.com/search?q...	98
1	de.wikipedia.org/wiki/A...	88
1	www.miniclip.com/ga...	-
2	www.yahoo.com/	9
2	search.yahoo.com/sear...	27
2	sports.yahoo.com/mlb/	94
2	en.wikipedia.org/wiki/Ba...	41
2	espn.go.com/mlb/	
3	www.nfl.com/	-

The webpages (www.nfl.com/) accessed by user #1 in Table V show that the proposed application recognized that a new user, user #3, accessed the webpage. This was because the "Referer:" property of its HTTP 1.1 header was missing and because the host name of this webpage was different from the previously accessed webpage. The proposed application recognized that a new user accessed the webpage based on this evidence.

This misrecognition caused a different problem. The viewing time of a webpage (www.bing.com/search?q...) was extended to 98 s because the webpage access (www.nfl.com/) was lost and the original separate viewing times were merged into a single access. Despite these failures to detect the viewing time or to identify users, the failure rate was sufficiently low to appreciate the overall web access trend. For example, the viewing rate of a TV program was based only on a limited sample. Thus, if the TV is on, it is not known whether someone is actually watching the TV. However, this is regarded as a reliable method for measuring the correct viewing rate of a TV program and it has the power to affect the market. From this viewpoint, the measured webpage viewing rates can be used to provide services.

As described above, the application needs to ignore accesses caused by the downloading of pictures, advertisements, etc., which follow webpage accesses. Technically, these unnecessary accesses can be detected by analyzing the HTML access. NEGI can capture entire HTML pages and analyze all of the links in the HTML pages. If the subsequent unnecessary accesses are issued by links, the application can ignore these access based on recognizing the viewing time. However, this process is too intensive to implement on an Internet router. As a simplified method, we can exploit the fact that subsequent accesses issued in a short period are usually unnecessary downloads.

Alternatively, if the files downloaded after the target HTML access do not have an HTML header, they can be regarded as unnecessary files such as pictures, movies, etc. These improvements will be considered in our future work.

5.2 Effectiveness of recommendation

Table VII shows the result of the A/B test. The results for proposed recommendation application that considered the viewing time are shown as method A. The recommendation application that did not consider the viewing time is shown as method B. Method A received more votes than method B, so users preferred method A to method B. The result shows that the proposed recommendation application delivered more effective and important webpages than the conventional recommendation application that did not consider viewing time.

5.3 Merits of the proposed recommendation service

The results of the analysis were based on actual user access rather than the link structures of webpages. It is clear that they express user preferences. A conventional crawler-based recommendation application might recommend a webpage that is rarely visited.

Additional functions of this application include recommending locations to users where a server or a client exists. To determine these locations, we can use the Whois database and Google Maps. Thus, our application can provide access to where and when, as well as recommending webpages. The user can know whether a query keyword is a hot topic and for whom or where the relevant area is familiar. All of services provided by the recommendation application are based on an on-the-fly analysis in real-time using SoR. This is a major merit because the results can change dynamically depending on transactions that occur on the Internet.

TABLE VII. ACCESSED URLS

Recommendation application	Votes
A (viewing time considered)	6
B (viewing time not considered)	4

6 Conclusions

In this paper, we proposed a novel recommendation application based on a viewing rate of webpages captured by an Internet router. This application recommends the URLs of webpages and the locations where information related to a query keyword is available. The SoR capture process occurs passively on a router and it does not cause any congestion on the Internet because it does not generate any additional packets, unlike conventional crawling methods. The recommendation score is calculated based on the similarity index between the query keyword and the contents of webpages. It is also based on the viewing frequencies of webpages and viewing times of webpages. In particular, the viewing time difference between hosts can be obtained using information captured by the network router. Using the HTTP header, the proposed method can identify users who are located inside an NAT and those with the same global IP. The effectiveness of the viewing time was verified using an A/B test, which demonstrated that the proposed method was superior to a conventional method. The proposed application allows Internet users to reach relevant information more quickly.

7 Acknowledgement

This work was partially supported by Funds for integrated promotion of social system reform and research and development, MEXT, Japan, by Low Carbon Technology Research and Development Program for "Practical Study on Energy Management to Reduce CO2 emissions from University Campuses" from Ministry of the Environment, Japan and by MEXT/JSPSKAKENHI Grant (B) Number 25280033.

8 References

[1] K. Inoue, D. Akashi, M. Koibuchi, and H. Nishi. "Semantic router using data stream to enrich services". In 3rd International Conference on Future Internet (CFI), pp. 20-23, June 2008.

[2] K. Mihara, M. Terabe, and K. Hashimoto. "A Proposal of Web Log Mining Method Considering Page Browsing Time". In 148th Intelligent Computing Systems (ICS), July 2007.

[3] P. Biswas and S. Rahim. Pagemap: "A Dynamic User Guiding Approach to the Most Relevant and Popular Pages in a Website". In 13th International Conference on Computer and Information Technology (ICCIT), December 2010.

[4] L. Xu, B. Xu, Z. Chen, and H. Chen. "Website evaluation based on statistic data". Distributed Computing Systems, 2003. FTDCS 2003. Proceeding of the 9th IEEE Workshop on Future Trends, pp. 301-306, May 2003.

[5] T. Takayama, K. Kato, H. Sasaki, and A. Shikoda. "Proficiency Evaluation for Engineering Experimentation Utilizing Web Log Analysis". Educational Technology (ET), July 2008.

[6] Y. Shimizu. "An examination of relations between user interests and reading time on WWW". In 57th Journal of Information Processing Society of Japan, vol. 3, pp. 3.191-3.192, October 1998.

[7] S. Ishida, S. Harashima, M. Koibuchi, H. Kawashima, and H. Nishi. "A Memory-efficient Method of TCP Reconstruction using Context Switch on Internet Router". In 190th Computer Architecture (ARC), August 2010.

[8] C. D. Manning, P. Raghavan, and H. Schuetze. "Introduction to Information Retrieval. Cambridge University Press". 2008. Chapters 4 and 6.

A Best Controlled Method for Very Large K-th Order Systems

Daniel Yuh Chao[1],
[1]Department of Managment Information Systems, National Chengchi University,
No. 64, Sec. 2, Zhinan Road, Taipei, Taiwan.
email: yuhyaw@gmail.com

Abstract— *Lately, a revolutionary method to synthesize maximally permissive with fewest monitors has emerged. It relies on reachability analysis to find minimal sets of legal and forbidden markings. A number of linear constraints are constructed [by solving an integer linear programming problem (ILPP)] to forbid all forbidden markings in the set, while guaranteeing all legal markings reachable. Due to the state explosion problem, it cannot handle very large systems. We propose earlier a method without reachability analysis and minimal siphon extraction; hence it is scalable to large systems. This paper illustrates such by applying the method to very large k-th order systems.*

Keywords: Petri net, flexible manufacturing system (FMS), deadlock prevention.

1. Introduction

Petri nets have been popular [1], [4], [13], [15], [16], [22] in modelling parallel programs, flexible manufacturing systems (FMS), etc. The fierce competition toward resources (such as data locks, machines, robots, machines, etc) leads to deadlocks, thwarting the usage of multiple processors and concurrent programming paradigm. The main cause of deadlocks are that some siphons become insufficiently unmarked. A siphon [2] is a set of places that tokens leak out are no less than tokens get trapped. It can become insufficiently marked so that output transitions of places in the siphon can never be fired and the net is not live. Therefore, supervisory control methods enforce the liveness by identifying all the minimal siphons and preventing them from becoming insufficiently marked. If a siphon contains a trap, then tokens in it cannot leak out completely. A strict minimal siphon (SMS) is a minimum siphon that does not contain a trap.

Deadlock prevention prevents deadlocks from occurring by adding control places (monitors) upon the original net model to make all SMS always sufficiently marked. An optimal liveness-enforcing supervisor should tackle the three issues: behavioral permissiveness, computational complexity and structural complexity. Traditional liveness enforcing supervisors such as FBM [22] and elementary-siphon [1], [4], [16], [17], [18], [20], [28] cannot guarantee maximal permissiveness by employing ordinary control arcs for structure simplicity.

Recently, Chen *et al.* [9] develop a novel method that prevents all the FBM from being reached and ensure that all legal markings be reached. Computation burden is much reduced the by considering only a minimal covering set of legal markings and a minimal covered set of FBM via a vector covering approach.

In summary, traditional optimal design [5], [25], [19]of a liveness-enforcing supervisor strives for efficient computation, least cost, and maximally permissiveness, but not concerning with minimal structure complexity of employing fewest monitors.

Later on, Chen *et al.* [8] pioneer a linear programming method (ILP) to allow a plant to forbid as many FBM as possible to achieve the minimal configuration or least structure complexity among all former approaches. They [10] further reduce the number of monitors by solving an ILPP at each iteration, when a place invariant (PI) for a control place is constructed to forbid FBMs as many as possible and to allow the reachability of all markings in the minimal covering set of legal markings. Cordone *et al.* [26] speeds up the method in [8] by the strategy of branch-and-bound. They also propose an algorithm to design monitors considering the various control objectives with significant improvements over known benchmark problems. Nazeem *et al.* [24] revise some linear constraints in the iteration-based heuristic by replacing the notorious big M with n and adding a small positive parameter ϵ.

We propose in [27] to optimize the number of monitors (good states as well) if one adds monitors in the normal sequence of basic, compound, control, and other types of siphons. It is shown that among all 2-dependent siphons (depending on two basic siphons), only one (called critical) siphon needs to be controlled by adding a monitor. This greatly simplifies the synthesis as well as minimizes the number of monitors required while making the controlled net near maximally permissive.

Most importantly, we [7] discover that a single called unmarked pattern (UP) of distribution of tokens in unmarked siphons unify all different types of critical siphons. However, the resulting control is not maximally permissive since there are forbidden states that do fit into the above UP. These states necessarily evolve into UP by firing some transitions. They also need to be controlled by adding monitors to avoid the loss of legal states. We propose a method to merge several monitors into a single one while not losing states. It solves a linear set of equations, resulting in some formula of some parameters of the monitors of the controlled net.

The total time complexity is linear to the size of the net compared with the exponential one of the current most advanced approaches. It achieves the same best results in the literature while avoiding the time-consuming reachability analysis and complete siphon computation which does not scale well with the size of the nets.

This paper illustrates the above claim by applying the proposed method to a k-th order system (a special case of Gadara net employed by Nazeem *et al.* [23] in their approach), where MIP (mixed integer programming) [3] is employed and hence cannot handle very large Gadara net.

The rest of this paper is organized as follows. Section 2 presents the preliminaries. The theory of critical siphon and control policy are reviewed in Sections 3 an 4, respectively. Section 5 concludes the paper.

2. Preliminaries

Here only the definitions used in this paper are presented. The reader may refer to [1], [21] for more Petri net details.

A *P-vector* (place vector) is a column vector Y: $P \to Z$ indexed by P where Z is the set of integers. The *incidence matrix* of N is a matrix $[N]$: $P \times T \to Z$ indexed by P and T such that $[N] = [N]^+ - [N]^-$ where $[N]^+(p, t) = F(t, p)$ and $[N]^-(p, t) = F(p, t)$. We denote column vectors where every entry equals 0 by $\mathbf{0}$. Y^T and $[N]^T$ are the transposed versions of a vector Y and a matrix $[N]$, respectively. Y is a *P-invariant* (place invariant) if and only if $Y \neq \mathbf{0}$ and $Y^T \bullet [N] = \mathbf{0}^T$ hold where '$\bullet$' means a vector or matrix multiplication. $\|Y\| = \{p \in P \mid Y(p) \neq 0\}$ is the *support* of Y. A *minimal P-invariant* does not contain another P-invariant as a proper subset.

Definition 1: [11] A System of Simple Sequential Process with Resources (S^3PR) is a Petri net $N = (P_A \cup P^0 \cup P_R, T, F)$ defined as the union of a set of nets $N_i = (P_{A_i} \cup \{p_i^0\} \cup P_{R_i}, T_i, F_i)$ sharing common places, where the following statements are true:

1) p_i^0 is called the process idle place of N_i. Elements in P_{A_i} and P_{R_i} are called activity and resource places, respectively. A resource place is called a resource for short in case of no confusion.
2) $P_{R_i} \neq \emptyset$; $P_{A_i} \neq \emptyset$; $p_i^0 \notin P_{A_i}$; $(P_{A_i} \cup \{p_i^0\}) \cap P_{R_i} = \emptyset$; $\forall p \in P_{A_i}, \forall t \in {}^\bullet p, \forall t' \in p^\bullet, \exists r_p \in P_{R_i}, {}^\bullet t \cap P_{R_i} = t'^\bullet \cap P_{R_i} = \{r_p\}$; $\forall r \in P_{R_i}, {}^{\bullet\bullet}r \cap P_{A_i} = r^{\bullet\bullet} \cap P_{A_i} \neq \emptyset$; $\forall r \in P_{R_i}, {}^\bullet r \cap r^\bullet = \emptyset$; and ${}^{\bullet\bullet}(p_i^0) \cap P_{R_i} = \emptyset$.
3) N_i' is a strongly connected state machine, where $N_i' = (P_{A_i} \cup \{p_i^0\}, T_i, F_i)$ is the resulting net after the places in P_{R_i} and related arcs are removed from N_i.
4) Every circuit of N_i' contains place p_i^0.
5) Any two N_i's are composable when they share a set of common places. Every shared place must be a resource.
6) $H(r) = {}^{\bullet\bullet}r \cap P_A$ denotes the set of holders of r (operation places that use r). Any resource r is associated with a minimal P-invariant whose support is denoted by $\rho_r = \{r\} \cup H(r)$.

Definition 2: A k-th order system is a subclass of S^3PR with k resource places $r_1, r_2, \ldots, r_k$ shared between two processes N_1 and N_2.

$M_0(r_1) = M_0(r_2) = \ldots M_0(r_k) = 1$.

N_1 (resp. N_2) uses $r_1, r_2, \ldots, r_k$ (resp. $r_k, r_{k-1}, \ldots, r_1$) in that order.

Each of N_1 and N_2 is an elementary circuit. $M_0(p_1^0) = M_0(p_2^0)$=kq, where p_1^0 and p_2^0 are the idle places in processes N_1 and N_2, respectively.

Holder places of r_j in N_1 and N_2 are denoted as p_j and p'_j respectively.

The net in Fig. 1a is an example of the controlled 3-rd order system. After removing all dashed objects (controlled arcs and places) from the net, it is a 3-rd order system. In the sequel, all the nets referred to are S^3PR. For a net system (N, M_0), a non-empty subset S (resp. τ) of places is called a *siphon* (resp. *trap*) if ${}^\bullet S \subseteq S^\bullet$ (resp. $\tau^\bullet \subseteq {}^\bullet\tau$), i.e., every transition having an output (resp. input) place in S has an input (resp. output) place in S (resp. τ). In [1], we show that an SMS in an S^3PR can be synthesized from a strongly connected circuit; such a circuit is called a *core* circuit.

S is called an *empty siphon* at M_0 If $M_0(S) = \sum_{p \in S} M_0(p) = 0$. A *minimal siphon* does not contain a siphon as a proper subset. It is called an SMS (Strict Minimal Siphon), denoted by S, if it does not contain a trap. Wang *et al.* develops a fast method [28] to compute SMS.

If a siphon $S \subset \|Y\|$, then $[S] = \|Y\| \backslash S$ is called the *complementary siphon* of S and $S \cup [S] = \bigcup_{r \in S} \rho_r$ is the *support* of a P-invariant.

Tokens in a siphon S of an ordinary Petri net can either leak out to the complementary set $[S]$ of S or stay in S. Thus the sum of tokens in $S \cup [S]$ is a constant. $S \cup [S]$ forms the support of a minimal P-invariant (PI).

Definition 3: An elementary resource circuit is called a basic circuit, denoted by c_b. The siphon constructed from c_b is called a basic siphon. A n-compound circuit c is a circuit consisting of multiply interconnected elementary circuits $c_{b_1}, c_{b_2}, \ldots, c_{b_n}$ extending between two processes and $c_{b_i} \cap c_{b_j} \neq \emptyset$ iff $j = i+1, i = 1, 2, \ldots, n-1$. $c = c_{b_1} \circ c_{b_2} \circ \cdots \circ c_{b_{n-1}} \circ c_{b_n}$ if $c_{b_i} \cap c_{b_j} = \{r_i\}$, $r_i \in P_R$; i.e., c_{b_i} and $c_{b_{i+1}}$ intersects at a resource place r_i. The SMS S synthesized from compound circuit c using the Handle-Construction Procedure in [1] is $S = S_1 \circ S_2 \circ \cdots \circ S_{n-1} \circ S_n$, where S_i is the basic siphon synthesized from c_{b_i}. Each siphon S^* such that $[S^*] \cap [B] \neq \emptyset$ is called an n-dependent one, where $B = S_1$ or S_n and $S_R^* = R(S_0)$ (the set of resource places in S_0). The set of n-dependent siphons is denoted as $\pounds(S_0)$. The monitor for S^* (resp. S_i) is called an n-monitor (resp. 1-monitor).

3. Critical Siphons

We [27] propose to optimize the number of monitors (good states as well) if one adds monitors in the normal sequence of basic, compound, control, and other types of siphons. It is shown that among all 2-dependent siphons (depending on two

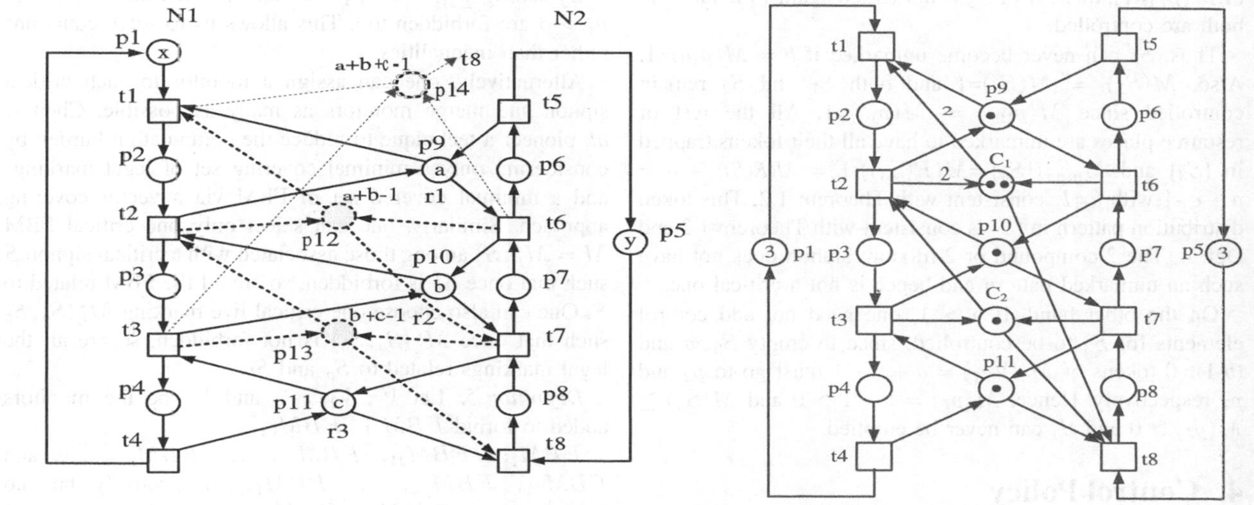

(a) The controlled model of a 3-rd order system (when $a = b = c = 1$). $S_1 = \{p_3, p_6, p_9, p_{10}\}$, $S_2 = \{p_4, p_7, p_{10}, p_{11}\}$, S_3=$\{p_4, p_6, p_9, p_{10}, p_{11}\}$, and $S_4 = \{p_{12}, p_{13}, p_3, p_7\}$.

(b) optimally controlled system $S_4 = \{V_{S_1}, p_3, V_{S_2}, p_6\}$ V_{S_1} (resp. $C_2 = V_{S_2}$) monitor for S_1 (resp. S_2). V_{S_1} and V_{S_4} merged into C_1.

Fig. 1: Petri net model of a manufacturing system.

component siphons), only one (called critical) siphon needs to be controlled by adding a monitor. This avoids redundant monitors and the unnecessary associated computational burden. Neither reachability graph nor minimal siphon needs to be computed achieving polynomial complexity—essential for large systems. As a result, there is no need to enumerate all siphons and the time complexity involved is polynomial.

We extend the result to n-dependent siphons with $n > 2$. It shows that in the set B of n-dependent siphons, there is only one emptiable (called critical) siphon (analyzed to be the one with the minimal number of tokens in the unmarked set of operations places) needs to be controlled while the rest of siphons are also controlled accordingly.

Definition 4: Let $S_0 = S_1 \circ S_2 \circ \ldots S_{n-1} \circ S_n$ be a compound siphon. The token distribution (called unmarked) pattern M is as follows: (1) For each singular place r_i, $M(r_i) = 1$, $M(H(r_i) \cap [S_0]) = 0$; and (2) For other r in S_0, $M(r) = 0$, $M(H(r) \cap [S_0] \cap^{\bullet} (V^{\bullet})) = M_0(r)$, where $H(r)$ is the set of holder places of r (places that use r) and V is a monitor or control place. The unmarked n-dependent siphon S with the above unmarked pattern (UP) is called a critical siphon.

Theorem 1: [7] 1) Once the critical siphon S for M in Def. 4 is controlled, so are the rest of siphons S' with $M([S']) \neq M([S])$ in $\mathcal{L}(S_0)$, and

2) when S is unmarked, $M([S]) = M_0(R(S_0)) - \theta$, where θ is the number of singular places and $R(S_0)$ the set of resource places in S_0.

In Fig. 1a, there are 3 SMS: S_1= $\{p_9, p_{10}, p_3, p_6\}$, $S_2 = \{p_{10}, p_{11}, p_4, p_7\}$, $R(S_1)$=$\{p_9, p_{10}\}$, $R(S_2)$= $\{p_{10}, p_{11}\}$, $S_0 = S_3$ =$\{p_9, p_{10}, p_6, p_{11}, p_4\}$. $R(S_3)$= $\{p_9, p_{10}, p_{11}\} \Rightarrow R(S_3) = R(S_1) \cup R(S_2)$. S_1 and S_2 (resp. S_0) are basic (resp. compound) siphons; both are optimally controlled since $M(V_{S_1}) = M(p_{12}) = a + b - 1$ and $M(V_{S_2}) = M(p_{13}) = b + c - 1$. $M(S_0) = a + b + c$. S_3 is optimally-controlled (no need for control elements) *iff* b=$M(S_1 \cap S_2) = M(p_{10}) = 1$ explained as follows.

If $b > 1$, S_3 can become unmarked when the tokens at each resource place are trapped in $[S_3]$; i.e., $M(p_9) = M(p_{10}) = M(p_{11})$=0, $M(p_3)$>0 (S_1 is controlled) and $M(p_7)$ >0 (S_2 is controlled), $M(p_2) = M_0(p_9)$, and $M(p_7) = M_0(p_{10})$. We need to add control elements for S_3 to be optimally-controlled. Note that in this case, all resource places are unmarked and $M_{max}([S])$=$M_0(R(S)) - \theta$ with θ=0 consistent with Theorem 1.2 . A monitor V is added so that $[V]$=$[S]$ and $M(V) = M(R(S))$ –1=$a+b+c-1$. This token distribution pattern in $[S]$ is consistent with Theorem 1. The 2-control or 2-mixture siphon does not have such unmarked patterns and hence is not a critical one.

If $b = 1$, then $M(V_{S1}) = M(p_{12}) = a$ and $M(V_{S2}) = M(p_{13}) = c$ and the control siphon S_4 =$\{p_{12}, p_{13}, p_3, p_7\}$ ($[S_4]$=$\{p_2, p_8\}$) generated by circuit $[p_{12}t_7p_{13}t_2p_{12}]$ in Fig. 1a can be emptied when all tokens in $M(V_{S1})$ and $M(V_{S2})$ sink to p_2 and p_8, respectively. Thus, to avoid empty S_4, we need to add control elements for S_4. If S_3 becomes unmarked [i.e., $M(p_9) = M(p_{10}) = M(p_{11})$=0, $M(p_3)$=1 or $M(p_7)$=1], then S_1 or S_2 is unmarked against the fact that both are controlled.

Thus, S_3 can never become unmarked if $b = M(p_{10})$=1. Also, $M(S_1) = M(S_2)$=1 and both S_1 and S_2 remain controlled since $M(p_{10}) = M(p_{10})$=1. All the rest of resource places are unmarked to have all their tokens trapped in $[S_3]$ and $M_{max}([S_3])$=$M(R(S_3))$-1 = $M(R(S))$ − θ = $a+c$ -1 with θ=1 consistent with Theorem 1.2. This token distribution pattern in $[S]$ is consistent with Theorem 1.2 and Def. 4. The 2-compound or 2-mixture siphon does not have such an unmarked pattern and hence is not a critical one.

On the other hand, if $b > 1$, one need not add control elements for S_3 to be controlled, since to empty S_3, a and (b-1)>0 tokens of $M_0(V_{S1}) = a + b - 1$ must go to p_2 and p_7 respectively. Hence, $M(p_7) = b - 1 > 0$ and $M(S_3) \geq M(p_7) > 0$ and S_3 can never be emptied.

4. Control Policy

This section reviews the control policy in [9]. Similar to [9], only the tokens in operation places are considered to obtain a PI to prevent an FBM (First met Bad Marking) from being reached since all places in $[S]$ are operation ones. By controlling the maximal amount of tokens in these operation places, S can never become empty of tokens. Following that in [9], $\mathbb{N}_A$ is defined as $\mathbb{N}_A = \{i|p_i \in P_A\}$, where P_A is the set of operation places. Thus, the relations between different markings are simplified to study the number of tokens in these operation places.

To forbid an FBM M', the plant is enforced to satisfy the following P-invariant constraint:

$$(G(M) = \sum_{i\in\mathbb{N}_A} l_i \cdot \mu_i) \leq \beta,\ \mu_i = M(p_i) \quad (1)$$

where

$$\beta = \sum_{i\in\mathbb{N}_A} l_i \cdot M'(p_i) - 1 \quad (2)$$

Constraint (1) is called the forbidding condition.

For maximally permissive control purpose, all legal markings should be kept after a control place is added. To ensure that every live marking M' cannot be prevented from being reached, coefficients l_i ($i \in \mathbb{N}_A$) should satisfy

$$\sum_{i\in\mathbb{N}_A} l_i \cdot M'(p_i) \leq \beta,\quad \forall M' \in \mathcal{M}_L, \quad (3)$$

where $\mathcal{M}_L$ is the set of all legal markings. Constraint (3) determines the feasible values for coefficients l_i ($i \in \mathbb{N}_A$). Thus, for an FBM M, if coefficients l_i ($i \in \mathbb{N}_A$) satisfy Constraint (3), a PI designed for Constraint (1) can guarantee the reachability of all the legal markings and forbid M. Therefore, a control place computed for the PI can ensure all the legal markings be reached. In this case, the control place is said to be optimal.

By setting $\sum_{i\in\mathbb{N}_A} l_i \cdot \mu_i = \beta$, all M' such that $\sum_{i\in\mathbb{N}_A} l_i \cdot \mu_i > \beta$ are forbidden too. This allows us to solve equations rather than inequalities.

Alternatively, one can assign a monitor to each critical siphon and merge monitors as many as possible. Chen *et al.* pioneer a technique to reduce the computation burden by considering only a minimal covering set of legal markings and a minimal covered set of FBM via a vector covering approach. Similarly, one can select only one critical FBM $M = M_F^\star(S)$ among those associated with a critical siphon S such that once M is forbidden, so are all the FBM related to S. One can also choose one critical live marking $M_L^\star(S_a, S_b$ such that once $M_L^\star(S_a, S_b)$ is not forbidden, so are all the legal markings related to S_a and S_b.

Definition 5: Let V_1, V_2, ..., and V_f be the monitors added to forbid FBM_{11}, FBM_{12}, ... , FBM_{1i_1}, FBM_{21}, FBM_{22}, ..., FBM_{2i_2}, ..., and FBM_{f1}, FBM_{f2}, ..., FBM_{fi_f}, respectively but no live states are forbidden. V_1, V_2, ..., and V_f are said to merge into a single monitor V if the corresponding PI constraint forbids each of FBM_{11}, FBM_{12}, ..., FBM_{1i_1}, FBM_{21}, FBM_{22}, ..., FBM_{2i_2}, ..., and FBM_{f1}, FBM_{f2}, ..., FBM_{fi_f}, but none of any live state.

Theorem 2: Let V_a and V_b be two monitors added to control S_a and S_b, respectively and $M_F^\star(S_i)$ (resp. $M_L^\star(S_a, S_b)$), the critical FBM (resp. legal) defined above. Let L ($l_i = 0, \forall p_i \notin [S_a] \cup [S_b]$) be the solution to the following equations.

$$L \cdot M_F^\star(S_i) = \beta + 1 = k, i = a, b, \text{and} \quad (4)$$

$$L \cdot M_L^\star(S_a, S_b) = \beta = k - 1. \quad (5)$$

Then the PI

$$L \cdot M \leq \beta, \forall M \in R(N, M_0), \quad (6)$$

does not forbid any live state and controls both S_a and S_b; that is, V_a and V_b can be merged into a single monitor.

This theorem allows to find the PI constraint by solving a set of linear first order equations.

Example 1: In Fig. 1a, $S_1 = \{p_3, p_6, p_9, p_{10}\}$ ($[S_1] = \{p_2, p_7\}$), $S_2 = \{p_4, p_7, p_{10}, p_{11}\}$ ($[S_2] = \{p_3, p_8\}$), and Control siphon $S_3 = \{V_1(p_{12}), p_3, V_2(p_{13}), p_7\}$ ($[S_3] = \{p_2, p_6\}$) is synthesized from Control circuit $[t_2p_{12}t_7p_{13}]$ where all places are monitor ones. Control siphon S_3 is a critical one (since $S_1 \cap S_2$=$\{p_{10}\}$ and $M_0(p_{10})$ =1 based on the theory in [27]) in the sense that once S_3 is controlled, S_4 and the rest of siphons containing at least one of V_1 and V_2 is also controlled.

Considering merging V_1 and V_3 (monitors for S_1 and S_3, respectively) where $[S_1] \cap [S_3] = \{p_2\} \neq \emptyset$. $[S] = [S_1] \cup [S_3] = \{p_2, p_7, p_8\}$. Hence, the constraint to control both S_1 and S_3 is: $l_2 \cdot \mu_2 + l_7 \cdot \mu_7 + l_8 \cdot \mu_8 < \beta + 1$=$k$, $l_i = 0$, $\forall p_i \notin [S]$. S_1 (resp. S_3) is unmarked at $M_1 = p_2 + p_7$

(resp. $M_3 = p_2 + p_8$), and $M^* = p_7 + p_8 = M_d - p_2$ is a live marking since $M^*(S_1) = M^*(S_3) = M^*(S) = 1$ where $M_d = p_7 + p_8 + p_2$ (=M' in Eq. (2)) is an FBM to be forbidden, $M_d(S) = 0$. We have

$$l_2 + l_7 = k, \quad (to\ forbid\ M_1)$$
$$l_2 + l_8 = k, \quad (to\ forbid\ M_3), \quad \text{and}$$
$$l_7 + l_8 = k - 1\ (to\ not\ forbid\ M^*)$$

Solving the above two equations, we have $l_2 = 2$, $l_7 = l_8 = 1$, $k = 3$, and the constraint that controls the two siphons is

$$2\mu_2 + \mu_7 + \mu_8 \leq 2 \tag{7}$$

By Theorem 2 in [6], V_{S_1} and V_{S_2} cannot be merged (since $[S_1] \cap [S_2] = \emptyset$). Thus, a separate monitor must be added for S_2. The resulting controlled model is shown in Fig. 1b and maximally permissive.

5. Supervisor Control

First, it is easy to see that a k-th order system is a special case of α-S^{3}PR (defined below) and the initial markings of resource places is one (Fig. 2a).

Definition 6: [6] An $\alpha-$S^{3}PR is an S^{3}PR where if any two basic circuits c_{b_1} and c_{b_2} intersect, they must intersect at a single resource place r.
The net in Fig. 1a is $\alpha-$S^{3}PR (also a k-th order system, k=3) defined above.

Theorem 3: [6] The number of monitors for an $\alpha-$S^{3}PR obtained using the methods in [10] is lower bounded by the number of basic siphons .
Hence, a minimal configuration of a k-th order system has k monitors, where k is the total number of basic siphons.

All control siphons are emptiable. There are 4 ($k = 4$) basic siphons S_1, S_2, S_3, S_4 (Fig. 2a) with monitors $V_{S_1}, V_{S_2}, V_{S_3}$, and V_{S_4} . There is a control circuit (Fig. 2b) containing every two adjacent monitor places; e.g., V_{S_2} and V_{S_3}. The corresponding 2-control siphons are critical ones. Monitors for these 2-control siphons are shown in Fig. 2c.

Again, there is a control circuit (Fig. 2c) containing every two adjacent monitor places; e.g., V_{22} [$M_0(V_{22})$=1] and V_{23}[$M_0(V_{23})$=2]. The resulting 3-control siphon is emptiable and critical since the unmarked pattern is $M(p_8) = M(p_{13}) = 0$ and $M(p_9) = M(p_{10}) = 1$. Monitor V_{32} is added with $M_0(V_{32})$=2 and [V_{32}]={p_2, p'_6} as shown in Fig. 2d. Similar conclusion applies to other level control or monitor places shown in Figs. 2d. and 2e, respectively.

In general, there are n basic siphons $S_1, S_2, \ldots, S_n$ (Fig. 2a), n-1 2-control siphons V_{11} o V_{12}, V_{12} o V_{13}, ..., $V_{1(n-1)}$ o $V_{1(n)}$ (Fig. 2b), n-2 3-control siphons V_{21} o V_{22}, V_{22} o V_{23} , ..., $V_{2(n-2)}$ o$V_{2(n-1)}$ (Fig. 2c), ... 1 n-compound siphon $V_{(n-1)1}$ o $V_{(n-1)2}$ (Fig. 2d), where V_{ij} is the jth monitor in Level i. The total number of emptiable siphons or monitors is also $n+(n-1)+(n-2)+\ldots+1 = n(n+1)/2$. Based on Theorem 3, the minimal configuration employs n monitors.

These monitors can be grouped into the following n sets and each set can be merged into one monitor.

1) V_1, V_{11}, V_{12}, V_{13}, ..., $V_{1(n-1)}$, $V_{1(n)}$ (n monitors),
2) V_2, V_{21}, V_{22}, V_{23}, ..., $V_{2(n-1)}$, $V_{2(n)}$ (n-1 monitors),
3) V_3, V_{31}, V_{32}, V_{33}, ..., $V_{3(n-1)}$, $V_{3(n)}$ (n-2 monitors),
4) ...,
5) $V_{(n-1)(n-1)}$, $V_{(n-1)(n)}$ (2 monitors)
6) V_n, (1 monitor)

We now consider merging the first set based on Theorem 2. The rest can be done similarly. First, the plant is enforced to satisfy the following P-invariant constraint:

$$(G(M) = \sum_{i \in \mathbb{N}_{A_1}} l_i \cdot \mu_i + \sum_{i \in \mathbb{N}_{A_2}} l'_i \cdot \mu'_i) \leq \beta,\ \mu_i = M(p_i),\ \mu'_i = M(p'_i) \tag{8}$$

where $\mathbb{N}_{A_j} = \{i | p_i \in P_{A_j}\}$, $j = 1, 2$. We are to solve l_i, l'_i, and β.

$$L \cdot FBM_1 = l_1 M_F(p_1) + l'_2 M_F(p'_2) = \beta,$$

......

$$L \cdot FBM_2 = l_1 M_F(p_1) + l'_3 M_F(p'_3) = \beta,$$

$$L \cdot FBM_n = l_1 M_F(p_1) + l'_{n+1} M_F(p'_{n+1}) = \beta, \text{and}$$

$$L \cdot M_L = l'_2 M_L(p'_2) + l'_3 M_L(p'_3) + \ldots + l'_{n+1} M_L(p'_{n+1}) = \beta - 1,$$

where $p_i \in N_1$ and $p'_i \in N_2$ belong to the holder set of a resource place $r \in P_R$. Setting $M_F(p_1) = M_F(p'_2) = M_F(p'_3) = \ldots = M_F(p'_{n+1}) = 1$ and $l_1 = a$, $l'_2 = b_2$, $l'_3 = b_3$, ..., $l'_{n+1} = b_{n+1}$, we have

$$a + b_2 = \beta,$$

$$a + b_3 = \beta,$$

......

$$a + b_{n+1} = \beta, \text{and}$$

$$b_2 + b_3 + \ldots + b_{n+1} = \beta - 1.$$

Solving the above equations, we have

$$b_2 = b_3 = \ldots = b_{n+1} = 1, \text{ and } a = \beta - 1 = n$$

.

The resulting constraint is

$$n\mu_1 + \mu'_2 + \mu'_3 + \ldots + \mu'_n + \mu'_{n+1} \leq n + 1. \tag{9}$$

When $n = 2$, we have

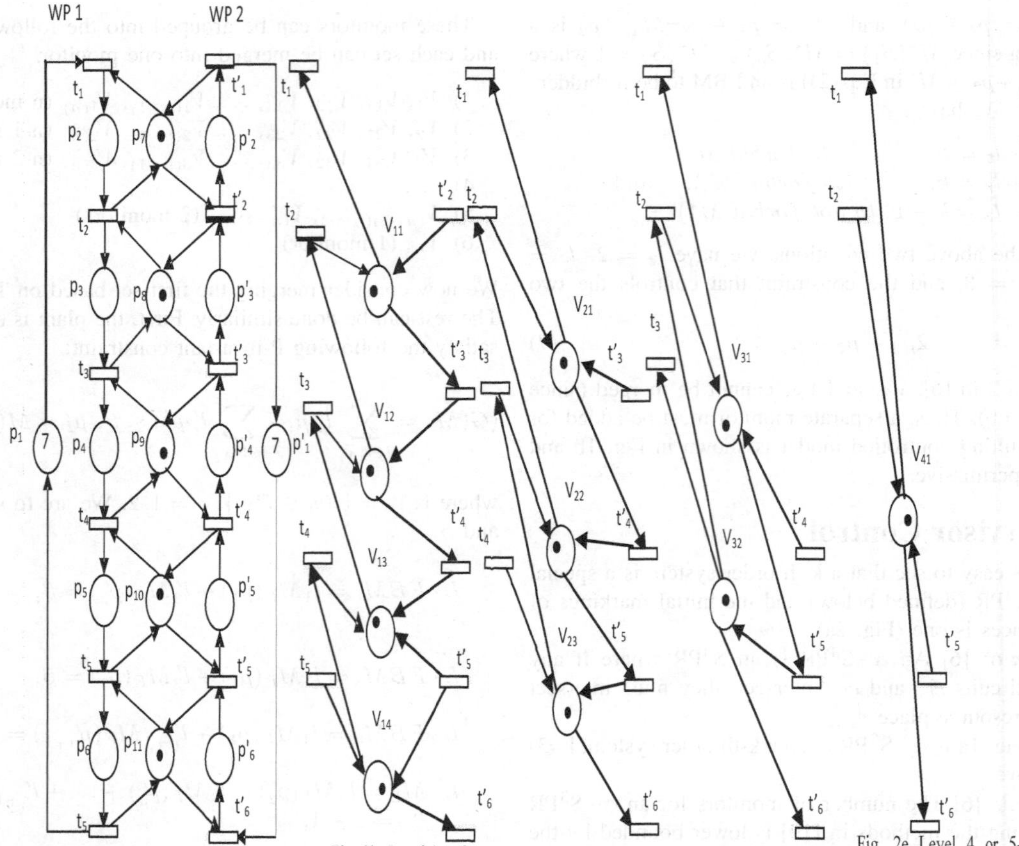

Fig. 2a. All critical siphons are control ones.

Fig. 2b Level 1 or 2-control monitor

Fig. 2c Level 2 or 3-control monitor

Fig.2d Level 3 or 4-control monitor

Fig. 2e Level 4 or 5-control monitor

Fig. 2: Petri net model of an FMS.

$$a + b_2 = \beta,$$

$$a + b_3 = \beta, \text{and}$$

$$b_2 + b_3 = \beta - 1.$$

Solving the above equations, we have $a = 2$ and $\beta = 3$ and the linear constraint is $2\mu_1 + \mu'_2 + \mu'_3 \leq 3$.

When $n = 3$, we have

$b_2 + b_3 + b_4 = \beta - 1$; b_4 is added to the left side compared with the case of $n = 3$. Hence, β is increased by one (to 4 from 3), so is a based on the equation $a+b_2 = \beta$.

Similarly, for the second set, we have

$$(n-1)\mu_2 + \mu'_3 + \mu'_4 + \ldots + \mu'_{n-1} + \mu'_n \leq n.$$

Clearly, the time complexity involved is $O(n)$, where where n is the total number of basic siphons. This is much faster than the exponential amount of time to solve the ILP problem for the current most advanced approaches.

6. Conclusions

We have illustrated a simple method to synthesize supervisors for very large k-th order system. The vector covering method by Chen *et al.* [8] and the more advanced version of it cannot handle such large systems since they cannot overcome the state explosion problem involved in the reachability analysis. Our method first identify all critical siphons (inferring from patterns M of unmarked siphons and the derived markings necessarily evolving into M) and the associated monitors. Second, we merge as many monitors as possible without losing any legal states. For k-th order systems, this amount to solving a set of linear equation. The time complexity is linear to the basic circuits (or elementary circuits containing only resource places), much faster than the exponential time for solving integer linear programming problems.

However, k-th order systems is just a special case of S^3PR. The extension requires further research as to the condition of merging two monitors for non-α systems. The critical siphons can again be inferred from patterns M of unmarked siphons, although it may be slightly more complicated. The task remains interesting and challenging.

One would expect the scheduling for k-th order system should be also much simpler than that for S^3PR since this paper has developed a closed form solution for the controller. In prior work, Petri net supervisors were synthesized without considering the temporal dimension. Hu et al. [12], [14] pioneer to address this difficult issue to synthesize an optimal deadlock-free timed supervisor. Future work should adapt Hu's work to k-th order system for its scheduling.

Acknowledgments

This work was supported by the National Science Council under Grant NSC 100-2221-E-004.

References

[1] D. Y. Chao, "Computation of elementary siphons in Petri nets for deadlock control," *Computer Journal*, (British Computer Society), vol. 49, no. 4, pp. 470-479, 2006.

[2] D. Y. Chao, "An incremental approach to extract minimal bad siphons," *Journal of Information Science and Engineering*, vol. 23, no. 1, pp. 203-214, Jan. 2007.

[3] D. Y. Chao, "Technical Note - MIP iteration-reductions for deadlock prevention of flexible manufacturing systems," *International Journal of Advanced Manufacturing Technology*, vol. 41, no. 3, pp. 343-346. 2009, doi: 10.1007/s00170-008-1473-x.

[4] Chao, D. Y., 'Improved controllability test for dependent siphons in S^3PR based on elementary siphons," *Asian Journal of Control*, vol. 12, no. 3, pp. 377-391, doi:10.1002/asjc.217, 2010.

[5] D. Y. Chao, "Improvement of suboptimal siphon- and FBM-based control model of a well-known S^3PR," *IEEE Transactions on Automation Science and Engineering*, vol. 8, no. 2, pp. 404-411, 2011.

[6] Daniel Yuh Chao, "On the Lower Bounds of Monitor Solutions of Maximally Permissive Supervisors for A Subclass ĉS3PR of Flexible Manufacturing Systems," *International Journal of Systems Science*, DOI:10.1080/00207721.2013.783946, 2013.

[7] Gaiyun Liu, Daniel Yuh Chao, and, Y. F, Fang, "A Control Policy for a Subclass of Petri Nets without Reachability Analysis," *IET Control Theory & Applications*, 2013, accepted to appear.

[8] Y. F. Chen and Z. W. Li, "Design of a maximally permissive liveness-enforcing supervisor with compressed supervisory structure for flexible manufacturing systems," *Automatica*, vol. 47, no. 5, pp. 1028-1034.

[9] Y. F. Chen, Z. W. Li, M. Khalgui, and O. Moshabi, "Design of maximally permissive liveness-enforcing petri net supervisor for flexible manufacturing systems," *IEEE Transactions on Automation Science and Engineering*, vol. 8, no. 2, pp. 374–393, 2011.

[10] Y. F. Chen, Z W. Li, and M. C. Zhou, "Behavior Optimal and Structural Simple liveness-enforcing supervisor for flexible manufacturing systems," *IEEE Transactions on Systems, Man, and Cybernetics, Part A*, vol. 42, nc. 3, pp. 615-629, 2012.

[11] J. Ezpeleta and L. Recalde, "A Deadlock Avoidance Approach for Non-sequential Resource Allocation Systems," *IEEE Transactions on Systems, Man, and Cybernetics, Part A: Systems and Humans*, vol. 11, pp. 173-184, 1995.

[12] H. Hu, M.C. Zhou, Z. W. Li, "Algebraic synthesis of timed supervisor for automated manufacturing systems using Petri nets," *IEEE Transactions on Automation Science and Engineering*, vol. 7, no. 3, pp. 549–557, July 2010.

[13] Hesuan Hu, Mengchu Zhou, and Zhiwu Li, "Supervisor optimization for deadlock resolution in automated manufacturing systems with Petri nets," *IEEE Transactions on Automation Science and Engineering*, vol. 8, no. 4, pp. 794-804, October 2011.

[14] Hesuan Hu, Mengchu Zhou, and Zhiwu Li, "Liveness and ratio-enforcing supervision of automated manufacturing systems using Petri nets," *IEEE Transactions on Systems, Man, and Cybernetics-Part A: Systems and Humans*, vol. 42, no. 2, pp. 392-403, February 2012.

[15] Hesuan Hu, Mengchu Zhou, Zhiwu Li, and Ying Tang, "Deadlock-free control of automated manufacturing systems with flexible routes and assembly operations using Petri nets," *IEEE Transactions on Industrial Informatics*, vol. 9, no. 1, pp. 109-121, February 2013.

[16] Z. Li and M. Zhou, "Elementary Siphons of Petri Nets and Their Application to Deadlock Prevention in Flexible Manufacturing Systems," *IEEE Trans. Syst., Man, Cybern. A.*, vol. 34, no. 1, Jan. 2004, pp. 38-51.

[17] Li, ZhiWu and Zhou, MengChu, "Two-stage method for synthesizing liveness-enforcing supervisors for flexible manufacturing systems using Petri nets," *IEEE Transactions on Industrial Informatics*, vol. 2, no. 4, pp. 313-325, November, 2006.

[18] Li, Z.W. and Zhou, M.C., "On Controllability of Dependent Siphons for Deadlock Prevention in Generalized Petri Nets," *IEEE Trans. Syst., Man, Cybern., A.*, vol. 38, no. 2, pp. 369-384, 2008.

[19] Z. W. Li, M. C. Zhou, and M. D. Jeng, "A maximally permissive deadlock prevention policy for FMS based on Petri net siphon control and the theory of regions," *IEEE Transactions on Automation Science and Engineering*, vol.5, no.1, pp. 182-188, 2008.

[20] Li, Z.W. and Zhou, M.C., "Control of Elementary and Dependent Siphons in Petri Nets and their Application," *IEEE Trans. Syst., Man, Cybern., A.*, vol. 38, no. 1, pp. 133-148, 2008.

[21] Li, Z.W. and Zhou, M.C., "Deadlock Resolution in Automated Manufacturing Systems: A Novel Petri Net Approach," Springer-Verlag, London, 2009.

[22] M. Uzam, "An optimal deadlock prevention policy for flexible manufacturing systems using Petri net models with resources and the theory of regions," *International Journal of Advanced Manufacturing Technology*, vol. 19, no. 3, pp. 192-208, 2002.

[23] Yin Wang, Hongwei Liao, Ahmed Nazeem, Spyros A. Reveliotis, Terence Kelly, Scott A. Mahlke, and Stephane Lafortune, "Maximally permissive deadlock avoidance for multithreaded computer programs (Extended abstract)," *IEEE Conference on Automation Science and Engineering*, pp. 37-41 CASE 2009, Bangalore, India, 22-25 August, 2009.

[24] A. Nazeem, S. Reveliotis, "Designing maximally permissive deadlock avoidance policies for sequential resource allocation systems through classification theory," *IEEE Conference on Automation Science and Engineering*, pp. 405 - 412, CASE 2011, Trieste, Italy, Aug. 24-27, 2011.

[25] L. Piroddi, R. Cordone, and I. Fumagalli, "Combined Siphon and Marking Generation for Deadlock Prevention in Petri Nets," *IEEE Transactions on Systems, Man and Cybernetics - Part A*, vol. 39, no. 3, pp. 650-661, May 2009.

[26] R. Cordone abd L. Piroddi, "Parsimonious monitor control of Petri net models of flexible manufacturing systems," *IEEE Transactions on Systems, Man and Cybernetics: Systems*, vol. 43, no. 1, pp. 215-221, 2013.

[27] Y. Y. Shih and D. Y. Chao, "Sequence of control in S3PMR," *Computer Journal*, vol. 53, no.10, pp. 1691-1703, 2010.

[28] ShouGuang Wang, ChengYing Wang, and MengChu Zhou, "Necessary and Sufficient Conditions for Resultant Siphons to be Controlled," 2011 American Control Conference. pp. 4484-4489.

Efficient Packet Cache Utilization of a Network Node for Traffic Reduction

Yuki Otaka and Akiko Narita
Graduate school of Science and Technology, Hirosaki University, Hirosaki, Aomori, Japan

Abstract - *In recent years, large amounts of redundant data are often delivered in a short time. For example, a video streaming sender sends data to multiple receivers concurrently. We proposed network nodes in order to reduce such redundant traffic in TCP/IP network with packet cache. An upstream node compresses data into a small identifier and a downstream node reconstructs. In this paper, we present format of a packet and cache, techniques and strategies to search and replace elements in the cache. We implemented the method to computer network for experiment and carried out measurements. We obtained enough hit rates and high reduction rates that agree with ideal case.*

Keywords: traffic reduction; network node; packet cache; TCP

1 Introduction

In recent years, large amounts of data are transmitted in computer networks. They are often redundant, that is, the same contents are transferred multiply. For example, a host machine serves video streaming to multiple receivers. If we can reduce redundant traffic, we can utilize limited bandwidth of computer network effectively.

When redundant data are generated concurrently, the most powerful techniques to eliminate redundancy of traffic is IP multicast, with which routers at branch points duplicate datagrams. However, some difficulties discourage IP multicast from prevailing. One is requirement to equipment. All equipment for communications including routers and hosts on the routes must be applicable to IP multicast to utilize it. The other is lack of reliability. IP multicast is based on connection less communications. Application level multicast is not constrained by such limitations. The end hosts constructs multicast tree in the overlay network and duplicate packets so that sophisticated routers are unnecessary. Disadvantages of application level multicast are poorer efficiency of utilization of bandwidth and overhead of constructing the multicast tree especially when one of the hosts leaves.

On the other hand, caching has been implemented to eliminate redundant traffic of data requested repeatedly. If a proxy server at a relaying point caches data, the server can inhibits traffic between a receiver and it. Another type of caching is compression and reconstruction by two or more nodes. An upstream node encodes received redundant data and a downstream node decodes it. The upstream node refers the cache to exam whether it should encode, and the downstream node use to reproduce. Though not only routers but also hosts can cache and forward, caching enables to reduce redundant traffic transparently without hosts on the endpoint. Furthermore, the latter method is more flexible than using proxy server at the point of location of the node. This advantage extends mechanism to introduce as proposed in [1]. Moreover, it is possible to combine other function for networking, for example, utilization of lightweight protocol near the low-end host [2].

Caching with secondary storage has been offered since early stage of data delivering with computer network. However, I/O time of the secondary storage is not enough short to be responsible for real time applications. We have studied the network nodes for compression and reconstruction with network cache using the primary storage in order to reduce redundant traffic generated concurrently. We obtained enough reduction rates experimentally for traffic of only redundant data [3] [4]. Furthermore, modified procedures for searching data in the cache [5] [6], and replacement of cache elements [7]. In this paper, we present procedures and improved experimental results.

2 Method for Traffic Reduction

2.1 Basic Method for Traffic Reduction

We designed our method to reduce traffic for TCP. We implemented our method for the network with Ethernet, IP, and TCP for data link layer, internet layer, transport layer protocol, respectively. It is easy to replace Ethernet with the other data link layer protocol. However, our method has a few dependencies on IP and TCP.

Fig. 1 shows conceptual diagram of our method. The sender generates redundant traffic because of multiple requests by the receivers. The node U and D reduce traffic cooperatively. They have the same data in their communications caches shown by Fig. 2 using main memory. When the node U does not find the same data as received ones in its cache, it writes the data and modifies the packet to request the node D to hold the data. If the node U finds the same data as in the packet in its cache, it sends record identifier of it and request to reconstruct data to the node D. Size of the identifier is much smaller than that of original data so that traffic is reduced. To notify the request, the node U alters IP header as shown in Table I. We proposed three types of requests. The node U modifies TCP data field of the received frame as shown in Fig. 3. Note that a frame with code FC in the protocol field in its IP header has the same data field as that server sends.

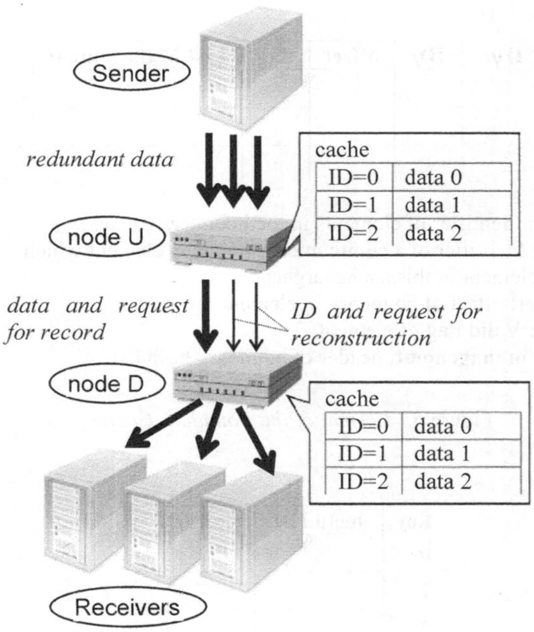

Figure 1. *Redundunt Traffic and Reduction.*

ID*f*	**property**				**List management**
	data	**length**	**stream**	**flag**	
0					
1					
2					

ID*f*: Identifier of elements in the communications cache.
data: Payload of TCP.
length: valid length of the data field of element.
stream: IP addresses and port numbers of source and destination, and sequence number of element
flag: Valid flag of element.
List management: Identifiers of forward and backword elements of data hash list, FIFO list, non-redundant list, and boundary hash list, and header of boundary list.

Figure 2. *Format of the Communications Cache.*

The communications cache holds substantial data for coding and encoding. Size of the field is enough large to store the whole data transmitted per frame. Maximum length of payload of the Ether is 1500 bytes, minimum length of IP and TCP headers are 20 bytes respectively, so that we ensured 1460 bytes for each data field. Data in the stream fields are used to distinguish redundant data as explained later. The list management field is used to construct linked lists. Table II gives the linked list constructed in our system. Details are shown later. Required size for an element is 1496 bytes.

TABLE I. ALTERED IP HEADER

IP header	**Altered IP header**	
Total length	Cache element number	
Protocol	instruction for nodes at down stream	
	code	***Request***
	FC	record
	FD	reconstruct
	FE	reconstruct and partially record

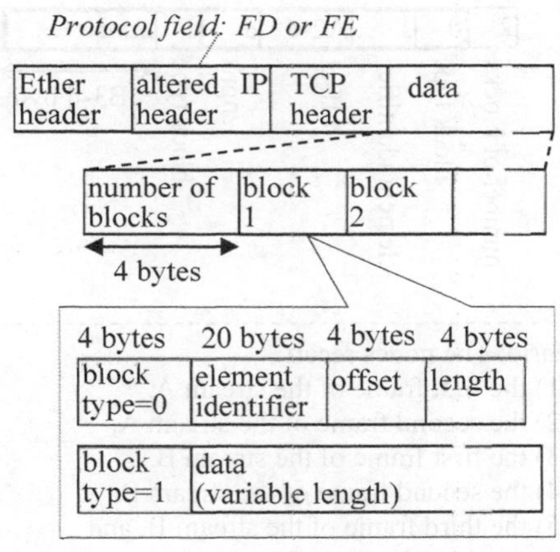

Figure 3. *Packet Format used beween the node U and D.*

TABLE II. ORGANAIZED LISTS

List Name	**node**	**List header**	**ordering**
Data Hash	**ID*f***	Hash Table	Search
FIFO	**ID*f***	Hit Table	Replace
Non-Redundant	**ID*f***	Hit Table	Replace
Boundary Hash	**ID*p***	Boundary Hash Table	Search with Boundary
Boundary	**ID*p***	Communications Cache	Replace

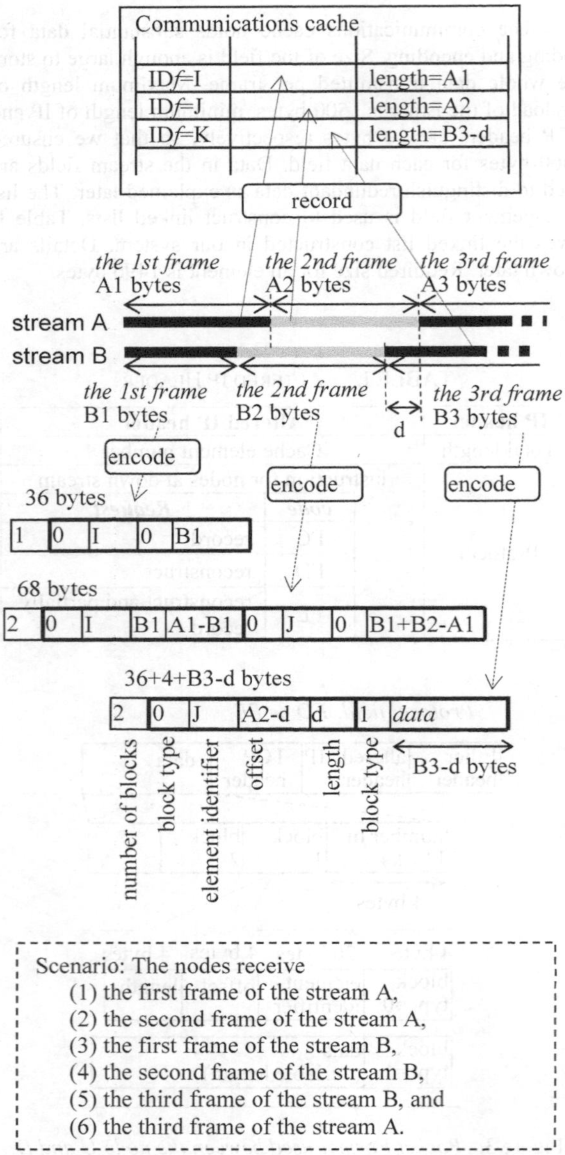

Figure 4. *Fragment and Offset of the TCP streams.*

Sizes of payload of TCP are not necessarily the same among different TCP streams. Fig. 4 is an illustrative example of two redundant streams and different position of division. Under the scenario in this figure, the nodes record data when they receive the first and second frames of the stream A, and the third frame of the stream B. The node U changes their protocol fields of IP headers into code FC. Sizes of them are the same as received ones. When the node U receives the first and second frames of the stream B, it finds the same data in the data field of a cache element I and K. It compresses the frame as shown in the figure. The node U changes the protocol field into code FD. The node U makes a block for the first frame but two blocks for the second frame. When the node U receives the third frame of the stream B, it can compress partially since only leading d bytes of the data of it exists in the cache. The node adds a new element of the cache. The node U writes residual data region of the frame in the data field of the element. Converted frame by the node U has code FE in its protocol field.

ID*p*	**ID*f***	**offset**	**flag**	**List Management**
0				
1				
2				

ID*p*: Identifier of elements in the boundary cache.
ID*f*: Identifier of a communications cache element which the element in this cache targets.
offset: offset of boundary in element
flag: Valid flag of element.
List management: header of boundary hash list.

Figure 5. *Format of the Boundary Cache.*

key	**head ID*f***	**tail ID*f***
0		
1		
2		

Figure 6. *Hash Table for searchin Data.*

2.2 Effective Replace of Element

In both points of views from cost for resource and searching time, it is important to hold only effective data in the communications cache. However, it is difficult to predict whether if a particular data received will hit or not in future. Then we abandon to avoid to record non-redundant data but intend to replace it preferentially. We arrange connection table of Fig. 7 and lists for replacement given in the Fig. 8 to get characteristic and classify redundant data.

Roughly speaking, there are two types of storage for caching as mentioned before. The secondary storage has much larger storage capacity instead of much longer I/O time. Characteristics of the primary and secondary storages lead to different applications and strategies of caching. Large capacity of the secondary storage enables to leverage various attributions. Frequency of access, data size and so on, are also index for replacing cache elements [8], and even static cache brings reasonable results [9]. On the other hand, criterions of temporal property are adoptive. FIFO and LRU strategies are used in [10] and [11], respectively.

stream	Hit Flags		Valid Flag
	Most Recently	Recently	

Figure 7. *Connection Table*

List name	IDf of head	IDf of tail
FIFO		
No-Hit		

Figure 8. *Header of Lists for Replacement*

Our method for effective replacement of the communications cache elements is similar to LRU (Least Recently Used) algorithm. An element holding non-redundant data never hits so that it becomes to be least recently used element faster than that holding redundant data. We compared LRU to FIFO in the previous study [7]. We implemented LRU with linked list in which a matched element located at the head position of it. We obtained similar results to those without no-hit list, in other words, FIFO. A particular stream rarely reuses a part of a stream that LRU and FIFO give nearly the same results. This result agrees with reported in [10].

Hence, we adopt strategy that is more aggressive. Elements holding redundant data moves more slowly than replacement with LRU. No-hit list can put off the elements before they match receives data referring connection information rapidly. When the node receives a packet whose stream is not recorded in the connection table yet, the node adds the property of the stream in the table. This registration is for stream but not data so that it is not concerned with hit in the communications cache. If whole or a part of the received data found in the communications cache, that is to say hit, most recently hit flag of both stream of the received data and record in the communications cache are set. At a time, elements that belong to the stream are removed from no-hit list. All elements of the communications cache compose the FIFO list in Fig. 8. The elements queue in order of arrival at the cache. On the other hand, elements that are probably non-redundant data remain in the no-hit list. When the node add new element to the communications cache that is full of valid data, it selects the oldest element of the non-hit list. If the list has no member, the node replaces the oldest element of the FIFO list.

At the beginning of the period of M seconds, the most recently hit flags are moved to fields of recently hit flag and reset. If both of most recently and recently hit frags of a particular stream is reset, cache elements that belong to the stream are inserted non-hit list again. Refresh and monitoring with the period M helps replacing of elements of closed connection. We used M = 30 in experiments.

3 Performance Evaluations

3.1 Ideal Case

Here, we define a reduction rate R with amount received redundant data D_r and that of sent after conversion by the node D_c as

$$R = \frac{D_r - D_c}{D_r}. \quad (1)$$

Ideal case of traffic reduction is following:

- All Redundant data are transported with the shortest headers length of H. That is, IP and TCP headers have no option.
- All Redundant data are divided at the same offset of the TCP streams. Then all compressed data have minimum length S.
- Length of the all of redundant data is upper limit L.
- Elements in the communications cache are not replaced until it becomes unnecessary.

Under these conditions, length of all received packets of redundant data equals to $(H + L)$. If number of redundant stream is N, $1/N$ of all packets have code FC in protocol field of altered IP header. Their length is also $(H + L)$ bytes. $(N - 1)/N$ of the packets have code FD in H-byte header and S-byte data. Then ideal value of R is given as

$$R_{ideal} = \frac{\left((H+L)\cdot N - (H+L) + (N-1)\cdot(H+S)\right)}{(H+L)\cdot N}$$
$$= 1 - \frac{1}{N} - \frac{(H+S)}{(H+L)}\cdot\frac{(N-1)}{N}. \quad (2)$$

R_{ideal} for large value of N is about 0.94 for $H = 54$, $S = 36$, and $L = 1460$. In our experiment shown later, we examined $N = 5$. Then R was about 0.75.

Fig. 9 exhibits the reduction rate R for number of redundant streams N. Note that Element identifier of the encoded packet presented in Fig. 3 contains unnecessary 16 bytes for compatibility. However, effect for R is very small.

3.2 Implementation and Measurement

We built a computer network for evaluation of the proposed method with machines given in Table III. Basic topology of the network is the same as Fig. 1 but two sender machines and a receiver machine. One of the senders (sender A) sends redundant data of pseudo-random numbers and the other (sender B) does non-redundant data. The sender A and B generates pseudo-random numbers with different seed each other. Ratio of the redundant data and non-redundant data was changed varying transfer rate of the sender B. The sender A transmits data as much and fast as it can. Total transfer rate of the two senders uses whole bandwidth. The receiver machine substitutes six machines with six processes on it. One of them establishes connection with a process on the sender B and receives non-redundant data, and the other five receives redundant data from the sender A. The node U acquires experimental data. It counts packets from the sender A as redundant data and those from the sender B as non-redundant ones. Measurements were carried out during 3000 seconds with which experimental results were stable.

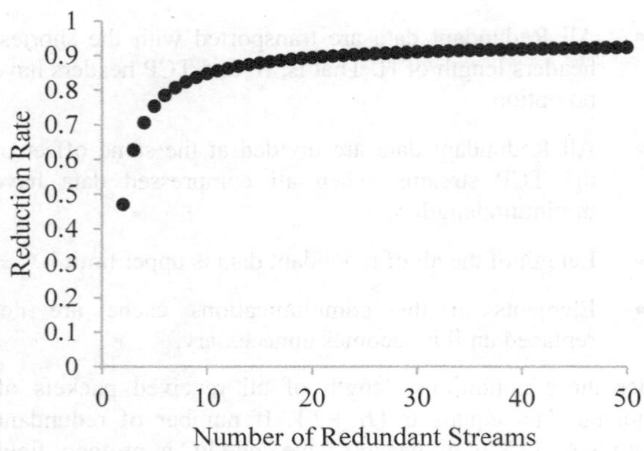

Figure 9. *Ideal Traffic Reduction Rate*

TABLE III. HARDWARE AND SOFTWARE SPECIFICATION OF THE EXPERIMENTAL SYSTEM

	Sender A, Nodes, Receiver	Sender B
CPU	Opteron1210 (1.8GHz)	Intel Celeron CPU (2.66GHz) AMD
OS	Debian 4.0 Linux 2.6.18-6-486	Ubuntu 11.04 (Linux 2.6.38-11-generic)
Memory Size	1024 MB	512 MB
Network	100BASE-TX	

3.3 Experimental Results

Fig. 10 shows dependency on the communications cache size. Reduction rate for redundant data is defined by (1). For our experimental condition, 500 elements, that is, about 750 M bytes are required for the cache to read benefits of cache avoiding replacement of redundant data with the other redundant data. At the same time, large size cache can prevent replacement of redundant data with even non-redundant data to some extent. Utilization of no-hit list can realize high reduction rate with small cache size if the node U receives redundant data together with non-redundant data. It is important not only for cost but also for performance. Because searching large size cache containing unnecessary data cause overheads usually. Furthermore, such overheads enlarge transmission delay, which may lead to packet lost in the node and congestion may occur. Then congestion control of TCP inhibits packet transfer rate and throughput of the route becomes lower than that without function of traffic reduction. In fact, such congestion was observed with previous version of the node program that employed linear search algorithm for searching the communications cache. Elimination of overhead is significant to achieve efficient traffic reduction with not expensive machine.

Effects of presence of non- redundant data are given in Fig. 11 and Fig. 12. Measurements for these figures were performed with the 1000-element communications cache. Hit rate and occupancy are given as followings, respectively.

$$occupancy = \frac{number\ of\ elements\ holding\ redundant\ data}{number\ of\ total\ elements}, \quad (3)$$

$$hit\ rate = \frac{number\ of\ packets\ element[s]\ matched}{number\ of\ received\ packes}. \quad (4)$$

Even redundant data must forwarded at least one time so that maximum value of hit rate is 1/N=0.8.

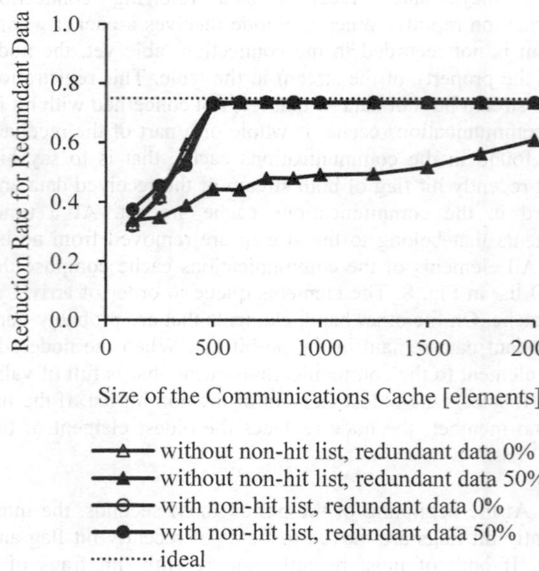

Figure 10. *Experimental Traffic Reduction Rate*

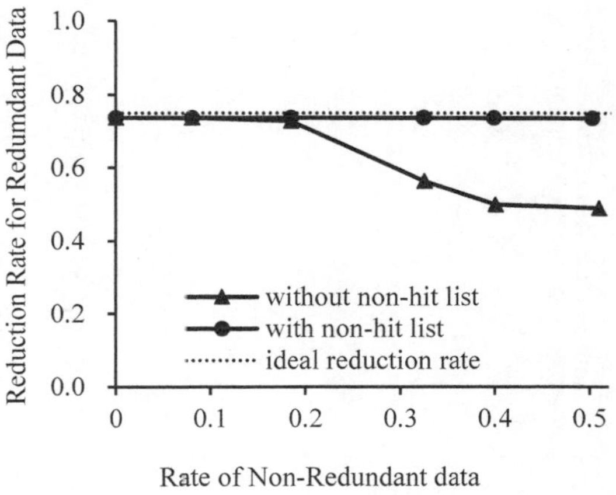

Figure 11. *Recuction Rate for the Redumdant Data with the Communications Cache of 1000-element.*

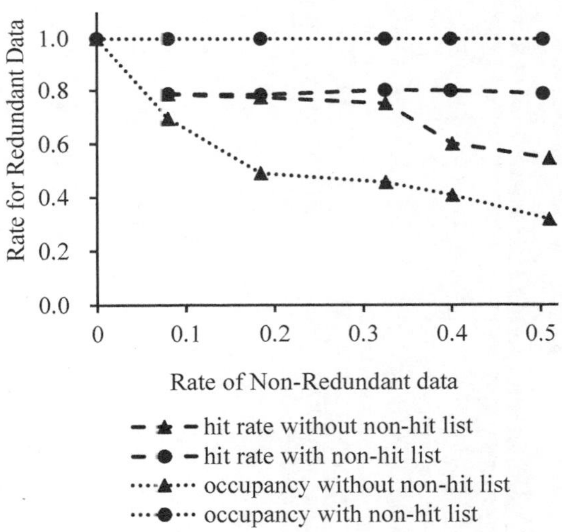

Figure 12. *Redundant Data Occupation and Hit Rate of the Communications Cache of 1000-element.*

If an element in the communications cache replaced using no-hit list, reduction rate for redundant data is high for increasing rate of non-redundant data. High occupancy of redundant data in the cache shown in Fig. 12 brings in this accomplishment. Configured cache size is enough large for rate of non-redundant data lower than about 0.2 as shown in Fig. 11. Then occupancy of redundant data is about 0.5 without no-hit list. This result means that about 500 elements holds valid data, and consistent with Fig. 10 which suggest the size is enough for purely redundant data transmission. Roughly speaking, 1 for N (N=5) packets of redundant data cause replacement in the cache. At the same time, N for N packets of non-redundant data replace old elements because they never hit. Therefore, occupancy of redundant data is low for its rate in received data. If rate of non-redundant data is about 0.3, in spite of not so low comparing to maximum value of 0.8, reduction rate for redundant data decreases noticeably. This means that hit rate is not suitable for criterion of performance evaluation of the present system. Hit rate here gives same value whether if whole data of the received packet matches an element or partially matches. However, only the former case yields the ideal compression.

4 Conclusions and Future Works

In this paper, we proposed network nodes to reduce traffic of redundant TCP stream with packet cache. We implemented our method for the network with Ethernet, IP, and TCP for data link layer, internet layer, transport layer protocol, respectively. The nodes record received packets if their data have not been held in the caches. Otherwise, an upstream node compresses them and sends small identifiers, and a downstream node reconstructs it. Traces of boundary of the redundant streams are used for effective search of the cache. Elements that belong to connections transmitting redundant data are deselected from candidates of replacement. Cache elements construct multiply linked list for effective search of redundant data in their cache and replacement. We built a computer network system for experiment and evaluated the proposed method. Almost ideal reduction rates are obtained.

We consider that the proposed method is the most efficient for such applications that generate highly temporally redundant traffic and require real time communications, for example, videoconference system or live broadcast. We are currently working to implement for more applicative topology for mentioned applications, and evaluate using real traffic. At the same time, optimizations of encoding/decoding procedure and memory usage are necessary to improve throughput and achieve high applicability with low cost.

5 References

[1] Jae Woo Lee, Roberto Francescangeli, Jan Janak, Suman Srinivasan, SalmanAbdul Baset, Henning Schulzrinne, Zoran Despotovic, Wolfgang Kellerer. "Net-Serv: Active Networking2.0"; IEEE ICC 2011, pp.37-42, Jun 2011,.

[2] Koji Funayama and Akiko Narita. "Implementation and Evaluation of a Lightweight Protocol for a Home Network"; Journal of INFORMATION, to be published.

[3] Yasuyuki Saito, Kenji Ichijo, Akiko Narita, and Yoshio Yoshioka. " Data reduction with cache in TCP/IP network"; Tohoku-Section Joint Convention of Institutes of Electrical and Information Engineers, pp.110, Aug 2007.

[4] Yasuyuki Saito, Kenji Ichijo, Akiko Narita, and Yoshio Yoshioka. "Reduction of video traffic of TCP stream with cache"; Tohoku-Section Joint Convention of Institutes of Electrical and Information Engineers, Japan, 2008. pp.110

[5] Koji Funayama, Sayuri Yamamoto, Yasuyuki Saito, Kenji Ichijo, Akiko Narita, and Yoshio Yoshioka, "Speed-up of a TCP/IP data reduction program"; Tohoku-Section Joint Convention of Institutes of Electrical and Information Engineers, pp.72, Aug 2009.

[6] Tomoya Shikanai, Kengo Kimura, Sayuri Yamamoto, Yasuyuki Saito, Kenji Ichijo, Akiko Narita, and Yoshio Yoshioka. "Modification and evaluation of a network node for traffic reduction"; Tohoku-Section Joint Convention of Institutes of Electrical and Information Engineers, pp.138, Aug 2010,.

[7] Yuki Otaka, Yasuyuki Saito, Akiko Narita. "Efficient packet cache utilization of a network node for traffic reduction"; Proceedings of 2012 Annual Conference of Electgronics, Information and Systems Society, I.E.E. of Japan, pp.1867-1868, Sep 2012.

[8] Adam Wierzbicki, Nathaniel Leibowitz, Matei Ripeanu, Rafal Wozniak. "Cache replacement policies revisited: the case of P2P traffic"; Proceedings of the IEEE International Symposium on Cluster Computing and the Grid (CCGrid) 2004, pp.182-189, Apr 2004

[9] Meeyoung Cha, Haewoon Kwak, Pablo Rodriguez, Yong-Yeol Ahn, and Sue Moon. "I tube, you tube, everybody tubes: analyzing the world's largest user generated content video system"; Proceedings of the 7th ACM SIGCOMM conference on Internet measurement, pp. 1–14, Oct 2007

[10] Ashok Anand, Archit Gupta, Aditya Akella. "Packet Caches on Routers: The Implications of Universal Redundant Traffic Elimination". Proceedings of the ACM SIGCOMM 2008 conference on Data communication, pp.219-230, Oct 2008

[11] Shu Yamamoto, Akihiro Nakao. "P2P packet cache router for network-wide traffic redundancy elimination"; Proceedings of International Conference on Computing, Networking and Communications (ICNC), 2012, pp.830-834, Feb 2012

[12] Mohamed Hefeeda, Cheng-Hsin Hsu, Kianoosh Mokhtarian. "Design and Evaluation of a Proxy Cache for Peer-to-Peer Traffic"; IEEE Transactions on Computers, Vol. 60, No.7, pp.964-977, Jul 2011

[13] Ashok Anand, Vyas Sekar, and Aditya Akella. "SmartRE: an architecture for co-ordinated network-wide redundancy elimination"; SIGCOMM Comput. Commun. Rev., 39(4):87-98, Oct 2009.

SESSION

SOCIAL NETWORKS + BLOGS + TEXT MESSAGING SYSTEMS AND RELATED ISSUES

Chair(s)

TBA

Text Interpretation and Mood: Is Happiness an Indicator?

Laurie J. Patterson
Department of Computer Science, University of North Carolina Wilmington, Wilmington NC USA

Abstract - *Text and e-mail are widely open to (mis)interpretation by the recipient. It is widely accepted that humor, sarcasm, double entendres do not work well or are interpreted correctly without the smile, tone, or expression given by the sender. This paper looks at the "mood" or level of happiness of the recipient in the correct interpretation of a text or email message.*

Keywords: Emotion, happiness, interpretation, mood, text e-mail.

1 Introduction

The United States Department of Commerce predicted in 2001 that almost half of the U.S. population used e-mail to the extent that e-mail messages now outnumber the number of letters sent through the U.S. Postal Service [21]. For 2010, Internet World Stats, shows that 77.3% of the U.S. population used the Internet [14]. Gatz and Hirt suggest that email is used daily, and in some cases, even hourly [7]. The Radicati Group, in 2010, estimated the total number of emails sent per day to be approximately 294 billion [22].

The Pew Internet & American Life Project states that approximately 83% of the U.S. population own cell phones and, of this group, 73% send and receive text messages. That means that daily, at a minimum, almost 240 million emails are sent in the US. If only one text message is sent by each cell phone user, approximately 145,351,532 texts are sent daily. Combined, that means that, at a minimum, 385,245,132 electronic messages are sent daily.

1.1 Message Interpretation

With that number of messages being sent, there is a chance that messages may be misinterpreted. Because messages arrive without the benefit of seeing or hearing the sender, the recipient may not receive the message in the tone in which it was meant. Nonverbal cues, in a conversation, provide clues to the meaning of the message [10]. Humor, sarcasm, or simple requests for information, when done in person, are frequently presented with a smile, a nudge, or some other form of body language or vocal cue [18].

The sender of a message "hears" the tone of a message in their head as they type it. The recipient, however, does not hear that tone. Sarcasm, for example, is defined as a sharply ironical taunt or cutting remark [4]. That definition, in itself, strongly suggests verbal cues are associated with sarcasm. Sarcasm, therefore, does not fare well in e-mail [2]. Without hearing the "tone" of the message, recipients may choose to ignore or delete the message [17]. E-mail, as a form of writing, is not usually reviewed or edited and particularly not for possible tone interpretation.

1.2 Message Tone

E-mail has tone, even though the message is not heard by the recipient. All text has tone. The writer of a book/poem/article carefully chooses their words and presents them in a way meant to convey a meaning to the message [14]. Tone is the attitude or feeling the writer wishes to deliver [13] or convey toward the message's topic [17].

The problem for most writers is that they expect the recipient of their message to understand exactly what the writer meant to convey, tone included [10]. Readers, however, take the message literally, with no understanding of what the writer means to say, especially if acronyms are included and the reader does not understand the meaning [17]. In a study conducted using Cornell University students, Kruger et al. found that only half the time was the tone of a message correctly identified by the recipient; however, 80% of the time, the sender believed the recipient would get the tone correct [11].

A Canadian company, The Strategic Counsel, conducted an opinion poll for Microsoft Canada that supports the above study. In their 2007 polling of Canadians, they found:

- 66% worried about the possibility of their emails being misinterpreted or misunderstood;
- 37% experienced work problems due to email misinterpretation;
- 30% retrieved an email because they were afraid it would be misinterpreted [1].

In a study at the University of Vermont Extension, Deziel collected responses from the extension employees on the successful interpretation of e-mail messages. A majority of respondents had experienced a misinterpretation of at least one of their messages [3]. His results for the number of e-mails that have been misinterpreted are shown in Figure 1.

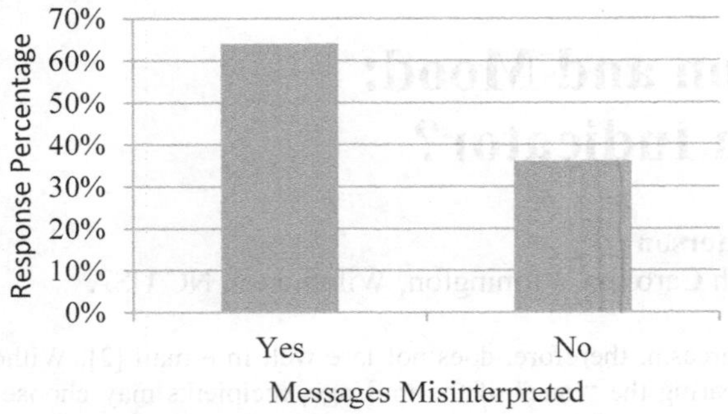

Figure 1. Percent of survey participants who have had an e-mail message misinterpreted [3].

2 Mood

How people evaluate events that occur in their lives depends on two things: cognition and affect (or mood). Mood influences the "instant evaluation" of an event [6]. For most people, terms such as "happy" and "unhappy" are words that are used to describe their mood.

2.1 Measuring Mood

Psychologists identify three types of happiness: emotional, moral, and judgmental [9]. Of these three, it is emotional happiness that most people identify; however, emotional happiness is considered subjective [9]. Despite the subjective nature of emotional happiness, there are ways to measure its levels and these methods can be scientific [19]. The most frequently used method of happiness measurement is by asking individuals, through surveys, if they are happy and how happy they feel. Other methods of measurement include physiological indicators, observed behaviors, and nonverbal behaviors. As a subjective concept, each individual tends to be the best judge of their level of happiness [6]. Figure 2 shows objective vs. subjective happiness and how the two are measured.

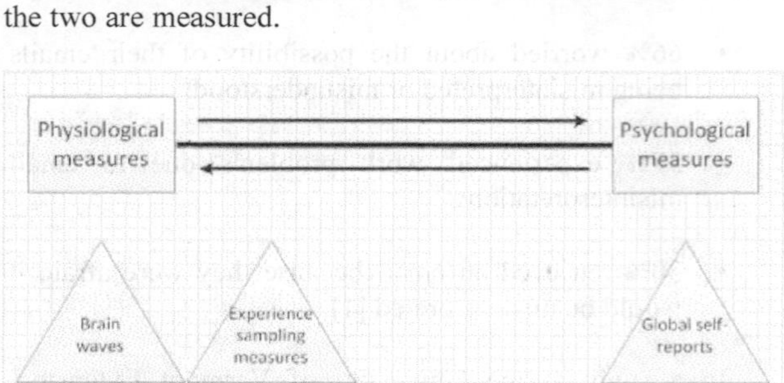

Figure 2. Concepts of happiness and how they are measured [6].

When surveying for happiness, psychologists have identified five main factors that determine an individual's level of happiness: personality, socio-demographic, economic, situational, and institutional [6]. An issue with identifying happiness, however, is that respondents often give answers focusing on joy or satisfaction. Joy is a term used to define an emotion. Satisfaction is a term used to define a perception [19].

2.2 Measuring Happiness

One survey, the Subjective Happiness Scale (SHS), was created by Sonja Lyubomirsky and Heidi Lepper [12]. Their survey, through several different studies meant to validate it, was reduced to four simple questions. Answers to the four questions, using a 7-point Likert scale, are averaged. Happiness scores range from 1.0 to 7.0; the higher the score, the higher the level of reported happiness [12]. The questions are:

- In general, I consider myself (with 1 corresponding to "not a very happy person" and 7 corresponding to "a very happy person").

- Compared to most of my peers, I consider myself (with 1 corresponding to "less happy" and 7 corresponding to "more happy).

- Some people are generally very happy. They enjoy life regardless of what is going on, getting the most out of everything. To what extent does this characterization describe you? (with 1 corresponding to "not at all" and 7 corresponding to "a great deal").

- Some people are generally not very happy. Although they are not depressed, they never seem as happy as they might be. To what extend does this characterization describe you? (with 1 corresponding to "not at all" and 7 corresponding to "a great deal") [12].

3 Mood and Message Interpretation

There is an abundance of anecdotal evidence regarding the "mood" of the sender and the "tone" of the message. Frequently, one will hear that the "sender" must have been in a bad mood to send that message. Rarely is it heard that the recipient is the one with the bad mood. This, in part, may explain the Facebook page developed (2011) and titled "Bad-mood-DONT-text-Shutup-No-one-was-going-to-text-you-anyway." The page is no longer available.

To assist with mood and tone, many social network sites provide users with an opportunity to signal their mood with a status. Facebook recently announced that they were going to test a "status update composer" that would let you use an emoticon and add a mood to accompany your post [15]. E-mails and texts have for many years used emoticons to soften or strengthen the message's interpretation [20]. The problem with emoticons is that the user may not understand its meaning, thus further frustrating the reader [17]. Another issue with the use of emoticons is that it suggests an unprofessional writer. This is especially an issue when the message comes with a business email [8].

This study attempts to connect, not the writer's mood, but the recipient's mood with how an e-mail is interpreted.

4 Influence of Mood on Message Interpretation: The Study

To determine if there is a connection between the recipients' current mood and their interpretation of a text message, a study was conducted using the SHS and several text scenarios. The SHS was selected for use in this study because of its simplicity.

4.1 Research Hypotheses

The purpose of this study was to determine whether there was a correlation to the mood (or happiness level) of an e-mail reader to the perceived tone of an e-mail. To this end, the following null research hypothesis was created:

> There will be no difference between the happiness levels of an e-mail recipient and how they view the tone of the email message.

4.2 Scenario Development

To reflect messages that individuals might receive, six general topics were selected. Each of the topics was then written with three perspectives in mind: neutral, friendly or "warm fuzzy," and unfriendly or "cold prickly." The topics were:

- Cat having kittens
- Upcoming football game
- Going out for dinner
- Upcoming exam for a course
- Acceptance of a poem for publication
- Day trip to the beach

These topics were developed using a small formative committee of three individuals. The neutral scenario was created first, and then was modified to give more extreme "warm" positive or "cold" negative responses.

The 18 developed scenarios were then submitted to a group of seven individuals who were asked to evaluate the scenarios on whether they felt "warm," "cold" or "neutral" towards the message sender. In addition, this group was asked how they would modify each question to get a response closer to "neutral." The scenarios were then modified to move the overall feeling of each of them closer to neutral.

4.3 Survey Submission

These final scenarios were combined with the SHS questions and submitted to students attending the University of North Carolina Wilmington. Students in these courses were asked to voluntarily participate in the survey. Standard IRB protocols were used with regard to the survey submission.

At the writing of this ongoing research, 42 students responded. The survey remains open and additional data continues to be collected.

4.4 Happiness Results

Responses to the four SHS questions were based on a seven point Likert scale. Happiness levels are determined by averaging the four scores. Survey results were divided into three groups: happier than average, average, unhappier than average. Lyubomirsky and Lepper's results show the average score for college students to be slightly below 5.0 [5]. Current results from this study of college students show an average of 4.69; the mean, however, is 4.77. For the respondents, happiness scores ranged from 3.00 to 6.25. Plotted, the scores have a modified bell curve. Figure 3 shows the modified bell curve.

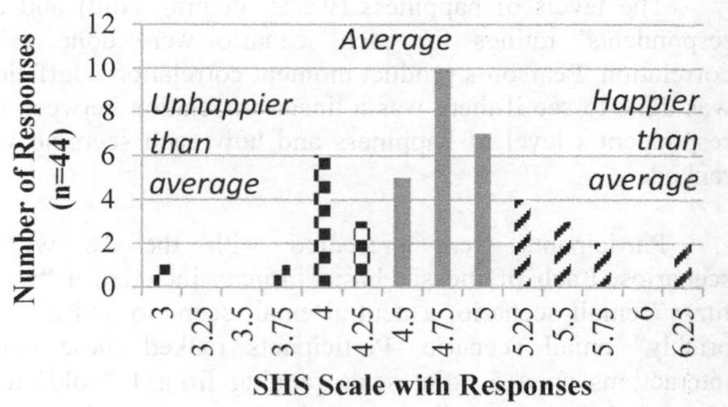

Fig. 3. Levels of respondent happiness.

The bell curve results were used to determine which respondents would be considered happier than average, average in happiness, and unhappier than average. The columns on the right (slash markings) (n=11) are sorted into "happier than average," the middle section (n=22) are those individuals sorted into "average happiness," and the columns to the right (checkered) (n=11) are those individuals sorted into "unhappier than average."

4.4.1 General Happiness Demographic Results

Of the 35 responses, 25 (59.5%) are female and 17 (40.5%) are male. Males, on average, identified that they were happy individuals. With '7' as the happiest, men averaged a score of 4.88 ('4' is neutral). Females averaged a score of 4.51.

When reviewing question one, identifying the level of happiness felt at the given moment, males are slightly more happy (5.588) than females (5.52). The overall average to this question, across genders, was 5.548.

When compared to their peers (question two), however, females identified themselves as slightly more happy (5.08) than males did (4.94). The overall average to this question, across genders, was 5.024.

The third question, whether the respondents enjoyed life "regardless of what is going on," females were slightly lower than males with a score of 5.080 compared to the male average score of 5.118. The overall average to this question, across genders, was 5.095.

With the fourth question, referencing that some people just are not happy people, females had a stronger negative response to this characterization of them with an average score of 3.120 ('1' corresponds to "not at all") than males did. Males rated themselves, on average, with a score of 3.882. The overall average to this question, across genders, was 3.429.

4.4.2 Specific Results

The levels of happiness (warm, neutral, cold) and the respondents' ratings for each scenario were done using correlation. Pearson's product moment correlation coefficient was done to see if there was a linear association between the respondent's level of happiness and how each scenario was ranked.

Participants were presented with the 18 written scenarios. Each of the six basic formats included a "warm fuzzy" email scenario, a neutral email scenario and a "cold prickly" email scenario. Participants ranked these email interactions on a 5 point scale ranging from 1 "cold" to 5 "warm". Scores from all 18 scenarios were averaged to give a final score. These general rankings will be termed "civility scores."

Happiness scores ranged from 3.000 to 6.250 with a mean of 4.774 and standard deviation of .662. Civility scores averaged from a range of 1.929 to 4.762 with a mean of 3.025 and a standard deviation of .239.

A Pearson's correlation coefficient was calculated for happiness by civility, resulting in a significant positive correlation of .476 ($p < .001$). These results suggest that happier respondents are more likely to perceive email responses as civil, than are less happy respondents. r^2 suggests that 23% of the variation in civility judgment is due to the level of happiness felt by the recipient.

In reviewing the data, there is some evidence to suggest that this effect is consistent across the "cold prickly," neutral and "warm fuzzy" response scenarios. Similar bivariate correlations appear when comparing each of the three separate scenario groups with the level of happiness. The results, from "cold prickly" to neutral to "warm fuzzy" are $r = .347$, $r = .364$, and $r = .350$ respectively. There was not difference, however, between how males and females responded to the scenarios. Their overall results mirrored the results of that of the combined genders.

5 Conclusion and Future Work

It appears that it is the mood, or level of happiness, of the recipient appears to significantly determine how an electronic message is interpreted. There is a connection between the recipients' current mood and their interpretation of a text message.

The survey and subsequent evaluation continues to attract more participants. With this initial result, other variables or influences could also be evaluated, such as other ages (non-college students) or settings (businesses,

6 References

[1] Bell Media. (October 17, 2007). "Email rife with regret, misinterpretation: study." [Online]. Available: http://www.ctv.ca/CTVNews/CanadaAM/20071016/email_issues_071016 /

[2] Business Email Etiquette. (May 8, 2008)." Emoticons in Business E-mail." [Online]. Available: http://www.businessemailetiquette.com/emoticons-in-business-e-mail

[3] G. Deziel, "E-Mail Use and Communication Perceptions of University of Vermont Extension Employees," Journal of Extension, Volume 42, Number 3, June, 2004.

[4] Dictionary.com. (2012). "Sarcasm." [Online]. Available: http://dictionary.reference.com/browse/sarcasm

[5] The Dr. Oz Show. (04/02/2010). "Subjective Happiness Scale." [Online]. Available: http://www.doctoro 04/02/2010 z.com/dr-oz-total-body-reboot-contest

[6] B. S. Frey, and A. Stutzer, Happiness and Economics: How the Economy and Institutions affect Well-Being. Princeton University Press, Princeton NJ, 2002.

[7] L. G. Gatz, and J. B. Hirt, "Academic and social integration in cyberspace: Students and e-mail," Review of Higher Education, 23, 299-318, 2000.

[8] P. Gil. (January, 2013). "Emoticons and Smileys 101 An Introduction to 21st Century Hieroglyphs." [Online]. Available: http://netforbeginners.about.com/cs/netiquette101/a/bl_emoticons101.htm

[9] D. Gilbert, Stumbling on Happiness, Vintage books, New York, NY, 2007.

[10] J. Kruger, N. Epley, J. Parker, and N. Zhi-Wen, "Egocentrism Over E-Mail: Can We Communicate as Well as We Think?,' Journal of Personality & Social Psychology. Vol. 89 Issue 6, 925-936, December, 2005.

[11] Stephen Leahy. (02.13.06). "The Secret Cause of Flame Wars." [Online]. Available: http://www.wired.com/science/discoveries/news/2006/02/70179 retrieved 2/8/11

[12] S. Lyubomirsky and H. S. Lepper, "A Measure of subjective measure of subjective happiness: Preliminary reliability and construct validation," Social Indicators Research 46, 137-155, 1999.

[13] Microsoft Developer Network. (2012). "Style and Tone." [Online]. Available: http://msdn.microsoft.com/en-us/library/aa974175(d=printer).aspx

[14] Miniwatts Marketing Group. (2012)." Internet World Stats, Usage and Population Statistics, Internet Usage and Population Growth." [Online]. Available: http://www.internetworldstats.com/am/us.htm

[15] A. Moscaritolo. (February 1, 2013). "Facebook Channels Vintage MySpace with New 'Mood Status'." [Online]. Available: http://www.pcmag.com/article2/0,2817,2415024,00.asp

[16] NetM@nners.Com. (2011). "Are Your E-mails Tone Deaf?" [Online]. Available: http://www.netmanners.com/email-etiquette/are-your-e-mails-tone-deaf/?/

[17] M. Rudick, and L. O'Flahavan. (2001). "Set The Tone In E-Mail: How You Say It IS As Important As What You Say." [Online]. Available: http://www.hodu.com/email-tone.shtml retrieved 2/8/11

[18] S. Schafer, "E-Mail's Impersonal Tone Easily Misunderstood Conflicts can arise from mistyped, misperceived messages," San Francisco Chronicle (reprinted), November 3, 2000.

[19] F. Strack, M. Aargyle, and N. Schwarz, (Eds), Subjective Well-Being: An Interdisciplinary Perspective. Pergamon Press, Oxford, 1991.

[20] L. Tiffany. (January 29, 2008). "Control Your Emoticons." [Online]. Available: http://www.pcworld.com/businesscenter/article/141882/control_your_emoticons.html

[21] L. L. Thompson, The mind and heart of the negotiator (2nd ed.), Upper Saddle River, NJ: Prentice Hall, 2001.

[22] H. Tschabitscher. (2010). "How Many Emails Are Sent Every Day?" [Online]. Available: http://email.about.com/od/emailtrivia/f/emails_per_day.htm

Design of an Interactive Text Messaging Platform for Problem Alcohol Use Intervention in College Students

Thomas Way[1], **Michael Mason**[2], **Eric Benotsch**[3], **Hannah Kim**[3], **Daniel Snipes**[3]
[1] Dept. of Computing Sciences, Applied Computing Tech. Lab, Villanova University, Villanova, PA, USA
[2] Department of Psychiatry, Virginia Commonwealth University, Richmond, Virginia, USA
[3] Department of Psychology, Virginia Commonwealth University, Richmond, Virginia, USA

Abstract - *College students are a highly connected population, and also one with a potential for problem alcohol use. Young adults of college age frequently have cell phones and other mobile electronic devices and spend significant time maintaining their social networks of friends via Facebook, Instagram, Twitter and other instantaneous means of communication such as text messaging. Alcohol use is not uncommon among this same group, and the newfound freedoms experienced in a college environment can lead some young adults to develop problems with alcohol use that go beyond occasional social drinking. This paper reports on the design of an interactive text messaging platform that enables therapeutic alcohol use intervention treatment to go beyond the counselor's office and directly into the mobile devices students typically carry and use. The design of this interactive system is detailed, technology decisions are discussed, and a summary of the results of a pilot study using the system is presented. Future plans for extension of the platform onto smart phone technology and with a higher degree of interactivity are explored.*

Keywords: Interactive text messaging, parsing, SMS, alcohol use treatment, server-based text message processing.

1 Introduction

Interactive technology such as text messaging and other features of smart phones and older feature phones provides an appealing way for young adults to maintain interpersonal connections with a circle of friends. Because mobile device technology, and the quick communication it facilitates, is so prevalent, opportunities abound for making use of this technology in innovative ways. One intriguing possibility is as a support tool for interactive, text messaging based interventions as a therapeutic technique for reducing substance abuse in of various forms by young adults. Although generally too complex and proprietary to develop as part of a single research study, there are a number of platforms that implement a cloud application architecture and can facilitate development of an interactive, text-based protocol, including Twilio [22] and Tropo [21] (Figure 1).

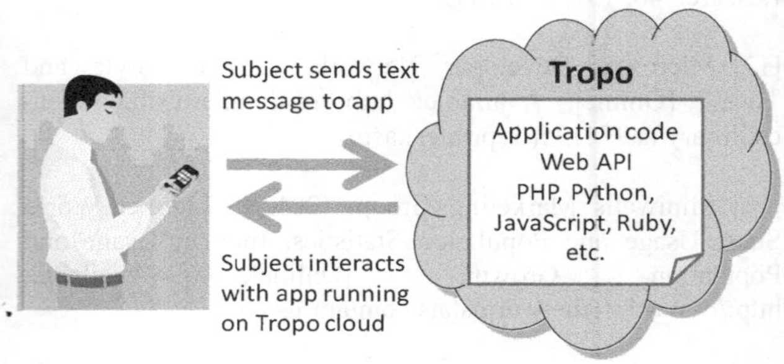

Figure 1. Tropo Cloud Application Architecture [21].

Young adults are a high risk group for many health problems including substance use, suicide, and drinking. For example, full time college students (ages 18 to 22) were more likely than their peers not enrolled full time to use alcohol in the past month, binge drink, and drink heavily [15]. Heavy alcohol consumption and the resulting negative consequences are significant risk factors for college students in the United States [8,10], with one in four college students having met alcohol abuse or dependency diagnostic criteria in the past year [16]. In 2011, over 60 percent of full-time college students consumed alcohol on a regular basis, nearly 40 percent were binge drinkers, and 13 percent were heavy drinkers. Among those not enrolled full time in college, these rates were 52, 35, and 10 percent, respectively [5,20]. Thus, not only are young adults drinking, but the way in which they drink put them at high risk for alcohol-related problems.

Motivational interviewing (MI) techniques which make use of brief and supportive interactions have shown promise for reducing alcohol-related problems [1,15,18], smoking [2,9], marijuana use [4], and substance use and drinking [11]. These MI approaches tend to focus on the goal of reducing use, rather than leading to complete abstinence. Thus, MI often serves as a stimulus to contemplation about current and future use, which is an important and necessary precursor to eventual abstinence, or in some cases, more responsible use [13,14;19].

In a previous study, the efficacy of a preventive intervention using MI for substance use and associated risk behaviors among adolescent patients was measured. A 20 minute, evidence-based session with a social network component was performed in a study of 28 teen subjects who were recruited, provided consent/assent, screened, and randomly assigned to a treatment or control (no treatment) group. After one month, a follow-up survey showed that teens in the treatment group reported getting into less trouble related to substance abuse and were more prepared to begin substance abuse counseling than teens in the control group [14]. The success of this earlier study led to the development of a protocol for a text messaging based MI approach.

In this paper, we present the motivating factors and technological foundations of an automated, interactive, text messaging system that implements an MI-based therapeutic treatment protocol. The system is designed to be easily retargeted to other domains, and in this instance is used for alcohol use intervention. The design is described using a system architecture design and accompanying detailed explanation of software design, technology decisions, messaging protocol, and message content. The results of a pilot study using the system are summarized, and future plans for extension of the platform onto smart phone technology and with a higher degree of interactivity are explored.

2 Suitability of Text Messaging

Traditionally, motivational interviewing is performed by a trained clinical psychologist as part of a treatment and intervention program [7]. It has long been used as a technique for the treatment of problem drinkers, though it has shown benefits in many other forms of motivation-dependent counseling [1,2,4,9,11,15,18]. As a technique, motivational interviewing is a client-centered counseling style that helps clients to make positive changes in their behavior by uncovering varying degrees of readiness and other internal motivation within a client in order to facilitate the desired change [1].

At the outset of this research, it was unknown if a motivational interviewing protocol using automated text messaging would be successful as an intervention technique within an overall treatment protocol, although recent research has indicated strong potential [3]. Guiding our application of text messaging as an MI approach was the Transtheoretical Model of Behavior Change (TTM), which organizes behavior change through a series of stages [17].

In accordance with what the literature suggests, and due to the ready availability of a college student population, we envisioned that our study would target heavy drinkers in the young adult population at Virginia Commonwealth University. Specifically, we hoped to be able to identify what stage of change each subject was in via interactive questions such as "Do U think it will be hard for U to reduce or stop drinking?"

During the study and based on subject responses, each subject was classified as being in one of the accepted TTM stages that are precursors to active change: precontemplative, contemplative, or preparation. The interactive nature of the text messages allowed for the integration of consciousness raising (educated each of the participants on how much they drank in comparison with other young adults), self-reevaluation, environmental reevaluation, and self-liberation (participants were asked if they were willing to make adjustments to their drinking habits, were asked to commit to an adjustment, and then sent encouragement that they could fulfill their commitments). Although the text messages were sent via a computer program, they were designed to make the participant feel as if they had a helping relationship.

According to early work in this area, consciousness raising and environmental reevaluation are effective change processes for individuals in the precontemplative stage [17]. Self-reevaluation is an effective change process for those in the contemplative stage, and self-liberation is a helpful change process during the preparation stage. Although, a helping relationship is a change process that is not effective in moving participants to the consecutive stage of health behavior change unless they are in the action stage, this aspect of the text-messaging was a component of integrating MI with social network counseling.

Thus, based on an analysis of previous research, the prevalence and availability of text messaging capable cell phones among college students, and the highly interactive nature of text messaging as a communication medium, it became clear that there was merit in conducting a study using a text based approach to motivational interviewing. Equally important to this research was the need to evaluate the feasibility and efficacy of this text based approach as part of the overall intervention goals of the study.

3 Interactive Platform Design

The framework that was designed, implemented and deployed for this interactive, text-based approach relies on popular Linux, Apache, MySQL and PHP (LAMP) computer server technology [12] and the Tropo cloud-based platform for text-enabled applications [21], with design direction taken from several well-studied software engineering design patterns [6]. Figure 2 illustrates the architecture of this system, including cell phones, cloud-based texting platform, server and database components, and support for management, subject enrollment and system status monitoring. At a fundamental level, the solution to this design is creation of a parsing technique that is driven by a database and responds to incoming text messaging events.

3.1 Server Technology

The web server that hosted the texting application software was configured using the popular LAMP configuration [12]. This configuration is designed for efficient and cost-effective web servers, enabling a wide variety of power web-based applications.

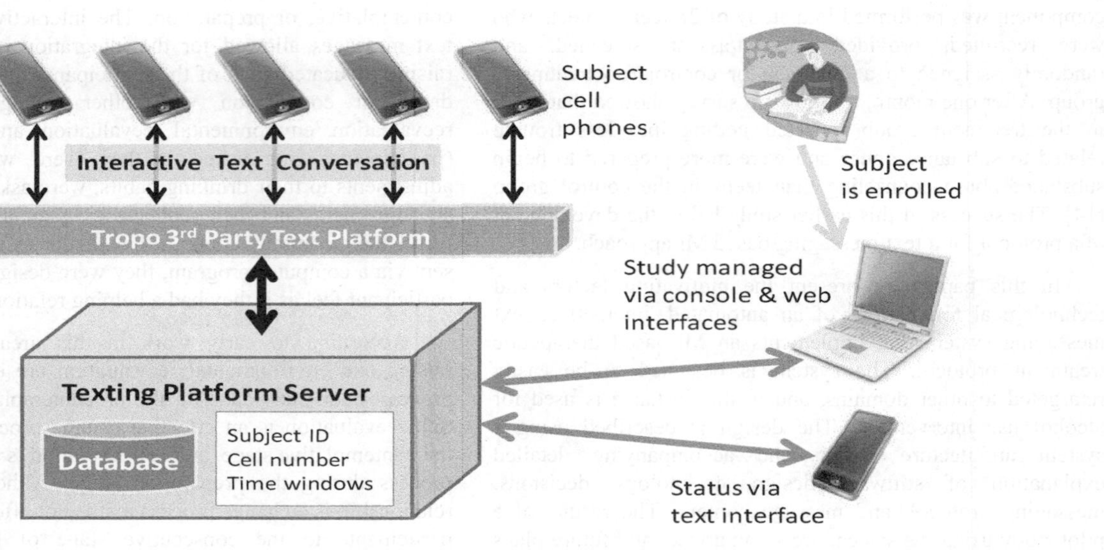

Figure 2. Design of interactive text messaging platform.

The text-based software that drives our study was implemented in the PHP programming language, which is widely used for web-based application development. PHP was selected for its broad adoption, availability of example programs, and support within Tropo, the cloud-based, text messaging platform that was selected for this project. The server was configured to use a high level of security to insure that data integrity was maintained.

3.2 Software System Design

The overall design of the text messaging software system was engineered using three well-known design patterns [6] to describe the structural, behavioral and concurrency aspects of the system. The Front Controller structural design pattern was used to centralize control of this combined web-based and server-based application. The State behavior design pattern was used to guide development of the state-machine algorithm that tracked progress of each subject within the study, including which of the many possible messages was the next appropriate message to be sent to each subject. To support the significant concurrently used in the application, the Event-based Asynchronous concurrency pattern was implemented in order to marshal incoming requests and manage the corresponding system state changes.

3.3 SMS System Design

The Short Message Service (SMS), or text messaging service, component of the system was implemented using a commercial cloud-based Application Programmer Interface (API) called Tropo. Tropo provides web-application developers an API for designing software that supports voice and SMS communication in a variety of popular programming languages [21]. The Tropo system enables unlimited, free use of the text-messaging platform for web-applications during the development and testing phase and a cost-effective pricing structure during the production phase of a project. Tropo was selected over its main competitor, Twilio [22], because of its more favorable pricing structure and comparable feature set.

Application design began with an event and data parsing algorithm definition phase, during which appropriate design patterns were identified and implemented and test programs were developed to experiment with the features of the Tropo platform. Because the initial proof-of-concept was designed to be easily modified, a text-based approach for storing data and tracking subject progress was used to enable more convenient data collection management and data-format changes. Due to numerous modifications made to the data collection strategy and data management needs, the choice to use a text-based approach was fortuitous as database table modifications can be cumbersome when data management is complex.

The production version of the text-based software system used this less complex text-based data system, consisting of individual comma-separated-value files for each subject to support this ease of support during ongoing development. In future uses of this platform, the MySQL database platform will be incorporated to provide more flexible and robust programmer support for data management.

Subjects were entered into the study on a rolling basis, resulting in subjects being in various states of the study simultaneously. To enter a new subject into the study, the subject's unique subject ID and cell phone number were inserted into the database. Note that subject IDs were used to identify subjects on the web server in order to maintain and protect the privacy of each subject. No identifying information was stored on the web server, and it was only after data was gathered and securely downloaded by researchers that data could be linked with subject identities for further analysis.

Text message sequences were sent over four days, with the initial message of each day sent to each subject initiated using a daily, time-triggered "cron" job. Table 1 describes the breakdown of text messages for each day, and how the messages were designed to support a particular approach and motivational interviewing focus. For each day, Table 1 also explains the intent of each model component of the text messages for each day.

The initial text message sent to each subject was done so during an individualized time permission window during which the subject indicated it was okay to receive a text message. Subsequent message interactions were handled asynchronously based on individualized interactions with each subject. When a subject replied to a given message, the text-messaging platform prepared a customized, outgoing message based on that subject's current progress, or state, within the study. Figure 3 shows the sequence of text messages sent each day, including placeholders where a subject's first name (SUBJECT_NAME), typical of number of days per month the subject drinks alcohol (NUMBER_OF_DAYS), percentile raking of alcohol use as compared with peers (ALCOHOL_USE_PERCENT), risk level of the subject's peer network (RISK_LEVEL), and finally email (EMAIL_CONTACT) and telephone (PHONE_CONTACT) contact information.

Once the day's defined messages for a given subject were exhausted, any subsequent messages from that subject were responded to with a generic message reminding the subject that additional messages of support were available. All of these interactions were gathered in per-subject logging files and an overall study logging file to enable both individual and summary post mortem analysis of interactions and to provide data redundancy.

At any time, a subject could request a "booster" message by simply texting back the word "boost." These booster messages (Figure 4) were designed to be simple messages of encouragement and support, written in the form of interactions used in motivational interviewing.

Upon completion of the four day sequence, subjects were sent reminder text messages at days 23, 29 and 30 after they entered the study. These reminders provided information to subjects about the online follow-up survey they were asked to complete in order to conclude their involvement in the study and to receive a small stipend. Subjects were encouraged to complete the online follow-up survey one month after entering the study, and were sent a single, daily text message reminder each day after that point until they completed the survey.

For study administrators, text-based system support was implemented. By texting single word commands such as "help," "start," "stop," or "status," the text messaging system respectively would provide a summary of available commands, start the system to enable sending of messages, stop the system to disable sending of messages, and report on the current status of the system including a summary of progress of the enrolled subjects. This simple administrative interface was also available from the Linux command-line and provided administrators with a straightforward way to control the system and verify its status. Two web-based interfaces were developed to enable researchers to verify each subject's cell phone during the initial interview phase of the study, and to indicate when a given subject had officially completed the study, thereby stopping any reminder messages that were being sent.

Table 1. Description of text message design and model components based on focus of Motivational Interviewing stages.

Day	Texts	Approach & *MI Focus*	Model Components
1	6 texts boost texts	Rapport building *MI acceptance & engagement*	Asked about general well-being Asked about difficulty to stop/reduce drinking Asked what they like and dislike about drinking
2	4 texts boost texts	Presenting feedback *MI acceptance*	Drinking is reviewed & compared to national norms Asked to reflect and consider future in light of current drinking
3	5 texts boost texts	Presenting information & feedback *MI acceptance*	Information about social networks is presented Personal social network quality is reviewed Asked to reflect on their social network
4	4 texts boost texts	Summary of session *MI encouragement*	Texts are summarized Asked if they would consider making small changes in their social network Asked to consider with whom in their network they would like to increase or decrease time with & where Reminded about follow-up telephone interview

Day 1
Message 1: "Hi SUBJECT_NAME. This is the VCU Psych Study. What up? How U feeling today? Txt back: good, ok, bad."
Message 2: "B-4 we start, do U think it will be hard for U to reduce or stop drinkin? Txt back: no way, maybe, or def."
Message 3: "Let's talk about sum of your responses from the survey. U reported drinkin NUMBER_OF_DAYS days in past 30 days. Can U tell me what U like about drinkin?"
Message 4: "OK, thanks I appreciate it. Can U also tell me what U dislike about drinkin?"
Message 5: "Sometimes there are pluses & minuses to drinkin. What are U doing now?"
Message 6: "Thanks for your responses. I appreciate it. I hope U can think over what we discussed. Bye. Need some extra support? Txt: boost"

Day 2
Message 1: "Hey SUBJECT_NAME. How are U feeling? Txt back: good, ok, bad."
Message 2: "Let's talk more about ur drinkin. Did U know that ALCOHOL_USE_PERCENT of other 18-23 year olds drink less than you? How's that for you? Txt: surprised, unsure, upset."
Message 3: "Can U tell me how U see your life in light of your current drinkin?"
Message 4: "Ok, thanks for Ur response, I really appreciate it. Need some extra support? Txt: boost"

Day 3
Message 1: "Hey SUBJECT_NAME. How r u doing? Txt back: good, ok, bad. Then, let's talk about your friends."
Message 2: "Your network is RISK_LEVEL risk to affect your drinkin. How do U feel about Ur network? Txt back: ok, need to change, need lots of change."
Message 3: "How would U rate Ur craving right now? Txt back: Intense, pretty strong, under control."
Message 4: "Remember, very small adjustments in ur network can have big effects w/ ur drinkin. What are U doing now?"
Message 5: "K, thx. I hope U can think over what we discussed. Hang in there, bye. Need some extra support? Txt: boost"

Day 4
Message 1: "Hey SUBJECT_NAME. Howz life? Txt back: good, ok, bad."
Message 2: "Based on what we have been texting about, would U consider making any small adjustments to Ur drinking at this time?"
Message 3: "An option is to spend slightly more time with non-drinkers and less with drinkers, and spending more time at non-drinking locations. What do U think?"
Message 4: "What do you think U would like to do about your drinkin?"
Message 5: "Thx for Ur texts. Hope U can think over what we discussed. Questions? EMAIL_CONTACT PHONE_CONTACT. Complete follow-up survey in 1 mnth & get $20"

Figure 3. Text messages

Booster messages
Boost 1: "Ask for support from a non-drinking friend, find out what they are doing tonight."
Boost 2: "Mix up Ur routine so U won't be tempted to drink, do different things."
Boost 3: "Try to spend less time at places that remind U of drinking. U can do this!"
Boost 4: "Hang in there, U are doing great! Go work out, see a movie, have a meal."
Boost 5: "Go to a coffee shop, go to a bookstore, study, improve Ur GPA!"
Boost 6: "Hang in there, there are lots of students who are interesting, fun, cool, and sober, like U!"

Figure 4. Booster messages

4 Results

Our primary feasibility finding centered on the development and application of our computer program that organized, scheduled, maintained, and delivered our text-messaging intervention. We found that the automated and individualized text messaging protocol was successful in delivering text messages to the correct individual (97%), in the correct sequence (100%), with appropriate responsiveness to each participant's replies (98%). The sequencing of text messages was accurate in the day sequence as well as within day interactive texts based upon participant response.

To determine the efficacy of the text-based approach to delivering motivational interviewing support, we analyzed the response data collected during interactive sessions as well as pre- and post-study survey assessments. In comparing the results for the intervention and control groups, we found two promising trends. The intervention group had increased intentions to reduce alcohol use in three months following the text protocol, while the control group had decreased intentions to reduce alcohol use the same period. Due to the pilot nature of the study and a relative small population, statistical significance was marginal ($p<0.10$). However, texting responses and other interactions with both groups of subjects provided qualitative support for these results. Similar results were seen in actual steps taken to reduce alcohol use, with the intervention group showing a slight increase while the control group showed a decrease.

The results from this small feasibility trial are promising on multiple fronts. First, the strong negative correlation between readiness to change and perceived difficulty stopping drinking provides support that our measures fit our unique intervention. This could also be evidence that we are accurately tapping into the readiness for change construct with this initial text item. Although we did not see significant changes in social stress outcome scores between groups, the strong positive correlation between anxiety and need to change their social network due to drinking issues provides support for further exploring the social-psychological consequences of college student problem drinking. These findings mirror other social network research that has demonstrated strong relationships between mental health outcomes such as anxiety and depression and social network quality among adolescents [13]. Socially based interventions that can address peers, mental health, and drinking behavior may be warranted.

5 Conclusions

The development of an automated computer program that can accurately remind, send, respond, track, and maintain a text-messaging intervention is a promising finding. Having the ability to reach populations of interest at an extremely low cost has implications for a public health approach towards substance use prevention and treatment. Effect sizes would not have to be large to justify the further testing on this type on intervention on problem alcohol use for a high-risk population such as college students. The cost-benefit ratio is fairly clear, even from this small trial. This entire program can now be tested for accuracy in a larger scale trial as well as to continue to evaluation implementation improvements.

In all, this trial piloted an innovative study that utilized automated text-messaging computer programming and evidence-based text intervention and produced promising enough results to warrant further study. The future of mobile behavioral health interventions has just begun with an exponential increase of text-based interventions over the last 7 years. It is clear that for the young adult population, mobile phones will continue to be a very close part of their lives, and thus integrating interventions into this platform makes good scientific sense.

In the future, the system will migrate the data collection component to a true database system rather than the current text-file-based approach. Other uses of this system will be explored, including use in similar health behavior intervention studies as well as more general information and customer support systems that can use artificial intelligence techniques to respond to user interactions.

6 Acknowledgment

The work reported in this paper was partially supported by the Institute on Drug and Alcohol Studies, Virginia Commonwealth University.

7 References

[1] Barnett, N. P., Monti, P. M., & Wood, M. D. (2001). Motivational interviewing for alcohol-involved adolescents in the emergency room. Innovations in adolescent substance abuse intervention, 143-168.

[2] Colby, S. M., Monti, P. M., Tevyaw, T. O.L., Barnett, N. P., Spirito, A., Rohsenow, D. J., & Lewander, W. (2005). Brief motivational intervention for adolescent smokers in medical settings. Addictive behaviors.

[3] Cunningham, J. A., Kypri, K., & McCabridge, J. (2011). The use of emerging technologies in alcohol treatment. Alcohol and Health, 33, 320-325.

[4] D'Amico, E. J., Miles, J. N., Stern, S. A., & Meredith, L. S. (2008). Brief motivational interviewing for teens at risk of substance use consequences: a randomized pilot study in a primary care clinic. Journal of substance abuse treatment, 35, 53-61.

[5] Dawson, D.A., Grant, B.F., & Li, T.K. (2005). Quantifying the risks associated with exceeding recommended drinking limits. Alcoholism: Clinical and Experimental Research, 29, 902–908.

[6] Erich Gamma, Richard Helm, Ralph Johnson, and John Vlissides. 2002. Design patterns: abstraction and reuse of object-oriented design. In Software pioneers, Manfred Broy and Ernst Denert (Eds.). Springer-Verlag New York, Inc., New York, NY, USA 701-717.

[7] Hettema, J., Steele, J., & Miller, W. R. (2005). Motivational interviewing. Annu. Rev. Clin. Psychol., 1, 91-111.

[8] Hingson, R. W., Zha, W., & Weitzman, E. R. (2009). Magnitude of and trends in alcohol-related mortality and morbidity among US college students ages 18-24, 1998-2005. Journal of studies on alcohol and drugs. Supplement, (16), 12.

[9] Hollis, J. F., Polen, M. R., Whitlock, E. P., Lichtenstein, E., Mullooly, J. P., Velicer, W. F., & Redding, C. A. (2005). Teen reach: outcomes from a randomized, controlled trial of a tobacco reduction program for teens seen in primary medical care. Pediatrics, 115, 981-989.

[10] Johnston, L. D., O'Malley, P. M., Bachman, J. G., & Schulenberg, J. E. (2009). Monitoring the future national survey results on drug use, 1975–2008: Volume II, college students and adults ages 19–50. Bethesda, MD: National Institute on Drug Abuse.

[11] Knight, J. R., Sherritt, L., Van Hook, S., Gates, E. C., Levy, S., & Chang, G. (2005). Motivational interviewing for adolescent substance use: a pilot study.Journal of adolescent health, 37, 167-169.

[12] Lee, James; Brent Ware (December 2002). Open Source Web Development with LAMP: Using Linux, Apache, MySQL, Perl, and PHP. Addison Wesley.

[13] Mason, M. J. (2009). Social Network Characteristics of Urban Adolescents in Brief Substance Abuse Treatment. Journal of Child and Adolescent Substance Abuse, 18, 72-84.

[14] Mason, M., Pate, P., Drapkin, M., & Sozinho, K. (2011). Motivational interviewing integrated with social network counseling for female adolescents: A randomized pilot study in urban primary care. Journal of substance abuse treatment, 41, 148-155.

[15] Monti, P. M., Colby, S. M., Barnett, N. P., Spirito, A., Rohsenow, D. J., Myers, M. & Lewander, W. (1999). Brief intervention for harm reduction with alcohol-positive older adolescents in a hospital emergency department. Journal of consulting and clinical psychology, 67, 989-994.

[16] Naimi, T.S., Brewer, R.D., Mokdad, A., et al. (2003). Binge drinking among US adults. JAMA, 289, 70–75.

[17] Office of Applied Studies. (2003, October 31). The NSDUH Report: Alcohol use and risks among young adults by college enrollment status. Rockville, MD: Substance Abuse and Mental Health Services Administration. Retrieved from http://www.samhsa.gov/data/nsduh/2k4mrb/ShortRptCollege.pdf

[18] Prochaska, J. O. , & DiClemente, C.C. (1983). Stages and processes of self-change of smoking: Toward an integrative model of change. Journal of Consulting and Clinical Psychology, 51, 390-395.

[19] Spirito, A., Monti, P. M., Barnett, N. P., Colby, S. M., Sindelar, H., Rohsenow, D. J. & Myers, M. (2004). A randomized clinical trial of a brief motivational intervention for alcohol-positive adolescents treated in an emergency department. The Journal of pediatrics, 145, 396-402.

[20] Strang, J., & McCambridge, J. (2004). Can the practitioner correctly predict outcome in motivational interviewing?. Journal of substance abuse treatment, 27, 83-88.

[21] Abuse and Mental Health Services Administration. (2011). Results from the 2010 National Survey on Drug Use and Health: Summary of National Findings, NSDUH Series H-41, HHS Publication No.(SMA) 11-4658. Rockville, MD: Substance Abuse and Mental Health Services Administration.

[22] Tropo voice and text messaging cloud service (2013). Free and commercial platform, web site documentation. Available at: http://www.tropo.com.

[23] Twilio cloud framework for business communication applications. Simplified commercial platform, web site documentation. Available at: http://www.twilio.com.

Sentimental versus Impact of Blogs

Sadi Evren SEKER
Dept. of Business Administration
Istanbul Medeniyet University
academic@sadievrenseker.com

ABSTRACT

Sentimental analysis on web-mined data has an increasing impact on most of the studies. Sentimental influence of any content on the web is one of the most curios questions by the content creators and publishers. Also the impact of the web-mined data is completely another issue than the sentiments. For example categorizing a blog post into positive or negative sentiment is a parameter and measuring the like and dislike numbers of the blog post is completely another issue. In this study, the impact and sentimental of the comments collected from five different web sites in Turkish with more than 300,000 comments in total. The web sites are from newspapers; movie reviews, e-marketing web site and a literature web site. All the comments are mixed into a single file. The comments have a like or dislike number, which are used as ground proof of the impact of the comment. The ground proof of the sentiment of the blog is the smileys in the post text. Also the sentiments are spread to the rest of the blogs without smileys by using the bag of words. The correlation is implemented by using the support vector machine classifier and success rates are 50.7% similarity between the sentiment and the impact of the comment.

Keywords

Data Mining, Sentimental Analysis, Big Data, Text Mining

Acknowledgement

This study is supported by Istanbul University, research projects department under project number YADOP-27254

1. INTRODUCTION

The data set on this study is collected from internet for one of the high-circulating newspapers, a movie review web page with highest comments, an e-marketing web site with highest comments and a literature web site holding poems and novels all in Turkish. The properties of the dataset will be explained in the experiments section. Some of the comments hold the smileys and depending on the emotion of the sentiment, the post is categorized as positive or negative. For example a positive smiley is ":-)" and a negative smiley is ":-(". Only a few of the posts holding smileys are considered as neutral since they have both positive and negative smileys. The sentiment of positive or negative posts are spread to the rest of the posts in the data set, which will be explained in the background and experiments sections.

On the other hand, the numbers of likes or dislikes are considered as the ground proof of the impact of the comments. After feature extraction from both sentiment and impact, the correlation between impact and sentiment is investigated by using the support vector machine (SVM), k nearest neighborhoods (KNN), decision tree (C4.5) and majority vote learning (MaVL) on top of them as classifiers. This paper also holds the implementation details and the methodology of evaluation of smileys, which are held in the evaluation section.

2. PROBLEM STATEMENT

This study is the first time to address the correlation of sentiments built on the smileys and the impact built on the like / dislike count of comments for Turkish data sources.

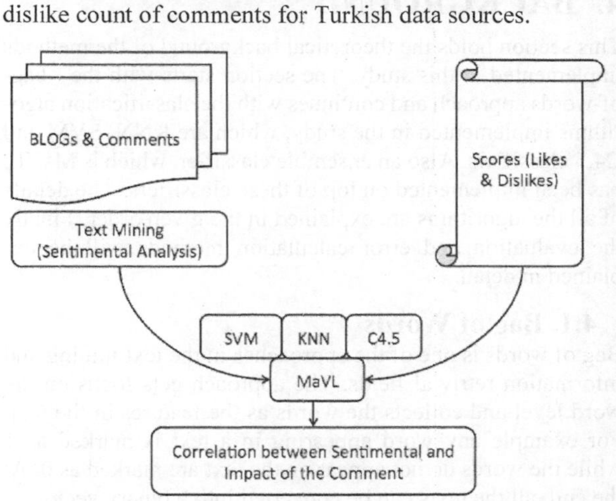

Figure 1. Overview of Study

One of the difficulties in this study is dealing with natural language data source, which requires a feature extraction. The other difficulty is dealing with large number of comments, which can be accepted as big data problem. The dataset holds 131,248 distinct words and when the feature vector of each economy news item is collected, the total size of the feature vector is over 32.5 GByte, which is beyond the computation capacity of a single computer with these classification algorithms. For a simple SVM implementation the required RAM is slightly more than 1TB.

3. RELATED WORK

Current studies on sentimental analysis on web-mined data has a great impact for the both content authors and publishers. For example the impact of a politician's speech can now be monitored real-time by the help of current studies[1]. For example, the researchs on Arabic Spring and the effect of social media on the Tunisian case [1] or French Presidental Election and social media research [2] or Iran Green Movement from the twitter data [3] or research on UK 2010 election and effect of social media [4] are only a few researches on the topic.

In most of the researches, the data is collected from the social media like Twitter [1-4] or Facebook [5] or e-learning environments mixed with social networks[6]. All of these studies have a text mining part. Zhai[7] shows that the studies based on TF-IDF has a higher success than suffix tress or n-gram based approaches for Chinese case with the SVM classifier.

Some of the reserachers prefers using the metrics built on the social network itself. For example in Twitter, it is possible to get the number of followers and following and such information may be useful to calculate the political views of people depending on who they follow as in UK Election research [4] where the feature extraction is built on the followers/following. Or on some other researches, text mining approaches like bag of words, interjection of emotics, part of speech tagging methods are implemented together [6].

4. BACKGROUND

This section holds the theoretical background of the methods implemented in this study. The section starts with the bag-of-words approach and continues with the classification algorithms implemented in the study, which are KNN, SVM and C4.5 classifiers. Also an ensemble classifier, which is MaVL, has been implemented on top of these classifiers. The details of all the algorithms are explained in the given order. Finally the evaluation and error calculation methods will be explained in detail.

4.1. Bag of Words

Bag of words is one of the approaches in the text mining and information retrivial fields. The approach gets focus on the word level and collects the words as the features in the text. For example any word appearing in a text is marked as 1 while the words do not appear on the text are marked as 0. At the end, all the texts can be converted into a binary vector.

Let P be the corupus of posts and W be the set of words in the corpus.

Feature vector k, which is the feature extracted for the post number k, *feature* (P_k) will hold 1 for any $w_i \in W$ if and only if $w_i \in P_i$ and will hold 0 for any $w_i \in W \wedge w_i \notin P_i$.

Also it can be assumed that the sentimental of a post is built over the words in the post, which means, some of the words can be considered as postive and some can be considered as negative. [Satyn paper]

4.2. K- Nearest Neighborhood (KNN)

The k, c-neighborhood (or k, c(x) in short) of an U-outlier x is the set of k class c instances that are nearest to x (k-nearest class c neighbors of x). U-outlier is any instance which can not be considered within the boundaries of any classes.

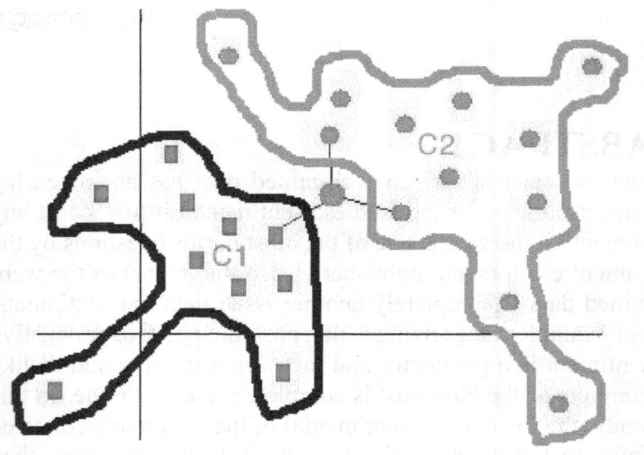

Figure 2. Visualization of K-NN

The K-NN [14] is explained in Figure 2. Here k is a user defined parameter. For example, k , $c_1(x)$ of an U-outliers x is the k-nearest class c_1 neighbors of x.

Let $\overline{D}_{Cout,q}(x)$ be the mean distance of a U-outlier x to its k-nearest U-outlier neighbors. Also, let $\overline{D}_{C,q}(x)$ be the mean distance from x to its $k,c(x)$, and let $\overline{D}_{Cmin,q}(x)$ be the minimum among all $\overline{D}_{C,q}(x)$, c $\in$ {Set of existing classes}. In order words, k , c_{min} is the nearest existing class neighborhood of x. Then k-NSC of x is given in equation (1).

$$k-NSC(x) = \frac{\overline{D}_{C\min,q}(x) - \overline{D}_{Cout,q}(x)}{\max(\overline{D}_{C\min,q}(x), \overline{D}_{Cout,q}(x))} \quad (1)$$

4.3. Support Vector Machine (SVM)

The reason of applying SVM method as in Figure 3 over the dataset is determining the boundaries between classes [18].

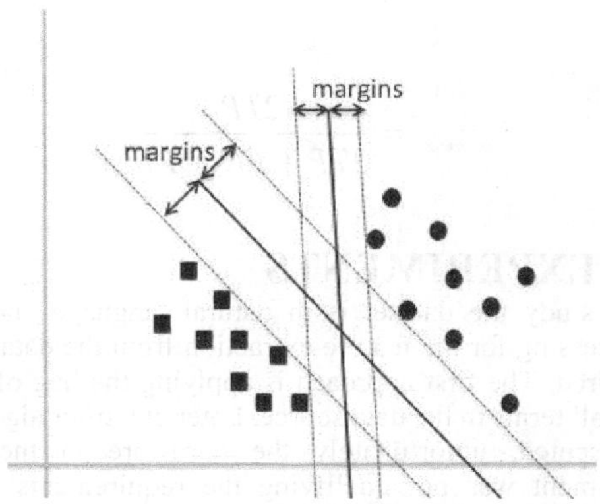

Figure 3. SVM boundary and margins

SVM aims to classify the samples into groups and define a boundary between the groups. SVM also tries to find out the maximum margin possibility between the groups [18].

$$\| \omega \|^* = \sum_{i=1}^{n} \alpha_i y_i x_i \quad (2)$$

The margin between the classes is symbolized by ω symbol in equation (2) and SVM seeks to maximize the value of ω. The above formula can be rewritten as below for the linearly separable classes [19].

$$\| \omega \|^2 = \sum_{i=1}^{l} \alpha_i = \sum_{iSVs} \alpha_i = \sum_{iSVs} \sum_{iSVs} \alpha_i \alpha_j y_i y_j \langle x_i, x_j \rangle \quad (3)$$

In the equation (3), all the possible cases of i and j are considered. Also SVM can use a radial basis function and one of the options is the Gaussian kernel function, quoted in equation (4) [19].

$$K(x, x') = \exp\left(-\frac{\| x - x' \|^2}{2\sigma^2} \right) \quad (4)$$

Finally, the class is determined by the result achieved from K function.

4.4. C4.5 Tree

C4.5 method [17] is a decision tree based classification algorithm. The tree is built by using the information gain of each feature in the feature vector.

The algorithm starts with a training data set S where S= { s_1, s_2 , … s_n } where each sample s_i has a p dimensional feature vector, FV.

For each sample s_i, FV = { x_{1i}, x_{2i}, … x_{pi} } and the information gain of each values would be IG = { ig(x_{1i}), ig(x_{2i}), … ig(x_{pi}) }.

The algorithm creates a decision tree where each node defines a decision to either side.

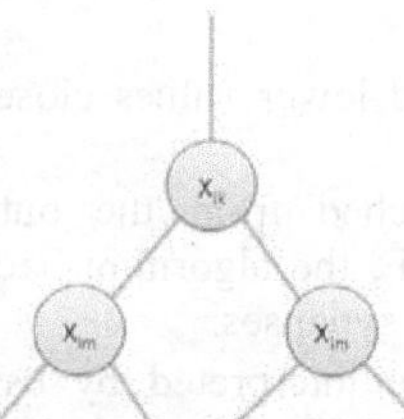

Figure 4. C4.5 Tree Demonstration

The highest information gain value is selected for the top most decision node and the second is get the decision criteria on the next level. Let ig(x_{ik})> ig(x_{im}) for the figure 4. The tree is constructed by following the similar approach for the next levels. Finally at the leav es, the samples are placed after the training.

In the time of testing, the features extracted from test samples are questioned via the decision nodes in the tree from root to leaves. The final leaf is accepted as the class of the test sample.

C4.5 has an advantage on other decision trees, since it uses the information gain and normalization and also it uses the prunning for the time performance.

4.5. Ensemble Classification

The majority vote learning (MaVL or Marvel) [16] has been implemented on this study, which can be considered as a based ensemble method to combine three different classification methods. MaVL can be considered as a meta classifier which works over the classifiers like KNN, C4.5 or SVM in our case.

Let $S_i \in S$ where S is the set of classifiers and let $C_i \in C$ where C is the set of classes,

$$C(x) = argmax_i \sum_{j=1}^{B} w_j I(S_j(x) = i) \quad (5)$$

Where w_j is the weight of each indicator function I(•) which is added into the equation for normalization and the weights of each classifier is equal in our model.

Marvel, gets the summation for each of the classifier's vote and the sample is classified into the class with the highest vote.

4.6. Error Rate Calculation

The error rate of the system is calculated through root mean square error (RMSE). The calculation of RMSE is given in equation (6) [20].

$$x_{rmse} = \frac{\sqrt{x_1^2 + x_2^2 + \ldots + x_n^2}}{n} \quad (6)$$

For this study, above x values are the results achieved from the implementation of the algorithm. The RMSE result of 0 is considered ideal and lower values close to 0 are relatively better.

By the results fetched from the output layer and the calculation of RMSE, the algorithm back propagates to the weight values of the synapses.

Also the results are interpreted by using a second error calculation method RRSE (Root Relative Squared Error) and the calculation is given in equation (7) [15].

$$x_{rrse} = \sqrt{\frac{\sum_{j=1}^{n}(P_{ij} - T_j)}{\sum_{j=1}^{n}(T_j - \bar{T})^2}} \quad (7)$$

Where P_{ij} is the value predicted for the sample case j, T_j is the target value for sample case j and $\bar{T}$ is calculated by equation (8) [17].

$$\bar{T} = \frac{1}{n}\sum_{j=1}^{n} T_j \quad (8)$$

The RRSE value ranges from 0 to ∞, with 0 corresponding to ideal.

The third error calculation method is RAE (Relative Absolute Error) and the calculation is given in equation (9) [15].

$$E_i = \frac{\sum_{j=1}^{n}|P_{(ij)} - T_j|}{\sum_{j=1}^{n}|T_j - \bar{T}|} \quad (9)$$

$P_{(ij)}$ is the value predicted by the individual program i for sample case j (out of n sample cases), T_j is the target value for sample case j, and $\bar{T}$ is given by the equation (10) [15]:

$$\bar{T} = \frac{1}{n}\sum_{j=1}^{n} T_j \quad (10)$$

For a perfect fit, the numerator is equal to 0 and E_i=0 So, the E_i index ranges from 0 to infinity, with 0 corresponding to the ideal.

Also the success rate of prediction and expectation can be measured as the f-measure method. The f-measure method is built on the Table 1.

Table 1. f-measure method

Expectations	Predictions		
		Positive	Negative
	True	True Positive	True Negative
	False	False Positive	False Negative

The calculation of f-measure can be given as in equation (11) depending on the Table 1.

$$F_{measure} = \frac{2TP}{2TP + FN + FP} \quad (11)$$

5. EXPERIMENTS

In this study the dataset is in natural language and some preprocessing for the feature extraction from the data source is required. The first approach is applying the bag of words for the all terms in the data source. Later classifier algorithms are executed, unfortunately the hardware in the study environment was not qualifying the requirements for the feature extraction of all the terms in data source which is 139,434.

5.1. Dataset

We have implemented our approach and Table 2 demonstrates the features of the datasets.

Table 2. Properties of the Dataset

	News
# of posts	303,108
Average word length	~6.7

The above dataset is collected from the web site of a high-circulating newspaper in Turkey. The data is collected directly from a database so the noisy parts on the web page like ads, comments, links to other news, etc. are avoided. Another problem is the noise of HTML tags in the database entries for formatting the text of news. The data has preprocessed and all the HTML tags are removed from the news and also all punctuations and stop words are removed in the preprocessing phase.

5.2. Feature Extraction

Feature extraction requires determining the sentimental analysis on the posts. The bag of words approach has been implemented to spread the sentimental effect collected from smileys to the rest of the data preset. The problem is handled in the word level and it is assumed that each word has a sentimental effect of positive, negative or neutral. For example word "good" has a positive sentiment while word "bad" has a negative sentiment.

Obviously handling the problem in word level has advantages and disadvantages, for example loosing the phrase, sentence and pragmatics level is one of the drawbacks of the approach. On the other hand the performance is higher than the approaches with natural language processing techniques. In a research, with high amount of data, the performance is kept as a primary issue and the implementation is selected in the word level. The algorithm implemented, takes the words from positive or negative sentiments and each word has a tagging from the training set with the smileys. Those labeled words are carried to the rest of the blogs and each blog is categorized within this manner.

Algorithm: Spreading Sentiments from Smileys

1. *Let S_+, S_- and S_0 be sentiment classes,*
2. *For each $P_i \in$ Posts*

```
Let wi∈ set of Words ∧ wi∈ Pi
    if(Pi ∈ S+) increase score (wi)
    if(Pi ∈ S-) decrease score (wi)
    if(Pi ∈ S0) no change (wi)
V ←(Pi ,Sum scores of all wi∈ set of Words ∧ wi∈ Pi)
```

During the execution of algorithm, the execution requires more memory than the available hardware, where we run the algorithms on a intel i7 cpu and 8GByte of RAM. The required memory is calculated in equation (26).

$$\text{Memory Requirement} = 139{,}434 \text{ words} \times 303108 \text{ posts} \times 6.7 \text{ average word length} \times 2 \text{ bytes for each character} = \sim 283\text{GByte} \quad (26)$$

As a solution we have limited the number of words with the highest occurences. The number of occurences on our implementation is 30 and a word is taken into consideration after this number of occurences. The words appearing above this threshold value are 2878 and the memory required is reduced to 700MByte which is easier to handle in the RAM.

The feature vector extraction is about 56 minutes on average for the economy news.

5.3. Evaluation

The results of executions can be summarized in Table 3.

Table 3. Error and Success Rates of Classification Methods

	f-measure Average	RMSE	RAE	Correctly Classified
Classification Before Spread (12,412 posts)	0.491	0.4174	0.9892	52.52%
Classification After Spread (303,108)	0.501	0.4404	0.9930	50.70%

The correctly classification rate in Table 3 is the percentage of correlation between two feature vectors. The success has been measured in two different times. The first row, which is the classification before spread, measures only 12421 posts which holds the smileys in the corpus. So, at that level the bag of words approach has not been executed yet.

The second row of Table 3 holds the success rate after spreading the sentiments to the rest of the posts without sentiments. There is a slight loss of success since the spreading algorithm is not perfect.

6. CONCLUSION

This study claims the lossly correlation between sentiments and the impact of the posts on the web. This claim has been proven by using text mining and classification methods. Also the data is collected from the web using the web crawlers and it is first time researched the correlation on a Turkish corpus. Furthermore the research may have an importance on understanding and forecasting the impact of any post before it has been published in the future.

The results shows that at least there are 50% correlation between two feature vectors.

7. REFERENCES

[1] Younus, A.; Qureshi, M.A.; Asar, F.F.; Azam, M.; Saeed, M.; Touheed, N., "What Do the Average Twitter-ers Say: A Twitter Model for Public Opinion Analysis in the Face of Major Political Events," Advances in Social Networks Analysis and Mining (ASONAM), 2011 International Conference on , vol., no., pp.618,623, 25-27 July 2011
doi: 10.1109/ASONAM.2011.85 [2] Braun, H. 1987. Predicting stock market behavior through rule induction: an application of the learning-fromexample approach. Decision Sciences, vol. 18, no. 3, pp. 415-429.

[2] Wegrzyn-Wolska, K.; Bougueroua, L., "Tweets mining for French Presidential Election," Computational Aspects of Social Networks (CASoN), 2012 Fourth International Conference on , vol., no., pp.138,143, 21-23 Nov. 2012
doi: 10.1109/CASoN.2012.6412392

[3] Khonsari, K.K.; Nayeri, Z.A.; Fathalian, A.; Fathalian, L., "Social Network Analysis of Iran's Green Movement Opposition Groups Using Twitter," Advances in Social Networks Analysis and Mining (ASONAM), 2010 International Conference on , vol., no., pp.414,415, 9-11 Aug. 2010
doi: 10.1109/ASONAM.2010.75

[4] Boutet, A.; Hyoungshick Kim; Yoneki, E., "What's in Twitter: I Know What Parties are Popular and Who You are Supporting Now!," Advances in Social Networks Analysis and Mining (ASONAM), 2012 IEEE/ACM International Conference on , vol., no., pp.132,139, 26-29 Aug. 2012
doi: 10.1109/ASONAM.2012.32

[5] Neri, F.; Aliprandi, C.; Capeci, F.; Cuadros, M.; By, T., "Sentiment Analysis on Social Media," Advances in Social Networks Analysis and Mining (ASONAM), 2012 IEEE/ACM International Conference on , vol., no., pp.919,926, 26-29 Aug. 2012
doi: 10.1109/ASONAM.2012.164

[6] Martin, J.M.; Ortigosa, A.; Carro, R.M., "SentBuk: Sentiment analysis for e-learning environments," Computers in Education (SIIE), 2012 International Symposium on , vol., no., pp.1,6, 29-31 Oct. 2012

[7] Zhongwu Zhai; Hua Xu; Jun Li; Peifa Jia, "Sentiment classification for Chinese reviews based on key substring features," Natural Language Processing and Knowledge Engineering, 2009. NLP-KE 2009. International Conference on , vol., no., pp.1,8, 24-27 Sept. 2009 doi: 10.1109/NLPKE.2009.5313782

[8] Zhai, Y., Hsu, A., and Halgamuge, S. 2007.Combining News and Technical Indicators in Daily Stock Price Trends Prediction. Lecture Notes in Computer Science. 1087-1096.

[9] Fung, G., Yu, J., and Lam, W.2002. News sensitive stock trend prediction. Lecture Notes in Computer Science, vol. Volume 233, 481– 493.

[10] Keikha, M., Carman, M. J., and Crestani, F. 2009.Blog distillation using random walks. In *Proceedings of 32nd international ACM SIGIR conference on Research and development in information retrieval. SIGIR'09*. 639-639. DOI= 10.1145/1571941.1572054

[11] Karaman, A.S., Altiok, T. 2004. An experimental study on forecasting using TES processes., In *Proceedings of the 36th conference on Winter simulation, WSC'04*. 437-442.

[12] Wilder, J. W. 1978. New Concepts in Technical Trading Systems. ISBN 0-89459-027-8

[13] Asia Pac, finance portal, Technical Analysis web page, http://www.asiapacfinance.com/trading-strategies/technicalindicators, retrieved, Feb, 2013

[14] Masud, M. M., Al-Khateeb, T. M., Khan, L., Aggarwal, C. C., Gao, J., Han, J., and Thuraisingham, B. M.2011. Detecting recurring and novel classes in concept-drifting data streams. In *Proceedings of the 2011 IEEE 11th International Conference on Data Mining*.(Vancouver, Canada, December 11-14, 2011)IEEE Computer Society Washington, DC, USA , 1176–1181. DOI= http://dx.doi.org/10.1109/ICDM.2011.49

[15] Qureshi, S.A., Mirza, S.M., and Arif, M. 2006. Fitness function evaluation for image reconstruction using binary genetic algorithm for parallel ray transmission tomography, emerging technologies. In *Proceedings of Emerging Technologies, 2006. ICET '06. International Conference on.* (Islamabad, Pakistan, November 13-14,2006). 196–201. DOI= http://dx.doi.org/10.1109/ICET.2006.336012

[16] Mahmoud, S. A. and El-Melegy, M.T. 2004. Evaluation of diversity measures for multiple classifier fusion by majority voting. In *Proceedings of Electrical, Electronic and Computer Engineering, 2004. ICEEC'04. 2004 International Conference on.* (September 5-7, 2004). 169 – 172. DOI= http://dx.doi.org/10.1109/ICEEC.2004.1374412

[17] Yahia, M.E. and Ibrahim, B. A. 2003. K-nearest neighbor and C4.5 algorithms as data mining methods: advantages and difficulties. In Proceedings of Computer Systems and Applications, 2003. Book of Abstracts. ACS/IEEE International Conference on. (Tunis, Tunisia, July 14-18, 2003). DOI= http://dx.doi.org/10.1109/AICCSA.2003.1227535

[18] W. H. Press, S. A. Teukolsky, W. T. Vetterlinga and B. P. Flannery , Numerical recipes: the art of scientific computing, Cambridge University Press, New York, 2007.

[19] S. R. Gunn, Support vector machines for classification and regression, University of Southamtpon, Technical Report, 1998.

[20] K. V. Cartwright, Determining the effective or RMS voltage of various waveforms without calculus, Ph.D. Thesis, School of Sciences and Technology College of the Bahamas, Bahamas, 2007.

Reader's Emotion Prediction Based on Partitioned Latent Dirichlet Allocation Model

Ruifeng Xu, Chengtian Zou, Jun Xu
Key Laboratory of Network Oriented Intelligent Computation,
Shenzhen Graduate School, Harbin Institute of Technology,
Shen Zhen, China

Abstract—*Different from traditional emotion analysis which focuses on the identification of emotions from the text, this research aims to predict the reader's emotion for given text. Regarding reader emotion as the response to the text, emotion prediction may be transferred to a classification problem which classifies the text into the categories causing different emotions. In this study, we propose an emotion prediction approach based on Partitioned Latent Dirichlet Allocation (PLDA) model. Through providing the supervised information to the training process of LDA model, PLDA model associates the words from one certain type of emotion to one certain partition of topics. The outputs of PLDA model are used as the features of a multi-label classifier for predicating the reader's emotion. Evaluations on a large community emotion corpus show that PLDA model achieves much better performance compared to bag of words model and LDA model.*

Keywords: Reader's Emotion Prediction, LDA model

1. Introduction

Recently, with the development of Web 2.0 and social network, the social community emotion analysis becomes more and more attractive. Many websites allow users voting their reactions to the news articles, which makes the study of reader's emotion predication feasible. Up to now, most researches in emotion analysis area focus on the understanding of writer's emotion in the text while few works on reader's emotion. These two types of emotion are not always the same, even in contrary, in some cases. Consequently, the emotion analysis techniques from writer's perspective cannot be applied to reader's emotion prediction directly. The existing works in this area are few and most of which are based on the single-label classification method [1][2][3][4], which classifies the document to only one category within several basic emotion categories. However, the single-label classification approach is conflict to the fact that community readers' reaction always contains more than one dominant emotion types, which is observed from reader emotion voting results among many news website. Obviously, regarding the reader emotion prediction problem as a multi-label classification task is more reasonable.

Many previous works on emotion analysis and predication are majorly based on supervised machine learning approach. Most of them represents a document as a Bag of Words (BOW) and uses words vector as the classification features. The studies mainly focus on choosing appropriate word vectors to represent the content of the document. Document frequency (DF) and chi-square statics (CHI)[5] and so on were adopted as the selecting metrics. However, these purely statistic-based methods usually generate a large dimension word vectors with much noises. Meanwhile, these vectors always cannot reflect the content of the text effectively as each terms is considered as independent. With the development of topic model such as Latent Dirichlet Allocation [6], some research use the topics instead of words to represent a document for predicating the reader's emotion. A better performance is achieved. However, there are still some disadvantages in the researches based on the LDA model. Since LDA employs an unsupervised learning method while the supervised information, i.e. readers' voting information are not used.

In this paper, we propose to apply Partitioned Latent Dirichlet Allocation (PLDA) model to topic modeling, which makes all of the words from one certain type of emotion only associated to one certain partition of topics through introducing the supervised information into the training process of LDA model. Then, we employ the output of PLDA as features to do the multi-label classification for predicting the reader's emotion. Evaluations on a large user-generated community emotion corpus show that the proposed method achieves a better performance compared to BOW model, LDA model and weighted LDA model.

The rest of this paper is organized as follows. Section 2 reviews the related work. Section 3 presents the emotion prediction approach based on PLDA and multi-label classification. Evaluations are given in Section 4. Finally, Section 5 concludes.

2. Related Works

This section reviews some of the related work on reader's emotion prediction. As our major approach is based on the topic model, some of the important works related to this is also introduced. Finally, some method concerns with the multi-label classification is reviewed.

2.1 Reader's Emotion Prediction

With the rapid increase of user labeled emotions on the news website, the study tries to analyze and predicate the reader's emotion of the news article becoming available. With the help of corpus from Yahoo! Kimo News, Lin et al.[7] used five different strategies to select features for predicting readers emotions. The employed features include bigram, Chinese words, news meta data and so on. Later, they employed PLM (Pairwise Loss Minimization) and EDR (Emotional Distribution Regression) algorithms to rank the reader emotions. Ye et al.[5] took document frequency(DF), chi-square statistic(CHI) and some other criteria such as POS tags as features and applies Multi-Label K-nearest Neighbor(MLKNN)[8] and RAkEL [9] algorithm to make the emotion prediction, respectively. The results show that RAkEL com-bined with the intersection of chi-square statis-tics and document frequency achieve better results.

2.2 Topic Modeling

There are many approaches for modeling docu-ments topic. Among them the Latent Dirichlet Allocation(LDA) model has been applied to many areas such as information retrieval and text category for its flexibilities and complete-ness. As the traditional LDA model employs unsupervised machine-learning method, many studies try to adding the supervised information into the training process of LDA model, or some other improvement. Ramage et al.[10] pro-posed a Labeled LDA which could be consider as extension of both LDA and Multinomial Naive Bayes. They associate each user tag with topics generate from the model, and use this model to label individual words as well as providing interpretable snippets for document summarization. Zhu et al.[11] proposed a maximum entropy discrimination LDA topic model(MedLDA) which utilizes the max-margin prin-ciple in the training process as a supervised topic models. Wilson et al.[12] 2010 proves that of each term in the LDA model should be weighted and give a scheme for this.

2.3 Incorporate Topic Model to Emotion Prediction

Recently, many studies of emotion prediction are based on the topic of text. Normally, they got a better performance. Lin et al.[13] proposed an unsupervised joint sentiment/topic model (JST) based on LDA which may deal with both sentiment and topic at the same time. Bao et al. [14][15] proposed a joint emotion-topic model to predict reader's emotion. The main idea of their model is to add another emotion layer into traditional LDA model which appends emotion generation step for the generation process of the model. However, all these models output only one emotion prediction. Xu et al.[16] gave every term different weights of topics to expand the LDA model. They used the Multi-Label k-Nearest Neighbour (MLkNN) to do the emotion predication. The achieved performance is higher than BOW model and LDA model.

3. Reader Emotion Prediction Based on PLDA

3.1 Partitioned Latent Dirichlet Allocation Model

LDA model is proposed by Blei et al.[6] It may be considered as a three-level hierarchical Bayesian model.After Griffiths et al.[17] brought a Dirichlet prior distribution on parameter, LDA changes into a complete generative model. For generating a word of a document, LDA firstly choose a topic from the polynomial distribution of the document and then choose a word from the polynomial distribution of the topic. The generating process is shown in fig1.

A document is treated as a mixture of topics instead a bag

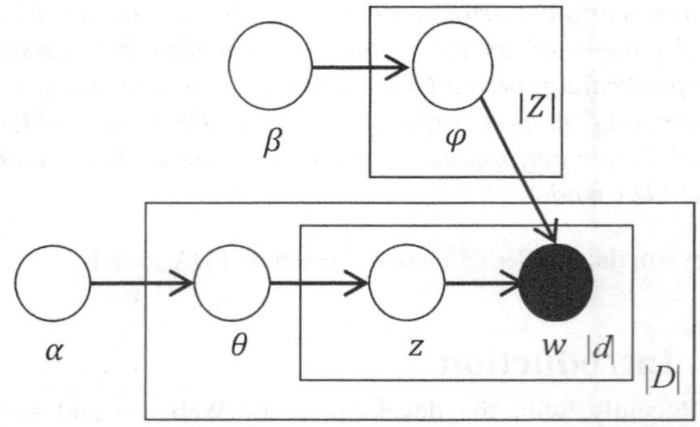

Fig. 1: Framework of Latent Dirichlet Allocation topic model

of words, while a topic is treated as a mixture of words. It is reasonable to treat a document in this way because reader's emotions are usually connected with certain types of topics or events.

The two important parameters which shows the topics distribution of each document and words distribution of each topic could be estimated by many algorithms. Since the Gibbs sampling is shown simple and computationally efficient in the previous studies, it is adopted in this study. The detailed procedures of Gibbs sampling for our method is presented in Xu et al. [16].

During the parameter estimation process, terms from document are assigned to any topic without considering the category information of documents. The two parameters θ and β are then updated. The analysis on the topic distribution of a document shows that each topic takes a certain proportion. However, a better topic model should have a large disparity between topics, and document should shows obvious disparity on every topics. More specifically, in the emotion prediction task, documents belong to one certain type of emotion should have a larger proportion on the topics which could be connected with that type of emotion. For this purpose, in our study, an improved model is proposed which takes the labeled emotion category of each document into account. In this way, the traditional unsupervised LDA model is transferred to a supervised one. The generate process of this model is shown in Fig 2. Where c_j means the j_{th} type of emotion, |K| is the

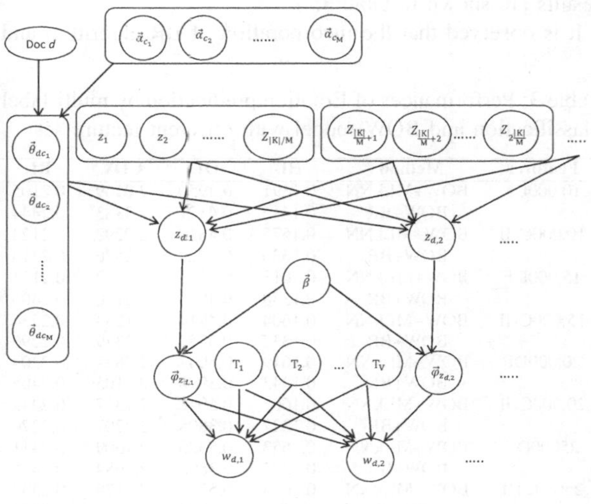

Fig. 2: Framework of Latent Dirichlet Allocation topic model

total count of topics, M is the total number of emotions categories. The only step different from the traditional LDA model is that when generating a word of one document, a certain category of emotions should be chosen first, then the topic chosen could only be from this emotion category. It can be observed that the topics Z are partitioned by the category of emotions.

When deal with the input training documents with reader's emotion label, during each iteration of the parameter estimating process, each word of document is assigned to the topics which is connected to the certain type of emotion of this document. For example, suppose there are 80 topics and 8 emotion category in total. Thus, each emotion category is associated with 10 topics. The "touched" emotion is connected with topic 0-9, "sympathy" emotion is connected with topic 10-19, and so on. During the training process, all the words from "touched" document are distributed in topic 0-9 and the "sympathy" ones are distributed in topic 10-19, the probability for any other topics are 0. Thus, the documents with the same emotion label are distributed in the same topics while the documents with different emotion label can't affect each other. This makes the model just like constructed by 8 independent small partitions.

In the prediction period, after input the document without emotion label, the model will output the topic distribution of document and word distribution of topic, the first one of which could be used to make the multi-label classification on reader's emotion.

3.2 Multi-label Classification

As the distribution of one document on every topic has already been calculated by the model and the connection between topics and emotion types is known, the probability of the document belongs to one specific type of emotion could be calculated, as shown in equation 1:

$$P(d_i \in c_j) = \sum_{k=(j-1)*(|K|/M)}^{(j+1)*(|K|/M)-1} \theta_{ik} \qquad (1)$$

where d_i is the input document, c_j means the j_{th} type of emotion, $|K|$ is the total count of topics, M is the total type count of emotions, θ_{ik} means the probability of document i belonging to topic k. For each group of $|K|/M$ topics which could be associated with one single emotion, the corresponding probabilities may be computed. Thus, M values which shows the probabilities of the document belongs to each type of emotions are obtained. Then, the M values are normalized. The one or several of them if bigger than 0.3, an empirical threshold, the emotion labels which they belong to will be set as the document's emotion predication labels.

4. Experiments and Discussions

4.1 Dataset and Evaluation Metrics

A community-based reader votes corpus is used to evaluate the proposed method. The news articles and corresponding reader's emotion votes are collected form sina.com. We adopted eight types of emotion in total with the labels Touched, Empathy, Boredom, Anger, Amusement, Sadness, Surprise and Warmness. The votes of articles which are lower than empirical threshold are filtered out. Finally, 8,802 articles with 1,454,912 emotional votes are obtained in total. There are about 165 votes for each article on the average. The detailed statistics for each emotion category is shown in table 1.

We determined the majority emotion categories based on the statistics of original votes, in which there are 5,745 articles with one emotion labels, 2,770 ones with two emotion labels and 287 ones with three labels. This means that there are totally about 35 percent of articles with more than one label, which shows that the multi-label classification is important. Table 2 shows the number of aricles for each combination of emotion types. More information about this dataset are presented in[5].

Table 1: Number of news articles with different number of labels

Emotions	News Articles	Votes
Touched	1352	154357
Empathy	414	105089
Boredom	481	116065
Anger	2919	555609
Amusement	2000	245919
Sadness	835	142253
Surprise	715	91662
Warmness	86	43958

Table 2: Number of news articles with different number of labels

Labels	Labels combination	News Articles
	Anger	2375
1	Touched	1189
	Amusement	1032
	Surprise	440
	Anger Amusement	560
2	Empathy Sadness	394
	Boredom Amusement	374
	Anger Sadness	271
	Boredom Anger Amusement	65
3	Empathy Anger Sadness	47
	Touched Empathy Sadness	26
	Boredom Amusement Surprise	65

In this study, the commonly used metrics for single-label classification are replaced by those for multi-label classification due to the inherent differences of the classification problem.

- **Hamming Loss (HL):** it measures the inconsistency between the predicted sets of labels and the actual over the examples.
- **Hamming Loss (HL):** it measures the inconsistency between the predicted sets of labels and the actual over the examples.
- **One-error (OE):** it evaluates how many times the top-ranked label is not in the set of relevant labels of the instance, and it could evolve into general classification error rate in the single-label classification.
- **Coverage (COV):** it measures in the ranked list, from the category of the top-ranked to start, how many labels are needed to cover all the relevant labels of the example.
- **Ranking Loss (RL):** it shows the probability that the irrelevant labels are ranked higher than the relevant.
- **Average Precision (AVP):** it reflects the average precision of the predicted labels.

We take 75 percent of articles with their votes as training and the others as test set in the experiments.

4.2 Baseline Systems

In the experiment, we adopted two groups of baselines. The multi-label classification algorithms, namely MLkNN and BR are combined with BOW model and regular LDA model, as one group of baselines. Another one is the MLkNN combined with regular LDA model and Weighted LDA(WLDA) which is presented in [16].

4.3 Experiment Results and Discussions

Firstly, the performance of emotion prediction based on multi-label classification algorithms and BOW model are evaluated. The classification features set differs in the dimensions of words chosen by DF or CHI criteria. The results are shown in table 3.

It is observed that the incorporation of BR algorithm and BOW model with the 25000 features selected by CHI-test achieves better results. The average precision is 0.7009. Meanwhile, it is shown that more features are helpful.

In the second experiment, LDA and WLDA model

Table 3: Performances of Emotion predication by multi-label classification and BOW model with different feature set

Features	Methods	HL	OE	COV	RL	AVP
10,000DF	BOW+MLkNN	0.1591	0.4950	2.0169	0.2105	0.6606
	BOW+BR	0.1415	0.4121	2.3383	0.2444	0.6726
10,000CHI	BOW+MLkNN	0.1575	0.4818	2.0292	0.2124	0.6691
	BOW+BR	0.1330	0.3820	2.2576	0.2313	0.6913
15,000DF	BOW+MLkNN	0.1613	0.5032	2.0602	0.2171	0.6562
	BOW+BR	0.1358	0.4008	2.3100	0.2406	0.6785
15,000CHI	BOW+MLkNN	0.1604	0.4914	2.1234	0.2234	0.6576
	BOW+BR	0.1332	0.3785	2.2379	0.2296	0.6933
20,000DF	BOW+MLkNN	0.1619	0.5042	2.0827	0.2204	0.6534
	BOW+BR	0.1343	0.3970	2.3105	0.2405	0.6803
20,000CHI	BOW+MLkNN	0.1604	0.5018	2.1317	0.2242	0.6522
	BOW+BR	0.1327	0.3808	2.2207	0.2270	0.6940
25000DF	BOW+MLkNN	0.1653	0.5320	2.1609	0.2311	0.6351
	BOW+BR	0.1323	0.3893	2.3084	0.2405	0.6840
25000CHI	BOW+MLkNN	0.1674	0.5023	2.1179	0.2237	0.6519
	BOW+BR	0.1290	0.3675	2.2027	0.2247	0.7009

Table 4: Performances of Emotion predication by LDA and WLDA with different feature set

Topic	Methods	HL	OE	COV	RL	AVP
20	LDA+MLkNN	0.1395	0.3956	1.5807	0.1539	0.7354
	WLDA+MLkNN	0.1349	0.3690	1.5220	0.1451	0.7529
30	LDA+MLkNN	0.1395	0.3912	1.5728	0.1525	0.7368
	WLDA+MLkNN	0.1323	0.3565	1.5098	0.1436	0.7576
40	LDA+MLkNN	0.1381	0.3970	1.5958	0.1555	0.7337
	WLDA+MLkNN	0.1331	0.3592	1.5192	0.1449	0.7560
50	LDA+MLkNN	0.1387	0.3917	1.5944	0.1557	0.7360
	WLDA+MLkNN	0.1355	0.3686	1.5328	0.1471	0.7515
60	LDA+MLkNN	0.1389	0.3887	1.5954	0.1549	0.7371
	WLDA+MLkNN	0.1356	0.3696	1.5378	0.1472	0.7503
70	LDA+MLkNN	0.1383	0.3884	1.5825	0.1542	0.7368
	WLDA+MLkNN	0.1343	0.3680	1.5575	0.1496	0.7493
80	LDA+MLkNN	0.1394	0.3912	1.5983	0.1551	0.7350
	WLDA+MLkNN	0.1352	0.3721	1.5608	0.1507	0.7474

Table 5: Performance of PLDA model on multi-label predicting.

Topic	HL	OE	COV	RL	AVP
40	0.1214	0.2079	1.6398	0.1899	0.8431
48	0.1127	0.1867	1.6346	0.1863	0.8531
56	0.1106	0.1768	1.5955	0.1849	0.8626
64	0.1132	0.1683	1.6082	0.1825	0.8651
72	0.1094	0.1561	1.5738	0.1791	0.8755
80	0.1066	0.1485	1.5879	0.1777	0.8779
88	0.1036	0.1513	1.5540	0.1750	0.8797
96	0.1043	0.1513	1.5809	0.1774	0.8779
104	0.1057	0.1476	1.5747	0.1735	0.8806
112	0.1005	0.1513	1.5969	0.1733	0.8774
120	0.0997	0.1320	1.5912	0.1688	0.8909
128	0.1022	0.1348	1.6365	0.1713	0.8866
136	0.0997	0.1344	1.6153	0.1698	0.8876
144	0.1005	0.1268	1.6568	0.1658	0.8916
152	0.1002	0.1419	1.6677	0.1673	0.8852
200	0.1004	0.1438	1.7431	0.1639	0.8848
240	0.0987	0.1315	1.8831	0.1582	0.8897

are incorporated with MLkNN classification algorithm, respectively. The Document-topic distributions with different number of topics generated from the model are used as feature vectors. The achieved performances are shown in table 4.

In this experiment, MLkNN with topic models achieve better performance compared with BOW model. WLDA combined with MLkNN under the situation of 30 topics achieved the best performance. These results shows the advantage of topic model over BOW model. This also shows that WLDA model performs better than regular LDA model in readers emotion predication.

In the third experiment, the PLDA model with multi-label classification is adopted. Table 5 gives the performances. The experiment begin with 40 topics, and add 8 topics each time. When topic number is less than 100, the performance keeps on increasing with the topic number. As the topic number is more than 100, the performance stabilized at about AVP 88 percent. It is observed that the performance with PLDA is much better than the base line systems on any metrics.

5. Conclusion

In this paper, we propose a new topic model for reader's emotion prediction problem by incorporating the supervised information into the regular LDA model and change it into a supervised machine-learning model. The evaluations on the dataset of a large-scale community reader emotion votes show that PLDA achieves a rather encouraged result.

Acknowledgement

This research is supported by MOE Specialized Research Fund for the Doctoral Program of Higher Education20122302120070, Shenzhen Foundational Research Funding JCYJ20120613152557576, and Shenzhen Interna-tional Cooperation Research Funding GJHZ20120613110641217.

References

[1] Z. Kozareva, B. Navarro, S. Vazquez, and A. Montoyo. UA-ZBSA: a headline emotion classification through web information. In Proceedings of the 4th International Workshop on Semantic Evaluations (SemEval-2007), pages 334-337, 2007.

[2] F. R. Chaumartin. UPAR7: a knowledge-based system for headline sentiment tagging. In Proceedings of the 4th International Workshop on Semantic Evaluations (SemEval-2007), pages 422-425, 2007.

[3] P. Katz, M. Singleton, and R. Wicentowski. SWAT-MP: the semeval-2007 systems for task 5 and task 14. In Proceedings of the 4th International Workshop on Semantic Evaluations (SemEval-2007), pages 308-313, 2007.

[4] K. H. Y. Lin, C. Yang, and H. H. Chen. Emotion classification of online news articles from the reader's perspective. In Proceedings of Web Intelligence, pages 220-226, 2008.

[5] L. Ye, R. F. Xu, and J. Xu. Emotion prediction of news articles from reader's perspective based on multi-label classification. In Proceedings of IWWIP 2012.

[6] D. M. Blei, A. Y. Ng, and M. I. Jordan. Latent dirichlet allocation. The Journal of Machine Learning Research, 3: 993-1022, 2003.

[7] K. H. Y. Lin, and H. H. Chen. Ranking reader emotions using pairwise loss minimization and emotional distribution regression. In Proceedings of the 2008 Conference on Empirical Methods in Natural Language Processing, pages 136-144, 2008.

[8] M. L. Zhang, and Z. H. Zhou. A k-nearest neighbor based algorithm for multi-label classification. In Proceedings of the 1st IEEE International Conference on Granular Computing (GrC 2005), pages 718-721, 2005.

[9] P. K. Bhowmick, A. Basu, and P. Mitra. Reader perspective emotion analysis in text through ensemble based multi-Label classification framework. Computer and Information Science, 2(4):64-74, 2009.

[10] D. Ramage, D. Hall, R. Nallapati and C. D. Manning. Labeled LDA: a supervised topic model for credit attribution in multi-labeled corpora. In Proceedings of the 2009 conference on Empirical Methods in Natural Language Processing, pages 248-256, 2009.

[11] J. Zhu, A. Ahmed, et al. MedLDA: maximum margin supervised topic models for regression and classification. ACM, 2009.

[12] A. T. Wilson and P. A. Chew. Term weighting schemes for Lantent Dirichlet Allocation. The 2010 Annual Conference of the North American Chapter of the ACL, pages 465-473, 2010.

[13] C, Lin and Y. He. Joint sentiment/topic model for sentiment analysis. ACM, 2009.

[14] S. Bao, S. Xu, et al. Joint emotion-topic modeling for social affective text mining. In Proceedings of the 2009 Ninth IEEE International Conference on Data Mining, IEEE Computer Society, pages 699-704, 2009.

[15] S. Bao, S. Xu, et al. Mining social emotions from affective text. IEEE Transactions on Knowledge and Data Engineering, 2011.

[16] Ruifeng Xu, Lu Ye, Jun Xu. Reader's Emotion Prediction Based on Weighted Latent Dirichlet Allocation and Multi-Label k-Nearest Neighbor Model. Journal of Computational Information Systems 9: 1 (2013) 1–8

[17] T. L. Griffiths, and M. Steyvers. Finding scientific topics. In Proceedings of the National Academy of Sciences, 101(suppl. 1): 5228-5235, 2004.

The Effect of Social Media on Student's Engagement and Collaboration: *a case study of University of Venda using Facebook*

Munienge Mbodila[1], Bassey Isong[2] and Kikunga Muhandji[2]
[1]Science Foundation Unit - Computer Science Unit, University of Venda, Thohoyandou, South Africa.
[2]Department of Computer Science, University of Venda, Thohoyandou, South Africa

Abstract *- In today's e-society, the role of the social media is increasingly gaining momentum. It is known to play a vital role in collaboration, community building, participation, and sharing of information. As digital applications, several social media exist and vary in their purposes. In particular, the educational section is one giant beneficiary of this development involving impact creation on students and instructors. However, despite the widespread use of social media by students and instructors, very little empirical evidence exist regarding its impact on student's collaboration and engagement. In this study, a case study was performed in University of Venda where students offering the module Foundation Information Technology (FIT) were used as participant. Facebook social network was the platform for various academic activities and questionnaires were designed and used in collecting data from the students. The goal of our study is to investigate the impact of the social media on students, specifically, the level of collaboration between them while using facebook during in and out of classroom. The results obtained showed that facebook uses has a significantly increased impact on student's collaboration and engagement than face to face contact. Our analysis indicated that students, tutors, and instructor were highly engaged in the learning process in ways that transcended traditional classroom activities. This study provides experimental evidence that social media can be used as an educational tool to help students to collaborate and engage.*

Keywords: Social media, Facebook, student, collaboration, engagement, FIT

1 Introduction

In today's e-society, the role of the social media is increasingly gaining momentum. Social media can be defined as a group of Internet-based applications built on the ideological and technology of Web 2.0 which allow the creation and exchange of user generated content [1]. It is known to play essential role in collaboration, community building, participation, and sharing. One vital aspect of social media is that it uses mobile and web-based technologies to create highly interactive platforms through which individuals and communities share, discuss, and modify user-generated content [2]. This technology exist in different forms such as internet forums, web-logs, social-blogs, micro blogging, wikis, podcasts, rating, social bookmarking and social networks [3]. Examples of existing social networks which are popular and gained widespread use are Facebook, Skype, MySpace. Social media has found huge application in many areas in which the educational sector is one of the beneficiaries.

The Foundation Information Technology (FIT) or simply FIT1540 is a module offered at Science Foundation Unit of University of Venda, South Africa (SA). The foundation programmes was designed for students whose do not meet the requirements for direct entry into an undergraduate degree programme. In other words, it is a pre-degree program that runs for a year, designed to provide students with potential who have not met the normal admission criteria with knowledge and skills to succeed in science or science related degrees and bridge the gap between their highest education qualification and the academic qualifications accepted. The FIT module is aimed at developing interest and familiarity with modern computer technologies as well as encouraging their productive use. The module has no prerequisites and was designed specifically for students with little or no prior computing background to provide them with computer skills, understanding and gaining confidence to use the hardware and software critical for their education or professional development. However, the main challenge faced by the programme is high demand for admission access which in turn, give rise to exponential growth of student's number in many courses and subjects offered and FIT is not an exception. This however poses a serious teaching challenge involving large number of students in a small class. Consequently, we found it difficult getting students to collaborate and engage inside or outside the classroom since the University has no e-learning platform. In addition, this situation goes a long way affecting the performances of the students.

In other get rid of this impending challenge, we introduced an online blog using facebook as a platform for various academic discussions, posting of all information about the course including tutorial, test-memos, feedback and communiqués about the course between the students, tutors and their instructor. To access the impact of the platform on the students in terms of collaboration and engagement to see if it has positive or nagative effects on the students as against face to face contact, a sample was drawn and questionnaire was designed and used in collecting data from the students. The results obtained showed that the use of facebook in the module has significantly increased impact on student's collaboration and engagement than face to face contact. Our analysis indicated that students, tutors, and instructor were highly engaged in the learning process in ways that transcended traditional classroom activities. The experimental evidence shows that that social media can be used as an educational tool to help students to collaborate and engage. Therefore, the objective of this study is to investigate the impact of the social media on students, specifically, the level of collaboration between them while using facebook in the module during in and out of classroom.

The paper is organized as follows; section 1 is the introduction, section 2 provides information on students engagement and collaborations, section 3 gives the challenges faced by the FIT1540 class, section 4 explain the solution approach, while sections 5 and 6 gives the research goal and methodology respectively. Section 7 presents the research results and discussions while section is the paper conclusion.

2 Student Engagement and Collaborations

Student engagement is of the buzzword identified in the educational sector in 1996 and is considered a major topic in higher education [11]. The phrase is frequently used to denote the readiness, need, desire and compulsion of students to actively participate in everyday school activities involving things like attending classes, adherence to instructor's directives in the class, and submitted required course works or assignments [10,11]. It is aimed at achieving success in the learning process as well as promoting high-level thinking for lasting comprehension. The term at large is used to describe significant student participation throughout their learning environments as well as in extra- curricular activities in the campus life that binds a school, college or university which are beneficial to their curricular studies.

Student engagement is usefully a term considered to be ambiguous since it includes both psychological and behavioral component. In one way, it be can view as the way students behaves and in other way, it can viewed as a psychological investment in learning in order to understand their studies material and incorporate them in to their lives. Many researches have been carried out on student engagement in the literature and analysis showed it is critical to the quality of the system. For instance, one study suggested that student engagement could be used as teaching quality indicator of an institution. Other have defined it in terms of effort, motivation, time-on-task with a suggestion that there is a casual relationship between the engaged times and academic achievement [7]. For student engagement to be established and sustained, it requires that instructors or teachers actively seek to create the conditions that foster this reaction.

Accordingly, for the past decades till date, collaboration has played a critical role in the success of teams, organizations, to mention but a few. In the education circles, educators have recognized the value of collaborative learning. They widely recognize that students do not learn well when they are isolated and collaboration has to be fostered. Indeed, students must overcome isolation in order to collaborate in their learning such as peer review workshops, collaborative research assignments, group presentations, collaborative papers, discussion groups, and so on for active learning to exist. With this act, students are opportune to become more deeply engaged with learning, and with one another [4]. In general, collaboration between students leads to a better understanding of the learning activities which is evidenced in many existing empirical studies. Collaboration can be achieved in many ways. Social network services (SNS) such as Facebook, Skype, Twitter, MySpace, etc. are among such ways. These platforms can be used to host events, debates, reviews, aggregate resources, support courses and reading circles as well as providing space for discussing ideas for learning.

Our intuition is that when students are allowed to actively engage and collaborate, it will make whole lots of difference in achieving their academic successes. Based on the challenges faced by our science foundation programme which drastically affects the level of student engagement and collaborations, our goal here is to evaluate the use of Facebook that tries to bridge the gap created. We aim to evaluate the daily activities inside and outside the classroom to see the level of engagement and collaboration between student's communities, tutors and their lecturers in the teaching and learning process in FIT 1540 module.

3 Challenges Faced by FIT Class

In our foundation programme, the main drive in the use of Facebook blog is the large-enrolment atmosphere that resulted to having large classes in small rooms. One immediate consequence of this large class is that students often become disengaged or cut-off from the class. In addition, interaction between students and the lecturer is difficult to achieve. This impending challenge emanates from the fact that in large classes, though some students may show good peer group adjustment and social interaction ability with the lecturer, but they may display communication anxiety when asked to answer questions, presentation, or engage in an activity that can be evaluated. Individual response to lecturer impromptu questions is limited and sometimes the students feel intimidated. Another important issue is the collaboration between students when carried out their course work. As we know, collaboration plays a vital role of helping students to understand learning as a process, learn from one another and increase their sense of mastery of what is often a complex and difficult task. Like we know, the best way to learn something is to teach it. Also with the large class, the issues of passing information from time to time for some changes such as assignment submission date, time table change, cancellation of lecture or test dates, corrections of marks, etc. to all students at the same time poses also poses a big challenge. Due to the above mentioned challenges, we decided to use Facebook to deal with these challenges through a device the student used the most in class or outside the classroom which is the mobile cell phones.

4 Our Solution Approach

SNSs such as Facebook, Twitter, and MySpace are the typical application of Web 2.0 technology which has gained huge popularity and widespread use among multiple age groups in same or different educational institutions, places, and countries over the past few years. In the educational perspective, students and employees differ in their level of education, access to resources and age group. However, what is common among the two is actually their level of connection and use with the social networks integrated in their phones. In the same vein, teachers and students are not left out. Social networks offer them the opportunities to cultivate the student teacher relationship, which can ultimately create a positive learning experience for both parties [3]. For changes to happen, it will take time for both students and the teacher to develop new skills.

Therefore, our approach is to use the facebook blog as a means of engaging and collaborating between students and instructors in order to develop new skills and rid the existing challenges. Mobile phones are used to access the Facebook by students in order to enable them directly collaborate, engaged by exchange questions with their lecturer and getting feedback posting on the wall. Furthermore, it will enable them to browses our blog for additional information, and instructions for test and practical.

5 Research Goal

Evaluation plays a significant role in accessing or measuring the effectiveness of processes and products. It has found huge application in all existing disciplines such software engineering, social sciences, engineering, etc. The basis of evaluation is to support effective decision making process. We have introduced the use of facebook in our science foundation FIT 1540 module. and has been used by the students and the instructor for quite some times but we do not know if is creating the expected impacts on the student lives. In order to make decisions on either to improve it use or discontinue it use, evaluation has to be performed. Therefore, our goal in this study is the measure the level of engagement and collaborations between students, tutors, and instructor in and out of the classroom while using facebook.

6 Research Methodology

In this section, we shall present the methodology used in performing our study.

6.1 Participants

The target participants of this include all the students offering the FIT 1540 module of the foundation programme at the school of mathematical and natural sciences, University of Venda. The statistics of the participants are 70% female and 30% male. With these percentages, majority of the students were known to come from different places around the Limpopo province while 65% of them are in full foundation programme and 35% enrichment programme. See Table 1.

Table1: Distribution of Participants (Male and female)

Gender	G1	G2	G3	G4	G5	Total
Male	16	16	3	10	15	60

6.2 Data collection

As stated above, we designed an evaluation questionnaire which we used in collecting data from the students. The setup of questionnaire was based on a diversified method of finding out the time spend on Facebook inside and outside the classroom, the level of collaboration between students in using Facebook in the FIT 1540/1640 modules during the 2012 academic year. In more details, the questions consisted of information about the participants place of residence (i.e. in campus or out of campus), their access to the internet, the type of devices used (Computer or cellphone), their attitudes towards the use of their device to access internet, and finally the use of Facebook in their day-to-day lives and its impact in the module FIT 1540/1640. Some of these questions were to find the needed information and others to elicit suggestion and comments from the students.

The data were collected and analysed by the instructor responsible. A sample of 150 students from both foundation and enrichment offering FIT1540/1640 modules was drawn up from student's population and used for the study. The genders of students who participate were 90 females and 60 males as shown in the table1 above.

7 Research Results and Discussions

In this section, we present the results obtained from the study which is based on the data collected as discussed above. Results were analyzed and presented in various sections below such as information about participants, program in which they are registered (full foundation or enrichment), the age's group of participants, type of mobile phones that they are using (normal phone, smart phone or PDA), whether they have a Facebook account and lastly between mobile phone and Computer which device they mostly prefers to use. From answers collected, the students appeared to be very confident especially for most questions regarding the usage of Facebook in their day-to-day life, either inside or outside the classroom.

7.1.1 Participant age group

Today's young people are called "Digital Native" generation since they can get use to these new technologies Web 2.0, mobile phone technologies, social networks etc in a short time. In this question, we were interested in knowing the age group of these students. As shown from the chart diagram in Fig. 1, majority of the participants were between 15-19 years old of age.

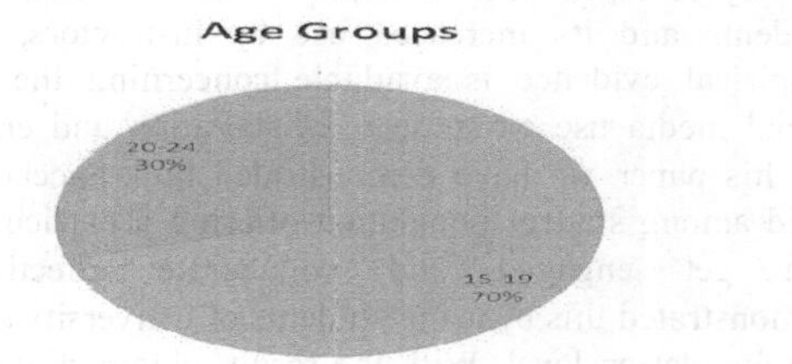

Figure 1: Age group

7.1.2 Do you have a mobile phone?

Two scales were included in the questionnaire which requires knowing the type or model of devices they owned. For instance, we asked about a mobile phone and which type of mobile phone (e.g. smart phone or normal phone). The chart below demonstrates the result obtained. It shows that 99% of the classroom had a mobile phone and 71% of those devices are smart phone with the capabilities of accessing the internet, send instant message, receive radio or TV programmes, and other applications. This signifies that most of students had a small computer in their pockets, purses and backpacks not only as their primary means of communication but also as a mean of studying and learning.

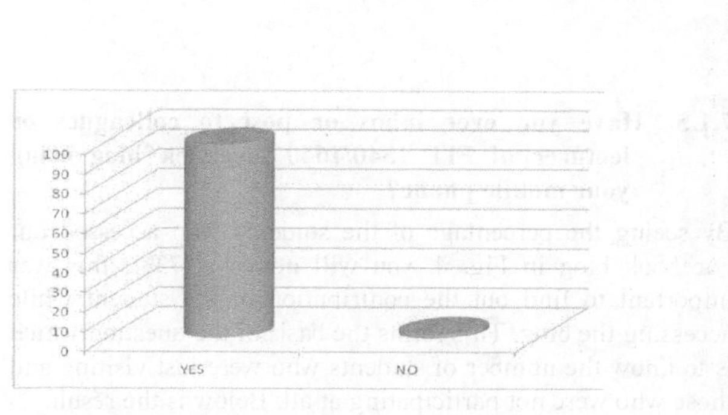

Figure 2: mobile phone owners

7.1.3 Do you have a facebook account?

With our study platform, it was imperative to find out the average number of participants that had Facebook account and applications on their mobile phone. As represented in Fig. 3, the data shows that 90% of the participants have Facebook account and 20% do not have and don't use Facebook for personal reasons.

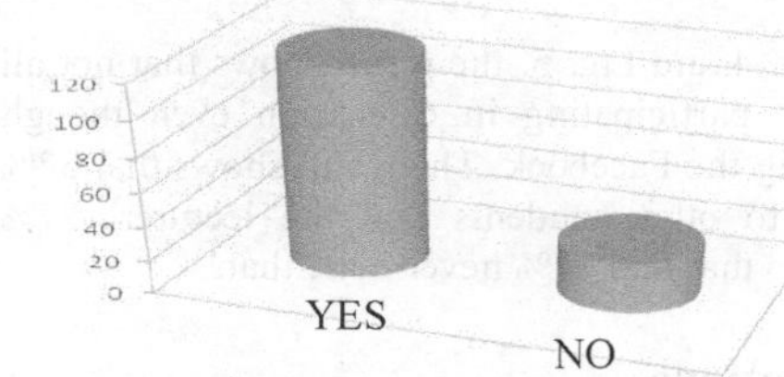

Figure 3: People having Facebook account

7.1.4 How often do you use your mobile phone for FIT 1540/1640 Facebook blog?

This question was directed at finding out how often students use their mobiles to access Facebook for class-related matters. The diagram below illustrates the results obtained from the participants.

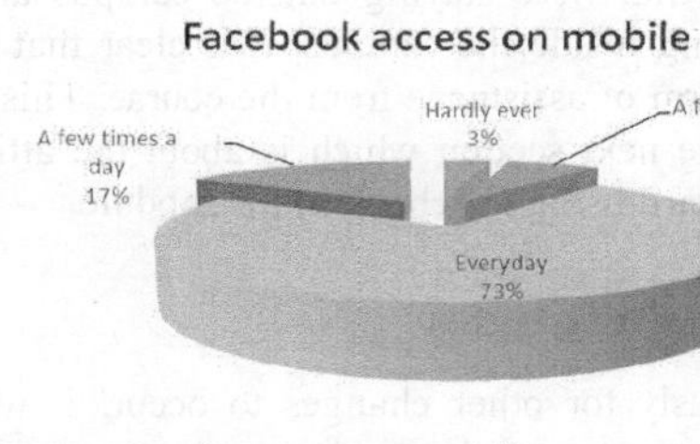

Figure 4: Facebook access on mobile

As shown in Fig. 4, about 73% of the students who offered FIT 1540/1640 used their mobile phone every day to see the update in our blog as opposed to 17% who used it a few times a day and the rest is 7% a few times a week or hardly ever represent by 3%.

7.1.5 Have you ever inbox or post to colleagues or lecturer of FIT 1540/1640 facebook blog using your mobile phone?

By seeing the percentage of the students who accessed our Facebook blog in Fig. 4, you will notice is 73%, this was important to find out the contribution of the student while accessing the blog. This forms the basis of the question which is to know the number of students who were just visiting and those who were not participating at all. Below is the result.

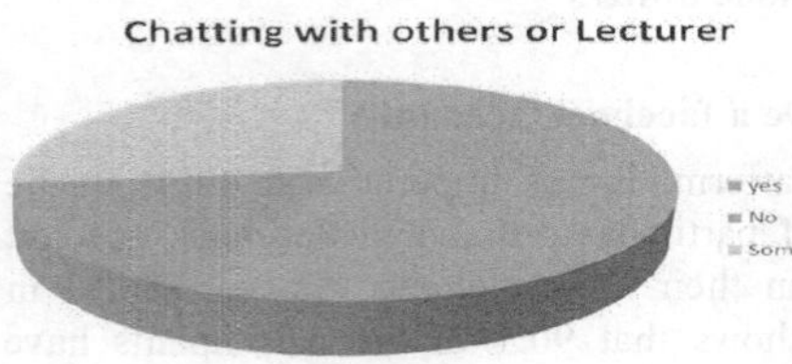

Figure 5: Chatting with others or Lecturer

By comparing Fig. 4 and Fig. 5, the result shows that not all the students were participating in discussion even though they were accessing the Facebook. The result shows that 57% manage to chat to other students and the lecturer, 27% sometime use to do that and 17% never done that.

7.2 Other findings

Participants were asked to indicate whether they stay in or off campus to see the impact of this study in assisting students with information about the module and feedback for their tests, practical and assignments. Since you know student who stay inside the campus may have more advantages in term of getting information on time and the ability to see the lecturer during the class and after the class than those who stay outside the campus. The finding here show that 62% of the foundation students were staying outside campus and only 38% were staying inside the campus, it is clear that student did benefit in term of assistance from the course. This will be confirmed in the next section which is about the attitude of the students toward using Facebook in the module.

7.3 Students' attitudes

As said previously for other changes to occur, it will take time for both students and the teacher to develop new skills. By using this technology the students were asked to specify their scale of agreements or disagreements to measure their attitudes and perceptive vis-à-vis the use of Facebook integration using mobile phone in learning for this module and in general.

The result is presented in Table 2 in the appendix and it displays the attitude of the participants toward the use of their mobile in learning. This result is basically what students have experienced by using this technology during FIT module. With the result, 70% agreed that the mobile phone help them to get the needed information in our Facebook blog, 7% disagreed. Accordingly, 80% of participant agreed that the use of mobile help them to interact and get feedback from the lecturer as against 10% who disagreed with them. One interesting fact is that 85% of the participants used their mobile phone to access the class Facebook blog which was helpful and 2% disagreed in that fact. It is also shown that 82% of participants found it easier to communicate with the lecturer and other students as against 13% who disagreed.

Furthermore, a large number of about 83% of the participants believed that the technology helped them to engage and be informed about the module in and outside the classroom and 3% disagreed in that fact. Finally, 80% participants believe that the technology must be used in the entire foundation and enrichment programme while 4% disagreed. By comparing the data in Table 2 and Fig. 5, you will notice that 87% of the class participants were actually engaged.

8 Conclusions

The use of social network has dominated our life in the 21st century. Despite the widespread use of social media by students and its increased use by instructors, very little empirical evidence is available concerning the impact of social media use on student collaboration and engagement. In this paper we have demonstrated how Facebook can be used among student population offering a particular module can get engaged and collaborate effectively. We demonstrated this by using students of University of Venda at the foundation level. With the result obtained, it shows that majority of the students had mobile phone to access the Facebook which helped them to engaged and collaborated with peers, tutors, and lecturer. We therefore conclude that, social media could be an effective tool for students to engage and collaborate as well as succeed in their academic activities. At this point, we recommend that further research have to be carried out to validate this claim.

9 References

[1] Kaplan Andreas M., Haenlein M (2010) Users of the world, united! The challenges and opportunities of Social Media, Businnes Horizons, 53(1).

[2] H. Kietzmann, Jan; Kristopher Hermkens (2011). "Social media? Get serious! Understanding the functional building blocks of social media". Business Horizons 54: 241–251)

[3] Mazer, J.P., Murphy, R.E., and Simonds, C.J. (2007) 'I'll See You On "Facebook": The Effects of Computer Mediated Teacher Self-Disclosure on Student Motivation, Affective Learning, and Classroom Climate'

[4]http://www.dartmouth.edu/~writing/materials/faculty/methods/collaborative.html

[5] Barber M, Njus D (2007) Clicker evolution: seeking intelligent design. Cell Biol Educ—Life Sci Educ 6:1–8

[6] Buckingham, D. (2007), Beyond Technology: Children's Learning in the Age of Digital Culture, Malden: Blackwell Publishing.

[7] Bulger, M.E., Mayer, R.E. Almeroth, K.C & Blau, S.D (2008), Measuring Learner Engagement in Computer Equipped College Classrooms. 17(2), 129-143

[8] Caldwell JE (2007) Clickers in the large classroom: current research and best-practice tips. Cell BiolEduc—Life Sci Educ 6:9–20

[9] Carbone E, Greenberg J (1998) Teaching large classes: unpacking the problem and responding creatively. In: Kaplan M (ed) To improve the academy 17. New Forums Press and The Professional and Organizational Development Network in Higher Education, Stillwater, OK, pp 311–326

[10] Coates, H(2006). Student Engagement in campus-based and online Education. Retrieve Oct 10, 2012 from http://www.cqu.eblis.com.ezproxy.cqu.edu.au/EBLWeb/patron/

[11] Kenny, G. Kenny, D. and Dumont, R. (1995) Mission and Place: Strengthening Learning and Community Through Campus Design. Oryx/Greenwood. p. 37

Appendix

Table 2: Student's Attitudes

	Strongly Agree	Agree	Disagree	Strongly Disagree
1. Was the information in our facebook blog helpful to you in this module by using your phone	17%	70%	7%	8%
2. The use of mobile help you to interact and get feedback from the lecturer	7%	80%	10%	3%
3. The FIT 1540/1640 Facebook blog was it helpful using your phone	2%	85%	2%	11%
4. I find it easy to communicate with the lecturer and other students using your phone	5%	82%	13%	5%
5. I was engage and inform about module with my mobile in and outside the classroom	4%	83%	3%	14%
6. It will be good to use this technology for other module	7%	80%	4%	13%

SESSION
POSTERS

Chair(s)

TBA

Research Roadmap: Big Data in Healthcare

Joseph M. Woodside[1]
[1]Department of Decision and Information Sciences, Stetson University, DeLand, Florida, US

Abstract - *Healthcare generates 30 percent of the world's data with a value of $300 billion in the next decade. Despite this, many healthcare providers have not developed a strategy for handling this data, and realizing the full set of opportunities to reduce costs and improve quality of care delivery. This Research Roadmap is set in major sections of structured and unstructured data and incorporates analytical decision making to improve the healthcare industry through Big Data.*

Keywords: Big Data, Healthcare, Structured Data, Unstructured Data

1 Big Data in Healthcare

Healthcare generates 30 percent of the world's data according to estimates, with 65 percent of survey respondents indicating their data storage will grow at a rate between 25-50 percent per year, driven by imaging files, electronic health records, personal health records, and scanned documents. Big Data in healthcare reflects the volume, growth, and types of data, as well as the tremendous opportunities available to unlock the potential value. In one report Big Data in healthcare was expected to be valued at $300 billion in the next decade, with annual growth between 1.2 – 2.4 Exabytes per year. Despite this growth, full integration and coordination has yet to occur and few healthcare providers have developed a formal strategy for handling the increasing amounts of data [1,2,3].

Healthcare organizations are under both industry and government pressure to reduce costs and improve quality of care delivery. With ever increasing amounts of data healthcare organizations are identifying the importance of business intelligence and analytics for decision making. Gartner recognized this as one of the fastest growing areas despite minimal economic growth, as organizations seek to compete and differentiate themselves through data based decisions [4,5]. The Big Data in Healthcare knowledge and research roadmap represents an opportunity to take advantage of the growing healthcare field and big data sources. The research stream seeks to develop innovate research, theory-building, publications, and grant funding.

This research output can be utilized to provide the management methods to improve the healthcare industry through Big Data decision making aimed at reducing costs and improving quality through use of information systems and technology. The research stream incorporates business intelligence, data analysis, and data mining to develop fact based decision making, through analysis and major research sections of structured and unstructured data.

2 Structured Data

Structured healthcare data is typically available in real-time, and includes established systems such as medical claims, pharmacy, lab, and financial data. Data is stored in data warehouses, and typically range from terabytes to petabytes in size. Decision making may take the form of reporting, alerts, performance management, and financials [6,7]. Future research streams include:

- Hospital Readmission – identify the factors leading to hospital readmission, predictive modeling of readmission, and successful methods to reduce readmission rates.
- Machine Learning Outcomes – development of machine learning algorithms to learn and predict outcomes automatically, significantly reducing costs and increasing quality.
- Geographic Information Systems – identify the spatial and temporal trends through cluster analysis to predict healthcare utilization/costs. This research is able to be applied to new to population management and database applications.
- Pay for Performance – formulation of incentive programs that can be utilized for providers and healthcare entities as a cloud service.
- Fraud Detection – neural network and pattern detection of patients, providers, and healthcare entities for fraud as well as training or errors improvement.

3 Unstructured Data

Unstructured healthcare data is typically available in non real-time, and includes data sources such as electronic medical records, radiology images, and clinical notes. Data is stored outside of the data warehouse in file systems, and commonly larger in size than structured systems ranging from terabytes to petabytes in size. Decision making may take the form of data mining, text mining, and other batch analysis methods [6,7]. Future research streams include:

- Risk Management – through classification validate existing and identify potential future care management needs for patient conditions based on imaging, notes, and historical medical records.
- Wellness – application architecture for a patient centric framework, to improve virtual health management and monitoring.
- Social Media – development of social media tools and evaluation of current tools for improving member's general health and condition specific areas.
- Workflow – monitoring of clinical and non-clinical activities, for improving process intelligence through best practices, and efficiency of care.
- Communities of Care – analysis of web logs and outcomes information for measuring self-management of conditions by the patient and community of patients.

4 References

[1] Healthcare IT News survey on healthcare data growth: Miliard, M. "'Deluge of data' has hospitals swimming upstream" H.I. News, 2012.

[2] Healthcare Informatics survey results on data and migration: DeGaspari, J. "Healthcare Data Experiencing Explosive Growth" Healthcare-Informatics, 2010.

[3] Description of healthcare Big Data estimates: Hughes, G. "How big is 'Big Data ' in healthcare," SAS, 2011.

[4] Description of Big Data: "Big Data in Healthcare - where does one start?" Schick, C. IBM, 2012.

[5] Description of Growth: "Gartner Forecasts Global Business Intelligence Market to Grow 9.7 Percent in 2011" Gartner, 2011.

[6] Description of Data: "Healthcare Data's Perfect Storm." Burns, W. Hitachi, 2013.

[7] Description of Data: "Big Data in Healthcare - where does one start?" Schick, C. IBM, 2012.

NoC-aware Adaptive Loop Tiling for Explicit Data Transfers in Many Core Systems

Keni Qiu, Mengying Zhao, Chun Jason Xue
Department of Computer Science, City University of Hong Kong, Hong Kong, China
qiukeni2015@gmail.com, my19900808@gmail.com, jasonxue@cityu.edu.hk

***Abstract*—SPM+DMA architecture is commonly employed in many core systems. Loop tiling is an effective way to partition data space for SPM+DMA based data blocking transfers. We observe that DMA based data transfer may induce heavy NoC congestion when the data block is very large. Furthermore, the NoC delay under congestion presents significant differential for the cores in different NoC locations. This paper considers the unbalanced distance-to-data property in the NoC and proposes a NoC-aware adaptive loop tiling (NALT) scheme to improve DMA transfer performance. In the NALT scheme, cores are grouped into different core families taking into account their distance-to-data in the NoC. Then tiling sizes are determined for different core families accordingly. On one hand, the NALT scheme can adaptively hide DMA transfer cost into computation cost and reduce the overall execution time. On the other hand, it can avoid bulk DMA data blocks bursting at the same time and thus mitigate NoC congestion. We evaluate the NALT scheme on the NIRGAM platform. The results show that it achieves an average of 21% execution time improvement compared to the uniform loop tiling method in DMA transfer.**

***Keywords*-DMA, adaptive loop tiling, many-core system, cost model**

I. Introduction

In many core systems, SPM+DMA architecture is often adopted to parallel computation and data transfer to alleviate the *memory wall* problem. In this SPM+DMA architecture, SPM specifically denotes the local memory and DMA denotes the explicit data transfer between local SPMs or between local SPM and low-level shared memory. Computation and memory communication can be effectively overlapped using *double buffering* or *asynchronous data movement* mechanisms, with which, the core can work on data residing in the local SPM while at the same time DMA is loading the next batch of data to the SPM or writing the previous completed data from SPM to other memory [1]. In the ideal situation, data transfer time should be totally concealed in CPU computation time except the first read (referred as *prologue*) and the last write (referred as *epilogue*) cost.

Loop tiling is a loop transformation way to partition the iteration space as well as data space into smaller blocks, thus fitting data array elements into local memory size and enhancing data reuse [2]. Loop tiling has been applied in the SPM+DMA architecture to indicate DMA operation granularity and meanwhile improve data reuse in SPMs [3].

We have two interesting observations in terms of Network on Chip (NoC) in a many core system. First, the DMA based data transfer may exhibit heavy NoC congestion when transferring bulk data blocks. Second, cores with different memory access path lengths have unbalanced NoC latencies.

Motivated by these observations, we take into account the critical issue of the unbalanced NoC latency due to the different core locations in the NoC. First, a fine-grained DMA transfer cost model is derived considering the location of each core in a many core system. Then a NoC-aware Adaptive Loop Tiling (NALT) scheme is proposed to determine adaptive loop tiling size for the cores.

To the best of our knowledge, this is the first work that analyzes the unbalanced latency property in the NoC under the SPM+DMA architecture in many core systems. The major contributions of this paper include:

- A fine-grained DMA transfer time cost model considering NoC latency differential is formulated. It points out the DMA-based data transfer exhibits unbalanced NoC latency among the cores due to their different distance-to-data lengths.
- A NALT scheme is proposed to minimize the DMA transfer cost. In the NALT solution, considering different NoC latencies of different core families, loop tiling size is adaptively determined to effectively hide memory access latency and mitigate NoC congestion.

II. DMA Cost Modeling and Problem Formulation

In the SPM+DMA architecture, each local SPM is not equipped with explicit dedicated DMA channel to communicate with shared memory or remote SPMs. Instead, DMA transfer should traverse the NoC and then access the desitination. In the NoC, data transfer links vary with different locations of cores, resulting in unbalanced NoC latencies. To this end, we develop a fine-grained DMA cost model considering core locations in the NoC.

A. DMA Cost Modeling

DMA-based data transfer between local SPM and shared memory consists of three stages: (i) DMA request setup; (ii) data traverse in the NoC; and (iii) access the shared memory banks.

In the first stage, the setup cost for a single DMA operation is a constant. It can be represented as: $t_{setup\_latency} = t_{base}$.

In the second stage, assuming the wormhole switching mechanism is adopted, the NoC traverse cost $t_{NoC\_latency}$ can be divided into three parts: t_{NoC_head}, t_{NoC_data} and t_{info}. The first item denotes the transfer time of the head flit of the DMA data block with congestion. The second item denotes the transfer time of the rest contiguous flits with no congestion. The last item denotes the transfer time of delivering request/return information.

Definitions *(Distance-to-Data (DD) and Average Distance-to-Data (ADD))* *The term DD means the path length measured by hops between the shared memory bank where a data block is stored and the core accessing the data in the NoC. The term ADD is the expectation value of all DDs of the local SPM of a core to the shared memory banks.*

The average ADD of $Core_{i,j}$ can be calculated as $ADD_{i,j} = \frac{1}{n}\sum DD$ where the item n denotes the memory bank number connected to the the NoC and DD denotes the link hops traversed in the NoC when $Core_{i,j}$ has access request to a memory bank.

The head flit and request/return information may encounter NoC congestion. Therefore, both of the items t_{NoC} and t_{info} can be represented as $(t\_switch + t_{congestion}) \cdot ADD_{i,j}$. The items

t_switch, $t_{congestion}$ and $ADD_{i,j}$ denote the average time cost of a data block passing a switch node, the average time cost of queuing on a switch and the average DD of $Core_{i,j}$ respectively.

The item t_{NoC_data} can be represented as $t_{NoC\_data} = \frac{Size^{tile}}{BW}$ where the item $Size^{tile}$ denotes the data block size of a single DMA transfer and the item BW stands for the network bandwidth.

Thus, the NoC latency for $Core_{i,j}$ can be represented as:

$$t^{i,j}_{NoC\_latency} = t_{NoC\_head} + t_{NoC\_data} + t_{info}$$
$$= 2(t\_switch + t_{congestion}) \cdot ADD_{i,j} + \frac{Size^{tile}}{BW}$$

In the third stage, DRAM memory bank access cost can be represented as $t_{bank\_latency} = C \cdot Size^{tile}$ where C is a constant.

Putting all together, the DMA cost model for a loop can be represented as:

$$T^{i,j}_{DMA} = n_{i,j} \cdot (t_{base} + (2(t_{switch} + t_{NoC\_congestion}) \cdot ADD_{i,j} + \frac{Size^{tile}}{BW_{NoC}}) + C \cdot Size^{tile})$$

The item $n_{i,j}$ denotes DMA operation number for the $Core_{i,j}$. Furthermore, this equation can be simplified as:

$$T^{i,j}_{DMA} = n_{i,j} \cdot (\alpha + \beta \cdot ADD_{i,j} + \gamma \cdot Size^{tile})$$

The items α, β, γ are all positive constants and can be measured given a many core system. It can be seen that the DMA transfer cost of a core correlates with not only the DMA data block size, but also the ADD of the core.

B. Problem Formulation

The objective of the SPM+DMA architecture is to maximize the overlap of computing and data transferring. The problem can be formulated as:

Objective: $t_{DMA} < t_{cmp}$

Subject to: $Size_{lb} \leq Size^{tile} \leq Size_{ub}$ *where* $Size_{lb}$ *and* $Size_{ub}$ *denote the lower bound and upper bound of a single DMA transfer size respectively.*

III. NoC-Aware Adaptive Loop Tiling Scheme

To solve the above problem, one naive approach is to enumerate and compare all tiling plans for each core and choose the best solution. However, it results in a very huge searching space. This paper proposes an adaptive loop tiling scheme to solve tiling solution for the cores with very low searching complexity. The NALT scheme consists of three steps in sequence.

Step 1 *Determining the value of* α, β *and* γ. These values can be obtained by measurements on the target many core platform.

Step 2 *Core family grouping*. The cores are grouped into clusters based on their ADDs. First, the ADD for each core is calculated. Then a bottom-up hierarchical clustering analysis is employed to group the cores into different *Final Core Family (FCF)* based on a prespecified similarity. Each FCF has a new average distance-to-data of ADD_f which is the expectation value of all the ADDs of the cores in this FCF.

Step 3 *Selecting tiling size*. It is assumed that $t_{cmp} = \delta \cdot Size^{tile}$ where t_{cmp} denotes the computing time for the tile size assigned to a FCF and δ is a constant. There exist three possible cases when determining the adaptive tiling size for each FCF.

Case 1: For any tiling size, there always exists $t_{DMA} \leq t_{cmp}$. It implies that there is no intersection in the reasonable range for the computing function $t_{cmp} = \delta \cdot Size_{tile}$ and the single DMA transfer function $t_{DMA} = \alpha + \beta \cdot ADD_f + \gamma \cdot Size^{tile}$ as shown in Fig. 1(a). So the objective $t_{DMA} \leq t_{cmp}$ is always true. In this case, we should select the optimal tile size $(Size^{tile})^{op} = Size_{lb}$ to obtain the minimal prologue and epilogue in DMA double buffering transfer.

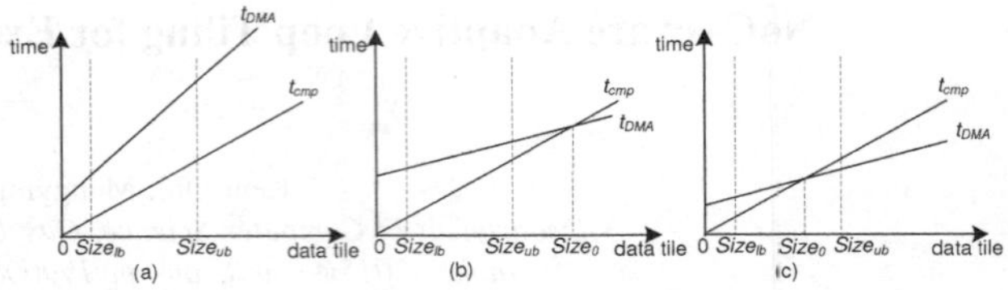

Figure 1. Three cases for tiling size selection

Case 2: For any tiling size, there always exists $t_{DMA} > t_{cmp}$. This also implies there is no intersection in the reasonable range for the computing function and the DMA transfer function as shown in Fig. 1(b), so the objective always fails. In this case, we should select $(Size^{tile})^{op} = Size_{ub}$ to obtain the minimal DMA operation number and guarantee the DMA setup time and NoC delay is more amortized for large tile size.

Case 3: For different tiling size, there exists either $t_{DMA} \leq t_{cmp}$ or $t_{DMA} > t_{cmp}$. This implies there exists an intersection point $Size_0$ in the reasonable range for the computing function and the DMA transfer function as shown in Fig. 1(c). Targeting on the objective, it should satisfy: $\alpha + \beta \cdot ADD_f + \gamma \cdot Size^{tile} < \delta \cdot Size^{tile}$. Hence $Size^{tile}$ should satisfy: $Size_{ub} > Size^{tile} \geq \frac{\alpha+\beta \cdot ADD_f}{\delta-\gamma}$.

So far the objective is satisfied, in order to obtain the minimal prologue and epilogue, we should choose the minimal reasonable value that $(Size^{tile})^{op} = max(\frac{\alpha+\beta \cdot ADD_f}{\delta-\gamma}, Size_{lb})$.

We evaluate the proposed NALT scheme on the NIRGAM simulator configured in Bursty mode [4]. Core numbers are set as 25, 36 and 64 to build 5×5, 6×6 and 8×8 mesh NoC configurations respectively. The FCF number is assigned to 2. The proposed NALT scheme is applied to determine the non-uniform tiling sizes for different core families. The results show that the overall execution latency has an average of 21% improvement with the NALT approach over the uniform tiling approach.

IV. Conclusions

This paper proposes the NALT scheme to adaptively assign variable loop tiling sizes to different cores during DMA transferring in many core systems, so that the NoC congestion and delay is mitigated, and thus the overall execution time is improved.

Acknowledgment

This work was partially supported by the Research Grants Council of the Hong Kong Special Administrative Region, China [CityU 123811].

References

[1] S. Saidi, P. Tendulkar, T. Lepley, and O. Maler, "Optimizing explicit data transfers for data parallel applications on the CELL architecture," *ACM Trans. Archit. Code Optim.*, vol. 8, no. 4, pp. 37:1–37:20, 2012.

[2] M. S. Lam and M. E. Wolf, "A data locality optimizing algorithm," *SIGPLAN Not.*, vol. 39, pp. 442–459, 2004.

[3] H. Lin, T. Liu, L. Renganarayana, H. Li, T. Chen, K. O'Brien, and L. Shao, "Automatic loop tiling for direct memory access," in *IPDPS*, 2011, pp. 479 –489.

[4] "Nirgam: http://nirgam.ecs.soton.ac.uk/."

SESSION

LATE BREAKING PAPERS: GAME TECHNOLOGIES, BIG DATA, WEB MINING, DATABASES, RESOURCE DISCOVERY AND WEB SERVICES, TIME-SERIES ANALYSIS, AND DATA WAREHOUSES

Chair(s)

Prof. Hamid Arabnia
University of Georgia

Accelerometer and Spatial-Orientation Interfaces to Maze Games on Tablets and Mobile Devices

S.A. Innes, B.J. Kennedy, E. P. Clarkson, L.J. Edmonds and K.A. Hawick
Computer Science, Massey University, North Shore 102-904, Auckland, New Zealand
email: redmansteve2@hotmail.co.uk, benkennedy50@gmail.com
{elliot.clarkson,leuan.edmonds}@gmail.com, k.a.hawick@massey.ac.nz
Tel: +64 9 414 0800 Fax: +64 9 441 8181

June 2013

ABSTRACT

Computer games on mobile platforms are increasingly popular and modern devices offer games developers unconventional user interface technologies based on device orientation. We describe a maze game implemented both for Android mobile phone and tablet devices that supports navigation though a generated landscape using tilt motions accessed via the devices accelerometer sensors. We report on implementation issues including device sensitivity, resolution and appropriate ways to utilise tilt motion in a practical game or simulation. We discuss future directions for this technology and possible uses in simulations as well as games.

KEY WORDS
computer games; mobile game; accelerometer; maze game; tilt navigation.

1 Introduction

Human Computer Interaction(HCI) [6] for computer games [27] and other highly interactive simulation or navigation programs is an important field with the potential to make use of new devices and interaction idioms for highly mobile devices such as tablet computers or mobile phones [8].

Interfaces [23] for modern computer games [17] can make use of the sensors such as tilt accelerometers that are now commonly available in both tablet and mobile phones. While touch screen interfaces are becoming widely used by various programs for tablets, uptake of the accelerometer sensor information has been slower. Touch sensitive devices have had a slow route to adoption [28] but the commodity pricing and now widespread availability of programmable devices such as Android or IOS enabled tablets or phones has led to an increasing market and demand for game Apps for such platforms.

A great deal of work has been reported on conventional HCI techniques [5, 24], but these new devices require new interaction metaphors and idioms that go beyond conventional graphical user interfaces [12]. There is considerable scope for new HCI frameworks [1] that can make use of development trends [10] in personal digital assistant(PDA) [25] technologies such as touch screens and other sensors.

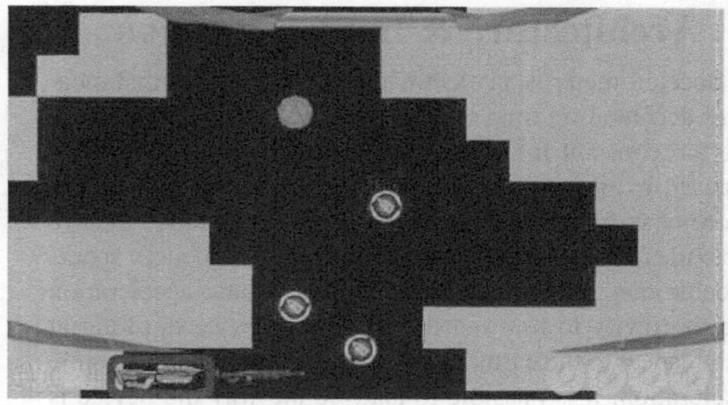

Figure 1: **Screen-shot of the prototype Androrbs game.**

Computer games are an important market for Apps that use these ideas [15], but there are also important applications areas such as education [16, 22] or training systems as well as more serious simulations [19, 20] and model demonstrators [18] that can also use them [9].

In this paper we describe how accelerometer sensor information can be used in a maze navigation game where the user tilts the whole device - tablet or phone - to make the player entity move around. Furthermore sensor fusion techniques can combine new touch gestures or multi-finger clicks [21] with the accelerometer orientation information to provide new game-player modes of interaction.

We also discuss a number of software architectural issues such as how to calibrate the tilting response to avoid the game or simulation appearing sluggish, and generation and manipulation of feasible maze maps that make use of the tilt sensor information.

Figure 1 shows a screen-shot from the Androrbs game showing three players within a generated map.

Tilt sensors [3, 13] are not new although they have only recently become widely available in commodity proceed devices [2]. Work has been reported on use of tilt sensors for navigation of geophysical map data, health applications [14], floating raft navigation [26] and other serious applications [7] as well as games [11].

Our article is structured as follows: In Section 2 we describe how we used the accelerometer in various devices. We present some results concerning sensor control and sensitivity in Section 3 and discuss tablet orientation issues and comparable games on similar platforms in Section 4. In Section 5 we summarise our conclusions and offer some suggested areas for further investigation.

2 Architecture & Implementation

An accelerometer is an electro-mechanical device that measures acceleration forces. These forces can either be static, like the constant force of gravity, or they can be dynamic - caused by moving or vibrating the accelerometer. An accelerometer allows the device in which it is installed to have some idea about its own orientation and movement in space. Accelerometers measure the amount of static acceleration due to gravity to find out the angle the device is tilting at with respect to the earth. By sensing the amount of dynamic acceleration, it is possible to analyse the way the device is moving. The output of the accelerometer can help the device know if it is being dropped, tilted, or shaken.

Accelerometers have heavy use in many industries today. As well as being a staple addition to most tablets, the accelerometer sees use in laptops. Using the accelerometer a laptop is able to detect if it is falling and temporarily turns off the hard drive, protecting the head from crashing onto the platters. In a similar fashion, High-G accelerometers are the industry standard way of detecting car crashes and deploying airbags at just the right time. Because of the way most accelerometers are implemented, they suffer from high frequency noise.

In contrast to an accelerometer which measures acceleration, a gyroscope measures the rate of rotation around an axis and suffers from low frequency noise. Gyroscopes are useful because its output can be used to minimise the effects of noise from an accelerometer. Likewise, the output of an accelerometer can be used to minimise the long-term drifting effect that a gyroscope suffers from. This is known as sensor fusion and results in a more accurate output, which can greatly enhance the feeling of control by the user.

Accelerometer/Gyroscope sensor fusion is done automatically by Android since API level 9 [4] in the virtual sensors 'Linear Acceleration' and 'Gravity', but their presence depends on available hardware and device API level. Despite these sensors resulting in a clearer, more useful signal, they were not further examined due to a priority on compatibility with older devices.

2.1 Obtaining Accelerometer Data

Androrbs uses the AndEngine framework, which provides its own interface `IAccelerationListener`. However, this is entirely unnecessary and simply builds on Android's already existing sensor listeners.

Obtaining accelerometer data in Android 1.5 or above without a third party framework involves creating a `SensorManager`, obtaining a `Sensor` from it, and supplying that `Sensor` with a `SensorEventListener` instance to report its data to.

```
sensorManager = (SensorManager)
  getSystemService(Context.SENSOR_SERVICE);
Sensor asensor =
        sensorManager.getDefaultSensor(
                Sensor.TYPE_ACCELEROMETER);
sensorManager.registerListener(
        this,
        asensor,
        SensorManager.SENSOR_DELAY_GAME);

@Override
public void onSensorChanged(SensorEvent ev)
{
    if (ev.sensor.getType() ==
            Sensor.TYPE_ACCELEROMETER)
    {
        Log.i("Accelerometer Example",
              "Accelerometer data: " +
               ev.values[0] + " " +
               ev.values[1] + " " +
               ev.values[2]);
    }
}
```

Figure 2: Obtaining acceleration data in Android Version 1.5 or later.

2.2 Movement Algorithms

```
final Vector2 velocity = Vector2Pool.obtain(
        pAccelerationData.getX() * 5,
        pAccelerationData.getY() * 5);
playerBody.setLinearVelocity(velocity);
Vector2Pool.recycle(velocity);
```

Figure 3: Initial movement algorithm.

Figure 3 shows the first attempt to control the player entity, by simply applying the forces obtained from the accelerometer directly as velocity. This results in a mathematically incorrect but extremely responsive control scheme. Because acceleration is completely bypassed and a force is never applied, the entity responds as quickly as the device can be tilted. This feels bizarre, but not entirely unpleasant. We felt this was not appropriate for our game, but interesting enough to note.

```
Vector2 f = Vector2Pool.obtain(
        pAccelerationData.getX() * accel,
        pAccelerationData.getY() * accel);
orb.getBody().applyForce(f,
        orb.getBody().getWorldCenter());
Vector2Pool.recycle(f);
```

Figure 4: Secondary movement algorithm.

Figure 4 shows the second attempt at moving the player entity via a function of accelerometer output. This time, actual forces are applied to the player entity to move it. This is the most mathematically accurate algorithm and the entity responds as it would in reality if the equivalent forces were applied. However, mathematical accuracy does not necessarily guarantee a pleasant experience. The entity seemed unresponsive, and felt out of place for a fast-paced game such as Androrbs.

```
accel = 5.0f, counterAccel = 4.0f.
Vector2 f = Vector2Pool.obtain(
        pAccelerationData.getX() * accel,
        pAccelerationData.getY() * accel);
Vector2 v = Vector2Pool.obtain(
        orb.getBody().getLinearVelocity());
// If we are trying to accelerate in an
// opposite direction to movement, compensate
if (f.x * v.x < 0)
        f.x -= v.x * counterAccel;
if (f.y * v.y < 0)
        f.y -= v.y * counterAccel;

orb.getBody().applyForce(f,
        orb.getBody().getWorldCenter());
Vector2Pool.recycle(v);
Vector2Pool.recycle(f);
```

Figure 5: Movement algorithm 3

Figure 5 shows the third iteration of the movement algorithm. To try to compensate for the unsatisfying motion of the previous code iteration, if the player tries to accelerate in the opposite direction to their current motion, they receive a boost to their newly applied force by their current velocity magnified by a 'counter-acceleration' constant.

Figure 6 shows an updated version of the movement algorithm with much more accurate calculation of friction.

2.3 Interfacing with the game

We wanted the game to behave ("feel") like a ball bearing puzzle (Figure 7), in which you navigate ball bearings

```
final static float friction=0.3;
Vector2 f = Vector2Pool.obtain(
        pAccelerationData.getX() * accel,
        pAccelerationData.getY() * accel);
Vector2 v = Vector2Pool.obtain(
        orb.getBody().getLinearVelocity());
f += friction*-v; // Apply friction

orb.getBody().applyForce(f,
        orb.getBody().getWorldCenter());
Vector2Pool.recycle(v);
Vector2Pool.recycle(f);
```

Figure 6: Movement algorithm 4

Figure 7: **A ball bearing puzzle game, must be tilted to solve.**

through a maze to a desired location by tilting the board. The maze is randomly generated in our levels see 2.6 for details. The tilting gesture is used in the game to move the players "orb", allowing the user to navigate a maze and attack opposition players.

2.4 How it is implemented

Android being the Operating System of choice requires the use of the Java programming language for applications. The open source game engine AndEngine was used to build our game upon. This gave us easy access to the Box2D physics engine and interfaced with the Android motion sensors. AndEngine scales the game to different resolutions automatically so no extra work was required to make the game work correctly on a tablet or mobile phone.

2.5 Accelerometer limits

Accelerometers give us an interesting method of input for a tablet or phone device, but when using such methods of control, there are considerations one should take into account with regards to the resultant simulated motion of player entities. Unlike using a directional pad or on-screen control method, the input cannot change instantaneously from one extreme to another.

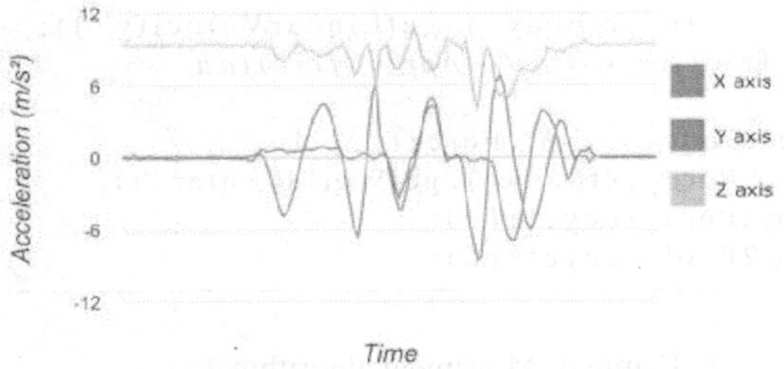

Figure 8: Smoothing of player intent signal by accelerometer over a period of two seconds.

Instead, input is always a gradual arc, as demonstrated in Figure 8. The smoothing of the original signal of player intent becomes more destructive as their input device is heavier, and gains more momentum with motion. This effect is magnified over long use periods, as the natural inclination of the player is to use a more relaxed grip.

Care should be taken to account for this on a game design level.

2.6 Maze generation

Because of the accelerometer limits discussed in the previous section, some environments could prove difficult to navigate. Unless the challenge is specifically to navigate difficult terrain, it may be wiser to provide players with natural, sweeping terrain, which mimics the input gathered from the accelerometer and levels the playing field for those on larger tablet devices.

There are a variety of signal processing techniques which could be applied to existing landscapes to improve their appropriateness for traversal with an accelerometer or similar device. Here, a cellular automata approach will be discussed for procedural generation of map data. One of the most famous rule tables for cellular automata is Conway's Game Of Life due to the highly dynamic patterns that can emerge. There are other rule sets in existence which are less dynamic and unpredictable which can be used to generate interesting structures. One such rule is the 4-5 rule, valid for any 2 dimensional grid of wall and floor tiles. This rule is interesting because after a few iterations on a grid filled with a random selection of floor and wall in some proportion as a function of cavern density, natural and organic flowing form emerges. This rule is described thusly, using a self-inclusive Moore neighbourhood:

- A tile becomes a wall if:
  - It was previously a wall and 4 or more of its 9 neighbours were walls
  - It was previously not a wall and 5 or more of its 9 neighbours were walls
- Otherwise, the tile becomes a floor.

This rule is capable of generating organic, cave-like structures of any size, as demonstrated in Figure 9.

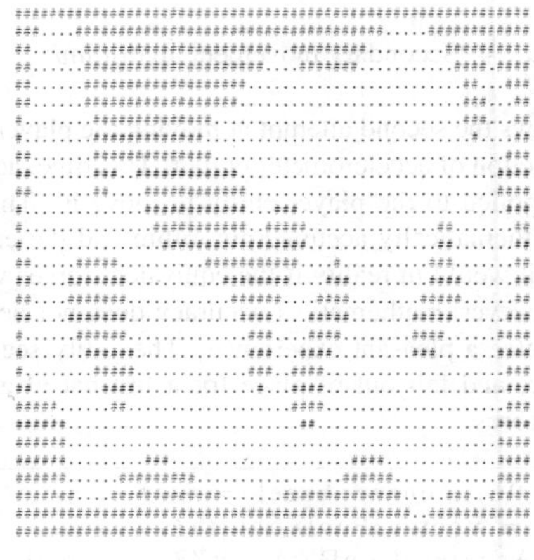

Figure 9: A sample generated map using the 4-5 rule. Note the flowing, natural curves.

2.7 Map Optimization

Sometimes the map generator would produce a map that was not particularly fun to play. These include maps almost entirely made of wall or floor, and maps with disconnected, unreachable segments. To deal with these situations, some checks are done before the map is selected for play. If any of these checks fail, the map is discarded, and another one is produced. This ensures entertaining maps every time.

First, disconnected areas must be dealt with. There is no guarantee that all areas of the map will be accessible by the player, and if care is not taken with start point selection, players may find themselves trapped in a small area. The approach taken here was to fill all but the largest connected area of floor with wall, effectively removing any smaller pockets that may have emerged. However, this reduces the number of floor tiles present in the map. It is recommended that after this elimination pass is complete, the number of floor tiles is evaluated, and the map discarded and regenerated if the proportion of wall to floor falls below a certain threshold.

While this approach does generate smooth curves, it does so in a rather uncontrolled manner. It is, however, possible to 'seed' the generated structure to adhere to a rough design. A technique considered was to generate a small maze with another algorithm such as Prim's algorithm or a simple

Depth-first search. The generated tiles were then scaled up, so that for each tile of output, an area of 7x7 random tiles are created, with probabilities weighted towards the original tile type. The 4-5 rule is then run on this field. Because of the non-random input to 4-5, the resulting output is fitted to the weighted maze probabilities, biasing the system to following the previously generated structure.

Figure 10: The disconnected map problem.

Note that this approach becomes significantly more complicated when the player entity is larger than one tile, as it is difficult to guarantee that all areas of the generated landscape are accessible. When the player entity is large, choke points could emerge - Segments of the landscape which are too narrow for the player to pass through, yet mean that the map is still actually connected. These are difficult and expensive to detect, so generating fine resolution landscapes this way comes at a downside.

3 Experimental Results

There are various aspects of the tilt sensor behaviour that arise from the user example as shown in Figure 11.

The first iteration of the movement algorithm (applying the forces of the accelerometer directly as the velocity of the player) proved very effective. The movement was alarmingly responsive. Unfortunately the movement proved too responsive; the player entity moving much too fast for a user to accurately control in the close quarters of the maze, most of the time leaving the user crashing into walls. In order to counteract this the speed was modified in order to make the player orb easier to control. Because the player orb only used velocity for movement, no matter how the speed was adjusted the motion did not seem natural.

The second iteration of the movement algorithm used the acceleration given by the accelerometer to equate force to apply to the orb. This lead the user to have much better control over the player orb, however turning became an issue without the snappy reactiveness of the other algorithm. As speed was a factor in Androrbs, the algorithm needed to be improved upon to optimise game-play.

The third iteration of the movement algorithm built upon the second by utilising a 'counter-acceleration' constant. This had the effect of amplifying movements made in the opposite direction of which the user was originally traveling. This brought back the reactiveness of the first algorithm while allowing the speed of the player orb to not get out of hand.

The fourth iteration of the movement algorithm is a finely polished version of the third. It gave the user enough speed to allow them to run around the maze easily without having to hug a wall. It also gave the user the right amount of control in order to hide in the maze and traverse some of the more narrow passages that might develop.

Because of the high frequency noise the accelerometer is exposed to, there is a decent amount of extra input the user does not deliberately make. This became evident in development as the player orb would casually roll to a corner when placed on a flat table. Occasionally, it would also shuffle slightly in one position when balanced in the middle of the screen. In order to stop this from happening the algorithms were changed in order to filter out small inputs and eradicate noise. This proved to be successful but made the player orb harder to control in tight spaces, eliminating the small degrees of motion needed to accurately roll through. This decision was later revoked in order to keep the player orb as easy to control as possible. It was also evident that as the main control scheme was the tilting motion of the accelerometer, and the game was designed to be fast paced, there would not be many times a user would want to remain perfectly still, finding it much more beneficial to roll away as fast as possible than staying still and hoping not to be found.

As mentioned previously, the accelerometer suffers from high frequency noise. Steps were taken in order to minimize this and improve the overall stability of the accelerometer, but overall this hindered game-play by restricting the finer movements. Inputs differ from devices depending on how well the accelerometer is made. If the Android device contains a gyroscope this can be remedied with the help of sensor fusion. If the device contains both a gyroscope and an accelerometer the input is smoothed out, removing the majority of noise, allowing for a much more stable signal and a much more pleasing experience. On development of the application, phones with gyroscopes were not as common and most could not utilise sensor fusion, making the

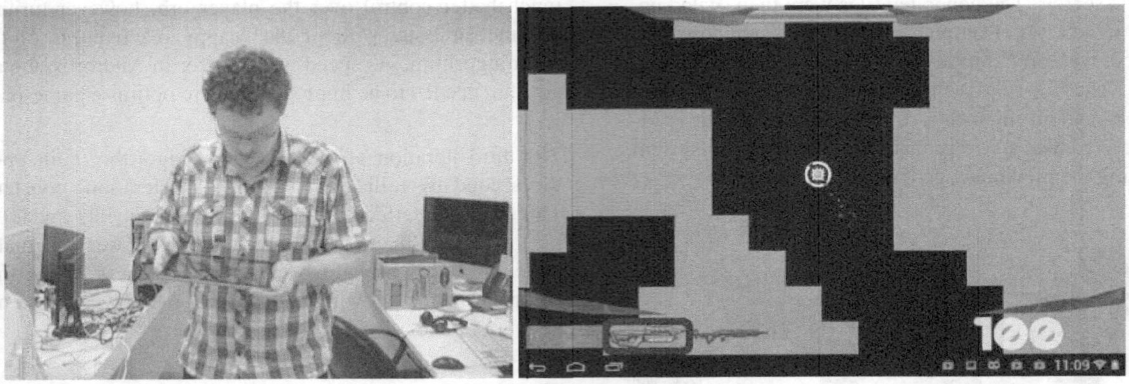

Figure 11: Tilting the top left corner of the tablet resulting in a movement towards the top left corner of the in-game screen.

tablet-controlled versions of the App a lot more enjoyable with the controls feeling a lot more stable.

4 Discussion

The control scheme of the game needed the player to keep the tablet mostly flat and held above the ground. This was not very intuitive to new players and needed to be explained before the game could be played properly. If the game was to be developed further, a useful option would be to calibrate the game with a default orientation. This would allow a player to hold the device more comfortably in front of them, rather than having to keep it flat and below the head, which may prove to be uncomfortable for long periods of time. This may also prove to be counter-productive as it may be confusing for a user to comprehend the adjusted orientation. It is easy to think about moving a surface with your hands and having the ball roll down it, but if that surface was in front of the player horizontally it would effectively make the player have to grasp the concept of rolling up a wall.

4.1 Other games and platforms

A game similar in concept to ours is “MadBalls in Babo Invasion” in which the player controls spherical characters that resemble the “MadBalls” toys. The game is almost identical to our own in that the players move through a maze using an orb like character in order to find and defeat other players who are trying to accomplish the same of you. This game is a lot more graphically impressive than ours as it has been commercially made with a much wider development team. The game is developed for the PC which had a lot more graphical power behind it when the game was made. The game uses the ‘WASD’ control scheme on a keyboard. Comparatively, Androrbs seems to be more natural to control than ‘MadBalls’ as it feels more physically accurate using an accelerometer-based control scheme. That being said, the ‘WASD’ control scheme does not suffer from the high frequency noise problem that plagues the accelerometer, leading to a much more accurate sense of control.

Because the App was written in Java it would be very simple to move it from one platform to another. The main challenge would be replacing the components we used from the AndEngine to suit another platform. When developing the App, one of the main goals was to make something that both older and newer devices could play. Because so many mobile platforms come equipped with an accelerometer as standard, the App can be played with a plethora of devices.

5 Conclusions

We made an App that uses the accelerometer on an Android device, a standard in the majority of mobile platforms, as its main control scheme in order to cater for the broadest market possible. We took the limits of the input device into account when designing traversable landscapes using a cellular automata, and discussed methods of map optimization such as initial seeding with non-random values and avoidance of disconnected areas.

We found that using the accelerometer as a control scheme is not only simple and easy to do, but also relatively accurate. This accuracy is further improved with that of a gyroscope. The developer can use sensor fusion in order to smooth out the noise of the accelerometer. Accelerometer movement can be considered superior to traditional methods of input in terms of intuitiveness and ease of use, but may be tiring for prolonged play.

We believe the accelerometer could be used to make multi-platform games with little to no hassle, provided its limits are respected and elements of the game which closely interact with accelerometer data are designed appropriately.

Whenever a correctly configured sensor-fused virtual input is available which makes use of the accelerometer as an input, it will always provide a less noisy signal than the accelerometer alone. There is scope for further research on exactly how this newfound accuracy could be leveraged. In addition, the z-axis is largely ignored in our investigation, and could be used to provide additional input.

References

[1] Ali, S.I., Jain, S., Lal, B., Sharma, N.: A framework for modeling and designing of intelligent and adaptive interfaces for human computer interaction. Int. J. Applied Information Systems 1(2), 20–25 (January 2012)

[2] Browne, K., Anand, C.: An empirical evaluation of user interfaces for a mobile video game. Entertainment Computing 3, 1–10 (2012)

[3] Chatting, D.J.: Action and reaction for physical map interfaces. In: Proc. Second Int. Conf. on Tangible and Embedded Interaction (TEI'08). pp. 187–190. Bonn, Germany (18-20 Feb 2008)

[4] Developers, A.: Software development kit (February 2012), http://developer.android.com/sdk, android SDK

[5] Diaper, D., Stanton, N. (eds.): The Handbook of Task Analysis for Human-Computer Interaction. IEA (2004)

[6] Dix, A., Finlay, J., Abowd, G., Beale, R.: Human-Computer Interaction. Prentice Hall (1993)

[7] Elmaghraby, A., Mendez, A., Zapirain, B.G.: Serious games and health informatics: A unified framework. In: Proc. 17th IEEE Int. Conf. on Computer Games (CGAMES 2012). pp. 35–38 (2012)

[8] Furio, D., Gonzalez-Gancedo, S., Juan, M.C., Segui, I., Costa, M.: The effects of the size and weight of a mobile device on an educational game. Computers and Education 64, 24–41 (2013)

[9] Gerdelan, A.P., Hawick, K.A., Leist, A., Playne, D.P.: Simulation frameworks for virtual environments. In: Proc. International Conference on Internet Computing (ICOMP'11). pp. 272–278. No. ICM4087, CSREA, Las Vegas, USA (18-21 July 2011)

[10] Gouin, D., Lavigue, V.: Trends in human-computer interaction to support future intelligence analysis capabilities. In: Proc. 16th Int. Command and Control Research and Technology Symposium No. Paper 130, Quebec City, Canada (21-23 June 2010)

[11] Hwang, I., Lee, Y., Park, T., Song, J.: Toward a mobile platform for pervasive games. In: Proc. ACM MobiGames'12. pp. 19–24. Helsinki, Finland (2012)

[12] Kortum, P.: HCI Beyond the GUI - Design for Hapric, Speech, Olfactory and other Nontraditional Interfaces. Morgan Kaufmann (2008)

[13] MacKenzie, I.S , Teather, R.J.: Fittstilt: The application of fitts? law to tilt-based interaction. In: Proc. 7th Nordic Conference on Hman-Computer Interaction (NordCHI'12). pp. 568–577. Copenhagen, Denmark (14-17 October 2012)

[14] McCallum, S.: Gamification and serious games for personalized health. In: Proc. 9th Int. Conf. on Wearable Micro and Nano Technologies for Personalized Health (pHealth'12). Porto, Portugal (26-28 June 2012)

[15] Muehl, W., Novak, J.: Game Development Essentials - Game Simulation Development. Delmar (2008), iSBn 978-1-4180-6439-6

[16] Narayan, M.A., Chen, J., Perez-Quinones, M.A.: Usability of tablet pc as a remote control device for biomedical data visualization applications. Tech. Rep. TR04-26, Virginia Tech (2004), http://eprints.cs.vt.edu/archive/00000703/01/TR04-26-Jian-Michael.pdf

[17] Novak, J.: Game Development Essentials - An Introduction. Delmar, 3rd edn. (2012)

[18] Pearce, B.T., Hawick, K.A.: Interactive simulation and visualisation of falling sand pictures on tablet computers. In: Proc. 10th International Conference on Modeling, Simulation and Visualization Methods)MSV'13). p. MSV2341. No. CSTN-196, WorldComp, Las Vegas, USA (22-25 July 2013)

[19] Preez, V.D., Pearce, B., Hawick, K.A., McMullen, T.H.: Human-computer interaction on touch screen tablets for highly interactive computational simulations. In: Proc. International Conference on Human-Computer Interaction. pp. 258–265. IASTED, Baltimore, USA. (14-16 May 2012)

[20] Preez, V.D., Pearce, B., Hawick, K.A., McMullen, T.H.: Software engineering a family of complex systems simulation model apps on android tablets. In: Proc. Int. Conf. on Software Engineering Research and Practice (SERP'12). pp. 215–221. SERP12-authors.pdf, CSREA, Las Vegas, USA (16-19 July 2012)

[21] Rautaray, S.S., Agrawal, A.: Real time multiple hand gesture recognition system for human computer interaction. Int. J. Intelligent Systems and Applications 5, 56–64 (2012)

[22] Reed, R.H., Berque, D.A. (eds.): The Impact of Tablet PCs and Pen-based Technology on Education. Purdue Univ. press (2010)

[23] Saunders, K.D., Novak, J.: Game Development Essentials - Game Interface Design. Delmar, 2nd edn. (2013), iSBN 978-1-111-64288-4

[24] Scogings, C.J.: The Integration of Task and Dialogue Modelling in the Early Stages of User Interface Design. Ph.D. thesis, Massey University (2003)

[25] Tesoriero, R., Montero, F., Lozano, M.D., Gallud, J.A.: Hci design patterns for pda running space structured applications. In: Proc. 12th Int. Conf. on Human-Computer Interaction: Interaction Design and Usability (2007)

[26] Tomlinson, B., Yau, M.L., O'Connell, J., Williams, K., Yamaoka, S.: The virtual raft project: A mobile interface for interacting with communities of autonomous characters. In: Proc. ACM CHI '05. pp. 1150–1151. Portland, Oregon, USA (2-7 April 2005)

[27] Turner, J., Browning, D.: Workshop on hci and game interfaces: A long romance. In: Proc. OZCHI 2010 : Design, Interaction, Participation. Queensland University of Technology, Brisbane, Queensland, Australia (22-26 November 2010 2010)

[28] Yarow, J.: Tablet computing: A history of failure. Business Insider Online, 1–3 (January 2010)

The Big Data User-Centric Model

Asta Zelenkauskaite[1], **Bruno Simões**[2]
[1]Drexel University, Philadelphia, Pennsylvania, USA
[2]Fondazione Graphitech, Trento, Trentino, Italy

Abstract— *With a myriad of new opportunities arising from the Big Data paradigm, we propose a model to enhance user experience. Our adaptive user-centric model capitalizes on fluidity of online and offline realms and autonomous environments that are sensitive to the changing data fluxes. This model is based on a prototype of an ad hoc media company which for a more than a decade has been using social media to enhance user experience. We propose a prototype that expands an existing vision of Big Data by interlinking fluctuating social media streams and external web information with the media company's data. Theoretically we focused on the veracity and value as the Big Data constructs being the most pertinent to argue for a user-centric perspective.*

Keywords: user-centric approach, enhance user experience, big data

1. Introduction

The concept of Big Data has challenged the notion of data and its relevance to myriad of new opportunities. With the explosion of social media outlets in particular, Big Data conceptualizes a new vision on media and entertainment, which is primarily driven by the increasing amounts of user-generated content (UGC) which is contrasted with the professionally-produced content. Media and entertainment, are in fact, some of the best candidates to Big Data, among many others such as surveillance, embedded and medical contexts, data processing, consumer images, and voice-based content [1].

Social media, promoting a greater user-created content visibility provides an emerging, yet underresearched area of studies. Changing mass media landscape emphasizes the hope for new opportunities of user-generated content, yet presents us with uncertainties [2]:

> Prior to digitalization it might be said that the demand for interactive modes of communication was frustrated by the rigid control architectures of modern mass media. With the attachment of mobile devices and networks to television receivers, recording devices, and broadcasting networks there has been a circumscribed and narrow but definite and potentially significant opening for cultural expression and exchange–the future of which is uncertain. (p. 327)

Social media has been primarily interpreted as a source of additional revenue, by providing a new lens to meaningfully extract insights from proprietary data and solve complex problems that so far were impossible to address [3]. Even if value creation is one of the central components of user-generated content [4], [5], as for now, solutions on materialized value from social media, especially considering multiplatform environments, are still underexplored.

As new opportunities for Big Data applications arise, this study collocates Big Data in the mass media context. The need of a meaningful UGC integration to media contexts is evident not only because it provides the foundation for better products and services, but also because media companies struggle to integrate user content across multiple platforms meaningfully. We gear Big Data towards an adaptive user-centric model that facilitates cross-platform user interaction and enhances user experience [6].

Specifically, we expanded an existing ad hoc media company's model that is based on user participation through social media in mass media context. To understand the underpinnings of Big Data, which can generate value for users, we analyzed social media-based back-channels as well as considered multiplatform content distribution via an integratory prototype. Based on the parameters of Big Data, we proposed a model that enhances experiences of diverse types of users.

We employed functional reasoning to Big Data. The functional definition of data states that it serves as "a basis for reasoning, discussion, or calculation" [7]. We considered the first part of the definition–the reasoning–as new potential ways to think about multiple streams of inhomogeneous data integration. The second part of definition–the calculation–served as a the foundation for analysis and decision-making mechanisms. We proposed calculation as a sense-making mechanism that extracts correlations between complex components of data.

The paper is structured as follows. We start with explaining the parameters of Big Data applied towards an adaptive user-centric model by underlying the challenges inherent in the definition of Big Data and the opportunities that arise from a user-centric approach. Subsequently, we discuss the relevance of Big Data for a multiplatform media context by exemplifying it with a contextually-embedded Italian use-case RTL 102.5 and by introducing an adaptive user-centric model. In section four, we have proposed an architecture that supports one possible vision for our user-centric model.

Given that our model operates with data owned by a single media company, we reflect on a future vision of Big Data that expands user experience by navigating within user-generated data across various streams of UGC through various media companies. We conclude with final remarks and practical implications.

2. Big Data Properties

In the past decade, we have been witnessing an unprecedented growth of digital data on the World Wide Web [1], which is further increasing with the rapid growth of portable devices and social media. The concept of Big Data has emerged based on dilemmas of data abundance to provide companies with the foundation for creating new levels of business value.

With integrated storage, analytics, and applications, Big Data helps companies to drive efficiency, quality, and personalized products and services, thus producing better user satisfaction and experience. The concept of Big Data is characterized by a set of properties that are very difficult to handle by existing database management systems–volume, variety, and velocity.

This section discusses Big Data based on five properties: properties that pose challenges inherent in database management systems–volume, variety, velocity, [8] and by conceptual properties–veracity, and value [9]. Volume concerns with huge amounts of data. Variety refers to sets of uncorrelated data sources and their unstructured nature [10]. Velocity refers to gained advantage in a timely manner. Veracity refers to trust associated with inhomogenous data. Big Data, constrained by the volume, variety, and velocity, can be gathered from unverified sources. User-generated content, driven by crowdsourcing culture, compared to professional content, is not subject to verifiability, neither has to adhere to predefined structure-based parameters.

The definition of 'value' comprises multiple constructs such as "the monetary value of something", the market value, or "something intrinsically valuable or desirable" [11]. As the definition suggests, the value depends on the context and involved parties. In social media contexts, we propose user value through the construct of adaptability, increased choices, and flexibility, resulting in higher degrees of autonomy [12] and interactivity [13].

2.1 Value creation with Big Data

Even though volume remains an important challenge, variety and velocity emerged as the most critical Big Data challenges [8] as these characteristics influence how the value is discovered. Big Data is unlike conventional business intelligence, where the simple summing of a known value reveals a result. With Big Data, the value is discovered through a refining modeling process, a narrative, where the data itself is the story.

In this section we explore two opposed facets of Big Data value in media contexts. The first facet–henceforth known as Business-oriented value–considers multiple data sources within a given business model or a company that is geared to generating profit. The second one focuses on a user gain and explores requirements necessary to Big Data to maximize user experience. In fact, we proposed the latter one as a user-centric view to Big Data.

Big Data fames for its advantages and new arising opportunities positioned as a defining cornerstone of a business-oriented value. The advantageous contexts from Big Data get created through a fast and meaningful data analysis. Thus, business-oriented value gets created by a meaningful data interpretation and management.

Business-oriented value has been strategically complemented with the user-centric approach focusing on users. For example, media companies emphasized interactive technological affordances even if most of them provided very limited ways of user interaction. Concurrently, such user-centric approach has been highly beneficial for the companies in areas such as product and service innovation. User-centric approach diminished product or service failure rates and rewarded companies by promoting user-acceptance. Customers, lead users especially, have been utilized as testers of the system [14]. In media contexts, users were crucial of media business models through demographic advertising as well.

With the rise of social media technologies, "the responsibility towards users" and business-oriented value generation has been further intensified given that social media products provide increased choice-based impressions [15]. Furthermore, users became generators of value for companies that serve to strengthen the brand [16]. As a result, media companies increasingly started to integrate interactive applications. Interactive tools were conceptualized as leading to greater levels of user exchange, resulting in enhanced experience [17]. In media, interactivity also was proposed as ways to shift user roles from passive ones to active roles. In the radio contexts, listeners become active participants and in televised programming viewers who merely watched the program become active contributors in their favorite programs in television as described in Figure 1:

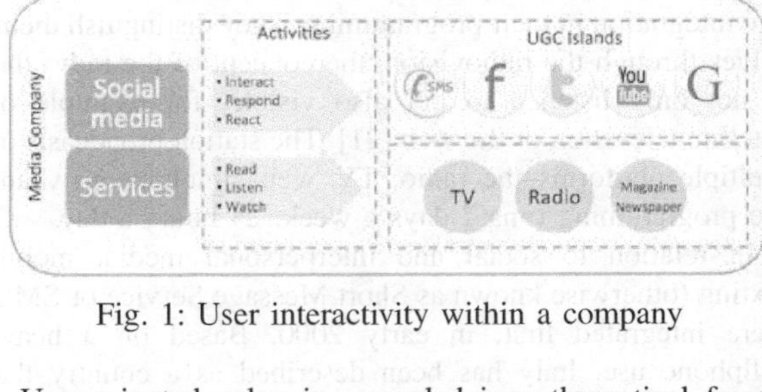

Fig. 1: User interactivity within a company

User-oriented value is grounded in a theoretical framework of interactivity as ways to enhance user engagement. Interactivity can be achieved through user-to-content, user-to-context, and user-to-user engagement and content exchange in a networked environment [13]. By interacting with the content and the others, users are enabled to be engaged in a dialog rather than in a passive content consumption. Degrees of interactivity vary contextually and as a theoretical construct interactivity is viewed as a technological property or/and as a psychological construct based on an individual perception [18].

In recent years, the promise of increased interactivity is reaching its peak. Through social media tools, such as Facebook, mobile texting, or Twitter users are provided with the back-channel based on which they can react to the comments or prompts of the companies and interact with the program and with the others. Despite that user-generated content becomes prevalent through a myriad of diversified content and services, interactive environments have been criticized as illusionary for their limiting, pre-established, rigid hierarchical structures and limited interaction or just merely reaction [19]. Regardless the promise of user-generated content and interactive applications, control of the content is still in hands of the companies since they control over 80% of the content, even if half is produced by users who become co-producers of the content [20].

Enhanced user experience is eclipsed by limited ways to interact for the users. Interactivity has been proposed to foster a two-way communication, while most of the media companies use a reactive communication model, which is based on a prompt solicited by a media company and a reactive response reserved to a user. Moreover, the decisional power of the products is still held by media companies and commercial logics dominate the orientation towards revenue gathering.

2.2 RTL 102.5 Use-Case

We have foregrounded our Big Data user-centric model on an existing forward-looking private media company RTL 102.5, which has been experimenting with various interactive back-channels for more than a decade.

Established in 1975, RTL 102.5 is one of the top commercial radio stations' in Italy with an average of five million listeners a day; also leading in social networking site integration in their programming. They distinguish themselves through the radiovision, the concept of the radio that is not only listened to but also visible, for example on satellite television or the web [21]. The station broadcasts on multiple platforms–the radio, TV, web–simultaneously and the programming runs 7 days a week, 24 hours a day.

In relation to social and interpersonal media, mobile texting (otherwise known as Short Message Service or SMS) were integrated first, in early 2000. Based on a heavy cellphone use, Italy has been described as a country that is "in love with mobiles" [22], where the cellphone are considered not only as a communication tools but also as a fashion gadgets [23]. Worldwide, Italy has a cellphone penetration rate of 92.65%, ranking as number four out of 43 countries [24]. Due to cellphone popularity, an agreement between the Acotel group and RTL 102.5 resulted in a multiplatform user integration by activating the back-channels of communication [25].

RTL 102.5's Facebook fan base is ranked as number 11 among all Italian brands; it is number two among radio stations [26]. Facebook messages were incorporated into the station's programming in 2009. Anyone wishing to post a message or read the RTL 102.5 Facebook wall's "youONair" section must first confirm it by clicking the "like" button. Audience base continuously grow along with increasing amounts of generated data. As of April 1 2013, user activity statistics comprised 986,056 likes compared to three times smaller "like" base with 300,954 likes in 2010 December 12. Users are encouraged to interact by posting their messages to RTL 102.5 since user content can be displayed on TV and stored temporarily on the web.

Figure 2 shows the message distribution within a given program for a random day, April 26, 2011, and it includes Facebook and SMS messages.

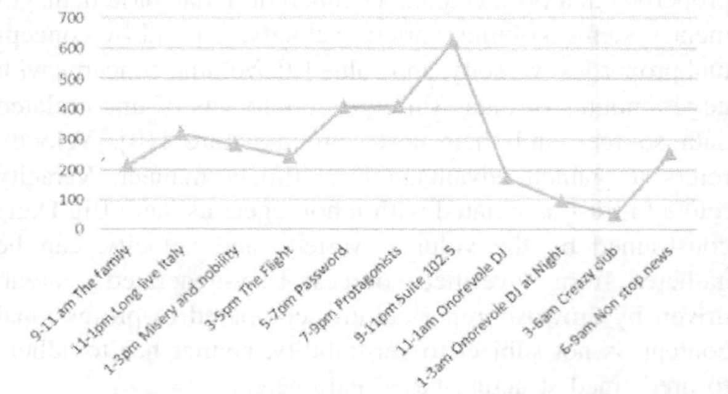

Fig. 2: Total number of SMS and Facebook messages by program

The most active user participation occurred from 9-11pm during the Suite 102.5 program, followed by 5-7pm The Password program and finally lead by 11am-1pm Long Live Italy. This graph also identifies user-driven variability, which has been segmented by the program.

RTL 102.5 also has a Twitter channel, where it tweets the question of the day to its audience members as well as informs them about any important news. RTL 102.5 Twitter has 112,807 followers ranking as number 46 among media companies [26]. RTL 102.5 broadcasts specialized contents on Google+. Also, it is possible to download an application that allow connecting to the radio station via cellphones (smartphones). RTL 102.5 has also created a YouTube channel on November 7th, 2006, which remains strongly active.

Existing social media back-channels implemented by RTL.105 have several limitations. First, only a small percentage (30%) of user-generated content goes through due to time and space constraints of some of the platforms (e.g. TV). Filtering process requires the presence of a dedicated operator, who has to read all the content originated from multiple data sources, in real-time, and intuitively decide the best fit to the actual time slot. This leads to large amount of data being simply discarded; thus eliminating a possibility of an added value if combined with other selection criteria– topic, context, proper timing, or interlinked external Big Data sources.

3. Adaptive User-Centric Model

We focused on advancing existing social media back-channel capacities by using the concept of Big Data to further enhance user experience through a flexible and adaptive environment. Our adaptive user-centric model capitalizes on fluidity of online and offline realms, flexible environments, sensitive to the changing data fluxes. Flexibility provides users with the possibility to acquire more choices. More importantly, environment adapts to accommodate users' behavior and changing roles. Flexible adaptive environment is vital for our model because of pervasiveness of user-generated content.

We conceptualize user value through the following parameters geared towards users: 1) the experience that foster increased audience engagement by fluidity of user roles; 2) visibility; 3) a sense of a community; 4) provide more autonomy; 5) opportunistic benefits. The value proposed here is based on user experience rather than the interactivity, embedded in a service or a product. The core value of the user-centric model is based on enhanced user experience in a flexible and context-sensitive environment that gathers data sources from multiple platforms, resulting in an opportunistic context for the user. In this model user levels of engagement is self-selected with fluid boundaries between various activities.

Our user-centric model is based on Grounded theory [27], in which established parameters emerge from the context. We have extracted key recurrent constituents situated in our use-case, instead of foregrounding research on pre-established parameters. Such data-driven approach has been proposed as a recommended ways to establish meaings from Big Data contexts [28]. In addition to backchannel content analysis, interviews with key actors at RTL 102.5 comprised media producers, technicians, and innovation department of RTL 102.5 were conducted [29].

3.1 Proposed Model

In addition to the ability of distributing UGC along a temporal dimension, our model focuses on user role fluidity that bridges online and offline environments through a visual representation of user location and interests. UGC that is collected by RTL 102.5 may serve as a rich data source from which multiple types of information can be extracted. For example, generic messages such as "Hello from Rome!" may be discarded by the operator. However, they provide important bits of information about the user location. For example, the users who watch TV or listen to the radio online, can be mapped based on their IP location. Any bits of information would lead to a better understanding of the user demographics or can interface with other keyword-based data streams, which are part of Big Data repository. Nevertheless, user location represents just a small percentage of information that can be extracted from UGC content.

Social networks can also be used to gather information about users' interests either by parsing the *user profile* section or by performing network analysis by using triangulated data as proposed by Donath [30]. We suggest maps as an interface for an enhanced user experience. Maps are among the most efficient visualization techniques of spatial knowledge [31], [32]. When information is presented visually, efficient innate human capabilities can be used to perceive and process complex data relations at nearly 9,000 kilobits per second [33], therefore it reduces search times, improves recognition of patterns, increases inference making, and monitoring scope. Moreover, the same advantageous principles are also applied to large virtual worlds [34].

Maps are also advantageous due to user-distribution visualization given that each of media outlet has its own market. In our specific case study RTL 102.5 represents a national radio station and broadcasts its content exclusively in Italian. Even if the content can be accessible via digital terrestrial, its main audience is localized within clearly defined geographical boundaries of Italy. From that perspective, by considering an enhanced user experience, we propose user visibility through the map of Italy as ways to represent user activity in a specific geographical location; yet location can be expanded once user base extends to a larger global community. At the same time, geographical maps can provide interelational data that connects user data with other activities.

To account for veracity of the UGC, we propose to apply the network analysis theory, which can assign trust indicators to the different pieces of information [30]. Specifically, network-based trust can be achieved by gathering information through interlinked nodes, that are linked via weak ties which refer to occasional interaction or information flows between the nodes. Weak ties that represent infrequent and often distant relations produce interest-free evaluations [30]. It is the data, gathered through the weak ties, that has been considered as crucial referrals of trustworthy information. Social network analysis has been proven to be a successful analytical tool for real-time data analysis in the context of Internet of Things [35].

User centric model emphasizes fluid user roles. Although

most of the RTL 102.5 audience's members roles are passive, based on interactive applications implemented by the station, a small percentage of users react to launched topics of interests or prompts [29]. These users considered as reactive users. The map representation, which has the goal of strengthening the user experience, would also incorporate content generated by these reactive users, in addition to their location. Not only the map would allow users to explore this temporal dimensional of the data, but also to react to those users that did not get their content exposed through the TV. Hence, freeing them from program time constraints.

Finally, users who currently interact with other users or with the radio (e.g. via SMS), and that are referred as to interactive ones, would benefit from a richer interaction platform. Additionally, the map would provide an anonymous interface that would allow users to subscribe to specific topics or addressees by selecting the user or a set of keywords. The proposed model and roles are not static, users can shift roles or have multiple concurrent roles at any given time. Given that user roles differ, proposedodel accounts for diversified experience to different segments of the users. In addition to users, media company itself, and external companies could also be involved into the triangulated model.

Media company's role thus gets projected as carriers' role, where it interlinks users and external companies for the mutual benefit, yet without exercising central hierarchical control. Environments supporting these communities (e.g. restaurants and pubs), which are on the infrastructure of a given media company, would be responsible for delivering some occasional benefits to their users. By merely being on the infrastructure, users would be able to take advantages of this opportunistic network, thus coupling their media entertainment experience. Such an adaptive network would support shared experiences with the other users through additional Big Data sources, in addition to above mentioned ones.

4. Big Data Architecture

Our proposed Big Data architecture aims at transforming user-generated content into insights that can serve the enhanced user experience through a refining modeling process: make a hypothesis, create visual and semantic models, validate, and then make new hypotheses. It either takes a person interpreting and making interactive knowledge-based transformation queries (e.g. editorial logics or users), or by implementing algorithms based on machine learning of semantic relations, to discover meaning from the increasing channels and variety of data received.

To maximize the value that can be discovered through analytics, one has to combine growing volumes of traditional data, such as professionally-produced media company's data, with time-sensitive and unstructured user-generated content. Additionally, one has to cover a wide range of different services, platforms, applications and tools, such as those found within a unified data architecture (UDA) environment.

In our use-case, some of the data sources that need to be collected, stored, and correlated comprise social websites (e.g. Facebook, Twitter, and Google+), the RTL 102.5 website (e.g. video and audio), and data gathered from mobile devices (e.g. SMS and RTL 102.5 mobile application).

Hence, the process of data correlation requires a specialized architecture that not only handles large amounts of continuously growing data in real-time, but also enables users to discover and find their own interests. Hence, can users model the environment that surrounds them to the degree that the behavior predefines the architecture of the environment itself.

The logical components of our architecture are: data source, transformation, integration, and visualization.

Data Source. This component provides access to structured and heterogeneous data, stored in SQL and NoSQL databases such as radio, video, news, logs (user clicks, user visits, activity, user location, etc), and to semi/un-structured user generated data.

Data Transformation. Transformation of data from one form to another is part of the ETL (Extract, Transform and Load) process, which is primarily conducted by means of data extracting and parsing tools. This component follows the graphical principles introduced in [36], [37] and features a distributed parallel processing framework capable of parsing large and complex sets of data.

Data Integration. As various data are captured and transformed, they are stored and processed in traditional database management systems (DBMS) across a distributed-clustered system. Hadoop is our choice for acquisition and reduction of user-generated data since it provides a robust, fault-tolerant Hadoop Distributed File System (HDFS), inspired by Google's file system [38], as well as a Java-based API, specifically designed to permit large-scale distributed data analysis across the nodes of a computing cluster, by using the MapReduce paradigm, which is utilized to filter data according to a specific data discovery strategy.

Machine learning and semantic algorithms are then integrated to do further reasoning. They analyze user-generated content, such as SMS and check-ins (e.g. to extract addressees, user location, and context), to perform network analysis and assign trust. A recent seminal article by [39] highlighted a number of standard techniques that can be computed in a data-parallel fashion via summations. The Apache Mahout project represents an effort in this direction, which we use to implement our techniques in the open-source Hadoop MapReduce engine.

Data Visualization and Interaction. Data visualization and integration components features a rich user interaction that is constructed over a map representation, and enhanced with advanced analytics, in-database statistical analysis, and collaborative tools.

Apart from four logical components, monitoring plays a crucial role in detecting any failure within the data pipeline along with threshold changes to identify any bottlenecks in terms of performance, scalability, and overall throughput. The Figure 3 describes a framework built on top of a set of specialized open source tools that implement all these components.

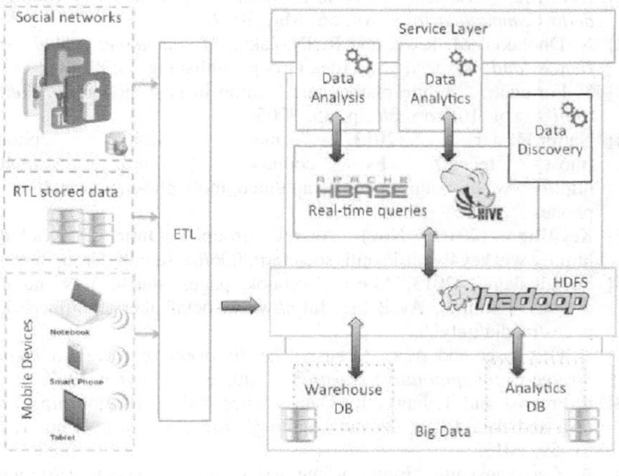

Fig. 3: User-Centric Big Data Framework

With this architecture, users do not see a divide between data and intelligence. They do not even need to be made aware of the difference between traditional transaction data and Big Data. The data and analysis flow would be seamless as they navigate and interact through various data and information sets.

5. Conclusion

This paper contributes to the discussion of Big Data in multiplatform media by providing additional solutions for a user-centric approach of content management. Proposed here is a prototype that focuses on fluid roles of the users within mass media contexts. In contrast to hierarchy-based structures, inherent to media, we proposed flexible environments that enhance user experiences.

In this data analytics part we focused to enhance user-environment interaction, by further enhancing RTL 102.5 extended model since it allows users to modify the environment based on their specific interests. In practical terms, an expanded understanding of Big Data paradigm has to reconsider the concept of the maps proposed as tools of visualization. Given that the geographical networks are no longer relevant for UGC data streams from multiple media companies', the maps gets conceptualized through visual representation as ways to organize and understand multiple streams of information. Similarly, this model assists content filtering process. Content flows could be redirected for those times of the day where user participation is less intensive, or where it fits better the context.

By capitalizing on the value creation to a user-centric approach, future studies should explore additional models that would fulfill diverse needs of users through user segmentation to assess multiple facets of needs. User experience levels through levels of activity and use of diverse sources, satisfaction with the fluid roles could be tested. The perception of user-sensitive, adaptive environment should be analyzed in different media contexts to identify station-specific issues and compare them with Big Data-specific issues. Furthermore, even if this model has been based on the previously identified user value creation, a more fine-grained user value should be continuously assessed. To account for diversified and changing user values, further studies are need to test the validity and success of the proposed model.

It is worth to highlight that the current user-centric model operates based on constraints through which users access Big Data. Big Data assumes content fluidity within a given company's data, while it is highly restrictive to external data sources because of intellectual property liability. From this perspective, users' experience can be only enhanced within the Big Data present in a given context. We proposed our model considering the existing Big Data model of RTL 102.5, thus explicating its limits. The future vision of Big Data for a user-centric approach should overcome these limitations. For example, users would be able to access all UGC streams from multiple media companies. By being exposed to multiple media platforms concurrently, users could easily navigate across various UGC streams generated by other users similar to them. One way of conceptualizing such aggregation of streams is by taking an example of multiple applications developed by media companies to foster UGC and access all of them with a single ID, which would account for data volume and veracity.

In a future vision of user-centric Big Data users would be given an access to multiple companies' UGC data that could be streamed in synergy. Big Data analytics would be used to filter data streams by large or narrow interest categories. For example, users could select "all radios", "commercial radios", "public radios" as broad categories or filter down to specific categories such as "rock music" or "Björk" as specific content or a "topic of the day."

User-centric Big Data paradigm as of now is subject to constraints – currently UGC content flows get distributed through a single company's space. Even if the visionary value user-centric future conceptually has no obstacles, yet, companies tend to create innovation that generates profit within its own boundaries. Also, some of the companies create profit by providing duplicates of existing services. Accessibility of cross-company data is another obstacle to Big Data for User-centric approach. In recent years the direction towards fluid data has been taken with convergence and consolidation. In such case, companies share data and share profits. However, convergence has not necessarily benefited users. From Big Data perspective, users are not yet able to freely navigate through a myriad of user-generated content across various services and tools. No cross-integration of the tools has been proposed as a finite benefit to the users. Yet, with a user-centric approach of Big Data, we argue that users should be able to access data stored outside company boundaries to map and personalize data to their own needs and goals. We position the user-centric scenario to fully explore the fluidity of Big Data and even ability to model the surrounding environment.

6. Acknowledgments

This research has been supported by the European Commission under the project i-Tour (Grant Agreement nr. 234239) and SUNSHINE (Grant Agreement nr. 325161). We are also greatful to RTL 102.5 that has inspired the use-case for our user-centric Big Data model.

References

[1] J. Gantz and D. Reinsel, "The digital universe in 2020: Big data, bigger digital shadows, and biggest growth in the far east," Technical report, IDC, Tech. Rep., 2012.

[2] C. Spurgeon and G. Goggin, "Mobiles into media: Premium rate sms and the adaptation of television to interactive communication cultures," *Continuum: Journal of Media & Cultural Studies*, vol. 21, no. 2, pp. 317–329, 2007.

[3] R. Higdon, W. Haynes, L. Stanberry, E. Stewart, G. Yandl, C. Howard, W. Broomall, N. Kolker, and E. Kolker, "Unraveling the complexities of life sciences data," *Big Data*, vol. 1, no. 1, pp. 42–50, March 2013.

[4] P. J. McKenzie, J. Burkell, L. Wong, C. Whippey, S. E. Trosow, and M. B. McNally, "User-generated online content 1: overview, current state and context," *First Monday*, vol. 17, no. 6-4, 2012.

[5] F. Provost and T. Fawcett, *Data science for Business*. Sebastopol, CA: O'Reilly Media, 2013.

[6] P. Mui, Chief Product and Engineering Officer, Acxiom. Personal communication, 2012.

[7] data. (2013, May) Merriam-webster.com. [Online]. Available: http://www.merriam-webster.com/dictionary/data

[8] D. Laney, "3-d data management: Controlling data volume, velocity and variety," META Group," Research Note, February 2001, http://blogs.gartner.com/doug-laney/files/2012/01/ad949-3D-Data-Management-Controlling-Data-Volume-Velocity-and-Variety.pdf.

[9] TDWI. (2012, July 24) Big data – why the 3vs just don't make sense. [Online]. Available: http://tdwi.org/Articles/2012/07/24/Big-Data-4th-V.aspx?Page=1

[10] A. Cuzzocrea, I.-Y. Song, and K. C. Davis, "Analytics over large-scale multidimensional data: the big data revolution!" in *Proceedings of the ACM 14th international workshop on Data Warehousing and OLAP*, ser. DOLAP '11. New York, NY, USA: ACM, 2011, pp. 101–104. [Online]. Available: http://doi.acm.org/10.1145/2064676.2064695

[11] value. (2013, May) Merriam-webster.com. [Online]. Available: http://www.merriam-webster.com/dictionary/value

[12] M. Castells, *Communication power*. OUP Oxford, 2009.

[13] S. Rafaeli and F. Sudweeks, "Networked interactivity," *Journal of Computer-Mediated Communication*, vol. 2, no. 4, pp. 0–0, 1997.

[14] V. Bilgram, A. Brem, and K.-I. Voigt, "User-centric innovations in new product development - systematic identification of lead users harnessing interactive and collaborative online-tools," *International Journal of Innovation Management*, vol. 12, no. 03, pp. 419–458, 2008. [Online]. Available: http://www.worldscientific.com/doi/abs/10.1142/S1363919608002096

[15] M. Proulx and S. Shepatin, *Social TV: How Marketers Can Reach and Engage Audiences by Connecting Television to the Web, Social Media, and Mobile*. Wiley & Sons, 2012.

[16] C. Shih, *The Facebook era: tapping online social networks to market, sell, and innovate*. Addison-Wesley Professional, 2010.

[17] J. F. Jensen, "Interactivity: tracking a new concept," 1998.

[18] S. Kiousis, "Interactivity: a concept explication," *New Media & Society*, vol. 4, no. 3, pp. 355–383, 2002.

[19] J. Van Dijck, "Users like you? theorizing agency in user-generated content," *Media, Culture, and Society*, vol. 31, no. 1, p. 41, 2009.

[20] I. A. the future. (2010, December) Consumers and the digital universe. [Online]. Available: http://www.emc.com/infographics/digital-universe-consumer-infographic.htm

[21] RTL 102.5, "La radio secondo rtl 102.5," *Supplemento ai Quaderni della Communicazione*, vol. 56, May 2007.

[22] N. Dholakia, M. Rask, and R. Dholakia, *M-commerce: global experiences and perspectives*. Idea Group Publishing, 2006.

[23] L. Fortunati, "Mobile phones and fashion in post-modernity," *Telektronikk*, vol. 101, no. 3/4, p. 35, 2005.

[24] NationMaster. (2013, may) Mobile phones (most recent) by country. [Online]. Available: http://www.nationmaster.com/graph/med_mob_pho-media-mobile-phones

[25] Key4Biz. (2010, Nov) Acotel group. [Online]. Available: http://www.key4biz.it/Profili_societari/2006/05/Acotel_Group.html

[26] Socialbakers. (2013, May) Facebook pages statistics & number of fans. [Online]. Available: http://www.socialbakers.com/facebook-pages/media/italy/

[27] B. G. Glaser and A. L. Strauss, *The discovery of grounded theory: Strategies for qualitative research*. Aldine de Gruyter, 1967.

[28] F. Provost and T. Fawcett, "Data science and its relationship to big data and data-driven decision making," *Big Data*, vol. 1, no. 1, pp. 51–59, 2013.

[29] A. Zelenkauskaite, "Between interactivity and gatekeeping: Audience participation via mobile texting and facebook in italian radiovision rtl 102.5," Bloomington, IN, USA, September 2012.

[30] J. Donath, "Signals in social supernets," *Journal of Computer-Mediated Communication*, vol. 13, no. 1, pp. 231–251, 2007.

[31] P. Thorndyke, "Differences in spatial knowledge acquired from maps and navigation," *Cognitive Psychology*, vol. 14, no. 4, pp. 560–589, October 1982.

[32] B. G. Witmer, J. H. Bailey, B. W. Knerr, and K. C. Parsons, "Virtual spaces and real world places: transfer of route knowledge," *International Journal of Human-Computer Studies*, vol. 45, no. 4, pp. 413–428, 1996.

[33] S. M. J. Card and B. Shneiderman, *Readings in Information Visualization*. San Francisco, CA: Morgan Kaufmann Publishers, 1999.

[34] M. J. Kraak and A. M. MacEachren, "Visualization for exploration of spatial data," *International Journal of Geographical Information Science*, vol. 13, no. 4, pp. 285–287, 1999.

[35] A. Zelenkauskaite, N. Bessis, S. Sotiriadis, and E. Asimakopoulou, "Interconnectedness of complex systems of internet of things through social network analysis for disaster management," in *Intelligent Networking and Collaborative Systems (INCoS), 2012 4th International Conference on*. IEEE, 2012, pp. 503–508.

[36] B. Simões and R. D. Amicis, "User-friendly interfaces for web gis," in *The 2011 World Congress in Computer Science, Computer Engineering, and Applied Computing*, July 2011.

[37] B. Simões, G. Conti, S. Piffer, and R. de Amicis, "Enterprise-level architecture for interactive web-based 3d visualization of geo-referenced repositories," in *Web3D'09: Proceedings of the 14th International Conference on 3D Web Technology*. New York, NY, USA: ACM, 2009, pp. 147–154.

[38] S. Ghemawat, H. Gobioff, and S.-T. Leung, "The google file system," in *ACM SIGOPS Operating Systems Review*, vol. 37, no. 5. ACM, 2003, pp. 29–43.

[39] C. Chu, S. K. Kim, Y.-A. Lin, Y. Yu, G. Bradski, A. Ng, and K. Olukotun, "Map-reduce for machine learning on multicore," *Advances in Neural Information Processing Systems*, vol. 19, p. 281, 2007.

A Fuzzy, Incremental, Hierachical Approach of Clustering Huge Collections of Web Documents

Patrick Hennig[1], Philipp Berger[1], Christian Godde[2], Daniel Hoffmann[2] and Christoph Meinel[3]
Hasso-Plattner-Institut
University of Potsdam, Germany
[1]Email: {patrick.hennig, philipp.berger}@hpi.uni-potsdam.de
[2]Email: {christian.godde, daniel.hoffmann}@student.hpi.uni-potsdam.de
[2]Email: office-meinel@hpi.uni-potsdam.de

Abstract— *Since every day millions of posts are published inside the blogosphere a huge collection of web documents develops. Clustering this ever-changing collection is a very time consuming task. Therefore some certain challenges has to be accomplished because a clustering cannot be executed from scratch all the time. The presented fuzzy, incremental and hierarchical clustering algorithm tries to succeed these challenges with both, clustering terms and documents in a meaningful way and keep them up-to-date all the time. Furthermore we take a critical look at the performance, which is crucial on such a live data collection.*

Keywords: Web Mining, Data Mining, Blog Mining, Clustering, Blogs, Unstructured Data

1. Introduction

With a tremendous circulation of several hundred million blogs worldwide, the ever changing collection of weblogs are getting bigger and bigger every day. For mining, modeling and presenting this think tank of open-source intelligence a very intelligent and fast clustering method is needed. This incorporates some very important and as well very difficult challenges.

Since a clustering of an ever-changing huge corpus consumes a lot of computing power, it cannot be calculated from scratch every time a new document is added. Therefore the first challenge is to keep the clustering up-to-date. In addition, the number of clusters cannot be fixed in the beginning, since different granularity levels should be covered. As a consequence, it has to be a hierarchical clustering. Furthermore, since we know a lot about the ambiguity from semantic web it is not appropriate to force documents and terms to fit into exactly one strict cluster. This means, the clustering algorithm has to consider fuzziness.

In the next Section the overall project, the presented work is integrated, is explained in more detail before some related work for such clustering techniques are introduced. In Section 5, we describe the basic challenges for the presented clustering. Afterwards the main algorithm and its characteristics is described in more detail.

In addition, the presented algorithm gets evaluated in Section 7. Furthermore the performance is evaluated and decisions are explained in order to improve the performance of the presented algorithm. Finally, some future work that can be conducted is highlighted before the paper is summarized in the last Section.

2. Project Scope

With a wide circulation of more than 200 million *weblogs* worldwide, weblogs with good reason are one of the most important data streams in the World Wide Web. Therefore, weblogs offer access to latest information discussed in the real world. Since writing posts in weblogs goes along with a high editorial effort, the available information is of major interest. However, for a user it is becoming harder and harder to gain an overview of all discussions in the blogosphere. It is almost impossible for a user to extract information from the web, especially from the blogosphere. Hence, a system that collects information from the blogosphere and presents it to the user in a very meaningful way would be of great use.

Therefore, mining, analyzing, modeling and presenting this enormous amount of data is the overall aim of the project the presented work is integrated in. This enables the user to detect technical trends, political climates or news articles about a specific topic. Most approaches to mining and analyzing such a huge amount of data focus on offline algorithms which use pre-aggregated results. This is in contrast to the continuously growing nature of the World Wide Web. As a result, including the latest data is one of the key aspects of data mining on the web. This is exactly the topic covered by the *BlogIntelligence*[1] project. Since BlogIntelligence usees different text mining analytics a clustering is a fundamental factor of success.

[1]BlogIntelligence is a tool the extract and analyze data such as content and links from weblogs of the German blogosphere in order to visualize this information and provide a tool to explore and discover the world of social media. More information on: http://www.blog-intelligence.com/

3. Related Work

As the field of cluster analysis is very complicated and algorithms heavily depend on the specific domain, there are as many different papers on clustering as there are possible use-cases. In this section we mention some of them that are closely related to our own work.

The initial idea for an incremental clustering was introduced by Arnaud Ribert et al. [1]. They explain an efficient way of inserting new elements into existing hierarchical clusterings and give a brief overview of hierarchical clustering itself. In their evaluation they show that the required memory and number of computations can be significantly reduced with an incremental algorithm.

Among other improvements in our algorithm we mainly focused on the efficiency of the distance matrix calculations. The map reduce technique that is now in use and described in the implementation section is based on the work of Elsayed et al. [2].

With the objective that the algorithm should perform in reasonable time the focus moves towards building up a hierarchy tree. Therefore we looked at different approaches for preparing the data in order to improve efficiency of clustering. Dash et al. [3] relies on partitioning the items beforehand.

The 'BIRCH' algorithm by Zhang et al. [4] would be an alternative that uses a different tree structure for a first rough clustering. It can be computed in quadratic time and thereby reduces the time that has to be spent for the final clustering. Unfortunately the time complexity even for these sophisticated techniques can not be better than $O(n^2)$.

4. Clustering Techniques

a) Partitional Clustering: The most prominent representative of the first class is the k-means algorithm. Partitional clusters divide a database into a specific amount of clusters. In general this number of clusters (k) has to be given in advance and it is not possible to change it later on. The problem is to find the optimal k if the exact composition of the data is not well known before.

b) Hierarchical Clustering: A Hierarchical clustering does not produce a partition into a specified number of clusters. It produces aso called dendrogram. This dendogram can be build either top-down or bottom-up. The first type is called divisive clustering. Starting with the whole data set and splitting it into two subsets until every item is represented by a leaf node. The top-down clustering is called agglomerative clustering. Starting with each item in a separate node and combining two nodes until the root includes the whole data set.

In both cases, when finished, the dendrogram forms a hierarchical binary tree with each item of the given database as leaf node and the root representing the whole database. Every node in the tree represents a subset of the database and thereby a sub-cluster. The greater the difference between the two sub-nodes, the higher the node is in the hierarchy. Knowing this, we can get few big clusters as well as many small clusters from the same dendrogram without recomputing the clustering. The biggest disadvantage of hierarchical clustering versus partitional cluster techniques is the higher computational time.

c) Hard and Fuzzy Clustering: In general, each item is assigned to exactly one cluster it fits best (e.g. the average distance to the other cluster members is the smallest). This is called hard clustering. If we want to express that an item can be quite similar to different other items we have to introduce a fuzzy clustering. In fuzzy clustering techniques the membership of an item to a cluster is expressed as a probability value which in total sums up to 1. That way any item can appear in multiple clusters.

d) Incremental Clustering: Incremental clustering has to be taken into account either if the corpus to be clustered is too big to keep the information about all items at the same time in memory or if the corpus is increasing over time and we do not want to repeat the clustering every time a new item is added. Incremental clustering has the advantage that we can add the items of the database one by one and therefore reduce time and space complexity. A huge disadvantage is the order-dependence of the resulting clustering. We might get completely different results if the order of the items added to the clusters is changed. Thus, it is very difficult to guarantee the quality of the clustering.

5. Clustering the Blogosphere

The goal of the system that is described in this paper is to improve and add new functionality to *BlogIntelligence*. Inside the blogosphere cluster analysis faces a lot of old and new problems. The first question to be answered is: Where do we want to find clusters? This question can be answered in two ways. On the one hand, blogs and their post can be clustered. These represent documents in a more classical view on cluster analysis. So the goal is to find groups of blogs that might cover the same topic like politics or computer science. This is important because it helps finding new links between different blogs and thereby helps authors and users to explore the Web 2.0.

On the other hand, we are also interested in clustering features of blogs and posts. These are terms or also tags of blog posts. By clustering terms it gets necessary to find words that together best describe specific topics. So we are able to categorize blogs even better and again improve the possibility to explore the blogosphere. These term clusters can be used for further analysis like trend detection and visualization.

The main challenge the blogosphere imposes on clustering is its size. The user might dive into the blogosphere from the top and narrow the search down to parts of the blogosphere he is interested in. Hence, the clustering should provide a way of getting a very rough division as well as a very detailed one.

The size of the blogosphere also pushes the need for the efficiency of the clustering algorithm. Another characteristic of the blogosphere is that new documents are added continuously. Because of this, it is not applicable to constantly recompute the clustering. It has to be possible to change the existing one if a new item has to be integrated.

All in all, a system is needed that clusters both, documents and terms, that is capable of adding new documents to an existing cluster, that returns clusters of variable size and amounts, and that assigns terms and documents to multiple topics and groups. This leads to a hierarchical, incremental, fuzzy clustering.

6. Implementation

6.1 General Idea

Before the main algorithm is described in detail we first have to define the most important terms concerning cluster analysis within blog posts.

6.1.1 Post term matrix

The post term matrix describes the distribution of terms across all blog posts. For every post a list contains the frequency of each possible term. The optimal case provides normalized tf-idf values as described in the next Section. The other way around, it is also possible to get a list that for a specific term containing all frequencies among all blog posts. The number of terms defines the dimensionality of a document vector and the other way round. Typically, the post term matrix is sparse because for each blog post only the most representing terms (terms with the highest tfidf) are stored.

6.1.2 Term frequency - inverse document frequency

The *tf-idf* value [5] describes the frequency of a term in a document in comparison to its frequency in the whole corpus. A term that appears in all available documents is not very descriptive for a single document and therefore has a low *tf-idf* score for every document. On the other hand, a term that only occurs in one document has a high score for this specific document even if its frequency is low and therefore has a high meaning for this document. The general formula for calculating the tf-idf is given as follows:

$$tfidf(t_i, d_j) = tf(t_i, d_j) * \log \frac{N}{n_i}$$

$tf(t_i, d_j)$ is the frequency of term t_i in document d_j. N is the number of documents in the corpus. And n_i is the number of documents that contain term t_i.

6.1.3 Similarity measure

To measure the similarity between documents and terms, we use the cosine similarity. It measures the inner angle between two tf-idf vectors.

$$sim(d_1, d_2) = \frac{d_1 \cdot d_2}{|d_1||d_2|}$$

To accelerate similarity computation normalized tf-idf vectors can be used. That way the cosine similarity becomes a simple inner product

$$sim(d_1, d_2) = d_1 \cdot d_2 = \sum_{i=0}^{n} w(t_i, d_1) w(t_i, d_2)$$

where $w(t, d)$ is the tf-idf of term t in document d.

6.1.4 Initial Clustering

Initially a common agglomerative clustering algorithm is used. To determine how many documents should be taken into account at the initial clustering, we take a look at *Heaps' law* [6]. This helps to reduce the computational effort enormously. Heaps' law describes how the size of the vocabulary V_R grows depending on the document size n:

$$V_R(n) = Kn^\beta$$

For English language normally K is between 10 and 100 and β is between 0.4 and 0.6. The vertical line in 1 shows a possible cut to cover sufficient terms of the existing corpus. This ensures that most terms are covered in the cluster and the clustering runs still in an acceptable time.

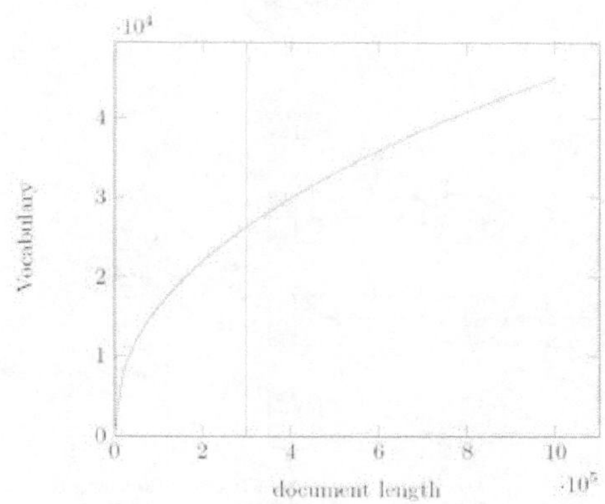

Fig. 1: Example plot for Heaps law $V_R(n) = Kn^\beta$

6.2 Approaching Fuzzyness

Since a term can appear in several contexts, a fuzzy clustering should be used as well. Thus a term can be contained in several clusters. To achieve this, we search for all pairs of items that have a similarity above a certain threshold. These pairs constitute the leaves in the clustering tree. In order to reduce the computational effort, the calculation of the similarity can be limited to terms that have been occurred with each other in the same document once.

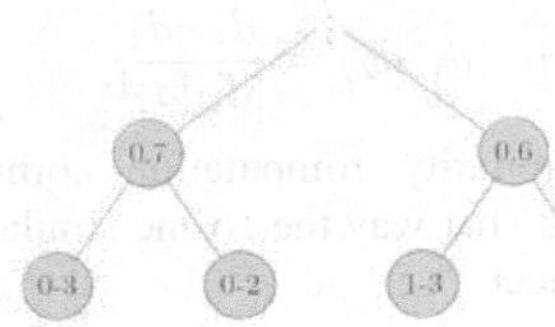

Fig. 2: Two clusters: $\{0, 2, 3\}$ and $\{1, 3, 4\}$

6.3 Algorithm

The initial clustering algorithm consists of three steps: finding the items that have a high similarity and associate them in leaves, adjusting the distance matrix and computing the hierarchical clustering.

1) **Finding leaves** For efficient similarity calculation a MapReduce [7] approach fits to our needs. MapReduce is a framework that allows parallel execution of an algorithm on several CPUs or machines. The *map* functions map a list of key-value pairs from one domain to another, the *shuffle* function groups the results and the *reduce* function computes the results for each group (see Figure 3).

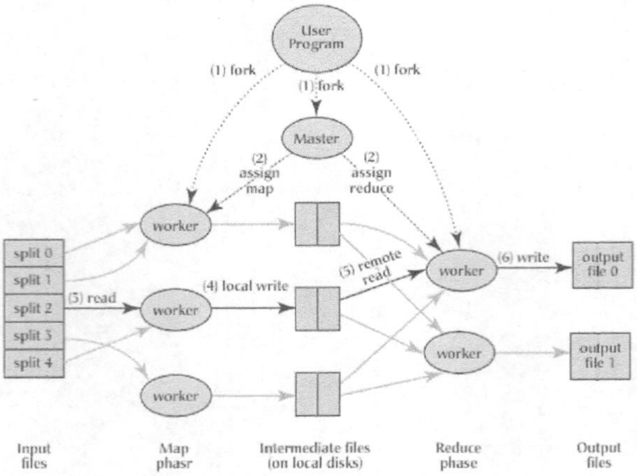

Fig. 3: General MapReduce architecture (taken from [7])

This method is used for computing document similarity with the approach described in [8]. For each term a list of the documents it appears in and its tf-idf value in this document is constructed. The *map* task multiplies the term weights for each pair of documents in the posting. The output is sorted by the keys, resulting in a list of pairs of documents as keys and a list of products computed in the *map* step. *Reduce* sums up the products and outputs the similarity values for the pairs of documents (see Figure 4). While this method is much faster than calculating the cosine similarity by iterating over the vectors, it uses more memory. Nevertheless, since the MapReduce approach allows simple distributed computing and main memory gets cheap we favor the faster version.

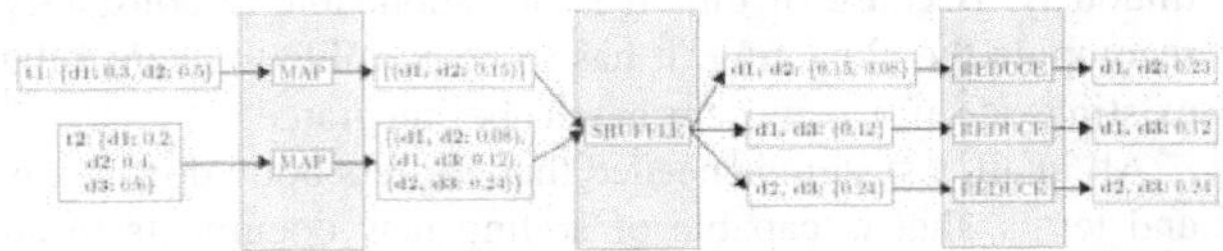

Fig. 4: Computing document similarities with MapReduce

After computing the similarity values, each pair having a similarity above a certain threshold is associated in a leaf node. The tf-idf vector for this pair is the average of the two tf-idf vectors of the associated items.

2) **Calculating the distance matrix** To compute a matrix of distances between these new leaves, we use the similar *map* and *reduce* function mentioned before with the new tf-idf vectors.
3) **Hierarchical Clustering** The implementation makes use of the *Efficient HAC* [9, 368] (Algorithm 1), which uses priority queues. For each row of the distance matrix a priority queue keeps the entries sorted in decreasing order. The maximum value of $P[k]$ consists of the similarity and index of the cluster most similar to the cluster with index k.
   Since the C++ standard library priority queue does not allow erasing other elements than the top, we implemented a suitable version using the *std::make_heap*, *std::push_heap* and *std::pop_heap* functions. In this algorithm I stores the clusters that are still active, A stores the clustering as a sequence of merges. With these optimization the time complexity becomes $O(n^2 \log n)$.

6.4 Adding and removing documents/terms

6.4.1 Adding

To add an element into the cluster tree it is compared with each existing element as shown in Algorithm 2. If the similarity is above the threshold mentioned in Section 6.3, a new leaf is constructed with this pair of elements. For each new leaf its place in the clustering hierarchy is determined by starting at the root node and following the path with the highest similarity. To accelerate this procedure, each centroid of a cluster is cached. If a leaf is reached, a new inner node with this leaf and the new leaf as children is inserted. Its centroid is computed and the similarity values up to the root are refreshed.

```
Input: d_1, ..., d_n
for n = 1 to N do
    for i = 1 to N do
        C[n][i].sim = d_n · d_i;
        C[n][i].index = i;
    end
    I[n] = 1;
    P[n] = priority queue for C[n] sorted on sim;
    P[n].DELETE(C[n][n]) (don't want
    self-similarities);
end
A = [ ];
for k = 1 to N - 1 do
    k1 = arg maxk: I[k]=1 P[k].MAX().sim;
    k2 = P[k1].MAX().index;
    A.APPEND(k1, k2);
    I[k2] = 0;
    P[k1] = [ ];
    forall the i with I[i] = 1 and i = k1 do
        P[i].DELETE(C[i][k1]);
        P[i].DELETE(C[i][k2]);
        C[i][k1].sim = SIM(i, k1, k2);
        P[i].INSERT(C[i][k1]);
        C [k1][i].sim = SIM(i, k1, k2);
        P[k1].INSERT (C[k1][i]);
    end
end
return A;
```

Algorithm 1: Efficient HAC algorithm using priority queues (from [9, 386])

```
Input: element e' to add
foreach other element e do
    if similarity(e', e) > threshold then
        construct new leaf(e', e);
    end
end
foreach new leaf l' do
    node = root;
    while !node.isLeaf() do
        node =
        arg max_{n∈{node.left,node.right}} sim(l', n);
    end
    construct new inner node(leaf, node);
end
refresh similarity up to root;
```

Algorithm 2: Add element to clustering tree

6.4.2 Removing

When removing an element from the tree each leaf containing this element is inspected as shown in Algorithm 3. In order to not remove an element that is just contained in one leaf, we need to keep track of the number of leaves an element appears in. Suppose we want to delete it from the tree. If a leaf (e, e') is the only one containing the element e' that is not deleted, e is deleted from the node. Otherwise the father node of the node to be deleted is replaced by its sibling node. Finally, the similarities of the nodes up in the hierarchy get refreshed.

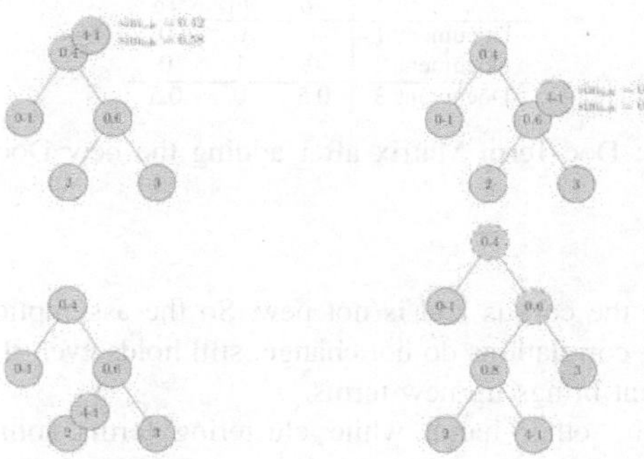

Fig. 5: Inserting a new leaf into the cluster tree, following the path of highest similarity. The similarity values in the dashed nodes needs to be refreshed.

```
Input: element e to delete
foreach leaves (e,e') containing e do
    if number of leaves containing e' > 1 or
    the leaf contains only one element then
        replace father node with brother node ;
    else
        delete element from leaf;
    end
    refresh similarity up to root;
end
```

Algorithm 3: Remove element from clustering tree

6.5 Differences between Document and Term Clustering

When we talk about adding a new element to the cluster, regarding our use-case, this means generally adding a new blog post and thereby a new document to the corpus. Adding a new term independently is rather impossible. This leads to the following observation.

While clustering documents, the insertion of a new item does not raise any complications. Table 1 shows a simple document-term matrix after document 3 was added to. Because the new document does not change the correlations of all other documents, the new document can simply be compared to the existing documents and a new base nodes can be added accordingly.

When adding a document, there might also be new terms, but the frequencies for these in the existing documents will always be zero. Otherwise the term must have already

	T_0	T_1	T_2
Document 1	1	0	0
Document 2	0	1	0
Document 3	0.5	0	0.5

Table 1: Doc-Term Matrix after adding the new Document 3

been in the corpus and is not new. So the assumption that existing correlations do not change, still holds even if a new document brings up new terms.

On the other hand, while clustering terms some new challenges has to be faced. As shown in Table 1, the terms T_0 and T_2 get more similar because they are now used together in the same document. The same way a new document might as well decrease the similarity of two existing terms. Taking this into account we adjust our algorithm for adding elements as follows:

For all terms in the new document

1) find all base nodes that include the term as one of their elements
2) remove all those base nodes
3) find and add new base node according to Section 6.4

This ensures that changes in the increasing or decreasing similarity between existing items are propagated to the cluster without recomputing the clustering as a whole. Nevertheless the number of nodes that has to be removed and added can be quite huge, depending on the composition of the clustering and the new document. As a side-effect the cluster tree might get smaller although a new document is added.

6.6 Runtime versus Correctness

The presented method for adding new elements does not always produce a correct cluster tree, but it is much faster than computing a new cluster tree. Additionally, the clustering is very heavily order-dependent as already pointed out. Therefore the more documents are added incrementally the more inaccurate the cluster becomes. To maintain an at least proximate correct partitioning, the clustering algorithm can be performed in background periodically. And the currently active cluster can be replaced by the latest computed one.

7. Evaluation

7.1 Improvements Through Parallelization

For parallelization, OpenMP [10] allows simple multi-platform parallel programming. Compiler directives indicate the code parts that are executed in parallel. *#pragma omp parallel* denotes a parallelized section. Then, as many threads are created as there are CPUs. OpenMP takes over the whole work of thread creation and management. *#pragma omp for* distributes the iterations of a for loop to these threads. Critical sections are marked with *#pragma omp critical section*. If a compiler does not understand these directives, the code still compiles and the for loop is executed sequentially.

The part that profits the most of parallelization is the pair-wise similarity computation which is used for example for creating the distance matrix. By using map reduce as pointed out in Section 6.3, a high degree of parallelization can be achieved. Parallelizing the construction of the dendogram has to be done carefully because we are looking for the global most similar items and not for the one in a subset of the dataset. This requires a high amount of inter-thread communication.

7.2 Runtime

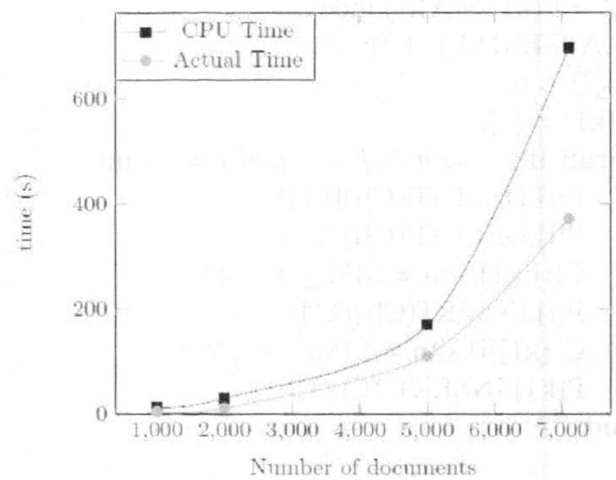

Fig. 6: Runtime of the initial clustering algorithm for different corpus sizes

For evaluation purposes we used the Classic collection of documents called Classic3 published by Cornell University[1]. This collection of documents is often used as benchmark in text mining. It consists of 7095 documents and 5896 terms.

Figure 6 shows the results of the presented clustering algorithm with this collection. It ran on a 4-core 64bit Linux-System with 8GB main memory. The similarity threshold for combining elements into one base node was set to 0.8 which resulted in approximately 25% combined base nodes and 75% single base nodes while clustering documents. The CPU Time is the aggregated time of all cores working while the actual time is the time the program actually runs. The results show that the presented algorithm has a complexity of about $O(n^3)$. Which is the general complexity of hierarchical clustering algorithms. However these figures do not entirely represent the proposed algorithm. The documents in the classic collection have the characteristic that documents with a lower ID also only use terms with lower IDs. This leads to considerably shorter term vectors for smaller corpus sizes

[1] You can find more information about the document collection at http://www.dataminingresearch.com/index.php/2010/09/classic3-classic4-datasets/ and download it at ftp://ftp.cs.cornell.edu/pub/smart/

and longer vectors for the whole corpus. So the numbers are not unbiased and in practice the complexity is better than $O(n^3)$.

8. Future Work

a) Memory versus Time Complexity: A big step in the direction of reasonable performance was the decision to use map reduce for pairwise similarity computation. This reduced the calculation time of the distance matrix by 80%. Tthe downside of this is the fact that our implementation of the map reduce tasks extremely increases the memory consumption. This is due to the fact that during the map step all values in the document-term matrix are emitted before they are combined during the reduce step. However, as the whole environment is based on main memory computation and runs on systems offering a lot of main memory the advantage of better performance outweighs this disadvantage.

b) Distributed Hierarchical Clustering: In Section 7.1 we pointed out that parallelizing the hierarchy construction is not easy because every time time all distance values are needed. Dash et al. [3] introduced a way to compute the hierarchy in a distributed manner called 'partially overlapping partitioning (POP)'. The algorithm is split into two parts. At first the data is distributed into p partitions with p given by the number of processors available and clustered into sub-clusters. In the second phase the p sub-clusters have to be combined and further clustered. This approach can be combined with the approach presented in this paper to reduce the execution time.

9. Conclusion

With this paper we presented an approach of a fuzzy, hierarchical, incremental clustering. The initial step of finding items that have a high similarity and combining them into one base node enables a fuzzy clustering. Hereby, terms representing different topics can be grouped together.

The hierarchical characteristic provides the user with different levels of granularity for the composition of weblogs. By incrementally adding new documents we can cover the fact that bloggers publishes new blog posts all the time. As we showed, the performance of the presented algorithm is already pretty good, but can be boosted with some smaller improvements. Finally, the algorithm is able to deal with all challenges that are imposed by the overall use-case of clustering the blogosphere.

References

[1] A. Ribert, A. Ennaji, and Y. Lecourtier, "An incremental hierarchical clustering," in *IAPR-VI'99*, Trois Rivières, Québec, Canada, 1999, pp. 586–591.

[2] T. Elsayed, J. Lin, and D. W. Oard, "Pairwise document similarity in large collections with mapreduce," 1999, pp. 265–268.

[3] M. Dash and P. Scheuermann, "Efficient parallel hierarchical clustering," in *In International Europar Conference (EURO-PARŠ04*, 2004.

[4] T. Zhang, R. Ramakrishnan, and M. Livny, "Birch: an efficient data clustering method for very large databases," in *Proceedings of the 1996 ACM SIGMOD international conference on Management of data*, ser. SIGMOD '96. New York, NY, USA: ACM, 1996, pp. 103–114. [Online]. Available: http://doi.acm.org/10.1145/233269.233324

[5] K. Sparck Jones, "A statistical interpretation of term specificity and its application in retrieval," pp. 132–142, Dec. 1988.

[6] H. S. Heaps, *Information Retrieval: Computational and Theoretical Aspects*. Orlando, FL, USA: Academic Press, Inc., 1978.

[7] J. Dean and S. Ghemawat, "Mapreduce: simplified data processing on large clusters," *Commun. ACM*, vol. 51, no. 1, pp. 107–113, Jan. 2008. [Online]. Available: http://doi.acm.org/10.1145/1327452.1327492

[8] T. Elsayed, J. Lin, and D. W. Oard, "Pairwise document similarity in large collections with mapreduce," in *Proceedings of the 46th Annual Meeting of the Association for Computational Linguistics on Human Language Technologies: Short Papers*. Association for Computational Linguistics, 2008, pp. 265–268.

[9] C. D. Manning, P. Raghavan, and H. Schtze, *Introduction to Information Retrieval*. New York, NY, USA: Cambridge University Press, 2008.

[10] OpenMP Architecture Review Board. (2011) OpenMP application program interface version 3.1. [Online]. Available: http://www.openmp.org/mp-documents/OpenMP3.1.pdf

Clinical Database applications in hospital

Mo Sun, Ye Lin, Roger Yim Lee

sun2m, lin2y, lee1ry@cmich.edu
Department of Computer Science
Central Michigan University

Abstract

Database applications are used in many fields, for example, in education, mathematics, and hospitals. Clinical database is one type of database. It is often used in hospitals, medicine factories, and colleges of medicine. Some clinical databases include patients symptoms and prescriptions. Since clinical databases cover such important information, they help researchers develop new theories and methods of using drugs. At the same time, they are used to predict the risk of death; however, few of the databases are combined to be considered in single cases of patients. In this paper, we create a relational clinical database used by doctors choosing drugs for a patient. The results of comparing testing cases by using either single clinical database or the relational databases will be reported in this paper. They show that the relational databases provide more details to be considered in each case.

Keywords: clinical database, hypertension

1 Introduction

With the rapid development of contemporary society, people have to accelerate their pace to catch up to avoid falling behind others. The same situation happened to databases too. Several decades ago, it developed so fast that not only was it applied in storing as well as managing the data, but also it turned to a method that user need to manage all kinds of data. Nowadays, an increasing number of people have already had or tend to have healthy problem, such as cancer, heart attack. It is necessary to pay attention on peoples' health. Thus, it is essential to establish a database for it. It is an application of clinical database in hospitals.

This database is really meaningful for peoples' health. First of all, the clinical database can improve the relationship between patients and hospitals. This database records statistics about some treatments as well as the death rate of some diseases like hypertension. It is much easier for doctors to check the related data between the treatments and the diseases. Furthermore, the clinical database reduces the difficulties of searching the information of the disease. The clinical database provides a platform for doctors to learn more on diseases. Doctors can use this database to record the disease whether they cured it or not. This is benefit for both doctors and patients.

In this research paper, the clinical database is based on the existing databases which contain diseases recorded in hospital database. However, it is not as same as the existing databases we found in other journals and research papers. It's actually much more specific and convenient than the existing databases when it is applied to hospitals. This clinical database selects some exiting database, then it picks some useful information. The last step is to create a new database based on these past databases' attributes we collected.

2 Bacground

2.1 Death rate

The death rate of specific disease was collected[1][4][6]. Hospitals used those clinical databases and analyzed part of hospital statistics of inpatients. The results showed that the collected data can be used to monitor health care performance and complement the clinical databases[1].

2.2 prescription

Besides, there exists other article about Traditional Chinese Medicine (TCM). In 2006, Chen[2] and his colleagues published an article about TCM. They gather the information like prescriptions, constituent herbs and so on about TCM. This article demonstrates the usage of TCM in many drugs and multiple targets in single treatment.

2.3 drug use

One research studied in using drugs on specific diseases[5]. They took the records which show how many percentage of people having this diseases take a specific drug at every single period of the treating. They use these records to analyze whether the specific drug should be used in each period for every patient.

3 Method

3.1 Research Question and Answer

In this research paper, the goal of the study is to find a link for tables of clinical databases, then use the relationship to create a new database. Since there exists different types of clinical databases, combining several of them, the function of the new database is different. Thus, this result several question:

Question 1: How many databases should be considered?

Answer: Two or three of different types of databases are better. Once there are too many databases, it's difficult to analysis and select useful information. In the other hand, if the databases are too little, there also exist problems. Less information can be used in the new database.

Question 2: Which type of databases can be combined with?

Answer: Different but related types of databases are better to combine. If the databases have no relationship, it's hard to put the attributes in the same, new database. On the contrary, if the databases are of the same types, there is no need to select them.

Question 3: What kind of databases we choose?

Answer: We chose three clinical databases. All of them are used for different purposes [1][2][5]. One is about the death rate of a specific disease, one presents the detail information of drugs, and another one is about the rate of a drug used among patients.

3.2 Research Table

In this study, three kinds of tables are used. The first table regarding the death rate of isolated coronary artery bypass is used to predict the risk of patients[1].

Table 1 | Odds ratios (95% confidence intervals) for mortality in hospital for isolated coronary artery bypass (CABG), repair of ruptured abdominal aortic aneurysm (AAA), repair of unruptured AAA, and colorectal excision procedures for cancer for variables applying to all four index procedures

Variable and value	Isolated CABG	AAA with rupture	AAA without rupture	Colorectal excision
No of cases in training and validation set	152 523	12 781	31 705	144 370
No (%) of deaths in training and validation set	3247 (2.1)	5987 (46.8)	3246 (10.2)	10 424 (7.2)
Age (years):				
≥85	20.1 (12.5 to 32.42)	8.18 (5.17 to 12.96)	8.49 (5.55 to 13)	19.00 (14.43 to 25.02)
80-84	9.97 (6.90 to 14.41)	5.87 (3.79 to 9.08)	6.40 (4.3 to 9.51)	12.23 (9.3 to 16.1)
75-79	5.40 (3.89 to 7.77)	4.43 (2.88 to 6.80)	4.69 (3.18 to 6.94)	8.23 (6.26 to 10.83)
70-74	3.43 (2.44 to 4.84)	3.33 (2.17 to 5.12)	3.59 (2.43 to 5.31)	5.65 (4.29 to 7.44)
65-69	2.42 (1.72 to 3.42)	2.34 (1.52 to 3.61)	2.48 (1.67 to 3.69)	3.67 (2.78 to 4.86)
60-64	1.72 (1.22 to 2.44)	1.66 (1.07 to 2.58)	1.97 (1.31 to 2.97)	2.83 (2.13 to 3.76)
55-59	1.22 (0.85 to 1.75)	1.89 (1.19 to 2.99)	1.76 (1.13 to 2.74)	1.74 (1.29 to 2.34)
50-54	1.00 (0.68 to 1.47)	1.71 (1.02 to 2.86)	1.05 (0.6 to 1.84)	1.69 (1.23 to 2.32)
45-49	1.11 (0.73 to 1.68)	0.76 (0.37 to 1.60)	1.79 (1 to 3.22)	1.36 (0.94 to 1.97)
≤44	1	1	1	1
Sex:				
Female	1.39 (1.29 to 1.51)	1.06 (0.96 to 1.16)	1.23 (1.12 to 1.35)	0.77 (0.74 to 0.80)
Male	1	1	1	1

Figure 1: predict the risk of patients

source:[1]

This table divides the patients into 10 groups by their age, and it also divides the patients by gender. Four kinds of treatments are given in this table. Thus, the table shows the death rate of different age of people adopting different treatments, and the death rate of different gender of people adopting different treatments.

The second table shows detailed medicine informations. One typical example is a prescription of a Chinese traditional medicine[2].

TCMID Result(Formula)	
Chinese Name	Wu Ji Bai Feng Wan (乌鸡白凤丸)
Common Name	White Phoenix Bolus of Black-bone Chicken
Function	"To repenish qi and nourish blood, regulate menstruation and arrest leukorrhagia."
Herbal Components	Wu Ji; Lu Rong Jiao; Bie Jia; Mu Li; Sang Piao Xiao; Ren shen; Huang qi; Dang gui; Bai shao; Xiang fu; Tian Dong; Gan cao; Sheng Di Huang; Shu Di Huang; Chuan xiong; Yin Chai Hu; Dan Shen; huai Shan Yao; Qian shi; Lu Jiao Shuang;

Figure 2: prescription

source:[2]

This table includes the name, common name, function, and components of the medicine.

The third table is about the use rate of disease modifying anti-rheumatic drugs.

Table II. Use of disease modifying anti-rheumatic drugs in 251 patients with early rheumatoid arthritis of less than one year's duration from the Western Consortium of Practicing Rheumatologists (CPR) between 1993 and 1996 at baseline, and 6 months, 12 months, and 24 months after baseline.

Drug	Baseline	6 months	1 year	2 years
Methotrexate	35.7%	53.6%	55.3%	57.4%
Hydroxychloroquine	16.7%	30.0%	30.2%	31.2%
Injectable gold	3.6%	2.7%	2.0%	0%
Sulfasalazine	7.1%	9.1%	13.1%	12.1%
Prednisone	40.1%	43.2%	44.2%	45.4%

Source: (22)

Figure 3: Drug use

source:[5]

It shows different drugs' rate of use used to treat a same disease in different period.

3.3 Research direction decision

Since we choose three tables for different purposes, and they are used for analyzing different diseases, we cannot simply combine these three tables. We selected a specific field "hypertensio" to do the research.

3.4 Data collection

Since we chose hypertension as our topic, we collected the data we needed from many articles and databases. Three kinds of data we need in our research include: death rate of hypertension, drugs used for treating hypertension, the rate of use these drugs for treating hypertension.

3.5 The schema of new tables

First of all, we create a table of disease:

attribute	type	constraint
disease	char	primary key

Table 1: Disease

3.5.1 death rate table schema

attribute	type	constraint
disease	char	foreign key
year	int	primary key
age	char	key
death rate	float	not null

Table 2: The schema of death rate

We chose year, age, and death rate for each combination of year and age. For the limited data we could find, the table only contains data in three years: 1995, 2000, 2005, and we changed the age range to four group: 20-34, 35-49, 50-64, older than 65[6].

3.5.2 medicine prescription table schema

attribute	type	constraint
name	char	primary key
function	string	not null
warning	string	
side effect	string	
disease	char	foreign key

Table 3: The schema of use rate for drugs

Learning the prescription from Figure 2, we get rid of "common name" in our new table, and add "warning" ,"side effect" and "disease."

3.5.3 The schema of use rate for drugs

We only use name and use rate in this table to show how frequently a certain drug is being used, and we do not discuss it in each period of a disease.

3.6 Result

Since we did research on hypertension, we found two typical drugs which are used to treat high blood pressure. Table 5 is the drug table. It contains many drugs. In Table 5, we only present three examples:

To create the death rate table, we collect data and reorganize it as Figure 4 shows[1]. Death rate of hypertension for different age range are shown.

	hypertension			
year	20-34	35-49	50-64	older than 65
1995	0.0019	0.0033	0.0094	0.043
2000	0.0014	0.003	0.008	0.0457
2005	0.0012	0.0026	0.007	0.0434

Figure 4: death rate of hypertension

source:[1]

As we can see in Figure 4, the death rate become higher when the age is larger. Especially for the elders who have hypertension, they have the most probability of death although the number death is still a very small part of the whole patients.

The prescription of medicine are like Table 6. Table 6 is the prescription of beta-blockers[8].

Death rate are collected as Table 7 as shown below

We used beta-blockers as a sample to test these tables. For example, a patient who has hypertension sees a doctor, and the doctor wants to know whether he should include beta-blockers in the prescription for this specific patient.

First of all he should check the detail information about beta-block are like that in Table 6. Then, he knows that it cannot be used with propranolol or pindolol with thioridazine or chlorpromazine because they

attribute	type	constraint
name	char	foreign key
use rate	float	primary key

Table 4: The schema of use rate for drugs

name
Beta-blockers
Thiazides
Aspirin

Table 5: drugs

name	beta-blockers
function	beta blockers reduce heart rate; reduce blood pressure by dilating blood vessels
warning	Combining propranolol or pindolol with thioridazine or chlorpromazine may result in low blood pressure
side effect	diarrhea, stomach cramps, nausea, vomiting

Table 6: prescription of beta-blockers

name	Use rate
Beta-blockers	36.9%
Nitrates	32.1%
Spironolactone	20.5%

Table 7: drug use rate

source[2]

may result in low blood pressure. If the patient has other diseases at the same time and using any of the drugs above, the doctor should reconsider whether he should include beta-blockers in this prescription. The warning in Table 8 is the most important part for either this drug or patients.

If the patient does not use ant of the drugs above, the doctor should check the use rate (Table 7) and death rate (Figure 4) next. If the use rate is decreasing in recent years, it means doctor should use the drug carefully. It may be because the side effects are so strong which hurts patients in recent years. The third thing the doctor should consider is the patient's age; if the patient is under 65, meaning the death rate is very low, the effect of age can be ignored in this case, but if the patient is older than 65, the doctor may be more careful using drugs and consult for the history of the drugs used in other case of elders who have hypertension.

4 Conclusion and Future Work

A single table like Figure 4 is only used to make a guess of a certain group of patients' death rate for current year[6]. A single table like Table 6 only used for develop drugs[2]. Compared to a single table, the relation database shows more details to be considered when choosing drugs for a specific patient. Each of these tables are important for either patients or hospital. The age of a patient, the warning and side effect of a drug, and the drug use rate should not be ignored in every single case.

The limitation of our work is that we did not have use rate for each year, and we did not design a table of the history record for patients. If we have this information, doctors may get more convenience form this database we created. Another limitation of our work is that we did not analyze any reason for drugs' use rate decreasing and increasing, so we cannot check whether the increasing or decreasing have effect on choosing drugs.

In the future, we hope a more exhaustive clinical database used to choose drugs can be created, which includes what we did not contain in ours.

Reference

[1]Aylin, P., Bottle, A., Majeed, A. (2007). Use of administrative data or clinical databases as predictors of risk of death in hospital: comparison of models.*Bmj, 334*(7602), 1044.

[2]Chen, X., Zhou, H., Liu, Y. B., Wang, J. F., Li, H., Ung, C. Y., ... Chen, Y. Z. (2006). Database of traditional Chinese medicine and its application to studies of mechanism and to prescription validation. *British journal of pharmacology, 149*(8), 1092-1103.

[3]Komajda, M., Follath, F., Swedberg, K., Cleland, J., Aguilar, J. C., Cohen-Solal, A., ... Mason, J. (2003). The EuroHeart Failure Survey programmea survey on the quality of care among patients with heart failure in Europe Part 2: treatment. *European Heart Journal, 24*(5), 464-474.

[4]Roger, V. L., Go, A. S., Lloyd-Jones, D. M., Benjamin, E. J., Berry, J. D., Borden, W. B., ... Turner, M. B. (2012). Heart Disease and Stroke Statistics2012 Update A Report From the American Heart Association. *Circulation, 125*(1), e2-e220.

[5]Sokka, T., Willoughby, J., Yazici, Y., Pincus, T. (2003). Databases of patients with early rheumatoid arthritis in the USA. *Clinical and experimental rheumatology, 21*(5; SUPP 31), 146-153.

[6]Tu, K., Chen, Z., Lipscombe, L. L. (2008). Mortality among patients with hypertension from 1995 to 2005: a population-based study. *Canadian Medical Association Journal, 178*(11), 1436-1440.

[7]www.en.wikipedia.org/wiki/Clinical_data_management_system, Wekipedia

[8]www.medicinenet.com. NedicineNet - Health and Medical Information Produced by Doctors

Storage Matters: Evaluating the Impact of Big Data Transfer Techniques on Storage Performance

(Submitted to the 2013 International Conference on Internet Computing and Big Data, ICOMP'13)

Adam H. Villa
Providence College
Providence, Rhode Island 02918
Email: avilla@providence.edu

Abstract—**When it comes to transferring Big Data, there are two main areas of concern: network performance and storage performance. The primary focus of recent work has been devoted to the problems of network connectivity and bandwidth. Different transfer techniques have been proposed to quickly move massive amounts of data between computers. The goal of these techniques is to maximize bandwidth consumption by any means necessary. The network performance of these techniques has been analyzed; however their impact on storage performance is not thoroughly investigated. In this study, Big Data transfers are evaluated from the storage viewpoint. Particular attention is focused on the granularity of request sizes issued to a storage node. This paper illustrates that there is a significant impact on performance when small portions of a data set are requested in place of a single large request.**

I. Introduction

The amount of data being produced every day is growing at a tremendous rate. Both academic and corporate entities are creating massive data sets and sharing these files with users around the world. The pinnacle of scientific data creation is CERN's large hadron collider experiments, which have generated thousands of terabytes of data [5]. CERN uses a well-defined data grid to distribute the data around the world [1]. Users are able to connect to one or more servers to retrieve the desired data sets. The user is tasked with creating, monitoring, managing and maintaining the data transfer [12], [13]. Other scientific fields, such as DNA sequencing, have also created massive data sets and share them using clouds or other distributed systems [2].

One of the major concerns for users is the ability to download these data sets for personal use. When it comes to file transfers there are two key concepts that should be of concern to users: networking and storage. Due to limited bandwidth and utilization of public networks, the main focus is typically network based. Storage is often not examined since it is assumed that it will be able to provide adequate performance. Since the focus of performance improvement studies have been isolated to networking, many of the techniques developed for Big Data transfers are engineered to maximize throughput of network connections. Studies examine how these techniques impact network performance on a large scale [11], however the impact of these techniques on storage systems is not fully understood. This paper attempts to examine their impact on simple storage systems to by simulating shared storage systems with a varying number of concurrent users.

When users retrieve these massive data sets, they are typically moving them across shared networks and the Internet. Due to the intense demand for available bandwidth, users on shared connections must compete for bandwidth in order to retrieve the desired data sets as quickly as possible. On residential and campus networks, users will find themselves competing with predominately streaming multimedia. A study of network traffic on a campus network illustrated the demands placed on shared Internet connections for thousands of users and identified that Netflix and other streaming video services consumed large portions of available bandwidth throughout a typical day [15]. Users must compete with this demand during peak periods in order to successfully transfer their desired data sets [14].

It is because of this intense competition for shared network resources that researchers have developed various transfer techniques to greedily consume as much bandwidth as possible for Big Data transfers. Recent studies examine various techniques for maximizing the throughput of a user's internet connection in order to reduce transfer times. There are many different techniques, but the main idea behind all of these techniques is to open multiple, simultaneous connections to one or more data servers. The user would then download portions of the data sets using multiple data streams that are optimized to maximize bandwidth usage. Section 2 presents a summary of the key works in this area.

Network performance is an important and crucial component of data transfer performance, however storage performance is equally important. Storage systems are closely monitored and engineered for high availability and low latency by system administrators. Users, however, do not immediately consider how their requests are impacted by the storage system. As most storage systems still use magnetic, hard disk drives for primary storage, the physical access times for disk requests are critical components of a user response times. Traditional hard disk drives are orders of magnitude slower than other devices and therefore they must be properly utilized in order to reduce physical access times. There have been many studies that examine the performance of disks and storage systems [8]. This paper does not examine or evaluate a specific storage device or system. The focus of this paper is to evaluate the impact that data transfer techniques have on storage system performance and consequentially on the performance of user requests. The rest of the paper is organized as follows. The next section details some of the techniques that have been designed for Big Data transfers. Evaluations of storage performance under varying user workloads is presented in Section 3. Section 4 summarizes the findings of this study and provides motivation for future work.

II. Related Work

This section presents several Big Data transfer techniques developed specifically for retrieving extremely large files over shared network connections and the Internet (highlighted in boldface). Many large data sets are often replicated amongst multiple servers distributed around the world. Users can then retrieve data from any of these replica servers. The transfer techniques are grouped based on how they retrieve data from the servers that store the data. These studies evaluate their various transfer techniques solely from a network perspective. Their impact on storage performance is evaluated using a simulated environment in Section 3.

A. Basic Technique

The basic, **brute-force**, parallel download technique [9] issues a request for equal sized portions of the file from all available servers. Every replica that contains the file is utilized and each is responsible for servicing an equal amount of data. There is no consideration given to the performance of servers or network conditions. Many studies include this technique as a baseline for comparison with other co-allocation strategies.

B. Predictive Techniques - History Based

In the brute-force technique, the performance of each transfer is not analyzed. Depending on network and server workload, each transfer will have varying performance. The following algorithms take into account the performance metrics of each server interaction when dividing the workload amongst all replicas in order to minimize the transfer completion time. Vazhkudai presents a **history-based data co-allocation technique** [9], [10]. This technique adjusts the amount of data retrieved from each replica by predicting the expected transfer rate for each replica. Zhou et al. also develop a history-based data co-allocation technique. They develop **Replica Convoy (ReCon)** [21], a tool for retrieving data from multiple replicas simultaneously where replicas that are predicted to deliver data faster are assigned a larger portion to service.

C. Predictive Techniques - Network Probes

Feng and Humphrey develop data retrieval techniques that utilize Network Weather Service (NWS) [17] predictions to specify the amount of data to be requested from replica servers [7]. The NWS is a distributed system that detects the network status at periodical intervals. Other mechanisms can be used to determine the status of connections between users and servers. Zhou et al. present a **probe-based data retrieval technique** [21], where a fixed sized pinging mechanism is used to probe network connections and determine network output. Based on the data returned by the probes, varying amounts of data are assigned to each replica.

D. Dynamic Techniques - Equal Request Sizes

The following retrieval techniques dynamically adapt to changing network conditions by requesting small, equally sized, portions of a file from multiple replicas. Vazhkudai develops a **conservative load balancing technique** that dynamically adapts to changing network and system conditions [9], [10]. The amount of data requested for a given server is decided dynamically instead of being based on previous history. The desired data file is divided into equal sized, disjoint blocks. Each available server is initially assigned one block to service in parallel. Once a server delivers the block, another block is assigned until the entire file is retrieved. Faster servers will transfer larger portions of the file. Feng and Humphrey also develop a similar dynamic data co-allocation algorithm called, **NoObserve** [7].

E. Dynamic Techniques - Varying Request Sizes

The techniques described in the previous section divide the desired data file into equal sized disjoint blocks. Other data retrieval techniques try to improve performance by varying the size of the blocks based on the performance of the replica servers. Faster servers are assigned larger blocks.

Vazhkudai develops an **aggressive load-balancing technique** [9], [10], which is a modified version his conservative load-balancing technique that was discussed in the previous section. Instead of requesting a single block from each replica, the amount of data requested from faster servers is progressively increased. The amount of data requested from slower servers is decreased or stopped completely.

The **recursively-adjusting co-allocation technique** [18]–[20] developed by Yang et al. is a combination of dynamic and predictive techniques, since it utilizes Network Weather Service forecasts. This technique works by continually adjusting the amount of data requested from each replica server to correspond to its real-time bandwidth during file transfers. The technique begins by dividing the desired data file into several sections. Each of these sections is then sub-divided into varying sized blocks that are individually assigned to all replicas. The number and size of the larger sections is variable and can be adjusted by the user. The size of each section is a percentage of the remaining file size to be retrieved. Each section size will therefore be progressively smaller than previous sections. The user can select the smallest section size that is used.

Another dynamic data retrieval technique, similar to the previous recursive mechanism, which varies the amount of data requested from each server while still dividing the data file into blocks is the **MSDT algorithm** [16] developed by Wang et al. The MSDT algorithm is a combination of dynamic and predictive techniques, as it utilizes the past transfer histories for predictions. The algorithm uses the overhead and bandwidth of previous segment transfers to predict the future performance of a replica. The amount of segments that are assigned varies depending on the transfer history for the particular replica.

F. Dynamic Techniques - Preemptive Measures

The dynamic techniques in the two previous sections retrieve portions of the data file from multiple replica servers. The amount of data retrieved may vary depending on the algorithm, however there is the possibility that a client will end up waiting for slower servers to deliver portions of the file. The previous techniques do not preempt transfers or redistribute the workload to other servers when replicas become unresponsive.

The ReCon data retrieval service [21] designed by Zhou et al. offers a **Greedy retrieval algorithm** where the desired data file is divided into equal sized segments. Each replica is initially assigned one segment. As servers complete their segments, they are assigned additional segments to service. A recursive scheduling mechanism handles any errors that occur. If a transfer fails, the mechanism automatically reschedules the failed data request to another replica that is currently transferring data.

Bhuvan et al. develop a different preemptive data co-allocation mechanism, the **Dynamic Co-allocation Scheme with Duplicate Assignments (DCDA)** [3]. This technique is used to cope with highly inconsistent network performance of replica servers. In their algorithm, the desired data file is divided into disjoint blocks of equal size. Each server is initially assigned one block to service. When a server completes a request, it is assigned another outstanding block. The algorithm continues until all blocks have been assigned. If a server delivers a block and there are no blocks remaining that have not been initially assigned, the server will be given an outstanding block request that has not been completed. There will now be several servers working on the same request. When a server delivers a request, all other servers are notified to stop serving this request.

Chang et al. [6] develop an advanced preemptive technique, **Multiple Parallel Downloads with Bandwidth Considerations technique**, that considers both server output throughput and client input bandwidth when assigning workloads to the replica servers. This paper is the first to discuss their technique in terms of multiple users. They realize that when everyone uses parallel downloads, they will compete for system resources that causes a degradation of system efficiency and unfairness for the users. They also determine that a server should not outdo its capacity by serving too many clients and a client should not download from too many servers with its limited incoming bandwidth. The authors discuss a multiple user environment and provide an example of how their technique would work with six users accessing a small number of files. Their experiments however, do not show the performance of their algorithm when many users are simultaneously utilizing their technique.

III. Evaluations

In order to evaluate the impact of Big Data transfer techniques on storage performance, the DiskSim storage simulator is utilized to emulate real workloads. DiskSim has been proven to correctly emulate real storage devices [4]. The hard disk drive model selected for the DiskSim simulations is the Seagate Cheetah 9LP, which provides fast disk service times due to its high-end configuration. The most recent iteration of the Cheetah drive similarly provides high performance and the results of the simulations are scaled to match the most recent drive specification.

Metric	Cheetah9LP	Cheetah15K.7
Capacity	9.10 GB	600 GB
Avg. Seek Time	5.4 msec	3.4 msec
Transfer Rate	23.95 MByte/sec	204 MByte/sec
Rotation Speed	10,025 RPM	15,000 RPM
Rotate Latency	2.99 ms	2.0 ms

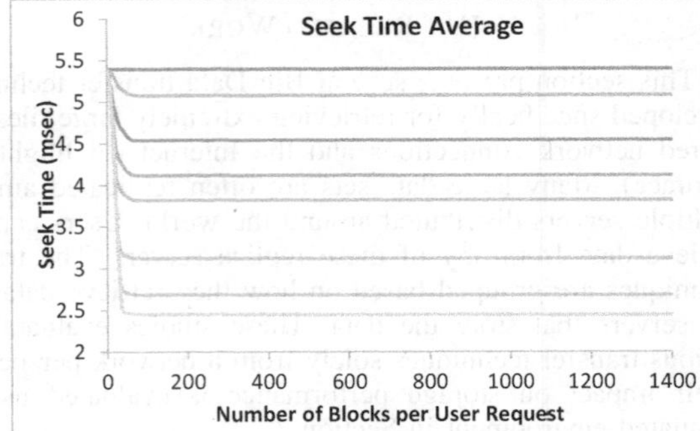

Fig. 1. Changes in the average seek time as the number of blocks per request increases. The top line represents 1 user and the bottom line represents 20 users.

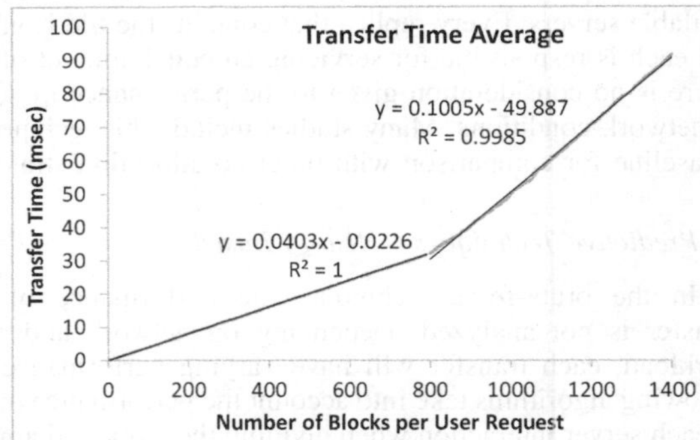

Fig. 2. Changes in the average transfer time as the number of blocks per request increases.

A. Initial Evaluations

In the initial evaluations, a varying number of users are configured in the simulator for a restricted number of blocks per disk request. Experiments are run for the following number of concurrent storage users: 1, 2, 3, 5, 6, 10, 15, and 20. The size of each request is fixed for each experiment and the number blocks requested is varied from 1 to 1400 blocks throughout the series of experiments. Several performance metrics are monitored and evaluated for each experiment. Metrics for the physical disk performance, as well as all users requests, are carefully monitored.

The physical disk metrics are examined for all of the experiments. Figure 1 shows the changes in the average seek time as the number of blocks per request increases. The average seek time actually reduces as the number of users in the system increases. This is due to the larger number of requests being serviced and likelihood that the next request to be serviced is close to the current location of the read/write head of the disk. The changes in transfer time are demonstrated in Figure 2. The average transfer time was almost identical for any number of concurrent users. The determining factor for the transfer time is solely the number of blocks being requested. The shape of the graph is interesting in that the transfer time increases at a slower rate until 800 blocks and after that point there is a marked increase in the transfer rate for larger request

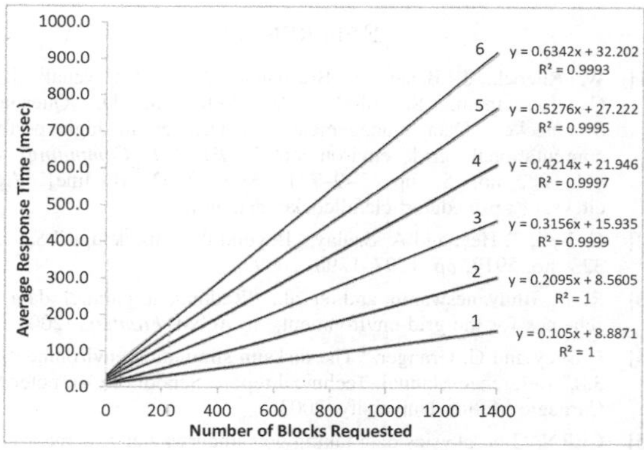

Fig. 3. Changes in the average system response time as the number of blocks per request increases. The bottom line represents 1 user and the top line represents 6 users.

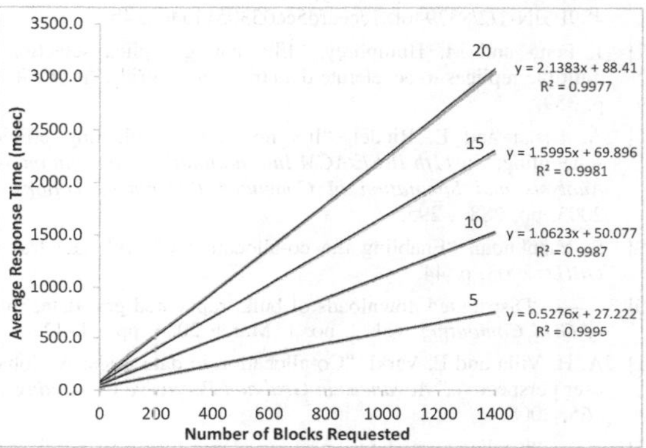

Fig. 4. Changes in the average system response time as the number of blocks per request increases. The bottom line represents 5 users and the top line represents 20 users.

sizes. This is confirmed by the larger coefficient on the trend lines for each section of the graph.

After examining the physical disk access metrics, the user request response times are evaluated. Figure 3 illustrates the system response time for the various sized requests when there are between 1 and 6 concurrent users utilizing the disk. The system response time is the total time that it takes to service a user's request and includes both disk access time and queue time. The graph shows that the average system response time increases as the number of blocks being requested increases. As one would expect, larger requests have larger response times. The increase in response time is linear and can be approximated using trend lines. The graph also indicates well-fitting trend lines, r squared values close to 1.

Figure 4 illustrates the system response time for the various sized requests when there are 5, 10, 15, and 20 concurrent users utilizing the disk. Similar to the previous graph, the increase in response time is linear. As the number of concurrent users grows, the average system response time also increases at a linear rate.

B. Big Data Transfers

Using the extremely well fitting trend lines that were calculated in the initial evaluations, the simulations can be scaled to emulate Big Data transfers that represent terabytes of data being requested from a storage system. In the next group of experiments, the size of the total data set being requested from the storage system is varied from 1 TB to 100 TB using the scaled DiskSim results in a custom designed simulation system.

When a user requests multiple terabytes of data, this type of request requires reading from multiple disks. In these simulations, a user's request is serviced in a serial, one disk at a time fashion. The request could be serviced by multiple hard disks in parallel, but it is unlikely that the user would have the bandwidth required to support the read rate supplied by simultaneous disk transfers. It is because of this rationale that the users' requests are serviced in a serial fashion and can be viewed as one request to a very large, logical disk.

The individual request sizes sent by the users are also varied in the evaluations from 1MB to 10GB. As described in the related work section, Big Data transfer techniques often divide the entire data set into chunks that are systematically retrieved from multiple replicas. The size of these chunks can vary depending on the algorithm and user configuration. These evaluations represent a set of possible file sizes that could be utilized by these Big Data transfer techniques.

In the following results, the total response time for retrieving a Big Data set is evaluated by comparing two approaches to Big Data transfers: single request and multiple requests. The single request approach issues only one request to the storage system for the entire data set. The multiple request approach issues multiple, smaller requests for the entire data set. In all of the evaluations, it was found that issuing a single request never incurred a penalty and frequently provided marked performance improvements over multiple, smaller requests. In order to better illustrate the performance differences between these two approaches, the **extra time** required when using the multiple request approach is graphed. The following graphs show how much longer a user would have to wait to retrieve the entire data set from the disk when using multiple, smaller requests instead of a single, large request.

Figure 5 demonstrates the significant performance impact of using a very small request size (1 MB) to retrieve a large data set. The lines on the graph represent a varying number of users in the system. The bottom line represents 1 user and the top line represents 20 users. As the size of the total data set increases and the number of users sharing the disk increases, the amount of additional time required retrieve the entire data set greatly increases. In the most extreme case, a user could potentially spend an additional 2500 hours (104 days) trying to retrieve a 100TB data set using 1 MB request sizes with 19 other users in the system performing the same task. For a single user, the impact is not as severe, especially for smaller total data set sizes. A 10TB data set would take a day longer using only 1MB requests, however retrieving a 100TB using the same technique would take almost 11 days longer than issuing a single request.

In reality, most users would not attempt to retrieve a large data set 1MB at a time; however some of the algorithms specified in the related work section in theory could be configured to issue requests of this granularity. The next group of evaluations have the user request sizes fixed at 10MB and Figure 6 illustrates the time increase when issuing these 10MB requests for the large data sets. The overall time increases for retrieving the entire data set are less than the 1MB file requests, but the increases are still significant. With 10 users in the system, a 50TB data set would take an additional 73 hours to transfer the data from the storage system using 10MB sized requests.

The next two groups of evaluations examine the extra time that it would take to retrieve the entire data set when the file request sizes are raised. Figure 7 shows the time increases for 100MB file requests. A 100TB data set would take 26 hours longer using the 100MB file request size with 19 other users accessing the system. The time increase is reduced to 3 hours when the user is the sole workload in the system. Figure 8 shows the time increases for 500MB file requests. With the larger request size, the 100TB data set would only take an hour longer than retrieving the entire data set in a single request with only 1 user in the system.

The final three groups of evaluations raise the individual file requests to 1GB, 5GB and 10GB. Figure 9 shows the time increases for 1GB file requests and Figure 10 shows the time increases for 5GB file requests. As the user issues requests for larger portions of the data set, the extra time required is decreased. With 5GB file requests, the extra time for issuing multiple requests is reduced to minutes instead of hours. A final group of evaluations are run with 10GB file requests and the increase in total time is further reduced to less than 15 minutes even with 20 concurrent user requests in the system.

IV. Summary and Future Work

From the evaluations, it is evident that user request sizes have an enormous impact on storage performance when retrieving Big Data sets. When the number of concurrent users sharing the storage system increases, this impact only grows more important. As the file size of the individual storage requests increased, the extra time required for multiple request based Big Data transfer techniques decreased. Requests that represent a larger percentage of the total data set performed significantly better than smaller percentage requests. This is a clear indication that users should always attempt to retrieve the largest possible subset of data from each server involved in a transfer. Another aspect to storage, which is not specifically examined in any of the graphs, is prefetching. Storage systems will often pre-fetch and cache data when sequential data streams are detected. By issuing larger requests, the system can potentially decrease the physical access penalties of the storage system for the user.

Big Data transfers are becoming more commonplace amongst users around the world. As more Big Data sets are created, the need for efficient transfers of these massive file sets will grow. Research studies must consider both network and storage impacts when evaluating transfer performance. For future work, an examination of Big Data transfers workloads from a live storage system should be conducted in order to assess typical user request sizes. Big Data transfer techniques that consider both network and storage performance should also be developed and investigated further.

References

[1] W. Allcock, J. Bester, J. Bresnahan, A. L. Chervenak, I. Foster, C. Kesselman, S. Meder, V. Nefedova, D. Quesnel, and S. Tuecke, "Data management and transfer in high performance computational grid environments," *Parallel Computing Journal*, vol. 28, no. 5, pp. 749–771, May 2002. [Online]. Available: citeseer.ist.psu.edu/article/allcock01data.html

[2] G. Bell, T. Hey, and A. Szalay, "Beyond the data deluge," *Science*, vol. 323, no. 5919, pp. 1297–1298, 2009.

[3] R. S. Bhuvaneswaran and et al., "Redundant parallel data transfer schemes for the grid environment," in *ACSW Frontiers*, 2006.

[4] J. Bucy and G. Granger, "The disksim simulation environment, version 3.0," Reference Manual. Technical report, School of Computer Science, Carnegie Mellon University, 2003.

[5] CERN, "Lhc physics data taking gets underway at new record collision energy of 8tev," *http://press.web.cern.ch*, 2012.

[6] R.-S. Chang, M.-H. Guo, and H.-C. Lin, "A multiple parallel download scheme with server throughput and client bandwidth considerations for data grids," *Future Generation Computer Systems*, vol. 24, no. 8, pp. 798–805, 2008. [Online]. Available: http://www.sciencedirect.com/science/article/B6V06-4S9P5JN-1/2/837940f81cceafd5ec0530511a40834b

[7] J. Feng and M. Humphrey, "Eliminating replica selection - using multiple replicas to accelerate data transfer on grids," in *ICPADS*, 2004, p. 359.

[8] A. Riska and E. Riedel, "It's not fair - evaluating efficient disk scheduling," in *11th IEEE/ACM International Symposium on Modeling, Analysis and Simulation of Computer Telecommunications Systems*, 2003, pp. 288 – 295.

[9] S. Vazhkudai, "Enabling the co-allocation of grid data transfers," in *GRID*, 2003, p. 44.

[10] ——, "Distributed downloads of bulk, replicated grid data," in *Journal of Grid Computing*, vol. 2, no. 1, March 2004, pp. 31–42.

[11] A. H. Villa and E. Varki, "Co-allocation in data grids: A global, multi-user perspective," *Advances in Grid and Pervasive Computing*, pp. 152–165, 2008.

[12] ——, "It takes know-how to retrieve large files over public networks," in *1st International Conference on Advanced Computing and Communications (ACC)*, 2010.

[13] ——, "The feasibility of moving terabyte files between campus and cloud," in *23rd IASTED International Conference on Parallel and Distributed Computing and Systems (PDCS)*, December 2011.

[14] ——, "Automating large file transfers," in *13th International Conference on Internet Computing (ICOMP'12)*, July 2012.

[15] ——, "Characterization of a campus internet workload," in *27th International Conference on Computers and their Applications (CATA)*, March 2012.

[16] C.-M. Wang, C.-C. Hsu, H.-M. Chen, and J.-J. Wu, "Efficient multi-source data transfer in data grids," in *CCGRID*, 2006, pp. 421–424.

[17] R. Wolski, N. T. Spring, and J. Hayes, "The network weather service: a distributed resource performance forecasting service for metacomputing," *Future Gener. Comput. Syst.*, vol. 15, no. 5-6, pp. 757–768, 1999.

[18] C.-T. Yang, Y.-C. Chi, and C.-P. Fu, "Redundant parallel file transfer with anticipative adjustment mechanism in data grids," in *Journal of Information Technology and Applications*, vol. Vol. 1, no. No. 4, March 2007, pp. 305–313.

[19] C.-T. Yang, I.-H. Yang, C.-H. Chen, and S.-Y. Wang, "Implementation of a dynamic adjustment mechanism with efficient replica selection in data grid environments," in *SAC '06: Proceedings of the 2006 ACM symposium on Applied computing*, 2006, pp. 797–804.

[20] C.-T. Yang, I.-H. Yang, K.-C. Li, and S.-Y. Wang, "Improvements on dynamic adjustment mechanism in co-allocation data grid environments," *The Journal of Supercomputing*, vol. 40, no. 3, pp. 269–280, 2007.

[21] X. Zhou, E. Kim, J. W. Kim, and H. Y. Yeom, "Recon: A fast and reliable replica retrieval service for the data grid," in *CCGRID*, 2006, pp. 446–453.

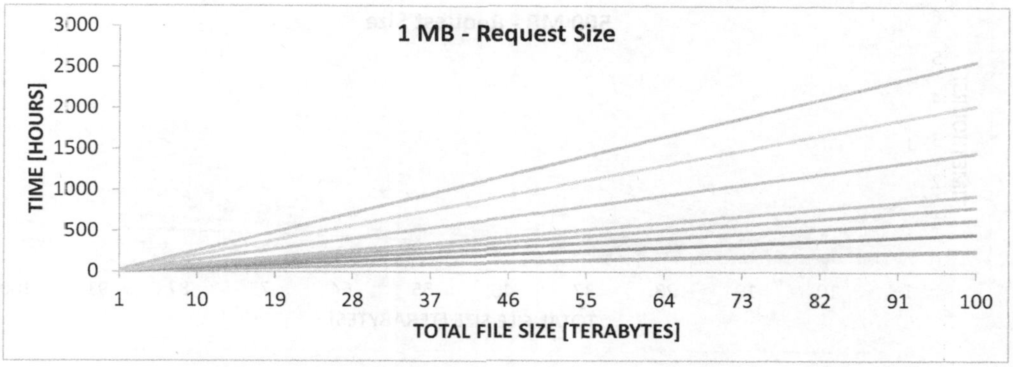

Fig. 5. This graph illustrates the extra time required (in hours) that would be required when issuing multiple smaller requests (1MB in size) instead of issuing a single request for the entire data set, as the size of the data set increases. The bottom line represents 1 user and the top line represents 20 concurrent users.

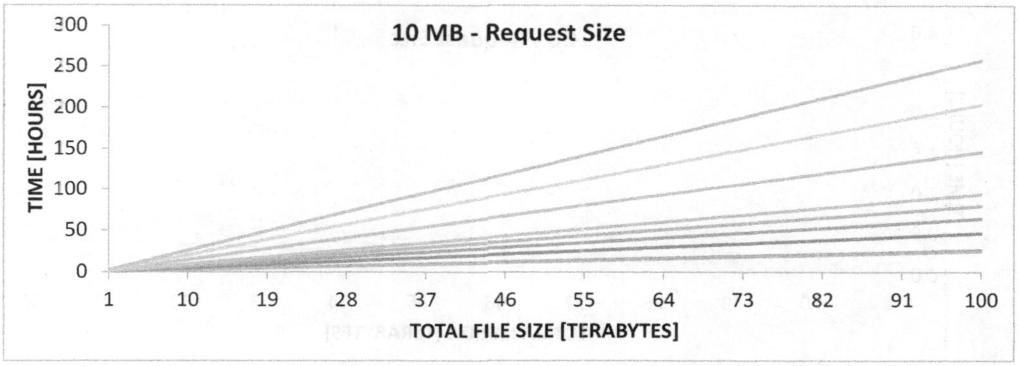

Fig. 6. This graph illustrates the extra time required (in hours) that would be required when issuing multiple smaller requests (10MB in size) instead of issuing a single request for the entire data set, as the size of the data set increases. The bottom line represents 1 user and the top line represents 20 concurrent users.

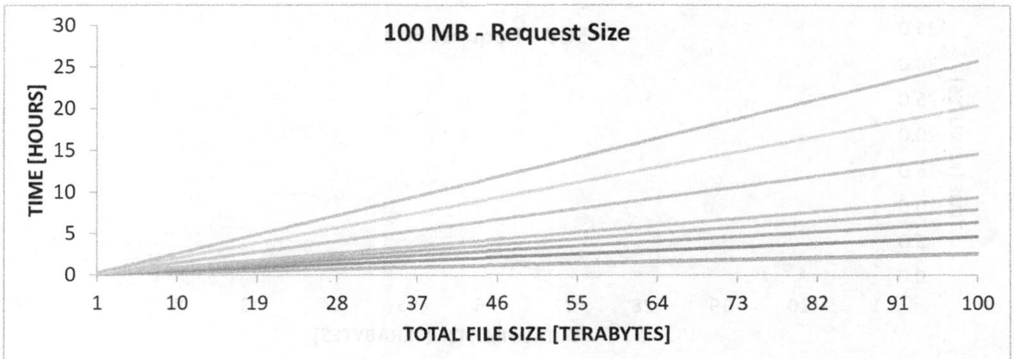

Fig. 7. This graph illustrates the extra time required (in hours) that would be required when issuing multiple smaller requests (100MB in size) instead of issuing a single request for the entire data set, as the size of the data set increases. The bottom line represents 1 user and the top line represents 20 concurrent users.

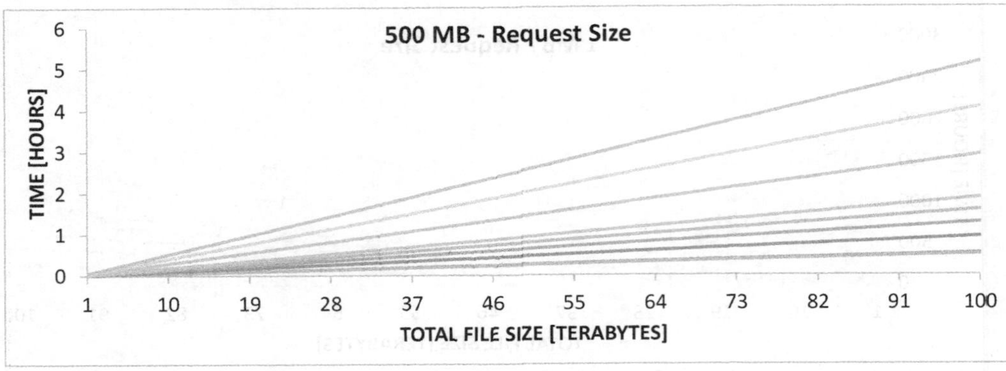

Fig. 8. This graph illustrates the extra time required (in hours) that would be required when issuing multiple smaller requests (500MB in size) instead of issuing a single request for the entire data set, as the size of the data set increases. The bottom line represents 1 user and the top line represents 20 concurrent users.

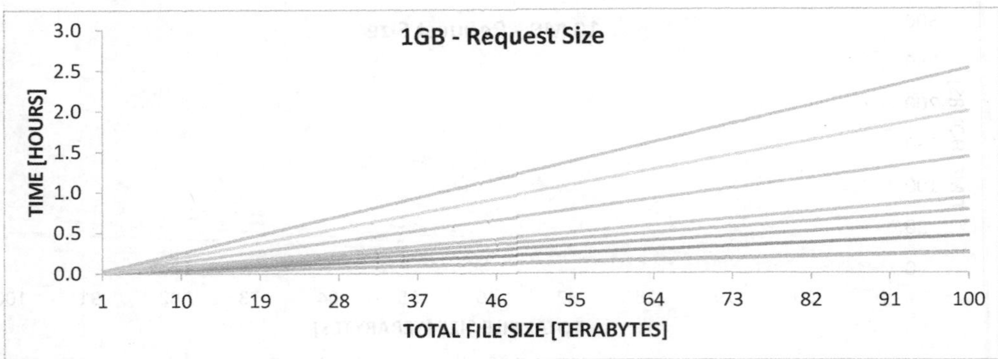

Fig. 9. This graph illustrates the extra time required (in hours) that would be required when issuing multiple smaller requests (1GB in size) instead of issuing a single request for the entire data set, as the size of the data set increases. The bottom line represents 1 user and the top line represents 20 concurrent users.

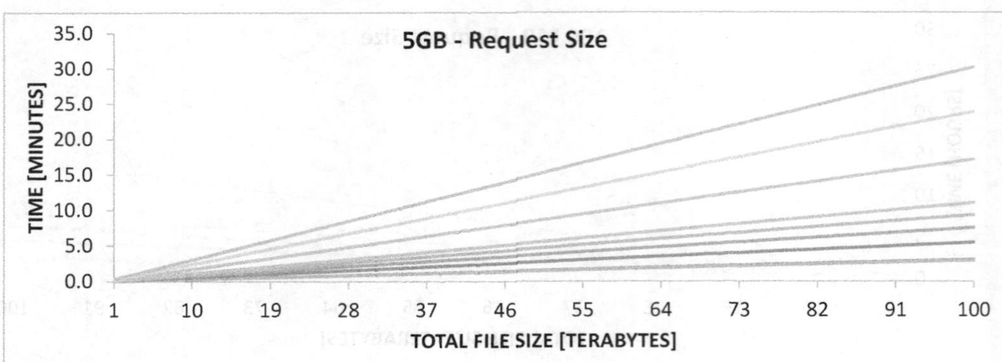

Fig. 10. This graph illustrates the extra time required (in hours) that would be required when issuing multiple smaller requests (5GB in size) instead of issuing a single request for the entire data set, as the size of the data set increases. The bottom line represents 1 user and the top line represents 20 concurrent users.

Small-World Networks, Distributed Hash Tables and the e-Resource Discovery Problem

A. Leist and K.A. Hawick
Massey University, North Shore 102-904, Auckland, New Zealand
Email: { a.leist, k.a.hawick }@massey.ac.nz
Tel: +64 9 414 0800 Fax: +64 9 441 8181

Abstract—*Resource discovery is one of the most important underpinning problems behind producing a scalable, robust and efficient global infrastructure for e-Science. A number of approaches to the resource discovery and management problem have been suggested in various computational grid environments and prototypes over the last decade. Computational resources and services in modern grid and cloud environments can be modelled as an overlay network superposed on the physical network structure of the Internet and World Wide Web. We discuss some of the main approaches to resource discovery in the context of the general properties of such an overlay network, and present performance data and predicted properties based on algorithmic approaches, such as distributed hash table resource discovery and management. We describe a prototype system and use its model to explore some of the known key graph aspects of the global resource overlay network – including small-world and scale-free properties.*

Keywords—Small-World Networks; DHT; P2P; Routing Algorithms; Semantic Web

1. Introduction

The general notion of e-Science is the use of connected computational data, services and resources to enable and accelerate the mission of science in all sorts of disciplinary areas beyond those associated with the development of the computational infrastructure. As e-Science ideas are increasingly used and up-taken, the support infrastructure for scientists to collect data, share data, process and analyse data has to be scalable, robust and efficient. In general, "successful e-Science" requires a global support infrastructure comprising both appropriate hardware but also distributed computing software.

The e-Science infrastructure problem has grown out of networked super-computing and parallel computing [1], broadband networking [2], meta-computing [3] and latterly grid [4] and cloud [5] computing research communities. It appears that e-Science has been embraced by the whole scientific community in a very natural way as global computing infrastructure has become widely available and easily used by all scientists.

Apart from the general software and systems complexity issues behind setting up global e-Science prototypes, one of the most challenging specific problems has been to find a way for users, software agents and components of the e-Science endeavour to discover resources. Resources might be computational services, data, analysis sub-systems, reduced data, provenance systems, bulk storage engines, supercomputers or indeed other human users.

There continues to be particular interest in small-world [6] and related community network problems [7] that arise from socio-technical applications. In the context of e-Science support, the resource discovery issue is at the vanguard of these application problems in that it represents a global-scale application of widespread interest, and it also involves computer scientists as both users and as those most likely to be able to contribute theoretically and practically to solutions.

Some typical e-Science scenarios involve arbitrary searches for resources, or more typically searches for details within a partially known sub-community of users, such as: the astronomical community; the particle physics community; or indeed some other well-defined sub-groups of users and service suppliers. Resource matching [8], [9] is required at a number of levels, since a search might initially pick up some suitable short-list of resources that might require subsequent refinement by secondary criteria, such as cost, availability, speed of response and so forth.

In addition to the core resource discovery problem, there are also specific problems associated with naming resources, but good frameworks such as RDF and XML-based [10], [11] systems for this have emerged from research work on prototypes. The resource discovery problem itself is still not completely solved, although some successful ideas and approaches have emerged in recent years.

In Section 2, we review some of the main approaches to resource discovery and its critical role in e-Science support infrastructure. As discussed above, resource discovery needs to be supported by some sort of distributed meta-data infrastructure. In Section 3, we discuss the main overlay network ideas for a distributed meta-data storage system, including scalability, efficiency and robustness. We describe our prototype implementation and ideas for a distributed meta-data storage system in Section 4, including the use and role of RDF, domain management and routing table management strategies. In Section 5, we present network analysis results covering routing table configurations, domain sizes, scaling and clustering. We offer a discussion of our results and findings in the context of present and future resource discovery for e-Science support infrastructure in Section 6 and some general conclusions in Section 7.

2. Approaches to Resource Discovery

Resource discovery can be modelled as a graph or network problem, whereby a partially connected graph of resources can be modelled as a set of overlapping overlay networks [12] superposed on the network infrastructure of the global Internet and World Wide Web. The problem then becomes how to match resources to user and agent requests [13]. This problem has some interesting implications for the way socio-technical scientific communities form and interact globally. Abstracting the general resource discovery notion into a more general graph problem allows us to study the problem in its generality and think in terms of global patterns and trends without needing to know the details of particular infrastructure grids or the usage needs of particular communities.

Approaches to storing, distributing and matching against resource description information and resource requests has been tackled in a number of interesting ways. In the early stages of e-Science in the 1990's, simple approaches such as flat data bases, simple gossip protocols [14], search agents and other ideas borrowed from Internet Domain Name Systems (DNS) [15] searching have been used. Existing software technologies such as the lightweight directory access protocol (LDAP) have also been employed [16]. A number of prototype grid and e-Science infrastructure projects [17], [18], [19] have provided an experimental basis for different resource discovery algorithms and some simulations have also thrown light on the problem [20], [21]

Over the last decade, it has become clear that simpler algorithms and ideas are no longer adequate and do not scale well, nor support the very dynamic changes required for resource discovery on a robust e-Science support infrastructure [22]. A number of investigations have been made using agent-based approaches [23], [24] and these have opened up the possibilities for loosely coupled wide area distributed discovery systems. Decentralised resource discovery approaches [25], [26] involving sophisticated distributed hash tables (DHT) and communicating peer-to-peer (P2P) [27] and hierarchical peer-based systems [28] are now being widely adopted [29]. There are a number of algorithmic variations possible within such a framework, including various forms of cache duplication and distributed management [30] to optimise speed and performance. We discuss DHT ideas more fully in the remainder of this paper.

3. Network Properties

The underlying network structure of a distributed metadata storage system has to fulfil certain requirements. These are *scalability* to large amounts of data and messages querying, storing or updating this information; *efficiency* when it comes to the delivery of messages and the maintenance of the network infrastructure; as well as *robustness* against churn—"the continuous process of node arrival and departure" [31]—and deliberate attacks. We are especially interested in networks that show the characteristics of small-world [32] or scale-free [33] graphs to tackle these problems.

3.1 Scalability

A network that is supposed to support large amounts of data and varying numbers of concurrent users, possibly in the millions, has to scale well with the current requirements. Distributed peer-to-peer based systems are more flexible than centralised networks and much cheaper to maintain. One such system is the open source distributed hash table Bamboo [34], which we use in modified form for our overlay network. The Bamboo DHT does not require any centralised services. Every node in the system acts as a gateway for new nodes. The available resources grow with the system size, since every participant is not only a consumer but also a provider of storage space and can act as a router for messages that are addressed to other nodes.

Section 5.3 shows how our system scales with increasing network size in regards to the actual number of hops needed to deliver messages, as well as the number of hops that would be needed if the whole network structure was known to every node (i.e. the theoretical minimum for the given network structure).

3.2 Efficiency

In a P2P system, messages can usually not be sent directly from the source node to the destination node, because there is no global registry that can be queried for the IP address of a certain node in the namespace of the overlay network. The message has to be routed towards the destination based on the local knowledge of the node currently processing it. To maximise performance and reduce network usage, the number of hops and the latencies of the nodes in the chosen route have to be minimised.

The maintenance of the network infrastructure is mainly done by the original implementation of the Bamboo DHT. This includes the protocols used to join the overlay network, keep the basic ring substrate maintained and manage the stored data. Bamboo maintains a ring substrate to ensure that every message can be routed towards its destination even if no suitable entry can be found in the routing table. Every node keeps track of its nearest neighbours in the namespace of the DHT up to a distance that can be specified in the configuration. This set of neighbours is called the leaf set of a node. The goal is to minimise the communication overhead needed for these tasks while still keeping the system's infrastructure up and the stored data accessible.

Section 4 explains how the routing is done in our system and Section 5 analyses how it performs in a simulated environment.

3.3 Robustness

Decentralised P2P networks have no single point of failure, which is an advantage over centralised networks. However, that does not mean that they are necessarily more robust against churn or deliberate attacks. Due to the lack of a global registry, the task of keeping track of available resources is more complex than in a centralised system and more sophisticated mechanisms are necessary to route messages between nodes. Especially under high churn, with many nodes only participating for a short amount of time, quick failure recovery from broken routes and nodes that are no longer available is important.

Decentralised networks can break apart into disjoint clusters when the number of random failures is high or if they are the subject of targeted attacks. The network structure plays an important role in the vulnerability of the network. Previous research [35], [36], [37] has shown that scale-free networks that consist of many nodes with low degrees and very few highly connected hub nodes are robust against random failures, because the likelihood that a hub node fails by random chance is low. However, attacks targeting the hub nodes can be devastating to such a network, as the network diameter rises sharply until the network fragments into isolated clusters if enough hub nodes fail. Both scale-free networks and small-world networks have also been shown to be vulnerable to bridge attacks. Bridges are nodes with a high betweenness centrality, i.e., nodes through which pass many shortest paths.

4. The Prototype System

This article builds upon our previous work in [38], which describes the implementation of the prototype system. Here, building upon our previous results, we analyse the routing algorithm in significantly more depth. This section gives a brief overview of the system.

The implementation is based on Atlas [18], which itself is based on the Bamboo DHT. Atlas can store metadata from Resource Description Framework (RDF) [10] and RDF Schema (RDFS) [11] documents in the DHT. The RDF Query Language (RQL) is supported to describe and execute queries on the stored metadata.

Atlas uses the Query Chain (QC) algorithm [19] to store RDF triples in the DHT. Each triple is stored on three nodes using three different keys: the hash values generated from the subject, the predicate and the object of the triple. This makes it possible to find matching triples when only one or two parts of it are specified in the query.

We have replaced the Bamboo routing table, which maintains the adjacency-list of a node, with an implementation that is based on the concepts of small-world network models.

4.0.1 Domains

Our prototype introduces the concept of domains and extends the QC algorithm accordingly. Every node in the network is a member of one domain, which is specified as a parameter when the node is started. The domains represent the clusters that are characteristic for small-world environments [39]. The idea is to group nodes that have a semantic relationship, for example web services that offer computing or storage resources to interested customers, as well as the nodes of customers that are mainly interested in these types of services, into the same domain. As sections 5.2 and 5.3 will show, the performance of the network can be increased substantially when messages are sent within the same domain.

The goal is to store related triples, which are likely to be part of the same query, in the same domain. This reduces the distance between these triples in the identifier namespace of the DHT and allows queries to be executed faster due to a decreased number of hops needed to route the messages to the relevant nodes in the domain.

When a new RDF document is to be stored, then the system first determines the types (a resource can be an instance of multiple classes in RDF) of each subject. Non-typed resources are discouraged, but we will describe how the system handles

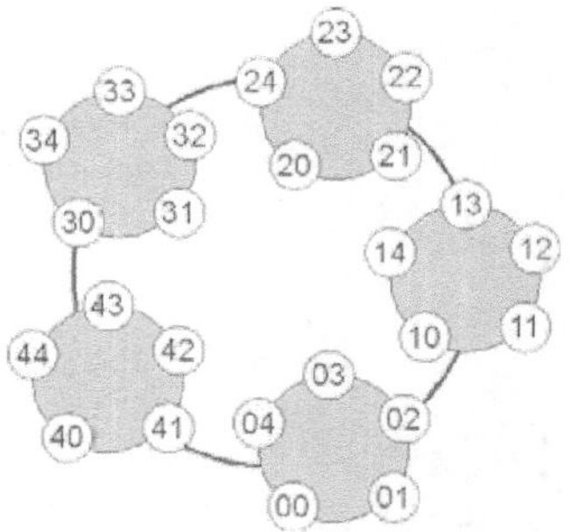

Fig. 1: The prototype system introduces domains to the DHT. Every node has a domain (or global) identifier as well as a local identifier. In this example, the first digit of the node ID identifies the domain and the second one identifies the local node. In the actual implementation, the identifiers are each 160 bits long, and the total namespace is 320 bits.

such triples later on. For now we assume that the resource is typed and select any one of the found types. The current implementation expects that the class is identified by an http-address. The protocol and domain part of the URI are used as the domain identifier. This means that the system currently assumes that related concepts are defined under the same domain name. The domain identifier `http://example.com` would be extracted from the class URI `http://example.com/terms/Person`. Unrelated concepts that are defined under the same second-level domain can be distinguished by using sub-domains or by modifying the generator of the domain identifiers to include parts of the directory path.

In the next step, the domain identifiers of all other types of the subject, the subjects themselves and the predicates are extracted as well. A reference triple has to be generated for each of these domain identifiers that is distinct from the one extracted from the chosen type URI. They are needed in order to be able to evaluate query path expressions that do not specify the type of the subject or that only specify types that were not used to extract the main domain identifier. The reference triples declare that the respective resource *R* is used in domain *D* of the previously selected main type. The reference triples have the following form:

```
R <http://example.com/terms/usedInDomain> D
```

These reference triples are then stored in the domains identified by the domain identifiers, which were extracted from the respective resources.

When triples with non-typed subjects have to be stored, then they are grouped by subject and the domain identifiers of the respective predicate URIs are extracted. If one domain identifier is extracted more often then others, then that one is selected to identify the main domain for this group of triples. Otherwise, it has to be selected randomly. Reference triples for distinct domain identifiers extracted from subjects and predicates are generated as described before. It may appear strange to choose the predicate over the subject URI when the subject is not typed. The reason for this is that a subject can be a blank node in the RDF graph , and blank nodes do not have a URI.

4.0.2 Storing and Querying RDF Metadata

This section describes how the following sample RDF document is stored in the DHT and how the information can be queried.

```
<?xml version="1.0"?>
<rdf:RDF
  xmlns:rdf="http://www.w3.org/.../22-rdf-syntax-ns#"
  xmlns:contact="http://www.w3.org/.../contact#">
  <contact:Person
    rdf:about="http://example.com/contact#me">
    <contact:firstName>Arno</contact:firstName>
    <contact:lastName>Leist</contact:lastName>
    <contact:mailbox
        rdf:resource="mailto:a.leist@massey.ac.nz"/>
  </contact:Person>
</rdf:RDF>
```

This RDF/XML document can be passed to the storage system, which extracts the RDF triples from it. It determines the types of the subject (`http://example.com/contact#me`), in this case the single super-class is identified by the URI `http://www.w3.org/.../contact#Person`. This URI is used to extract the target domain `http://www.w3.org`. All extracted triples are stored in this domain:

```
<http://example.com/contact#me>
  <http://www.w3.org/.../contact#firstName>
    "Arno" .

<http://example.com/contact#me>
  <http://www.w3.org/.../contact#lastName>
    "Leist" .

<http://example.com/contact#me>
  <http://www.w3.org/.../contact#mailbox>
    <mailto:a.leist@massey.ac.nz> .

<http://example.com/contact#me>
  <http://www.w3.org/.../22-rdf-syntax-ns#type>
    <http://www.w3.org/.../contact#Person> .
```

The system needs to perform one last step. It detects that the domain identifier extracted from the subject URI differs from the domain identifier used to store the triples. It therefore needs to create the following reference triple and store it in the domain `http://example.com`.

```
<http://example.com/contact#me>
  <http://example.com/terms/usedInDomain>
    <http://www.w3.org> .
```

Now that the information has been stored in the DHT, it can be queried. A query consists of query path expressions, which must provide at least one constant value. If the constant value can not be used to extract a domain identifier, which can be the case if the only constant is a literal object, then the user has to provide the domain identifier explicitly. The following query is automatically created and executed to look-up if any relevant reference triples are stored in the domain:

```
select REFERENCE
from <[URI]> ns:usedInDomain {REFERENCE}
using namespace ns=&http://example.com/terms/
```

The placeholder *[URI]* is replaced with the URI of the constant value. The system then checks this domain, and any other domains referred to by reference triples found in the previous step, for intermediate results. This procedure is repeated until all query path expressions have been evaluated. Finally, the results are returned to the node that issued the query.

4.1 The Routing Table

The routing table manages two adjacency-lists, one for nodes that are in the same domain and one for nodes in other domains. They are accordingly referred to as the *near* and the *far* routing tables. This enables the routing table to easily differentiate between nodes that are close in terms of the DHT namespace and nodes that are further away. Nodes that are closer are more likely to be the target of messages routed by this node than nodes that are further away.

A node always forwards a message on a best effort basis. If the destination node is in one of the routing tables, then it can deliver it directly. Otherwise, it determines if the receiver is in the same domain or in a different domain. If the latter is the case, then it uses the far routing table to send the message to a node as close to the destination domain as possible. If, however, the recipient is in the same domain, then it uses the near routing table to determine the next hop. If none of the neighbours is closer to the destination node than the node itself, then it uses its leaf set to determine the next hop. The leaf set guarantees that a message can always be routed closer to its destination node, assuming that the leaf set is consistent and up-to-date. We use a leaf set size of 8 (4 on either side of the node) for the simulations. The ratio of the number of nodes in either one

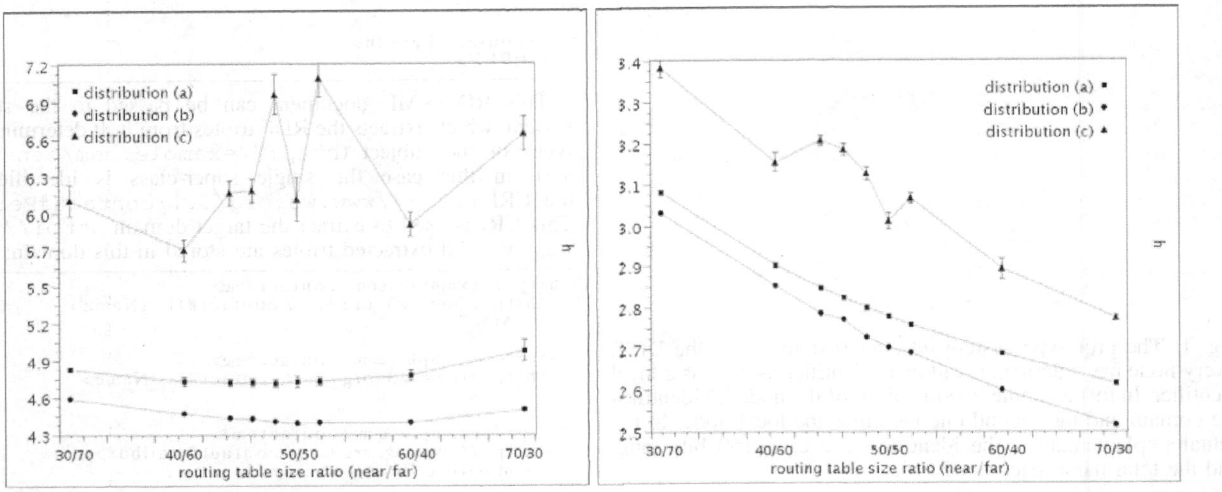

Fig. 2: The graph on the left shows the mean number of hops h needed to deliver a message to a randomly chosen destination node, whereas the destination nodes for the graph on the right are chosen from the same domain as the source node. The results were measured for varying near and far routing table size ratios and the three distinct neighbour distributions described in the main text. The combined routing table size is always $k_{near} + k_{far} = k = 100$ and the network size is $N = 100,000$. The nodes are approximately evenly spread over $d = 100$ domains and $m \sim 1,600,000$ messages were generated per simulation for each destination node selection method. The results are averaged over 40 simulation runs; the error bars represent the standard deviations.

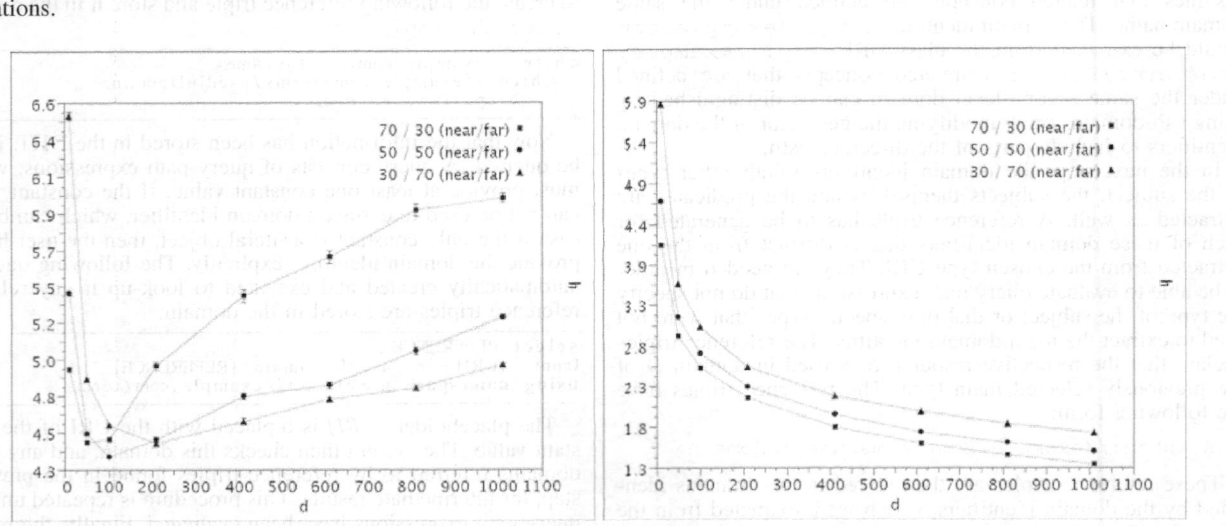

Fig. 3: The two graphs illustrate how the number of hops h varies with the number of domains d in the network (ranging from $d = \{10, \ldots, 1010\}$) for three routing table size ratios. The destination nodes were chosen randomly from the whole network for the plot on the left, whereas they were chosen from the same domain as the source node for the plot on the right. The network size $N = 100,000$ is constant, and therefore the number of nodes in each domain decreases with increasing d. The degree $k = 100$ and the neighbours are selected according to distribution (b). Roughly $m \sim 1,600,000$ messages were generated per simulation for each destination node selection method. The results are averaged over 100 simulation runs; the error bars represent the standard deviations and are too small to be visible for some of the data points.

of the routing tables can be adjusted. Section 5.1 analyses how different ratios influence the routing performance.

Another configuration option is to specify the optimal neighbour distributions for the near and far routing tables. The routing table then attempts to find the entries for the adjacency-lists based on these distributions. For example, it is possible to specify that neighbours closer to the node itself, in terms of the domain namespace for the near routing table and in terms of the global namespace for the far routing table, are to be preferred. The distributions are expressed as lists of integers and must contain an odd number of elements. The distribution $\{1,2,3,2,1\}$ means that the respective namespace is split up into 5 segments. The local node always considers itself to be in the centre of the namespace. This is possible because the namespaces are viewed as rings, with their own upper and lower boundaries connected. In this example, the implementation would attempt to fill the respective routing table with $\frac{3}{9}$ of the neighbours from the middle segment of the namespace as seen from the node, $\frac{2}{9}$ of the neighbours from the next namespace segments on either side and $\frac{1}{9}$ of the neighbours from the outermost namespace segments. The following sections analyse how different routing table distributions affect the routing performance and network structure.

5. Network Analysis

We have developed a simulator that allows us to analyse the performance of the routing table in a large scale environment. We have analysed the generated network instances and the performance of the system in a number of ways. The results are presented in this section.

5.1 Properties of the Routing Table

Figure 2 shows how well different ratios of the near and far routing table sizes work in terms of the mean number of hops needed to deliver a message to its destination node. It also compares the three distinct neighbour distributions $\{1\}$ (a), $\{2,5,10,15,20,15,10,5,2\}$ (b) and $\{20,15,10,5,2,5,10,15,20\}$ (c). The results for distribution (a) and (b) do not vary much for the different routing table size ratios when the destination node is randomly chosen from all nodes in the network, whereas the results for distribution (c) are much more noisy and less consistent. This is not surprising, since the routing implementation expects an increased density of neighbour connections between nodes the closer they are to each other in the namespace of the DHT. Therefore, it was to be expected that distribution (b) performs better than (c) with (a) being somewhere in between. The stronger deviations from the mean values in the results of distribution (c) can also be found in the graphs described in the following sections.

Also not surprising is that an increase in the near routing table size leads to a steady decrease in the number of hops needed to deliver a message to the same domain as the source node. The far routing table is not used at all in this scenario, thus, a larger near routing table equals a bigger pool of relevant connections. The results for distribution (c) look rather strange, but are most likely deceptive due to the increased number of data points between the ratios 40/60 and 60/40. We expect that further simulations will reveal that the lines in the lower and upper areas would not be as straight either if more data points were available.

5.2 Domains

So far, the number of domains was fixed and the nodes were evenly spread over all the domains. Here, we analyse how the domain size affects the results. Figure 3 shows the simulation results for networks with a constant number of nodes but with an increasing number of domains. More domains means smaller domains, and therefore the results for delivering messages within the same domain are not further surprising. When the destination nodes are selected randomly from all the nodes in the network, then the choice of the right domain size is more interesting. The results show that the introduction of domains had a positive effect, as as very small number of domains performs poorly. However, too many small domains do not perform well either, especially when the size of the far routing table is small. It is thus important to find a good balance for the given network size. In this case, a domain size of approximately 1,000 vertices ($d \approx 100$) appears to be a good value.

5.3 Scaling

As stated in Section 3.1, scalability is an important property for our system. Figure 4 shows how the implementation deals with networks ranging from 1,000 to 101,000 nodes. At size $N = 1,000$, the results are the same for the two destination node selection methods, because the domain size is set to 1,000, and, thus, only one domain exists in the networks generated with these properties. Even when selecting the destination node randomly from all the nodes in the network, it merely takes ≈ 4.5 hops on average to deliver the message for the largest network generated so far. The total network size does not affect the delivery time for messages sent within the same domain, which shows how useful it can be to arrange the nodes in a way that most of the messages they send are addressed to their own domain. The result values even decrease slightly for (2) with increasing network size. The most likely explanation for this is that, even though the number of messages increases linearly with the network size, more messages are routed through the network in total, which means the system has more opportunities to optimise the routing tables.

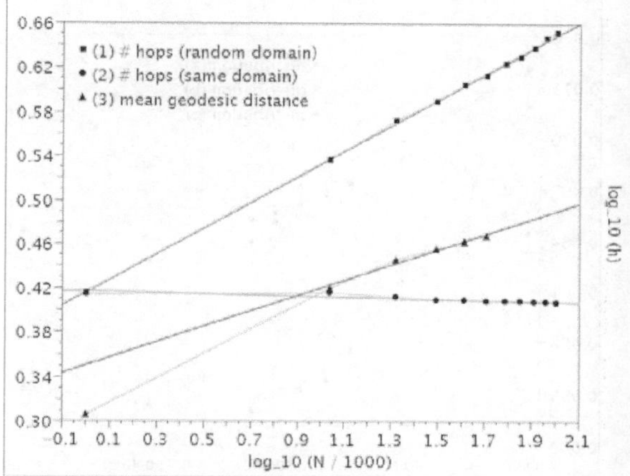

Fig. 4: This plot shows the mean number of hops h needed to deliver a message to a destination node either randomly chosen (1) or from the same domain as the source node (2) for increasing network size ($N = \{1000, \ldots, 101000\}$). (3) shows the mean geodesic distance between any two vertices in the network for networks up to 51000 nodes. Note the double log-scale used to more clearly represent the scaling. The straight lines are the least square linear fits with a slope of ≈ 0.117 for (1), ≈ -0.005 for (2) and ≈ 0.070 for (3). The number of nodes in each domain is always 1,000, and, therefore, the number of domains $d = \{1, 11, \ldots, 101\}$ increases with the network size. The degree $k = 100$ and the neighbours are selected according to distribution (b). The routing table size ratio is 70/30 for the near/far routing tables. Roughly $m \sim N * 16$ messages were generated per simulation for each of the destination node selection methods. The results are averaged over 100 simulation runs for (1) and (2) and over 40 network instances for (3); error bars representing the standard deviations are printed but smaller than the symbol size.

The plot also shows the mean geodesic distances for the network instances (3). These are the mean shortest paths between any two nodes in the networks, and, thus, the absolute minimum number of hops, on average, needed to route a message from a source node to its destination in the given network structure. This is an expensive metric to compute, and even though we were utilising the highly parallel processing power of a graphics processing unit [40], we were only able to compute it for networks with up to 51,000 nodes within the given time.

One of the characteristic properties of small-world networks is that the mean geodesic distance scales logarithmically or slower with the network size for fixed degree k. The plot in Figure 4 shows that, as far the data available to us suggests, our network model fulfils this requirement both for the geodesic distance and for the actual hops needed to route messages to randomly chosen nodes.

5.4 Clustering

Small-world networks exhibit larger clustering coefficients than random graphs. We use two different definitions to determine the clustering behaviour of the networks. Figure 5 shows the results for these clustering coefficients, each for varying routing table size ratios and neighbour distributions. The graph on the left shows the clustering coefficient γ as defined by Watts and Strogatz [32].

As expected, networks generated with distribution (c) have a lower clustering coefficient than the other networks. The values for distribution (a) and (b) are more interesting. When the routing table size ratio is in favour of the far routing table, then distribution (b) yields slightly higher results than distribution (a), which is what we expected to be the case. However, once the ratio changes in favour of the near routing table, distribution

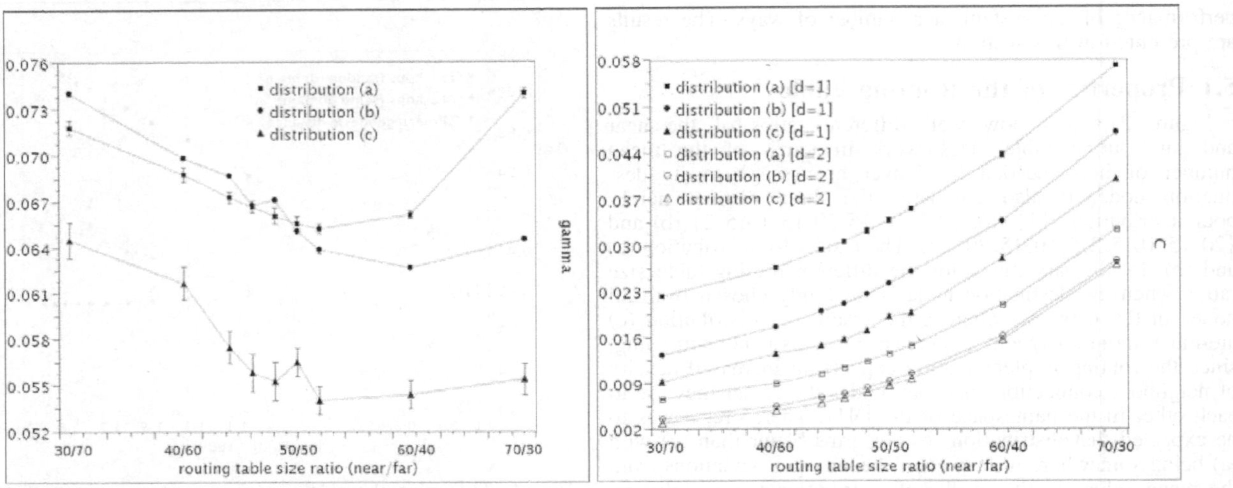

Fig. 5: The graphs show the results for two different definitions of the clustering coefficient for varying routing table size ratios and the three distinct neighbour distributions. The results γ calculated with Watts' clustering coefficient are illustrated by the plot on the left and the clustering profile C by the plot on the right. The combined routing table size is always $k = 100$ and the network size is $N = 100,000$. The nodes are approximately evenly spread over $d = 100$ domains. The results are averaged over 40 networks; the error bars representing the standard deviations are too small to be visible for some of the data points.

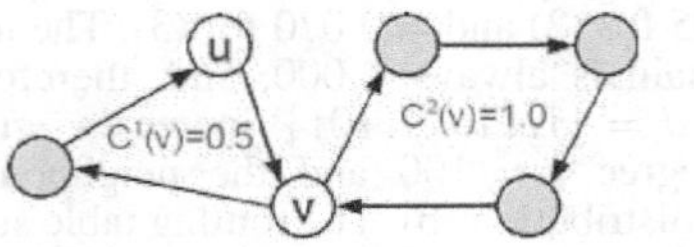

Fig. 6: Higher orders of clustering in a directed graph G. The clustering profiles for G by degree C_k^d are $C_1^1 = 0.3$, $C_2^1 = 0.5$, $C_1^2 = 0.4$ and $C_2^2 = 1.0$. The total clustering profiles averaged over all vertices are $C^1 \approx 0.33$ and $C^2 = 0.5$.

(a) shows a clearly higher clustering than distribution (b). It is also not clear why the clustering coefficients for all distributions decrease the more the routing table size ratio favours the near routing table, until they begin to increase again more or less significantly around the time the near routing table is actually larger than the far routing table. We expected that a proportionally larger near routing table would yield higher clustering coefficients.

The graph on the right of Figure 5 shows the clustering profile [41]. The clustering profile $C^d(v)$ for a vertex $v \in V$ was originally defined as the number of neighbours of v connected by a shortest path of length d that does not pass through v, divided by the total number of pairs of neighbours of v. Or in other words, $C^d(v)$ is the number of neighbours of v whose smallest cycle shared with it has length $d+2$, divided by the total number of pairs of neighbours of v.

However, this definition only works for undirected graphs. In the case of directed graphs, like the ones in our simulations, a vertex u can have v in its adjacency-list without itself being in the adjacency-list of v. Thus, we modified the definition to work with directed graphs as the one in Figure 6. The number of cycles of length $d+2$ that contain v and the number of paths of length $d+1$ that start from v (a vertex may only appear once in each cycle and path) are counted. The fraction of vertices at distance $d+1$ from v that have v in their adjacency-list—and are thus closing a cycle—is the clustering profile $C^d(v)$.

$$C^d(v) = \frac{\text{cycles of length } d+2 \text{ containing } v}{\text{paths of length } d+1 \text{ starting from } v} \quad (1)$$

In this definition, the clustering profile with $d = 1$ is the same as the clustering coefficient defined by Newman [42], [43]. It can therefore be considered an extended version of it.

The clustering profile can be used to gain more information about the network than the definition by Watts, as it makes it possible to determine a more in depth clustering behaviour. Unfortunately, with networks of size $N = 100,000$ vertices and degree $k = 100$, the number of cycles of a certain length increases dramatically (see Figure 7) with every increase in cycle length, restricting us to cycles of up to length 4 only.

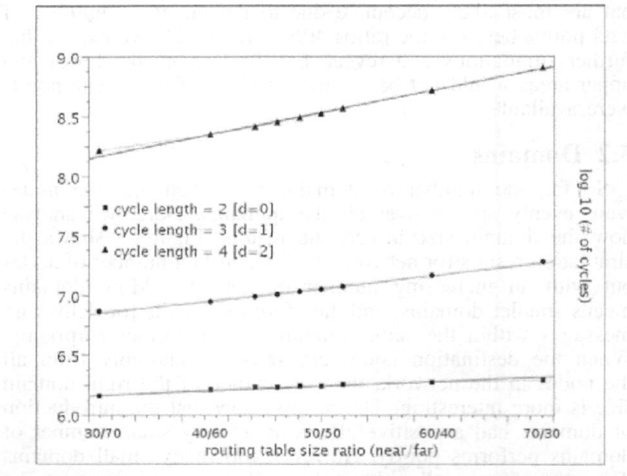

Fig. 7: This plot illustrates the number of cycles of length 2, 3 and 4 found in the networks generated with distribution (a) on a log-y scale. The slope of the least square linear fit for cycle length 2 is ≈ 0.004, for length 3 it is ≈ 0.010 and for length 4 it is ≈ 0.018.

The results given by this second definition look much more like what we expected to see. They consistently increase with the routing table size ratio changing in favour of the near routing table. But like in the previous results, distribution (a) again yields the largest values for the clustering profile and not distribution (b).

6. Discussion & Future Directions

We have analysed a variety of metrics relevant to a distributed peer-to-peer system and small-world graphs, using different configuration sets to show their effects on the system performance. We have not yet analysed the network robustness, which is another important property of a reliable system.

We are planning to perform additional simulations to gain further insights into the network structure and the effects that different parameter values have. For example, so far the routing table size has always been constant (degree $k = 100$), but it would be interesting to find out how the system performance changes with smaller and larger degrees.

The neighbour selection algorithm does not only take the neighbour distribution, but also the latency between the nodes into account when it chooses a new neighbour. This is an important feature to improve the performance in a real-world deployment scenario. However, this has not been incorporated into the network analysis yet. It will be interesting to observe how the neighbour "quality" changes over time, how this affects the geodesic distance over time when the arcs are weighted with the latency, and how the actual message delivery times change.

Further areas of improvement to the routing table include the use of preferential attachment to increase the cluster formation in the network, such that the probability to add a node as a neighbour increases with the number of current neighbours that already have that node in their routing tables. Preferential attachment can also be based on the number of messages routed to a certain node, increasing the probability to add a new neighbour based on how often it is the destination of messages from the local node.

7. Conclusions

We have given an overview over previously published resource discovery material and described our own prototype system for the distributed peer-to-peer storage of semantic metadata. The underlying network model is based on a distributed hash table that was modified to create a network that possesses the characteristic properties of small-world graphs. Especially the scaling behaviour of the small-world network model is important for a resource discovery system that is supposed to be able to handle large scale deployments of many thousands or even millions of nodes. We introduced the concept of domains to store related information. Messages that are sent between nodes in the same domain are typically delivered within less hops than messages sent to an arbitrary destination node, and the number of hops grows with the domain size and not with the network size. We analysed a variety of network metrics in a simulated environment and showed that it does indeed scale logarithmically or slower with the network size. It seems likely that e-scientific user communities will continue to organise themselves into small-world structures that scale in this way.

References

[1] Fox, G.C., Williams, R.D., Messina, P.C.: Parallel Computing Works! Morgan Kaufmann Publishers, Inc. (1994) ISBN 1-55860-253-4.

[2] Kirkham, D.: Telstra's experimental broadband network. Telecommunications J. Australia **45**(2) (1995)

[3] Hawick, K.A., James, H.A., Silis, A.J., Grove, D.A., Kerry, K.E., Mathew, J.A., Coddington, P.D., Patten, C.J., Hercus, J.F., Vaughan, F.A.: DISCWorld: An environment for service-based metacomputing. Future Generation Computing Systems (FGCS) **15** (1999) 623

[4] Foster, I., Kesselman, C., eds.: The Grid: Blueprint for a New Computing Infrastructure. Morgan Kaufmann Publishers, Inc. (1999) ISBN 1-55860-475-8.

[5] Buyya, R., Yeo, C.S., Venugopal, S.: Market-Oriented Cloud Computing: Vision, Hype, and Reality for Delivering IT Services as Computing Utilities. In: Proceedings of the 10th IEEE International Conference on High Performance Computing and Communications (HPCC 2008). (2008) 5–13

[6] Milgram, S.: The Small-World Problem. Psychology Today **1** (1967) 61–67

[7] Hawick, K., James, H.: Managing community membership information in a small-world grid. Research Letters in the Information and Mathematical Sciences **7**(CSTN-002) (2005) 101–115 ISSN 1175-2777.

[8] Czajkowski, K., Foster, I., Karonis, N., Kesselman, C., Martin, S., Smith, W., Tuecke, S.: A resource management architecture for metacomputing systems. In Feitelson, D.G., Rudolph, L., eds.: JSSPP'98. Number 1459 in LNCS, Springer-Verlag Berlin Heidelberg (1998) 62–82

[9] Rana, O.F., Bunford-Jones, D., Hawick, K.A., Walker, D.W., Addis, M., Surridge, M.: Resource discovery for dynamic clusters in computational grids. In: Proceedings of the 15th International Parallel & Distributed Processing Symposium. (2001) 82

[10] W3C: RDF Primer. (February 2004)

[11] W3C: RDF Vocabulary Description Language 1.0: RDF Schema. (February 2004)

[12] Hauswirth, M., Schmidt, R.: An overlay network for resource discovery in grids. In: Proc Sixteenth International Workshop on Database and Expert Systems Applications. (2005) 343– 348 ISBN: 0-7695-2424-9.

[13] Rana, O.F., Bunford-Jones, D., Walker, D.W., Addis, M., Surridge, M., Hawick, K.: Agent-based resource discovery for dynamic clusters. In: Proc. Second IEEE International Conference on Cluster Computing (CLUSTER'00), Chemnitz, Germany (2000) 353 ISBN: 0-7695-0896-0.

[14] Hawick, K.A., James, H.A.: Modeling a gossip protocol for resource discovery in distributed systems. In: Proc. Int. Conf. on Parallel and Distributed Processing Techniques and Applications (PDPTA 2001), Las Vegas, USA (2001) DHPC-102.

[15] Mockapatris, P., Dunlap, K.: Development of the domain name system. ACM Computer Communications Review **18**(4) (August 1988) 123–133

[16] von Laszewski, G., Foster, I.: Usage of ldap in globus. Available from http://www.globus.org (1998)

[17] Foster, I., Kesselman, C.: Globus: A meta-computing infra-structure toolkit. Int. J. Supercomputer Applications (1996)

[18] Atlas Project: Atlas Distributed RDF Metadata Storage and Query System. `http://atlas.di.uoa.gr` (2008) Last accessed May 2013.

[19] Liarou, E., Idreos, S., Koubarakis, M.: Evaluating Conjunctive Triple Pattern Queries over Large Structured Overlay Networks. In: Proceedings of the Semantic Web - ISWC 2006: 5th International Semantic Web Conference, Athens, GA, Springer-Verlag (November 2006) 399–413

[20] Hawick, K., James, H.: Simulating resource trading and discovery in grid systems. In: IASTEd Conference on Modelling, Simulation and Optimisation (MSO 2003), Banff, Canada, IASTED (July 2003)

[21] Iamnitchi, A., Foster, I.: A peer-to-peer approach to resource location in grid environments. In Nabrzyski, J., Schopf, J., Weglarz, J., eds.: Grid Resource Management: State of the Art and Future Trends. Volume 64 of International Series In Operations Research & Management Science. Kluwer Academic Publishers (2003) 413–429

[22] Al-Dmour, N., Teahan, W.: Peer-to-peer protocols for resource discovery in the grid. In: IASTED International Conference on Parallel and Distributed Computing and Networks, Innsbruck, Austria, IASTED (February 2005)

[23] Chunlin, L., Layuan, L.: Agent framework to support the computational grid. The Journal of Systems and Software **70** (2004) 117–187

[24] Ding, S., Yuan, J., Ju, J., Hu, L.: A heuristic algorithm for agent-based grid resource discovery. In: Proceedings of the 2005 IEEE International Conference on e-Technology, e-Commerce and e-Service (EEE'05), IEEE (2005) 222–225 ISBN:0-7695-2274-2.

[25] Ranjan, R., Chan, L., Harwood, A., Karunasekera, S., Buyya, R.: Decentralised resource discovery service for large scale federated grids. In: Proc. Third IEEE International Conference on e-Science and Grid Computing. (2007) 379–387

[26] Iamnitchi, A., Foster, I.T.: On fully decentralized resource discovery in grid environments. In: Proceedings of the Second International Workshop on Grid Computing, London, UK., Springer-Verlag (2001) 51–62

[27] Iamnitchi, A., Foster, I., Nurmi, D.C.: A peer-to-peer approach to resource discovery in grid environments. In: High Performance Distributed Computing, IEEE (2002)

[28] Mastroianni, C., Talia, D., Verta, O.: A super-peer model for resource discovery services in large-scale grids. Future Generation Computer Systems **21** (2005) 1235–1248

[29] Naseer, A., Stergioulas, L.K.: Resource discovery in grids and other distributed environments: States of the art. Multiagent and Grid Systems - An International Journal **2**(ISSN 1574-1702/06) (2006) 163–182

[30] Filali, I., Huet, F., Vergoni, C.: A simple cache based mechanism for peer to peer resource discovery in grid environments. In: Proc. Eighth IEEE International Symposium on Cluster Computing and the Grid, IEEE (2008) 602–608

[31] Rhea, S., Geels, D., Roscoe, T., Kubiatowicz, J.: Handling Churn in a DHT. In: Proceedings of the General Track 2004 USENIX Annual Technical Conference, Boston, MD, USENIX Association, Berkeley (June 2004) 127–140

[32] Watts, D.J., Strogatz, S.H.: Collective dynamics of 'small-world' networks. Nature **393**(6684) (June 1998) 440–442

[33] Barabsi, A.L., Albert, R.: Emergence of scaling in random networks. Science **286**(5439) (October 1999) 509–512

[34] Bamboo Project: Bamboo Distributed Hash Table. `http://www.bamboo-dht.org` (2008) Last accessed May 2013.

[35] Albert, R., Jeong, H., Barabsi, A.L.: Error and attack tolerance of complex networks. Nature **406**(6794) (July 2000) 378–382

[36] Holme, P., Kim, B.J., Yoon, C.N., Han, S.K.: Attack vulnerability of complex networks. Physical Review E **65**(5) (May 2002)

[37] Xu, J., Chen, H.: The Topology of Dark Networks. Communications of the ACM **51**(10) (October 2008) 58–65

[38] Leist, A., Hawick, K.: A Small-World Network Model for Distributed Storage of Semantic Metadata. In Kelly, W., Roe, P., eds.: Proc. 7th Australasian Symposium on Grid Computing and e-Research (AUSGRID 2009). Volume 99 of Conferences in Research and Practice in Information Technology (CRPIT). (January 2009)

[39] Newman, M.E.J.: The Structure and Function of Complex Networks. SIAM Review **45**(2) (June 2003) 167–256

[40] Leist, A., Playne, D., Hawick, K.: Exploiting Graphical Processing Units for Data-Parallel Scientific Applications. Concurrency and Computation: Practice and Experience **21** (December 2009) 2400–2437 CSTN-065.

[41] Abdo, A.H., de Moura, A.P.S.: Clustering as a measure of the local topology of networks. Technical report, Universidade de São Paulo, University of Aberdeen (February 2008)

[42] Newman, M.E.J., Strogatz, S.H., Watts, D.J.: Random graphs with arbitrary degree distributions and their applications. Physical Review E **64**(2) (July 2001) 026118

[43] Newman, M.E.J.: Ego-centered networks and the ripple effect. Social Networks **25**(1) (January 2003) 83–95

Mining Dynamic Association Rules From Multiple Time-series Data Streams

Chunkai Zhang, Yulong Hu
School of Shenzhen Graduate, Harbin Institute of Technology, Shenzhen, China

Abstract-Multiple time-series data streams exist in industrial processes, commercial activities, etc. A method of mining dynamic association rules which change over time and whose meta-patterns which have only one item maybe have different length of time slot in different rules in a sliding window from multiple time-series data streams is proposed. As streams flow, the contents of streams are preprocessed for rule discovery. The preprocessing includes piecewise linear approximation, segmenting linearized time series to let each stream have only one line segment in one time slot, and then increamental cluster these line segments, symbolic representation of the data, and merging preprocessed streams into transactions from which rules are mined. After preprocessing we use a rule finding method to obtain rules. Through periodically pruning the obsolete and infrequent patterns are deleted. To differentiate the patterns of the latest generated transactions from those of historic transactions, decay factor is introduced.

Keywords-multiple time-series data streams; dynamic association rules; sliding window; decay factor

I. INTRODUCTION

Time-series exists widely in the field of science, engineering and business, etc. A time-series[1] is formally defined as a sequence of values that are recorded in one of the following manners:

o at equal time intervals

o at random points in time by also recording the time of measurement or recording

The proposed method uses the first definition above of time-series data with numerical value. In real life many time-series data is presented in the form of the stream. Unlike the static time-series data time-series data stream has similar characteristics with data stream which is generated continuously in a dynamic environment, with huge volume, infinite flow, and fast changing behavior. Therefore, the mining of time-series data streams has the similar challenges[2]:

1. The data elements in the stream arrive online.
2. The system has no control over the order in which data elements arrive to be processed, either within a data stream or across data streams.
3. Data streams are potentially unbounded in size.
4. Once an element from a data stream has been processed it is discarded or archived.

Time-series data stream also has its own characteristics. It can be regarded as a special data stream with time property. In this paper data mining is over multiple time-series data streams.

So far there are a number of association rules mining researches over time-series data. In [3], a method is proposed to mine rules over time series. The type of rules of multiple time series is like if A_1 and A_2 and ... and A_h occur within V units of time, then B occurs within time T in which $A_1...A_h$ and B represent subsequences. The method uses a fixed-size sliding window to discrete time-series to get subsequences, which is regarded as the basic elements of the rules. In [4], a novel method is proposed to extract time-correlations among multiple time-series data streams. The type of rules is like A increases more than 5% then B will increase more than 10% within 2 days in which A and B represent different streams.

Both of the methods mine the rules whose meta-patterns having the same length of the time slot. And they also do not consider the case that sometimes knowledge in the new data may be more interesting than that in old.

In this paper a method is proposed to mine dynamic association rules in a sliding window whose conditions refer to patterns which maybe have different length of the time slot in different rules,like in a certain time slot whose length can be calculated if A has the pattern like increased by 10% and B has the pattern like increased by 5% then C has the pattern like decreased by 10% (20%,80%). The time-delayed cause-effect relationships may be occurred because of different time granularity. And the effect may be appeared in rules which are not the true reflection of the relationships between time series and should be deleted in the final result.

The rest of this paper is organized as follows. Section 2 introduces the basic concepts of the method. Section 3 presents the preprocessing of the time-series data streams. Section 4 and 5 presents data storage structure and the dynamic rules discovery method. Section 6 presents experimental results. Section 7 concludes the paper.

II. PRELIMINARY

The basic concepts of the method and the time-decayed model are introduced.

A. Related concepts

Definition 1. Assume a set of multiple time-series data streams $S=\{S_1, S_2,..., S_i, ...,S_n\}(1\le i\le n)$, S_i represents one time-series stream. Time series in S are divided into parts with a fixed length of time. Every part in multiple time series streams is a basic window. And sling window consists of several basic windows. Sliding window $SW=\{SW_1,..., SW_i,..., SW_n\}(1\le i\le n)$, SW_i represents the ith part of the multiple time-series data streams.

Definition 2. Transaction $T=\{a_1,..,a_i,...,a_k\}$. Items of T are rearranged according to a total ordering relation and then get a new transaction $T'=\{a_1',..,a_i',...,a_k'\}$ which is a mapping of transaction T.

Definition 3. Given the minimum support threshold $\theta(0<\theta<1)$ and the maximum permissible error $\xi(0<\xi<\theta)$. Then for a pattern P in the sliding window SW whose size is N, if the supporting count of P ,$freq(P,SW)\ge\theta N$, then P is a frequent pattern; if $freq(P,SW)<\xi N$, then P is infrequent pattern; if $\xi N\le freq(P,SW)<\theta N$, then P is critical frequent pattern.

The definitions above have a close relationship with the research in this paper. And they will be used in this paper.

B. Time-decayed model

Due to the features of time-series stream, mobility and continuity, the knowledge of time-series stream changes over time. In practical applications, people are more interested in the knowledge which is contained in the latest data. Therefore, in order to mine the latest frequent patterns in the data and reduce the influence of historical data, decay factor λ $(0 <\lambda <1)$[5] is used in the algorithm.When a new part is being processed, the supporting count of historical patterns should be reduced once in my method. When the ith data streams part enter into the sliding window to be analyzed, the supporting count of the pattern P can be got by the following equation:

$$count = count'*\lambda + r \qquad (1)$$

where count' indicates the old supporting count before updating, if i is 1, then the count'= 0, r represents the supporting count of the pattern P in the ith data streams part.

III. PREPROCESSING

Through the following three steps the part of multiple time-series data streams are transformed into transaction dataset.

A. Piecewise linear approximation of time series

To overcome the feature, too many different values, of the data in time series, it is often used in the analysis of multiple time series that compressing time series. In this paper we use piecewise linear approximation method which can also smooth the data. Linearization method can transform time series into different line segment according to the changes in morphology of time series. Each line segment can visually represent the characteristics of changes of the time series in the time slot of the line segment. It can be roughly divided into three types, such as rising, falling and smoothing according to the changing trend. And different line segments have different morphologies. Thus time series are compressed into several line segments. The time series are greatly compressed. In this paper time-series streams will be divided into parts which are basic windows. The sliding window is consist of several basic windows.Therefore, when a new part is captured, piecewise linear approximation processing of the new time series part is beginning.

In this paper a simple bottom-up algorithm mentioned in [6] is used to do piecewise linear approximation of time-series streams.

B. Getting meta-patterns and symbolic representation of the streams

After doing piecewise linear approximation to the latest part which entering into the sliding window, we segment linearized time series to let each part of streams have only one line segment in one time slot. The similar line segments are clustered by using a clustering method. For data stream the clustering method is incremental. And for each cluster we introduce a symbol. Thus time series are composed of symbols. In my method the symbols of time series after segmenting are the basic elements of the association rules, that is meta-patterns.

Due to the unpredictability of the values of the data in time-series streams, the number of clusters cannot specified in advance. Therefore, a greedy method mentioned in [3] is improved for clustering. Treat each meta-pattern as a point in R^2 and use the following equation which we propose according to the characteristics of the vector to calculate the similarity of meta-patterns:

$$SIM_{i,j}=\begin{cases} \cos(\theta)*w_1+\dfrac{1}{2|x_i-x_j|}*w_2 & |x_i-x_j|\ge 1 \\ \cos(\theta)*w_1+(1-\dfrac{|x_i-x_j|}{2})*w_2 & 0\le|x_i-x_j|<1 \end{cases} \quad (2)$$

where θ is the angle of the vector i and j corresponding to the point i and j, x_i and x_j are the size of the vetor i and j, and w_1 and w_2 are the weights of the similarity of direction and size of vectors respectively where $w_1+w_2=1$.

Cosine similarity, cos(θ) is often used to calculate the similarity of vectors, which only considers the direction of vectors. However, in this paper we need to consider both of the direction and the size of vectors to determine the similarity. So when the vectors have the same size the similarity of the size of vectors is 1. The equation of the similarity of the size of vectors is show below:

$$Sim_{i,j}=\begin{cases} \dfrac{1}{2|x_i-x_j|} & |x_i-x_j|\ge 1 \\ 1-\dfrac{|x_i-x_j|}{2} & 0\le|x_i-x_j|<1 \end{cases} \quad (3)$$

Through calculating cos(θ) and $Sim_{i,j}$ we can get the equation (2) which can be used to calculate the similarity of vectors and take both direction and size of vectors into account. We can get that the value of $Sim_{i,j}$ is (0,1] and cos(θ) is [-1,1]. So $SIM_{i,j}$ is (-1,1], And when it is closer to 1 the similarity is greater.

The clustering method is that add the point which has a maximum similarity that is greater than a specified parameter r with a cluster center p to the cluster whose center is p, otherwise a new cluster with the center which is the point is formed. In order to determine a good value of r, in this paper a method is used that randomly sample several parts of data from the historical dataset of the time-series streams and preprocess them and then randomly sample some line segments which have been segmented for clustering. And the concept of total-error is proposed. Between elements of a cluster and center of the cluster there exists error which is defined as the value of 1 minus the similarity of these elements to the cluster center. The total-error is defined as the sum of the error of each cluster. And the upper bound of the number of clusters, d, is given. It cannot be too many or too few. Through the analysis of the results of several experiments we can determine a good value for d. When the total-error is minimum and the number of clusters satisfy the requirements, the value of r can be used when the algorithm runs.

C. Merging time-series streams into transactions

Assume a part of multiple time-series streams S = {S_1, S_2, ..., S_n}. After S is preprocessed the elements in S are composed of meta-patterns and each meta-pattern maybe have different length of time slot. If there is a meta-pattern in S_1 in a time slot i (i=1,2...) then in the time slot i there exists only one meta-pattern in other elements of S, and we can get a set T_i={S_1(i), S_2(i),...,S_n(i)} in which S_k(i) (k=1,2...,n) represents a meta-pattern. After the merging of S we can get D = {T_1, T_2, and ...}. Each set in D is a transaction, and assigned an identifier TID.

In order to explain the above processing an example of merging is shown below:

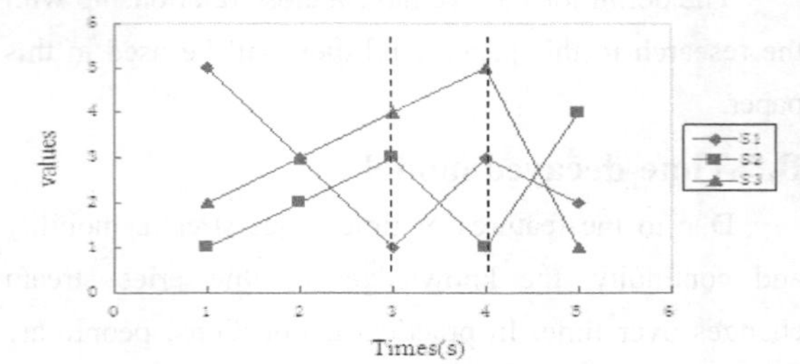

Figure 1. A part of time-series streams

The part of time-series streams in Figure 1 have been preprocessed by the first two steps. After that S1= a, b, c, S2 = d, c, e, S3 = d, b, f in which each lowercase letter correspond to one meta-pattern.

Transaction dataset D is shown below:

Table 1. Transaction dataset

TID	ITEMS
0	S1.a,S2.d,S3.d
1	S1.b,S2.c,S3.b
2	S1.c,S2.e,S3.f

From Table 1 we can get that after the merging of the data, time-series streams in the basic window have been transformed into transaction dataset to which we apply a mining discovery method.

IV. SLIDING WINDOW FREQUENT ITEMSETS TREE

A. The summary data structure-SWFI-tree

Definition 4. An SWFI-tree (Sliding Window Frequent Itemsets Tree) is a tree structure that multiplexes the prefix of patterns and its structure is defined as follows:

(1) Except the root of the SWFI-tree, the other nodes consist of six data fields: item_name, count, segnum, nodelink, parentnode and childnodes.

(a) count is the supporting count of the pattern which contains elements in the path from the root to the node.

(b) segnum is the serial number of the part of time series which is assigned with the values 0,1... according to the order of the process of the parts.

(c) nodelink is a pointer that point to the node in the tree which have the same field of item_name.

(d) parentnode is a pointer that point to the parent node in the path.

(e) childnodes are set of pointers that point to its child nodes.

(2) SWFI-tree and its item header table are arranged according to a pre-defined total order relation. In this paper the total order relation is the order of the serial number of time series that are assigned to them and within the same serial number the order of the lowercase english letters in alphabet.

After preprocessing of the data definition 2 with the total order relation defined above is applied to the transaction dataset. In FP-tree, items are arranged in descending order of the supporting count. And that allows more patterns share common prefixes. However, due to the unpredictable feature of the data of time-series streams, the supporting count always change over time. This will make FP-tree modified frequently and cost a lot of time.

Through the improvement based on FP-tree structure,the new storage structure, SWFI-tree can be used to maintain patterns information of the time-series streams.

Because SWFI-tree is a structure that multiplexes the prefix of patterns the supporting count and the segnum of nodes in the tree except the root will be greater than or equal to its descendant nodes' supporting count and segnum.

B. Construction and maintenance of SWFI-tree

In my algorithm one global SWFI-tree is constructed to maintain the potential frequent patterns in the sliding window which are likely to become frequent patterns and one local SWFI-tree is constructed for each part of time-series streams being analyzed which is deleted after adding the new information of the local SWFI-tree to the global SWFI-tree.

An example is given in the following to introduce the details of SWFI-tree structure. As is shown in Figure 2.

The transaction dataset in Table 1 after applying the total order relation is used to construct a local SWFI-tree, assuming the segnum is 1. We can construct the local SWFI-tree in Figure 2.

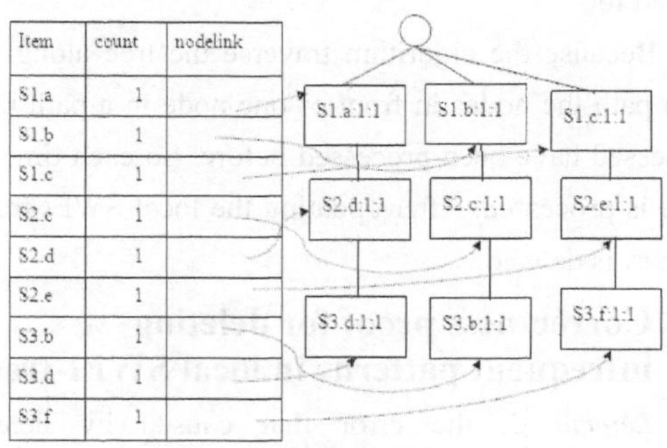

Figure 2. SWFI-tree structure

It can be seen from Figure 2, the number of clusters of time-series streams and time-series streams should be appropriate.

Through pruning local SWFI-tree, infrequent patterns of the basic window are removed and potential patterns are retained. It can be proved that the error of deleting infrequent patterns of the local SWFI-tree will not exceed the maximum permissible error ξ which is defined in definition 3 when mining is over a sliding window. And the proof is in the lemma 2.

Then the information of the local SWFI-tree after pruning is added to the global SWFI-tree. These steps can reduce the scale of the global SWFI-tree when the amount of data is increasing and memory consumption. Algorithm 1 presents the pseudo code for adding the new information of the local SWFI-tree to global SWFI-tree.

Algorithm 1. Updating global SWFI-tree

```
Input: local SWFI-tree
Output: global SWFI-tree
Update(local SWFI-tree)
1. for each path in local SWFI-tree
2. for each node of the path
3.   if(the item_name of the node not exist along with
     the same path in global SWFI-tree)
4.      add the node to the global SWFI-tree along
        with the path
5.   else
6.      node1->count=node1->count*pow(λ,node->
        segnum-node1->segnum)+node->count   //assume the
        node in global SWFI-tree having the same item_name
        along with the same path is node1.
7.   node1->segnum=node->segnum
8.   end if
9. end for
10.end for
```

Because the algorithm traverse the tree along with each path the nodes in front of one node in a path being processed have been processed before. So each time one node is processed. After updating the local SWFI-tree of the part is deleted.

C. Correctness proof for deleting infrequent patterns in local SWFI-tree

Lemma 2: the error that caused by deleting infrequent patterns in local SWFI-tree will be not greater than the given maximum permitted error ε defined in definition 3 for mining association rule in sliding window.

Proof: Assume the size of the sliding window is |N| and the number of the basic windows in the sliding window is n, SW_i ($1 \le i \le n$) represents the ith basic window. Infrequent pattern, p in the local SWFI-tree of SW_i meets $P.count_i < \varepsilon |SW_i|$ and assume that P's actual supporting count within the entire sliding window is freq (P, SW), $freq(P, SW) = \sum_{i=1}^{n} P.cont_i * \lambda^{segn-segi}$, in which segi is the segnum of the ith part of data streams. If P is infrequent in the local SWFI-tree of SW_j, SW_k ..., delete P in these local SWFI-trees and then we can get the approximate supporting count of P in sliding window is freq'(P, SW), satisfying freq (P, SW)-freq' (P, SW) $= P.count_j * \lambda^{segn-segj} + P.count_k * \lambda^{segn-segk} \ldots < \varepsilon |SW_j| + \varepsilon |SW_k| + \ldots < \varepsilon \sum_{i=1}^{n} SW_i = \varepsilon |N|$. Therefore, after deleting infrequent patterns in local SWFI-tree, the error between the actual supporting count and the approximate supporting count does not exceed ε. Thus the lemma is proved.

It can be obtained from the above proof that the actual supporting count and approximate supporting count of infrequent patterns does not exceed the permitted error ε. Therefore, (θ-ε) can be used as the minimum support threshold to mining frequent patterns in sliding window, which can ensure mining all frequent patterns even if deleting infrequent patterns in time-series streams,that is there is no false negative in the mining of data streams in sliding window.

V. DYNAMIC RULES DISCOVERY METHOD

A. Periodically pruning strategy

With the data of time-series streams arriving Continuously, the count of transactions is increasing. The scale of global SWFI-tree is constantly increasing over time. And this results in an increase of the space complexity of global SWFI-tree and the cost of maintenance being greatly increased. In the global SWFI-tree infrequent patterns and obsolete patterns are also constantly increasing over time. And these patterns have no contribution to the results of the mining, only increase the scale of the storage structure and make it difficult to maintain. Therefore, periodically pruning of global SWFI-tree can remove infrequent patterns and obsolete patterns, and store frequent patterns and potential patterns in the global SWFI-tree. For each time the method process one part of time-series streams. So the pruning cycle should be the integral multiple of basic window.

Assume the size of sliding window SW is N 、the number of basic windows in SW is m and the segnum of the current part of time-series streams when the pruning is starting is n. The specific pruning strategy is as follows:

a. for node in global SWFI-tree, if |n-node.segnum| ≥m, then this node and its descendant nodes are recorded obsolete patterns. the sub-tree whose root is the node can be directly deleted. Meanwhile update the value of the count field in the item header table of the global SWFI-tree and nodelink field in the item header table and the global tree.

b. for every item in the item header table, if the nodelink filed is not null, and |item.count|<εN, then all nodes in the tree which have the same item_name are recorded infrequent patterns. These nodes can be directly deleted. And at the same time update the value of nodelink field null in the item header table.

Algorithm 2 is used to prune the global SWFI-tree. It prunes by traversing the global item header table from top to bottom.

Algorithm 2. Pruning global SWFI-tree

Input: global SWFI-tree, N, m, n

Output: global SWFI-tree after pruning

```
Pruning(global SWFI-tree)
1. for each item in item header table of global tree
2.    node=item->nodelink
3.    while(node)
4.       if((n-node->segnum)≥m)
5.          delete node
6.       end if
7.       node=node->nodelink
8.    end while
9.  end for
10. updata count field of the items whose nodelink is not null in the item header table
11. for each item whose nodelink is not null in item header table
12.    if(item->count<ε*N)
13.       delete all items whose item_name field are the same with item.item_name in the tree
14.       set nodelink field of the item null
15.    end if
16. end for
```

Step 1-9 is to delete obsolete patterns. Step 11-16 is to delete infrequent patterns.

B. Association rules generation

Association rules generation consist of two steps which are shown as follows:

Step1: frequent patterns generation

Step2: generate association rules from frequent patterns

Storage structure of the algorithm is improved based on FP-tree. Therefore, the method of patterns generation in my algorithm is similar to the FP-growth. But there exits frequent patterns and critical frequent patterns in global SWFI-tree. So when outputting, it is necessary to determine whether the patterns are frequent. Meanwhile, the time of output should be after periodically pruning. After pruning the global SWFI-tree is smaller, and there are no obsolete patterns and infrequent patterns. Therefore, less time is spent for output patterns after pruning. Specific method of association rules generation are as follows:sequentially scan each item in the global SWFI-tree's item header table, if the value of nodelink field is not null, and |count|≥(θ-ε)N, then construct the conditional pattern base and generate the frequent patterns which contain the item. Association rules are generated based on the frequent patterns.

VI. EXPERIMENTAL RESULTS

Some stock datasets downloaded from the website (http://www.wstock.net/wstock/hholiday.htm) are used to test the effectiveness of the algorithm. By running the algorithm we can mine dynamic association rules of the type mentioned in the first part of the paper.

Three stock datasets are selected with close price. Each stock dataset has 20000 records. Use the algorithm to mine the rules of close price of the three stock datasets. And we set the size of basic window 500,that is, it contains 500 transactions. Sliding window contain 3 basic windows. Pruning cycle of global SWFI-tree is 3 basic windows. The weight of similarity of direction of vectors, w_1 is 0.75 and w_2 is 0.25. And the parameter of clustering, r is 0.8.

Result is shown in Figure 3.

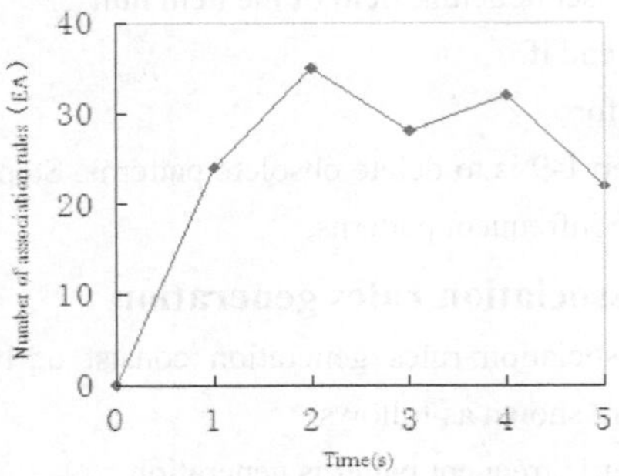

Figure 3. Number of rules in different time

It ban be seen from Figure 3 that because we mine the dynamic association rules the count of association rules changes over time.

VII. CONCLUSION

In this paper a method is proposed to mine dynamic association rules having the type that in a certain time slot whose length can be calculated if A has the pattern like increased by 10% and B has the pattern like increased by 5% then C has the pattern like decreased by 10% (20%,80%) from multiple time-series data streams. It considers the case that rules in the new data maybe more interesting. The knowledge of time series changes over time and rules also changes over time. Through preprocessing, simple rule discovery method we can mine dynamic association rules of the above type from multiple time-series data streams. Experimental results show that the algorithm is effective.

REFERENCE

[1] Fayyad U M, Piatetsky-Shapiro G, Smyth P, et al. Advances in knowledge discovery and data mining[J]. 1996.

[2] Babcock B, Babu S, Datar M, et al. Models and issues in data stream systems[C]//Proceedings of the twenty-first ACM SIGMOD-SIGACT-SIGART symposium on Principles of database systems. ACM, 2002: 1-16.

[3] Das G, Lin K I, Mannila H, et al. Rule discovery from time series[J]. Knowledge Discovery and Data Mining, 1998: 16-22.

[4] Sayal M. Detecting time correlations in time-series data streams[J]. Hewlett-Packard Company, 2004.

[5] Chen Y, Tu L. Density-based clustering for real-time stream data[C]//Proceedings of the 13th ACM SIGKDD international conference on Knowledge discovery and data mining. ACM, 2007: 133-142.

[6] Keogh E, Chu S, Hart D, et al. An online algorithm for segmenting time series[C]//Data Mining, 2001. ICDM 2001, Proceedings IEEE International Conference on. IEEE, 2001: 289-296.

Apply Service Oriented Architecture and Web 2.0 Application in Web Services

Ming-Chang Huang
Department of Business Information Systems / Operation Management
University of North Carolina at Charlotte
mhuang5@uncc.edu

Abstract

It is important how wireless hosts find other hosts efficiently for load and web service purposes because hosts in an ad-hoc network moves dynamically. This paper proposes a three-tier architecture, which includes content network, social network and service network. It presents a new structure for web and load services in ad-hoc computer networks, which is a new system architecture using SOA (Service Oriented Architecture) and Web 2.0 concepts to implement functions for web and load services. It is a three-tier system structure based on Web service functions to implement services seeking and load distribution. Furthermore, this project would construct a knowledge sharing and learning platform based on the mentioned three-tier architecture. Different communities can provide their services to each other using our new knowledge platform and this forms a "virtual community." This will leads to our desired accomplishments of "service reusability" and "service innovation" too. In addition, it can also propose the frameworks of new SOA, and evolve in other application in web2.0 style, and further more provides a platform and more resources in order to enhance the interactions between academia and industry.

Keywords: Web Services, Web 2.0, SOA, Service Oriented Architecture, Ad-hoc computer network, Load service and distribution

1. Introduction

Computer networks can provide parallel computation and services. It is important that hosts find services form other hosts, and send loads to other hosts for some certain function implementation through network transfer. With the increasing popularity of mobile communications and mobile computing, the demand for web and load services grows. When a computer is overloaded or it needs special services from other computers, it may send requests to other computers for web and load services. For example, a computer may need some jobs to be executed with higher quality of services or it needs some jobs to be done with a short period of time that its processor is too slow to perform the jobs; therefore, it may send part those jobs to other computers with higher speeds of processors. Since wireless networks have been wild used in recent years, how a host finds services it needs or how it transfers loads to other nodes has becomes a very important issue because not all wireless hosts have the ability to manipulate all their loads. For instance, a host with low battery power cannot finish all its jobs on time and should ask other nodes to provide services to finish the jobs, or it should transfer some of them to other hosts.

Before a wireless host transfers its loads to other hosts or asks for load services from other hosts, it has to find available hosts using resource allocation algorithms. There are several resource allocation protocols been developed, for example, IEFT Service Location Protocol (SLP) [8] and Jini [25] software package from Microsystems. However, these protocols address how to find the resources in wired networks, not in wireless networks. Maab [15] develops a location information server for location-aware applications based on the X.500 directory service and the lightweight directory access protocol LDAP [26]; while it does not cover some important issues about the movements of mobile hosts, for example, how to generate a new directory service and how a host gets the new services, when a directory agent moves away its original region. In an Ad-Hoc network, system structure is dynamic and hosts can join or leave any time. Therefore, how to provide load services and how to find available hosts providing load services become importance issues in an Ad-Hoc network system. The goal of this paper is that users can easily find and share resources based on the concepts of "service reusability" and "service innovation"

In this paper, a new architecture is proposed, which uses SOA model with Web 2.0 [8, 11] for web services. By using Web 2.0 with SOA, the network resources should be easily found by the hosts which need services. Based on XML, the SOA load service system can be used in any computer system platform [1, 2, 3]. This is a very important characteristic for hosts to share or request services in different systems. With the help of Web 2.0, hosts can find the required services easily from the Internet [4].

Figure 1 shows the basic SOA structure [5, 6, 7], which is built by three major components – the Directory, Service consumer, and Service provider. SQA is operated by the following: The Directory provides a platform for information that a service provider can register in the Directory for providing services; a service consumer can find its desired service it needs in the Directory. Once the Directory finds services that a service consumer needs, it sends a query response back to the service consumer to notify it the result. At this time, the service consumer has the information about the hosts which can provide services; therefore the consumer contacts the service provider directory by sending requests. The service provider now will send responses back to the consumer for the services the consumer needs. This is also called the "invoke" process.

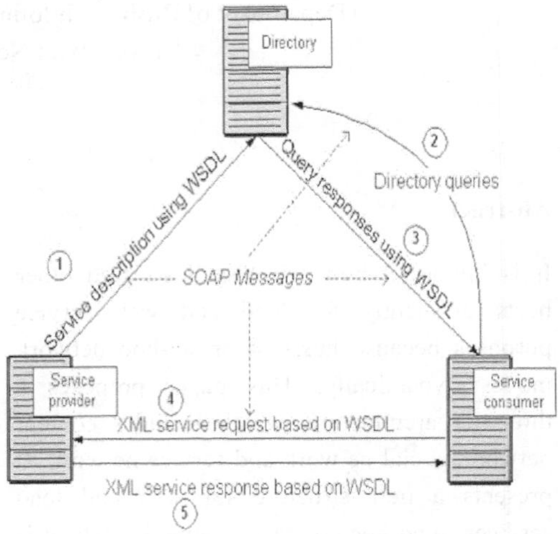

Figure 1: SOA structure

2. System structure

The system structure for the SOA model is illustrated in Figure 2. There are two layers in this structure – the Service Network layer, and the Service Logic layer.

The Service Network layer is the main network that connects to the internet using the regular network protocols. It receives requests from internet and forwards requests to the Service Logic layer in Web Service (WS) object forms. Each WS object is based on the SOA model which can communicate each other in social network way. The Service Logic layer is the main layer that uses WS objects to communicate each other in the sub-network under the Service Network layer. Different WS object has different objectives, for example, some WS objects are used for social network communication, while other WS objects are used for accessing contents in Content Networks. Since they are in SOA form, it is easy for them to find the resources they need for different purposes. Inside the Service Logic layer, there are sub-networks for different purposes and functions. For example, nodes can form social networks; storage devices can also form a content network for data accessing. All these operations are managed by the WS objects under the SOA model. For the service reusability purpose, most WS objects are generated by the Service Network layer for data and object consistency.

In Figure 2, all the services and requests are in the forms of Web Service objects which are defined and implemented by XML. For users who need services, requests are sent by the users to the Service Network Layer. The Service Network is the gateway for accepting requests and sending back requesting results to the requesters.

All the requests are processed by the Service Logic Layer, which finds the required information and applications for requests. The Content Network is a network which communicates databases. The Social Network contains the relations for social communities. The following procedure illustrates how it works.

1. Users send requests to a Service Network.
2. The Service Network forwards requests to Service Logic Layer via Web service functions.

   In this step, requests are transferred to objects that can communicate with the Service Logic layer.
3. When users send requests, Service Network has the ability to generate the desired WS objects according to the requests forwarded by the Service Network.
4. Service Logic Layer performs the required functions for the requests. It accesses data and information from Content Network using Web service functions. A User can also contact other users using WS objects under the Service Logic Layer.
5. After the Service Logic Layer has the results for the requests, it sends the results back to the Service Network using Web service functions.
6. Service Network then sends the results back to the users who sent initial requests.

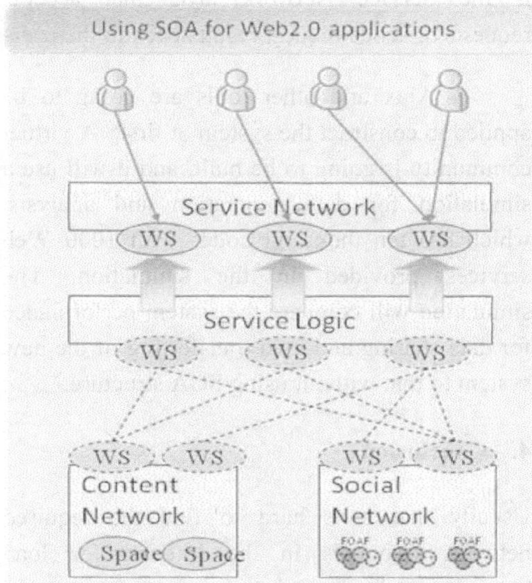

Figure 2: Using SOA for Web2.0 applications

There are several advantages with the design structure.

1. With the system structure, users can join the desired networks anywhere once they connect to the Internet.
2. With the characteristics of Web 2.0 with SOA model, users can join the desired networks they need to share or find resources easily they need.
3. Using WS objects for the communication makes it easy for service reusability and service innovation. Users do not need to construct special system or programs for data accessing and analysis.
4. Different Service Networks communicate with each other to find and share available resources.

3. Implementation and Simulation

Based on the structure of SOA model with Web 2.0 application, the system can be built in a three-tier structure. The lowest level is the sub-networks including Content Network, Social Network, which provides resources for data sharing. The middle level is the Service Logic layer, which provides WS objects. The top level is the Service Network layer that accepts requests or sends request results back to the users.

Ajax and other tools are going to be applied to construct the system at first. A virtual community is going to be built, and it will use a simulation for data generation and analysis, which has ten thousand nodes with 1000 Web services provided in the simulation. The simulation will compare the system performance for data sharing and load transferring of the new system to that without using SOA structure.

4. Conclusion

Usually that it is hard to find the required network resources in the Internet for load balance and load service purposes. Because of this, a new structure is proposed for hosts in the computer networks to find the resources for web services. This new structure provides new way that finds resources easily for web services. Especially, when a user needs services which are not very commonly provided in the Internet, with the help of Web 2.0 and SOA, users can find what they need because of the "long tail" property of Web 2.0 and the platform free property of SOA. With this system, uses can find and use the services easily since all the requests and services are constructed with the same web service structure. This can also improves the system performance for the network systems.

This system performance will be evaluated by using a simulation. Usually it is very hard to evaluate the performance for Web 2.0; therefore this project should have great helps in finding the performances for the usage of Web 2.0 and SOA.

References

[1] Ross J. Anderson, "The eternity service," *Pragocrypt* 1996, 1996.

[2] Stephanos Androutsellis-Theotokis and Diomidis Spinellis, "A survey of peer-to-peer content distribution technologies," *ACM Computing Surveys*, 36(4):335–371, December 2004. doi:10.1145/1041680.1041681.

[3] Yvonne Balzer, "Improve your SOA project plans," *IBM*, 16 July 2004

[4] Biddle, Peter, Paul England, Marcus Peinado, and Bryan Willman, "The Darknet and the Future of Content Distribution," *2002 ACM Workshop on Digital Rights Management*, 18 November 2002.

[5] Jason Bloomberg, "Mashups and SOBAs: Which is the Tail and Which is the Dog?," *Zapthink*

[6] Channabasavaiah, Holley and Tuggle, "Migrating to a service-oriented architecture," *IBM DeveloperWorks*, 16 Dec 2003

[7] Thomas Erl, "About the Principles," *Serviceorientation.org*, 2005-2006

[8] E. Guttman, C. Perkins, J. Veizades and M. Day, "Service Location Protocol," Version 2, IEFT, RFC 2165, November 1998.

[9] Dion Hinchcliffe, "Is Web 2.0 The Global SOA?," *SOA Web Services Journal*, 28 October 2005

[10] Huang, M., S. H. Hosseini, and K. Vairavan, *Load Balancing in Computer Networks*, Proceedings of ISCA 15th International Conference on Parallel and Distributed Computing Systems (PDCS-2002), Special session in Network Communication and Protocols. Held in the GALT HOUSE Hotel, Louisville, Kentucky, Sep. 19 - 21.

[11] Kim, A.J. (2000), "Community Building on the Web: Secret Strategies for Successful

Online Communities," *London: Addison Wesley (ISBN 0-201-87484-9)*.

[12] Christopher Koch, "A New Blueprint For The Enterprise," *CIO Magazine*, Mar 1 2005

[13] Peter Kollock (1999), "The Economies of Online Cooperation: Gifts and Public Goods in Cyberspace," *Communities in Cyberspace*, Marc Smith and Peter Kollock (editors). London: Routledge.

[14] Paul Krill, "Make way for SOA 2.0," *InfoWorld* , May 17, 2006

[15] H. Maab, "Location-Aware Mobile Application Based on Directory Services," MOBICOM 97, pp23-33.

[16] Joe McKendrick, "Anti-SOA 2.0 petition nears 400," *ZDNet.com*, June 29, 2006

[17] Yefim Natis & Roy Schulte, "Advanced SOA for Advanced Enterprise Projects," *Gartner*, July 13, 2006

[18] Andy Oram et al., "Peer-to-Peer:Harnessing the Power of Disruptive Technologies," Oreilly 2001

[19] Howard Rheingold (2000), "The Virtual Community: Homesteading on the Electronic Frontier," *London: MIT Press. (ISBN 0-262-68121-8)*.

[20] Ross, T. J., Fuzzy Logic with Engineering Applications, McGraw Hill, 1995.

[21] Antony Rowstron and Peter Druschel, "Pastry: Scalable, Decentralized Object Location, and Routing for Large-Scale Peer-to-Peer Systems," *Proceedings Middleware 2001 : IFIP/ACM International Conference on Distributed Systems Platforms*, Heidelberg, Germany, November 12-16, 2001. Lecture Notes in Computer Science, Volume 2218, Jan 2001, Page 329.

[22] Ralf Steinmetz, Klaus Wehrle (Eds), "Peer-to-Peer Systems and Applications," *ISBN: 3-540-29192-X,* Lecture Notes in Computer Science, Volume 3485, Sep 2005

[23] Smith, M. "Voices from the WELL: The Logic of the Virtual Commons," *UCLA Department of Sociology*.

[24] I. Stoica, R. Morris, D. Karger, M. F. Kaashoek, and H. Balakrishnan, "Chord: A scalable peer-to-peer lookup service for internet applications," *Proceedings of SIGCOMM 2001*, August 2001.

[25] J. Waldo, "The Jini Architecture for network-centric computing," Communication of the ACM, pp 76-82, July 1999.

[26] W. Yeong, T. Howes, and S. Kille, "Lightweight Directory Access Protocol," RFC 1777, March 1995.

[27] http://opengroup.org/projects/soa/doc.tpl?gdid=10632

Agent Based Dynamic Data Splitting In Relationnals Data Warehouses

Nader KOLSI[1], Abdelaziz ABDELLATIF[2] and Khaled GHEDIRA[3]
[1]Business School of Tunis - University Campus of Manouba - Tunisia
[2]University of Sciences of Tunis - University Campus of El Manar – Tunisia
[3] Higher Institute of Management of Tunis - Tunis University – Tunisia
nader.kolsi@topnet.tn, abdelaziz.abdellatif@fst.rnu.tn, khaled.ghedira@isg.rnu.tn

Keywords: Relationnal data warehouse, Dynamic data splitting, Scalability, Branch and Bound algorithm, Multi-agent system.

Abstract: In this paper, we propose a new approach to manage data distribution in a relationnal data warehouse environment. This approach deals with the dynamic data splitting on a set of interconnected machines. The data distribution that we consider is different from the "classical" one which depends on the data use. The distribution in our approach consists in splitting data when the machine reaches his storage capacity limit. This distribution assures the scalability and exploits the storage and processing resources available in the organization using the data warehouse. It is worth noting that our approach is based on a multi-agent model mixed with the scalability distribution proposed by the Scalable Distributed Data Structures. In this paper, we focus on the global dynamic for the data splitting operation based on Branch and Bound algorithm.

1 INTRODUCTION

A Data Warehouse (DW) is a principal component of the information systems in the organizations. It is, as defined by its inventor W. H. Inmon (Inmon, 1992), a collection of data which are subject-oriented, integrated, stamped, non-volatile, and used as a support of decision making. It is considered as a deposit of data that have been collected from heterogeneous and autonomous distributed sources. It is used for analytical tasks in business. These taskes are grouped in OLAP systems (OnLine Analytical Processing) which given the ability to the decision-makers to interactively explore the DW.

The relationnal DW is usually presented as a centralized database. However, it is rare to find machines which can cope with the continuous growth of these data volumes. Moreover, the improvements provoted to the existing data management systems concerning the management of a large volume of data are not sufficient to meet the needs caused by the increasing data volumes of the relationnal DW. In addition, the static data distribution schemas which are currently used in these systems constitute a major handicap. Indeed, the static data distribution creates, possibly, a large imbalances data load, which can cause a drop in performance (Imadali and chabane, 2010).

Our work, presented in this paper, aims at solving the problems of storage space and performance through: (1) developing a dynamic and scalable system that can manage the DW automatically (data storage, data distribution on a set of machines, and data access), (2) taking advantage of the storage and processing resources available in the organization (processors, memory, hard disks, etc.), (3) getting better data storage time, and (4) improving the query response time.

This paper is organized as follows: Section 2 gives an overview of related works and discusses the problems related to distribution topics. In section 3, we present the multi-agent system. In section 4, we describe the proposed multi-agent model. Section 5 details the global dynamic of the data splitting operation. Finally, in section 6, a conclusion and an outlook to future works are made.

2 RELATED WORK

Most of researches in literature working in optimization topics propose solutions based on a centralized DW or a model of partitioning which consist of storing the facts-table in pieces, instead of a large monolithic object, on a multiprocessors machine with a set of I/O devices or on a centralized database. These researches are based on the data partitioning. There are three types of partitioning: (1) vertical partitioning, (2) horizontal partitioning and (3) hybrid partitioning. The most used type, in the DW context, is the second one which consists in dividing the rows a table into separate subsets of rows, called horizontal partitions, each one is defined by a restriction operation applied to the source table (Bellatreche, 2003). This type of partitioning preserves the features of the star schema as the data hierarchy, the data granularity of the fact table and the semantic links between the fact table and the dimension tables (Ben Tekaya, 2011). In addition, it is the most suitable for OLAP queries which contain multiple join operations. There are two modes of horizontal partitioning: (1) the primary horizontal partitioning: which consists in dividing a table using restrction defined on the attributes of the table itself, (2) the referential horizontal partitioning: which consists in dividing a table using horizontal partitions of on one or more other (s) table(s).

In (Boukhalfa and al., 2008), the authors apply horizontal partitioning to the DW star schema (primary mode to the dimensional tables and referential mode to the fact table) based on a set of used queries. This approach is based on genetic algorithms and aims to control the number of partitions in order to optimize their maintenance cost. In (Barr and Bellatreche, 2012), the authors have mapped the problem of selecting an horizontal partitioning schema in a DW to the knapsack problem and they solved this problem by using ant colony optimization algorithm. In these works, the authors use a model cost to select the optimal horizontal partitioning schema. In (Mahboubi, 2008), the author proposes a partitioning method based on data mining technique. This method uses the classification algorithm "k-means" and aims to control the number of partitions. Unlike previous methods, the proposed one allows to merge the two modes of horizontal partitioning (primary and referential) in a single step. In (Drabant and Drabant, 2011), the authors have used the classification algorithms: k-means, fuzzy and hierarchical c-means, and they have proven the improvement of the quality of the obtained partitioning schema.

However, the use of DW with distributed structure has appeared with the data marts. Although the use of small data marts (data warehouses) was the first attempt to solve the problems of space and performance, data marts are basically stand-alone and have data integration problems in a global data warehouse context. In addition, the performance of many distributed queries is normally poor, mainly due to the load balance problems. Furthermore, each individual data mart is primarily designed and tuned to answer the queries related to its own subject area, whereas the response to global queries depends on the global system tuning and the network speed.

In literature, we can find several ways to partition horizontally the relation. Typically, it can be divided using a round-robin, random, range, or hash-based scheme. In (Almeida and al., 2008), (Bernardino and al., 2002) and (Furtado, 2004), the papers authors use the Data Warehouse Striping (DWS) technique. The latter is a round-robin data partitioning approach especially designed for distributed data warehouse environments. By using the DWS, the fact table will be distributed into an arbitrary number of machines which is fixed at the beginning. Consequently, the queries will be executed in parallel by all of the machines (Almeida and al., 2008). The round-robin distribution is simple to use and guaranties the load balancing, although its major disadvantage is that we must have machines with the same treatment and storage capacities. Otherwise, some machines will be too busy and the others will be under used. In (Zhao, 2007), the author proposes a distributed architecture of DW based on the separation between the initial production database and the OLAP applications. Indeed, the author uses three-tier network architecture: a production database tier, a DW tier and an OLAP operations tier. He has treated the behavior of the presentation component and the impact of the distribution on the collection and the integration components. However, he has not presented an approach to data distribution according to needs of OLAP applications. Other researches (Zhao and Ma, 2004), (Zhao and Schewe, 2004) use the abstract state machines as a flexible and quality-oriented formal method to design and optimize a distributed DWH and OLAP applications. In (Ben Tekaya, 2011), the author proposes a methodology for relational distributed DW design. For this purpose, he develops a set of matrix: 'Matrix of data partitioning', 'matrix of data allocation' and a 'matrix of data source'.

Obviously, most researches, in the literature, that work on the data warehouse distribution propose solutions based on the studies made on the production databases under the name of very large data bases. These solutions are based on the "classic" data distribution which depends on the data use and has a static distribution plan. Furthermore, this type of distribution is defined at the design phase.

These researches have deeply studied the data partitioning, but they neglected the allocation problems due to its complexity. Indeed, the authors of this work: (1) either they consider that the database is centralized and the partitioning will be on one machine, (2) or they assign partition to machines to optimizing their cost functions (minimization of the communication between machines, minimizing the cost of query execution by minimizing the input / output operations, minimizing the cost of maintenance, etc. .) without give consideration to the storage capacity of each machine while assuming all used machines have the same capacity and can contain any amount of data. Indeed, the used cost functions not reflect the characteristics of different machines (storage capacity, memory, CPU speed, etc.)

We have to point out that, in our approach, the data distribution that we consider is different from the usual-used ones (Kolsi and al., 2003). That is, it is not defined at the design phase and not depended on the data use. However, it is imposed by the storage capacity. As a matter of fact, when a machine reaches its storage capacity limit, we add another one. Then, we distribute the data on the two machines to have a balanced load. This distribution assures the scalability and exploits the set of interconnected machines available in the organization using the data warehouse. These machines give an important storage and processing capacities. It is worth noting that our work is based on the computer cluster as network architecture. But, the machines are not used only for the parallel processing.

We have to note that, in our approach, we use the range partitioning (horizontal fragmentation). So, the queries are executed in parallel not by all the machines but only by those that contain the necessary partitions.

Furthermore, the data distribution is dynamic and automatic. In fact, at each time when one machine reaches its limit capacity, it starts up the data distribution operation without needing an external intervention (administrator). Moreover, the number of used machines, in our approach, is not fixed. Therefore, the storage capacity of the DWH tends theoretically to the infinite because we can, at any moment, add dynamically other machines. This infinite storage capacity and dynamic data distribution are guaranteed by the principles of the Scalable and Distributed Data Structures (SDDS) (Litwin and al., 1994).

We note, also, that there is no work in the literature has proposed a solution that controlling the size of the generated fragments. This can cause storage problems for these fragments. The only work that has raised this problem is (Barr and Bellatreche, 2012). The authors posed the problem of big fragments from the point of view data access and not seen the data storage problem. They noted that applications accessing these partitions will always put a lot of time to collect the required lines. However, they have not given a detailed approach for solving this problem. In our approch, the choose of the fragmentation plan is based on the size of the generated fragments.

In the rest of this paper, we consider that the two terms 'splitting' and 'distributing' have the same significance.

In the following section, we present the multi-agent system concepts.

3 MULTI-AGENT SYSTEM

The agent paradigm is currently in vogue within a lot of research domains. An agent can be a physical or virtual entity that acts autonomously (without the direct intervention of humans or others), on behalf of entities (person, organisation, etc.), in response to input from his environment. Agents have a social ability. They may communicate with the users, system resources and other agents as required in order achieving its goals and tendencies. Moreover, more advanced agents may cooperate with other agents to carry out tasks beyond the capability of a single agent. So, agents contain some level of intelligence, ranging from pre-defined rules up to self-learning artificial intelligence inference machines. This intelligence enables agents to act not only reactively, but sometimes also proactively.

An agent can be static or mobile. The latter is a particular class of agent with the ability during execution to migrate dynamically (code, data and execution state) from one machine to another, where it can resume its execution, in order to reach data or remote resources. It has been suggested that mobile agent technology, amongst other things, can help to reduce network traffic and to overcome network latencies. Moreover, the mobile agents have proved a high performance when we access to the data distributed on a set of interconnected machines (Arcangeli and al. 2002) and when we store these data (Kolsi and al., 2007).

A MAS is a system composed of multiple autonomous agents and comprises the following elements (Ferber, 1999): (i) An environment 'E' is a space which generally has volume, (ii) A set of situated objects 'O', that is to say, it is possible at a given moment to associate any object with a position in 'E', (iii) An assembly of agents 'A', which are specific objects (a subset of 'O'), represent the active entities in the system, (iv) An assembly of relations 'R', which link objects (and therefore, agents) to one another, (v) An assembly of operations 'Op', that allows the agents of 'A' to perceive, produce, transform, and manipulate objects in 'O', (vi) Operators with the task of representing the application of these operations and the reaction of the world to this attempt at modification, which we shall call the laws of the universe.

The following section reveals the data distribution principle and the proposed multi-agent model.

4 PROPOSED MODEL

The aim of our proposed model is to solve the problems in the DWH context using the available resources in the organization. These problems are related to the data storage, splitting and access.

According to the proposed approach, the DWH will be distributed on a set of machines. In this case, the data management needs the collaboration and the interaction between those machines in order to reply to the user's queries while assuring the parallel processing of these queries. Thus, we have chosen to use the Multi-Agent System (MAS) with the mobile agents as essential actors. In fact, the MAS allows following the progress of the dynamic data distribution, facilitates the collaboration, the interaction, and the independency of the different machines, and improves the parallel execution of the user queries. The use of mobile agents in the proposed solution seems to be very helpful because it allows: (1) decreasing the network loads, (2) liberating client machines during the results preparation that needs generally a very important execution-time, (3) and, essentially, securing the data that are transported in the network.

We use the SDDS principle based on data distribution through intervals (range partitioning) in order to distribute the data of the DWH on a set of machines. This type of distribution allows the decomposition of the DWH into a set of domains. Each domain can be stored on one or more machines according to its data size.

4.1 Principle of Data Distribution

The DWH is horizontally distributed on a set of machines that have the same DBMS and the same star schema. Furthermore, on each machine, we can use the materialized views and indexes to tune and to optimize the performance.

The principle is to start with a single machine for which we define: (1) the storage capacity limit of this machine for which the used DBMS gives its highest performance (for data access and storage), and (2) both the inferior bound mark and the superior one for each fact table key. When this machine reaches its limit, we add another one and we distribute the data on the two machines to obtain a balanced load. In most cases, the fact table undergoes the splitting operation, because of its important volume. The dimensional tables are distributed when their key constitutes a distribution criterion. Otherwise, they are duplicated.

To get a load balance storage between sites, taking into account their maximum capacity, we balance the filling rate (FR_{Si}) of sites, which is equal to: FR_{Si} = Size of data to be stored on Si * 100 / CAP_MAXSi.

For example, if we have a site S0 with CAP_MAX_{S0} = 100GB and we introduce two new machines S1 and S2 with CAP_MAX_{S1} = 80GB and CAP_MAX_{S2} = 150GB. Knowing that the data volume has reached the 100GB, S0 must burst data such way we have of approximately 30GB on S0, approximately 25GB on S1 and approximately 45Go on S2 and that to have a rate of filling on each site 30-31%

To evaluate this distribution, we use a cost function to calculate the cost of query execution for the DW. For this, we define a set of queries Q = {Q1, Q2, ..., Qp} for each query Qj we will take its frequency : FREQ (Qj) and the list of useful sites for its execution Liste_S (Qj).

Hence, the overall cost function to optimize is: Σ Qj ∈ Q * FREQ(Qj) * CET (Qj) with CET (Qj) is the total cost of executing the query Qj. To calculate the CET (Qj), we must, first of all, calculate the CET_Si (Qj) is the cost of executing the query Qj on each site listed in the Liste_S and then we add the cost of transferring the intermediate result (CTResInt) to the requesting site. Then we take the maximum CET_Si (Qj) and add the cost of producing the final result.

That is why, in our approach, we take into consideration the following characteristics: (1) Characteristics of each site: (i) The storage space allocated to the DW, (ii) The features of the used databases management system: block size, number of blocks used for the join, for sorting, etc., (2) Characteristics of the network: (i) Capacity: 10, 100, 1000 Mbit/s to 10Gbit/s, (ii) Quality of the network: it can deteriorate depending on network traffic and noise, (3) Formula for Speed Data Transmission: CTResInt seconds = (data size in MB)

/ (debit (in MB / sec) * 0.8 Degradation).

In our approach, we suggest to study the HF on the fact table while considering all the attributes of the dimension tables are part of the fact table. Since our goal is not control the number of fragments, but rather it is the control of the size of the fragments. It should be noted that the number of fragment obtained after each fragmentation is always equal to two.

4.1.1 Mapping the HF problem to the multiple Knapsack problem

Our problem is to solve the problem of data storage of DW. We assume that the data are initially stored on a single S0 site. Once the site reaches its maximum capacity, another site must be added in the system and we split the contents of the original site on the two sites. Therefore, we map our problem to the multiple knapsack problem and we apply the algorithm "branch and bound" search of the fragmentation pattern that guarantees the filling of the two sites, while maintaining load balancing, and optimizing the query execution time.

The Knapsack Problem (KP) is known as a combinatorial optimization problem. It is one of NP-complete problems classics. The problem KP is to fill a backpack capacity well determined by a set of objects such that the total weight of the objects in the bag is maximized, without exceeding the capacity of the knapsack and each object must provide a profit.

The Multiple-Knapsack Problem (MKP) is a more complex variant of the KP which is to allocate a set of objects in a number of backpacks of different capacities. The gain provided by an object now depends on the bag in which it is placed. For example, if we put money into a project X provides more gain than if we invest the same amount in project Y.

For this, we assume that we have a set of predicates P = {P1, P2, ..., Pk} where each predicate admits its selectivity factor, this corresponds to the set of objects to be distributed with their weight, and a set of locations S = {Si, Sj} where each site has a maximum capacity CAP_MAXSi, which corresponds to knapsack capacity. Our goal is to build fragments from all predicates P, calculate the volume of each fragment obtained and assign, if possible, to one of two sites while maintaining their maximum storage capacity and function while optimizing the data access cost.

Note that the size of each fragment is calculated from: (1) the total size of the fact table on the site to be distributed, (2) and selectivity factors which determines the predicates fragment.

The following part deals with the proposed multi-agent model architecture and the waiting database notion that we use in our approach.

4.1.2 Fragmentation Approach

The process to be followed for the HF data on the site has reached its maximum capacity and new site added to the system is : (1) determining the set of the most frequent queries QF, (2) collection of predicates selection from the set QF, (3) constructing the fragments progressively from the predicates (4) determining the size of each fragment, (5) assignment of the fragment obtained in the site that may contain and the bar of the resulting fragment will be assigned to another site (6) calculating the execution time of the query workload (7) choose the best fragmentation that can fill up the sites and optimizes access time data. As Exemple, we take the following predicates:

P1: Sex = 'M', P2: Sex = 'F', P3: Age <18,
P4: Age> = 18 and Age <= 40, P5: Age> 40,
P6: Region = 'Tunis', P7: Region = 'Sousse'
P8: Region = 'Sfax'.

With the following selectivities:

Sel (P1) = 0.5, Sel (P2) = 0.5, Sel (P3) = 0.3,
Sel (P4) = 0.5, Sel (P5) = 0.2, Sel (P6) = 0.33,
Sel (P7) = 0.33, Sel (P8) = 0.34.

The first step is to build the fragments with a single attribute where the predicates are associated with the operator 'OR':

FSEX: {FSEX1 (P1, 0.5); FSEX2 (P2, 0.5); FSEX3 (P1 OR P2, 1)}

FAGE: {FAGE1 (P3, 0.3); FAGE2 (P4, 0.5); FAGE3 (P5, 0.2); FAGE4 (P3 OR P4, 0.8); FAGE5 (P3 OR P5, 0.5); FAGE6 (P4 OR P5, 0.7); FAGE7 (P3 OR P4 OR P5, 1)}.

FREGION: {FREG1: (P6, 0.33); FREG2: (P7, 0.33); FREG3 (P8, 0.34); FREG4 (P6 OR P7, 0.66); FREG5 (P6 OR P8, 0.67); FREG6 (P7 OR P8, 0.67); FREG7 (P6 OR P7 OR P8, 1)}.

Then we order FSEX, FAGE, FREG in descending order of selectivities. We remove fragments with selectivity factor is equal to 1.

From this point, we can look for solutions of fragmentation with a single attribute.

To build two fragments with different attributes we use the logical operator 'AND' between predicates. Eg F_SEX_AGE: FSEX1 AND FAGE1 with a selectivity factor, which corresponds to product selectivity factors FSEX1 AND FAGE1 to be equal to 0.15. Like so that large fragments will be divided into sub fragments. The total number of possible fragments is equal to 2 * 6 * 6 = 72. Hence the number of possible fragments increases with the number of attributes and the number of predicates defined on each attribute.

So with the B & B algorithm, we visit all the possible solutions, we minimize the absolute value of the difference between the size of the fragments obtained and the ability of each site to ensure maximum filling each site. This difference is used as the threshold for not visiting all the options and only to analyze the solutions that can improve the threshold.

At the end and choose the optimal fragmentation pattern, we take the list of solutions obtained by the algorithm B & B and load queries and we estimate the cost of executing the load for each scheme and we choose the scheme which gives the optimal access cost.

We have developed a program to determine the overall fragmentation patterns with a rate optimum filling. We tested our program on a set of 12 attributes with more than 16 million of fragmentation patterns possible and we got the result in a fairly reasonable time.

4.2 The proposed Multi-agent model

The proposed model consists of five static agent classes (Client, Dispatcher, Splitting, Domain and Server) and a mobile agent class (Messenger). Each agent class is defined by its knowledge (static or dynamic), its acquaintances (agents that it knows and with which it can communicate), and its behavior.

Figure 1 illustrates the interaction between the different agents.

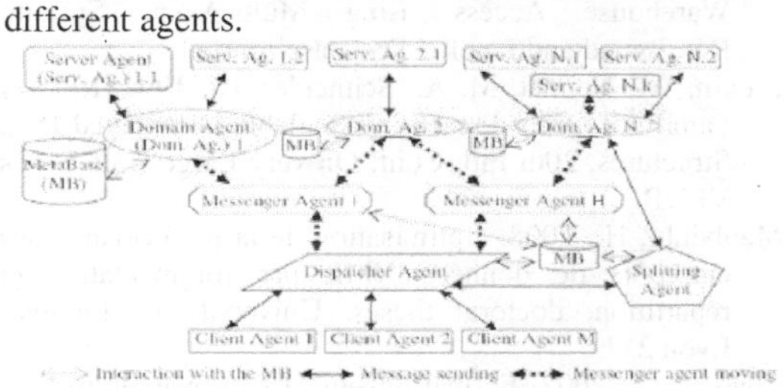

Fig. 1: the proposed Multi-agent model architecture.

For more detail about this model and the different agent classes, you can see the papers (Kolsi and al., 2009) and (Kolsi and al., 2007).

In the following section, we detail the dynamic of the proposed model for the data splitting operation.

5 DATA SPLITTING

The agents contributing in the data splitting operation are: the Server agent, the Domain agent, the Splitting agent, the Messenger agent and the Dispatcher agent.

The splitting operation will be automatically started up when the Domain agent detects that the available space at the Server agent cannot support entirely the data amount received at the storage operation. This operation does not necessitate the modification of both the treatments (agents) and the data structures.

Each Domain agent is characterized by a maximum number of Server agents that it can control. If the Domain agent does not reach this number, the splitting operation will be managed by the split Domain agent and a new Server agent will be created. Otherwise, the splitting operation will be managed by the Splitting agent and a new Domain agent will be created.

The afore-mentioned agents exchange different messages in order to achieve the splitting operation which involves the creation of a new Domain agent.

When the Server agent detects that the available space can not support the total amount of the received data, it sends a message informing the Domain agent that it reaches its capacity limit and it needs to split its data. This message contains, also, the data that are not inserted. Then, the Domain agent sends a message to the Splitting agent. This message contains the new values of both the superior bound mark and the inferior one. To determine these bounds, the Domain agent computes its records and determines the key values which allow dividing these records into two balanced parts.

When the Splitting agent receives the spilling request, it informs the Dispatcher agent that the Domain agent i will start up a splitting operation. Thus, the Dispatcher agent stops momentarily the operations sent to this agent. The Splitting agent is responsible for preparing the new Domain agent. Once the new agent is created, the Splitting agent informs the Domain agent asking for splitting of the new-created agent address as well as the bound marks of each dimensional table. According to these bound marks, the split Domain agent selects the data from the Server agents and sends them to the Messenger agent. Then, it informs the Splitting agent that the splitting operation is terminated and updates its descendants list. The Messenger agent moves to the new Domain agent and gives it the received data. This new agent achieves the storage operation as described in § 4.1.

When the Splitting agent is informed that the splitting operation is terminated, it sends message informing the Dispatcher agent that the new Domain agent and the split Domain agent are ready to receive operations. So, The Dispatcher agent updates its domain agents list according to the received information.

6 CONCLUSION

In this article, we presented a new approach to the selection of a fragmentation pattern spread that controls the size of the fragments generated and guaranteed optimization of data access time. To do this, we simulated our problem to the problem of multiple bags back and we have applied the algorithm "branch and bound" to search for the optimal solution. The prospect of this work, we can try to generalize the process of fragmentation of data on a sample of sites at the same time and not be limited to two sites.

It should be noted that this work is part of our research that uses multi-agent systems (MAS) as well as mobile agents for data management data warehouse. The use of such technology ensures transparency in the distribution of data from users, monitoring the dynamic distribution of data, the collaboration between different sites and their independence, security in the transfer of data, decrease the load of networks and the parallel execution of multiple operations.

REFERENCES

Almeida, R., Vieira, J., Vieira, M., Madeira, H., Bernardino, J., 2008. Efficient Data Distribution for DWS, in Proc. of the Lecture Notes in Computer Science 5182 Springer 2008, ISBN 978-3-540-85835-5, 10th International Conference on Data Warehousing and Knowledge Discovery (DaWaK '08), Turin, Italy.

Arcangeli, J., Hameurlain, A., Migeon, F., Morvan, F., 2002. Apport des agents mobiles à l'évaluation et l'optimisation de requêtes bases de données réparties à grande échelle. Technical Report, laboratory IRIT, Université Paul Sabatier.

Barr, M., Bellatreche, L., 2012. Approche dirigée par les fourmis pour la FH dans les entrepôts de données relationnels, Revue "Nature & Technologie", n° 06, pp 16 – 24.

Bellatreche, L., 2003. Techniques d'optimisation des requêtes dans les data warehouses, Sixth International Symposium on Programming and Systems, p. 81-98.

Ben Tekaya K., 2011. Fragmentation et Allocation Dynamiques des Entrepôts de Données, Doctoral thesis, University of Sciences of Tunis.

Bernardino, J., Furtado, P. S., Madeira, H. C., 2002. Approximate Query Answering Using Data Warehouse Striping. Journal of Intelligent Information Systems, 19:2, 145–167.

Boukhalfa, K., Bellatreche, L., Richard P., 2008. Fragmentation Primaire et Dérivée: Étude de Complexité, Algorithmes de Sélection et Validation sous ORACLE10g, research report N° 01.

Darabant, A. S., Darabant, L., 2011. Clustering methods in data fragmentation, Romanian Journal Of Information Science And Technology, Volume 14, Number 1, pp. 81–97.

Ferber, J., 1999. Multi-Agent System: An Introduction to Distributed Artificial Intelligence. Harlow: Addison Wesley Longman.

Furtado, P., 2004. Experimental Evidence on Partitioning in Parallel Data Warehouses. DOLAP 04 - WORKSHOP of the Int'l Conference on Information and Knowledge Management (CIKM), Washington.

Imadali, S., Chabane, F., 2010. Système transactionnel dans PBST*, Senior thesis, Higher National School for Computer Science-Algeria.

Inmon, W., 1992. Building the Data Warehouse, QED Technical Publishing Group.

Kolsi, N., Ghedira, K., Abdellatif, A., 2003. Utilisation d'un Système Multi-Agents pour la Répartition et la Scalabilité des Données d'un Data Warehouse, in *Acts of the Fourth Scientific Days*, Borj El Amri Aviation School, Tunis, Tunisia, Tome 1, pp. 118-129.

Kolsi, N., Abdellatif, A., Ghedira, K., 2007. Agent Based Dynamic Data Storage and Distribution in Data Warehouses. KES-AMSTA.

Kolsi, N., Abdellatif, A., Ghedira, K., 2009. Data Warehouse Access using Multi-Agent System. Distributed and Parallel Database Journal.

Litwin, W., Neimat, M. A., Schneider, D., 1994. RP*: A Family of Order-Preserving Scalable Distributed Data Structures, 20th Intl. Conf. On very Large Data Bases VLDB.

Mahboubi, H., 2008. Optimisation de la performance des entrepôts de données XML par fragmentation et répartition, doctoral theses, University of Lumière Lyon 2.

Zhao, J. Q., 2007. Formal design of data warehouse and OLAP systems. PhD thesis, Massey University, Palmerston North, New Zealand.

Zhao, J., Ma., H., 2004. Quality-assured design of on-line analytical processing systems using abstract state machines. In Proceedings of the Fourth International Conference on Quality Software (QSIC), Braunschweig, Germany.

Zhao, J., Schewe, K.-D., 2004. Using abstract state machines for distributed data warehouse design. In Conceptual Modelling. First Asia-Pacific Conference on Conceptual Modelling, vol. 31 of CRPIT, pp.49 – 58.Dunedin, New Zealand.

Opportunities and Challenges of Big Data Analytics

Faruk Bagci
Department of Computer
Engineering
Kuwait University
Kuwait City, Kuwait
dr.faruk.bagci@gmail.com

Abstract

In the era of information explosion, enormous amounts of data have become available on hand to decision makers. Big data refers to datasets that grow so huge that they become difficult to handle using traditional tools and techniques. Due to the rapid growth of such data, solutions need to be studied and provided in order to handle and extract value and knowledge from these datasets. Such value can only be provided by using big data analytics, which is the application of advanced analytics techniques on big data. This paper aims to analyze the different methods and tools which can be applied to big data, as well as the opportunities provided and the challenges which much be faced.

1. Introduction

Imagine a world without data storage; a place where every detail about a person or organization, every transaction performed, or every aspect which can be documented is lost directly after use. Organizations would thus lose the ability to extract valuable information and knowledge, perform detailed analyses, as well as provide new opportunities and advantages. Data is an essential part of our lives, and the ability to store and access such data has become a crucial task which we cannot live without. Anything ranging from customer names and addresses, to products available, to purchases made, to employees hired, etc. has become essential for day to day continuity. Data is the building block upon which any organization thrives.

Now imagine the extent of details and the surge of data and information provided nowadays through the advancements in technologies and the internet. With the increase in storage capabilities and methods of data collection, huge amounts of data have become easily available. Every second, more and more data is being created and needs to be stored and analyzed in order to extract value. Furthermore, data has become cheaper to store, so organizations need to get as much value as possible from the huge amounts of stored data. According to Gruenspecht [7], there has been a tremendous surge in the use of digital storage, as well as a drop in its price within the last twenty years. This has eliminated the requirement of clearing out previous data, increased the storage of metadata, or data about the data, as well as made backup storage a common practice against data loss. Additionally, companies and individuals possess more technologies and devices which create and capture more data in different categories. A single user nowadays, can own a desktop, laptop, smartphone, tablet, and more, where each device carries very large amounts of valuable data. Such sheer amounts of data need to be properly analyzed, and pertaining information should be extracted. Big data analytics is the operation of advanced analytic techniques on big data [14]. This paper will further examine the concept of big data analytics and how it can be applied on big data sets. The purpose of the paper is to discover some of the opportunities and challenges related to the field of big data, as well as the application of data analytics on big data.

The paper is organized as follows. The first section explains big data in details, as well as the characteristics which define big data, and the importance of storing and analyzing such voluminous data. The second section discusses big data analytics, starting with the data analytics lifecycle, followed by the possible advanced data analytics methods. It will also take a look at the theories and methods, as well as the technologies and tools for needed for big data analytics. Finally, we will conclude the paper by analyzing the challenges related to big data, and the need for future research in the field.

2. Big data

The term "Big Data" has recently been applied to datasets that grow so large that they become awkward to work with using traditional on-hand database management tools. They are data sets whose size is beyond the ability of commonly used software tools and storage systems to capture, store, manage, as well as process the data within a tolerable elapsed time. Big data also refers to databases which are measured in terabytes and above, and are too complex and large to be effectively used on conventional systems [21]. Big data sizes are a constantly moving target, currently ranging from a few dozen terabytes to many petabytes of data in a single data set. Consequently, some of the difficulties related to big data include capture, storage, search, sharing, analytics, and visualizing. Today, enterprises are exploring large volumes of highly detailed data so as to discover facts they didn't know before [14]. Business benefit can commonly be derived from analyzing larger and more complex data sets that require real time or near-real time capabilities, however, this leads to a need for new data architectures, analytical methods, and tools. In this section, we will discuss the characteristics of big data, as well the issues surround storing and analyzing such data.

2.1. Big data characteristics

Big data is data whose scale, distribution, diversity, and/or timeliness require the use of new technical architectures, analytics, and tools in order to enable insights that unlock new sources of business value. Big data is characterized by three main features: volume, variety, and velocity. The volume of the data is its size, and how enormous it is. Velocity refers to the rate with which data is changing, or how often it is created. Finally, variety includes the different formats and types of data, as well as the different kinds of uses and ways of analyzing the data [2].

Data volume is the primary attribute of big data. Big data can be quantified by size in terabytes or petabytes, as well as even the number of records, transactions, tables, or files. Additionally, one of the things that makes big data really big is that it's coming from a greater variety of sources than ever before, including logs, clickstreams, and social media. Using these sources for analytics means that common structured data is now joined by unstructured data, such as text and human language, and semi-structured data, such as XML or RSS feeds. There's also data which is hard to categorize since it comes from audio, video, and other devices. Furthermore, multidimensional data can be drawn from a data warehouse to add historic context to big data. Thus, with big data, variety is just as big as volume. Furthermore, big data can be described by its velocity or speed. This is basically the frequency of data generation or the frequency of data delivery. The leading edge of big data is streaming data, which is collected in real-time the websites [14]. So now that we know what big data is and what characterizes big data, we start asking ourselves why we need to consider such data with all its volume, variety, and velocity. In the following section, we will take a look at the importance of managing such data, and why it has become a recent trend.

2.2. Importance of managing big data

According to Manyika, et al. [8], there are five broad ways in which using big data can create value. First of all, big data can unlock significant value by making information transparent and usable at a much higher frequency. Second of all, as organizations create and store more and more transactional data in a digital form, they can collect more accurate and detailed performance information on everything from product inventories to sick days. This can therefore expose variability in the data and boost performance.

Third of all, big data allows a narrower segmentation of customers and therefore much more precisely tailored products or services to meet their needs and requirements. Fourth of all, sophisticated analytics performed on big data can substantially improve decision making. Finally, big data can also be used to improve the development of the next generation of products and services. For example, manufacturers are currently using data obtained from sensors which are embedded in products to create innovative after-sales service offerings such as proactive maintenance, which are preventive measures that take place before a failure occurs or is even noticed by the customer.

Nowadays, along with the increasing ubiquity of technology comes the increase in the amount of electronic data. Only a few years ago, corporate databases tended to be measured in the range of tens to hundreds of gigabytes. Now, however, multi-terabyte (TB) or even petabyte (PB) databases have become normal. According to Longbottom [1], the World Data Center for Climate (WDDC) stores over 6PB of data overall and the National Energy Research Scientific Computing Center (NERSC) has over 2.8PB of available data around atomic energy research, physics projects and so on. These are only a couple of examples of the enormous amounts of data which must be dealt with nowadays. Furthermore, even companies such as Amazon are running with databases in the tens of terabytes, and companies which wouldn't be expected to have to worry about such massive systems are dealing with databases with sizes of hundreds of terabytes. Additionally, other companies with large databases in place include telecom companies and service providers, as well as social media sites. For telecom companies, just dealing with log files of all the events happening and call logs can easily build up database sizes. Moreover, social media sites, even those that are primarily text, such as Twitter or Facebook, have big enough problems; and sites such as YouTube have to deal with massively expanding datasets. With such increasing amounts of big data, there arises an essential need to be able to analyze the datasets. Thus, big data analytics will be discussed in the subsequent section.

3. Big data analytics

Big data analytics is where advanced analytic techniques operate on big data sets. Analytics based on large data samples reveals and leverages business change. However, the larger the set of data, the more difficult it becomes to manage [14]. Sophisticated analytics can substantially improve decision making, minimize risks, and unearth valuable insights from the data that would otherwise remain hidden. Sometimes decisions do not necessarily need to be automated, but rather augmented by analyzing huge, entire datasets using big data techniques and technologies instead of just smaller samples that individuals with spreadsheets can handle and understand. Therefore, decision making may never be the same. Some organizations are already making better decisions by analyzing entire datasets from customers, employees, or even sensors embedded in products [8]. In this section, we will discuss the data analytics lifecycle, followed by some advanced data analytics methods, as well as some possible tools and methods for big data analytics in particular.

3.1. Advanced data analytics methods

With the evolution of technology and the increased multitudes of data flowing in and out of organizations daily, there has become a need for faster and more efficient ways of analyzing such data. Having piles of data on hand is no longer enough to make efficient decisions at the right time. As Oueslati and Akaichi [20] acknowledged, the acquired data must not only be accurate, consistent, and sufficient enough to base decisions upon, but it must also be integrated and subject-oriented, as well as non-volatile and variant with time. New tools and algorithms have been designed to aid decision makers in automatically filtering and analyzing these diverse pools of data.

Data analytics is the process of applying algorithms in order to analyze sets of data and extract useful and unknown patterns, relationships, and information [12]. Furthermore, data analytics are used to extract previously unknown, useful, valid, and hidden patterns and information from large data sets, as well as to detect important relationships among the stored variables [16]. Thus, analytics have had a significant impact on research and technologies, since decision makers have become more and more interested in learning from previous data, thus gaining competitive advantage [22]. Nowadays, people don't just want to collect data, they want to understand the meaning and importance of the data, and use it to aid them in making decisions. Data analytics have gained a great amount of interest from organizations throughout the years, and have been used for many diverse applications. Some of the applications of data analytics include science, such as particle physics, remote sensing, and bioinformatics, while other applications focus on commerce, such as customer relationship management, consumer finance, and fraud detection [12].

In this section, we will take a look at some of the most common data analytics methods. In order to fully grasp the concept of data analytics, we will take a look at some of the most common approaches as well as how they can be applied and what algorithms are frequently used. Three different data analytics approaches will be discussed: association rules, clustering, and decision trees.

3.2. Association rules

Association rules are one of the most popular data analytics tasks for discovering interesting relations between variables in large databases. It is an approach for pattern detection which finds the most common combinations of categorical variables [12]. Using association rules shows relationships between data items by identifying patterns of their co-occurrence [3]. Since so many various association rules can be derived from even a tiny dataset, the interest in such rules is restricted to those that apply to a reasonably large number of instances and have a reasonably high accuracy on the instances to which they apply to.

Association rule analytics discover interesting correlations between attributes of a database by using two measures, support and confidence. Support is the probability that two different attributes occur together in a single event, or the frequency of occurrence, while confidence is the probability that when one attribute occurs, the other will also occur in the same event [4]. Association rules are normally used in business applications to determine the items which are usually purchased together [22]. An example of an association rule would be the statement that people who buy cars also buy CD's 80% of the time, written as Car → CD. In this case the two attributes being associated are the car and the CD, while the confidence value is the 80% and the support value is how many times in the database both a car and a CD were bought together [3]. If a rule passes the minimum support then it is considered as a frequent rule, while rules which pass both support and confidence are considered strong rules.

One of the most common algorithms for association rule analytics is the Apriori algorithm. Like most association rule algorithms, it splits the problem into two major tasks. The first task is frequent itemset generation, in which the objective is to find all the itemsets which satisfy the minimum support threshold and are thus frequent itemsets. The formula for calculating support is:

$$Supp\left(A \Rightarrow B\right) = \frac{\#\ of\ instances\ containing\ A\ \cup B}{Total\ \#\ of\ instances}$$

The second task is rule generation, in which the objective is to extract the high confidence, or strong, rules from the previously found frequent itemsets [19]. The formula for calculating confidence is:

$$Conf\left(A \Rightarrow B\right) = \frac{\#\ of\ instances\ containing\ A\ \cup B}{\#\ of\ instances\ containing\ A}$$

Since the first step is computationally expensive and requires the generation of all combinations of itemsets, the Apriori algorithm provides a principle for guiding itemset generation and reducing computational requirements. The Apriori principle states that a subset of a frequent itemset must also be frequent. In this case, if an itemset is not frequent, then it will be discarded and will not be used as a subset for the generation of another itemset [5]. The algorithm uses a breadth first search strategy and a tree structure, as shown in Figure 1, to count candidate itemsets efficiently.

Each level in the tree contains all the k-itemsets, where k is the number of items in the itemset. For example level 1 contains all 1-itemsets, level 2 all 2-itemsets, and so forth. Instead of ending up with so many itemsets through all possible combinations of items, the Apriori algorithm only considers the frequent itemsets. So in the first level, the algorithm calculates the support of each itemset. Frequent itemsets which pass the minimum support are taken to the next level, and all possible 2-itemset combinations are made only out of these frequent sets, while all others are discarded. Finally, rules are extracted from the frequent itemsets in the form of A → B (if A then B). The confidence for each rule is calculated, and rules which pass the minimum confidence are taken as strong rules.

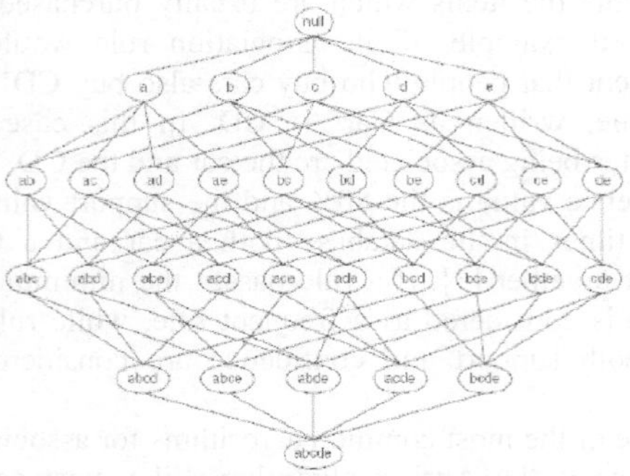

Figure 1: An itemset lattice [19]

3.3. Clustering

Data clustering is a technique which uses unsupervised learning, or in other words discovers unknown structures [12]. Clustering is the process of grouping sets of objects together into classes based on similarity measures and the behavior of the group. Instances within the same group are similar to each other, and are dissimilar to instances in other groups [4]. Clustering is similar to classification in that it groups data into classes; however the main difference is that clustering is unsupervised, and the classes are defined by the data alone, hence they are not predefined. Therefore, data to be analyzed is not compared to a model built from training data, but is rather compared to other data and clustered according to the level of similarity between them [3]. Several representations of clusters are depicted in Figure 5 [6].

Figure 2(a) portrays how instances fall into different clusters by partitioning the space to show each cluster. Some algorithms allow for one instance to belong to more than one cluster, so the diagram can lay out all the instances and draw overlapping subsets in a Venn diagram which represent each cluster as shown in Figure 2(b). Additionally, some clustering algorithms associate the instances with clusters probabilistically rather than categorically. As depicted in Figure 2(c), for every instance there is a probability, or a degree of membership, to which it belongs with each cluster. Furthermore, other clustering algorithms produce a hierarchical structure of clusters such that the top level the instance space is divided into a few clusters, each of which keeps dividing into its own sub-cluster at the next level down. Elements which are joined together in clusters at lower levels are more tightly clustered than those joined together at higher levels. Such diagrams, as shown in Figure 2(d), are called dendrograms [6].

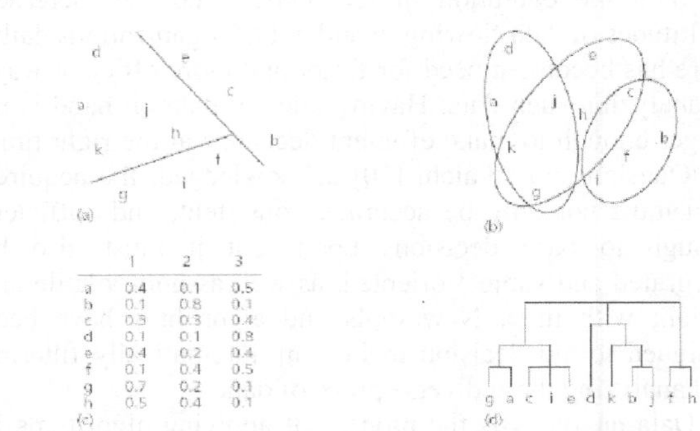

Figure 2: Different Ways of Representing Clusters [6]

The k-means algorithm is one of the most popular clustering techniques. The principle of k-mean is to assign members to the same group according to their score of similarity. It relies on a similarity or difference measurement to group relevant data values to the same cluster. K-means uses an iterative looping method to group data into a predetermined k number of clusters. If, for instance, k = 3 then that means we want to algorithms to return 3 different clusters of similar instances. Then, the k-means algorithms starts the iterative process by randomly selecting k points from the raw data to represent the initial centroids, or center points, of the k cluster. So in our example, 3 random points will be selected as the initial representative centroids of the 3 clusters [13].

Next, the similarity or distance measure chosen is used to assign each of the remaining data points to its most similar cluster. The Euclidean distance is the most commonly used proximity measure to calculate the distance between each data point and each centroid, and to assign the point to the nearest, or most similar, group which is the one closest in distance. The Euclidean distance between two n-dimensional points p and q, where p = (p1, p2,…,pn) and q = (q1, q2,…, qn), is calculated as follows:

$$dist\,(p,q) = \sqrt{\sum_{i=1}^{n}(pi - qi)^2}$$

Subsequently, after assigning all the points to clusters, the algorithm calculates the average of each cluster and assigns that value to the new representative centroid. The previous steps are repeated, and each of the data points is reassigned to the cluster of the nearest centroid. The new centroids are again calculated and the process continues iteratively until each cluster has a stable centroid and cluster members do not change their groups [10]. Furthermore, other stopping criteria, such as number of iterations or percentage of movement of members, can be set. The result of the k-means algorithm is a k number of similar clusters, where each data point is grouped with only one cluster based on its similarity to the other points in the cluster.

3.4. Decision trees

Another type of data analytics technique is the decision tree. Decision trees are used as predictive models to map observations about an attribute to conclusions about an attribute's target value. A decision tree is a hierarchical structure of nodes and directed edges which consists of three types of nodes. The root node is a node with no incoming edges and zero or more outgoing edges to other nodes. An internal node is a node in the middle levels of the tree, and consists of one incoming edge and two or more outgoing edges. Finally, the leaf node has exactly one incoming edge and no outgoing edges, and is assigned a class label which provided the decision of the tree [15].

Each of the tree's nodes specifies a test of a certain attribute of the instance, and each descending branch from the node corresponds to one of the attribute's possible values. An instance is classified by moving down the tree by starting at the root node, testing the attribute specified by that node, and moving down the branch which corresponds to the value of the given attribute to a new node. The same process is repeated at that node, until a leaf node providing a decision is finally reached [18].

The C4.5 algorithm is a commonly used extension to the previously used ID3 algorithm. Like ID3, it is also built upon Hunt's algorithm for decision tree induction. In Hunt's algorithm, the decision tree is grown recursively by partitioning the training records into successively purer subsets. If all records at a certain node belong to the same class, then that node is declared a leaf node labeled with the name of the class. However, if the node contains records that belong to more than one class, an attribute test condition is selected to partition the records into smaller subsets. A child node is then created for each outcome of the test condition, and the records at the parent node are distributed to the children nodes based on their outcome. The algorithm is then recursively applied to each child node until all records in the training set of data have been classified, all attributes have been split upon, or a specified criterion has been met [15].

C4.5 builds decision trees from data using the concept of information entropy. C4.5 chooses one attribute at each node in the tree which most effectively splits the set of sample data at the node into subsets enriched in a particular class. In other words, it chooses the attribute which provides the split with the highest information gain [17]. Therefore, at each node it calculates the information gain using the following formula, and makes its decision for the attribute split based on the highest result:

$$GAIN_{split} = Entropy(p) - \left(\sum_{i=1}^{k} \frac{n_i}{n} Entropy(i)\right)$$

P is the parent node which is split into k partitions, and ni is the number of records in partition i. The entropy measures the homogeneity of a node. Entropy of 0 implies that all records belong to one class and provides the most information. The higher the entropy, the more records are distributed among classes, implying the least information [15]. The entropy is calculated as follows, where p(j/t) is the frequency of class j at node t:

$$Entropy(t) = -\sum_{j} p\left(\frac{j}{t}\right) \log p\left(\frac{j}{t}\right)$$

The C4.5 algorithm differs from the ID3 algorithm in that it can handle both continuous and discrete attributes, as opposed to only handling discrete values, by creating a threshold and splitting the list of values into those who are greater than the threshold, and those who are less than or equal to it. Furthermore, C4.5 can handle data with missing attribute values by allowing them to be marked by a question mark, and not using them in entropy and gain calculations [9]. Finally, C4.5 also prunes the resulting trees by going back through the tree after its creation and removing useless branches of no help by replacing them with leaf nodes. This simplifies the tree, and removes unneeded checks and space [6].

4. Big data analytics tools and methods

Big data is too large to be handled by conventional means, and the larger the data grows, the more organizations purchase more powerful hardware and computational resources. However, the data keeps on growing and performance needs increase, but the available resources have a maximum capacity and capability. According to EMC [2], the MapReduce paradigm is based on adding more computers or resources, rather than increasing the power or storage capacity of a single computer; in other words, scaling out rather than scaling up. The fundamental idea of MapReduce is breaking a task down into stages and executing the stages in parallel in order to reduce the time needed to complete the task.

Map Reduce is a parallel programming model which is suitable for big data processing. It is built on Hadoop, which is a concrete platform which implements MapReduce. In MapReduce, data is split into distributable chunks, which are called shards. The steps to process those chunks are defined, and the big data processing is run in parallel on the chunks. This model is scalable, in that the bigger the data processing becomes, or the more computational resources are the required, the more machines can be added to process the chunks.

The first phase of the MapReduce job is to map input values to a set of key/value pairs as output. Thus, unstructured data such as text can be mapped to a structured key/value pair, where, in this case, the key could be the word in the text and the value is the number of occurrences of the word. This output is then the input to the "Reduce" function. Reduce then performs the collection and combination of this output. So assuming we have millions of text documents and would like to count the occurrence of a certain word. The text documents would be divided upon several workers, or machines, which will perform parallel processing. These workers will act as mappers and map the desired word to the number of occurrences in the text documents given to it for processing in parallel. The reducers will then aggregate these counts, thus giving the total count in the millions of text documents.

Hadoop is a framework for performing big data analytics which provides reliability, scalability, and manageability by providing an implementation for the MapReduce paradigm as well as gluing the storage and analytics together. Hadoop consists of two main components: the Hadoop Distributed File System (HDFS) for the big data storage, and MapReduce for big data analytics. The HDFS storage function provides a redundant and reliable distributed file system which is optimized for large files. Data is stored in replicated file blocks across the multiple Data Nodes, and the Name Node acts as a regulator between the client and the Data Node, directing the client to the particular Data Node which contains the requested data. Additionally, the data processing and analytics functions are performed by MapReduce which consists of a java API as well as software in order to implement the services which Hadoop needs to function. The MapReduce function within Hadoop depends on two different nodes: the Job Tracker and the Task Tracker nodes. The Job Tracker nodes are the ones which are responsible for distributing the Mapper and Reducer functions to the available Task Trackers, as well as monitoring the results. On the other hand, the Task Tracker nodes actually run the jobs and communicate results back to the Job Tracker. That communication between nodes is often through files and directories in HDFS so inter-node communication is minimized.

Figure 3 shows how the MapReduce nodes and the HDFS work together. At step 1, there is a very large dataset including log files, sensor data, or anything of the sorts. The HDFS stores replicas of the data, represented by the blue, yellow, beige, and pink icons, across the Data Nodes. In step 2, the client defines and executes a map job and a reduce job on a particular data set, and sends them both to the JobTracker. The Job Tracker then distributes the jobs across the Task Trackers in step 3. The TaskTracker runs the mapper, and the mapper produces output that is then stored in the HDFS file system. Finally, in step 4, the reduce job runs across the mapped data in order to produce the result.

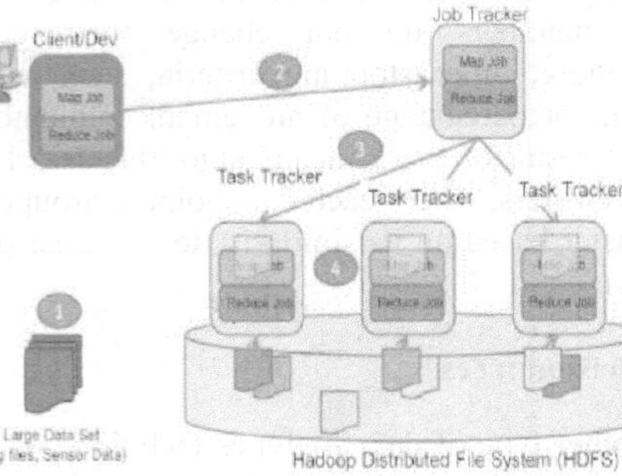

Figure 3: MapReduce and HDFS [2]

5. Big Data Challenges

Several issues will have to be addressed in order to capture the full potential of big data. Policies related to privacy, security, intellectual property, and even liability all need to be addressed in a big data world. Organizations need to put the right talent and technology in place, as well as additionally structure workflows and incentives to optimize the use of big data. Access to data is critical, and companies will need to increasingly integrate information from multiple data sources, often from third parties or different locations. Furthermore, questions on how to store and analyze data with volume, variety, and velocity have arisen, and current research lacks the capability for providing an answer. Consequently, the biggest problem has become not only the sheer volume of data, but the fact that the type of data companies must deal with is changing. In order to accommodate for the change in data, the approaches for storing data have changed throughout the years. Data storage started with data warehouses, data marts, data cubes, and then moved on to master data management, data federation and other techniques such as in-memory databases. However, database suppliers are still struggling to cope with enormous amounts of data, and the emergence of interest in big data has led to a need for storing and managing such large amounts of data.

Several consultants and organizations have tried coming up with solutions in order to be able to store and manage big data. Thus, Longbottom [1], recommends that organizations carefully research the following aspects regarding suggested big data solutions before adopting one:

- Can this solution deal with different data types, including text, image, video and sound?
- Can this solution deal with disparate data sources, both within and outside of the organization's environment?
- Will the solution create a new, massive data warehouse that will only make existing problems worse, or will it use metadata and pointers to minimize data replication and redundancy?

• How can, and will, the solution present findings back to the organization, and will this only be based on what has already happened, or can it predict with some degree of certainty what may happen in the future?

• How will the solution deal with back-up and restore of data? Is it inherently fault tolerant and can more resource easily be applied to the system as required?

Thus, from the challenges of big data is finding or creating a solution which meets the above criteria in regards to the organization.

6. Conclusion

In this paper we examined the concept of big data, as well as some of its different opportunities and challenges. In the first section of the paper, we discussed big data in general, as well as some of its common characteristics. After looking at the importance of big data and its management within organizations, and the value it can add, we discussed big data analytics as an option for data management and the extraction of essential information from such large amounts of data. Association rules, clustering, and decision trees were covered. However, with enormous amounts of data, performing typical analytics is not enough. Thus, in the following section, we discussed Hadoop which consists of the HDFS and MapReduce. This facilitates the storage of big data as well as parallel processing. Finally, we covered the challenges which arise when dealing with big data, and still need further research. Future research can include applying the big data analytics methods discussed on real business cases within organizations facing big data problems. Furthermore, the challenges related to big data previously discussed can be tackled or studied in more detail. Thus, we have seen that big data is a very important concept nowadays with comes with many opportunities and challenges. Organizations need to seize these opportunities and face the challenges in order to get the most value and knowledge out of their massive data piles.

7. References

[1] C. Longbottom, "Big Data: Large Problems or Huge Opportunities?", *Quocirca White Papers*, Quocirca, 2011, pp. 1-3.

[2] EMC, "Data Science and Big Data Analytics", *EMC Education Services*, EMC, 2012. http://education.emc.com/guest/certification/framework/stf/data_science.aspx

[3] F.J., Braz, "Warehousing and Mining Aggregate Measures Over Trajectories of Moving Objects", *PhD Thesis,* Universit`a Ca' Foscari di Venezia, Date, pp. 116.

[4] G.D. Marketos, "Data Warehousing & Mining Techniques for Moving Object Databases", *PhD Thesis*, University of Piraeus, 2009, pp. 131.

[5] G.I., Webb, "Efficient search for association rules", *Proc. ACM SIGKDD International Conference Knowledge Discovery and Data Mining*, ACM, 2000, pp. 99-107.

[6] I.H., Witten, and E., Frank, *Data Mining: Practical Machine Learning Tools and Techniques, 2nd edition*, Morgan Kauffman Publishers, 2005.

[7] J., Gruenspecht, ""Reasonable" Grand Jury Subpoenas: Asking for Information in the Age of Big Data", *Harvard Journal of Law & Technology*, 2011, pp. 543-562.

[8] J., Manyika, J., M., Chui, B., Brown, J., Bughin, R., Dobbs, C., Roxburgh, and A.H., Byers, "Big Data: The Next Frontier for Innovation, Competition, and Productivity", *McKinsey Global Institute Reports*, McKinsey Global Institute, 2011, pp. 1-156.

[9] J.R., Quinlan, *C4.5: Programs for Machine Learning*, Morgan Kaufmann Publishers, 1993.

[10] K., Prasanna, M.S.P.., Kumar, and G.S., Narayana, "A Novel Benchmark K-Means Clustering on Continuous Data", *International Journal on Computer Science and Engineering*, 2011, pp. 2974-2977.

[11] M., Bohanec, and V., Rajkovic, "Expert system for decision making", *Sistemica*, 1990, pp. 145-157.

[12] N.M. Adams, "Perspectives on Data Mining", *International Journal of Market Research*, The Market Research Society, 2010, pp. 11-19.

[13] P., Prabhu, and N., Anbazhagan, "Improving the Performance of K-Means Clustering for High Dimensional Data Set", *International Journal on Computer Science and Engineering*, 2011, pp. 2317-2322.

[14] P., Russom, "Big Data Analytics", *TDWI Best Practices Report*, TDWI, 2011, pp. 1-40.

[15] R.J., Roiger, and M.W., Geatz, *Data Mining: A Tutorial Based Primer*, Addison Wesley, 2003.

[16] S., Ayesha, T., Mustafa, A.R., Sattar, and M.I., Khan, *Data Mining Model for Higher Education System*, European Journal of Scientific Research, EuroJournals Publishing, 2010, pp. 24-29.

[17] S.B., Kotsiantis, "Supervised Machine Learning: A Review of Classification Techniques", *Informatics*, 2007, pp. 249-268.

[18] T., Mitchell, *Machine Learning*, McGraw Hill, 1997.

[19] T., Pang-Ning, M., Steinbach, and K., Vipin, *Association Analysis: Basic Concepts and Algorithms*, Addison-Wesley, 2005.

[20] W., Oueslati, and J. Akaichi, "Mobile Information Collectors Trajectory Data Warehouse Design", *International Journal of Managing Information Technology (IJMIT)*, 2010, pp. 1-20.

[21] W.R. Kubick, "Big Data, Information and Meaning", *Clinical Trial Insights*, Applied Clinical Trials, 2012, pp. 26-28.

[22] Z., Song, and A., Kusiak, "Optimizing Product Configurations with a Data Mining Approach", *International Journal of Production Research*, 2009, pp. 1733-1751.

Incorporating Singular Ratings into Collaborative Filtering

Ruzhi Xu, Shuaiqiang Wang, Xuwei Zheng
School of Computer Science and Technology
Shandong University of Finance and Economics
7366 East 2nd Ring Road, Jinan, 250014 China
{xrz,swang,zxw}@sdufe.edu.cn

Abstract— *Collaborative filtering (CF) is an effective technique addressing the information overload problem, where each user is represented as a set of rating scores on items. Given a target user, conventional CF algorithms measure similarity between two users by utilizing each pair of rating scores on common rated items but discarding scores rated by either of them. In this paper, we called the former as* dual ratings *while the latter as* singular ratings. *Our experiments show that only about 10% ratings are dual ones and can be used for similarity evaluation while the left 90% are singular ones and discarded. For making full use of the limited data resource, in this paper, we present SingCF, which attempts to incorporate singular ratings for accuracy improvement of CF algorithms. In particular, we first estimate the unrated scores for singular ratings and transform them into dual ones. Then we perform a CF process to discover neighborhood users and make predictions for each user. Experiments in comparison with the state-of-the-art methods demonstrate the promise of our approach.*

Keywords: Collaborative Filtering, Ranking-Oriented CF, Recommender Systems

1. Introduction

Ever since the thriving of the Web, the world has been flooded with an overwhelming amount of information, which represents one of today's major challenges on the Web. As an effective technique addressing the problem, recommender systems attempt to make predictions and recommendations based on a large collection of users' historical ratings, and become a de facto standard and must-own tool for e-commerce to promote business and help customers find products [1]. Prominent examples include eBay, Amazon, Last.fm, Netflix, Facebook, and LinkedIn.

Collaborative filtering (CF) is one of the most successful approaches to build recommender systems. CF algorithms are based on the assumption that users will rate or act on other items similarly if they have rated items similarly or had similar behaviors [2], [3]. CF utilizes the user-item rating matrix to make predictions and recommendations, avoiding the need of collecting extensive information about items and users. In addition, CF can be easily adopted in different recommender systems without requiring any domain knowledge [4].

Given the effectiveness and convenience, many CF methods have been proposed, which fall into two categories: memory-based [3], [5], [4], [6] and model-based [7], [8], [9], [10]. Memory-based methods make predictions based on similarities between users or items, while model-based methods estimate or learn a model to make predictions.

In this study, we focus on memory-based CF. In comparison with model-based CF, memory-based algorithms are relatively easy to implement with strong robustness and comparable effectiveness [11]. Besides, many commercial systems such as Amazon.com are memory-based.

Memory-based CF algorithms can be rating-oriented or ranking-oriented [6]. Rating-oriented methods predict rating scores for items based on users' historical rating scores on items, while ranking-oriented techniques predict a ranking of items based on users' preferences on items.

Generally, memory-based CF, either rating-oriented or ranking-oriented, works in the following two phases: (I) discovery of neighborhood users and (II) prediction for recommendation. For each user, Phase I discovers a set of most similar users as the neighborhood users, based on which Phase II predicts rating scores or preferences on items for recommendation purpose.

In existing memory-based CF algorithms, each user is represented as a set of scores on rated objects, either items or preferences. Phase I measures similarity between users by utilizing each pair of rating scores on common rated objects but discarding scores rated by either of them. In this paper, we called the former as *dual ratings* while the latter as *singular ratings*.

For example, Pearson correlation coefficient [3], [12], a widely used similarity measure in rating-oriented CF, is based on two users' rating scores on the set of common items [3], [5]. Kendall tau correlation coefficient [13], a popular similarity measure in ranking-oriented CF, is based on two users' preferences on the same set of items [4], [6].

Our experimental results on two movie rating datasets show that only about 10% ratings are dual ones and can be used for similarity evaluation in CF algorithms, while the left 90% are singular ones and discarded. Since data sparsity is one of the most acute challenges in CF [14], it merged to be an important issue to explore a practical way of making full use of the limited data resource, especially the singular ratings.

In light of this, in this study, we present SingCF, which attempts to incorporate singular ratings for accuracy improvement of CF algorithms. In particular, we first estimate the unrated scores for singular ratings and transform them into dual ones. Then we perform a CF process to discover neighborhood users and make predictions for each user. Besides, we prove the equivalence of the similarity measure and the prediction formula between rating-oriented and ranking-oriented CF algorithms, with which ranking-oriented algorithms can be directly built based on rating-oriented techniques. Then we implement two versions of our SingCF algorithms for validation, a rating-oriented and a ranking-oriented. Experiments in comparison with the state-of-the-art methods demonstrate the promise of our approach.

Why can SingCF achieve improvement in recommendation accuracy? Among the additional data introduced by SingCF, half of them are the ground truth scores rated by users, i.e., the singular ratings. Besides, the mean error of the estimated scores in the other half group are quite low, which is only less than 20% higher than that of the final predictions. Resulting from the additional high-quality data, SingCF can achieve more accurate performance.

The effectiveness of SingCF can be understood from another perspective. The unrated ratings of the singular ones are the missing values. Data cleaning is an essential technique in data mining, and one possible step is to attempt to fill in the missing values automatically with a measure of central tendency [15]. SingCF proposes an effective method to fill in the missing values for singular ratings and effects on predicting accuracy, as it would for recommendation accuracy.

We make the following contributions. (1) We propose SingCF, a collaborative filtering algorithm which incorporates singular ratings for making full use of the limited data resource and improving recommendation accuracy. (2) We prove the equivalence of the similarity measure and the prediction formula between ranking-oriented and rating-oriented CF, with which ranking-oriented algorithms can be directly built based on rating-oriented techniques.

The rest of the paper is organized as follows. Section 2 reviews the related work. Section 3 presents the preliminaries on memory-based collaborative filtering. Section 4 proposed the SingCF algorithm. Section 5 reports the experimental results. Section 6 concludes the paper.

2. Related Work

Given the effectiveness and convenience, many collaborative filtering (CF) algorithms have been proposed, which fall into two categories: memory-based or model-based. Memory-based methods make predictions based on similarities between users or items, while Model-based methods estimate or learn a model to make predictions.

2.1 Memory-based CF

Memory-based CF algorithms can be rating-oriented or ranking-oriented. Rating-oriented methods recommend items for users based on their historical rating scores on items. The user-based paradigm [3], [5] is more common, which estimates the unknown ratings of a target user based on the ratings by a set of neighboring users that tend to rate similarly to the target user. In the item-based paradigm [16], [17], item-item similarity is used to select a set of neighboring items that have been rated by the target user and the ratings on the unrated items are predicted based on his ratings on the neighboring items. Since the number of items is usually much less than the number of users in most applications, item-item similarities are less sensitive to the data sparsity problem.

Ranking-oriented methods are able to capture the preference similarity between users even if their rating scores differ significantly. Recently, the formulation of recommendation problem is shifting away from rating-oriented to ranking-oriented [18]. EigenRank [4] measured the similarity between users with Kendall tau rank correlation coefficient for neighborhood selection, predicted the relative preferences of items with the preference function, and aggregated these preferences into a total ranking. VSRank [6] introduced a novel degree-specialty weighting scheme to ranking-oriented CF based on vector space model.

Many commercial systems such as Amazon.com are memory-based since they are relatively easy to implement with strong robustness and comparable effectiveness [11]. In this study, we focus on memory-based CF, incorporating singular ratings to seek accuracy improvement of CF algorithms.

2.2 Model-based CF

Model-based CF algorithms can also be classified into rating-oriented and ranking-oriented. As a conventional CF paradigm, many rating-oriented algorithms have been proposed. For example, Shani et al. [7] used a Markov decision processes (MDPs) model for recommender systems, which viewed the recommendation process as a sequential optimization problem. Si and Jin [8] presented a flexible mixture model (FMM) for collaborative filtering. FMM is an extension of partitioning/clustering algorithms, which clusters both users and items together simultaneously without assuming that each user and item should only belong to a single cluster. Comprehensive surveys of rating-oriented CF can be found in [19], [20], [14].

As a new CF paradigm, Ranking-oriented techniques also received attentions recently. For example, Weimer et al. [9] used maximum margin matrix factorization to optimize ranking of items for collaborative filtering. Liu et al. [10]

adopted a probabilistic latent preference analysis model that made ranking predictions by directly modeling user preferences with respect to a set of items rather than the rating scores on individual items. Rendle et al. [21] proposed a Bayesian probabilistic model for personalized ranking from implicit feedback. Sun et al. [22] defined novel content-based and rating-oriented meta-level features, and adapted learning to rank to hybrid recommender systems.

3. Memory-based Collaborative Filtering

Memory-based collaborative filtering (CF) algorithms can be classified into two categories: rating-oriented and ranking-oriented.

3.1 Rating-Oriented CF

Let U be a set of users and I be a set of items. In a recommender system, each user $u \in U$ rates scores on a set of items $I_u \subseteq I$, and each item $i \in I$ is rated by a set of users $U_i \subseteq U$. Let $R_{m\times n}$ be a user-item rating matrix with m users and n items, where each element $r_{u,i} \in \mathbb{N}$ is the rating score of the item i with respect to u, and $\mathbb{N}$ is the natural number set indicating different relevance scores. $\overline{r}_u$ is the mean score of user u over all the items rated by u. For a target user u, a set of neighborhood users $N_u \subset U$ are selected according to their similarity to u, based on which the rating scores on the unrated items are predicted.

Rating-oriented CF recommends items based on historical rating scores of items. User-user paradigm is a widely model for rating-oriented CF, where the Pearson correlation coefficient is used to evaluate the similarity $s_{u,v}$ between two users u and v with their normalized ratings on the set of common items $I_{u,v} = I_u \cap I_v$:

$$s_{u,v} = \frac{\sum\limits_{i\in I_{u,v}} (r_{u,i} - \overline{r}_u)(r_{v,i} - \overline{r}_v)}{\sqrt{\sum\limits_{i\in I_{u,v}} (r_{u,i} - \overline{r}_u)^2}\sqrt{\sum\limits_{i\in I_{u,v}} (r_{v,i} - \overline{r}_v)^2}} \quad (1)$$

The rating of item i for user u can be predicted by the scores of i rated by a set of neighborhood users N_u of u:

$$r^{(P)}_{u,i} = \overline{r}_u + \frac{\sum\limits_{v\in N_u} s_{u,v}(r_{v,i} - \overline{r}_v)}{\sum\limits_{v\in N_u} s_{u,v}} \quad (2)$$

Item-item paradigm is an alternative model for rating-based CF, where the similarity between items can also be measured with Pearson correlation coefficient. The rating of item i for user u can be predicted by the scores of a set of neighborhood items I_u of i rated by u:

$$r^{(P)}_{u,i} = \frac{\sum\limits_{j\in I_u} s_{i,j} r_{u,i}}{\sum\limits_{j\in I_u} s_{i,j}} \quad (3)$$

3.2 Ranking-Oriented CF

Ranking-oriented CF predicts users' preference ranking on items to make recommendations based on their relative preferences on common pairs of items [4], [6].

In ranking-oriented CF, Kendall tau correlation coefficient [13] is a common measure for evaluating similarity between two users based on users' preference scores on the same set of the pairwise preferences on items:

$$s_{u,v} = \frac{N_c - N_d}{\frac{1}{2}k(k-1)} \quad (4)$$

where N_c and N_d are the numbers of the concordant pairs and discordant pairs respectively, and $N_c + N_d = \frac{1}{2}k(k-1)$.

Let $p_{u,(i,j)} \in \{+1, -1\}$ be the preference function, where $p_{u,(i,j)} = +1$ indicates user u prefers item i to j while $p_{u,(i,j)} = -1$ indicates u prefers j to i, formally:

$$p_{u,(i,j)} = \begin{cases} +1, & \text{if } r_{u,i} > r_{u_j} \\ -1, & \text{if } r_{u,i} < r_{u_j} \end{cases} \quad (5)$$

Let $N_{u,(i,j)}$ is the set of neighborhood users of u who hold certain preferences on the pair of items i and j. For user u, the preference on a pair of items (i,j) can be predicted with a preference function $\Psi_u(i,j)$ as follows.

$$\Psi_u(i,j) = \frac{\sum\limits_{v\in N_{u,(i,j)}} s_{u,v} p_{u,(i,j)}}{\sum\limits_{v\in N_{u,(i,j)}} s_{u,v}} \quad (6)$$

Based on the predicted pairwise preferences, a total ranking of items for user u can be obtained by applying a preference aggregation algorithm.

4. The SingCF Algorithm

In this section, we first investigate the equivalence between two paradigms of CF algorithms, rating-oriented and ranking-oriented. Then we mainly introduce our algorithm SingCF based on rating-oriented CF. The ranking-oriented version of SingCF can be easily implemented resulting from the equivalence between two CF paradigms.

4.1 Ranking-Oriented CF vs. Rating-Oriented CF

In ranking-oriented CF, each user u is represented as a set of relative preferences on pairs of items. In this study we propose another representation based on user-(item-item) preference matrix, which is defined as follows:

Definition 1: Let $R_{m\times n}$ be the user-item score matrix with m users and n items. The matrix $P_{m\times n(n-1)}$ is called a ***user-(item-item) preference matrix*** *with m users and $n(n-1)$ preferences on all possible pairs of items, where each element $p_{u,(i,j)} = \{+1, -1\}$ indicates the preference of the target user u on the pair of items i and j, as shown in Equation (5).*

According the definition of the user-(item-item) preference matrix $P_{m\times n(n-1)}$, the following corollary is satisfied:

Corollary 1: The average rating scores of each user is 0, formally $\forall u \in U : \overline{p}_u = 0$.

Since for each user $u \in U$ who has rated a pair of items i and j, $p_{u,(i,j)} + p_{u,(j,i)} = 0$, and thus Corollary 1 holds.

Theorem 1: The ranking-oriented similarity measure of the Kendall tau correlation coefficient based on the common preference sets is equivalent to the Pearson correlation coefficient based on the representation of the user-(item-item) preference matrix.

Proof: According to the definition of the user-(item-item) preference matrix $P_{m\times n(n-1)}$, $p^2_{u,(i,j)} = 1$.
Let I_C be the set of items where both u and v hold certain preference on each pair of items, formally, $I_C \subseteq I_{u,v} \wedge \forall i,j \in I_C \rightarrow p_{u,(i,j)}p_{v,(i,j)} \neq 0$. Based on Corollary 1, the Pearson correlation coefficient (Equation 1) can be rewritten as follows:

$$s_{u,v} = \frac{\sum\limits_{i,j\in I_C} (p_{u,(i,j)} - \overline{p}_u)(p_{v,(i,j)} - \overline{p}_v)}{\sqrt{\sum\limits_{i,j\in I_C} (p_{u,(i,j)} - \overline{p}_u)^2}\sqrt{\sum\limits_{i,j\in I_C} (p_{v,(i,j)} - \overline{p}_v)^2}}$$

$$= \frac{\sum\limits_{i,j\in I_C} p_{u,(i,j)}p_{v,(i,j)}}{\sqrt{\sum\limits_{i,j\in I_C} p^2_{u,(i,j)}}\sqrt{\sum\limits_{i,j\in I_C} p^2_{v,(i,j)}}}$$

$$= \frac{\sum\limits_{i,j\in I_C} p_{u,(i,j)}p_{v,(i,j)}}{k(k-1)}$$

For a target pair of items (i, v) and two users u and v, $p_{u,(i,j)}p_{v,(i,j)}$ can be considered as an indicator function, such that it is equal to $+1$ if the preference on items i and j is concordant in users u and v while -1 if the preference is discordant. Formally,

$$p_{u,(i,j)}p_{v,(i,j)} = \begin{cases} +1, & \text{if } (r_{u,i} - r_{u,j})(r_{v,i} - r_{v,j}) > 0 \\ -1, & \text{if } (r_{u,i} - r_{u,j})(r_{v,i} - r_{v,j}) < 0 \end{cases}$$

Thus the sum of $p_{u,(i,j)}p_{v,(i,j)}$ for all possible item pairs is $2(N_c - N_d)$, and $s_{u,v}$ can be rewritten as follows:

$$s_{u,v} = \frac{2(N_c - N_d)}{k(k-1)},$$

which is equivalent to the Kendall tau correlation coefficient based on the common preference sets (Equation 4). ■

Theorem 2: The ranking-oriented prediction formula based on the common preference sets is equivalent to the rating-oriented prediction formula based on the representation of the user-(item-item) preference matrix.

Proof: Based on Corollary 1, the rating-oriented prediction formula based on $P_{m\times n(n-1)}$ (Equation 2) can be rewritten as follows:

$$r^{(P)}_{u,(i,j)} = \overline{r}_u + \frac{\sum\limits_{v\in N_u} s_{u,v}(r_{v,(i,j)} - \overline{r}_v)}{\sum\limits_{v\in N_u} s_{u,v}}$$

$$= \frac{\sum\limits_{v\in N_u} s_{u,v}r_{v,(i,j)}}{\sum\limits_{v\in N_u} s_{u,v}},$$

which is the very formula of the rating-oriented prediction formula based on the common preference sets (Equation 6). ■

Besides, for memory-based algorithms, ranking-oriented CF performs same as rating-oriented CF, where a set of most similar users are discovered as the neighborhood users, based on which the scores/relationships of the unrated items/preferences are predicted for recommendation.

Thus, a ranking-oriented CF is equivalent to a rating-oriented CF based on user-(item-item) preference matrix.

In this section, we mainly introduce our algorithm SingCF based on the rating-oriented CF. The ranking-oriented version can be easily implemented resulting from the equivalence of the similarity measure and the prediction formula between ranking-oriented and rating-oriented CF algorithms.

4.2 Estimation for Singular Rating

In existing memory-based CF algorithms, the similarity between users is evaluated by with *dual* ratings without considering any *singular* one. The dual ratings are pairs of scores on certain items rated by a pair of users, and the singular ratings are scores rated by either of two users.

Definition 2: Let I_u and I_v be two sets of items rated by user u and v respectively. Let $I_{u,v} = I_u \cap I_v = \{i_1, i_2, \ldots, i_k\}$ be the common set of items *rated by users u and v. All pairwise rating scores rated by u and v on $I_{u,v}$ are called* ***dual ratings****, i.e.,* $\{(r_{u,i_1}, r_{v,i_1}), (r_{u,i_2}, r_{v,i_2}), \ldots, (r_{u,i_k}, r_{v,i_k})\}$. *The rating scores rated by u on items $I_u \backslash I_{u,v}$ and those by v on $I_v \backslash I_{u,v}$ are called* ***singular ratings****.*

Example 1: Let $\{i_1, i_2, i_3, i_4\}$ be four items. Let $\{u, v\}$ be two users, where their rating scores are listed as follows:

$$\begin{cases} r_{u,i_1} = 0, r_{u,i_2} = 1, r_{u,i_3} = 2. \\ \qquad r_{v,i_2} = 3, r_{v,i_3} = 4, r_{v,i_4} = 5. \end{cases}$$

According to our definitions, $(r_{u,i_2}, r_{v,i_2}) = (1,3)$ and $(r_{u,i_3}, r_{v,i_3}) = (2,4)$ are dual ratings. $r_{u,i_1} = 0$ and $r_{v,i_4} = 5$ are singular ones.

For incorporating singular ratings, a most straightforward way is to estimate their corresponding unrated scores and transform the singular ratings into dual ones. In Example 1, r_{v,i_1} and r_{u,i_4} are corresponding unrated scores of r_{u,i_1} and r_{v,i_4} respectively.

In doing this, accurate estimation is very important in SingCF, which can avoid introducing plenty of noises into the rating matrix R.

In this study, we fully consider the historical rating scores assigned by the target user u to items I_u, and the scores assigned by users U_i to the target item i:

$$\hat{r}_{u,i} = \overline{r}_u + \frac{\sum_{v \in U_i} (r_{v,i} - \overline{r}_v)}{|U_i|} \tag{7}$$

$$\tilde{r}_{u,i} = \frac{\sum_{i \in I_u} r_{u,i}}{|I_u|} = \overline{r}_u \tag{8}$$

In particular, Equations (7) and (8) are special cases of Equations (2) and (3) respectively, where all users U_i who have rated i are considered as the neighborhood users of u, all items I_u rated by u as the neighborhood items of i, and all similarities are 1.

In SingCF, we linearly combine $\hat{r}_{u,c}$ and $\tilde{r}_{u,c}$ to estimate the unrated ratings for singular data:

$$\begin{aligned} r^{(E)}_{u,i} &= \alpha \cdot \hat{r}_{u,i} + (1-\alpha) \cdot \tilde{r}_{u,i} \\ &= \alpha \cdot \left(\overline{r}_u + \frac{\sum_{v \in U_i} (r_{v,c} - \overline{r}_v)}{|U_i|} \right) + (1-\alpha) \cdot \overline{r}_u \\ &= \overline{r}_u + \alpha \cdot \frac{\sum_{v \in U_i} (r_{v,i} - \overline{r}_v)}{|U_i|} \end{aligned} \tag{9}$$

where U_i is the set of users who has rated i, α is a real number and $0 \le \alpha \le 1$.

A very interesting observation is that Equation (9) is very similar to Equation (2), where the first part measures the average scores assigned by u, and the second part evaluates the quality of i, whether its rating is higher than the average score or lower. These two equations are the same when the following conditions hold:

- The similarity between u and each user who has rated i is "1", formally, $\forall v \in U_i : s_{u,v} = 1$.
- Each user who has rated i is considered as a neighborhood user of u, formally, $\forall v \in U_i : v \in N_u$, and $N_u \equiv U_i$.
- The parameter α in Equation (9) is "1".

The first two conditions are easily understood. We have no prior knowledge on similarity between users, and have to assign each to "1". Thus each user who has rated i is considered as a neighbor of u.

Since not all of users in U_i are similar to the target user u, we lack full confidence on the quality estimation on i, and α can be regarded as a *confidence rate*.

Thus if the first two conditions are satisfied, Equation (9) generalizes (2), and they are the same if the confidence rate $\alpha = 1$.

Similarly, for ranking-oriented CF, let $U_{(i,j)}$ be is the set of users who hold certain preferences on items i and j, i.e., $U_{(i,j)} \subseteq U_i \cap U_j \wedge \forall u \in U_{(i,j)} \rightarrow p_{u,(i,j)} \neq 0$. According to Corollary 1, for each user, $\overline{p}_u = 0$. The estimating formula of Equation (9) can be rewritten as follows:

$$f(U_{(i,j)}) = \alpha \cdot \frac{\sum_{v \in U_{(i,j)}} p_{v,(i,j)}}{|U_{(i,j)}|} \tag{10}$$

$f(U_{(i,j)})$ returns a real number while the preference on i, j should be $+1$ or -1. Let θ be a threshold where $0 \le \theta \le 1$. The preference on (i, j) can be estimated as follows:

$$p^{(E)}_{u,(i,j)} = \begin{cases} +1, & \text{if } f(U_{(i,j)}) > \theta \\ -1, & \text{if } f(U_{(i,j)}) < -\theta \end{cases} \tag{11}$$

4.3 Discussion

The effectiveness of SingCF can be understood from the following two perspectives.

- **Utilizing additional high-quality data.** Among the additional data introduced by SingCF, half of them are the ground truth scores rated by users, i.e., the singular ratings. Besides, the mean error of the estimated scores in the other half group are quite low, which is only less than 20% higher than that of the final predictions. Resulting from the additional high-quality data, SingCF can achieve more accurate performance.
- **Data cleaning.** The unrated ratings of the singular ones are the missing values. Data cleaning is an essential technique in data mining, and one possible step is to attempt to fill in the missing values automatically with

a measure of central tendency [15]. SingCF proposes an effective method to fill in the missing values for singular ratings and effects on predicting accuracy, as it would for recommendation accuracy.

Thus SingCF works in three phases: (I) data cleaning, (II) neighbor discovery and (III) rating prediction. First of all, Phase I estimates the unrated rating scores and transforms singular ratings into dual ones. Then for each user, Phase II discovers a set of most similar users as the neighborhood users. Then Phase III makes predictions and recommendations based on the rating scores of the neighborhood users.

5. Experiments

We used MovieLens[1], a real movie rating datasets in our experiments. In our experiments, we randomly selected 80% rated items for training and used the remaining 20% for testing. In order to guarantee that there are adequate number of common rating items between each neighborhood user and the target user, we filtered those users who have rated less than 50 items. We ran each algorithm 5 times and reported the average performance.

5.1 Rating-Oriented CF

For rating-oriented collaborative filtering (CF), we used two standard evaluation criterions, Mean Absolute Error (MAE) and Root Mean Squared Error (RMSE), to evaluate our algorithm.

MAE is the most widely used evaluation metric in CF research literature. Let R_T be the test data, where each element $r_{u,i}^{(T)} \in R_T$ is the score assigned by user u to item i. MAE computes the average of the absolute difference between the predictions and true ratings:

$$MAE = \frac{\sum_{r_{u,i}^{(T)} \in R_T} |r_{u,i}^{(T)} - r_{u,i}^{(P)}|}{|R_T|}$$

RMSE is another popular metric, which was used in the Netflix prize[2] for movie recommendation performance:

$$RMSE = \sqrt{\frac{\sum_{r_{u,i}^{(T)} \in R_T} \left(r_{u,i}^{(T)} - r_{u,i}^{(P)}\right)^2}{|R_T|}}$$

We chose a conventional user-based CF method as our comparison partner, which measured similarity between users using the Pearson correlation coefficient, predicted ratings using Equation (2). Our implementation of SingCF was based on the conventional CF. A direct comparison of the two will provide valuable and irreplaceable insights.

Table 1 shows the performance comparisons under the MAE and RMSE measures. From the table we can see that our proposed SingCF algorithm can achieve significant accuracy improvement, resulting from effectively incorporate singular ratings.

[1]http://www.grouplens.org/
[2]http://www.netflixprize.com/

Table 1: Performance comparison on MovieLens

Algorithm	MAE	RMSE
CF	**0.8199**	**1.0546**
SingCF	0.8798	3.8339

5.2 Ranking-Oriented CF

For ranking-oriented CF, the wildly used measure is the Normalized Discounted Cumulative Gain (NDCG) [23] metric, which is popular in information retrieval for evaluating ranked document results.

In the context of collaborative filtering, item ratings assigned by users can naturally serve as graded relevance judgements. Specifically, the NDCG metric is evaluated over some number n of the top items on the ranked item list. Let U be the set of users and $r_{u,p}$ be the rating score assigned by user u to the item at the pth position of the ranked list from u. The average NDCG at the nth position with respect to all users U is defined as follows.

$$NDCG_{avg}@n = \frac{1}{|U|}\sum_{u \in U} Z_u \sum_{p=1}^{n} \frac{2^{r_{u,p}} - 1}{\log(1+p)}$$

The value of NDCG ranges from 0 to 1. A higher value indicates better ranking effectiveness. NDCG is very sensitive to the ratings of the highest ranked items. This is modeled by the discounting factor $\log(1+p)$ that increases with the position in the ranking. This is a highly desirable characteristic for evaluating ranking quality in recommender systems. This is because, just as in Web search, most users only examine the first few items from the recommended list. The relevance of top-ranked items are far more important than other items [4].

We used EigenRank [4], a state-of-the-art ranking-based CF algorithm, as our main comparison partner. Our implementation of SingCF was based EigenRank. A direct comparison of the two will provide valuable and irreplaceable insights. Besides, we also used CoFiRank, another state-of-the-art ranking-based collaborative filtering algorithms as our comparison partner. In particular, EigenRank measured similarity between users with Kendall tau rank correlation coefficient for neighborhood selection, predicted pairwise preferences of items with a preference function, and aggregated the predicted preferences into a total ranking with a greedy algorithm. CoFiRank used Maximum Margin Matrix Factorization and employed structured output prediction to directly optimize ranking scores instead of ratings. In addition, we also included comparisons with UPR, a conventional user-based CF method, which measured similarity between users using the Pearson correlation coefficient, predicted ratings using Equation (2), and then ranked the items for each user according to their predicted rating scores for the purpose of obtaining a ranking of items.

Figure 1 shows the performance comparisons under the NDCG measure. From the figure we can see that

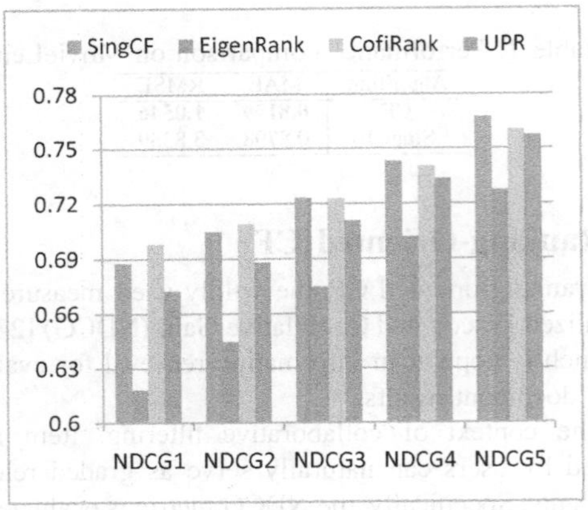

Fig. 1: Performance comparison on MovieLens.

our proposed SingCF outperformed all comparison partners. In particular, SingCF achieved the best performances on NDCG@3–5, and the second best performances on NDCG@1–2, only slightly lower than CoFiRank but significantly higher than EigenRank and UPR.

6. Conclusion

In this paper, we have proposed SingCF, a collaborative filtering (CF) algorithm which incorporates singular ratings for making full use of the limited data resource and improving recommendation accuracy. In particular, we first estimate the unrated ratings and transform the singular ratings into dual ones. Then we perform the CF process to discover neighborhood users and make predictions for recommendations. There are two paradigms for CF algorithms: rating-oriented and ranking-oriented. In this paper we prove the equivalence between the two paradigms, based on which we also provide two versions of SingCF for rating-oriented and ranking-oriented CF. Experiments have validated the effectiveness of our algorithm.

There are several interesting directions for future work. Firstly, we plan to perform a systematic study on SingCF, investigating the various factors that may affect its performance. Secondly, it is very interesting to study other possible formulae for estimating the unrated ratings for singular data. Last but not least, the proposed algorithm is not limited to ranking-based CF, and we plan to adapt it to model-based CF and examine its effectiveness.

References

[1] B. Sarwar, G. Karypis, J. Konstan, and J. Riedl, "Analysis of recommendation algorithms for e-commerce," in *Proceedings of the 2nd ACM Conference on Electronic Commerce (EC)*, 2000.

[2] D. Goldberg, D. Nichols, B. M. Oki, and D. Terry, "Using collaborative filtering to weave an information tapestry," *Communications of the ACM*, vol. 35, no. 12, pp. 61–70, 1992.

[3] P. Resnick, N. Iacovou, M. Suchak, P. Bergstrom, and J. Riedl, "GroupLens: An open architecture for collaborative filtering of netnews," in *Proceedings of the 1994 ACM Conference on Computer Supported Cooperative Work (CSCW)*, 1994.

[4] N. N. Liu and Q. Yang, "Eigenrank: A ranking-oriented approach to collaborative filtering," in *Proceedings of the 31st Annual International ACM SIGIR Conference on Research and Development in Information Retrieval (SIGIR)*, 2008.

[5] J. L. Herlocker, J. A. Konstan, A. Borchers, and J. Riedl, "An algorithmic framework for performing collaborative filtering," in *Proceedings of the 22nd Annual International ACM SIGIR Conference on Research and Development in Information Retrieval (SIGIR)*, 1999.

[6] S. Wang, J. Sun, B. J. Gao, and J. Ma, "Adapting vector space model to ranking-based collaborative filtering," in *Proceedings of the 21st ACM Conference on Information and Knowledge Management (CIKM)*, 2012.

[7] G. Shani, D. Heckerman, and R. I. Brafman, "An MDP-based recommender system," *Journal of Machine Learning Research*, vol. 6, pp. 1265–1295, 2005.

[8] L. Si and R. Jin, "Flexible mixture model for collaborative filtering," in *Proceedings of the 20th International Conference on Machine Learning (ICML)*, 2003.

[9] M. Weimer, A. Karatzoglou, Q. V. Le, and A. J. Smola, "Cofirank: Maximum margin matrix factorization for collaborative ranking," in *Proceedings of the 21st Annual Conference on Neural Information Processing Systems (NIPS)*, 2007.

[10] N. N. Liu, M. Zhao, and Q. Yang, "Probabilistic latent preference analysis for collaborative filtering," in *Proceedings of the 18th ACM conference on Information and Knowledge Management (CIKM)*, 2009.

[11] T. Hofmann, "Latent semantic models for collaborative filtering," *ACM Transactions on Information Systems*, vol. 22, pp. 89–115, 2004.

[12] J. Herlocker, J. A. Konstan, and J. Riedl, "An empirical analysis of design choices in neighborhood-based collaborative filtering algorithms," *ACM Transactions on Information Systems*, vol. 5, pp. 287–310, 2002.

[13] M. G. Kendall, "A new measure of rank corelation," *Biometrika*, vol. 30, p. 81, 1938.

[14] X. Su and T. M. Khoshgoftaar, "A survey of collaborative filtering techniques," *Advances in Artificial Intelligence*, vol. 2009, 2009.

[15] J. Han, M. Kamber, and J. Pei, *Data Mining: Concepts and Techniques*, 3rd ed. San Francisco, CA, USA: Morgan Kaufmann Publishers Inc., 2011.

[16] M. Deshpande and G. Karypis, "Item-based top-n recommendation algorithms," *ACM Transactions on Information Systems*, vol. 22, no. 1, pp. 143–177, 2004.

[17] B. M. Sarwar, G. Karypis, J. A. Konstan, and J. Riedl, "Item-based collaborative filtering recommendation algorithms," in *Proceedings of the 10th International Conference on World Wide Web (WWW)*, 2001.

[18] S. M. McNee, J. Riedl, and J. A. Konstan, "Being accurate is not enough: how accuracy metrics have hurt recommender systems," in *Extended Abstracts Proceedings of the 2006 Conference on Human Factors in Computing Systems (CHI)*, 2006.

[19] G. Adomavicius and A. Tuzhilin, "Toward the next generation of recommender systems: A survey of the state-of-the-art and possible extensions," *IEEE Transactions on Knowledge and Data Engineering*, vol. 17, no. 6, pp. 734–749, 2005.

[20] J. L. Herlocker, J. A. Konstan, L. G. Terveen, and J. T. Riedl, "Evaluating collaborative filtering recommender systems," *ACM Transactions on Information Systems*, vol. 22, no. 1, pp. 5–53, 2004.

[21] S. Rendle, C. Freudenthaler, Z. Gantner, and S.-T. Lars, "Bpr: Bayesian personalized ranking from implicit feedback," in *Proceedings of the 25th Conference on Uncertainty in Artificial Intelligence (UAI)*, 2009.

[22] J. Sun, S. Wang, B. J. Gao, and J. Ma, "Learning to rank for hybrid recommendation," in *Proceedings of the 21st ACM Conference on Information and Knowledge Management (CIKM)*, 2012.

[23] K. Järvelin and J. Kekäläinen, "Cumulated gain-based evaluation of IR techniques," *ACM Transactions on Information Systems*, vol. 20, no. 4, pp. 422–446, 2002.

A Mechanism to Prevent Side Channel Attacks in Cloud Computing Environments

Tzong-An Su
Fenh Chia University
Taichung, Taiwan

Abstract - Cloud computing provides the benefits of scalability, agility, reliability, security, performance, and maintenance to enterprises and has emerged to become a reality. While cloud computing brings in many benefits it also introduces several security issues. One of the most serious security issues is the side channel attacks which are attacks based on information gained from the physical implementation of a machine. In this paper, we aim at providing a platform to prevent various types of side channel attacks, e.g., cache-based and timing attacks.

Keywords – Side Channel Attack, Cloud Computing, Hardware Virtualization, Virtual Machine

1 Introduction

1.1 Background

Cloud Computing has been a buzzword for the pass few years. The concept combined technologies in networking and computing to provide various services to individuals and organizations. Services like SaaS (Software as a Service), Uaas (Utility as a Service), Iaas (Information as a Service), PaaS (Platform as a Service) and others are among those people are talking about. From the IT's point of view, it offers an approach to expand capacity and capability without investing in new equipment, hiring new personnel, training staff, and licensing new software and adds up to the most important business goal, i.e., cost reduction. In fact, some services like SaaS and PaaS have been out for some time and new services are kept coming. For example, Amazon's Elastic Compute Cloud (EC2) [1], Microsoft's Azure Service Platform [2], Google's App Engine [3], and HP's HP Cloud Services [4].

The technology supports behind cloud computing is not new at all. Two major ones are hardware virtualization and grid computing. Grid is a type of parallel and distributed system that enables the sharing, selection, and aggregation of distributed resources at runtime. Hardware virtualization creates a virtual machine (VM) acting like a real computer running some operating system on top of a physical computer to host a user's application. The software or firmware which performs the virtualization is call virtual machine monitor (VMM) or hypervisor, e.g., Xen [6] and VMware [7].

1.2 Side Channel Attacks in a Cloud

Original from cryptography, a side channel attack is any attack based on information gained from the physical implementation of a cryptosystem, rather than brute force or the theoretical weakness of the algorithm [25]. The term has been extended to apply to any computing system now. Common side channel attacks can be divided into the following categories:

- Timing Attack
- Power Consumption Attack

- Electromagnetic Attack
- Acoustic Cryptanalysis
- Differential Fault Analysis

In a cloud environment, we believe that only timing attack and differential fault analysis need to be paid attention to. In fact, there have been some research works done based on these two types of attacks in the past few years. We describe two of such works below.

1.2.1 Co-Residence Related Attacks

In [9], authors used the Amazon EC2 as a case study to demonstrate possible side channel attacks in a cloud computing environment. In this study, the network probing technique which uses some popular networking tools like nmap, hping, and wget to gather networking information is employed to collect the host interconnect information of the cloud. With the collected data, the infrastructure of the cloud can be mapped. Given a target instance (VM), the map can offer lots of knowledge of how to select launching parameters to launch attacking instances (VMs) with co-residence property (both target SM and attacking SMs are assigned to the same physical machine).

If attacking SMs can be co-resided with the target on the same physical machine, cross-VM information leakage could happen. After establishing the co-residence relationship with a target SM, attacking SMs can use side channels to steal information from the target.

1.2.2 Thief of Service Attacks

In [26], authors proposed another type of attack which takes advantage of the scheduler vulnerabilities of a VMM and steal the service time of a cloud. They demonstrated the attack on the Amazon EC2 cloud which uses the Xen VMM.

1.3 Research Goal

Side channel attacks have been extensively worked under the traditional computing environment, for example, timing attacks [32, 33], power consumption behavior [34], instruction or data cache behavior [11, 12, 13, 16, 22, 23, 24, 29, 30, 31], branch predictor behavior [14, 15], CPU pipelines (e.g., floating point units) [19, 28], DRAM memory bus [18], scheduling of CPU cores and time-slices, disk access [20]. Due to factors such as core migration, scheduling algorithm, double indirection of memory addresses, and varied CPU configuration parameters in a cloud computing environment, it is somewhat more difficult to realize a cross-VM attacks. But, these attacks are still feasible in a cloud computing environment because the same hardware channels exist. Therefore, on the way to the cloud, we have to pay attention to all these blocks and try to remove them away. Thus, our goal of this research is to find a general, practical, and easy-to – implement approach to counter the attacks described in Section 1.3.

2 Related Research

2.1 Security Mechanism for Virtual Machine Monitor

[36] proposed an architecture that enable administrators to configure virtual machine to satisfy prescribed security goal. [37] described an architecture that gives security tools the ability to do active monitoring while still benefiting from the increased security of an isolated virtual machine. [38] described the work of how to move the domain builder of Xen into a

minimal trusted compartment to make it a trusted computing base (TCB). [39] evaluated a new type of malicious software called virtual-machine-based rootkit, installs a virtual machine monitor underneath an existing operating system and hoists the original operating system into a virtual machine. [40] proposed two techniques to protect the integrity of control flow of a VMM. [41] described, implemented, and evaluated a VMM-based hidden process detection and identification service called Lycosid that is based on cross-view validation principle.

2.2 Side Channel Attacks

The following side channel attacks are found in a traditional computing environment, i.e., a single machine. Resource sharing related attacks might be applied to cloud environments.

The idea of timing attacks first appeared in [42]. [32] presented a timing attack on the OpenSSL's RSA. It used the timing difference of the processing time to derive the key value. [33] presented an implementation with improvement of [42]'s idea and successfully cracked the key of a smart card. [43] investigated how the modern x86 processors can leak timing information through side-channels that related to control flow and data flow. It also implemented a compiler backend to convert/eliminated key-dependent control flow and timing behavior. [19, 28] described functional unit e.g., parallel floating-point multiplier, sharing attacks in a multi-thread environment. [18] described the memory performance attacks in which unfair memory sharing could cause the denial of memory service in multi-core systems. [20] discovered side channels in disk I/O optimization scheme. [34] examined specific methods for analyzing power consumption measurements to find secret key from tamper resistance devices. [14, 15] present a new software side channel attack caused by the branch prediction capability common to all modern high performance CPUs. The extra cycle for a mis-predicted branch can be used for cryptanalysis of cryptographic primitives that employ a data dependent program flow. [44] described several solutions to the problems found in [14, 15].

2.3 Cache-Based Side Channel Attacks

Side channel attacks happen mostly in the cache sharing environment. Several types of attacks have been identified and countermeasures proposed in the traditional computing environment. We survey some works below. [23] proposed several methods to guard against the threats of two types of cache-based attacks, namely, trace-down and time-driven. [24] proposed a hardware cache architecture by using page concept to prevent cache-based attacks. [11] demonstrated complete AES key recovery from knowing plaintext timings of a network server on another computer and proposed advice for AES implementers. [13] demonstrated that in a multi-thread environment, the shared access to memory caches provides not only an easily used high bandwidth covert channel between threads, but also permits a malicious thread to monitor the execution of another thread, allowing thief of cryptographic keys. [16] studied the cache attacks in another type of cache memory, i.e., instruction cache or I-cache. [31] proposed some software-based methods to mitigate cache attacks. Many more attacks and countermeasures can be found in [12, 21, 22, 29, 30].

3 The Prevention Scheme

Cloud computing represents a new computation model and needs new thoughts to uncover its hidden security problems. Considering the above drawbacks existing in those countermeasures proposed before in a traditional computing environment we conclude that they are not practical and are not easy to apply to the cloud. Also, from related works surveyed in Section 2, we know that the side channel attacks mostly arise from the sharing of resources among processes. In a cloud environment, this situation is similar to the co-residence of VMs in a physical host. Since one of the major goals of cloud computing is to share resources, thus, co-residence of VMs is a necessary condition of cloud computing and it will not go away. With this thought and those drawbacks of known solutions described above in mind, our approach should allow co-residence of VMs and should be a general, practical, and easy-to-implement one.

Since co-residence of the attacking VM and the target VM is inevitable, instead of avoiding co-residence of the attacking VM and the target VM, we propose an approach called VM policing which consists of the following components:

- Police VM
- Capability of Police VM
- Scheduling / Dispatching policies of Police VM

In the VM policing approach, special VMs created by the cloud are launched by a physical host at a randomized frequency based on a special police VM scheduling policy. The police VMs are used to "confuse" the attacking VM by executing some clean-up or resource sharing instructions, e.g., cache flush or disk access.

3.1 Police VM

A police VM is a virtual machine launched by the physical host. Its job is to prevent, and handle side channel attacks. Refer to Figure 3.1.

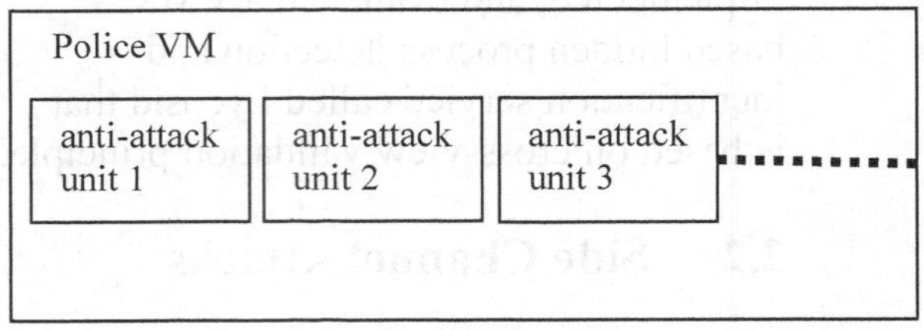

Figure 3.1 A Police VM

Inside a police VM, there could be none or more "anti-attack units". An anti-attack unit is a software component responsible for the prevention and handling of a specific type of side channel attacks, e.g., cache-based attacks. Anti-attack units are installed in a police VM dynamically depending on the needs of a situation. This structure has the following advantages:

- Scalability – The anti-attack units are installed only when necessary. When new types of attacks are found, new units can be developed and installed.
- Varied Execution Timing – The police VM could be used in timing need. Null police VMs (no anti-attack unit) could be created to stub or synchronize executions of VMs.

3.2 Capability of Police VMs

Other than the functionality of the installed anti-attack units, a police SM can also be launched by the physical host to mock the attacking VM by providing an illusion picture of the cloud. Adding "makeup" information to the cloud would make the probing efforts from attacking VM not accurate and useless.

3.3 Scheduling / Dispatching Policy of Police VMs

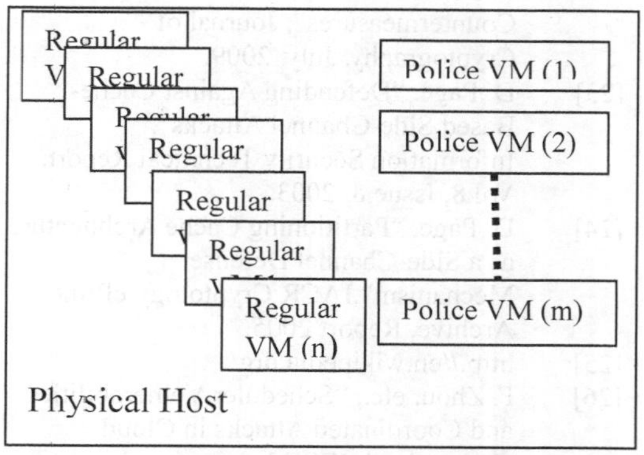

Figure 3.2 Running VMs in a VM Policing Physical

The number of police VMs running in a host (Figure 3.2) and how they are scheduled (Figure 3.3) could be guided by policies made according to the cloud environment. The factors should be considered are as following:

- the load of each host,
- special security request (e.g., running alone on a host),
- performance requirements of VMs,
- irregular VM launches (e.g., burst launches from same users), etc.

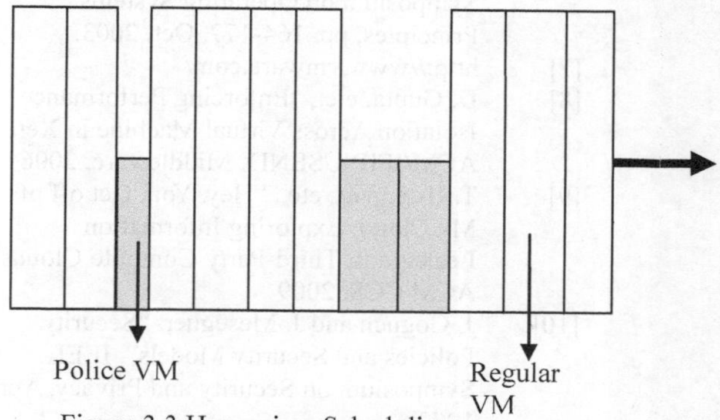

Figure 3.3 Hypervisor Scheduling

4. Conclusions

Cloud computing concept has evolved to become a reality. Not only enterprises begin to adopt this technology but also, some big companies have offer public cloud services. Cloud computing offers technology to consolidate servers, to utilize resources more efficiently, and to add or adjust computing capacity on demand faster. On the way to make cloud computing a more successful technology and let more people benefit from it, one of the major roadblocks is the security issues newly introduced in the cloud. Side channel attacks have been proved to be a type of serious and easy-to-implement attacks in a cloud. There is not much done in this area. We propose the VM policing technique to counter the attacks. It should be an effective countermeasure to the side channel attacks in the cloud and will cleanup some major obstacles in the promotion of cloud computing.

References

[1] http://aws.amazon.com/ec2/
[2] http://www.windowsazure.com/
[3] http://google.com/appengine/
[4] http://hpcloud.com/
[5] http ://gridcomputing.com/
[6] P.Barham, etc., "Xen and the Art of Virtualization", Proceedings of the ACM

Symposium on Operating Systems Principles, pp. 164-177, Oct. 2003.

[7] http://www.vmware.com/

[8] D. Gupta, etc., "Enforcing Performance Isolation Across Virtual Machine in Xen", ACM/IFIP/USENIX Middleware, 2006

[9] T.Ristenpart, etc., "Hey, You, Get off of My Cloud: Exploring Information Leakage in Third-Party Compute Clouds", ACM CCS, 2009

[10] J. Goguen and J. Meseguer, "Security Policies and Security Models", IEEE Symposium on Security and Privacy, Apr. 1982.

[11] D. Bernstein, "Cache-Timing Attacks on AES", http://cr.yp.to/antiforgery/cachetiming-20050414.pdf

[12] D. A. Osvik, A. Ahamir, and E. Tromer, "Cache Attacks and Countermeasures: The Case of AES", RSA Conference Cryptographers Track (CT-RSA) 2006.

[13] C. Percival, "Cache Missing for Fun and Profit", BSDCan, Ottawa, 2005.

[14] O. Aciicmez, C. Kaya Koc, and J. P. Seifert, "On the Power of Simple Branch Prediction Analysis", Proc. 2nd ACM Symposium on Information, Computer and Communication Security, 2007

[15] O. Aciicmez, C. Kaya Koc, and J. P. Seifert, "Predicting Secret Keys via Branch Prediction", RSA Conference Cryptographers Track CT-RSA 2007.

[16] O. Aciicmez, " Yet Another Microarchitectural Attack: Exploiting I-Cache", 14 th ACM Conference on Computer and Communications Security (ACM CCS'07) — Computer Security Architecture Workshop.

[17] D. Grunwald and S. Ghiasi, "Microarchitectural denial of service: insuring microarchitectural fairness", Proceedings of the 35th annual ACM/IEEE international symposium on Microarchitecture, 2002.

[18] T. Moscibroda and O. Mutlu, "Memoryy Performance Attacks: Denial of Memory Service in Multi-core Systems", USENIX Security Symposium, 2007.

[19] O. Aciicmez, and J. P. Seifert, "Cheap Hardware Parallelism implies Cheap Security", Workshop on Fault Diagnosis and Tolerance in Cryptography, FDTC, 2007.

[20] P. Karger and J. Wray, "Storage Channels in Disk Arm Optimization". IEEE Symposium on Security and Privacy, 1991.

[21] D. Hyuk Woo, and H. H. Lee, "Analyzing Performance Vulnerability due to Resource Denial Service Attack on Chip Multi-processors", Workshop on Chip Multiprocessor Memory Systems and Interconnects, 2007.

[22] E. Tromer, D. A. Osvik, and A. Shamir, "Efficient Cache Attacks on AES, and Countermeasures", Journal of Cryptography, July, 2009.

[23] D. Page, "Defending Against Cache-Based Side-Channel Attacks", Information Security Technical Report, Vol.8, Issue 8, 2003.

[24] D. Page, "Partitioning Cache Architecture as a Side-Channel Defense Mechanism",IACR Cryptology ePrint Archive, Report 2005.

[25] http://en.wikipedia.org/

[26] F. Zhou, etc., "Scheduler Vulnerabilities and Coordinated Attacks in Cloud Computing", IEEE International Symposium on Network Computing and Applications, Boston, MA USA, Aug., 2011.

[27] L. Cherkasova, D. Gupta, and A. Vahdat, "Comparison of the three CPU Schedulers in Xen", SIGMETERICS Performance Evaluation Review, 2007.

[28] Z. Wang and R. B. Lee, "Covert and Side Channels Due to Processor Architecture,"ACSAC 2006

[29] Z. Wang and R. B. Lee, "New Cache Designs for Thwarting Software Cache-Based Side Channel Attacks," SIGARCH Computer Architecture News, Vol 35, No. 2, pp.494-505, 2007

[30] J. Bonneau and I. Mironov, "Cache-Collision Timing Attacks Against AES," Cryptographic Hardware and Embeded Systems CHES 2006, LNCS 4249, Springer, 2006.

[31] E. Brickell, etc., "Software Mitigations to Hedge AES Against Cache-Based Software Side Channel Vulnerabilities", IACR ePrint Archive, Report 2006/052, 2006.

[32] D. Brumley, etc., "Remote Timing Attacks are Practical," Proceedings of the 12th Conference on USENIX Security Symposium, 2003

[33] J. F. Dhem, etc., "A Practical Implementation of the Timing Attack," CARDIS, 1998.

[34] P. Kocher, J. Jaffe, and B. Jun, "Differential Power Analysis," Advances in Cryptology – CRYPTO 99, LNCS 1666, Springer-Verlag, 1999.

[35] D. Ongaro, A. Cox, and S. Rixner, "Scheduling I/O in Virtual Machine Monitors," ACM, VEE, 2008.

[36] S. Reuda, Y. Sreenivasan, and T. Jaeger, "Flexible Security Configuration for Virtual Machines," ACM Workshop on Computer Security Architectures, 2008

[37] B. Payne, M. Carbone, M. Sharif, and W. Lee, "Lares: An Architecture for Secure Active Monitoring Using Virtualization," 2008 IEEE Symposium on Security and Privacy.

[38] D. Murray, G. Milos, and S. Hand, "Improving Xen Security through Disaggregation," ACM, VEE, 2008

[39] S. King, P. Chen, etc., "SubVirt: Implementing Malware with Virtual Machines," IEEE Symposium on Security and Privacy, 2006.

[40] Z. Wang and X. Jiang, "HyperSafe: A Lightweight Approach to provide Lifetime Hpervisor Control-Flow Integrity," IEEE Symposium on Security and Privacy, 2010.

[41] S. Jones, etc., "VMM-based Hidden Process Detection and Identification using Lycosid," ACM, VEE, 2008.

[42] P. Kocher, "Timing Attacks on Implementations of Diffie-Hellman, RSA, DSS, and Other Systems," Advances in Cryptography – CRYPTO '96, Vol. 1109 of LNCS, Springer, 1996

[43] B. Coppen, etc., "Practical Mitigations for Timing-Based Side-Channel Attacks on Modern x86 Processors," IEEE Symposium on Security and Privacy, 2009

[44] G. Agosta, etc., "Countermeasures Against Branch Target Buffer Attacks," 4 th Workshop on Fault Diagnosis and Tolerence in Cryptography (FDTC'07)

ICOMP: POSITION PAPER

Research on Cloud Service Community Constructing Approach for Personalized Tourism Service

Ruzhi Xu, Pengfei Zhao, Zhikun Zhao
School of Computer Science and Technology, Shandong University of Finance and Economics, Jinan, China
xuruzhi@sdufe.edu.cn

***Abstract*—The current tourism service is transferring from the passive mode to active one. More and more people expect to schedule the tourism plan by themselves according to the personalized requirements. This paper proposes a service organization approach of cloud community based on destination. The approach firstly classifies the tourism web services by destination and type etc. and clusters them by service function. Then by the aid of user preference model all the required services are gotten and clustered to be service pools with the same function. And the dynamic binding is also accomplished through service pool. To satisfy the requirement of service composition, the paper designs an individual service selecting algorithm based on the community. The experiments demonstrate that the approach of cloud service community can greatly improve service discovery efficiency and precision. And with the completion of the user preference library, the precision of service recommending also has a great improvement.**

Keywords—Personalized Requirements; Cloud Service Community; Cluster; Service Selecting Algorithm

I. INTRODUCTION

In the environment of modern Internet, more and more travel companies package their professional ability into web services and release them to the Web. Tourists can query the services needed and optimize the composition of the services. The web services related to tourism has a large number and covers the traffic, accommodations and scenic spots, and they are isolated. One time of tour the tourist needs is not just one web service, but a complete travel schedule that must be accomplished by a group of web services.

The core of constructing the tourism service flow is tourism service discovery and service composition. The problems about business process integration which is based on service composition mainly center on two aspects. One is selecting the required Web service set in the changing Web services according to the function need, which is called service discovery, while another is service selecting and optimizing which is to discover the service instance that can meet the user's quality of service from similar Web service set. In the environment of cloud computing, there is a great number of tourism service resource and they are distributed dispersedly, and the scope of services are far beyond the scope that the travel agency provides. Searching and matching in so many mixed Web services will make the computing scale very large.

Varieties of service organization frameworks have been put forward for ordinary Web services. The earlier one is Universal Description, Discovery, and Integration short for UDDI, which is supported by OASIS (Organization for the Advancement of Structured Information Standards), and provides keywords retrieval method through service registry and simple industry classification. From then on, many organization frameworks have been presented. For example, the distributed organizing framework[1], putting registry into Chord network and classifying the registries by domain ontology, has resolved the bottleneck problem brought by centralized service registry but increased the network load and decreased the efficiency of service discovery. Another distributed one is a P2P based hybrid collaborative model [2], which proposes the concept of ontology community. The framework connects the Web services and communities by the P2P structures. Although it has a good expansibility and satisfied the need of big data, the low efficiency problems still exist.

Researchers have attempted to take the method of service clustering to promote the query efficiency. The paper [3] puts forward a user driven method for Web services composition, which returns the required services that meet user's need to pools. The pools encapsulate the services and provide the same interface to users, which is the embryonic form of service cluster. The clustering method based on spanning tree [4] clusters the registered services as a form of spanning tree and the number of clusters is changing by the setting of threshold. But there appears difficulty to manage and govern the cluster that the method produces and the article has not provided the algorithm about clustering and matching.

Obviously, the existing web composing technology has no adequate consideration to the feature of tourism service and the flow feature of tourism service composition. And the excessive simple method of service discovering and organizing cannot be applied to complex tourism service business. According to the features of tourism services [5], this paper proposes an approach to tourism web service community organization for personalized tourism service which improves the service discovering efficiency. The community gets web service sets in which all the services have the same location attribute according to user's request and divides them into six basic types namely food, restaurant, traffic, sight, shop and entertainment. Then classifying and clustering are done in each type and the services are organized as tree structure. The service pool consists of web services with the same or similar function and is generated by the similarity matching algorithm based on ontology. Thus the pool can provide services with the same function but different performance. The web services are expressed by the service classifying format based on facet [6]. The community can present different view as the facet changes. As a result, the mechanism can provide the personalized service recommendation according to user's preference.

II. CLOUD SERVICE COMMUNITY ORGANIZATION BASED ON DESTINATION

2.1 Tourism web service representation

The paper represents services by facet. Facet is a set of words or phrase, describing certain aspect or viewpoint of service. Each facet has a group of terms, which are composed of a structure term space with the relationship among class layers and relationship between synonymies. The facet classifying model in this paper is extended from REBOOT (Reuse Based on Object-Oriented Technology) [7]. A complete service consists of facets of function, operation, I/O parameters, service relationship, service quality, service cost, and service time and so on. The function facet includes availability, reliability, service capability, addressing capability and load. Service relationship includes the name and location information of provider and tourism project ID.

2.2 Service classification and cluster

In consideration of the feature of tourism field, the community is divided into six parts according to six tourism factors, namely food, restaurant, traffic, sight, shop and entertainment. The services exist as tree structure and are classified and clustered by analyzing the function facet. Classifying is benefit to service query and composition while clustering contributes to the comparison between services, narrowing query space and increasing search efficiency. According to construction method of cloud service ontology from mOSAIC[8], the tourism field ontology O_T is built by adding the relative concepts of tourism field. The service classifying algorithm (CLA) and clustering algorithm (CLU) are all constructed based on O_T. Both take the similarity matching algorithm on ontology and cosine formula:

$$sim(a,b)=\begin{cases}\dfrac{\alpha\times(D(a)+D(b))}{(dist(a,b)+\alpha)\times D_{\max}\times\max(|D(a)-D(b)|,1)} & a\neq b\\ 1 & a=b\end{cases} \quad (1)$$

$Sim(a,b)$ is the similarity degree between a and b. $D(a)$ is the layer number of a in the tree of O_T. $dist(a,b)$ is the shortest path between a and b, which is also called ontology distance. $D_{\max}$ shows the deep of ontology tree. $\alpha\geq 0$ and it is a controllable parameter. Presuming A and B are text analytic vectors, the cosine formula is as (2):

$$sim(A,B)=\frac{\sum_{i=1}^{n} A_i\times B_i}{\sqrt{\sum_{i=1}^{n}(A_i)^2}\times\sqrt{\sum_{i=1}^{n}(B_i)^2}} \quad (2)$$

Supposing the function facet of S (service) is F_{func}, and parser is syntactic analyzer, CLA and CLU are showed as follows.

$$WS-CLA-0(s)$$
$$C:\{food,hotel,trip,sight,shop,joy\}$$
$$V:V_1,V_2,V_3,V_4,V_5,V_6\leftarrow\varnothing$$
$$s\xrightarrow{Paser}Set_{word}$$
$$for\ each\ ?w\in Set_{word}\ do$$
$$V_i=V_i+sim(C[i],w)$$
$$return\ MAX(V)\rightarrow C$$

$$WS\text{-}CLU\text{-}0(s,t)$$
$$CLU:\{C_1,C_2,\cdots,C_n\}$$
$$V[1\cdots n]\leftarrow\varnothing$$
$$s\xrightarrow{Paser}S$$
$$for\ each\ ?i\ C_i\neq\varnothing\ do$$
$$for\ each\ j,ws_j\ do$$
$$V[i]+=sim(S,paser(Face_f of\ ws_j))$$
$$V[i]=V[i]/(num\ of\ ws\ in\ C_i)$$
$$return\ MAX(V)\rightarrow CLU$$

The algorithm of CLA can be extended by adding classes, for example the child class of the six main classes.

2.3 Construction of cloud service oriented to personalized tourism service

Definition 1 TSCC (Tourism Service Cloud Community): It is a beforehand classified and clustered collection of available services, which is accord with user's requests and has location in the tourism destination. The web services with same or similar function facet are clustered to be a service pool. And the cloud service community is made up of the service pools. In a word, the tourism cloud service community is a tree structure organization that is composed by the clusters based on elements of tourism field. The formalization of TSCC is

$$TSCC=(SRC,CLAO,ServicePool,Algorithm) \quad (3)$$

Definition 2 Service Pool: It is a set of services with same or similar function. The services in the pool have the same function but different quality of service.

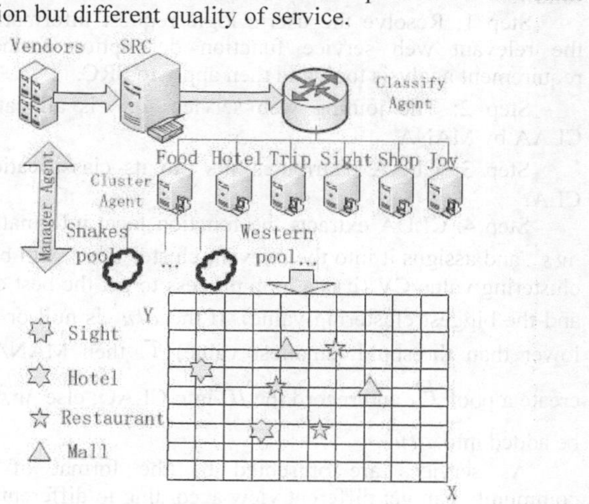

Figure 1 cloud service community framework

From the formula (3), the tourism cloud service community mainly consists of four parts, namely Service Register Center (SRC), Classifying Organization, Service Pool and Algorithm. SRC manages the process of service registering. The registering steps are as follows.

Firstly, vendors hand in the application of service registering to SRC according to the template of service information, such as OWS. After SRC received the application, it will check the information and test the connectivity to the vendors. If there have some problems, the vendor will receive the reply; else SRC records the service and makes it a legal service. The registering process is over.

The management of SRC is mainly to update the service information and check the connectivity frequently. Once the service is not supported by the vendors any longer, SRC will execute to remove the node in the service pool. CLAO is the relative organization structure of six tourism factors, recording the service pool ID and relative information. Service Pool is the cluster of similar services and indexes by different facet. Besides, service pool need to preserve the information of performance facet, so as to provide services with better performance and candidate services. Service pool is binding with the service flow that satisfy the dynamic service need. Algorithm mainly refers to the three agents: Classifying Agent(CLAA), Clustering Agent(CLUA), Management Agent(MANA). Their functions are as follows.

Table 1 Agent and its algorithm and function

Agent	Algorithm	Function
CLAA	CLA and its extensive algorithm	Dividing the registered services into classes.
CLUA	CLU algorithm	Clustering the registered services.
MANA	null	Managing the services and connecting CLA with CLUA。

Based on the structure and each part's duty of cloud service community, the steps of producing community are as follows.

Step 1: Resolve the user's logic request information to the relevant web service function description format by requirement analysis tool, and then apply to SRC.

Step 2: The joining web service ws' is allocated to CLAA by MANA.

Step 3: CLAA distributes ws' to its classification by CLA.

Step 4: CLUA extracts the function facet information of ws' and assigns it into the relevant cluster clu' with biggest clustering value CV (it is a loop process to get the best cluster and the biggest clustering value). If the clu' is null or CV is lower than threshold (smallest value) τ, then MANA will create a pool P_{ws} and record the *ID* into CLAO; else ws' will be added into clu'.

As services are presented by the format of facet, community can get different view according to different facet. Figure 1 is gotten by the service's location facet so that each service's location information can be recognized by the view.

III. SERVICE SELECTING ALGORITHM BASED ON CLOUD SERVICE COMMUNITY

3.1 Quality of service factors

The main factors that affect service selecting are service's function and QoS (quality of service). A complete service pool can be set up with the requested function by similarity matching algorithm. Thus how to choose the web service with the best QoS is the key factor. The elements that influence QoS can be divided into performance and field feature. Presuming $\mu, \nu > 0$ and are both controllable parameters, the quality of service's formula is as follows.

$$Q_s = \begin{cases} Q_d & Q_p > \mu \\ \nu Q_d & 0 < Q_p \le \mu \\ 0 & Q_p = 0 \end{cases} \quad (4)$$

Q_p is the value of performance while Q_d is the resultant value relative to the field. Use for reference of WSQM model, the qualitative service attributes can be quantified. The paper chooses the followed performance indexes: *Response time, Availability, SuccessRate, Accessibility, Maximum Throughput.*

Suppose $\iota, \kappa, \lambda, \eta, \sigma > 0$ and $\iota + \kappa + \lambda + \eta + \sigma = 1$, the resultant value of Q_p is as the formula (5) shows.

$$Q_p = \iota \times RT + \kappa \times Ava + \lambda \times Suc + \eta \times Acc + \sigma \times MT \quad (5)$$

But in the process of selecting and composing tourism services, the major factors are field features. According to the features of tourism field, the main influence factors are C (cost), T (time) and Q (quality). In order to compute conveniently, the unit of the three factors can be converted as the formula (6) shows.

$$1U_T = \varepsilon U_C, 1U_Q = \varphi U_C \quad (6)$$

ε and φ vary with users and they belong to the category of user's personalized requirements. *Q* is the average value of evaluations by general people. Thus the Q_d is gotten by the formula (7).

$$Q_d = U_C(C + \varepsilon T + \varphi Q) \quad (7)$$

Among which, *C*, *T* and *Q* are all signed numbers. To compute easily, time and cost would take the negative format.

3.2 Personalized service selecting algorithm

Definition 3 User Preferences: It is a bias choice made by users when they are measuring services and going to make a reasonable decision. It is a composite result through user's cognition, inside feeling and rational economics balancing, such as cost conservation or quality priority. In other words, priorities are based on variety of facets.

The UPM (User Preference Model)[10] is realized by clustering algorithm, and will be enriched by the users' operations. Directing against the user's different preferences through travelling, the paper divides them into conservation, efficiency and quality priority, the ratio of which can be gotten by UPM.

The following two functions can be achieved based on UPM. One is providing the services that meet user's preference and another is offering relative services, which is based on the fact that user not only chooses the single one, but maybe try the other composing services.

Presuming that a user chooses to travel the sight S in city A, now he looks for the restaurant services (actually the composition of restaurant service and traffic service). The time is the travel-time between the staying place and S. The cost is the price of restaurant and the quality is the degree of recognition to the restaurant's environment. The description of SSA (Service Selecting Algorithm) is shown as follows.

Step 1: According to user's description about where to stay (such as beside the lake), get the service pool $pool_x$ by matching the clusters under Hotel CLAO using the formula (2).

Step 2: Presuming that the tolerance of user to cost, time and quality is B_c, B_t and B_q. If the conversion ratio is preset by user, then go on Step 3; else switch to Step 5.

Step 3: Choose the location facet F_{loc} as the view V of the community, which only includes the sight S and the services in service set Set_1 with the feature of $C<B_c$,$T<B_t$ and $Q<B_Q$ in $pool_x$.

Step 4: Compose restaurant services and traffic services. Find all the traffic services from each service in Set_1 to S: $ws_{hotel} \rightarrow Set_{trip}$. According to formula (6), mark the value of restaurant services (C,Q) and traffic services (C,Q,T). Match each restaurant service with the traffic service with max quality value: $ws_{hotel} = ws_{hotel} + max(Set_{trip})$.

Step 5: Find the service with QoS_{max} or Set_2 by location information in V. Choose the service WS_{best} with the biggest value of F_{max} in the services with equal quality value; Return.

Step 6: Get preference ratios of the user's *CTQ* by UPM and the ratios are $\alpha, \beta, 1-\alpha-\beta$. Take the taxi's speed *speed* and the charge *price* of city A as the time and cost's conversion standard. We get $1U_T = \frac{\beta}{preferValue} speed \times price U_C$. Taking the price and quality standard of the hotel in A as the price and quality's conversion standard, the formula is $1U_Q = \frac{1-\alpha-\beta}{preferValue} \times \frac{price_{level+\Delta} - price_{level}}{\Delta} U_C$; Switch to Step 3.

After all, both of the above functions can be accomplished by SSA algorithm.

IV. Conclusion

Against the problems of the scattering resources and the large search space, this paper proposed a service organization approach of cloud community based on destination. The approach classifies and clusters the tourism services according to six tourism factors as a structure of tree, which is the service organizing framework that can dynamically binding to the personalized tourism service flow to provide services. The service selecting algorithm based on community offers services to services composing flow. Experiments show that cloud community has greatly improved service discovery efficiency and query precision ratio, at the same time it can provide recommending services that meet user's personalized requirements. The next step of the paper is to adjust the organizing structure of cloud community to flow style.

Reference

[1] Hongmei ZHAO, Yang XIA, Qiang ZHAO, et al. Research on Chord-Based Semantic Web Service Discovery and Composition [J]. Microelectronics & Computer, 2010,Vol.27(8): 161-164.

[2] Zhizhong LIU, HuaiMin WANG, Bin ZHOU. A Two Layered P2P Model for Semantic Service Discovery [J]. Journal of software, 2007,Vol.18(8),1922–1932.

[3] XuanZhe LIU, Gang HUANG, Hong MEI. Consumer-Centric Service Aggregation:Method and Its Supporting Framework [J]. Journal of software, 2007,Vol.18(8):1883-1895.

[4] ChunHua HU, Min WU, GuoPing LIU, DeZhi XU. An Approach to Constructing Web Service Workflow Based on Business Spanning Graph [J], 2007,Vol.18(8):1870–1882.

[5] Tourism services. Martin, Miguel-Angel Galindo, Gil-Pechuan et al. The Service Industries Journal.2011,Vol.31(10), 1561-1566.

[6] da Silva, S.T.F.,de Oliveira Apolonio et al. Ontoogle: Enhancing retrieval with ontologies and facets. CSCWD2011.

[7] Morel Jean-Marc, Faget Jean. The REBOOT environment [software reuse].Proceedings Advances in Software Reuse. 1993.

[8] Francesco Moscato, Rocco Aversa, Beniamino Di Martino. An Analysis of mOSAIC ontology for Cloud Resources annotation. Proceedings of the Federated Conference onComputer Science and Information Systems. 973–980.

[9] Lee Youngkon. Quality Control for Business Collaboration Based on SOA Framework. International Conference on Convergence Information Technology. 2007, 1963-1968.

[10] Cuiying WANG. Research Development of Folksonomy-based User Profile [J]. New Technology of Library and Information Service, 2009(6), 37-43.

[11] OWL-S/UDDI Matchmaker[EB/OL]. The Intelligent Software Agents Group The Robotics Institute Carnegie Mellon University, 2012, http://www.cs.cmu.edu/~softagents/atlas/matchmaker/inst-mm.htm#overview.

[12] RADA R, MILI H, BICKNELL E, et al. Development and Application of A Metric on Semantic Nets[J]. IEEE Transactions on Systems, Man, and Cybernetics, 1989, 19(1):17-30

[13] Elgazzar K, Hassan AE, Martin P. Clustering WSDL documents to bootstrap the discovery of Web services [C]//Proceedings of IEEE International Conference on Web Services (ICWS) 2010, IEEE Computer Society. Miami, Florida:Lisa O'Conner, 2010: 147-154.

[14] PAIK Hye-young, BENATALLAH B TOUMANI F. Towards Self-organizing Service Communities [J], IEEE Transactions on Systems, Man and Cybernetics, 2005, Vol.35(3).: 408 – 419.

[15]FAUTSCH C, SAVOY J. Adapting the tf idf Vector-space Model to Domain Specific Information Retrieval[C].SAC2010:1708-1712.

[16] ZENG L, NATALLAM B. QoS-aware Middleware for Web Service Composition [J]. IEEE Transactions on Software Engineering, 2004, Vol.30 (5):311-327.

[17] GOTTSCHALK K, GRAHAM S, KREGER H, et al. Introduction to Web Services Architecture [J]. IBM Systems Journal (IBMSJ), 2008, 41(2) : 170-177.

[18] AGGARWAL R, VERMA K, MILLER J, MILNOR W. Constraint Driven Web Service Composition in METEOR-S[C]//Proceedings of the 2004 IEEE International Conference on Services Computing Conference, 2004 23-30.

[19] YU Qi, LIU Xumin, BOUGUETTAYA A, et al. Deploying and Managing Web Services: Issues, Solutions and Directions [J]. Springer-Verlag New York, Inc. Secaucus, 2008, 17(3) : 537-572.

[20]PLATZER C, ROSENBERG F DUSTDAR S et al. Web Service Clustering Using Multidimensional Angles as Proximity Measures[J]. Association for Computing Machinery Transactions on Internet Technology, 2009, Vol.9 (3): 1552291-1552294.